The International Companion to Scottish Literature of the Long Eighteenth Century

INTERNATIONAL COMPANIONS TO SCOTTISH LITERATURE

Series Editors: Ian Brown and Thomas Owen Clancy

Titles in the series include:

International Companion to Lewis Grassic Gibbon
Edited by Scott Lyall
ISBN 978-1-908980-13-7

International Companion to Edwin Morgan
Edited by Alan Riach
ISBN 978-1-908980-14-4

International Companion to Scottish Poetry
Edited by Carla Sassi
ISBN 978-1-908980-15-1

International Companion to James Macpherson and The Poems of Ossian
Edited by Dafydd Moore
ISBN 978-1-908980-19-9

International Companion to John Galt
Edited by Gerard Carruthers and Colin Kidd
ISBN 978-1-908980-27-4

International Companion to Scottish Literature 1400–1650
Edited by Nicola Royan
ISBN 978-1-908980-23-6

International Companion to Scottish Literature of the Long Eighteenth Century
Edited by Leith Davis and Janet Sorensen
ISBN 978-1-908980-31-1

The International Companion to Scottish Literature of the Long Eighteenth Century

Edited by Leith Davis
and Janet Sorensen

Scottish Literature International

Published by
Scottish Literature International
Scottish Literature
7 University Gardens
University of Glasgow
Glasgow G12 8QH

Scottish Literature International is an imprint of
the Association for Scottish Literary Studies

www.asls.org.uk

ASLS is a registered charity no. SC006535

First published 2021

Text © ASLS and the individual contributors

All rights reserved. No part of this book may be
reproduced, stored in a retrieval system, or
transmitted in any form or means, electronic,
mechanical, photocopying, recording or otherwise,
without the prior permission of the
Association for Scottish Literary Studies.

A CIP catalogue for this title
is available from the British Library

ISBN 978-1-908980-31-1

Contents

Series Editors' Preface vii

Introduction 1
Leith Davis

PART 1: LANGUAGE, IDENTITY, AND HISTORY

1. Adaptation, Integration, and Renewal: Scottish Gaelic Literature, 1650–1750 24
   Domhnall Uilleam Stiùbhart
2. Poems in the Scots Register, 1650–1800 41
   Corey E. Andrews
3. Presenting the National Past: The Uses of History in Scottish Literature, 1650–1707 56
   Leith Davis
4. Literary Print Culture in Restoration Scotland, 1660–1688 73
   Holly Faith Nelson and Sharon Alker

PART 2: MEDIA AND MEDIATION

5. Gender and National Identity in Allan Ramsay's *The Tea-Table Miscellany* and Eighteenth-Century Scottish Song Culture . . . 96
   Emma Pink
6. Fierce Females and Male Pretenders: Gender, Cultural Memory and Anti-Jacobite Print Culture in the 1745 Rising. 117
   Leith Davis and Jasreen Kaur Janjua
7. How to Become an 'Authoress' in Provincial Scotland: Women's Poetry in Manuscript and Print 132
   Juliet Shields
8. Gaelic Enlightenment to Global Gaelosphere: Gaelic Literature, 1750–1800 149
   Domhnall Uilleam Stiùbhart

PART 3: POSSIBILITIES OF GENRE

9. Scottish Theatre in the Long Eighteenth Century 170
   Ian Brown

Contents (continued)

10. 'Will No One Tell Me What She Sings?': Scots Pastoral Poetry................................ 187
    David Radcliffe
11. Gaelic Women's Poetry........................ 199
    Kate Louise Mathis
12. Common Sense Philosophy and Sentimental Fiction: Eighteenth-Century Scottish Women Novelists......... 220
    JoEllen DeLucia
13. Scottish Enlightenment Inquiry in Gaelic Poetry: 'Air Fàsachadh na Gàidhealtachd Albannaich'........... 234
    Sìm Innes

PART 4: ENVIRONMENTS OF SPACE AND TIME

14. Eighteenth-Century Scottish Poetry and Ecology........ 246
    Eric Gidal
15. *The Poems of Ossian* and the Birth of Modern Geology..... 261
    Dafydd Moore
16. Crossing Borders: Travel Writing and Eighteenth-Century Scotland................................... 272
    Alex Deans
17. Scots and the Language of the Sea in Tobias Smollett's *Roderick Random* and William Falconer's *The Shipwreck*... 285
    Janet Sorensen
18. Ottobah Cugoano and Scotland's Minority Imperialist Culture.................................... 299
    Michael Morris

Endnotes 311
Further Reading 411
Notes on Contributors 417
Index 421

Series Editors' Preface

This volume, edited admirably by Leith Davis and Janet Sorensen to whom we are most grateful for their rigorous scholarship and positive vision, begins where that edited by Nicola Royan ended, the year of Cromwell's defeat of the Scottish army at Dunbar. The immediate impact on Scottish literature, its culture and politics, was, of course, powerful, but the reactions to and against its implications fuelled enormous changes in Scottish cultures and literatures over the following century and a half.

We were tempted at first to entitle this volume *Scottish Literature of the Enlightenment*. We have chosen, however, in consultation with the volume editors, to adopt the more neutral period term. Its start date marks our assertion that what is often called the Scottish Enlightenment was not something which suddenly emerged fully formed somewhere in the early eighteenth century. Rather, we suggest it developed out of older Scottish traditions of thinking and writing coming to fruition over a longer period, rooted at least as early as the mid-seventeenth century, if not before.

As this volume considers aspects of literature in all of Scotland's literary languages in that fruitful period, we welcome the volume editors' decision to explore the period under the headings of 'Language, Identity, and History', 'Media and Mediation', 'Possibilities of Genre', and 'Environments of Space and Time'. This arrangement of their material and that of our distinguished contributors allows us a fresh approach to the work and relationships of Scottish writers under discussion, avoiding the temptation to categorise work of the period in a potentially one-dimensional way.

Ian Brown
Thomas Owen Clancy

Introduction

Leith Davis

Background

The years 1650 to 1800 represent an era of unprecedented, as well as uneven, changes within Scotland in the interconnected areas of politics, religion, language, society and culture; these changes were reflected in, as well as influenced by, the literature produced during this time. During the first part of this 150-year-long period, the very borders of the nation were in flux. The 1603 Union of Crowns had created a politically complex situation whereby Scotland shared a monarch with England, but both nations maintained their own parliament.[1] Scotland subsequently became a key location during the Wars of the Three Kingdoms (1639–1652).[2] With the final victory of Oliver Cromwell over the Scots at Worcester in 1651 and the passing of the *Declaration of the Parliament of the Commonwealth of England, concerning the Settlement of Scotland*, Scotland was forcibly united (along with Ireland) into what was *de facto* an 'English empire'.[3] Although the 1660 Restoration of the Stuart monarchy reinstated Scotland's separate parliament, the English monarch essentially retained power over the nation.[4] Scotland's separate status became a pressing issue again during and after the 1688 Revolution.[5] After the flight of James VII/II and the accession of William III and Mary II, William desired a greater political union between Scotland and England. Although the English parliament initially resisted any such suggestion, the passing of the crown to the childless Queen Anne in 1702 prompted a change in English policy. Many Scottish politicians, too, were eager to embrace a union after the failure of the plans of the Company of Scotland Trading to Africa and the West Indies for a Scottish colony at Darien (1695–1700) and the famine years at the end of the seventeenth century.[6] A series of fraught negotiations took place between 1702 and 1707 before a political union was finally achieved in 1707 with the passing of Acts of Union in the parliaments of both Scotland and England.[7] In the subsequent united parliament of Great Britain, Scotland was allotted forty-five members out of 558 in the House of Commons and sixteen members out of a total of 168 in the House of Lords. Scotland maintained control over its legal and educational systems, however, and a separate act recognised Presbyterianism as the state religion.

Despite the outcome of the negotiations on union, the issue of Scotland's political position within the British islands was far from settled at this point, however. The union continued to be questioned, and a significant proportion of the early eighteenth-century population either actively or nominally supported the return of the Stuarts to the throne, particularly in the Gaelic-speaking Highlands and Islands.[8] The supporters of the Stuarts, or Jacobites, as they became known (after the Latin name for James, *Jacobus*), staged a number of risings and military plots in the first half of the eighteenth century, the most significant of which took place in 1708, 1715, 1719 and 1745.[9] Although the historical record, based from an early point in time upon government accounts, has tended to minimise the existence and the impact of Jacobitism, the threat to the establishment order was substantial, particularly during the Risings of 1715 and of 1745.[10] The final military event of the 1745 Rising, the Battle of Culloden (16 April 1746), marked the effective end of the Jacobite cause, however, and was followed by the violent suppression of Jacobites through mass transportation and execution as well as official attempts to eradicate Gaelic clan-based culture.[11]

The political union between Scotland and England and the Hanoverian monarchy became commonly accepted by the last half of the eighteenth century. But, at the century's end, Scotland, along with the rest of Britain, was affected by the political reverberations of the American and French Revolutions (1776 and 1789), and the political shape of the British Isles would change again with the Irish insurrection (1798) and the subsequent imposition in 1800 of another Act of Union, this time joining together Scotland, England, Wales and Ireland.

Throughout this politically complex period, Scotland was also transforming from within in terms of religion, economics, society and culture. Alasdair Raffe emphasises the fundamental impact that the religious controversies taking place during this time had on all subjects in Scotland: 'The period's religious upheavals mattered immensely to contemporaries [...] At stake were Scots' relationships with God, and their prospects of salvation'.[12] In the aftermath of the Wars of the Three Kingdoms and right through to the eighteenth century, religious beliefs were frequently a cause of tension and violence. The 1660 monarchical Restoration was accompanied by the restoration of bishops and the establishment of the Episcopalian church in Scotland (1661–1662).[13] As Kelsey Jackson Williams points out, 'radical Covenanters continued to fight their guerrilla war' in what became known as 'The Killing Time' and 'the government remained alert to instability, religious conflict, and the potentially disastrous consequences which could ensue'.[14] After the 1688 Revolution, however, Presbyterianism was established as the official religion of Scotland (1690), and it was the Episcopalians who found themselves disenfranchised. In the face of the prospect of the union with England, the Church of Scotland's official position was protected by the passing of the 'Act for Securing the Protestant Religion and Presbyterian Church Government' by the Scottish parliament in 1707. The Presbyterian church underwent a fundamental rift in 1733, however, in response to legislation passed by the British parliament, and it subdivided into what became known as 'Auld Licht' and 'New Licht', or evangelical and moderate, branches.[15]

In addition to grappling with spiritual concerns, Scots in the long eighteenth century also experienced significant alterations in their material existence. The population of the nation increased dramatically over the period, growing from 1,100,000 in 1700 to 1,625,000 in 1800.[16] As Sìm Innes notes, at mid-century, about twenty to twenty-five percent of that population lived in the Gaelic-speaking Highlands.[17] The spaces in which people lived and worked were also undergoing profound changes. Starting from the mid-seventeenth century, landowners in both the Highlands and Lowlands began investigating ways to increase the values of their holdings.[18] The drive for 'improvement' would develop into a national obsession, as Nicholas Phillipson suggests:

> 'Improvement' was the grab-all term used by contemporaries on the continent and in the Anglo-Saxon world to characterize a reformist, 'enlightened' interest in manners, morals, the arts and sciences and religion as well as in the business of wealth creation and the transformation of urban and rural environments, and it was generally assumed that improvement would help to serve the wider political and civilizational goal of creating governments that were more productive, and societies that were 'happier' and more 'polite'. What is striking about the experience of Scotland is that these goals were seen as having transformational possibilities for a small nation, faced with marginalization in an increasingly competitive, militaristic and imperialist world.[19]

Accordingly, Scotland embraced 'improvement' in all regards in the eighteenth century. Transportation and communication systems developed substantially over the period. After the Jacobite Risings, the Highlands became a particular focus, as roads and forts were constructed to preclude further Jacobite activity. As Alex Deans notes in his chapter in this volume, the forfeited Jacobite estates also became locations where 'new forms of agricultural practice and social organisation were attempted'.[20] The Lowlands were also transforming. By the second half of the eighteenth century, many people in the Lowlands were leaving the rural areas for urban locations as the Industrial Revolution was under way.[21] The national passion for improvement also affected cities in the Lowlands, as the capital of Edinburgh, for example, was transformed starting in 1767 with James Craig's plans for the construction of the New Town,[22] and Glasgow also increased in size and economic importance by the end of the century.[23] Hubs of sociability developed in cities around sites such as clubs, coffee-houses and, particularly for women, domestic tea-tables.[24]

The era also witnessed an astonishing efflorescence of intellectual activity, beginning with the late seventeenth-century climate of scientific inquiry and centred in the eighteenth century around a movement that became known as the Scottish Enlightenment. The individuals associated with the Scottish Enlightenment were connected to Scottish universities, the legal and medical professions, and the church, and were diverse in terms of their subjects of interest.[25] But although they pursued different intellectual areas, these thinkers shared a broad set of common beliefs, a reflection of what Alexander Broadie and Craig Smith refer to as the 'highly social' nature of the movement: 'The writers were held together by bonds of friendship; they argued and debated with each other and created many clubs and societies designed to facilitate discussion.'[26] One thread running through the work of the writers of the Scottish Enlightenment was a belief in the universal progressive nature of human society. Adam Smith famously described the stages of this progression in his *Lectures on Jurisprudence* (1763): 'first, the Age of Hunters; secondly, the Age of Shepherds; thirdly, the Age of Agriculture; and fourthly, the Age of Commerce.'[27] In addition, Scottish Enlightenment thinkers shared the conviction that human knowledge, too, was progressive, as well as the confidence that their own researches were contributing to a better and clearer understanding of the world. The impact of the Scottish Enlightenment on the literature in Scotland both at the time and subsequent to the eighteenth century was substantial. As Robert Crawford asserts, the same Scottish university system that encouraged these

Enlightenment thinkers was also responsible for the development of the discipline of English literature,[28] and, as Kenneth McNeil has recently observed, later Scottish writers 'took up a cultural preoccupation with progress in the modern age, offering to British Romanticism, and Britishness, a distinctive form of historicism that assumed a stadial model of human social development'.[29]

Richard Sher has investigated how the dissemination of Scottish Enlightenment ideas within the British archipelago – as well as in North America – was facilitated by the phenomenal growth of the print marketplace.[30] The expansion of print culture over the long eighteenth century (examined also in Volume II of the *Edinburgh History of the Book in Scotland*) allowed not only for the sharing of academic concepts through books and treatises, but also for the dissemination of popular works such as sermons, chapbooks and novels – and it also included the development of a robust periodical press.[31] As Rhona Brown points out in the context of the poet Robert Fergusson (1750–1774), the Scottish periodical press provided an important means of publication for aspiring writers of the time, and as Brown, Alex Benchimol and David Shuttleton have emphasised, Scottish periodicals enabled 'debate over a raft of indicative concerns with politics and religion, commercial and agricultural improvement, manners and civility, and literary language and values'.[32] Despite the growth of the marketplace for print, however, it is important to bear in mind that for Gaelic literature, orality and manuscript culture were the primary modes of cultural production during this time period, as Domhnall Uilleam Stiùbhart and Kate L. Mathis discuss in their chapters in this volume.[33] The first book of secular Gaelic poetry, *Ais-eiridh na Sean Chánoin Albannaich* (*The Resurrection of the Old Scottish Language*) by Alasdair mac Mhaighstir Alasdair / Alexander MacDonald (c. 1698–1770), was not published until the mid-eighteenth century (1751). But even for the non-Gaelic-speaking population, oral culture was still an important part of daily communication for all ranks, and manuscript culture remained a viable literary mode, especially for women writers, as Juliet Shields indicates in her contribution. Moreover, as a number of the chapters in this volume suggest, media do not work in isolation. As William Warner suggests, 'While it is conceptually possible to disentangle one media object from the larger aggregation of media, this analytical procedure seems to run counter to the way media actually worked in the seventeenth and eighteenth centuries, where a particular medium acquired its salience within a multimedia buzz of communication'.[34] Printed collections of ballads and songs, for example, served both to further disseminate oral cultural activity as well as to establish 'orality' as a category of mediation.[35] Conversely, a facility for what Eve Tavor Bannet calls 'letteracy' ('the collection of different skills, values and kinds of knowledge beyond mere literacy that were involved in achieving competency in the writing, reading and interpreting of letters') was required to interpret printed texts such as the verse epistles of Allan Ramsay and Robert Burns.[36]

While Scotland was changing internally in all of these crucial ways, the Scottish presence in the global arena was also changing. Although Scotland lost its chance to develop its own overseas empire after the failed Darien venture, due to a large extent to English government policies, eighteenth-century Scots, both Highlanders and Lowlanders, took on a disproportionately large role in the creation and maintenance of the expanding British empire.[37] Scots travelled to all locations of the globe in the service of the empire, from the East Indies to North America to the Caribbean. Douglas Mack suggests the cultural negotiation in which Scots wishing to participate in this 'British Imperial project' needed to engage: 'Scots who wished to seize the opportunities offered by the British Empire had to learn how to operate acceptably and successfully within Britain's Imperial power structures.'[38] Those opportunities frequently had a darker side, however. While recent work is revealing the vast extent to which Scotland as a whole profited from slavery due to a disproportionate investment in the manufacture of sugar and tobacco, and, later, cotton, Scottish interactions with Indigenous peoples around the globe demands further scrutiny.[39]

All of these transformations that took place in Scotland between 1650 and 1800 were reflected in and refracted through a complex linguistic and literary terrain that this volume seeks to represent. Key to any sense of Scottish literature in this period, however, is an understanding of how these important changes took place unevenly throughout Scotland due to the existence of divisions within the nation. Highland and Lowland societies remained distinct linguistically and culturally in the long eighteenth century, although, as Stiùbhart and Mathis note in their chapters, there was increasingly more interaction between the two toward the latter part of the eighteenth century. There were also divisions within both the Highlands and Lowlands, and it would be a mistake to present either one of them as homogeneous. In the Highlands, there were significant divisions of political allegiances, religion and desire for land improvement.[40] In the Lowlands, the rural/urban divide is important to recognise as well as differences of religion and station. Accordingly, this volume remains attentive to the fact that there were many different versions of Scotland existing within the nation's borders.

Aims of This Volume

Like the other volumes in this series, the *International Companion to Scottish Literature of the Long Eighteenth Century* recognises the richness and diversity of the literatures during the period. As Thomas Clancy suggests, 'the term Scottish Literature cannot naturally be made subservient to one linguistically determined literary tradition'.[41] Accordingly, we include chapters which discuss literatures in English, Gaelic, Latin and Scots in this collection, bearing in mind the extent to which the linguistic traditions sometimes overlapped with one another and also altered over the period in question. The literary situation of Gaelic was changing in the seventeenth and beginning of the eighteenth centuries due to the disappearance of classical Gaelic and the proliferation of 'regional variations in the dialects of Gaelic spoken, which could compromise the ability of Gaels from different parts of Gàidhealtachd to comprehend one another'.[42] Over the course of the eighteenth century, as print started to play a more important role in the transmission of Gaelic literary works, Gaelic literature became an object of antiquarian interest, too. The tradition of Scoto-Latin poetry was also changing. 1637 had seen the publication of what Gerard Carruthers terms the 'showcase of Scoto-Latinist pride', the *Delitiae Poetarum Scotorum*.[43] The Scoto-Latin literary tradition waned, however, in the early eighteenth century as Latin became associated with the Jacobite cause; it would eventually lose currency in the latter part of the eighteenth century.[44] In terms of literature composed in Scots, Robert McColl Millar points out that by the end of the seventeenth century, Scots had been 'thrust socio-linguistically underground in written domains', although women retained more 'local features' of Scots in their writing, possibly as a result of their domestic education in comparison to men.[45] Nevertheless, as Corey Andrews' chapter in this volume suggests, the eighteenth century witnessed a resurgence of literature in the vernacular register, beginning with the publication of the three volumes of James Watson's *A Choice Collection of Comic and Serious Scots Poems: Both Ancient and Modern* (1706–1711) and culminating in the celebrated poems and songs of Robert Burns at the end of the century.

While it acknowledges the important work that has been done by other scholars of the era, this volume also operates upon a set of unique critical assumptions. First, the editors of this volume seek to complicate the chronological divisions which have historically shaped the field of Scottish literature. Critical works and anthologies of eighteenth-century Scottish literature, for example, have typically bypassed the late seventeenth century, so much so that the editors of a recent collection of essays on Scottish literature have suggested that '[t]raditionally, Scotland's seventeenth century has been viewed as a cultural wasteland'.[46] Instead, many explorations of Scottish literature in the long eighteenth century, following in the critical footsteps of David Daiches's *The Paradox of Scottish Literature: The Eighteenth Century Experience*, have begun with 1707, the year of the passing of the Acts of Union, consciously or unconsciously representing it as a watershed moment.[47] In contrast, by beginning with the year 1650, the *International Companion to Scottish Literature of the Long Eighteenth Century* adopts a longer approach to the period, focusing more on the productions of the last fifty years of the seventeenth century and attending closer to the continuities of the Scottish literary landscape over this period of 150 years. Rather than seeing 1707 as a punctuating and defining moment after which a new kind of Scottish literature emerged, we draw attention to through-lines in poetry, drama and prose works in Gaelic, Scots and English before and after the Union. At the same time, by following the literary contours from 1650 through to the beginning of the nineteenth century, we also continue the project begun by Leith Davis, Ian Duncan and Janet Sorensen in *Scotland and the Borders of Romanticism* of calling into question the relevance of period divisions between Enlightenment and Romantic literature. Although these divisions have played an important role in helping to define the English literary tradition, a Scottish literary perspective reveals that elements associated with both modes are interwoven throughout the eighteenth century. As suggested in that work, 'In Scotland, "Classical" and "Romantic" cultural forms occupy the same historical moment and the same institutional base, rather than defining successive stages or periods'.[48] This current volume extends those claims, indicating ways in which 'Classical' and 'Romantic' literary modes can be traced further back as well as further forward from the eighteenth century.[49]

A second objective of the *International Companion to Scottish Literature of the Long Eighteenth Century* is to reconsider the relationship between eighteenth-century literature in Scotland and the Scottish Enlightenment. As indicated above, the intellectual climate within the linked circles of church, university and the professions in Scotland was richly nurturing from the seventeenth century through to the end of the eighteenth century. This 'hot-bed of genius', as it was dubbed by Tobias Smollett in 1771, has been the focus of much critical attention for over a century, since W. R. Scott first gave a name to the Scottish Enlightenment.[50] Dan Edelstein has suggested the difficulties associated with the use of the term 'Enlightenment' in general: 'the Enlightenment was a heterogeneous phenomenon, to the extent that some historians insist on speaking of it only in the plural.'[51] What is true for the general term is equally true for the particular case of the Enlightenment in Scotland, as critics have grappled with identifying and cataloguing the features of the Scottish Enlightenment in particular. The result has been a plethora of examinations of the philosophical and scientific writing connected with the Scottish Enlightenment. Strangely separated out from the more academic varieties of printed works, the literature of the eighteenth century has been seen as relatively less compelling. The editors of *The Scottish Enlightenment and Literary Culture* articulate this problem as they observe that '[w]hen viewed in relation to the remarkable output in polite letters during the Scottish Enlightenment and groundbreaking achievements in moral and natural philosophy, medicine and natural history, and the critical arts, the imaginative literature of the period is often seen as relatively barren'.[52]

More fundamentally, as Silvia Sebastiani points out, the critical focus on the Scottish Enlightenment thinkers of the eighteenth century has also perpetuated the categorical exclusions that are articulated within the Enlightenment's own discourse, exclusions of gender and race, in particular.[53] Enlightenment thinkers such as Hume, Smith and Ferguson used women and racialised peoples figuratively in the development of their concepts of civil society. Women were invested with civilising influence; their specialised role in society was a marker of civility. In contrast, the racialised peoples of the New World, for example, were used as speculative examples of pre-civil societies; as Silke Stroh suggests, this perspective also included the Highland Gaelic populations.[54] But neither women nor racialised individuals entered significantly into the church, university and professional circles during the eighteenth century. To view the works of the Enlightenment as representative of the writing of the eighteenth century therefore means necessarily to be exclusive. The 2003 edition of the *Cambridge Companion to the Scottish Enlightenment* makes the exclusion explicit in terms of gender, noting that '[t]he enlightenment everywhere was an urban movement and it was equally a movement dominated by men. In Scotland women shone only in the drawing room, at the keyboard and in the writing of poems and songs. They were in the background, and hardly formed any part of the intellectual gatherings, which were often in taverns.'[55] Responding to such historical exclusions both in Enlightenment writing and in the critical discussions of that writing, JoEllen DeLucia and Pamela Perkins have suggested the different ways in which women were participants in Enlightenment thought.[56] Contributors to *The Scottish Enlightenment and Literary Culture* also argue for a less exclusive Scottish Enlightenment, one that includes literary writing, by focusing on topics such as intersections between works of historiography, travel narrative, and rhetoric, for example, and imaginative writing.[57]

This volume adopts a different approach to the exclusive focus on Scottish Enlightenment writing in the eighteenth century and to the exclusions suggested within the writing of the Scottish Enlightenment. By choosing for its subject the literature 'of the long eighteenth century' instead of the literature 'of the Scottish Enlightenment', our volume looks afresh at the literary landscape of the time period between 1650 and 1800. Contributors have been free to reference Enlightenment ideas or not as they see fit within their arguments. A number of the chapters in this volume investigate how the ideas of the Scottish Enlightenment were represented, reconceptualised and sometimes challenged within the specific works of literature under consideration; an equal number of chapters choose not to engage specifically with the topic of Enlightenment thought. One important way in which we expand the scope of the literature of the long eighteenth century beyond the writing of the Enlightenment is by considering different literary media. The period from 1650 to 1800 saw profound changes in the media landscape as print moved to take 'center stage' in a complex media ecology.[58] The critical focus on printed works in the literary canon, however, has resulted in the narrowing of the record of literature. Our volume highlights the often marginalised literary activity of the Gaelic-speaking peoples during this time period by including four chapters devoted to oral, manuscript and print Gaelic literary productions. In addition, by including chapters that foreground the eighteenth-century persistence of oral performance and of manuscript culture in the Lowlands in the time period (Brown, Pink, Shields), this collection also aims to be more inclusive of other unacknowledged voices in this rich era of literary history.

In response to the relative dearth of research involving issues of gender during this time period, our collection also includes a number of chapters that specifically address women's writing in English, Scots and Gaelic. At the same time, we recognise that concerns of gender cannot be addressed merely by including separate chapters that feature the literary output of women. Accordingly, several other chapters offer models for considering the way that gender intersects with other concerns in the period. Emma Pink, for example, explores the gendering of voice in Allan Ramsay's *Tea-Table Miscellany* and Scottish song culture while Leith Davis and Jasreen Kaur Janjua examine the use of gendered perspectives in the anti-Jacobite print culture in the post-1745 Rising period. In terms of research that addresses critical perspectives on race, Michael Morris's chapter reveals the material and intellectual connections between Scotland and the transatlantic slave trade. We recognise that there is much more to be done in the areas of race, indigeneity and decolonisation, however, and this volume can only point to the importance of expanding the study of Scottish literature into those directions in the future and hope that scholars of all ranks will be inspired to take up the challenge. Sebastiani's comment on 'the profound ambivalences in the way the Enlightenment conceived and justified itself as part of an advanced stage of human progress' is important to bear in mind as it still informs our disciplinary thinking. As Sebastiani outlines, 'The Enlightenment discourse on man affirms and simultaneously denies the unity of humankind, to sustain, on one hand, the American and French revolutions, and, on the other, the practice of exploiting non-European populations'.[59]

The works that form the basis of this collection thus present a longer and wider eighteenth century than previously considered. Contributors cover a range of topics, from the underexplored corpus of works published in Restoration Scotland to poetry by Gaelic women to texts deeply embedded in awareness of the ecological changes occurring at the century's end. In attempting to broaden and deepen the focus, the volume also offers a reconsideration of the deployment of important genres of the era, including the ballad, pastoral, and epic. Instead of isolating major authors in specific chapters devoted to individual writers who have heretofore made up the canon of Scottish literature, the editors seek to situate those writers within the various complex cultural fields in which they worked; thus Allan Ramsay is considered in the context of the writing of Scots poetry (Andrews), Scottish drama (Brown), Scottish political history (Davis), and Scottish song culture (Pink); James Macpherson materialises in chapters on Scottish environmental literature (Gidal), Enlightenment geology (Moore), and Gaelic literature (Stiùbhart and Innes); and Robert Burns is examined in chapters on poetry in Scots (Andrews), Scottish song (Pink), and pastoral (Radcliffe), among others. Our focus on topics rather than major authors results, we hope, in a relative foregrounding of lesser-known writers: writers such as Màiri nighean Alasdair Ruaidh / Mary Macleod (c. 1615–c. 1705), Andrew Erskine (1740–1793), and Jean Marishall (fl. 1765–1788), as well as a focus on the anonymous writers who also contributed to the rich multi-lingual and multi-media stores of Scottish literature in the long eighteenth century.

Instead of attempting the impossible goal of comprehensiveness, we have opted instead to focus on a selection of important topics. Each of the chapters is designed not just to survey the topic under consideration for readers unfamiliar with the particular subject, but also to present new research findings, frequently adopting new theoretical perspectives in the process. Given the large chronological scope of the volume, rather than asking all contributors to cover the entire period, we have asked each of them to focus on the chronological subsection which makes the most sense for their subject and which reflects their own area of expertise. That said, the chapters proceed largely chronologically, with the first chapters addressing the earlier period and the later chapters providing a set of co-ordinates that help the reader navigate the complex literary terrain of the end of the eighteenth century. The aim is to chart a path through the complex literary landscape of this period. The word 'companion' literally means an individual with whom one breaks bread, often an individual who shares a journey, and this volume takes seriously the mandate of offering company and providing food for thought during a shared expedition. There are many other possible journeys that could have been taken through the Scottish literature of the long eighteenth century, of course, and we hope the selection presented here encourages readers to undertake further explorations of their own.

Contents of the Volume

The first group of chapters in the *International Companion to Scottish Literature of the Long Eighteenth Century* investigates the interconnected themes of 'Language, Identity, and History', beginning with Domhnall Uilleam Stiùbhart's comprehensive discussion of the trajectory of literary texts in Gaelic from 1650 to 1800. Focusing largely on traces of oral cultural productions, Stiùbhart emphasises the ongoing links between the Scottish Gàidhealtachd and other traditions throughout the time period. Taking up the story of Gaelic literature after the British Civil Wars, for example, he examines the shift away from classical Gaelic poetry to a more 'semi-bardic' tradition as well as the development of a vernacular style, noting in addition connections between seventeenth-century Gaelic songs and Lowland street ballads. In considering the literature of the Jacobite period, he points out similarities between Sìleas na Ceapaich's 'Còmhradh ris a' Bhàs' ('Conversation with Death') and the ballad 'Death and the Lady' as well as Alasdair mac Mhaighstir Alasdair's innovative use of English Augustan poetic forms. As Stiùbhart suggests, 'far from being timelessly traditional, early modern Scottish Gaelic culture was dynamic, endlessly changing and adaptive, the culture of a surprisingly cosmopolitan, increasingly hybrid nation.'[60]

Stiùbhart's overview of Gaelic literary production is complemented by Corey Andrews' examination of the development of poetry in the Scots register from seventeenth-century broadsides to the poems and songs of Robert Burns. For Andrews, 'register' indicates 'words or phrases that evoke an extratextual social dimension that colours a reader's interpretation'.[61] In Andrews's assessment, this 'extratextual social dimension' becomes more distinctly nationalist in tone over the course of the long eighteenth century with the work of Allan Ramsay, Robert Fergusson and, finally, Burns. As Andrews points out, however, the phenomenal success of Burns in employing the vernacular also had the effect of occluding the efforts of other writers attempting to establish their reputations by using Scots. Writers such as Janet Little, the 'Scotch milkmaid' (1759–1813); John Mayne (1759–1836); John Lapraik (1727–1807); David Sillar (1760–1830); Alexander Wilson (1766–1813); and Ebenezer Picken (1769–1816), for example, had their opportunities 'foreclosed' by Burns's stellar career. Furthermore, as Andrews argues, the nineteenth-century enshrining of Burns as 'Scotland's reigning bard' effectively suggested 'the vernacular revival [...] ended with the poet's death'.[62]

In 'Presenting the National Past: The Uses of History in Scottish Literature, 1650–1707', Leith Davis extends the theme of the relationship between literature and national identity as she explores the ways in which writers from the Cromwellian Union to the union of parliaments drew upon different tropes – ranging from 'mythic and biblical roots to classical literature and romance traditions' in order 'to lend authority to their national identity' in the present.[63] Davis examines a range of literary material: from the complex tomes of Thomas Urquhart (1611–1660) and George Mackenzie of Rosehaugh (1636–1691), to the popular pamphlets circulating regarding the colony at Darien, to the post-union collections of James Watson and Allan Ramsay. Key to her analysis is a consideration of how expressions of national identity are articulated within a context of transnational connections.

In the final contribution to this first group of chapters, Holly Faith Nelson and Sharon Alker share the results of their extensive research into 'Literary Print Culture in Restoration Scotland'. Utilising extensive database resources, Nelson and Alker point to the importance of understanding the complexities of the Scottish literary landscape from a print culture perspective, acknowledging that what they identify as a 'surge in publishing in Restoration Scotland' involved the printing of 'both Scottish and English works'.[64] Tracing through the literary works printed in Edinburgh, Glasgow, and Aberdeen from 1600 to 1688, Nelson and Alker suggest that 'Scottish publishers of poetry, prose fiction, and drama in the period privileged political conservatism, cultural tradition, virtuous living, and spirited (but not debauched) humour'. They also indicate the way in which Scottish literature of the Restoration engaged in the 'work of cultural mourning' as they attempted to re-imagine a Scottish nation which had been torn apart through civil divisions and whose ruptures were still starkly visible.[65]

Although they focus on works of print culture, by including works such as 'political speeches, proclamations, acts, orders, remonstrances, epistles, and panegyric, as well as religious treatises, declarations, confessions, commentaries, and covenants along with sermons and metrical psalters',[66] Nelson and Alker suggest the heterogeneous nature of the category of the literary at the time prior to the establishment of literature as a discipline. They also reflect the intermedial nature of print at the time as it drew from oral and manuscript forms at the same time as it encouraged further oral, manuscript and printed engagement from its consumers.

The next group of chapters in this volume, on 'Media and Mediation', highlights the importance of reflecting on the relationship between mediation and literary works. Emma Pink also focuses on issues of orality, remediation, and gender in her chapter on Allan Ramsay's *The Tea-Table Miscellany* and eighteenth-century Scottish song. Pink examines the way Ramsay's *Miscellany* was produced within a growing climate of interest in Scottish song, paying particular attention to 'the array of gendered perspectives' presented in the work.[67] Offering close analyses of Ramsay's 'Dedication' and a number of songs such as 'Dumbarton's *Drums*' and '*Norland* JOCKY *and Southland* JENNY', Pink argues that, instead of adhering to a specific concept of the imagined community of Scotland in the eighteenth century and the roles of men and women within that community, the *Miscellany* served 'to vex any simple understanding of female/male relations, family hierarchies of authority and obedience, and polarities such as lowland/highland, urban/rural, and local/national'.[68] Pink concludes by contrasting Ramsay's fluid presentation of contemporary issues involving gender and the nation in the early eighteenth century with the more nostalgic antiquarian pursuits of David Herd (1732–1810) in *Ancient and Modern Scots Songs* (1776), John Pinkerton (1758–1826) in *Scottish Tragic Ballads* (1781), and Joseph Ritson (1752–1803) in *Scotish* [sic] *Song* (1794), all of which suggest, in diverse ways, a connection between Scottish songs and a 'limited, nostalgic sense of Scottish identity'.[69]

Leith Davis and Jasreen Kaur Janjua, too, consider the way in which concerns regarding gender intersect with issues of national identity. In 'Fierce Females and Male Pretenders: Gender, Cultural Memory and Anti-Jacobite Print Culture During the 1745 Rising', they examine four representative works of anti-Jacobite print culture (visual and textual) published during and after the 1745 Rising: Richard Cooper's satirical engraving of Prince Charles Edward Stuart in 'disguise' (1745); John Williams's broadside engraving of *Prince Charles Edward Stuart Disguised as Betty Burke* (c. 1746); a pamphlet entitled *A Brief Account of the Life and Family of Miss Jenny Cameron* (1746) and *The Female Rebels: Being some remarkable Incidents of the Lives, Characters, and Families of the titular Duke and Duchess of Perth, the Lord and Lady Ogilvy, and of Miss Florence M'Donald* (1747). Within those works, 'unnatural' representations of gender reinforce 'unnatural' political behaviour, while characters' political beliefs also affect their ability to perform their expected gendered roles in society. At the same time, drawing on recent theories of cultural memory studies by scholars such as Michael Rothberg, Davis and Janjua also suggest the way that these texts serve as *noueds* (knots) of cultural memory that continue to circulate traces of Jacobite counter-memories even while serving the purpose of presenting a pro-Hanoverian perspective.[70]

Juliet Shields's 'How to Become an "Authoress" in Provincial Scotland: Women's Poetry in Manuscript and Print', makes a case for expanding the focus of literature in the long eighteenth century to include manuscript publication in order to feature the productions of more women. Shields examines the literary productions of two elite women, Elizabeth Rae Keir (1747–1834) and Frances Scott (1750–1817), and two working-class women, Christian Milne (1773–1816) and Anne Ross (fl. 1798), concluding that, while women of a working-class background were 'more likely to seek print publication by subscription', all four women 'appear to have considered poetry not as an elite literary form reserved for those with a classical education, but as an informal genre for entertaining and communicating with friends and relations'.[71] Shields's research offers an important revision of our understanding of women's roles as writers in eighteenth-century Scotland. As she suggests, 'expanding our own understandings of authorship [...] may reveal that women played a greater part in the literary culture of Enlightenment Scotland than we have hitherto recognised'.[72]

In Chapter Eight, 'Gaelic Literature, 1740–1800', Domhnall Uilleam Stiùbhart points out the creative entanglement of Gaelic, Scots and English influences toward the century's end in the midst of the fundamental changes occurring in land ownership, the clan system and agricultural labour. He examines in particular the development of a corpus of printed Scottish Gaelic literature in the second half of the eighteenth century, a phenomenon that occurred in tandem with attempts to produce a written standard more in keeping with the spoken language, eschewing some of the forms of classical Gaelic. While oral culture was still prominent in the Gàidhealtachd, numerous literary works were also created and printed for a new generation of literate Scottish Gaelic readers. Stiùbhart notes the impact that James Macpherson's *Poems of Ossian* had in encouraging an interest in Gaelic publishing. In addition, the project to translate the New Testament into Gaelic undertaken by Rev. Seumas Stiùbhart generated an interest in the creation of 'an ideal literary canon illustrative of the supposed essence of Gaelic culture'.[73] As Stiùbhart remarks, by the end of the eighteenth century, Scottish Gaelic culture was becoming increasingly hybrid, bilingual and print-oriented, but 'perhaps occasionally less adept when handling oral culture.'[74]

Together, this second group of chapters suggests that any assessment of the literature of this time period needs to take into account issues of mediation as well as to grapple with the fact that media can have different relative values and uses within different cultural contexts. Equally as important to our understanding of the literary landscape of the long eighteenth century is the question of the form in which writers sought to express their imaginative efforts. The third group of chapters in this volume explores 'Possibilities of Genre', considering what writers understood about the genres that were available to them, how they worked within them, but also how they adapted them to their own purposes. While there were numerous genres of literature produced in the eighteenth century, the chapters collected here serve as representative case studies for analysing both the limitations imposed by form and the creative possibilities for expanding beyond and rethinking those forms.

In 'Scottish Theatre in the Long Eighteenth Century', Ian Brown takes a long view of the various forms of drama produced in Scotland in the period, challenging the view that theatre in Scotland was suppressed by the Kirk. He discusses the playhouse productions that took place after the Restoration, from the establishment of the Tennis Court Theatre at Holyrood in 1662, to Aston's and Ramsay's attempts to develop theatres in the 1720s, to the establishment of playhouse theatre in Edinburgh in the 1740s and 1750s. But Brown also suggests 'that too much focus on patent theatres can lead one to miss the complexity of the theatre scene' in Scotland.[75] By examining various forms of entertainment such as popular ceremonies, amateur acting, private/public performances and printed dramas, and by drawing attention to the Gaelic theatrical traditions, Brown argues that theatre, if not primarily playhouse theatre, had 'deep roots in Scottish culture'.[76]

Meantime, in '"Will No One Tell Me What She Sings?": Scots Pastoral Poetry', David Radcliffe examines the development of another genre, the pastoral, noting how the form itself is bound up with the notion of stadial progress (as the first stage in a traditional generic progression from pastoral to georgic to epic), as well as dependent upon a gap between those stages (as it posits a fundamental distinction between simple characters of the narrative and the more sophisticated poetic voice). He considers how Scottish writers employing the pastoral mode draw from but also reconstitute Scottish Enlightenment ideas of stadial progress and improvement, suggesting that the 'juxtaposition of simplicity and sophistication' proved 'particularly attractive to Scottish poets writing about the effects of political economy on persons in humble life'.[77] Examining a wide selection of authors across the eighteenth century including Allan Ramsay, Andrew Erskine, James Macpherson, Alexander Ross (1699–1784), James Beattie, Robert Fergusson and Robert Burns, Radcliffe suggests that Scottish writers used the pastoral to question other distinctions: between local and cosmopolitan attitudes, between orality and literacy, and between Enlightenment and counter-Enlightenment views about civilisation and progress. Moreover, for early nineteenth-century writers like James Hogg, the pastoral becomes a way of unsettling 'conventional ideas about nature and art' as well as connecting back to earlier debates on the 'nature of culture and civilisation'.[78]

In the following chapter, Kate L. Mathis reconsiders forms of 'Gaelic Women's Poetry' as she notes the 'increasing visibility of Scottish Gaelic women poets' work' in the manuscript collections of the late eighteenth century as well as in works of print, including the publication of the first 'single-authored anthology assembled by a female poet' in 1785.[79] At the same time, however, she indicates the way that songs and poems by women were collected in manuscript and print forms only in retrospect; the works had often been circulating orally for a significant period of time before their appearance in those media. As a consequence, she suggests, 'the act of preservation in writing – or, thereafter, in print – tended to exclude the agency of poets themselves; even items of verse attributed to named women remained vulnerable to collectors' or editors' imprecision or lack of contemporary knowledge (and/or to subsequent singers' distance from attributed songs reshaped by years of circulation and performance in the oral tradition)'. While the 'gap between time of composition and time of mediated preservation'[80] became less wide toward the end of the eighteenth century, there remained a fundamental disconnect between women's productions that were circulating orally and those that were re-mediated into manuscript or print.[81] As Mathis concludes, for Gaelic women, 'the oral tradition was fundamental to ensuring preservation of poets' identities, reputations, and at least some of their work'.[82] In drawing attention to the uneasy relationship between forms of poetry in oral, manuscript and print, Mathis also reminds us of the way in which the development of the marketplace for print in the eighteenth century looks different when considered from the perspective of Gaelic culture.

While Mathis sheds new light on Gaelic women's poetic productions as well as on ways in which we think about poetic form, JoEllen DeLucia brings a similar defamiliarizing perspective to the novelistic productions of Lowland women writers of the later eighteenth century. In 'Common Sense Philosophy and Sentimental Fiction: Eighteenth-Century Scottish Women Novelists', DeLucia examines how women writers used the novel form to comment on ideas of sympathy and sentiment. As DeLucia suggests, writers such Jean Marishall, Elizabeth Hamilton (1756?–1816), and Mary Brunton (1778–1818) utilise the features of the commercially successful sentimental novel form (including 'formulaic plots', intertextuality, and a reworked 'virtue in distress' narrative), but redeploy them, thereby 'satisfying the desires of female consumers and codifying the morality of the emerging bourgeoisie'.[83] At the same time, however, these novelists also employ humour and ironic distance to draw attention to the limitations of the form. According to DeLucia, Scottish women novelists 'trade in laughter and derision instead of tears'.[84]

While DeLucia considers the shaping of the genre of the novel in response to changing market economics in the Lowlands, Sìm Innes examines the way poetry is used to explore effects of economic changes and social transformation in the Gaelic-speaking Highlands, drawing attention to the remarkable manuscript collection of Reverend James McLagan (1728–1805). Housed in the Special Collections of the Library of the University of Glasgow, the McLagan collection consists of 'around 630 items, mostly Gaelic songs and poetry'.[85] By providing an intensive close reading of one of the poems in that collection, 'Air Fàsachadh na Gàidhealtachd Albannaich' ('On the Desolation of the Scottish Highlands') and by offering a new translation of several of the lines in the poem, Innes positions its author in the context of Enlightenment ideas. While he avoids references to the by-then well-known *Poems of Ossian* of James Macpherson, the author of the 'Air Fàsachadh na Gàidhealtachd Albannaich' engages knowledgeably with discussions circulating in Enlightenment circles at the time, including the new geologic discoveries of James Hutton (1726–1797) and debates about stadial history and the role of 'luxury' in Highland economic development. Innes's contribution thus significantly re-positions the genre of Gaelic poetry as a contributor to rather than an object of Enlightenment inquiry.

With its focus on disruptions to the natural world in the Highlands, Innes's chapter also serves as a bridge to the next thematic group of chapters which examine 'Environments of Space and Time' in the long eighteenth century. These chapters consider a range of topics concerning the geopoetics of space during an era of unprecedented changes to Scotland's agricultural and urban environments as well as of expansion of its global activities, as suggested above. As we have also seen, such changes were also explained in Scottish Enlightenment discussions in terms of a stadial progress toward a commercial society. The introductory chapter in this group, Eric Gidal's 'Eighteenth-Century Scottish Poetry and Ecology', adopts a global ecocritical perspective as it considers the way in which Scottish poetry provides a record of perceptions of the changing eco-logical conditions in Scotland over the long eighteenth century. As Gidal posits, 'eighteenth-century Scottish poetry inevitably registers changes to the lands, airs, and waters through the no-less contested medium of language, be it English, Scots, or Gaelic'.[86] Gidal brings together Lowland poets such as Robert Burns and James Thomson and Gaelic poets Mac Mhaighstir Alasdair and Donnchadh Bàn Mac an t-Saoir / Duncan Bàn MacIntyre (c. 1723–1812) in order to suggest their commonality of approach to the environmental changes occurring around them. But Gidal's chapter also ranges beyond the borders of Scotland, as it positions the changes occurring in Scotland – and the poets who track those changes – within a wider world system that was moving toward ever more destructive means of energy extraction. For Gidal, these eighteenth-century Scottish poets can offer reflections for contemporary readers as we grapple with the legacy of those earlier changes.

Dafydd Moore also suggests the importance of looking to eighteenth-century Scottish poetry to understand twenty-first century experiences as he considers a work which, in its very form, suggests both the uncanny intersections of and unbridgeable distances between the past and the present: James Macpherson's *Poems of Ossian* (1760–1765). While he begins by referencing previous critical discussions of *Ossian*, Moore takes a different turn as he considers the poems' exploration of 'a changing understanding of geology and geological time'.[87] Following a cue from Stephen Jay Gould and echoing Innes's interests in Hutton, Moore examines how Hutton's ideas regarding uniformitarianism ('the principle that geological phenomena are the result of the same set of physical laws operating across and throughout time') introduced a new kind of understanding of 'deep time' into scientific and social scientific knowledge.[88] Regarded in the context of this 'deep time', human activities came to seem incalculably insignificant. While it is difficult to trace a direct line of influence from Hutton to Macpherson, Moore indicates nevertheless that, as a 'prolonged and insistent mediation on the passage of time', *Ossian* is 'part of the cultural sensibility that allows for the imaginative leap in the direction of the idea of "deep time"'.[89] At the same time, Moore suggests, *Ossian* also offers a sense of heroic resilience and the role of humans within the shifting natural world that mitigates a sense of the incomprehensibility of 'deep time' both in Macpherson's time, and, arguably, in ours.

The third chapter in this group, 'Crossing Borders: Travel Writing and Eighteenth-Century Scotland' by Alex Deans, examines ways in which writers of non-fictional journeys in Scotland contributed to the literary culture of the time period as well as to the eighteenth-century topographical and cultural identity of the nation. As Deans points out, there is a 'complex relationship between the forms and meanings of progress (historical and spatial)' in eighteenth-century travel writing about Scotland.[90] Travel confirms travellers' presuppositions regarding subjects such as the benefits of improvement, antiquarian researches, the relative civility of different regions of the nation, and, later, the aesthetics of the sublime, but it also poses the threat of 'the disruptive potential of encounter, and with it the radical diversity of place'.[91] Deans considers Scottish writers such as John Macky (d. 1726), the Gaelic-speaker Martin Martin (Màrtainn MacGilleMhàrtainn) (d. 1718) as well as English and Welsh writers who also exerted a powerful influence over perceptions regarding Scotland in the eighteenth century such as Daniel Defoe (c. 1660–1731), Joseph Banks (1743–1820), Thomas Pennant (1726–1798), and Samuel Johnson (1709–1784). Deans also sheds lights on writers such as John Lettice (1737–1832) and Sarah Murray (1744–1811) who, writing at the end of the eighteenth century, developed the idea of the Scottish tour as 'a leisure practice not necessarily linked to the Enlightenment concerns of knowledge production and improvement'.[92]

While Deans's chapter provides a perspective on how Scotland became understood to the wider English-speaking world through the discourses of improvement, travel and tourism, Janet Sorensen's 'Scots and the Language of the Sea in Tobias Smollett's *Roderick Random* and William Falconer's *The Shipwreck*' suggests the ways in which the imaginative discourse regarding travelling Scots helped situate the Scottish nation – and the Scottish linguistic register – within an expansive sense of Britishness at the end of the eighteenth century. Taking as its focus two 'mariner Scots writers', Sorensen suggests how, in the face of negative perceptions of mobile Scots 'on the make', Smollett and Falconer 'repurposed representations of distance and mobility in sailors and sea language to cultivate sympathetic relations with itinerant Scots characters'.[93]

Our volume ends with another chapter that focuses on mobile Scots and that provides a transnational perspective on the topic of 'Environments of Space and Time'. In 'Ottobah Cugoano and Scotland's Minority Imperialist Culture', Michael Morris provides a new theoretical perspective on the connections between Scotland and the transatlantic slave trade as he suggests the 'structural significance of Scots' in Cugoano's life.[94] As Morris reveals, the slave owner who eventually bought Cugoano and brought him to Britain was Alexander Campbell Esq., a Highland Scot. In addition, Cugoano's important *Thoughts and Sentiments on the Evil and Wicked Traffic of the Slavery and Commerce of the Human Species, Humbly Submitted to the Inhabitants of Great Britain, by Ottobah*

Cugoano, a Native of Africa (1787) was written in response to the debate that another Highlander, James Ramsay (1733–1789), provoked upon the publication of his *Essay on the Treatment and Conversion of African Slaves in the British Sugar Colonies* (1784). Morris also examines Cugoano's condemnation in his *Thoughts and Sentiments* of Scots in the West Indies as 'the most barbarous slave-holders',[95] unfolding Cugoano's observations into a wider analysis of a phenomenon which Morris calls Scotland's 'Minority Imperialist Culture'. Morris traces this 'Minority Imperialist Culture' back to the early eighteenth century, after the Darien venture, and he suggests the term refers to the historic and ongoing power imbalances both within Scotland and within Scotland's relationship to the British state and imperial projects. Morris's call is also an invitation to imagine a future, reconfigured Scottish Studies that includes research dedicated to decolonising the field. As he notes, 'Figures such as Cugoano must be at the centre of efforts to recover the memory of [Scotland's relationship to the transatlantic slave trade], and their discursive strategies deserve close attention, revealing as they do the shifting lines of inclusion and exclusion of the archipelago in an Atlantic context.'[96]

As is evident, the arc of the chapters in this volume moves from a focus on local and national identity and history toward a late-eighteenth-century shift in apprehensions of geological time and a recognition of archipelagic space, expanding far beyond Scotland's shores. Taken together, these contributions offer proof that this is an exciting time to be studying and researching the Scottish literatures of the long eighteenth century as the subject is changing even as this book goes through its long production process. New editions of Allan Ramsay and Robert Burns are scheduled to appear that will generate new perspectives on those writers and the milieux in which they wrote.[97] A host of new digital humanities projects are also offering innovative ways of conducting and sharing research on Scottish literature in the long eighteenth century.[98] The World Congress of Scottish Literatures has been through two iterations and plans are underway for the next two conferences, including significant contributions by scholars of the eighteenth century. Meanwhile, the Association for Scottish Literary Studies and the International Association for the Study of Scottish Literatures continue to play an important role in mobilising interest in eighteenth-century Scottish Studies, both within Scotland and in a global context, as new perspectives and lenses on Scottish literature continue to be developed. Crucial to any new work in the field will be not only acknowledgement but also efforts to redress the profoundly unequal relations of this world system and the understanding of what might count as Scottish literature that it produced. It is our hope that, along with these projects, this *Companion* can provide new sources of curiosity and offer new inspiration for rethinking what the study of the Scottish literatures of the long eighteenth century might look like in the future.

PART 1: LANGUAGE, IDENTITY, AND HISTORY

CHAPTER ONE

Adaptation, Integration, and Renewal: Scottish Gaelic Literature, 1650–1750

Domhnall Uilleam Stiùbhart

The subject of this chapter is the verbal art composed by the people of the Scottish Gàidhealtachd – that is, the northern and western half of Scotland, or the Highlands and Islands – between the mid-seventeenth and mid-eighteenth centuries. They, along with the inhabitants of the Isle of Man and most of Ireland, spoke various dialects of a great language continuum from Caithness in the north to Munster in the south: what scholars call Q-Celtic, from which were codified the languages known today as Manx, Irish, and Scottish Gaelic.[1] During this period Gaelic-language 'literature' remained predominantly oral in nature, fluid and hybrid. This presents formidable challenges for researchers and editors; for example, several decades might elapse between a song's original composition and its being recorded on paper. Meantime, multiple variant versions might have arisen, as the song passed from singer to singer. Performers could misunderstand, 'improve', censor, or entirely recreate the original text – as could songmakers themselves during their creative careers. Intentionally or not, they could 'contaminate' the text with words, phrases, or entire stanzas from similar songs. In the absence of sheet music, song airs could and did alter drastically from singer to singer.

Yet, it is important to remember that in the Highlands verbal art has always co-existed with written culture: manuscripts and, later, printed material. Written classical or semi-classical poetry and prose could filter through recitation into oral tradition, while, by the same channels, written texts of orally performed vernacular items could help to stabilise transmission and standardise canons within oral culture, not only of songs, but of anecdotes concerning authors. I shall focus upon evidence from a variety of media, suggesting that, far from being timelessly traditional, early modern Scottish Gaelic culture was dynamic, endlessly changing and adaptive, the culture of a surprisingly cosmopolitan, increasingly hybrid nation.

Oral Literature in the Scottish Gàidhealtachd

At the beginning of the period, most people in the Scottish Gàidhealtachd lived under the clan system. Clans comprised notional kin-groups and affiliated families, focused upon the figure of the chief, the personal protector and administrator of justice for his clanspeople. During the century under consideration, the system – if not the ideal – of clanship gradually withered: chiefs and clan elites increasingly managed estates commercially, treating erstwhile clanspeople as rent-paying tenants. Factors driving this process include state pressure, elite indebtedness, and wider commercial opportunities, firstly cattle-droving, and subsequently sheepfarming, kelping, fishing, and raising British army regiments. The Scottish Gàidhealtachd was drawn into the political, economic, and cultural ambit of Britain and the wider British imperial world.[2]

Across the Scottish Gàidhealtachd, verbal art was powerful and pervasive. Creatively patterned, connotative language – spoken, chanted, or sung – entertained, praised, inspired, provoked, censured, and educated; it structured and interpreted events and experiences; it maintained – or challenged – existing social networks and social norms. At everyday work, individually or communally, indoors or outdoors – herding, milking, churning, reaping, flailing, grinding, rowing, or waulking cloth – songs passed and marked time. During winter evenings, village cèilidh houses were communal workspaces, or even community factories, for spinning thread, twining ropes, mending nets, and weaving baskets and creels, as well as performance venues for songs, poetry, stories, and music, where history and politics were debated, anecdotes, riddles, and badinage exchanged, and social mores, values, and outlooks moulded and reinforced for young and old alike. Even the most casual everyday conversations could be textured with proverbs, quotes, and pointed allusions. Lived, embodied, performed, oral culture offered power, intensity, and vitality, but it was also evanescent: no song was ever sung the same, no story-tellings exactly alike. Corresponding to the art of speaking, of course, was the art of listening, by a discerning audience who valued and responded to spontaneous wit; to vivid, inspired, and succinct expressions; and to a sophisticated and nuanced shared rhetoric of imagery, conventions, and expectations. In a society attuned to verbal and musical art, poets, performers, audiences, and eventual recorders all helped to fashion and inform early modern Scottish Gaelic literature.

Performance was open to everyone. Under certain circumstances, it could be insisted upon. Adroitly composed verses gave ritual access over thresholds in order to participate, as community members, in hospitality and good cheer. Every year gangs of men or boys would bang on doors, reciting their *Rann Challuinn* or Hogmanay Rhyme; the chief's bard might offer a formal blessing – a *Beannachadh Bàird* – when visiting a house on a poetic circuit; or a dinner guest might have to recite a couplet in order to resume his place at a gentry table.[3] As an extreme example, the semi-legendary itinerant poet-band of the *Cliar Sheanchain* were said to have billeted themselves upon hapless hosts for so long as their sallies of caustic wit met with no fitting ripostes.[4]

Although verbal art was omnipresent, it was also the poets' special province, whether professional *filidhean* literate in classical Gaelic, vernacular clan bards, old women who keened the dead for a living, or township versifiers. Particularly prominent in the literature was what John MacInnes famously termed the panegyric code: a customary stylistic register of symbolic formulae, metaphors, motifs, and images focused on the chief as the clan's warrior protector, praising his prowess, his noble virtues and attractiveness, splendid, cultured household, generous hospitality, and compassionate provision for the vulnerable.[5] Though the panegyric code's ideology may have focused upon the chief as epitome for the Gaelic political community's social and moral expectations, it should be emphasised that it is never merely descriptive. No chief, no warriors, no court ever conformed to the code's ideals: a rhetorical construct, it was designed to influence, persuade, and convince its audience – clan chief first and foremost – to adopt a stance, to take action.

Chiefly eulogies moulded by the panegyric code parallel the *specula principum* or mirrors of princes genre popular throughout medieval and early-modern European literature.[6] We can fruitfully compare the challenges for early modern Gaelic poets addressing their chiefs while employing a customary panegyric framework of rhetorical conventions and expectations – *laudando praecipere* – with the dilemmas faced by those offering counsel to sovereigns and magnates elsewhere in these islands.[7] Inevitable disparities between the idealised heroic world articulated in their verses, and messy, compromised, crisis-ridden reality could raise difficult questions concerning authority and legitimation, sparking debate, dissension, estrangement, and, occasionally, suppression.

The Wars of the Three Kingdoms and the Rise of Vernacular Gaelic Poetry

The Wars of the Three Kingdoms fought during the 1640s appear to have stimulated crucial innovations in Scottish Gaelic poetry and song. Among these were the increasing prominence of poets employing more vernacular styles and metres, the adoption of regional and national perspectives looking beyond individual clans, and, perhaps, the reinvigoration of a Scottish Gaelic identity. The Highlands had been drawn into the intense, drawn-out, political conflict that raged across Britain and Ireland, itself fundamentally an offshoot of the horrifying struggles then devastating mainland Europe in the Thirty Years War. In the region, campaigns were not fought by the clan elite alone as had been the case in earlier clan feuds. Now, war was waged on a much wider scale, employing levies raised from among clansmen themselves. As a result, what may have previously been a specifically aristocratic warrior ethos – perhaps even a more widely held notion of clan consciousness *tout court* – now affected all levels of society, spread through songs, stories, and lived experiences. Supporters of the royalist Clan Donald in particular composed adversarial songs to mobilise popular political opinion, relating martial events from a partisan perspective. Significantly, these songs did not use the mandarin classical language of the *filidhean*, the hereditary professional poets; rather, it was much closer to the vernacular spoken by the people they were striving to persuade.[8]

Among a number of other bards, the polemical work of Iain Lom ('Bald-headed John': John MacDonald, c. 1624–c. 1710) stands out. Fervently anti-Campbell, imbued with an urgent, hectoring *terribilità*, Iain Lom's songs offer us an echo in Gaelic of the unruly torrent of political news-sheets and propaganda ballads of contemporary English literature, themselves an outgrowth of the pamphlets, tracts, and broadsheets flooding from the popular press in Germany and beyond in the wake of apocalyptic Reformation and Counter-Reformation conflicts:

> Sgeul a b' aite nuair a thigeadh
> Air Caimbeulaich nam beul sligneach:
> H-uile dream dhiubh mar a thigeadh
> Le bualadh lann 'n ceann 'gam briseadh.

The most pleasing news whenever it came / About the twisted-mouthed Campbells: / Every company of them as they arrived / Had their heads broken with sword-blows.[9]

Parallel to the upsurge of vernacular Gaelic poetry dating from this decade are the numerous prose traditions regarding the wars, especially those narrating the exploits of the great royalist hero Alasdair mac Colla, stories still recounted three hundred years after that warrior's death.[10] This was a pan-Gaelic oral literature arising from a pan-Gaelic war – not merely songs and stories commemorating individual clan feuds. In this literature, we can perceive the developing concept of a pan-Gaelic identity, and the notion of a pan-Gaelic public opinion, as attested in a motif that grows increasingly prominent in vernacular song during the later seventeenth century: the catalogue of clan allies. A good example is found in a eulogy to Sir Donald MacDonald of Sleat, Domhnall a' Chogaidh, possibly by Màiri nighean Alasdair Ruaidh (Mary MacLeod, c. 1625– c. 1705), a poet belonging to the neighbouring clan of the MacLeods of Dunvegan:

> Tha deagh ghàrd air th' ainmealachd:
> Do chàirdean an t-Iarla Earra-Ghàidhealach,
> MacCoinnich is Morair Tairbeirt leat,
> Fir Bhealach is Bhràghaid-Albann leat,
> Gleann Garadh 's fir nan Garbh-chrìoch leat
> 'S an Colla-s' – cha bu chearbach e –
>   'S na Camshronaich o Lòchaidh.
>
> MacAoidh nam bratach meanmnach leat,
> Sìol Airt is Chuinn is Charmaig leat,
> Na Collanan cìosal armailteach
> Len loingis luchdmhoir gheal-bhrèidich
>   Air fairge 's iad a' seòladh [...]

Your fame is well guarded: / Your friends the Earl of Argyll, / MacKenzie and Viscount Tarbat, / The men of Taymouth and Breadalbane, / Glengarry, and the men of the Rough Bounds with you / And this Colla [of Keppoch] – a skilful man – / And the Camerons from Lochy. // Mackay of the high-spirited banners with you, / The seed of Art and Conn and Cormac with you, / The descendants of Colla with their vast tributes, / With their heavy-laden white-sailed fleet / Voyaging over the ocean [...][11]

The upheavals of the 1640s also witnessed the final destruction of the schools of classical Gaelic learning in Ireland, which had catered to sons from literate, hereditary 'learned order' families in Scotland as well.

Prominent among these were the professional poets, some of whom at least would have undergone several years of arduous instruction in Ireland: the *filidhean* who have already been mentioned. This highest grade of poets composed their work in the technically exacting *dán* metre, characterised by a fixed number of syllables per line with varying stresses, in classical Gaelic, the standard literary language of both Irish and Scottish Gàidhealtachds. By the late seventeenth century, few in Scotland composed or indeed read such poetry, with its archaic diction, compressed syntax, and recondite allusions.[12]

Even in the late medieval period, however, it is likely that only the principal kindreds in the Scottish Gàidhealtachd were wealthy enough to support a family of *filidhean*. The relative paucity of the classical poets in Scotland may have enabled the rise of the *bàird*, a group of poets who, strictly speaking, were allotted a lower status in the professional poetic hierarchy than the *filidhean*. Traditionally, the *bàrd*'s primary responsibility was to recite or chant the syllabic poetry of the *filidh*, but he was also permitted to compose vernacular verses in stressed metres. In the latter half of the seventeenth century, however, we see both men and women who were certainly not professional *filidhean* asserting for themselves high literary status as poetic representatives of their clans, composing not classical but high-register vernacular verse, in rhythmical, declamatory, non-symmetrical strophic metres: the type of poetry, it seems, that was traditionally composed by the *bàrd*.[13]

As with Neo-Latin on a wider European stage, across Ireland and the Scottish Highlands classical Gaelic had hitherto been a passport to a vigorously intellectual territory – *rēspūblica litterārum Gadelicārum*, we might say, a notional Republic of Gaelic Letters. Now, however, with its institutions of higher education in ruins, its citizenship no longer offered prospects of courtly support and preferment. In both Scotland and Ireland, classical, written Gaelic literature gradually faded away.

We should, however, not ignore a still under-researched spectrum of 'semi-bardic' or semi-classical verse, a heterogeneous blend of vernacular and classically-inflected language in loose syllabic metre that was the province of educated Gaelic-speaking gentry in both Ireland and Scotland.[14] This informal poetry deals with a wide variety of subjects, such as religion, nature, and love, and its Scottish variety might be compared to the heavily Latin-inflected aureate poetry in vogue among Lowland makars of the Renaissance. But such verse was not just an ornate display of recondite antiquarianism for private coteries. Its linguistic register – effectively Scottish Gaelic vernacular with greater or lesser degrees of classical embellishments – would still have been understood by people throughout the Gàidhealtachd. This was the style of the celebrated heroic Ossianic lays, semi-vernacularised versions of late medieval syllabic ballads, as well as of the popular prose romances, some of which were still being composed in the late eighteenth century.[15] Also, elements of classical Gaelic vocabulary would perhaps be familiar to most Protestant Scottish Gaels from its use in printed religious texts, particularly the Irish Bible transliterated into Roman script and printed in 1690. In Scotland, this elite genre of poetry lasted well into the eighteenth century.[16]

Gaelic Oral Literature in a Time of Transition, 1660–1740

In the second half of the seventeenth century, there was a rise in prominence in vernacular poetry not directly engaged with politics, particularly what we might call proto-romantic love song, composed in stressed, stanzaic òran or amhran metre. This genre's origins would appear to lie in the medieval vogue for courtly love poetry in western Europe that variously blossomed in the work of *trobadors, trouvères*, and *Minnesänger*. It is likely that, as with these poets, the performers of Gaelic *amhrain* formerly accompanied themselves on a harp or other stringed instrument. Like the bardic metres discussed above, *amhran* was a stressed or accentual metre, but in this case with symmetrical stanzas, usually, as William Matheson explains, comprising four phrases with an arching melody rising at its opening and falling at its conclusion.[17] By the end of the seventeenth century, however, songs in this genre increasingly drew upon contemporary English and Lowland Scots models. To investigate this further, we might borrow from medieval song scholarship the notion of contrafacture: the notion that a later text sharing a metrical scheme and, perhaps, similar complex rhyme endings and semantic motifs with an earlier text, even if composed in a different language, may well have been influenced by its predecessor.[18] Thus we find a growing number of Gaelic songs from this period – predominantly popular love songs – being composed in iambic metres: that is, lines made up of feet with an unstressed syllable followed by a stressed syllable. Such metres are more suited to the rhythm of English rather than Gaelic, so it is likely that we have here examples of Gaelic songs being composed to tunes borrowed across the Highland Line from English ones.[19] Incidentally, we can compare these iambic love songs to a very different poetic genre: the Gaelic translation of the first fifty Psalms published by the Presbyterian Synod of Argyll in 1659. To make the translation accessible, its language was heavily influenced by the spoken vernacular, but the Psalms had to be set 'sa ghne Meadrachd sin a tha comhuighach anosach don teangaidh Ghaoidhlig, chum gum biodh iad freagrach do na fonnaibh gallta' ('in that kind of metre that is now foreign to the Gaelic tongue, in order that they suited the Lowland tunes'): that is, iambic verse.[20]

As well as metrical parallels, we also find similar motifs and imagery used in late seventeenth-century Gaelic songs and in contemporary Lowland street ballads, especially regarding the popular persona of the idealised Highland 'noble savage': the genesis of the enduring trope of the romantic Highlander. This figure seems to have been coopted into Gaelic song as propaganda by *ceathairne* or caterans, Highland cattle rustlers who enjoyed the same public esteem – not to mention notoriety – as contemporary social bandits elsewhere such as Irish rapparees or English highwaymen. For example, in various renderings of the extremely popular song 'The Bonny Highland Laddie', we have verses such as:

> O'er benty Hill with him I'll run
> And leave my Lawland Kin and Dady
> Frae Winter's Cauld and Summer's Sun
> He'll screen me with his Highland Plaidy

or:

> Thoul't row me in thy tartan plaidy[21]

In a song ascribed to the famous cattle raider Domhnall Donn, 'Thogainn fonn gun bhith trom' ('*I'd sing a tune that wasn't heavy*'), this imagery seems to have been remodelled into Gaelic:

> Lùib mi i 'nam breacan fhèin,
> Leam a b' èibhinn mar thachair.
>
> Biodh sneachd ann 's gaoth a tuath,
> Phaisginn suas i 'nam achlais.

I folded her in my own tartan plaid, / For me it was joyful what happened. // Let there be snow and a north wind, / I would fold her up under my arm.[22]

Some of the most infamous caterans were drawn from the Clan Gregor, a kindred who had been outlawed and dispossessed from their territories in Highland Perthshire at the beginning of the seventeenth century. MacGregor refugees were now dispersed widely across the Gàidhealtachd; it is likely that they were responsible for the remarkably extensive distribution and popularity of tragic love songs concerning their plight, songs paralleling and drawing upon the imagery of more formal elegies in the classical Gaelic tradition.[23]

In the late seventeenth century the *amhran* tradition was brought to a high degree of creative achievement by Ruairidh MacGilleMhoire, known as An Clàrsair Dall (Roderick Morrison, The Blind Poet, c. 1645–c. 1714). Probably trained in Ireland, Ruairidh later served as harper – and possibly clan bard as well – for the chief Iain Breac MacLeòid of Dunvegan. As William Matheson pointed out in his outstanding edition of the poet's work, now that older poetic conventions were breaking down, the Blind Harper was able to make innovative use of the flexibility and fluidity of sung *amhran* metre.[24] In the past, the metre was probably used for more informal subjects; MacGilleMhoire, however, used it to compose eulogies and elegies drawing upon the heroic imagery of the panegyric code, but modulated through a more subjective and reflective poetic voice. This gives an unusual personal depth and sincerity to his praise of his patron Iain Breac – and also sharpens his forthright indictment of the chief's spendthrift son in his celebrated 'Òran Mòr MhicLeòid' ('*The Great Song of MacLeod*'), effectively an elegy to the entire clan system:

> Chaidh a' chuibhle mun cuairt,
> Ghrad thionndaidh gu fuachd am blàths:
> Gum faca mi uair
> Dùn ratha nan cuach 'n seo thràigh,
> Far 'm biodh tathaich nan duan,
> Iomadh mathas gun chruas, gun chàs:
> Dh'fhalbh an latha sin uainn,
> 'S tha na taighean gu fuaraidh fàs.

The wheel of fortune has come round, / Suddenly the warmth has turned to cold: / But I once saw here / A prosperous castle, full of drinking cups now empty, / Once frequented by poems, / With much bounty given generously, readily: / That day has gone from us, / And the buildings are chill and deserted.[25]

The world of the Scottish Gàidhealtachd was indeed transforming. Against a background of ever more commercial estate management, absenteeism, conspicuous expenditure, and rising debt, power and patronage roles and relationships within kindreds were transformed. This led to a readjustment – or even an abdication altogether – of chiefly social responsibility.[26] Imbued with cultural perspectives arising from a Lowland or English education, increasingly acting as commercial landlords, chiefs no longer recognised poets' mandate to offer public counsel. This was especially the case when their songs, mourning loss and urging renewal, risked exacerbating already rising social and political tensions.

We can see comparable literary innovations to those of the Blind Harper – again synthesising heroic panegyric conventions with a passionate individual voice – in the work of the trio of great women poets of the late seventeenth and early eighteenth centuries. The songs of Màiri nighean Alasdair Ruaidh – like those of the Blind Harper – are primarily focused upon the clan she belonged to, the MacLeods of Dunvegan. Her most powerful eulogies, *Fuaim an Taibh* (*The Sound of the Ocean*) and *An Crònan* (*The Croon*), use the irregular strophic metre of the bàrd, gaining added emotional vigour from employing the diction, imagery, and intimate address of women's waulking songs, and the traditional women's genres of lullaby and ritual lament.[27] Màiri appears in the oral tradition as a nursemaid in the MacLeod household, as well as being associated with keening. Despite her claims to be composing *crònain*, or (private, domestic) croons, rather than (public) *amhrain*, oral tradition states that, as with the Blind Harper, Màiri's outspoken candour seems to have earned her several years in exile.[28]

In contrast to the Blind Harper and Màiri nighean Alasdair Ruaidh, from the later seventeenth century onwards several Maclean poets composed their work during their own chief's exile following the Campbell takeover of much of the Duart estate in Mull and Tiree. These poets were thus faced with the challenge of sustaining the tradition of clan poetry without the presence of the chief himself. They had to speak on behalf of the community (with necessary circumspection), conserve the memory of the lavishness and generosity of the erstwhile Maclean court – and keep hopes alive of a triumphant homecoming.[29] Prominent among the poetry of the Macleans are the songs of Mairearad nighean Lachlainn (Margaret Maclean, c. 1660–c. 1751), the best of which are characterised by an intimate, impassioned voice, above all in her lament for Sir John Maclean of Duart who had died in the final stages of the 1715 Jacobite Rising:

> 'S goirt leam gaoir nam ban Muileach,
> Iad ri caoineadh 's ri tuireadh
> Gun Sir Iain an Lunnainn
> Na san Fhraing air cheann turais:
> 'S trom an sac thug ort fuireach –
> Gun thu dh'fhalbh air an luingeas
> Gur h-e adhbhar ar dunach;
>   'S òg a choisinn thu an t-urram sna blàraibh.

The wailing of the Mull women is painful for me / As they weep and lament, / Sir John being neither in London / Nor on a visit to France: / Heavy is the burden that made you remain – / The cause of our woe / Is that you did not leave with the ships: / You earned honour on the battlefields when you were young.[30]

Oral traditions state that both Màiri nighean Alasdair Ruaidh and Mairearad nighean Lachlainn participated in ritual lament. If they were indeed adept in a genre which allowed women the opportunity publicly to articulate their grief and grievances, accomplishing 'emotional labour' in highly dramatic, compelling, and skilled performances, this might help us better to understand their situation, and better to appreciate their art.[31]

The third major Gaelic woman poet of this period, Sìleas na Ceapaich (Cicely or Giles MacDonald, c. 1660–c. 1729), daughter of Gilleasbaig, chief of the MacDonells of Keppoch, offers a further contrast. Sìleas spent most of her life on her husband's estates on the borders of the eastern Gàidhealtachd, far from her native Lochaber: a form of domestic exile doubtless all too common for women of gentry status in the region at the time. Unlike Mairearad nighean Lachlainn, Sìleas evidently knew English, and was acquainted with popular English literature: her *Còmhradh ris a' Bhàs* (*Conversation with Death*) is, as Colm Ó Baoill points out, indebted to the contemporary ballad *Death and the Lady*.[32] Sìleas's most striking work is her supercharged elegy, almost an apotheosis of the panegyric code, for Alasdair Dubh of Glengarry:

> Bu tu 'n loch nach fhaoidte thaomadh,
> Bu tu tobar faoilidh na slàinte,

Bu tu Beinn Nibheis thar gach aonach,
Bu tu chreag nach fhaoidte theàrnadh;
Bu tu clach uachdair a' chaisteil,
Bu tu leac leathann na sràide,
Bu tu leug lòghmhor nam buadhan,
Bu tu clach uasal an fhàinne.

You were the loch that could not be drained, / You were the generous well of health, / You were Ben Nevis above every ridge, / You were the cliff that could not be descended; / You were the keystone of the castle, / You were the broad flagstone of the street, / You were the bright crystal of virtues, / You were the noble jewel in the ring.[33]

Sìleas's songs demonstrate how, during the early eighteenth century, national, political and religious issues were increasingly preoccupying and polarising the people of the Gàidhealtachd. A Jacobite and a Catholic, she composed a biting satire on King George I, as well as a series of hymns teaching Counter-Reformation doctrine, notably a twenty-seven-stanza life of Christ that was still sung in Catholic districts within living memory.[34] Sìleas na Ceapaich comes across as a particularly vivid personality among her poetic contemporaries, in part because of the number of extant family lullabies and laments we have that were composed by her. This could, however, be a simple stroke of fortune: a single manuscript source derived from her own kindred preserved half of the twenty or so songs attributable to her, including the most private and personal.

Jacobite Poetry and the Genius of Alasdair mac Mhaighstir Alasdair

From the 1690s onwards, Jacobitism – the clandestine movement to restore by force the exiled Stuart kings to the British throne – played a significant role in the politics and culture of the Scottish Gàidhealtachd.[35] At different times during the first half of the eighteenth century, many Gaels at all levels of society were alienated from the British state, for many different reasons. Their disaffection is not necessarily due to mulish traditionalism and blind loyalty to the House of Stuart, excuses asserted as expiation for their rebelliousness by many Gaels themselves after Jacobite defeats and still tacitly assumed by some historians today. There were other pressing reasons for Gaels to be uneasy with political and economic circumstances in the Highlands, particularly in the years before the final Jacobite rising of 1745. On the one hand, centralising authoritarian landlords and their counsellors, eager to profit from commercial competition, were beginning to 'creatively disrupt' their estates by eliminating the tacksmen managerial class and so extracting increased rents directly from the tenantry.[36] On the other, the government in London, increasingly preoccupied with mercantile opportunities beyond the Atlantic, was neglecting earlier undertakings to promote regional development in the Highlands.[37] We might even portray the 1745 Rising as an attempted *coup d'état*, with some members of a relatively penurious elite seeking to thrust themselves from the periphery of empire into its core. For all the propagandist appeals to nativist Stuart loyalties, more hard-headed aspirations for financial security and land, in ever more discouraging circumstances, may have motivated many Gaels to rise for Charles. Similar considerations would later impel some of their descendants to emigrate to America and beyond. As an example, the poet's promise in an *òran brosnachaidh* or 'song of incitement' composed during the 1745 Rising by Alasdair mac Aonghais (c. 1665–c. 1745) from Glencoe, would be echoed in emigrant songs later in the century:

> Gheibh sibh pailteas gach dùthcha,
>   Chan e ur dùthchas as nì leibh,
> Agus ragha gach fearainn
>   Gun ghearradh gun chìs air.

You shall have plenty of every country, / More than the territory of your ancestors, / And the choice of every land / Without tribute or tax on it.[38]

One particular strand of Jacobite songs in the first half of the eighteenth century strongly echoes the royalist poetry already touched upon from the Wars of the Three Kingdoms. It urges murderous, pitiless exploits on the field, incites powerful anti-Campbell animus, and offers extended lists of allies in order to encourage refractory kindreds and forestall accusations of disorder and internal divisions. But fundamental to later Jacobite poetry, and also to subsequent poetry of the Clearances, are feelings of dispossession: resentment, nostalgia, internal exile, and hopes of restoration. These themes are anticipated in songs already referred to, composed and disseminated by MacGregors in the wake of that clan's persecution and proscription; and in works by bards on the Maclean of Duart estates following the expulsion of many gentry of that kindred by the Campbells of Argyll in the later seventeenth century.

Much later Jacobite poetry is a propagandist re-creation and reinvigoration of clan panegyric at a time when, as we have seen, the clan system itself was already clearly on the wane. It is already imbued with the Highland romanticism we have seen developing in popular song on both sides of the Highland Line since the end of the seventeenth century. Taken as a whole, poetry of the 1745 Rising offers us a plethora of different voices and perspectives on its events: optimism and calls to action during the campaign; bitterness and disorientation after Culloden; threats of bloodthirsty revenge following British atrocities throughout the region; modulating into later efforts to rally a united Gaelic front to avenge the humiliation of the heavy-handed Act of Proscription.[39] There are also songs offering other standpoints to the sorry affair: a ludicrous attempt to recast Simon Lord Lovat as a saintly martyr for the cause; the farcical chaos of the redcoat rout at Falkirk; the heart-breaking pathos of Caitrìona Fhearghasdan's lament for her husband William Chisholm, slain at Culloden:

> Och a Theàrlaich òig Stiùbhairt, 's e do chùis rinn mo lèireadh;
> Thug thu uam gach nì bh' agam ann an cogadh nad adhbhar;
> Cha chrodh is cha chaoraich tha mi caoidh ach mo chèile,
> Ged a dh'fhàgte mi 'm aonar gun sian san t-saoghal ach lèine,
> Mo rùn geal òg.

Och, young Charles Stuart, your cause has tormented me; / You took everything from me in the war on your behalf; / Not cattle nor sheep am I mourning, but my husband, / Although I was left alone with nothing in the world but my shirt, / My dear young love.[40]

Dominating Jacobite poetry, and eighteenth-century Gaelic culture as a whole, is the figure of Alasdair MacDhomhnaill, Alexander MacDonald (c. 1700–c. 1770) from Moidart, known to posterity as Alasdair mac Mhaighstir Alasdair, Alexander the son of the Reverend Alexander, his father being a redoubtable episcopalian clergyman. The modern language and culture carry Mac Mhaighstir Alasdair's stamp. He is a poet of protean talents, endless invention, and immense ambition; a pioneer song collector; a pioneer lexicographer and 'language planner'; and a man whose life reflects the events he lived through: university student in Glasgow; apprentice lawyer in Edinburgh; ill-advised 'Protestant' claimant to his Catholic chief's estate; catechist and teacher of English to Ardnamurchan schoolchildren on behalf of the Society in Scotland for Propagating

Christian Knowledge, the SSPCK; Gaelic tutor to Prince Charles; captain on Culloden field; factor on the Isle of Canna; author of the first secular printed book in Scottish Gaelic; internal émigré after the Jacobite fiasco. Possessing perspectives beyond most of his contemporaries, Mac Mhaighstir Alasdair played many different social roles – not always altogether adroitly – and these are mirrored in the many styles and poetic personae rehearsed in his work. One persona not adopted, however, was that of clan bard, a position to which he was suited neither by circumstance – he was apparently estranged from his Clan Ranald chief – nor by temperament. Of course, had events turned out otherwise, Mac Mhaighstir Alasdair might well – and deservedly so – have accepted the post of Gaelic poet laureate from the one man he did praise: Prince Charles Edward Stuart.[41]

His poetry is in turns ironic, frank, convivial, experimental, passionate, ebullient, often disconcertingly wayward: *càilein san fhiacail*, as it were, 'a husk in the teeth' (or, perhaps, 'grit in the oyster') of the Gaelic literature he did so much to establish. He was the first to try out Augustan poetic trends, diction, and voices, offering *Òran an t-Samhraidh* and *Òran a' Gheamhraidh*, songs of summer and of winter, as Highland responses to James Thomson's nature poetry.[42] His riotous exercises to pìobaireachd metre *Moladh Mòrag* and *Dìomholadh Mòrag*, praise and dispraise of the allegedly allegorical Morag, are contrasting poetic explorations of idealised romanticism on the one hand, and misogynistic obscene satire on the other. Mac Mhaighstir Alasdair's major work is *Birlinn Chlann Raghnaill* (*Clan Ranald's Galley*), a communal, masculine, vernacular epic rather than a classical panegyric focused upon a single individual, tellingly premised on an eventful voyage from Scotland to Carrickfergus in Ireland, whose epic storm-scene, as Ronald Black has suggested, may well recall the chaos of the Battle of Culloden, the final devastating defeat of the Jacobites in 1746:

> Dh'fhosgail a' mhuir gorm 'na chraosaibh
>   Farsaing cràcach,
> An glaicibh a chèile ri taosgadh,
>   'S caonnag bhàsmhor.
>
> Gum b' fhear-ghnìomh bhith ag amharc 'n aodann
>   Nam maoim teinntidh,
> Lasraichean sradanach sionnachain
>   Air gach beinn diubh.

Na beulanaich àrda liath-cheann
  Ri searbh-bheucail,
Na cùlanaich 's an cladh dùldaidh
  Ri fuaim-gheumnaich [...]

The blue sea opened up in great gullets / Wide and foaming, / Struggling with each other, overflowing, / In mortal contention. // A man's task it was to stare / The fiery torrents in the face, / Flashing flames of phosphorescence / On every mountain of them. // The high, grey-crested leading waves, / Bitterly roaring, / The hinder waves, and their gloomy trough / Noisily bellowing [...][43]

Mac Mhaighstir Alasdair also composed English prose accounts of the 1745 Rising, in both fact and fiction, and also recorded at least one tale in classical Gaelic. But although he could read and write classical Gaelic script, his book *Ais-eiridh na Sean Chánoin Albannaich* (*The Resurrection of the Ancient Scottish Language*, 1751) is a work emphatically of and for vernacular Scottish Gaelic. In the preface, Mac Mhaighstir Alasdair, 'a lover of his country', patriotically portrays the language as 'the depositary [sic] of the manners, customs, and notions of the earliest inhabitants of this land'. As he goes on to explain, he has refashioned the spelling of the language to make it as accessible to readers as possible. Finally, unlike his contemporaries, he does not describe this language as 'Irish' or 'Erse', as it were a tongue foreign to Scotland; rather, his poems are composed in 'the GALIC language', or as the title states, 'an t-seann chànan Albannach', 'the ancient Scottish language'.[44]

Conclusion

Although necessarily brief and allusive, this chapter has delineated certain key aspects of the history of song and poetry composed in the Scottish Gàidhealtachd between the mid-seventeenth and the mid-eighteenth centuries. It has emphasised two specific moments of political crisis, insecurity, and ideological confrontation opening and closing the period, when opposing sides struggled to rally the loyalty and secure the assent of the people of the Gàidhealtachd, making use of their own vernacular and culture to do so. In an effort to win popular support and legitimacy during the highly polarised conflicts of the 1640s, propagandists and adherents on both sides sidelined classical Gaelic literary norms in favour of vernacular registers of style, grammar, and vocabulary that were more comprehensible to ordinary people in the Gàidhealtachd, whether in songs acclaiming the Stuart cause, or in Presbyterian Psalms. A century later there was another political crisis in the region. This time, however, it took place in a society where an increasing number of young people were learning to read and write, particularly in the extensive network of charity schools teaching English, supervised by the SSPCK.[45] As before, both supporters of the House of Stuart and Presbyterian loyalists needed to inspire and motivate the people of the Highlands to accept their interpretation of past and present, and to take action to fulfil their vision of the future. Promulgating their message effectively among the people of the Gàidhealtachd required the adoption of an altogether more vernacular, accessible register in Gaelic, this time in written as well as in oral culture: the first steps towards the codification of the language we know today as Scottish Gaelic – and, in its wake, the creation of a Scottish Gaelic literary canon.

CHAPTER TWO

Poems in the Scots Register, 1650–1800

Corey E. Andrews

This chapter focuses on poems in the Scots register written from 1660 to 1800, seeking to assess continuity as well as gaps in this tradition of Scottish literature. An array of poets and works are examined in order to determine common formal and thematic traits, as well as the relationship of poems in the Scots register to questions of national identity. The chapter concludes with a brief discussion of the tradition of Scots verse in the early nineteenth century, with particular reference to the abiding influence of Robert Burns.

Preliminary Definition

It is important first to define the meaning of the term Scots register in the Scottish poetic tradition. Register is a literary term used to describe language usage in poetry, with singular attention to the influence of social factors on a poet's stylistic choices.[1] Register is related to tone, in that both can influence readers' interpretations of poetic works in ways often unrelated to the immediate subject matter.[2] Where register differs from tone is in specific linguistic choices evident throughout a poem, words or phrases that evoke an extratextual social dimension that colours a reader's interpretation. For instance, a poem composed of formal and slang English forces the reader to contend with not only the associations of the diction but also the social disparity evident in their juxtaposition. In the case of poems in the Scots register, this refers directly to the poet's use of Scots diction and/or phrasing; the poet's linguistic choices influence the reader's extratextual perceptions of social factors in the works, particularly in those poems composed with a blend of Scots and English diction. More generally, register in literary writing can also refer to a work's formality of address; in poems in the Scots register, this address is frequently perceived as informal and vernacular, an effect greatly influenced by the poet's usage of Scots diction and phrasing. As will be discussed, poems in the Scots register are often perceived as conveying a national means of address, whereby Scots language usage is regarded as a key marker of Scottish identity. This is conveyed to both poet and readers who are capable of understanding and appreciating Scots in addition to English. This national element of poetic register becomes increasingly prevalent during the eighteenth century, finding expression most notably in the works of Robert Burns.

Scots Verse in the Late Seventeenth Century

When compared to the abundance of Middle Scots verse by late medieval makars like Robert Henryson and William Dunbar, late seventeenth-century Scotland appears a rather barren terrain for poems in the Scots register. In many ways this reflects the deleterious effects of the Crown's removal from Edinburgh to London in 1603, which diminished opportunities for court patronage of Scottish poets. Of poets who remained in Scotland after the Union of Crowns, the work of William Drummond of Hawthornden (1585–1649) is a representative example of early to mid-seventeenth century poetic practice. A friend of Ben Jonson (1572–1637), Drummond wrote in English and Latin, employing many conventional poetic modes and genres with an 'almost complete absence of any Scottish markers in the language'.[3] In this respect, he resembled his English contemporary Jonson more than his Scottish predecessors; in addition, Drummond's wealth provided him with necessary resources for his literary endeavours that many fellow Scottish poets lacked.

However, in the late seventeenth century, a rich vein of poems in the Scots register remained in the form of ballads. The 'great wealth of traditional balladry' in Scotland provides a powerful counterpart at this time to the prevalence of English verse by Scottish poets.[4] Derived from the Norman French *balade* ('sung story'), Scottish ballads during this period were anonymously composed and transmitted orally, creating opportunities for textual variation once they were gathered and edited. Although most of the ballads from this time were collected in the eighteenth and nineteenth centuries, they were preserved in performance and often printed and distributed in handbills by the singers themselves.[5] Many of these ballads are narrative in form and content, providing a descriptive plot and characters, a single dramatic incident, and much dialogue. As with other specimens of orally composed narrative, the ballads use a 'common measure', a rhymed quatrain with alternating four- and three-stress lines.⁶ Common themes of ballads include tragedies created by treachery and deceit, often resulting in murder, as well as tragic love relationships ending in death. While these are themes common to ballads in other national traditions, Scottish ballads often 'use Scots language forms' and have 'Scottish backgrounds, contexts, and references', as well as 'Scottish historical topics, events, persons, [and] places'.⁷

Of the many ballads collected from this period, 'The Gaberlunzie Man' is a fine example of the Scottish tradition; the Scots ballad depicts the wiles of a 'gaberlunzie man' (beggar) who seeks the hospitality of a 'Gudewife' on a cold evening. Once invited in, the gaberlunzie man cosies up to the roaring fire with the gudewife's daughter, and he soon begins to woo her, begging her to go 'awa' wi' me'.⁸ She agrees to steal away with him that night, leaving the gudewife to panic the next morning and threaten to burn her daughter and kill the beggar. However, her efforts to find the couple come to naught. Meanwhile, the pair travels from town to town, begging and spinning yarn for sustenance, and the gaberlunzie man promises to teach the gudewife's daughter how to speak 'the beggar's tongue'⁹ and 'carry the gaberlunzie on'.¹⁰ A similar ballad from the period is 'The Jolly Beggar', which also recounts the seduction of a host's daughter by a cunning beggar; however, in this poem, deception is also practiced by the daughter upon the beggar. After their sexual encounter, the daughter is shocked to discover that the beggar is really a 'poor body' and not 'some gentleman, at least the laird of Brodie' that she had hoped.¹¹ The beggar gives her money to pay for a wet-nurse and leaves, only to reveal himself to the reader as a nobleman, 'the brawest gentleman' in the land.¹² In this respect 'The Jolly Beggar' resembles other popular works from this period that feature a king in disguise among common folk.¹³

In addition to the Scottish tradition of balladry at this time, there were two poets writing verse in the Scots register. The work of the Sempills of Beltrees (Renfrewshire) led the noted anthologist of Scottish poetry George Eyre-Todd to remark that 'the poetical annals of Scotland in the troublous latter half of the seventeenth century are illuminated almost solely by the productions of a single family'.¹⁴ The peculiarity of this feature of Scottish literary history is amplified by the fact that the work of the poets is 'written for the most part in the Scottish vernacular, and not in the fashionable English of the court'.¹⁵ The father Robert Sempill (c. 1595–c. 1665) is primarily remembered for a single poem entitled 'Habbie Simson', which provided the template for the 'standard Habbie stanza' used by many Scottish poets in the eighteenth century. While the 'Habbie stanza' is not unique to Sempill, his version – a sestet rhymed

AAABAB – was the primary model for the later Scots innovations of Allan Ramsay (1684–1758), Robert Fergusson (1750–1774) and Robert Burns (1759–1796). 'Habbie Simson' is a Scots elegy mourning the death of Kilbarchan's local piper who had 'played before the spear-men [soldiers]' in local fairs and 'gart [made] his pipe [...] / Baith skirl [shriek] and screed [scream]' at horse races.[16] The loss is felt throughout the community, emphasised by the repeated last line 'Sen Habbie's dead' of each stanza; given Simson's many contributions to civic harmony recounted throughout the poem's fourteen stanzas, Kilbarchan as a whole deeply mourns its fallen piper.

The Scots works of Sempill's son, Francis (c. 1616–1682), reveal a similar interest in social roles and communal experience, evident in poems like 'Maggie Lauder' and 'Hallow Fair'. The former poem narrates an encounter between the titular character and a poor piper named Rob the Ranter, who has heard of 'bonny Maggie Lauder' and is 'fidging fain' (anxious) to meet her.[17] Though she calls him a 'hallanshaker' (beggar) and a 'bladderskate' (foolish person), she informs Rob that 'I've heard o' you' and dances to his playing 'for brawly could she frisk it'.[18] This pleases Rob immensely, who remarks that it is 'worth my while to play indeed, / When I hae sic [such] a dancer'.[19] The poem ends with Maggie's compliment to Rob that 'there's nane in Scotland plays sae weel / Since we lost Habbie Simson'.[20] A source of inspiration for Robert Fergusson, Robert Burns and John Mayne, Sempill's poem 'Hallow Fair' uses the social event of the title to represent the drinking and frolicking of 'mony braw Jockies and Jennies'.[21] Assorted folk customs are recounted, as is the superstitious concern that 'Auld Nick' is prowling about; these features clearly influenced Burns's 'Halloween', in which Scottish courtship rituals associated with the night are represented at length.[22] Other poems of interest by Francis Sempill include his account of wedding customs in 'Fy, Let Us A' to the Bridal', a poem written in the persona of James, Duke of York and Albany (the future James VII/II) entitled 'The Banishment of Poverty' in which the duke provides a much-needed loan to the poet, and a ten-stanza version of the song 'Old Longsyne' that would be later adapted by both Allan Ramsay and Robert Burns.

The works of the father and son Sempills exhibit many strong characteristics of verse in the Scots register nearing the end of the seventeenth century, particularly in their persistent interest in local communities and social customs. Eyre-Todd observes that their work provides a 'picture of the character, manners, and merriment of ancient Scottish rural life' that was 'unsurpassed by anything in the popular literature of the country'.[23]

The Sempills' poetic representations of Scottish life are focused largely on rural communities that maintain social ties through local customs and rituals. Social roles are also represented as significant features of Scottish identity, embodied in gaberlunzie-men, local pipers like Habbie Simson, and strong women like Maggie Lauder. In all cases, poems in the Scots register from this period use Scots to mark and emphasise the distinctiveness of local communities and their role in delineating and defining Scottish identity.

Scots Verse in the Early Eighteenth Century

The association of Scots verse with the expression of national identity became intensified after the Act of Union in 1707. Scotland's loss of political independence was met with considerable popular resistance, and the event was memorably described by the Earl of Seafield, Lord Chancellor of Scotland as the 'end of an auld sang'.[24] In the year prior to the Act of Union, the Scottish printer James Watson sought to enshrine these 'auld sangs' in *A Choice Collection of Serious and Comic Scots Poems, Both Ancient and Modern*, described in its preface as 'the first of its nature which has been published in our own native Scots dialect'.[25] Watson's anthology contained Scots works not only from the medieval makars but also immediate predecessors like the Sempills of Beltree; in addition, numerous Scots ballads and songs were included in the collection. Watson definitely wished the volume to be seen in national terms, stating in the preface that 'the frequency of publishing collections of miscellaneous poems in neighbouring kingdoms and states, may, in great measure, justify an undertaking of this kind with us'.[26] T. F. Henderson links Watson's *Choice Collection* with other 'symptoms of awakening interest in Scottish vernacular verse' and describes the works in the collection as 'sufficiently noteworthy as the first important symptoms of the dawn of a great vernacular revival'.[27]

The first major Scots poet of the early eighteenth century was Allan Ramsay, a wigmaker turned poet, bookseller, and theatre impresario who continued the tradition of Scots verse found in Watson's *Choice Collection*. Ramsay was a resolutely urban poet who was well-versed in Edinburgh's local patois and shrewdly aware of the differing currents in the city's commercial and literary cultures. An intriguing feature of Ramsay's poetic development was his decision to devote equal attention to works in English and those in Scots, crafting verse that would cater to the demands of different communities of readers in Scotland and beyond. His first works to appear were broadsides modelled after Robert Sempill's 'Habbie Simson' elegy, designed to be sold and read in the city streets. Of these works, 'Lucky Spence's Last Advice' is presented as the dying words of 'a famous bawd who flourished for several years about the beginning of the eighteenth century' near Holyroodhouse.[28] In the 'Habbie stanza', Lucky offers words of consolation and hard-earned wisdom to her 'loving lasses',[29] urging them to take advantage of a drunken client by helping him 'drive at the jango [liquor] till he spew'[30] and then proceed to rob him for all he's worth. The 101-line elegy is written with abundant Scots diction, a feature which is also found in Ramsay's 'Elegy on Lucky Wood in the Canongate, May 1717'. This poem is clearly indebted to Robert Sempill's 'Habbie Simson', also employing the 'Habbie stanza' and mourning the loss of an alehouse keeper who kept the denizens of the Canongate as happy as Simson had with his piping in Kilbarchan. One key difference in Ramsay's approach to the mock-elegy is his comic use of hyperbole, evident in the following lines about Lucky Wood: 'She's dead and gane, / Left us and Willie burd alane, / To bleer [cry] and greet [weep], to sob and mane [moan], / And rugg [pull] our hair, / Because we'll ne'r see her again / For evermair'.[31] The mock-elegy in Scots becomes a subgenre of its own as the century continues, indebted to Ramsay's alert ironies in such lines praising Lucky's generous propensity to 'cram our wames [bellies] for naithing'.[32]

Ramsay composed other mock-elegies in Scots at this point in his career, including an 'Elegy on Maggie Johnston' (another alehouse keeper), an 'Elegy on Patie Birnie' (a Kinghorn fiddler in the mold of Habbie Simpson), and a satirical 'Elegy on John Cowper Kirk-Treasurer's Man' (a 'citizen respected for riches and honesty' who abuses his power to 'seize and imprison the girls that are too impatient to have on their green gown before it be hemmed').[33] Ramsay was also an avid anthologist of Scots verse and song, publishing the successful song collections *The Tea-Table Miscellany* (1724) and *The Evergreen: Being a Collection of Scots Poems, Wrote by the Ingenious before 1600* (1724), the latter of which also includes a Middle Scots poem of Ramsay's invention entitled 'The Vision'. He became best known as the author of the Scots pastoral drama *The Gentle Shepherd* (1725), as well as for being the father of Allan Ramsay the Younger (future Principal Painter in Ordinary to George III and friend of Samuel Johnson; 1713–1784). Ramsay's works in English include a Popean imitation 'The Morning Interview' (1719), a topical poem on the South Sea Bubble entitled 'Wealth, or the Woody' (1720), and a philosophical verse essay called 'Content' (1719).

When Ramsay began to prepare his own works for publication in the 1720s, he included a series of verse epistles in Scots written to fellow poets, Edinburgh notables, and London litterateurs. Among the recipients was William Hamilton of Gilbertfield (1670–1751), a Scots poet whose poem 'The Last Dying Words of Bonnie Heck, a Famous Greyhound in the Shire of Fife' added the animal to the repertory of the Scots mock-elegy. Showing the influence of Robert Sempill, Hamilton's elegy offers the perspective of the dying dog as a satirical lens on human affairs (a technique used later to great effect by Robert Burns). Bonnie Heck reflects on the passing of time, lamenting that 'because I'm cripple, auld, and lame', he can no longer do 'great feats I have done mysel' when 'I was souple, young, and fell [fierce]'.[34] Like Lucky Spence, Bonnie Heck has advice to dispense to the young, in this case puppies 'which I gat on a bonnie lady';[35] he exhorts his brood to be 'baith clever, keen, and beddy [eager to seize prey]'[36] and never to forget to 'clink [strike or thrash] it like their ancient daddy, / The famous Heck'.[37] Hamilton of Gilbertfield is best remembered, however, for *Wallace* (1722), his 'modernised' version of Blind Hary's Middle Scots epic; Burns in particular greatly praised Hamilton's Scots translation, stating that 'the story of Wallace poured a Scottish prejudice in my veins which will boil along there till the flood-gates of life shut in eternal rest'.[38] Henderson describes this work as 'the greatest, if not the best achievement of Hamilton', which 'commended itself by its subject to the patriotic Scot, and achieved an instant and lasting popularity'.[39]

Another contemporary Scots poet from this period, Lady Grizzel Bailie (1665–1746), wrote primarily in the ballad tradition of the tragic love affair ending in death. Her ballad 'There Ance Was a May' describes the reclusive life of a 'may' [maiden] who 'loo'd na men', owing to her embittered sister's prevention of her marriage to 'bonnie young Johnnie'.[40] The resulting disaffection plagues both the 'may' and Johnnie, who allows his family's desire for a wealthier bride to override his love for the 'may'. The last stanza highlights the final tragedy of this affair, which ends not in actual death but in a kind of living death; the speaker recognises that 'were I but young for thee, as I hae been, / We should hae been gallopin' doun on yon green, / And linkin'-it [arm in arm] on the lily-white lea'.[41] The speaker's nostalgia poignantly addresses the time that she has lost waiting, offering a decidedly bittersweet remembrance of things past.

Lady Elizabeth Wardlaw (1677–1727) also wrote in the ballad tradition, and her best-known poem 'Hardyknute' is a Scots folk ballad that was initially shrouded in notoriety. Represented by Wardlaw as a genuine 'ancient' poem found in a vault in Dunfermline, 'Hardyknute' recounts the battle between the Scottish warrior Hardyknute (in service to King Alexander III) against Norse invaders during the thirteenth-century battle at Largs.[42] The poem follows in the ballad tradition of works like 'Sir Patrick Spens', in which duty to the king and nation overrides all other concerns; it is also a tragic ballad, for Hardyknute's ultimate fate is a state of perpetual fear and anxiety created by his experiences in battle – 'Black fear he felt, but what to fear / He wist [knew] not yet with dread'.[43] Considerably predating James Macpherson's Ossian controversy, 'Hardyknute' appeared in several anthologies (including in later editions of Ramsay's *Evergreen* with additional stanzas by Ramsay) as an authentic work until it was finally acknowledged by Wardlaw as her own work.[44] Despite the ballad's knotted textual history, it depicts Hardyknute's battles as national victories, preserving Scottish independence from foreign rule: 'Let Scots, while Scots, praise Hardyknute, / Let Norse the name aye dread'.[45] However, the rebirth of the Scots verse tradition during this period would be short-lived, as many mid-century Scottish poets worked primarily in English with a British, rather than solely Scottish, audience in mind.

Scots Verse in the Mid-Eighteenth Century

The most famous Scottish poet of the mid-eighteenth century was the London-based writer James Thomson (1700–1748), still remembered for supplying the lyrics for 'Rule, Britannia!'. He also wrote *The Seasons* (1726–1730), a long discursive poem that exerted much influence on contemporary aesthetics and prosody, as well as *The Castle of Indolence* (1748) which harkened back to Spenser in subject and style. Thomson's verse was entirely in English, and his immense popularity encouraged many other Scottish poets to write in English rather than Scots. Poets who followed his example include Robert Blair, 1699–1746 (noted for his poem 'The Grave', published in 1743), David Mallet, 1705–1765 (who collaborated with Thomson on the masque 'Alfred', which premiered in 1740), James Beattie, 1735–1803 (philosopher and author of *The Minstrel*, published in 1771), and Dr John Armstrong (who wrote the medical treatise in verse 'The Art of Preserving Health'). There were other reasons than fame and money for this linguistic choice, particularly considering the vagaries of Scottish Jacobitism at the midpoint of the century. After two failed Jacobite risings (in 1715 and 1745), Scots who had engaged with them were suffering brutal reprisals from the British government, such as confiscation of estates and a ban on wearing tartan.[46] Novelist and poet Tobias Smollett published 'The Tears of Scotland' in 1746, a poem in English which expresses outrage at the cruel reprisals. However, Smollett does not seek to instigate another revolt, but instead to garner better treatment for 'hapless Caledonia' which fell due to 'civil rage and rancour'.[47] This state of affairs contributed greatly to the linguistic turn to English verse, with Scots poems falling out of favour with many practicing Scottish poets who sought to avoid controversy and appeal to a broader British audience.

The trend of writing in English largely continued until Robert Fergusson's urban Scots verse in the 1770s, although there were a few exceptions in the interim between Ramsay and Fergusson. Ballads in Scots continued to circulate, many with Jacobite themes such as 'The White Cockade' and 'The Campbells are Coming'. The song 'Johnnie Cope' by Adam Skirving (1719–1803) recounts the flight of the titular British commander from the forces of Bonnie Prince Charlie at the Battle of Prestonpans in 1745, depicting Cope's fear and cowardice. 'The Flowers of the Forest' by Jean Elliott (1727–1805) is another Scots song about war with the English, mourning the loss of Scottish soldiers in the lost battle of Flodden Field in 1513.[48] The song 'Tullochgorum' by John Skinner (1721–1807) offers the pleasure of fiddle music ('the reel o' Tullochgorum') as an antidote to the poison of Whig and Tory politics, particularly inspiring Fergusson and Burns about the importance of national music.[49] William Julius Mickle (1734–1788), famous in his day for his translation of *The Lusiad* by Luis de Camoes, wrote a single Scots poem entitled 'The Sailor's Wife', describing the household preparations for the return of the sailor Colin by his wife, punctuated by the refrain 'There's nae luck about the house, / There's nae luck ava; / There's little pleasure in the house / When our gudeman's awa'.[50] When compared with the bulk of Scottish verse in English at this time, however, this is a meagre sampling of poems in the Scots register.

One notable exception was Alexander Ross (1699–1733), who wrote primarily in Scots in a variety of styles and genres such as the ballad, lyric, and pastoral drama. Ross was a schoolteacher in Lochlee in Angus, and he had been writing verse for his own pleasure since the 1730s; in 1766, however, he decided to share his work with James Beattie, who not only assisted him in the publication of *Helenore; or, The Fortunate Shepherdess* (1768) but also wrote a prefatory Scots poem dedicated to Ross.[51] *Helenore*, described as a 'pastoral tale', was deliberately modelled after Ramsay's *Gentle Shepherd*, and Ross's intentions were decidedly national, as noted by Alexander Thomson: 'To the Scottish dialect he had contracted a great partiality from his early youth' and 'his opportunities of seeing some excellent Scottish poems which he said formed his taste [...] disposed him to try something of the same kind'.[52] Peter Zenzinger has described *Helenore* as among 'the "purest" Scots poems of the period', calling it 'one of the most consistent examples of a realistic pastoral'.[53] Despite its use of Doric Scots, the poem was immediately successful, providing Ross with a measure of literary fame and recognition. However, Zenzinger notes that *Helenore* was not written with 'the general Scottish, and even less the general British, reader in mind: his intended reading public seems to have been local and unsophisticated'.[54] Ross was also known at this time for his Scots songs, such as 'Woo'd and Married and A'', 'The Rock an' the Wee Pickle Tow', and 'The Braes of Flaviana'. Burns praised Ross's songs for expressing 'wild happiness of thought and expression peculiarly beautiful in the old Scottish song style'.[55]

After Ross, the Scots verse of Robert Fergusson (1750–1774) commands attention for its novelty and innovativeness in the Scottish poetic tradition. As with Ramsay, Fergusson was an Edinburgh poet, and his work was decisively grounded in the daily life of the city known as 'Auld Reikie'. He lived and worked in the city after leaving St. Andrews without graduating in 1768, finding employment as a clerk and copyist in the Commissary Records Office.[56] Fergusson quickly immersed himself in Edinburgh's active club culture and began writing verse for the Cape Club, a convivial Edinburgh club still in existence.[57] He also started to publish his poems in *The Weekly Magazine* in the early 1770s, and it was in this forum that many of his first Scots poems appeared, such as 'The Daft-Days' in 1772. Written in the 'standard Habbie' stanza, this poem celebrates the New Year holiday in wintry Edinburgh, where 'mirk December's dowie [sad] face / Glours owr the rigs [ridges] wi' sour grimace'.[58] In fact, it is so cold that 'From naked groves nae birdie sings, / To shepherd's pipe nae hillock [small mound] rings'.[59] In the midst of such frigid weather, 'Auld Reikie' appears as a rare place of warmth and ease, 'the canty [cheerful] hole, / A bield [shelter] for mony caldrife [very cold] soul, / Wha snugly at thine ingle [fireplace] loll, / Baith warm and couth [sociable]'.[60] The poem takes a convivial turn, where warmth derives from 'reaming ale' and pleasure is found in Scottish fiddle tunes, Highland reels, and Skinner's 'Tulloch Gorum'.[61] The choice of music is distinctly national, for the speaker seeks to 'banish vile Italian tricks'[62] in order to 'let mirth abound, let social cheer / Invest the dawning of the year'.[63] As the poem nears its close, however, the tone darkens as the speaker envisions the inevitable end of such carousing in possible arrest and punishment. Although the 'great god of Aqua Vitæ [...] sways the empire of this city',[64] 'auld Reikie' is still regulated by 'that black banditti, / The City Guard'.[65] MacLachlan explains that 'the City Guard was Edinburgh's police force, a semi-military body' that as 'a symbol of authority [...] was the object of insults from boys and the uproarious'. They were primarily recruited from Gaelic-speaking Highlanders and MacLachlan also notes that 'Fergusson frequently makes fun of their attempts to speak English'.[66]

Like Ramsay, Fergusson also wrote and published in English, creating verse that conformed in style and subject to popular modes and genres in British poetry.[67] He was greatly influenced by John Gay (1685–1732) and William Shenstone (1714–1763), and the former poet's *Trivia, or the Art of Walking the Streets of London* (1716) directly inspired Fergusson's own ambulatory poem 'Auld Reikie'. Composed in rhymed couplets, this Scots poem invites the reader to join the speaker in a walk-through of Edinburgh's many streets, beginning in the morning when 'servant lasses' are observed telling their 'lies and clashes [gossip]' at the break of day.[68] The speaker visits other labouring characters hard at work already, such as 'barefoot housemaids'[69] charged with emptying chamber pots that give 'auld Reikie' its 'snell [pungent]' aroma in the morning.[70] The shops at Luckenbooths are next visited, then schools, businesses, and law offices. After school is over and the businesses are closed, 'Night, that's cunzied [moneyed] chief for fun, / Is wi' her usual rites begun'.[71] These rites include the nocturnal journeys of errand-boys and thieves, the indolence of the 'lazy chairman',[72] and the mutual interchange of 'whores and culls [customers]'.[73] One particular prostitute is singled out for a tonally ambiguous moral rebuke: 'Whane'er we reputation loss— / Fair chastity's transparent gloss!— / Redemption seenil [seldom] kens [knows] the name, / But a's [all is] black misery and shame'.[74] The poem proceeds to narrate episode after debauched episode, as a drunken 'bruiser'[75] emerges from a tavern looking for a fight, a 'macaroni [young man of fashion]' lays 'drunk, / In pools or gutters aftimes sunk',[76] epic eaters follow 'auld Epicurus' line',[77] and the Cape Club 'knights' enjoy 'mirth, music, porter deepest dyed'.[78] While celebratory, Fergusson's poem is unflinching in its portrayal of the city's many nocturnal dangers that end in death in the streets: a morning worker finds himself 'among the regions of the dead' and 'straight a painted corp [corpse] he sees, / Lang streekit [stretched] 'neath its canopies'.[79]

Such unhappy discoveries lead the speaker to opine that 'when the dead-deal (awful shape!) / Makes frighted mankind girn [grimace] and gape, / Reflection then his reason sours, / For the neist [next] dead-deal may be ours'.[80] The poem reviews further the city's delights and hazards, arguing for its merit over contenders like Glasgow and lamenting the loss of the monarchs of both city and nation: 'Gie's [give us] our dignity again: / For o, waes [woe is] me, the thistle springs / In domicile of ancient kings, / Without a patriot to regret / Our palace, and our ancient state'.[81] 'Auld Reikie' is one of Fergusson's many memorable Scots poems, which include poems on social occasions ('Leith Races' and 'Hallow-Fair'), elegies and mock-elegies (on Dr David Gregory and the porter John Hogg), and eclogues ('The Ghaists'), among others. Fergusson's brilliance as a Scots poet is all the more remarkable when one takes into account his short and unhappy life; despite assertions in his verse about his enjoyment of the city's many convivial delights, Fergusson suffered from depression so severe that he was committed by his mother to a public asylum, where he died at the age of twenty-four in October 1774.[82] Subsequently, Fergusson's verse disappeared from the literary scene, leaving him almost forgotten in his native city by the end of the decade. However, his verse was greatly appreciated by the next major Scots poet in late eighteenth-century Scotland, Robert Burns, who not only testified to Fergusson's vital importance as a Scots predecessor but also purchased a gravestone for Fergusson's unmarked grave in Canongate Kirkyard.

Robert Burns and His Contemporaries

Robert Burns (1759–1796) towers above all other poets writing in the Scots register from 1650 to 1800, and his work has contributed as much to world literature as it has to the Scottish poetic tradition. His great talent was immediately recognised and celebrated, and his significance for later British poets (particularly William Wordsworth and John Keats) was paramount for the development of Romanticism as a literary movement. That said, Burns is among the most allusive and intertextual Scots poets, and he acknowledged his many debts to the Scots verse of predecessors such as Ramsay and Fergusson. He was also inspired by the Scottish song and ballad tradition and spent the last years of his life collecting, editing, and publishing the oral literature of his country. Clearly seeing his work in national terms, Burns sought to situate his writing within the Scottish poetic tradition, particularly in Scots verse and song. To this end, he drew on the strategies and perspectives of earlier Scots poets, ranging from Ramsay's mock-elegies in 'standard Habbie' stanzas to Fergusson's satirical verse; he also noted the significance of nationalist texts like Blind Hary's *Wallace* as well as mid-century Jacobite songs. Like Ramsay and Fergusson, Burns also wrote poems in English that asserted the influence of British writers such as Pope, Milton, and Shakespeare. After the unprecedented success of the Kilmarnock edition of *Poems, Chiefly in the Scottish Dialect* in 1786, Burns himself became a source of inspiration for many other Scottish poets seeking to gain recognition in the literary marketplace.[83] Their failure to do so speaks largely to the drastic changes that Burns made as the premier Scots poet of his day, resulting in both positive and negative consequences for the Scottish poetic tradition.

Among his many innovations, Burns contributed to the formal development of Scots verse, displaying great versatility with multiple modes and genres. In particular, his skillful use of the 'standard Habbie' stanza led to its renaming as the 'Burns stanza' by later poets and critics. He also excelled at satire, for which he drew inspiration from not only Ramsay and Fergusson but also Swift and Pope. For instance, in 'Holy Willie's Prayer', Burns employs Swiftian satire by fashioning an obtuse and hypocritical speaker (the ironically named 'Holy Willie'), who believes that his many sins will be forgiven due to his status as a 'chosen sample' of God's grace.[84] The poem is a tour de force of satirical characterisation, its unremitting exposure of religious hypocrisy inspiring later works like *Private Memoirs and Confessions of a Justified Sinner* (1824) by James Hogg (1770–1835). Other satires in this vein include 'Death and Dr. Hornbook' (a narrative which portrays Death in competition with the incompetent Doctor Hornbook), 'Address to the Unco Guid' (another skewering of religious hypocrisy), and 'The Holy Fair' (a humorous representation of the intended versus actual practices at a religious festival, where attenders have more fun than they should). Burns also worked in the modes of mock-elegy and verse epistle, creating many memorable works that innovated upon earlier Scots incarnations. For instance, 'The Death and Dying Words of Poor Mailie, the Author's Only Pet Yowe' reveals its indebtedness to 'Bonnie Heck', while also using the occasion to argue for the need for the humane treatment of domestic animals: 'Tell him, if e'er again he keep / As muckle [much] gear [possessions, money] as buy a sheep, / O, bid him never tye them mair [more], / Wi' wicked strings o' hemp or hair!'.[85] In his first 'Epistle to John Lapraik, an Old Scotch Bard', Burns expresses his admiration for the older poet and explains his own poetic status: 'I am nae poet, in a sense, / But just a rhymer like by chance, / An' hae [have] to learning nae pretence'.[86] In fact, he represents his lack of learning to the operation of Nature itself: 'Gie me ae [one] spark o' Nature's fire, / That's a' the learning I desire'.[87]

Such a statement of poetics found ready followers in the Romantic movement, as did his remarkable empathy with Nature's creatures as seen in 'To a Mouse'. This poem has an unlikely auditor, a mouse whose nest has been unearthed by the speaker with his plough. This unhappy event for the mouse provides the speaker with an opportunity to speculate on their commonalities as living creatures, as well as their obvious disparities. For the latter, the speaker apologises that 'I'm truly sorry Man's dominion / Has broken Nature's social union, / An' justifies that ill opinion, / Which makes thee startle, / At me, thy poor, earth-born companion, / An' fellow mortal!'.[88] The speaker seeks to bridge this separation wrought by dominion (nicely symbolised by the plough itself as agricultural implement), offering the mouse 'a daimen-icker [an ear of corn] in a thrave [payment of corn to the ploughman]'[89] as small compensation for the 'ruin' of its 'wee-bit housie'.[90] As in Fergusson's 'The Daft-Days', the approach of winter ('bleak December's winds ensuin''[91]) makes the mouse's prospects grim indeed, a situation leading to the poem's famous moral apothegm in the penultimate stanza: 'Mousie, thou art no thy-lane [alone], / In proving foresight may be vain: / The best-laid schemes o' mice an' men, / Gang [go] aft agley [awry]'.[92] However, the shared fates of mice and men separate as the speaker returns to human difference in the final stanza, where he asserts that the mouse is 'blest, compar'd with me! / The present only toucheth thee'.[93] In a style and tone prescient of Romantic concerns, consciousness of past sorrows and future peril defines the human animal, giving it a measure of suffering unknown by other species.

Burns explored similar themes in many of his other poems and songs, numbering over six hundred during the period from 1785 to 1796. Several of his works are standards of world literature, including 'To a Mouse', 'Tam o' Shanter' (a masterpiece of narrative Scots verse), 'Ae Fond Kiss' and 'A Red, Red Rose' (love lyrics), and 'Auld Lang Syne' (the definitive version sung every year the world over). He saw his work collecting Scottish songs in the last years of his life as a duty to Scotland's literary heritage performed by its national bard, for which he would accept no compensation.[94] By the end of his life, he had achieved lasting celebrity and respect from the next generation of British poets, many of whom sought to gain their own recognition as Scottish bards. Publication opportunities were available immediately after the proven sales of Burns's

1787 Edinburgh edition had created a market for Scots verse, leading to publications by such poets as Janet Little, the 'Scotch milkmaid' (1759–1813); John Mayne, a Glasgow printer and poet (1759–1836); John Lapraik (1727–1807) and David Sillar (1760–1830), recipients of Burns's epistles; Alexander Wilson, poet and future ornithologist (1766–1813); and Ebenezer Picken, a Paisley poet (1769–1816).[95] None of these works were successful, however, due to a variety of factors relating to shifting aesthetic tastes and market saturation.

It is an abundant irony in the history of poems in the Scots register that the poet most responsible for popularising the form inadvertently foreclosed opportunities for other Scots poets seeking to follow his lead. While the nineteenth century heralded notable Scots poets and songwriters like James Hogg (1720–1835) and Carolina Oliphant, Lady Nairne (1766–1845), there were to be no figures equal to Burns in terms of influence and authority in the Scottish poetic tradition. Indeed, because nineteenth-century Scotland enshrined Burns as Scotland's reigning bard, it effectively encapsulated Scots verse as an eighteenth-century revival that ended with the poet's death.[96] This unfortunate scenario greatly affected the terrain of nineteenth-century Scots verse, leading many later poets (such as Hugh MacDiarmid) to decry Burns's lasting influence as inhibiting and baneful. However, it is to Burns and his predecessors that Scots verse owes its continuing significance as a distinctive art form deeply meaningful in the history of Scottish literature.

CHAPTER THREE

Presenting the National Past: The Uses of History in Scottish Literature, 1650–1707

Leith Davis

This chapter examines the variety of ways in which Scottish writers responded to the changing political situation of their nation between 1650 and 1707 by creatively representing the nation's past in such a way as to shape its identity in the present. In keeping with this volume's intent to revise traditional period boundaries, I begin not with the events commonly seen as the political watershed for Scotland in the long eighteenth century, the 1707 Acts of Union (passed by the parliaments in both London and Edinburgh), however, but with an earlier union that was effected under the Cromwellian Commonwealth of the 1650s. I then follow a trajectory of writing that imagined different forms of Scottish national identity from the 1660 Restoration through the 1688 Revolution, ending with the post-Union period in the early eighteenth century. Within that time period, writers in Scotland drew on a variety of different historical tropes to lend authority to their national identity – from mythic and biblical roots to classical literature and romance traditions, sometimes creatively combining several of these. I conclude this examination by suggesting how the writing produced during and shortly after the 1707 Union debate both reiterated the historical tropes used by writers in the earlier decades as well as introducing new ways of conceptualising the past.

    This chapter is also concerned, however, with challenging the way in which, within the history of Scottish literary criticism, Scotland's identity has been considered largely in terms of its relationship with England.[1] In particular, the critical focus on the creation and contestation of national identity by Scottish writers in a British context after 1707 has often obscured our attention to the ways in which the articulation of Scottish national identity has always been bound up with the activities of the nation in the wider global arena. As Louisa Schein reminds us, however, the nation has a 'dialectical relation to the production of the transnational'; it is 'crystallized in part through its engagement with that which breaches its border control, its putative sovereignty'.[2] In examining the representation of Scottish national identity from 1650 to the post-1707 era, I draw attention to the transnational contexts within which writers situated their discussion of their nation's identity. This chapter aligns itself, then, with a turn toward the transnational, focusing on what Suvir Kaul has described as the relationship between the uneven and 'significantly contested' 'nationalizing and internationalizing processes'.[3] In fact, many of the representations of national history that I consider here were conceived of only in relation to the transnational, whether in terms of cosmic history, romance traditions or imperial ambitions. My secondary aim in this chapter, therefore, is to focus attention away from the dyadic relationship between Scotland and England and toward the transnational contexts that informed the articulation of Scottish identity during the long eighteenth century.

From the 1603 Union of the Crowns to the 'English Empire' of the 1650s

The outcome of the Wars of the Three Kingdoms (1639–1652) had dire consequences for Scotland's political identity. The victory of Oliver Cromwell's parliamentary forces at Dunbar in 1650 and Worcester in 1651 was followed by the *Declaration of the Parliament of the Commonwealth of England, concerning the Settlement of Scotland*, and the nation now found itself incorporated (along with Ireland) into what was essentially an 'English empire'.[4] Writers in mid-seventeenth-century Scotland were abruptly required to adapt to the circumstances of being subjects in a union that was 'imposed by military conquest'.[5] They adopted different specific strategies in their responses, but they shared a common bond in looking to the past for an affirmation of Scottish identity in the time of the current crisis. Many of them drew, if not directly then allusively, on texts by earlier Scottish writers, particularly those by John Fordun (died c. 1384) and Hector Boece (1465–1536) which commingled myth with chronicle. Fordun's *Chronica Gentis Scotorum*, for example, traces the legendary origins of the Scots back to Greece and Egypt and weaves together (as well as partially invents) a chronology of kings in Scotland from the time of the Picts.[6] Reiterating Fordun's chronology, Boece's *Scotorum Historia* uses the history of Scottish kings to consider the mutual obligations between subjects and their monarch. Also important influences for later seventeenth-century writers were the romance histories *The Bruce* (1375) by John Barbour (c. 1320–95) and *The Wallace* (1508) by Blind Hary (1465–1506) which continued to be printed throughout the long eighteenth century.[7] These earlier versions of Scottish nationhood had already been mobilised in the aftermath of the 1603 Union of Crowns as both supporters and detractors of the monarchical union had used them to establish a strong identity for Scotland.[8] They proved equally as compelling for writers working within the parameters of the enforced Commonwealth.

The Royalist writer Thomas Urquhart (1611–1660), for example, responded to the political situation of the 1650s by combining elements found in Fordun's and Boece's chronicles with Biblical references, classical literature and personal history, seeking to advance his own political position as well as to 'vindicate the reputation' of the nation of Scotland.[9] A minor aristocrat and landowner, Urquhart had supported Charles I at the beginning of the British Civil Wars and had joined the Royalist forces of Charles II after he was crowned at Scone. Urquhart was captured at the Battle of Worcester in September, 1651 and imprisoned in Windsor Castle.[10] In the years during his comfortable confinement, he produced some of his most important works, frequently suggesting a connection between Scotland and the transnational as he links his own personal history to that of the 'Honour of the Country, unto which I did owe my birth'.[11] In *Pantochronochanon: or, A Peculiar Promptuary of Time* (1652), Urquhart traces the 'lineal descent' of the Urquharts back to the time of Adam, weaving together the Urquhart family tree with the biblical account of Moses and stories from Ovid's *Metamorphosis*, as well as drawing on Scotland's legendary historiography as advanced by Fordun. Suggesting a transnational connection for Scotland and for his family, Urquhart notes, for example, that his ancestor, Mollin, came with Gathelus from Egypt to Portugal.[12]

In *Ekskybalauron: or, The Discovery of a Most Exquisite Jewel* (1652), Urquhart interlinks his plea for the restoration of his own rights and liberties with a request for greater political rights for Scotland within the united 'Isle of great *Britain*'.[13] *Ekskybalauron*, which, he claims, was hastily expanded from a few sheets of his papers that were salvaged from the battlefield at Worcester, begins with an Epistle Liminary in which Urquhart indicates his purpose: 'to intreat the honorable Parliament of this Commonwealth, with consent of the Council of State thereof, to grant to Sir Thomas Urquhart of Cromarty his former liberty, and the enjoyment of his own inheritance' and to provide 'honest men' with 'a better opinion of Scotish [sic] spirits'.[14] In the main text of this 'Heterogenean miscellany', written with his characteristic polysyllabic exuberance, Urquhart provides reflections on the history of language, religion and national identity in general, as well as a lengthy account of the specific 'martial and literary [sic] endowments of some natives of [Scotland]', dating chiefly from the period of the Union of Crowns onward.[15] He also makes a case for a more equal relationship between Scotland and England in the new union, arguing against what he calls a 'heterogeneal' union of conquest (which he likens to the way that 'timber and stone upon ice stick sometimes together' when they are 'bound by the frost of a conquering Sword') and in favour of a union 'homogeneated by naturalization, and the mutual enjoyment of the same priviledges & immunities'.[16]

In another work, *Logopandecteision, or, An Introduction to the Universal Language* (1653), Urquhart tries a different tack to promote his own case and that of his nation. He demonstrates what he has already been able to produce in the service of the Scottish nation and suggests that he can perform equally an important role for the Commonwealth. He asserts an intimate connection between his individual body and the national body politic: 'knowing that the welfare of the Body of a government, consisteth in the intirenes of its noble parts, I always endeavoured to employ the best of my Brain, and Heart towards the furtherance of the Honour of that Country, unto which I did owe my birth'.[17] Although he has devoted himself to the country of his birth up until now, however, he asserts that he can repurpose his skills in the service of the new governmental body as he suggests that 'betwixt what is printed, and what ready for the presse', he has the potential to create 'above a hundred severall Bookes, on Subjects never hitherto thought upon by any'.[18] Pointedly, what he offers as a sample of the many ingenious works he has employed his 'Brain' in devising in his role as representative of the Scottish body politic is a plan for a 'universal language' which would facilitate communication between people of all different kinds of native tongues. In *Logopandecteision*, Urquhart capitalises on his record as a writer in the service of the Scottish nation to advertise his potential service as a writer 'for the weal of the Publike' of a united 'Isle of great *Britain*'.[19] The effect, however, is to draw attention to the nation of Scotland as a source of literary endeavour and an inspiration for transnational linguistic communication. Urquhart is a powerful example of the interconnection between what Kaul refers to as 'nationalizing and internationalizing processes'. While he connects his endeavours to the interests of his

'Country', Urquhart's literary interests and style connect him to a wider transnational humanist tradition. Notably, he also published a translation of Rabelais in the same year as *Logopandecteision*.[20]

Urquhart drew parallels between his personal situation and the political events of the time, encouraging readers to see him as a walking body politic, a representative of Scotland's long illustrious and transnational history which would continue to have relevance in the present and future of the united kingdoms. His contemporary, Alexander Ross (1591–1654), however, responded to the political events of the day by minimising the contemporary conflicts in Britain by representing them in relation to the cosmic history of the world. Educated at Marischal College at the University of Aberdeen, Ross had moved to England to pursue his scholarly interests, becoming a teacher, writer and Anglican priest and eventually taking up a position as vicar of Carisbrooke Parish on the Isle of Wight. Although forced to leave his residence in Southampton due his support of the Royalists, he continued to have an active writing career during the Civil Wars, penning Latin poetry as well as tracts on astronomy, mythology and religion. In his *Som Animadversions and Observations Upon Sr Walter Raleigh's Historie of the World* (1648) and *The History of the World: The Second Part* (1652), Ross puts the recent history within the context of a chronology that stretches back beyond the time of Adam, the starting point of Urquhart's *Pantochronochanon*, to the time of the creation of 'the first matter'.[21] Although Ross's extensive history ends in 1638 before the outbreak of the civil wars, the last item he includes in his *History of the World: The Second Part* hints at the conflict to come: 'The English Lyturgie sent into Scotland, occasioned much mischief: The Scots Presbyterians enter into a Covenant, and raise Arms: Preparation in England and Ireland against them, both by Sea and Land'.[22] Ross's *History*, then, also represents as a prophecy of the future as seen in the past.

In fact, Ross intimates such a connection between past and future as he reflects self-consciously on his use of historical methodology, suggesting the 'Histories' provide a 'Compass to steer by' for those who 'sit at the Helm of Government', 'admonishing and reproving them' as necessary.[23] But he indicates that history is important for ordinary people as well as government officials to understand, as it represents a 'Microcosme of Mankinde' that allows anyone to 'see the whole world [...] as a Stage on which men of all sorts have acted their parts'.[24] From this detached historical position, individuals can discern the same patterns occurring over and over again:

if they will look upon the various Examples of Vertue and Vice; of Humane Imbecilities, of various Changes in Kingdoms, States, and all Governments, of the Mutabilitie that is in mens minds, of the Inconstancy in their affections, of the Cunning and Falshood that are in Promises and Covenants, and the Vanity that is in all Humane Felicitie: They will truely finde that there is no such Antidote against the Infection and Poyson of Sin, as the reading of Historie.[25]

Within the chapters of his *History*, Ross dissolves the particulars of the present conflicts within the accounts of other civil wars. He represents the separate histories of Scotland and England within a transnational framework stretching from the Holy Land to Helvetius, suggesting that unification is a universal paradigm. The extraordinary range of Ross's transnational interests is indicated by the fact that he produced the first English translation of the Qur'an.[26]

Although Scottish writers during the Commonwealth period who employed English were often forced to engage in complex intellectual sleights of hand or nods to the English Parliament in order to bring their work to press within the 'English Empire', individuals from the Gaelic tradition were freer to express their anti-Cromwellian perspectives without censorship as they circulated their work through oral recitation, song and manuscript. The late seventeenth century was a productive time for Gaelic verse, although the Gaelic literary tradition was undergoing its own transition as classical poetic modes were shifting to accommodate a more vernacular poetic practice associated not with courts, but with clans.[27] Gaelic poets, too, drew on history to ground their observations in the present. In 'Oran Cumhaidh air Cor na Rìoghachd', for example, Iain Lom MacDhomhnaill (John MacDonald, c. 1624–c. 1710), the most 'celebrated Gaelic poet of the seventeenth century',[28] sang in despair about the execution of Montrose and the sad state of the country of Scotland:

> Tha Alba dol fo chìoschain
> Aig farbhalaich gun fhìrinn
> Bhàrr a' chalpa dhìrich—
> 'S e cuid de m'dhìobhail ghoirt.

Scotland is under tribute / to foreigners without justice / above the right taxation— / that is part of my sore plight.[29]

Iain Lom suggests the special role that Scotland has played in the history of Charles II, as he was 'crown[ed]' in Scotland following his father's death, although he has now been turned out as 'a poor stripped vagrant / without guard or parliament or court' ('Na thaisdealach bochd rùisgte / Gun ghèard gun chùirt gun choist').[30] Like a number of his Lowland contemporaries, Iain Lom situates Scotland's history within a Biblical context as he equates 'the poor land' of Scotland to Israel when 'in bondage', implicitly depicting Cromwell as the 'King of Egypt':

> Tha Sasannaich gar fairgneadh,
> Gar creach, gar murt 's gar marbhadh;
> Gun ghabh ar n-Athair fearg ruinn—
> Gur dearmad dhuinn 's gur bochd.
>
> *We are plundered by the English, / despoiled, slain and murdered: / we must have caused our Father anger / for we are neglected and poor.*[31]

Iain Lom concludes his work not in sorrow but in anger, however, as he curses Macleod of Assynt who was responsible for Montrose's death, asserting that he has 'sold justice / for the sake of a boll of Leith-meal / with two thirds of it gone sour'.[32]

Restoration to Revolution

Iain Lom's 'poor stripped vagrant', Charles II, was returned to his throne in 1660. The Restoration of the monarchy also effected a restoration of Scotland's parliament, albeit a parliament that was designed to be obedient to the king. Works praising Charles and depicting the positive effects for Scotland of the return of the Stuart monarchy abounded. 'A Poem [...] upon his Majesties [*sic*] Happy Return', by George Mackenzie of Rosehaugh (1636–1691), for example, celebrates the monarch's return throughout Britain. Significantly, however, by identifying Scotland and England through their distinct symbols (the 'Thristle' and the 'Rose'), Mackenzie represents them as separate and equivalent entities:

> All shall our Thristle, the blessed Thristle call,
> And in fames Eden our Rose flourish shall,
> And of our Lillies we may Justly say,
> That Solomon ne're flourished as they;

> Let then our Harpe play, and our Lyons daunce,
> For joy that Heaven should thus our King advance.[33]

Attentive to the power of history, Mackenzie also turned his attention to the recent events of the Wars of the Three Kingdoms, depicting them in imaginative form in his anonymously published 'serious Romance', *Aretina* (1660). In his dedication 'To the Ladies of the Nation', Mackenzie justifies his use of the romance genre by suggesting that 'Romances' arguably play a more important role than 'History': 'where Romances are written by excellent wits, and perused by intelligent Readers [...] the judgement may pick more sound information from them, then from History, for the one teacheth us onely what was done, and the other what should be done'.[34] In fact, *Aretina* offers readers both a coded history of recent events in Britain to teach them 'what was done' and instructs them on the best form of national governance to ensure that they know 'what should be done' in the future. Set in a fictional landscape in Athens, Egypt, and Thrace, *Aretina* relates the story of the knights Megistus and Philarites as they struggle to find the right balance between passion and reason in their courtships and between action and restraint in their political lives.[35] While there are parallels to contemporary events in Britain suggested throughout this long work, Book Three in particular reads as a detailed account of the events of the Wars of the Three Kingdoms, albeit with fictional names for the kingdoms as Megistus recounts the recent events of the 'lunatick Country' of Lacedemon which he and Philarites have visited.[36] Lacedemon is, suggests Megistus, 'the stage whereon Fortune acted all her Tragedies', a nation which 'had pilgrimaged through all Governments, and seing [sic] it could not unload it self of Rules heavy burden, it did, like the Asse, fetch it from shoulder to shoulder, and so, contrarie to its expectation, past from evil to worse, and from worse to worst of all'.[37] In telling his story, Megistus shares the sentiment of Iain Lom about Montrose as he speaks disparagingly, but in coded terms, of the 'ignominious rascal' who sold a 'pricelesse Gentleman to the Athenian Senate, buying with his price perpetual infamy to himself and his posterity'.[38] Alluding to the death of Charles I, Megistus also movingly portrays the execution of the king of Lacedemon as a 'masterpiece' of 'wickedness', and celebrates the subsequent joy and fruitfulness following the reinstatement of the monarchy. In *Aretina*, the history of 'what was done' is presented as a testing ground for the nation from which it emerges with greater wisdom about 'what should be done'. At the conclusion of

Book Three, the Senate of Lacedemon consciously articulate the view that monarchy is the best mode of governance, a perspective which they indicate they have learned painfully as a result of their nation's past experiences. But they also acknowledge that in the restored king, they in fact have a monarch who is both 'hereditary' and 'elected': 'if there be any thing more desirable in elective Monarchy, than there is in hereditary, your Majesty may justly pretend to both'.[39] Clearly, while Mackenzie uses *Aretina* to promote monarchy, he also wants to satisfy all parties in the wake of the Wars of the Three Kingdoms. Mackenzie also uses the romance genre to suggest the transnational connections that exist between individual nations. Athens and Thrace, for example, experience some of the same political problems of rebellion and usurpation as Lacedemon. Moreover, the characters of Megistus and Philarites offer their guidance and military skill to other nations, suggesting their own transnational affiliations.

In *Aretina,* the story of Lacedemon ends positively with the restoration of the king and an increase in prosperity: 'The Nation now begin to look like a body reconvalescing after a feaver, which grows more fat than it was formerly, and like a woman brought to bed, did forget its former miseries'.[40] But in actuality in Scotland, the return of the Stuarts to the throne also contributed to a renewed wave of religious conflict and violence as Charles championed Episcopalianism over Presbyterianism. Mackenzie himself was involved in the prosecution of the minority Presbyterian group known as the Covenanters during the so-called 'Killing Time'.[41] Many Scottish writers between 1660 and 1689 concentrated more on the religious fractures within the nation than on the wider parameters of Scotland's identity.[42]

The Revolution of 1688 and the flight of James VII/II marked another profound realignment of the political and religious as well as the literary landscape of Scotland. While John Graham of Claverhouse, Viscount Dundee (1648–1689) led a number of clans in a military rising in support of the Stuart monarch, a hastily-gathered Convention of estates in April, 1689 offered William and Mary the crown. Dundee's rising was suppressed following his death at the battle of Killiecrankie on 27 July, 1689, but the accession of William and Mary prompted a further splitting of the Scottish nation down ideological and religious as well as linguistic lines.[43] The 1688 Revolution put power in the hands of the Presbyterians and Whigs at the same time as it 'reinvigorated the Buchanan version of national identity' which emphasised the right of the people of a nation to take action if a monarch were unjust.[44] The Revolution also marked 'the triumph of Presbyterianism' as it gave official voice to those adherents of Presbyterianism who acknowledged William and Mary as monarchs.[45] Despite the fact that the Whigs and Presbyterians wielded official power, those loyal to the Stuarts continued to voice support for what became known as the Jacobite cause of returning James and his family to the throne.[46] Such writers often made linguistic choices to compose in vernacular Scots, which they associated with the 'great, classic tradition of Middle Scots' or in Latin, which also connected them with the Scottish past in terms of the humanist tradition.[47] In fact, as Jack MacQueen suggests, writers promoting the Jacobite cause frequently chose to write in Latin such that 'After 1688, Latin poetry and Jacobitism became virtually synonymous'.[48] The physician Archibald Pitcairne (1652–1713), for example, penned Jacobite poetry in Latin, praising the Stuarts and depicting post-1688 Scotland as a fallen state. Pitcairne was jailed in 1700 for suspected Jacobitism, but his work continued to circulate in manuscript poems that were later published as *Poemata Selecta*.[49] As well as his Latin poems, Pitcairne also produced a biting anti-Presbyterian satirical play in English, *The Assembly: A Comedy by a Scots Gentleman*, written around 1692 but not published until 1722.[50]

James Philip (Philp) of Almerieclose (1656–1713) also circulated in manuscript form his unfinished five-book retelling of the story of Dundee's rising.[51] Like Mackenzie's *Aretina*, Philip's manuscript, entitled 'Panurgi Philocaballi Scoti Grameidos' (later referred to as *The Grameid*), reminds readers throughout Britain of the recent civil turmoils. Philip, however, aligns events with classical literary tradition as he writes in Latin in the style of Virgil's *Aeneid* and Lucan's *Pharsalia*: 'Oh! what new madness now excites the northern world, and tempts again the fierce Britons into barbarous wars, to burn their country in civil flames, to endure the calamities of a tragic contest. Is Britain so forgetful of her past misfortunes?'[52] Philip also reinforces the connections that Mackenzie had articulated between the Stuart monarch and Scotland's ancient identity as he reiterates the idea that Scotland was an unconquered nation in the past: 'Scotland, the illustrious, never obeyed democratic rule, nor came under the law of an enemy [...]. How often did she beat back the Britons, the Angles, and the Danes, whose hosts she broke, enriching her soil with their blood, and whitening her shores with their bones'.[53] At the same time as it asserts Scotland's independent past, however, *The Grameid* represents a federation of Scotland with the other nations of the British Isles in the present, representing the Stuarts as 'leaders of a united patriotic resistance'.[54] Drawing on foundation myths both of Scotland and of Britain,

Philip urges all Britons to unite in the cause of fighting a common enemy instead of wasting time in internecine struggles.[55] *The Grameid* puts struggles within the British Isles into a wider global perspective of religious warfare as it encourages the readers to 'go and drive the Tartar host from the besieged walls of Hungary, and carry her conquering banners among the Ethiopians and the fierce Moors', and to 'loosen the necks' of Christians from the 'Infidel' and come to the aid of 'the wearied state of Europe'.[56] *The Grameid* ends abruptly with a lengthy harangue regarding the hypocrisies and evils of Presbyterianism and the hopes that the success of Dundee's venture can reverse the course of the nation's future.

1688 also marked the year when Donnchadh MacRath (Duncan MacRae) of Inverinate (d. c. 1700) began his manuscript collection of poetry *Làmh-sgrìobhainn Fheàrnaig* (the Fernaig manuscript).[57] The Jacobite cause continued to be promoted in Gaelic from the 1688 Revolution to the final conflict in 1745 in oral culture by poets such as Sìleas na Ceapaich (Cicely Macdonald of Keppoch) (c. 1660–1729) and Iain Dubh (c. 1665–1725). Secular poetry from the Gaelic tradition would not appear in print, however, until after the final Jacobite conflict in 1745–46.

Darien and the 1707 Union

While it further exacerbated the political and religious schisms in Scotland, the 1688 Revolution also provided new, albeit constrained, opportunities for the Scottish economy in the new climate of financial speculation, including the creation of the Company of Scotland Trading to Africa and the Indies.[58] Shares in the joint stock company were eagerly bought up in Scotland itself after the Company was forced to abandon its plans to sell shares more widely in England, Scotland and Europe. Although it began as a transnational venture, the Company of Scotland quickly became a symbol of national association. As the memorial presented to King William in May, 1699, regarding the Company's establishment of a colony in Darien, suggested: 'there was never any Enterprize of a more National Concern, than the foresaid Plantation is to the Kingdom of *Scotland*'.[59] The initial apparent success of the Company led a number of Scottish writers to explore, at least briefly, the idea of a Scottish imperial identity within a monarchical union with England. 'An Ode Made on the Welcome News of the Safe Arrival and Kind Reception of the Scottish Collony at Darien in America', printed by James Watson, for example, imagines a Scottish national spiritual collectivity, calling upon all 'SCOTS' to give thanks to '*Heaven's Protecting Pow'r*' for the safe arrival of the colonists.⁶⁰ The 'Ode' also suggests the national economic benefits of imperial plunder: '*Indian Gold* shall soon release / The Nation from its *Tempral Grand Disease*' (the text includes a footnote indicating that '*Grand Disease*' translates as 'Poverty'). Alexander Pennecuik's *Caledonia triumphans: a Panegyrick to the King* similarly interconnects a sense of Scottish nationality with both a spiritual destiny and an imperial identity. The poem reinforces the cultural memory of Scotland as resistant to invasion and also projects the Scottish past into a future invulnerability: 'as our Valour flew all Europe round, / So now our Trade scarce both the Poles shall bound'.⁶¹ Anticipating the later motto of the British empire, *Caledonia triumphans* asserts, 'Our ships through all the World shal go and come, / Even from the Rising to the Setting Sun'.⁶² This vision of Scottish national and imperial identity was short-lived, however. Faced with disease, Spanish military attacks, and a proclamation preventing their trading with English colonies, the Scottish colonists surrendered their outpost at Darien in August, 1699. In the pamphlet debate that followed the disaster, the historical independence of Scotland that had been debated from 1603 onward became once more a contemporary point of contention. In *A Defence of the Scots Abdicating Darien*, Walter Herries, an erstwhile colonist who had also served as a spy for the English government, attacked the Company of Scotland and the nation itself, claiming that the Company Directors were not only inept, but also ungrateful, as, by complaining about the restrictions on their trade, they were forgetting the benefits that Scotland had enjoyed since the Union of Crowns: 'Your People now enjoy the Blessings of Heaven, and Product of the Earth, and Ocean without any interruption; and whereas formerly they liv'd on the Mountains, and under the Shelter of some strong Rocks or Castles, they are now come down to the Plains, and can sleep sound in Beds, without the least Apprehension of Blood and Rapine'.⁶³ *In Scotland's Grievances Relating to DARIEN*, George Ridpath refuted Herries and attempted to rescue the 'Honour and Interest of our Nation' that had been 'so much neglected and despised'. Ridpath argued that the only way of repairing the situation was 'by [the Scottish] Parliaments [sic] asserting our Independency and Freedom against all those Invasions and Neglects, and by making it appear to the World, that we are still a Sovereign Nation, and have as much Right to consult our own Interest, without any regard to that of England, as they have to do so by us'.⁶⁴

The economic losses of the Darien disaster, coupled with the agricultural failures of the 1690s, were substantial enough to convince many Scots that a more complete union with England rather than greater independence was the only way forward.[65] At the same time, the accession of the childless Queen Anne in 1702 also made the issue of union more urgent for the English. The complicated series of negotiations regarding parliamentary union between the two nations that took place between 1702 and 1707 was accompanied by another virulent printed pamphlet debate which reanimated earlier claims made during the Darien disaster debate.[66] Writers such as Andrew Fletcher, George Ridpath and James Hodges, for example, who had drawn on Scottish historiography in the Darien pamphlet debate, drew again on this discourse to make their case.[67] In arguing for greater balance of power under a constitutional monarchy, for example, Fletcher traced Scotland's current problems back to the failures of the Union of 1603:

> All our Affairs since the Union of Crowns, have been manag'd by the Advice of English Ministers, and the principal Offices of the Kingdom fill'd with such Men as the Court of England knew wou'd be subservient to their Designs: By which means they have had so visible an influence upon our whole Administration, that we have from that time appear'd to the rest of the World, more like a conquer'd Province, than a free and independent People.[68]

Like Urquhart earlier, who favoured a union which was 'homogeneated by naturalization, and the mutual enjoyment of the same priviledges & immunities', all three writers sought a federal union rather than an incorporating union which, they argued, would further erode Scottish 'Liberties, Privileges, and Independency'.[69]

Despite fierce opposition and a lack of popular support, however, a Treaty of Union was negotiated in 1706 and an incorporating Act of Union, ratifying the Treaty, was finally passed by both parliaments in early 1707: on 1 May 1707, the United Kingdom of Great Britain officially come into existence. Scotland was limited to forty-five members out of 558 in the new British House of Commons and sixteen members out of a total of 168 in the House of Lords. It did, however, maintain its separate legal and educational systems, as well as the protection of the Presbyterian religion. Christopher Whatley argues that a Scottish 'cultural nationalism' 'emerged as an important form of creative consolation to which many Scots were drawn as a result of the sense of loss of Scottish political nationhood caused by the union'.[70] While that is certainly true, it is also the case, as this chapter has suggested, that elements of this cultural nationalism had already been articulated by Scottish writers in the previous half century as they creatively drew upon – and frequently drew together – modes of national history ranging from mythic and cosmological origins to the classical and romance literary traditions to economic imperialism in order to construct a Scottish past that also situated the nation in relation to transnational forces.

Scottish Writing After the Union

Scottish writers in the aftermath of the 1707 Union, like those writing in the shadow of the Cromwellian union, drew upon Scotland's history in order to assert the continuing identity of their nation going forward into the new British future. James Watson, who had been imprisoned in the Edinburgh Tolbooth for publishing *The People of Scotland's Groans and Lamentable Complaints, Pour'd out before the High Court of Parliament*, published the first volume of his *Choice Collection of Comic and Serious Scots Poems* in the midst of the final debates on the Union in the Scottish capital.[71] Watson draws attention in his prefatory comments of the *Choice Collection* to his national project, noting that it is 'the first of its Nature which has been publish'd in our own Native Scots Dialect'.[72] The *Choice Collection* would be generative for the later eighteenth-century revival of Scots by writers such as Robert Fergusson, Robert Burns and Janet Little. But the *Choice Collection* is not just an anthology of poems written in Scots; rather it contains poems that suggest the linguistic diversity of Scottish writers. Watson includes a broad range of historical and contemporary texts in his miscellany, beginning with a poem written in Middle Scots, 'Christ's Kirk on the Green' which was, he asserts, 'Composed (as was supposed) by King James the Fifth', and including historical works by George Buchanan (tutor to James VI/I) and Alexander Montgomerie (James VI's court poet) as well as more recent works like 'The Life and Death of the Piper of Kilbarchan'.[73] The second and third parts of the *Choice Collection* were published after the Union had taken place in 1709 and 1711 respectively, but despite the different political situation, they, too, continue to keep the debate about Scotland's sovereignty alive. Part Two begins, for example, with '*ROBERT* the III. King of *Scotland*, His Answer to a Summons sent Him by *Henry* the IV. of *England*, to do Homage for the Crown of Scotland', a poem which argues for Scotland's historical independence from England: 'For our Heretage was ever Free, / Since *Scota* of *Ægypt* tuik the Sea'.[74]

As well as curating a collection of Scottish literature himself, Watson was also the printer for the *Lives and Characters of the Most Eminent*

Writers of the Scots Nation (1708–22) by the physician George Mackenzie. In that work, Mackenzie, like Urquhart before him, draws attention to the history of Scotland's literary luminaries as a way of asserting both the independence of the nation in the past as well as its creative vitality in the present. Commenting that 'our Nation has produc'd as Great Men as any other Nation in the World', Mackenzie laments that 'we have been so unjust to their Memories and to our Posterity, that hitherto there has not been made a Collection of their Lives'.[75] His work, he suggests, will serve as a 'Paper Monument' to Scotland's 'mighty Heroes in Learning'.[76]

The wigmaker turned bookseller Allan Ramsay also drew on the Scottish past to promote Scottish identity in the present. One of Ramsay's first works was a republication of 'Christis Kirk on the Green' that contains new verses by Ramsay himself.[77] Ramsay included this newly modified poem in his 1724 work, *The Ever Green, Being a Collection of Scots Poems, Wrote by the Ingenious Before 1600*, along with a number of other poems from Watson's *Choice Collection* and other sources. In the Dedication to *The Ever Green*, Ramsay refers more directly than Watson did to his project to promote Scotland, as he refers to the 'Spirit of Freedom' and 'Love of Liberty' demonstrated by the 'antient Heroes' of nation.[78] In the Preface, Ramsay further suggests that his work operates as a medium through which the 'OLD BARDS' can convey that 'Love of Liberty' to the present generation.[79] But, in keeping with those writers such as Fletcher who believed that Scotland had been but 'a conquer'd Province' since the Union of Crowns, Ramsay only features poems in *The Ever Green* which were written prior to that event: *before* 1600. In *Scots Songs*, first published in 1718, then expanded and republished throughout the eighteenth century as *The Tea-Table Miscellany*, Ramsay sets out not to produce a collection consisting solely of Scotland's past literary treasures, but to bring those treasures into the present by combining them with popular folk songs such as 'The Last Time I Came O'er the Moor' and 'The Lass of Peatie's Mill' as well as newly-minted lyrics for older tunes.[80]

It is crucial to remember that the Treaty of Union was conceived and first made operative within the context of a number of different commercial and military engagements between Scotland, England, Britain and the wider world: the Darien venture, the War of the Spanish Succession, the formation of the South Sea Company and the War of the Quadruple Alliance (1718–20). Accordingly, the Acts of Union also prompted not just a re-evaluation of Scotland's relationship with England, but also the re-imagining of Scotland's place in a transnational framework.

Unlike the Scottish writers after the union of 1650, however, Scottish writers after the 1707 union turned not to the frameworks of biblical and legendary time and global space, but to the transnational commercial connections of a Scotland within the present united nation of Britain. As well as attempting to preserve the literature of the past and to hybridise it with contemporary Scottish – and English – culture, Ramsay, for example, was also conscious of writing Scotland into a modern world of global mobility and finance. In his 'Edinburgh Address to the Country', published a short eleven years after the Union, Ramsay envisions a future for Scotland that connects it with global economic activity. Written as a speech by the erstwhile capital city to the 'Brave and Fair' urging them seek the pleasures and enlightenment of city life, the poem presents post-Union Edinburgh not as a peripheral outpost of empire, but as a hotbed of intellectual discussion and political debate about 'Affairs Home and Abroad':

>   What Pleasure can exceed to know what's Great,
> The Hinge of *War*, and winding Draughts of *State*?
> These in my *Coffee Shops* th' aspiring Youth
> May learn, with Pleasure, from the Sage's Mouth,
> While they full-fraughted Judgments do unload,
> Relating to Affairs Home and Abroad.[81]

The poem concludes by imagining instead 'a glorious Fate' for the city that includes the construction of 'new stately Structures on new Streets' as well as 'new built Churches'. The energy and novelty of the city will in turn draw people from all over Britain: 'From Utmost *Thule* to the *Dover Rock*, / *Britain's* best Blood in Crowds to me shall flock' (8). Moreover, Edinburgh is pictured as the centre of a new wave of international trade:

> A numerous Fleet shall be my *Fortha*'s Pride,
> While they in her calm Roads at Anchor ride:
> These from each Coast shall bring what's Great and Rare
> To animate the *Brave*, and please the *Fair*.[82]

The irony here, of course, is that the only reason that 'Great and Rare' goods are able to 'animate the *Brave*, and please the *Fair*' is that the Acts of Union made global markets available to the Scots who had been held back by navigation acts (as the disaster at Darien proved). *Edinburgh's Address to the Country* expresses ambiguity about Scotland's position in

1707, however. The Union ensured that the 'numerous Fleet' would be able to enter and leave Scottish ports calmly, but it also 'widowed' the nation leaving it only the 'distant Image of thy ancient Sire' and relegating it to a subordinate political status in a United Britain.[83] This was an ambiguity with which Scottish writers of the long eighteenth century would continue to grapple. Nevertheless, they would have the rich stores of Scottish history woven into the works of their literary predecessors as their 'Compass to steer by' in navigating this unknown terrain.

CHAPTER FOUR

Literary Print Culture in Restoration Scotland, 1660–1688

Holly Faith Nelson and Sharon Alker

Introduction

While single works of literature published in Restoration Scotland are periodically the subjects of critical attention, the literary output of Scottish presses as a whole during the reigns of Charles II (r. 1660–1685) and James VII/II (r. 1685–1688) has rarely been examined, likely because Restoration Scottish literature is often considered relatively insignificant in terms of major developments in aesthetic form and content. Scottish literature of the period is also regularly overlooked, seen as substandard in comparison to creative works written by earlier and later Scots or by English Restoration authors. A representative case is *The Cambridge Companion to Scottish Literature* in which the chapter on the literature of the 'Reformation and Renaissance' is immediately followed by one on 'The Aftermath of Union'; there is no analysis of Scottish literature composed or published between 1660 and 1700.[1] There are, of course, exceptions to this practice, as evidenced by the perceptive overview of Restoration Scottish literature in Roderick Watson's *The Literature of Scotland: The Middle Ages to the Nineteenth Century* and Robert Crawford's *Scotland's Books: A History of Scottish Literature*. However, given the general trend of bypassing the literature of Restoration Scotland, there is still much to be learned about the literary culture and aesthetics that emerged in Scotland after the Interregnum by examining the past works of literature that still held sway, the contemporary English authors to which the reading public were drawn, and the works of newly emerging Scottish creative writers. This chapter aims not only to fill a gap in the historical record, but also to shed light on the literary imagination of Scottish Restoration writers and publishers as they sought to reconceive their culture and national identity in a tumultuous period of change and to strengthen the cultural relationship with their English counterparts.

We focus on the poetry, drama, and prose fiction printed in Restoration Scotland between 1660 to 1688, the end date marking the major political and cultural shift that resulted from the Revolution and that complicated the robust royalism of published literature in the period.[2] After providing a brief historical context, we first adopt a macroscopic approach to determine what literary works were published in the printing hubs of Edinburgh, Glasgow, and Aberdeen, including those by non-Scottish authors, and to develop an accurate picture of the public literary climate in Restoration Scotland. We then adopt a microscopic perspective by turning to seven Restoration Scots who published original works of literature in Scotland between 1660 and 1688 in order to reveal how they attempted to come to terms with losses in the civil war and to help rebuild both Scottish and English culture after the Restoration. We demonstrate that in response to a volatile war, the instability of Interregnum life, and the sudden restoration of the monarchy, Scottish publishers of poetry, prose fiction, and drama in the period privileged political conservatism, cultural tradition, virtuous living, and spirited (but not debauched) humour. We also suggest that the Scots authors who were published during the Restoration often elected to engage in work of cultural mourning, assigning a transcendent grandeur to past traumatic events; re-enchanting the present moment by celebrating Scottish heroes across class and time; purging the nation of anti-Stuart sentiment; and rebuilding networks of literary patronage in North Britain. Along the way, it will become evident that by the 1680s, some of these emergent cultural trends in Scotland were coloured by a particularly close affiliation with the future James VII/II, who was seen not only as the progeny of Scottish kings but also as a monarch with an interest in promoting Scottish identity and culture.

The Historical Backdrop: Military and Political Discord

It has long been argued that post-civil war English literature was deeply influenced by the Wars of the Three Kingdoms (1639–1652), both in terms of content and form. Nigel Smith and Joad Raymond, for example, have theorised the ways in which genre was fractured and reconfigured in post-war England.[3] This reworking of literary form and content after the wars also occurred in Scotland, as this chapter reveals, a fact which is unsurprising given the active service of many Scotsmen and the violent conflicts that occurred in North Britain. John Morrill's calculations lead him to conclude that 'the proportion of adult male Scots […] in arms was almost certainly higher' than in England, and Charles Carlton estimates that there were an enormous number of civil-war related deaths in Scotland.[4] This brutal military experience among the Scots had a significant influence on the types of literature selected for publication in Restoration Scotland and on the perceptions and aesthetic works of Restoration Scottish authors, especially in light of the need to mourn past losses and to rebuild and stabilise culture.

The need for Restoration Scots to reconceptualise themselves as a stable, heroic, moral, and spirited nation was also necessary because of the ideological discord brought about by the Interregnum. As R. Scott Spurlock details, not long after the English secured Edinburgh for the Commonwealth in September 1650, 'a massive influx of alternative religious ideas' was 'introduced into Scotland for the first time'; English soldiers who were 'not ordained to preach publicly' gave sermons that affirmed the Commonwealth objective to impose 'religious toleration' in Scotland, deeply upsetting the Kirk; and the English forces 'quickly seized control of the capital's presses, and only one of the city's three major printing houses continued to operate'.[5] Throughout Cromwell's reign as Lord Protector, Spurlock maintains, these 'English-controlled presses of Scotland' continued to publish 'declarations and newsbooks for the benefit of the regime', many intended to undermine the Kirk.[6] As if this were not enough to thrust the Scots into disarray, the Rump Parliament, as David L. Smith reminds us, issued 'a declaration incorporating Scotland into a single Commonwealth with England' on 28 October 1651, effectively forcing a union on Scotland.[7] These and other events would have inevitably led to confusion and frustration among the Scots, inspiring Scottish publishers and authors to respond in ways that would reorient the nation's readers through print.

Printed Texts in Restoration Scotland: An Overview

Far more is known about the publishing industry in Scotland after the Restoration than before it. In his study of the early-modern Scottish book trade, Alastair J. Mann contends that '[t]he Covenanting and Cromwellian periods offer up the greatest degree of frustration for the historian of the early modern book' given the paucity of records.[8] He does establish, however, that 'in publishing activities, in the polite engagement with book culture and leisure, and in the desire for newssheets and diurnals, the late 1650s were crucial to the development of Restoration culture'.[9] Mann explains that after the Restoration, patronage, especially 'royal sponsorship', helped bolster and expand the 'Scottish book trade', particularly after James, Duke of York and Albany, became involved in the 1670s and early 1680s. James's acts of patronage were rooted in his 'desire to create a court of literati in Edinburgh based at Holyrood'.[10] Mann suggests that in addition to royal patronage, changes in government acts that permitted the 'naturalisation of skilled foreign workers, such as French paper makers and Dutch printers', advances in printing technologies, increases in literacy rates, and superior distribution networks ensured that the publishing sector became a potent space in which to reconfigure Scottish identity in this period.[11] However, this surge in publishing in Restoration Scotland involved printing both Scottish and English works: Scottish publishers were not isolationists and understood that rebuilding and re-enchanting Scottish culture meant integrating elements of all three kingdoms restored under Charles II.

To establish what works were published in Restoration Scotland, we rely on Early English Books Online (EEBO) and the updated *List of Books Printed in Scotland Before 1700* by H. G. Aldis. These resources do not provide an exhaustive list of all works published in Scotland during our period of study; however, they do offer a substantial and representative sample from which reasonable conclusions can be drawn about the Restoration Scottish literary climate. EEBO's and Aldis's records of works in English published in Scotland between the years 1660 and 1688 indicate that relatively few works of poetry, prose fiction, or drama were printed in the period. The vast majority of texts published in Edinburgh, Aberdeen, and Glasgow during this time were political or religious works of prose non-fiction; the dominant genres and modes were political speeches, proclamations, acts, orders, remonstrances, epistles, and panegyric, as well as religious treatises, declarations, confessions, commentaries, and covenants along with sermons and metrical psalters. Many of the religious works published were politically inflected, if not overtly political.[12] Almanacs, educational books, histories, travel narratives, accounts of crimes, trials, and executions, and works on aspects of natural philosophy, like literary works, appear here and there, but in a rather scattered fashion. This emphasis on the political and religious in Scottish Restoration works listed on EEBO and Aldis, if, for example, Steven N. Zwicker's random sample of imprints published in Britain in the 1660s is accurate, mirrors the focus of Restoration publications in Britain more generally. His research leads him to conclude that twenty-eight per cent of the works published in the 1660s, as recorded in the British Library's English Short Title Catalogue (ESTC), are on 'public affairs' while thirty-eight per cent take 'religion' as their primary subject, though he rightly reminds us that '[t]he borders' between many of our subject categories 'are [...] porous'.[13] While the attraction to religious material remained strong for both Scottish and English readers in our period of study, as Mann points out, the 1670s represented a watershed in Scottish publishing history as at that point '[f]or the first time in Scottish book history secular works outnumbered the religious as seen in the output of the Scottish press and in the inventories of booksellers'.[14]

With each new major political or religious turn of events, copious occasional works were published in Scotland that pertained to events in Scotland or in Britain as a whole. For example, in 1660 panegyrical texts in English and Latin across the genres abound on Charles II's restoration; in 1678, there is a sudden rise in pamphlets published on Quakerism; in 1679, a variety of works are issued on the Covenanters, notably on the suppression of Scots in 'the West of Scotland' in relation to the Battle of Bothwell Bridge; and in the late 1670s and early 1680s, works on the plot of Titus Oates, the danger of popery, the Church of Scotland, executions, and the succession issue come to the forefront of the Scottish publishing scene.

In terms of the languages of published works in Restoration Scotland, it is important to keep in mind Scotland's 'plural [...] linguistic heritage'.[15] As Crawford observes, 'Scotland [...] has always been keen on other tongues, and the continuing polylingual inflection of Scottish literature is the most obvious feature that sets it apart from conventional ideas of English literature'.[16] Gaelic and Latin had especially important places in Scottish society and culture in early modern Scotland. Only one work in Gaelic, however, is listed in EEBO and Aldis's *List of Books* during this period in Scotland: the Episcopal minister Robert Kirk's metrical psalter, *Psalma Dhaibhidh a nMeadrachd. Do reír an phriomh-chanamain* (1684). This is perhaps predictable since, as Jonquil Bevan tell us, in the early modern period 'the traditional forms of [Gaelic] literature were transmitted into manuscript, and this remained a largely manuscript culture for a considerable time to come'.[17] Of the 144 works in Latin that EEBO lists as published in Scotland between 1660 and 1688, about fifteen per cent might be classified as literary texts, excluding textbooks on language and rhetoric. Although, as Steven Reid has shown, 'the zenith of Scottish Latin literature was reached in the first four decades of the seventeenth century', after which it began to seriously decline, this percentage of Latin literature indicates that there was still an effort by some Restoration Scots to sustain it.[18]

Approximately nine per cent of the works published in English – in its various forms, though formal English, not the Scots register, dominates – during this period in Scotland is poetry (including ballads), prose fiction, or drama. About one-third of these literary works written in English are anonymous, the majority of which are political ballads and verse broadsides. Most of these texts would have been published in and circulated throughout Britain and are, thus, not unique to the literary marketplace of Restoration Scotland. However, some focus on contemporary Scottish subjects or experience, including, for instance, *The Chearfull Acclamation of the City of Edinburgh, for the Happy Return of His Sacred Majesty, Charles the Second* (1660); *Lætitiæ Caledonicæ, or, Scotlands Raptures, upon the Thrise Happy Return of her Sacred Soveraign Charles the Second* (1660); and *The Battell of Bodwell-bridge, or The Kings Cavileers Triumph* (c. 1680).

Most of these ballads and verse broadsides are royalist panegyric and are sometimes saccharine in their praise; in occasional cases, Whig policy and practices are directly attacked. Publication was clearly motivated by a desire to affirm the restored Stuart regime and its agents. This motivation is hardly surprising, especially when these works were issued by royal printers in Restoration Scotland, notably Evan Tyler between 1660 and 1671, Andrew Anderson between 1671 and 1676, and thereafter in our period by Anderson's widow Agnes Campbell, who assumed the role of king's printer of Scotland after her husband's death.[19] However, as Mann explains, there were certainly opportunities for a range of opinions to be expressed in print in Restoration Scotland, since 'no government or centralised limitation was placed on the proliferation of presses',[20] and copyright issues and censorship practices would only pertain to selected works. As Restoration publishers in Glasgow, Edinburgh, and Aberdeen worked to build up their offerings in literature, they frequently chose to republish works by Renaissance and Restoration English authors and Medieval and Renaissance Scots, works that would appeal to a distinctly Scottish readership. While it would be reductive, as Crawford has argued, to imagine that all Scottish writers, or for that matter publishers, were primarily or solely invested in imagining a nation for this readership, at this historical moment there was an urgent need to heal from the civil wars and address the religious, political, and cultural shifts that accompanied the Interregnum and Restoration.[21] Therefore, politically conservative literature that allowed the Scots to navigate and purge their communal grief and that promoted cultural tradition and continuity was highly appealing to the reading public.

Literature by English Authors Reprinted in Restoration Scotland

The literature authored by English writers that Restoration Scottish publishers chose to reprint tended toward the spiritual/moral, the folkloric, and the political. In the category of spiritual/moral literature we place one of the most significant English works reissued in Scotland from the perspective of literary history: *The Isle of Man: or, The Legal Proceeding in Man-shire against Sin* by the Puritan minister Richard Bernard (1568–1642). It was republished in Glasgow in 1674, several years before the 1678 publication of John Bunyan's (1628–1688) *Pilgrim's Progress* and the 1682 publication of *The Holy War*, on which it exerted considerable influence. Bernard, the Rector of Balcomb, Somerset, turned to allegory to expose, detail, and put on trial 'the chief Malefactors' or forms of sin 'disturbing both Church and Common-wealth' and to instruct readers that God had mercifully granted the believer, the '*new man*', the ability to recognise and '*curb sin*', through the use of his conscience.[22] This subject resonated so much with English and Scottish readers in general that it had run through sixteen editions by 1683.[23] Two other pre-Restoration English works republished in Scotland in the 1680s also sought to morally improve the reader, albeit with less religious fervour: Francis Quarles's (1592–1644) *Enchiridion* (repr. 1680), a collection of brief prose meditations on divine (contemplative and practical) and moral (economic and political) subject matter; and Francis Bacon's (1561–1626) *The Wisdom of the Ancients* (repr. 1681), which Bacon describes as a series of 'fables' and 'parables' in his preface to the anthology of thirty-one classical stories. These two works may have been especially useful in educational contexts and would have complemented the Renaissance Scottish Reformer David Ferguson's (c. 1533–1598) *Nine Hundred and Fourty Scottish Proverbs* published in Glasgow in 1667, since all three texts might be viewed as 'wisdom literature'. The moderate number of classical texts published in Latin in Restoration Scotland, most notably works by Aesop, Ovid, and Terence, would also likely have found a home in the classroom.

This inclination to publish earlier English works that focus on the virtuous Christian life or the classical good life dovetails with the publishing of two significant imaginative works by contemporary English writers in Restoration Scotland: *Pilgrim's Progress* and the dramatic prose dialogue on the benefits of holy Christian living by John Goodman (1592–1645), Rector of Hadham, and Chaplain in Ordinary to Charles II, *A Winter-Evening Conference Between Neighbours* (repr. 1684).[24] The fifth edition with additions to the first part of *Pilgrim's Progress* was published in Edinburgh in 1680 and 1681, and the sixth edition, with additions, was published in both Edinburgh and Glasgow in 1683. Though Bunyan and Goodman differed in confessional stance, both produced works that sought to guide readers toward religious truth and holy living.

While quite a few pre-Restoration and Restoration English works dedicated to spiritual or moral improvement were published in Scotland during the reigns of Charles II and James VII/II, fanciful folkloric English works from earlier periods were not wholly ignored. Although it is always difficult to identify the national origins of many folk tales in verse and prose, several of those published in Restoration Scotland – *The Frier and the Boy* (repr. 1668), *The History of Adam Bell, Clim of the Clough, and William of Cloudesley* (repr. 1668), and *Tom Thumb, His Life and Death* (repr. 1682) – appear to originate from Medieval or Renaissance England. Two of the three deal in some way with the question of authority and rebellion: the comic *Frier and the Boy* takes great pleasure in imagining a boy given three magical gifts that allow him to control and expose to ridicule those in authority over him; the 'outlaw narrative' *The History of Adam Bell, Clim of the Clough, and William of Cloudesley,* celebrates three English bandits, akin to Robin Hood, two of whom stealthily save the third from the noose;[25] and *Tom Thumb* amusingly relates the upbringing, childhood, courtly life, and death of Tom, a one-inch-tall knight in King Arthur's court created by Merlin and named by the Fairy Queen. Such playful folkloric works connected English readers to their storied pasts, but also appealed to Scottish readers.

The majority of original English literature composed between 1660 and 1688 that was reprinted in Restoration Scotland, however, was decidedly political: occasional royalist poetry in support of the monarchs, their offspring or agents, and their military achievements. This corpus includes a series of anonymous broadsides containing conventional panegyric and elegiac verse,[26] as well as poems by authors from Robert Wild (c. 1615–1679) and Sir John Birkenhead (1617–1679) in the 1660s to Elkanah Settle (1648–1724), Aphra Behn (1640–1689), and John Dryden (1631–1700) in the 1680s. Wild, a minister who labelled himself a 'loyal nonconformist', and Birkenhead, the royalist poet and journalist, celebrate in their poems the naval successes of the English forces during the Anglo-Dutch War.[27] In 1665, Wild published *A Gratulatory Verse upon our Late Glorious Victory over the Dutch*, in which, as Richard L. Greaves puts it, he 'effuse[s] patriotic fervour for James's naval triumph over the Dutch', while Birkenhead composed a broadside ballad on the Four Days' Battle in June 1666 during the Second Anglo-Dutch War (1665–1667), *A New Ballad of a Famous German Prince and a Renowned English Duke*, in which he warns the Dutch that their efforts, like those of the Rump Parliament after the regicide, would ultimately be in vain.[28]

About twenty years later, the royalist occasional verses of Settle, Behn, and Dryden made their way to the Edinburgh literary scene. Settle's six-page *An Heroick Poem on the Coronation of the High and Mighty Monarch, James II* (1685) gushes about '*Britannia's* sacred Nuptial Day' and envisions the dissipation of treasonous feeling.[29] The three Dryden poems published in Edinburgh all attempt to bolster the Stuart monarchy and stave off dissent, particularly as propagated by the Whig party: the satirical *Medall. A Satyre Against Sedition* (1682), the allegorical beast fable *The Hind and the Panther* (1687), and the panegyric *Britannia Rediviva: A Poem on the Birth of the Prince* (1688). In *Britannia Rediviva*, for example, with the characteristic excess that the genre of royal panegyric demands, Dryden describes his experience of looking upon the infant face of James Francis Stuart, Prince of Wales (much later the Old Pretender), in paradisiacal terms:

> [W]hen humbly on the Royal Babe we gaze,
> The Manly Lines of a Majestick Face
> Give awful joy: 'Tis Paradise to look
> On the fair Frontisepiece of Natur[e]'s Book;
> If the first opening Page so charms the sight,
> Think how the unfolded Volume will delight![30]

Dryden envisions this miraculous infant as capable of 'unit[ing]' the 'Three Realms' that make up Great Britain, the 'Mighty Trinity', on Trinity Sunday, the day of the baby's birth, 'stamp[ing] their Image, on the promis'd Seed [...] An Emblem of their Mystick Union'.[31] This mystical language is echoed in Aphra Behn's poem on the same event, with a focus on the prince's mother Mary of Modena: *A Congratulatory Poem to Her Most Sacred Majesty, on the Universal Hopes of All Loyal Persons, for a Prince of Wales* (1688). In this poem, Behn draws a shocking analogy between longing for the birth of James Francis Stuart and yearning for the birth of the Christ-child, which might strike some early modern Scottish readers as blasphemous; this child, like Christ, will 'call the wand'ring scatter'd Nations home': '*ALBION, HIBERNIA* and old *CALEDON*' will 'join their *Int'rests*, and no more dispute, / With sawcy Murmurs, who is *Absolute*'.[32]

The majority of pre-Restoration and Restoration English works reproduced in Restoration Scotland, therefore, convey a religious or ethical vision, revisit folkloric tradition, and/or give voice to a committed royalist platform. These works largely serve a conservative, steadying force in Scotland, reinforcing the wisdom of past knowledge and belief, reproducing traditional stories to ensure cultural continuity, and reaffirming, generally speaking, a monarchical worldview through the language of the mystical and the miraculous.[33] However, by the end of the late 1670s and into the 1680s, a variety of English literary texts that imaginatively engaged with the intense anxiety surrounding a Catholic threat (real or imagined) were reprinted by Scottish publishers, inevitably injecting into the Scottish literary marketplace a sense of instability and dread.

Medieval and Renaissance Scottish Literature Published in Restoration Scotland

The Medieval and Renaissance Scottish literary works republished in Restoration Scotland are more generically rich and varied than the English works reprinted, but, for the most part, they also similarly draw our attention to the importance of cultural tradition and the spiritual and/or moral life. Moreover, the spirited wit characteristic of a few of the republished English works is even more common in the early Scottish works reprinted. In reissuing these texts, Scottish Restoration publishers appealed to the reading public's attraction to a diverse range of intersecting imaginative modes – the heroic, historic, tragic, spiritual or moralising, and satirical. This emergent canon of Scottish literature reveals a definitive preference for early Scottish verse, often composed by courtiers, as opposed to drama and prose fiction. This trend may signify an attempt to revive and update the tradition of the courtly makars, thereby establishing a firm alliance between the Stuart court and Scottish producers of culture.

The most reproduced of the earlier Scottish works in Restoration Scotland was the heroic historic poem *The Wallace* by Blind Hary (c. 1440–1492), who was paid to perform in the court of James V (r. 1488–1513). In 1661, the work was published (twice) for the first time in thirteen years in Scotland; other editions or reprints followed in 1665, 1666, 1673, and 1685. Although the work was popular in Scotland before the Restoration, and may have been published with such frequency in this period simply because of its many enthusiasts, its revival would certainly have helped Scots work through the brutal military experience of civil war and re-establish a sense of heroic identity borne out of valiant self-sacrifice and loss overcome.[34] Such sentiments would also be conveyed by the earlier heroic romance in verse, *The Bruce* by John Barbour (c. 1320–1395), with its detailed account of military machinations (republished in Scotland in 1665, 1670, and 1672). Whether the reissuing of these works was meant to support the restored Stuart monarchy – since Charles II was a Scottish monarch – is difficult to say, given the anti-English sentiment they express and their emphasis on political resistance. However, it is also possible that, in the minds of Scottish Restoration readers, Charles I was a type of Wallace and Charles II a type of Bruce.

While the republication of *The Wallace* and *The Bruce* in Restoration Scotland points in part to the desire to re-establish the tradition of Scottish heroic literature, considered in its totality, the body of early Scots works published in Restoration Scotland might initially appear a rather motley assortment. Along with the heroic historic verse of Barbour and Blind Hary are published a revised version of *The Meire of Collingtoun* (repr. 1662),[35] a beast poem and mock testament in the Scottish register that tells the 'tragic' tale of a talking horse who, nearing death, endures physical abuse, sends a letter for relief from itinerancy, confesses her sins to a priest, and leaves a last will and testament (in which she distributes her body parts);[36] Robert Henryson's (fl. 1460–1500) gloomily tragic *The Testament of Cresseid* (repr. 1663) which traces the folly, abandonment, suffering, repentance, and death of Cresseid; Sir David Lyndsay's (c. 1486–1555) *Works* (repr. 1665, 1670, 1672, 1683, 1686), largely religious and political verse aimed at exposing sin and corruption and advising the monarch on right rule, as well as his semi-biographical verse romance *The History of the Noble and Valiant Squyer Meldrum* (repr. 1669, 1683) on love, war, and survival against all odds; a voluminous collection of George Buchanan's (1506–1582) neo-Latin poetry and drama, *Georgii Buchanani Scoti, Poetarum* (repr. 1677), which includes his psalm translations, two original biblical tragedies, and translations of Euripides's *Medea* and *Alcestis*; Alexander Montgomery's (1588–1661) fashionably written but moralising allegorical poem *The Cherrie and the Slae* (repr. 1668, 1675, 1680, 1682); Sir James Sempill's satirical anti-papist dramatic poem *A Pick-tooth for the Pope* (repr. 1669); Elizabeth Colville, Lady Melville's (fl. 1599–1631) Calvinist dream vision *Ane Godlie Dream* (repr. 1680, 1686) which reveals the hellish end of the reprobate and instructs that 'the way to Heaven is wondrous hard'; Patrick Anderson's (c. 1574–1624) dramatic verse satire *The Copie of a Barons Court* (repr. 1680?) which mocks the workings of the manorial court held by a landowner with the baillie, his representative, presiding over mostly tenant-related cases; David Dickson's (c. 1583–1662) 107-stanza scripturally dense song of worship *True Christian Love* (repr. 1680, 1686) which expresses his Christocentric Presbyterian vision; William Drummond of Hawthornden's (1585–1649) mock-heroic neo-Latin poem *Polemo-Middinia Inter Vitarvam et Nebernam* (repr. 1670?, 1684) that takes as its subject a feud between country tenants of two landowners; and *A Pleasant History of Roswall and Lillian* (repr. 1663) which features a steward who assumes his prince's identity to usurp his power only to be executed once the prince is revealed and restored (a tale that would surely resonate with readers shortly after the Restoration).

Despite the miscellaneous nature of this grouping, there are three dominant strains in Medieval and Renaissance Scottish literature reprinted in Restoration Scotland: the heroic, the homiletic, and the comic. *The Wallace* and *The Bruce* inscribe the Scottish heroic in the cultural imagination, as does *Roswall and Lillian*, in more chivalric terms, but this is balanced by a strong religious vision in a number of these early Scottish works, several by writers affiliated in some way with the court, in which the painful consequences of spiritual or moral failure are laid bare. A Calvinist perspective regularly comes to the fore, with an emphasis on human corruption and the redeeming love of a sovereign Christ. There is, however, also a real sense of play in some of the satirical and mock-heroic works, with that humour at times serving a greater moral or political imperative. The pre-Restoration Scottish literature reprinted on Scottish presses during the Restoration, like the pre-Restoration English literature reissued, stresses spiritual or moral instruction and highlights cultural tradition by mythologising heroic Scottish leaders and elevating the chivalric medieval past. The satiric bite of several of these earlier reprinted Scottish works also complements the satirical bent of some of the Restoration English works reproduced in Scotland during the Restoration. The literature of morality, mythology, and wit, therefore, might be viewed as the aesthetic context against which new works by Scots were produced and published in Scotland between 1660 and 1688.

Restoration Scottish Literature Published in Scotland

Literary works published by Scottish authors in North Britain between 1660 and 1688 include a prose romance, two plays, a dramatic dialogue, elegies, panegyrics, satirical poems, religious poetry, and a 'poetical essay'. Most of these works were published in the 1660s or 1680s, with a fairly rapid incline of new works appearing in the 1680s. The 1670s were a rather barren decade for original Scottish works of literature. Scottish authors attempted to enter the literary culture of Restoration Scotland from all angles and through a wide range of literary forms, mirroring, in some respect, the diversity and commitments of past English and Scottish works reprinted in the period and sharing an emphasis on the patriotic in Restoration English literature published in Scotland.

In the 1660s, a number of Scottish Restoration literary texts focused on bridging an earlier and contemporary royalist culture, often leading to a Janus-faced approach to their subject matter. They engage in both the work of mourning for the losses that resulted from civil war and regicide and the work of re-enchantment, demonstrating directly or indirectly the critical role to be played by the Scots in political and cultural recovery. *The Chearfull Acclamation of the City of Edinburgh* (1660) is representative of the congratulatory ballads and verse broadsides that exhibit both the element of mourning via the rehearsal of past events and re-enchantment via the deployment of the discourse of sacred mystery. '*Edina*', Scotland's capital personified, is depicted moving from immersion in 'seas of brynie tears' (having seen the king 'Martyr'd', his heir 'exyl'd', his subjects 'Murther'd', the land 'Ruin'd' and the 'worst of Monsters [...] usurp[ing] Command') to the assumption of a 'chearful countenance' when Charles II's 'Radiant Lustre' 'despell[s]' the worse than hellish 'Clouds' that loomed over the nation as he takes his rightful place at his 'Royal Shryne'. This is an occasion for 'All Natives' of Scotland or Britain to join in an enchanting sacred ritual that associates God and King and figures Charles II as a heavenly ray of light emerging out of the devilish darkness:

> All Natives come I pray
> And (with *Edina*) Solemnize this Day
> To CHARLES the Second, Men, and Angels sing,
> God save Great *Britains*, *France's*, and *Irelands* King.[37]

This type of work, composed and printed as it is in Scotland in particular, reflects a need to form and restate cultural ties between Scotland and the Stuart monarchy. After all, it was common for Scotland to be compared in royalist works with Judas who had sold out the Christ-like Charles I in exchange for 'thirty pieces of silver'.[38] Scottish panegyric verse on the Restoration of Charles II rewrites history, suggesting (falsely) that all Scots had been horrified by the regicide and the Commonwealth that followed, when 'the scum of men' 'usurped [...] The Throne [...] And Sacred Majestie / Was sacrifized to the Tyrannie / of worst of Vermin' (*Caledons Gratulatory Rapture*, 1660). It is not enough simply to reprint the numerous English celebratory poems: Scotland must participate in this ritual with its own voice, bearing in mind the absence of 'Scottish representation at the Convention parliament', leading the 'Scottish nobles' to become 'increasingly worried'.[39] Cultural production makes up in such cases for political loss.

The cultural work of mourning and re-enchantment is equally present, if less directly, in two works written by the young lawyers George Mackenzie of Rosehaugh (c. 1636–1691) and William Clark (sometimes spelled Clarke) of Penicuik (fl. 1663–1685),[40] the prose romance *Aretina* (1660) and the tragi-comedy *Marciano* (1663) respectively. Both authors defend older literary traditions, but also adapt genres to new circumstances as they insert themselves in cultural and political life. Mackenzie was known later in life for 'his rigorous pursuit of the law and its violators throughout his public life' as a 'King's Advocate' who 'earned the sobriquet of "Bluidy Mackenzie"' because he was a 'methodical exterminator of enemies to the Crown he served'.[41] But when he wrote *Aretina*, he was a young lawyer seeking to negotiate a place for himself at court which for him meant reimagining the complex and troubled network of relations between the king and his subjects, dwelling on the deceit of favourites and the dangers of factionalism. In contrast to Mackenzie, Clark largely faded into the background after the appearance of *Marciano*. The first original Scottish play performed and printed in Restoration Scotland, *Marciano* was staged by non-professionals 'at the Abby [sic] of *Holyrudhouse*' to an audience made up of John Leslie, seventh Earl of Rothes, 'His *Majesties* high Commissioner, and others of the Nobility'.[42]

Mackenzie and Clark rely on the language of ethics in defending their turn to romance and drama, often seen as morally suspect genres. Both royalist Scotsmen emphasise that they are dedicated to the cause of morality, Clark arguing that tragedy and comedy can reveal 'the fatal ends' of criminal behaviour, expose and deter 'Court vanity and prodigality', 'City covetousness', and 'Country-simplicity', and 'incite the youth to imitate the vertuous actions' of past heroes,[43] and Mackenzie insisting that men and women 'would be incited to vertue and generosity, by reading in Romances'.[44] These defenses might be directed in part at a Scottish Presbyterian audience, but might also serve to strengthen the tie between ethical discourse and a royalist worldview, which would, for example, appeal to the Earl of Rothes, the Scottish favourite of Charles II for whom the play was performed. In his preface ("To all humours") to the published version of *Marciano*, Clark establishes the relationship between the Earl as both 'a zealous propogator of the Royal Interest' and 'a very noble Patron to all true wit and gallantry whatsoever', stressing the need for Scottish patrons with significant influence at court to support the pro-Stuart Scottish literati.

Although radically different works in many respects, *Aretina* and *Marciano* both represent the threat to right rule, the hazards of courtly life, and the need for courageous and loyal noble military men to serve the legitimate ruler in order to protect him from rebellious plots and usurpation (the King of Egypt in *Aretina*) or to restore him to leadership after rebel success (the Duke of Florence in *Marciano*); and both demonstrate that rebellion never goes unpunished. While the allegorical signification of major figures and events is transparent in *Marciano* – Lord Barbaro representing Cromwell and Cleon, Duke of Florence, figuring Charles II, etc. – it is more complex in *Aretina* which is populated by a diverse array of characters and is rich in philosophical meditations.

Nevertheless, both works clearly recount and stage internecine conflict, mourn the consequences of rebellion and civil war, and mystify the legitimate ruler. In *Marciano*, for example, the eponymous hero laments at the beginning of Act I, Scene 3,

> O *Florence*! don't insult at this dayes success,
> This unnatural victory over thy lawfull Prince
> Will quickly make thee sensible of unnatural
> And intolerable Tyranny [...][45]

By Act V, Scene 5, however, the audience is gifted with a song of re-enchantment:

> *Now breaks our day,*
> *Fairies away,*
> *Pack hence, I say,*
> > *our power's undone.*
> *Room for Jov's progeny,*
> *Full of divinity*
> Cleon, *brave* Cleon, *natures Paragon,*
> *Rebellion breathless lyes,*

> *Hell sings, her obsequyes,*
> > *Usurping Traytors quick be gone.*
> *Now,* Cleon, *divine* Cleon *mounts His Throne,*
> *Room – room – room – room for Him alone.*[46]

While the substance of *Aretina* is more complex – since, as a 'mirror for princes', it includes a critique of court life, indirectly referencing past mistakes of Stuart monarchs – Mackenzie still mystifies the restored king, Theopemptus, a figure of Charles II:

> All things being thus prepared, *Theopemptus* enters the City of *Lacedemon*, in the greatest pomp that loyalty, or luxury could invent: Above him at the Gates stood clouds, as they seemed, which rained down Wines of all sorts […]. These and many other expressions of joy were presented to him.[47]

However, while Mackenzie gives voice to an unadulterated Scottish loyalty to the crown and justifies the monarchy in political terms, he is aware of systemic flaws.[48] The ability to balance the discourses of political mourning, re-enchantment, and reservation in *Aretina* renders Mackenzie a rhetorically compelling and politically useful Scot in Restoration Britain, which explains his rise to political heights.

Original works of mourning and re-enchantment by Restoration Scots were not limited to the secular genres of tragi-comedy and romance. Both William Clark's 'poetical essay' *The Grand Tryal, or, Poetical Exercitations upon the Book of Job* (1685), dedicated to the recent Catholic convert James, the fourth Earl of Perth and Lord High Chancellor of Scotland (1648–1716), and the poems on Job in *Divine Poems, in Three Parts* (1665) by Arthur Nasmyth (fl. 1665), dedicated to the royalist James Carnegie, second Earl of Southesk (c. 1583–1669), are caught up with images of paradise lost and restored.[49] Peter C. Herman explains that 'the Book of Job's marked rise in popularity' occurred during and after the civil war because it spoke to and 'symbolize[d] national catastrophe';[50] but for Restoration royalists, it also symbolised national renewal since Job's restoration seemed to parallel that of Charles II in 1660, perhaps carrying on to the succession of James VII/II in 1685.[51] It is very likely that both Clark and Nasmyth engaged in Jobean poetic exposition within a royalist political framework; and both also make it clear in their prefatory matter that they write with the intent of securing a Scottish nobleman for a patron, Nasmyth reflecting, for example, that:

> [...] its [the poem's] perfection
> Only depends upon your sweet Acception.
> O then, My LORD, admit this glorious guise,
> To see your Servant Penn, You Patronize.
>   Accept my *Mite*, most Noble, I do crave
> No more; *its much*, because its all I have.[52]

In alluding to his work as the biblical widow's mite, Nasmyth also aligns the noble Scottish earl with the divine, reinforcing royalist ideology, but also associating in the paratext and in the religious poems that follow, a royalist worldview and religious commitment. Therefore, these original poems on Job by Scottish poets, including the paratextual matter that frames them, work to solidify the patronage of Scottish earls whose political stars are rising or on full display, associating the discourse of virtue (especially loyalty) or the Christian faith with a royalist perspective and with Scottish nobility operating in courtly circles. They also reveal the ongoing commitment of the Scottish literary community to the discourses of wisdom and religious piety.

Like Mackenzie, Clark, and Nasmyth, Thomas Sydserf (1624–1689?),[53] the former soldier and possible royalist spy who became a journalist, playwright, and theatre manager, hoped to energise the cultural scene in North Britain in the 1660s and to build up networks of patronage there. This royalist Scot, however, took an alternative route, importing the saucy and satirical wit of Restoration English culture to Scotland.[54] Clark made a gesture in this direction by inserting a witty subplot in *Marciano*, defending this choice to balance seriousness and mirth in his preface. In addition to publishing the first (short-lived) Scottish newspaper, *Mercurius Caledonius*,[55] Sydserf bombards Scots readers with brief prose burlesques and Menippean satires including: *Bourlasque News from the Antipodes* (1661), *The Prince of Tartaria his Voyage to Cowper in Fife* (1661), *The Scout of Cockeny* (c. 1661), *The Work Goes Bonnely On* (1661), *The Remarkable Prophesies in Order to the Present Times* (1665), and *The New Claret-Club* (1669).[56] Often comprising odd bits and pieces of satirical prose stitched together into seven- or eight-page pamphlets, these works adopt some of the literary strategies found in the libertine Cyrano de Bergerac's (1619–1655) 1657 *L'Autre Monde* (which Sydserf translated and published in 1659 as *Selenarchia*) and anticipate some Swiftian satirical moves. Frequently taking the reader to foreign lands (e.g. Normandy, Holland) or into the cosmos (e.g. the moon), these works draw attention to human folly in Scotland and beyond. The literature of travel is a vehicle through which to wittily critique a range of figures and issues, including what Sydserf views as fanatical Covenanters and divisive sectarians.

Unlike Mackenzie, Clark, and Nasmyth, Sydserf felt no compunction to detail the virtuous ends of his satirical prose or of his play, *Tarugo's Wiles: or, The Coffee-House*. Largely a translation of the Spanish playwright Agustín Moreto's (1618–1669) *No puede ser* (c. 1660), *Tarugo's Wiles* was first performed in London in 1667 and then at the Tennis Court Theatre in Edinburgh in 1668. The play consists of the familiar comic plot of thwarted genteel lovers overcoming opposition to their love through trickery (Tarugo, the master of disguise, is the play's trickster figure). However, Sydserf inserts original material into Act III which is set in a vibrant urban '*Coffee-House*, where is presented a mixture of all kind of people' talking of such unrelated matters as 'the physiological properties of coffee, inane syllogisms, the transfusion of blood, utopian Harringtonian political philosophy, Italian painting, political allegiance, sexuality and military stratagems'.[57]

Although the play was performed in Edinburgh, it was never published in Scotland, only in London, though there is evidence that the London edition was 'to be sold by the Book-sellers in Edinburgh'.[58] Perhaps it was not published in Restoration Scotland because its dramatic form and status as a mere 'Comical Trifle',[59] as Sydserf calls it, made it unsuitable for print.[60] Elsewhere Sydserf, in the voice of Symon Scruple, acknowledged the difficulties of producing such a work in Scotland: 'I do not see a possibility to introduce the use of Comedies into this Countrey, for the following reasons. First, a general unwillingness in the People to hear them; Secondly, the scarcity of money to pay for them; Thirdly, the want of Actors to represent them'.[61] However, through his published satirical prose vignettes, Sydserf managed to playfully deconstruct old Scottish icons like the Solemn League and Covenant, to engage in topical criticism to support Charles II and subject his political enemies to ridicule, and to promote an anti-puritanical wit and laughter in his role as a pro-Stuart Scottish 'comedian'.

While Sydserf's attempt to recreate aspects of the London theatrical scene in Edinburgh was not ultimately successful, some Scottish creative writers that followed continued to define themselves in relation to English authors. At least one hoped to become the Dryden of North Britain, with a focus on bolstering the Stuart heroic from a Scottish perspective, defending the Stuarts during volatile political times of plots and crises often through religious scripts, and securing patronage from Scottish peers, including James Stuart himself. There was a shift, therefore, from the discourse of mourning and re-enchantment to the discourse of resolute loyalty in the face of fanaticism as well as a merging of the language of royalism and authentic religious faith in a great deal of the writing of the late 1670s through the mid-1680s. Three Scottish royalist poets who emerge in this period during the Popish Plot (1678–1681) and the Exclusion Crisis (1679–1681) with the aim of taking up this cultural function are Ninian Paterson (d. 1668), Mungo Murray (fl. 1679–1684), and Michael Livingston (fl. 1680–1682). They consistently link Scotland and the Stuarts through panegyric verse on James, Duke of York and Albany, rather than on his brother, the king. This is not surprising when we consider that in 1679, James and Mary of Modena had visited Edinburgh and in 1680, 'the duke returned to Edinburgh for what would become a year-and-a-half stint as Charles II's Lord High Commissioner in Scotland, lodging his family in Holyrood Palace and thereby establishing a quasi-royal court in that kingdom for the first time in thirty years'.[62] This was a remarkable opportunity for Scottish poets in particular to become courtly makars, once again, in their homeland.

A Glaswegian by birth, a resolute royalist, and an Episcopalian minister, Paterson produced a lengthy book of Latin poetry and at least sixteen separately published English or linguistically hybrid (English and Latin) works.[63] He was eventually deposed from the position of minister of the Kirk at Liberton for 'sundry misbehaviours; but mainly for having defamed his Bischop in severall companies and occasions', and his appeals to have 'his sentence relaxed' fell on deaf ears.[64] Before losing his position, Paterson's literary focus had been Latin poetry, notably epigrams on Scottish 'worthies' situated alongside biblical and moral epigrams and biblical paraphrases in *Epigrammatum Libri Octo* (1678). After he left the Kirk, he retained the desire to populate the literary landscape with 'heroic' Scottish figures, but did so in English verse, often published on broadsheets, while expanding the definition of heroism. His subjects ranged from tailors and tradesmen to the future King James VII/II and his infant son.

To privilege and defend James Stuart, Paterson wrote two contentious works: *The Fanatick Indulgence Granted, Anno 1679* (1683) and *A Poem on the Test* (1683). Drawing on the tradition of Juvenalian satire, the former is composed of a series of poems: a brief Latin dedicatory poem to James followed by a much lengthier one in English exposing the danger 'Fanatick[s]' pose to the state and the monarch's person; a poem giving political advice to Charles II and another that scathingly attacks those who threaten the Stuart succession; and a welcome poem to the future

James VII/II on his visit to Scotland in 1679. The thrust of *The Fanatick Indulgence* is Paterson's categorisation of English or Scottish subjects as either loyal or dangerously treacherous with the purpose of encouraging the king to use violence rather than indulgence to suppress opposition. Paterson opposes crazed '*Fanatick[s]*', 'nastie, hairbraind scum, / A furious spawn of fiends' with law-abiding and religiously committed 'Loyal Subjects' who, like suffering Job, have been 'vext' by 'distractions, and destructions' from these fiendish characters for almost two decades.[65] Since Presbyterian '*Fanatick[s]*' are likely to perpetrate 'bloody monstrous crimes', they should no longer be 'Indulg'd', since '*Indulgences* ar[e] *Popish* things' and these fanatics showed no such mercy to Charles II's father, revealing the horrors of which they are capable.[66]

In contrast to this lamentable scene is the arrival in Scotland of James, Duke of York and Albany, who is 'welcome as was the light / To *Chaos* after an eternal night', most comforting given North Britain's 'distance' from Charles II.[67] In this future king Paterson places his hopes, looking to him to 'Calm Church distractions, and cure states disease'.[68] Treating Scotland and England as distinct entities, Paterson makes a clear statement about where Scotland should stand on the Exclusion Crisis, offering himself up as a devoted spokesman for the future king. Paterson's *Poem on the Test* serves a similar purpose, affirming the king's absolute prerogative, in this case on matters of church, and revelling in the hope that this 'true Gospel *Test*' will ensure 'faithful Loyalty' of the clergy: the Test is 'the *fan* [that] will purge this soultrie Isle / And separat[e] the precious from the vile'.[69] Paterson offers up biblical proof texts to support his conclusion that subjects should submit to the king in matters of religion, not rebel against monarchs they deem 'Oppressi[ve]', 'Idolatrous', 'Heretical', or '*Erronious*', and warns that to remove the Test Act is to give fuel to the firebrand '*Fanaticks*'.[70]

In the other English or linguistically hybrid works Paterson published in Edinburgh, mostly broadside funeral elegies, he presents to the reader a gallery of 'heroic' Scottish subjects who have now passed away. As a case in point, in elegising Thomas Robertson (1592–1686), Edinburgh Baillie and builder, Paterson zeroes in on how the citizens depended on the builder for the reliable and handsome works he erected, thereby 'Inrich[ing] and Beautif[ying] the Town', but also for, as a magistrate, 'preserv[ing] our State' by 'Law and Building'. Paterson suggests that in carrying out these tasks and in charitable giving, Robertson proved himself a loyal subject to the monarch: 'And with a Sumptuous, Free Magnificence, / Made Donatives both to the State and Prince'.[71] Though from the middle class, such a man, Paterson exclaims, was a noble 'Subject [that] could oblidge a King', especially since he also practiced his faith at his home, 'a Temple', where his family 'Praye[d] and Praise[d]' God. While we imagine Paterson wrote such works to line his own pocket when he was unemployed, there is still a concerted effort in this poem to link loyal Scottish subjects across social stations with 'glorious virtues' and religious devotion.[72]

In the works of Michael Livingston (M. L.), who writes in imitation of Dryden, we observe a similar association of the future James VII/II with the Scots and a pantheon of modern heroic figures who inhabit Scotland, all of whom embody the virtues lost during the Interregnum, including loyalty to the king. Little is known about Michael Livingston of Pantasken (Bantaskin), but he was probably born in Falkirk on 22 June 1656 to David Levingston and Helein Elphingston and was related to Alexander Livingston, the Earl of Callendar, in whom he also found a patron. In addition to writing panegyrical verse on the Earl of Callendar (after 1653–1692), William Douglas, Duke of Hamilton (1634–1694), and George Livingston, third Earl of Linlithgow (1616–1690), Livingston wrote four poems to James in Edinburgh in 1680: *Albion's Elegie* and *Albion's Farewel* (printed together); *Augustis, ac Praepotentibus Heroibus, Jacobo & Mariæ, Albaniæ & Eboraci Ducibus*; and *Albion's Congratulatory*. Three of the four are on James's departure from or arrival at Scotland, events described with excessive rhetoric and dense classical allusion: he laments that James will '[d]esert' Scotland and longs for the future king to stay since he cannot imagine Scotland living without '*Caledon's Sun*';[73] yet he recognises that England and Scotland each claim half of him. Defending James's position on political and religious matters, Livingston encourages the Scots to praise him openly and assures James that all but a few Scots are devoted to him.[74] With encouragement from James to write such panegyrics, Livingston felt comfortable directly asking for patronage and protection from him (among others): 'Vouchsafe, therefore, ROYAL SIR, to accept the humble tender of an obsequious Muse; and, in these injurious and tempestuous times, daign to shrowd her under the hospitable shade of your *Protection*'.[75] All of Livingston's poems strive to produce networks of patronage and do so by working to define the post-Restoration Scottish heroic, particularly with respect to James Stuart.

Mungo Murray (M. M.) is also intent on painting portraits of Scottish heroes, though always in elegiac verse. The identity of Murray has not yet been established,[76] but we do know that he published four elegies between 1679 and 1684 on major Scottish political and religious figures:

David Wemyss, second Earl of Wemyss (1610–1679), a member of Charles II's Privy Council; James Sharp, Archbishop of St Andrews and Lord Primate of Scotland (1618–1679), brutally murdered by Covenanters in 1679; John Leslie, seventh Earl and first Duke of Rothes and Lord Chancellor of Scotland (1630–1681); and James Graham, third Marquess of Montrose (1657–1684). These Scottish men of high standing exhibit similar qualities, according to Murray, inasmuch as he depicts them as loyal subjects who despise sedition and are dedicated to virtuous living and/or religious faith. Scottishness, royalism, and virtue/belief are once again triangulated in this work, while any force that disrupts this stable relation is deemed an alien, unintelligible, or peculiar entity. In his broadside poem, *On the Death and Horrid Murther of the Most Reverend Father in God, James Archbishop of Saint-Andrews, Lord Primate of Scotland* (1679), for example, Murray renders the Scottish Episcopal Archbishop, an emblem of restored 'right religion', a holy martyr whose fate is akin to that of Abel and Charles I.[77] In contrast, the '*Independent-Presbyterians*' responsible for his death, 'Hells Cruel Band', are figured as monstrous beings, whose acts would even disturb the 'Turks, Pagans, Heths, [and] Jews'. In this way, Murray, like Paterson and Livingston, stabilises the relation of Scotland, the Stuarts, and the restored Episcopal Church.

Conclusion

Publishers in Restoration Scotland printed past and contemporary English and Scottish literature that undergirded a belief in the value of virtue and faith, cultural and political tradition, and jovial and instructive wit. They printed very few poems, plays, or works of prose fiction that might be negatively associated with 'the promiscuity and lawlessness of those close to the king [Charles II]', explaining in part their resistance to publishing plays in general, especially urbane comedies.[78] They often opted instead to publish Scottish works from the medieval period onward that supported a distinctly Caledonian heroic lineage that continued into the present, albeit with emergent modern qualities aligned with urban development and municipal management. In reissuing significant past Scottish literary texts, most often poems, and publishing the poems, plays, and prose fiction of emerging Scottish authors, these publishers also display a dedication to solidifying and promoting a canon of Scottish literature. Restoration Scottish authors took advantage of this opportunity to participate in rebuilding Scottish culture, working to negotiate a patronage network in North Britain with a focus on members of the Scottish nobility who were Stuart favourites, thereby encouraging the Court to invest in the production of Scottish culture. To bridge earlier and later Stuart culture, the majority of these Scottish writers engaged in the cultural work of mourning, re-enchantment, and resolute loyalty. Although at times Scots creative writers experimented with genres that did not gain traction in the moment, such as drama, most new cultural productions contributed to this goal of a Scotland reawakening to its potential. And yet, in the 1680s, there was increasing awareness of the fragility of that culture, given the alignment of Scotland's interests with those of James. In the years following 1688, therefore, Scottish writers would once again have to reformulate their culture in the face of radical change.

PART 2: MEDIA AND MEDIATION

CHAPTER FIVE

Gender and National Identity in Allan Ramsay's *The Tea-Table Miscellany* and Eighteenth-Century Scottish Song Culture

Emma Pink

This chapter considers popular eighteenth-century Scottish song culture through the lens of Allan Ramsay's (1686–1758) *Tea-Table Miscellany* (1723–37). Innovative and highly successful, the *Miscellany* paved the way for developments in Scots literary culture throughout the century, such as the Scots vernacular revival in poetry, and the adoption of a wide-ranging, inclusive approach to the production, editing, and collection of national songs.[1] This chapter locates the complexities of Ramsay's collection in relation to earlier and later characterisations of Scottish song. I begin with late-seventeenth-century broadsides and collections that refer to their contents as Scottish 'ballads' or 'songs'. Next, I consider the performativity of song culture and the tropological richness of the idea of 'voice' in the construction of the Scottish nation in the *Tea-Table Miscellany*. Scholars such as Murray Pittock, Steve Newman and Leith Davis have commented on Ramsay's concern to give Scotland, in Davis's words, 'a voice in a more inclusive kind of Britishness'.[2] While Davis uses the term 'voice' metaphorically to comment on Ramsay's editorial and poetic practices, this chapter explores the literal function of 'voice' as it relates to national identity and gender in Ramsay's *Tea-Table Miscellany*, noting in particular the array of gendered perspectives in the work that serve to vex any simple understanding of female/male relations, family hierarchies of authority and obedience, and polarities such as lowland/highland, urban/rural, and local/national.[3] Finally, this chapter considers Ramsay's *Miscellany* in relation to later works such as David Herd's (c. 1732–1810) *Ancient and Modern Scots Songs* (1769; 1776, expanded,

2 volumes), John Pinkerton's (1758–1826) *Scottish Tragic Ballads* (1769; 1776, expanded, 2 volumes, new title, *Ancient and Modern Scottish Songs, Heroic Ballads, Etc.*), and Joseph Ritson's (1752–1803) *Scotish [sic] Song* (1794), reflecting on how Scottish song at the end of the eighteenth century became synonymous with the 'affect' of national identity. The chapter concludes by noting how over time both Ramsay and Scottish songs became associated with a limited, nostalgic sense of Scottish identity.

Scottish Songs Before Ramsay

Ramsay brought out his *Miscellany* in a literary marketplace which was already familiar with printed Scottish songs. Throughout the seventeenth century, for example, songs signifying their 'Scottishness' through elements such as title, author, musical setting, language, topic, or place of origin had been published as broadsides. These songs, much like Ramsay's and, indeed, popular Scottish songs throughout the eighteenth century, covered a wide range of topics, including romantic love, social ritual, politics, and war. *An Excellent New Song, Intituled, Valiant Jockie: His Ladies Resolution* (1700?), for instance, features a female speaker whose beloved Jockie has been 'march'd away, / To fight a Battle with great *Mackay*'.[4] Regardless of the danger, she is determined to follow him into battle 'to guard his precious Life', as well as protect 'Our King's Right'.[5] *The Sorrowful Maiden for the Want of Tocher-good* (1700) details the anguish of a young woman whose gentleman father has squandered the family's fortune. Lacking a dowry, she is left with limited choices – 'An old Maiden if that I be, / no Man will of me make' – in a society in which marriage involves economic exchange.[6] The issue of dowry is again taken up in *A Dialogue between Ald [sic] John M'clatchy, and Young Willie Ha, about the Marriage of his Daughter Maggy M'clatchy*; however, unlike the female speaker in *The Sorrowful Maiden*, Maggy has a father who brokers the best deal he can for Maggy, but only after Maggy finds the suitor acceptable and grants her father permission to proceed with the negotiations.[7]

Scottish songs also appeared in books such as the English dramatist and songwriter Thomas D'Urfey's (1653?–1723) *Wit and Mirth; Or, Pills to Purge Melancholy* (1699–1720) and Scottish printer and bookseller James Watson's (1664?–1722) *A Choice Collection of Comic and Serious Scots Poems both Ancient and Modern* (1706–1711). Of D'Urfey's 'Scotch songs', late-eighteenth-century song collector and antiquarian Joseph Ritson claimed: 'it is hard to say whether wretchedness of poetry, ignorance of the Scotish [sic] dialect, or nastiness of ideas, is most evident or most despicable'.[8] Yet Ritson also noted the great popularity of D'Urfey's songs and how many of them were considered 'as genuine specimens of Scotish [sic] song; as indeed most of them are regarded even in Scotland'.[9] Many of D'Urfey's 'favourite [Scottish] songs' listed by Ritson are also found in Ramsay's *Miscellany*, some with revisions. For example, D'Urfey's 'A SONG' from volume one of *Wit and Mirth* appears in the *Miscellany* retitled as 'SONG' with a subtitle of 'She raise and loot me in', and the substitution of the Scots-language forms, 'bairn' (child) for D'Urfey's 'Bern' and 'loot' for D'Urfey's English verb 'let'. Revisions such as these suggest the 'Scottifying' of songs produced for a London-based market and their adoption as 'genuine' Scottish cultural forms within Scotland.[10]

Multi-mediation and *The Tea-Table Miscellany*

For the *Miscellany*, Ramsay collected and revised existing songs such as those circulating in broadsides and appearing in collections such as D'Urfey's. In addition, Ramsay wrote new songs, thereby representing Scottish song as both fluid and malleable.[11] The songs demonstrate Ramsay's sophisticated use of genre, as well as his thematic and linguistic complexity. Ramsay published the first volume of the *Tea-Table Miscellany* in duodecimo form in 1723. By that point, he was a bookseller and was involved in the Edinburgh theatre scene.[12] He had also established himself – in Edinburgh and beyond – as a popular poet and writer of Scottish songs. He had taken up that role twelve to fifteen years earlier when he was a member of the Easy Club, a group of young Scottish professionals who penned poems and letters and discussed national politics, particularly the relations between Scotland and England since the Acts of Union of 1707. The first volume of the *Miscellany* was followed by three more volumes;[13] by 1737 the *Miscellany* had gone through nine editions, and nineteen by the century's end, with reprintings of several editions throughout the century. By 1876, the *Miscellany* totalled thirty editions.[14]

Fundamental to a discussion of how Ramsay's *Miscellany* functioned in the eighteenth-century cultural field is a consideration of the ways in which oral, scribal and print cultures interact in the production of song culture. Eighteenth-century song collectors such as Ramsay did not simply collect songs; they revised, adapted, and produced the songs they published. Moreover, they drew on various sources – oral, scribal, and print – which were often involved in a complex cycle of mediation.¹⁵ While an oral source may be textualised in print, for instance, it can continue to engage with oral culture. This is demonstrated by the epigraph, 'Of Mrs. Arden', found on the imprint of the *Miscellany*. Written by the seventeenth-century Stuart poet and politician, Edmund Waller (1606–87), whose work was widely read throughout the seventeenth and early eighteenth centuries, the epigraph evokes the oral/aural, and other, senses in the first stanza:

> Behold, and listen, while the fair
> Breaks in sweet sounds the willing air;
> And with her own breath fans the fire
> Which her bright eyes do first inspire:
> What reason can that love controul,
> Which more than one way courts the soul?¹⁶

Directing the reader to 'listen' to the 'sweet sounds' of the 'fair', the speaker suggests a desire which, while initially inspired by the sight of the woman's 'bright eyes', is 'fanned' by the sound of her voice: multi-sensorial, desire arises from aural, oral and visual perceptions. This epigraph by Waller embodies the way that the *Miscellany* itself draws so heavily on multiple media to arouse its readers' desires.

At the same time that it recognises the power of multiple media, however, the epigraph also registers another important characteristic of the *Miscellany*: its complex alignment of gender and the nation, as the speaker sounds a cautionary note regarding the potential failure of reason to 'control' that 'love' which is stimulated by multiple senses. In his discussion of Ramsay's songs in *Ballad Collection, Lyric, and the Canon*, Newman points out that the sight and sound of a woman singing came to be understood by some eighteenth-century theorists as performing a civilising effect on society. Newman identifies several moments in the *Miscellany* in which a woman singing is figured 'as a privileged object of aesthesis. No mere object of sexual desire, she elicits desire in order to redirect it for the good of polite society'.¹⁷ I would argue, however, that song culture, gender, and national identity come together in a multifarious, often unstable polyphony in the text and paratexts of Ramsay's *Miscellany*, and many of the female voices within the *Miscellany* are articulating their own desires, expressing an agency directed toward the realisation of their own objectives rather than 'for the good of polite society'.

Gendering the National Song (Para)Text

In the 1740 London edition of the *Miscellany*, the gendering of the text and the nation begins with the frontispiece which features a full-page portrait of Ramsay.[18] A lone, male figure, he is captured in side-profile, looking to his left, toward the title page, typical of authors' portraits at this time. The portrait's frame features thistles on all four corners and tartan ribbons on the top two corners. The imprint continues the nationalist theme introduced by the frontispiece, with the title of the 1740 edition printed in large font at the top of the page, *The Tea-Table Miscellany: Or, A Collection of Choice Songs, Scots and English*. Furthermore, gender is never far from any page throughout the *Miscellany*, including the frontispiece and imprint, which feature an all-male cast of cultural producers, from the author, portrait painter, engraver, epigraph author (Allan Ramsay the Elder, Allan Ramsay the Younger, G. King, Waller) to those who print and sell the work listed at the bottom of the page (A[ndrew] Millar and J[ames] Hodges). The frontispiece and imprint imply a male-dominated field of cultural production; however, the other paratextual materials (such as the Dedication and the Preface) and the songs themselves involve a much more complicated treatment of gender, and serve to problematise, however subtly, what may initially appear to be a homogenous male authority. For example, Ramsay dedicates the *Miscellany* to every woman of all classes throughout Britain:

> *To ilka lovely* BRITISH *Lass,*
> *Frae Ladies* Charlotte, Anne *and* Jean,
> *Down to ilk bonny singing* Bess,
> *Wha dances barefoot on the Green.*[19]

Following these four lines is a six-stanza poem addressed to the 'Dear Lasses' (the dedicatees mentioned directly above). In the first stanza of the poem, Ramsay, speaking of himself in the third person, positions himself as their 'most humble slave', who, in seeking their acceptance, 'presents this sma' propine'.[20] Here Ramsay conflates vernacular and highly classical literature. In the second stanza, however, he switches from petitioner to director, instructing the women to take his work and 'Revive it with your tunefu' notes', as 'Its beauties will look sweet and fair, / Arising saftly through your throats'.[21] In the third stanza, he situates the women in the home, surrounded by their children whom they will amuse with their singing. The scene is domesticated, involving conversation and work, and Ramsay's songs have their place in it as entertainment. Though the Dedication initially appears to place women in an elevated position as 'dedicatees', in fact, it serves to position them under Ramsay's direction, within the domestic arena. Subject to male authority, their voices are co-opted, employed to further his aesthetic project (to 'Revive' and make 'Its beauties [...] look sweet and fair'), care for children ('The wanton wee thing will rejoice'), and fill empty time ('Thir sangs may ward you frae the sowr, / And gayly vacant minutes pass').[22]

Yet, while the Dedication may seem to ventriloquise women's voices, the songs themselves complicate this process. The theme of sensorial, sensual desire, or 'love' aroused orally/aurally by women that is suggested in the epigraph by Waller occurs repeatedly throughout the *Miscellany*, but in such a way as to question male power. For example, the unidentified speaker of 'SONG' describes 'BRIGHT *Cynthia*'s power' (Cynthia being the woman the speaker desires) as arising from her sensorial appeal:

> She seems the queen of love to reign;
> For she alone dispenses
> Such sweets as best can entertain
> The gust of all the senses.[23]

Appealing to sight ('Her face a charming prospect brings'), smell ('Her breath gives balmy blisses'), sound ('I hear an angel when she sings'), and taste ('And taste of heaven in kisses'), Cynthia constitutes an intensely alluring presence whose power ('divinely great'), which derives from 'nature's richest treasure', can more than satisfy sensorial appetites ('Four senses thus she feasts with joy').[24] Yet, while the speaker testifies to Cynthia's power, his portrayal of 'love', much like that of Waller's speaker, is not entirely unambiguous. The speaker in 'Song', in the final two lines ('Let me the other sense employ, / And I shall die with pleasure'), suggests the sixteenth- and seventeenth-century usage of 'die', as a poetical metaphor for experiencing sexual orgasm: through the fifth sense, touch, he will achieve orgasm and, thus, 'die with pleasure'.[25] At the same time, however, 'die' may be read as a warning regarding pleasure (especially excessive pleasure), in which 'die' signifies the suffering of death-like pains (such as implied by Addison in *Spectator* No. 86 [1711], in which he writes, 'Nothing is more common than for Lovers to [...] languish, despair, and dye in dumb Show').[26] If read in this way, this song, like many of the songs in the *Miscellany* which depict desiring bodies, evokes a sense of unease regarding the degree of desire and its containment, as well as the voicing of desire which is further complicated by gender, as the female figures in both 'Mrs. Auden' and 'SONG' stimulate a desire which is unstable and which threatens the male speakers' reason and control.

In later editions of the *Miscellany* Ramsay included additional paratextual commentary which serves to emphasise his alignment of gender and the nation. In the Preface of the tenth edition of the *Miscellany*, Ramsay tells his readers that his '*worthy friend Dr. Bannerman tells me from America*' that not only is Ramsay's work well received and in demand throughout Britain, America, and 'Round all the globe' by people of all classes, but his songs, here treated as composites of both lyric and music ('soft verse, made to a *Scottish* air') are performed by the 'fair', often at the expense of other music such as '*Camilla*'s warbling notes' and Italian operas.[27] According to Bannerman, as quoted by Ramsay, it is Ramsay's Scots songs (and Bannerman specifically lists '*Last time I came o'er the moor*', '*Mary Scot*', '*Tweed-side*', and '*Mary Gray*') that women are performing, again drawing on the image of women coming together in song; however, unlike the Dedication which places women and Ramsay's songs within the home, here the women and the appeal of the Scottish songs are imagined not within the domestic sphere; rather, they (both women and songs) are transnational and transatlantic in their positioning and influence.[28] This would suggest a markedly different role for women and song than that suggested in the Dedication. Given that, as Jeff Strabone has pointed out, in the period following the 1707 Union 'the loss of sovereignty and the rise of print-capitalism in Scotland combined to yield a new concept of the nation based not in political institutions but in culture', the imagining of women as the conveyers of Scottish culture throughout the world accords women an important role in the (re)forming of the Scottish nation.[29]

Moreover, while women were granted no political power, at least officially, their increasing commercial and critical influence is suggested by the *Miscellany*'s Preface, in which Ramsay writes:

> *IN my compositions and collections, I have kept out all smut and ribaldry, that the modest voice and ear of the fair singer might meet with no affront; the chief bent of all my studies being, to gain their good graces: and it shall always be my care, to ward off these frowns that would prove mortal to my muse.*[30]

Ramsay frames his concern regarding women's reception of his work within an economy of female modesty, suggesting that he has edited his works with a view to womanly sensibilities, yet the songs themselves caution against any simple understanding of female agency. As Kathleen Wilson notes, women were actively involved in the cultural field as consumers, producers, and critics.[31] That Ramsay's work would appeal to women is suggested by the relatively high number of women (32%) named in the subscription list of William Thomson's 1733 edition of his *Orpheus Caledonius: Or, A Collection of Scots Songs,* a work very similar in content to Ramsay's.[32] In fact, ninety-one of its one hundred songs had appeared earlier, in the first three volumes of the *Miscellany* (1723, 1726, 1727). Certainly, Ramsay's prefatory comments speak to his attempt to engage his female readers' support for his project while at the same time suggesting their ability to affect his symbolic, cultural and economic capital. Urging his 'little books, go your ways; be assured of favourable reception wherever the sun shines on the free-born chearful Briton', he tells them: '*steal your selves into the ladies bosoms.* [...] *please the ladies, and take care of my fame*'.[33] In doing so, he connects cultural production, pleasure, national identity, and the female body, suggesting his work as an intimate, perhaps even prurient, infiltration into the private arena of the nation, embodied in female form.

Within the songs, women's voices express a wide range of views on cultural, political, economic and sexual issues. A pervasive theme is love and its complex intersections with sex and money. While many of the women seek emotional fulfillment, women are also heard negotiating for their material security and sensual pleasure, often at the same time. The coming together of these various interests can be heard in 'DUMBARTON'S *Drums*', in which Annie sings of her beloved, Jonny, whose military career will improve their collective fortunes. Not only is he sensually appealing ('While he kisses and blesses his *Annie*—O! / 'Tis a soldier alone can delight me—O'), and handsome ('For his graceful looks do invite me—O'), but he will keep her safe:

> While guarded in his arms,
> I'll fear no wars alarms,
> Neither danger nor death shall e'er fright me—O.[34]

Sensual and aesthetic pleasure, safety, and security: the form of masculinity Annie constructs (and values) must provide a diverse range of benefits. In addition, she demonstrates a keen sensitivity to the connections between gender and class and actively pursues her and Jonny's mutual interests by planning to secure a commission for Jonny:

> My love is a handsome laddie—O,
> Genteel, but ne'er foppish nor gaudy—O:
> Tho' commissions are dear,
> Yet I'll buy him one this year;
> For he shall serve no longer a cadie—O.[35]

Here, Annie suggests the various ways in which Jonny will be well served by the procurement of a commission. Honourable and brave, 'Unacquainted with rogues and their knavery' (presumably the lower and ungentlemanly classes), a commissioned officer attends to 'the ladies or the king; / For every other care is but slavery—O'.[36] Liberated from the confines of the non-commissioned ranks, Jonny will be in the company of those through whom promotions and privileges are obtained. Moreover, Jonny is not the only one to benefit from his obtaining a commission. Annie recognises that the military provides opportunities for women as well as men; she will also be elevated through Jonny's military endeavours and position:

> Then I'll be the captain's lady—O,
> Farewell all my friends and my daddy—O;
> I'll wait no more at home,
> But I'll follow with the drum,
> And whene'er that beats, I'll be ready—O.[37]

Annie will obtain status ('the captain's lady'), freedom from her familial and domestic obligations, and a degree of autonomy. She will also be with the man she desires, one who pleases and values her.

Throughout the song, we hear only Annie's voice detailing her plans for both her and Jonny's professional and economic future. Jonny's voice is never heard, and we are left assuming a male agency which is pliable, accommodating, and willing to be led in contrast to the directing, politically and economically savvy female agency modelled by Annie.[38] She will buy the commission, however expensive, suggesting that she has economic capital to invest. While, indeed, Annie anticipates sexual pleasure, it is a pleasure for which *she* has planned and which she says will make *her* happy. Importantly, it is a pleasure for which, through her capital investment (buying Jonny's commission), she has provided the opportunity. She is no servant doing the bidding of others. She expresses sexual desire and professional ambition; she also demonstrates an awareness of the social and political hierarchies operating and develops a strategy by which to navigate them and succeed.

The *Miscellany* features many voices singing of the economic, social, political and sexual opportunities available through marriage. In 'MAGIE'S Tocher', two men (the wooer and Magie's father) hammer out the details of Magie's dowry, concluding a deal which is agreeable to both parties and which offers sufficient support for the young couple and any children who may come along.[39] The male speaker of '*Lass with a Lump of Land*' also suggests the prospects available through marriage, though, for him, the most important element is that of economic gain. Capital alone, in the form of money or land, will ensure an enduring union. He looks to the woman to provide such capital and explicitly states that in the economy of marriage, 'she that's rich, her market's made', and 'naithing can catch our modern sparks, / But well tocher'd lasses, or jointer'd widows'.[40]

A different kind of economy is proposed by the female speaker of '*This is no mine ain House*', who connects obedience with love, honour, and good treatment. Of her marital relations with her soon-to-be husband, and her obligation to obey him, she says,

> When *Hymen* moulds us into ane,
> My *Robie*'s nearer than my kin,
> And to refuse him were a sin,
> Sae lang's he kindly treats me.[41]

Importantly, she says that her obedience is conditional upon his good treatment of her and that the marriage is a contractual arrangement in which love dictates duty and is dependent on the partners fulfilling their obligations. The speaker gains her 'ain house', which means not only her own property, but also her own affective landscape, over which she is mistress.

> When I'm in mine ain house,
> True love shall be at hand ay,
> To make me still a prudent spouse,
> And let my man command ay;[42]

In the speaker's eyes, love is the catalyst, the agent directing her actions; because she loves, she is directed by love and love allows her husband's command over her. Moreover, though in legal terms she has no claim to Robie's (her husband's) house, she makes clear from the beginning that whereas in her father's house she has no standing, in Robie's house she is 'mistris of his fire-side' and can – and will – express agency in terms of the domestic power structure.[43]

A dissimilar form of female agency operates in '*Norland* JOCKY *and Southland* JENNY'. This song evokes issues of class and regionalism, while simultaneously operating as a test of the male (north) by the female (south). The first six lines of the song are in third person and set up the dialogue which follows between 'A Southland *Jenny*' and 'a norland *Johny*'. Johny (also referred to as Jocky), a suitor from the north, comes courting the 'right bonny' Jenny from the south. Johny, taken with the beautiful Jenny, is overwhelmed by shyness.[44] However, 'blinks of her beauty, and hopes o' her siller / Forc'd him at last to tell his mind till her', and, overcoming his shyness, he proposes marriage. Jenny agrees to marry him, though she admits to having 'neither gowd nor money', but will 'ware my beauty on thee'.[45] On hearing that she is without wealth, he seems to recant his proposal, evoking a simplistic form of regionalism, suggesting that whereas 'Ye lasses of the south, ye'r a' for dressing; / Lasses of the north, mind milking and threshing'.[46] He explains that his parents would disapprove of his marrying 'a lady' (though Jenny's status as a 'lady' did not seem to deter him when he held out hopes of a substantial dowry), and that he must marry a woman who can manage the physical labour as well as social networking required of a northern wife:

> For I maun hae a wife that will rise in the morning,
> Crudle a' the milk, and keep the house a scaulding,
> Toolie with her nibours, and learn at my minny,
> A norland *Jocky* maun hae a norland *Jenny*.

Jenny responds,

> My father's only daughter and twenty thousand pound,
> Shall never be bestow'd on sic a silly clown;
> For a' that I said was to try what was in ye.
> Gae hame, ye norland *Jock*, and court your norland *Jenny*.[47]

Revealing that she is an only daughter with a considerable fortune, she sends him on his way, but not before telling him that she had been testing him. The critical capacity needed to judge and the power to act on her judgment are located in the woman; the woman knows her own worth on the marriage market and will test those men who come wooing, sending away those whom she deems wanting. She is not attended by a male relative, nor does she invoke male authority. She can assess a man's worth, his value as a potential mate. Money empowers her but she is also no pawn without agency.[48]

The song evokes a binary of a southern, propertied female, and a northern, labouring male. The woman, Jenny, expects to be valued for her beauty and her inherent worth; she employs a marriage economy based on aesthetic value and affect, and rejects her suitor, Johny, on the grounds that he employs a different marriage economy and is unable (or unwilling) to operate within her value system. He is 'sic a silly clown' because he is unable to appreciate her aesthetic capital and engage with an economy of affect. His inability to do so means that he cannot function in her world; thus, the marriage economy he employs – which values female partners in terms of the economic capital (specifically, money and labour) they bring to the marriage – renders him, however ironically, incapable of realising the economic capital Jenny would bring to their marriage. Implicit in this song is a critique of the regionalism operating in eighteenth-century Scotland; just as Johny cannot move beyond his northern regionalism to inhabit, and benefit from, the social, cultural, and economic landscape of the south, so is the north condemned to remain economically undercapitalised if unable to participate in the increasingly industrial, commercial market economy of the nation.

A different type of regional critique is offered in *The Highland Laddie*. The female speaker, who self-identifies as a 'lawland lass', compares the 'lawland lads' to her 'highland laddie'. She begins with a critique of the men of the lowlands:

> THE lawland lads think they are fine;
> But O they're vain and idly gawdy!
> How much unlike that gracefu' mein,
> And manly looks of my highland laddie?[49]

As a Lowlander, she speaks from a position of knowledge. She knows the men of the Lowlands, is familiar with their ways and their self-deceptions. She claims that they are conceited and uselessly, tastelessly fine, and lack the grace and manliness of Donald, her Highlander. She posits a model of masculinity which involves a pleasing, elegant, courteous manner, and a strong, independent appearance. Her use of the word 'manly'[50] suggests that for her, the Highlander is the paradigm of masculinity, the model against which both womanliness and manliness may be judged. She claims that given the freedom to choose 'To be the wealthiest lawland lady', she would 'take young *Donald* without trews, / With bonnet blew, and belted plaidy'. Even the 'brawest beau in borrows-town, / In a' his airs, with art made ready', is 'but a clown' when compared to her Highlander, who is 'finer far in's tartan plaidy'.[51]

In the first three stanzas she speaks as a Lowlander within the Lowlands and centres her critique on a direct comparison of the Lowland men with the Highland Laddie. However, in the fourth stanza, she switches to a celebration of the Highland Laddie, located in the Highlands, with her by his side:

> O'er benty hill with him I'll run,
> And leave my lawland kin and dady,
> Frae winter's cauld, and summer's sun,
> He'll screen me with his highland plaidy.[52]

Imagining herself running through the Highlands with Donald, without her family, protected from the elements by the Highlander's 'plaidy', she constructs a moment of impossible freedom: freedom to run, freedom from familial obligations, freedom to be intimate without censure, freedom to be in nature and yet protected from its threatening aspects. In this imagined space, she is free of all physical, social, sexual strictures. In the fifth stanza she briefly returns to a Lowland scene, but only to compare it to the pleasures of the Highlands:

> A painted room, and silken bed,
> May please a lawland laird and lady;
> But I can kiss, and be as glad
> Behind a bush in's highland plaidy.[53]

Whereas the aesthetic and foreign elements associated with the urbanised culture of the Lowlands may appeal to the upper classes, the speaker positions herself within the natural landscape of the Scottish nation, which she associates with the Highlands. Both the Highlands and the Highlander are imagined as sources of wilderness and liberation, providing opportunities for intimacy and sensual/sexual pleasure without the social and cultural conventions of the more urban Lowlands. The speaker suggests, in the sixth stanza, that her speech with Donald is informal, intimate, and sensual, and she concludes, in the seventh stanza, with her declaration of endless love for her Highlander. Entangling gender, class, and regionalism, the song sets forth a complicated view of the nation. It presents multiple binaries, such as Lowland versus Highland, urban versus rural, art versus nature. The Lowlands are associated with art and artifice, which, together with its foreign elements ('A painted room, and silken bed'), constitute an emasculating influence on the nation's men. Only those men of the Highlands are beyond the urban, alien effects of the lowlands.

Yet, in the song 'SANDY *and* BETTY', Scottish masculinity is not associated with the Highlands, but with the nation more generally. In this song, an allegorical treatment of the 1707 unification of the English and Scottish parliaments under Queen Anne, Scotland is represented by a male lover, Sandy, a Lowlander born in Edinburgh, who is 'As blyth a lad as e'er gade thence'.[54] England is represented by a female lover Betty, who 'did *Stafford*-shire adorn / With all that's lovely to the sense'.[55] Alluding to the dissolution of the Scottish parliament and its post-union re-location in London, the song's unidentified speaker suggests that this re-location, and, more generally, the political unification with Britain, had an ameliorating effect on Scotland: 'Had *Sandy* still remain'd at hame, / He had not blinkt on *Betty*'s smile'.[56] While the move proves enriching to Sandy, Betty

> [...] like the fragrant violet,
> Still flourish'd in her native mead:
> He, like the stream, improving yet
> The further from his fountain-head.[57]

Unlike Betty (England), who thrives in her native environment, Sandy (Scotland) improves the further he travels from his place of origin, until, that is, he reaches Betty (England):

> The stream must now no further stray;
> A fountain fixt by *Venus*' power
> In his clear bosom, to display
> The beauties of his bord'ring flower.[58]

Union is portrayed as a love affair, decreed by the queen of Britain (Anne) and preserved by the 'queen of love' (Venus), which furthers both parties' interests:

> When gracious *Anna* did unite
> Two jarring nations into one,
> She bade them mutually unite,
> And make each other's good their own.
>
> Henceforth let each returning year
> The *rose* and *thistle* bear one stem:
> The *thistle* be the *rose*'s spear
> The *rose* the *thistle*'s diadem.[59]

While the rose (England) and the thistle (Scotland) will 'bear one stem', the song leaves no doubt that though 'The *thistle* will be the *rose*'s spear', the rose will be the '*thistle*'s diadem'. If 'spear' is understood to symbolise military power, and 'diadem' royal authority, then Scotland, here initially portrayed as a masculine presence (Sandy), transforms under the influence of England, a feminine presence (Betty), to become the armed force protecting and promoting British royal interests; here, however, Britain is England: the thistle (Scotland) remains distinct from the rose (England), however much grafted together through politics and desire.

Performance and/or Preservation

For Ramsay, a song became a song through the act of performance.[60] Many of the *Miscellany*'s songs include the title of an air to which it was to be sung, and a range of works featuring musical texts to the songs began appearing in print as early as 1725–26. Some of these works present music without words, while others include both music and song texts. William Thomson's first edition of *Orpheus Caledonius* (1725–26), and Allan Ramsay and Alexander Stuart's *Musick for Allan Ramsay's Collection of Scots Songs* (c. 1726), for example, contain musical texts without song texts, whereas William Thomson's second edition of *Orpheus Caledonius* (1733), and Robert Bremner's *Thirty Scots Songs for a Voice & Harpsichord. The Music taken from the Most genuine Sets extant, the Words from Allan Ramsay* (1757, c. 1770 [two books]) feature both musical and song texts. David McGuinness and Aaron McGregor, in their recent discussion of the music associated with the *Miscellany*, note that the variations in 'presentation and musical style' amongst these publications indicate a range of intended audiences.[61] Thomson's first edition of *Orpheus Caledonius*, for example, 'is clearly intended for an affluent readership: it is a high-quality folio edition, at the cost of one guinea, with an illustrious list of over three hundred mainly upper-class subscribers and a dedication to the Princess of Wales'.[62] Its 'vocal writing is technically demanding' and ornamented melody lines stand in contrast to Robert Bremner's *The Songs in the Gentle Shepherd, Adapted for the Guitar* (c. 1765) in which melodies 'are left almost undecorated, and […] their texts underlaid, giving the clear impression that Bremner's publication is a songbook intended for widespread amateur use'.[63]

The *Miscellany*'s songs were also adapted for public performances such as that listed on a playbill which appeared in the *World* newspaper, 17 August 1789. The theatre named in the playbill is Sadler's Wells, London, and the first act – 'a Favourite Piece, with Singing and Dancing' – is titled, '*Hooley and Fairly: or, The Highland Laddie*. The Songs chiefly compiled from the Works of Allan Ramsay'. Moreover, the *Miscellany*'s songs appeared in numerous chapbooks and song collections throughout the eighteenth century. Some of these collections cite Ramsay as evidence of the symbolic and cultural capital associated with his work as a writer and editor of Scottish songs;[64] others, however, do not. *The Merry Companion: or, Universal Songster* (1742), for example, makes no mention of Ramsay, though it features sixty-six Scottish songs – 'carefully chosen,' the editor tells us, 'from the best miscellanies' – fifty-four of which were printed in Ramsay's *Miscellany*.[65]

This distancing of authorial attribution, while common in song culture throughout the period, assumes a different kind of significance as Scottish songs become subject to efforts by antiquarians to preserve what they saw to be a national cultural form. As Paula McDowell notes, the 'historically unprecedented flood of print' created in the eighteenth century gave rise to 'new efforts to historicize communicative modes (print, script, voice, gesture, etc.)'.[66] In Scottish song culture we see this process of historicisation take shape in works such as David Herd's *Ancient and Modern Scottish Songs, Heroic Ballads, etc.*, John Pinkerton's *Scottish Tragic Ballads*, and Joseph Ritson's *Scotish [sic] Song*, in which songs – embedded in paratextual materials (prefaces, introductions, annotations, glossaries) – are explicated, categorised, and historicised in terms of the nation.[67] While each of these works engage with the historicity of Scottish songs, the songs selected and the paratextual framing signify diverse understandings of Scottish songs and their role as a national cultural form.

Pinkerton, in his introductory essays ('On the Oral Tradition of Poetry' and 'On the Tragic Ballad'), outlines his project as one of recovery and preservation, for which he draws on oral, manuscript and print sources in his search for 'monuments of ancient Scottish Poetry'.[68] Both the essays and the numerous annotations (in English, French, German, and Latin) that he appended to his volume, reveal his intended audience (scholarly men of the middling and upper classes), as well as his eccentric and at times inconsistent approach to his source materials. In a note to 'Hardyknute' (also discussed by Corey Andrews in chapter 2), for example, he explains his amendment of line 188: 'This is substituted in place of a line of consummate nonsense, which has stained all the former editions. Many such are corrected in this impression from comparing different rehearsals, and still more from conjecture'.[69] He corrects, substitutes, and omits his source material according to subjectively-laden and vague ideas such as 'common sense' and 'conjecture', imposing his contemporary interpretations on material he claims is authentic and uncorrupted by the passage of time. In another annotation to 'Hardyknute', in which he discusses a battle description, he observes, 'though perhaps not the most sublime, it is the most animated and interesting to be found in any poet'.[70] He cites a passage from Edmund Burke's (1729/30–1797) *A Philosophical Inquiry into the Origin of Our Ideas of the Sublime and Beautiful* (1757) in which Burke claims that the '"business"' of '"Poetry and Rhetoric"' is '"to effect rather by sympathy than imitation; to display rather the effect of things on the mind of the speaker, or of others, than to present a clear idea of the things themselves. This is their most extensive province, and that in which they succeed the best"'.[71] At the close of the Burke quotation, Pinkerton asks, 'Will [Burke] forgive me if I offer this rude Scottish Poem ['Hardyknute'] as an example sufficiently illustrative of this fine remark?'.[72] In aligning Burke's analysis of the effective and affective qualities of poetry with 'Hardyknute', Pinkerton troubles any easy understanding of Scottish song as purely historical. Instead, he suggests that the value of Scottish songs is not simply a function of their ancientness, but also of their aesthetic and affective qualities.

Certainly, Pinkerton's introductory materials emphasise the historicity of Scottish ballads, casting them as ancient relics which function only as evidence of a far distant past and offer no comment on the immediate present. This sense of stability in relation to history intersects with gender and takes form in the illustration on the work's title page, which depicts a medieval scene featuring three groups of people. The image suggests a calm, gendered ordering of men and women. On the (viewers') left stands a group of men and boys (one man wears military dress and holds a standard); on the (viewers') right stands a group of women; both groups talk amongst themselves and look towards the man and woman in the centre. The man in the centre stands erect, his legs set apart, balanced, as he supports the woman in an embrace; the woman, who, leaning into him, her head bowed (presumably in grief, given the work's title, *Scottish Tragic Ballads*), appears slightly off balance. The medieval style of the image suggests both the antiquity of Pinkerton's collection as well as the chivalric codes associated with medievalism (such as respecting the honour of women; protecting widows and orphans; being just, faithful, truthful, and valorous). However, the gender binaries which take visual form in this image – male stability / female instability; male power / female powerlessness; male militarism / female domesticity – are belied within the ballads themselves by the voices (female and male) which express rage, despair, grief, and love in response to (and, at times, despite of) the acts of treachery, deceit, and unimaginable violence perpetrated by those (women and men) around them.

Like Pinkerton, Ritson traces a history of Scottish song in his equally male-centric Preface and introductory essay to his *Scotish* [sic] *Song*.[73] Yet, his distrust of the oral tradition as a reliable source of information and his development of rigorous manuscript- and print-based authentication protocols suggest that for him, Scots songs are not malleable, ever-evolving cultural forms, but arise from, and are evidence of, a Scotland that no longer exists, and, as such, must be recovered in their pure and uncorrupted form and maintained as historical artefacts.[74] He applies his scrupulous sense of authenticity to the songs in performance. Publishing both song and music texts together (lyrics are embedded in musical scores in his collection), Ritson avows that the value of Scots songs lies in their capacity to evoke emotion. In his Preface, he quotes 'an ingenious writer': '"It were endless, […] to run through the many fine airs expressive of sentiment and passion in the number of our Scottish songs, which when sung in the genuine natural manner, must affect the heart of every person of feeling, whose taste is not vitiated and seduced by fashion and novelty"'. 'For these reasons', Ritson adds, 'the words and melody of a Scotish [sic] song should be ever inseparable'.[75] Notably, Ritson, not discriminating between female and male performers, allows for the possibilities of female and male voices raised in song and of a role for both women and men in the creation of the nation's culture as it takes shape in song in performance.

Ritson was not the first song collector to note the affective power of Scottish song. Sixty-five years earlier, in the Preface to his *Miscellany* (Dublin, 1729), Ramsay claimed that Scottish songs 'are for the most part so cheerful, that on hearing them well play'd or sung, we find a difficulty to keep ourselves from dancing'.[76] David Herd was to develop this idea more fully in the 1776 edition of *Ancient and Modern Scottish Songs*. As Janet Sorensen explains, Herd, influenced by 'Scottish Enlightenment theories of sense and cognition', drew a connection between affect and Scottish song culture and developed a new understanding of the role of song in the life of the nation as providing an opportunity for association between Scots.[77] Herd, 'Less invested in a separate ancient tradition and in essential distinctions between print and orality',[78] saw songs as a mutable, fluid cultural form, subject to change over time. Herd adopted an inclusive approach to collecting and publishing songs. Throughout his Preface, he employs arguably non-gender-specific language, using the term of address 'people' rather than 'men' or 'women', and alternative forms, such as 'the Gay', 'the Chearful' [sic], 'the Speculative and Refined'.[79] He represents Scottish songs as an ever-evolving cultural form and invites his readers (albeit, 'classical' readers) to amend song lyrics as they deem necessary; he notes that while many of the lyrics in his collection 'may appear much below mediocrity', some of the songs had new words which had been supplied by 'eminent modern Scots poets; and the classical reader may easily substitute more'.[80]

Performative, adaptable, and mutable: Robert Burns was to take these characteristics of song culture identified and promoted by Ramsay (and others such as Herd) and employ them in his work with Scottish songs. Burns differentiated between Scottish and English songs based on the 'wildness' of the Scottish songs, their capacity to move the emotions, to produce an affective response.[81] He linked aesthetic effect and national identity (specifically, Scottishness) to argue that a nation's song culture – as an expression of its members – takes its shape and assumes its power (cultural, political, social) in performance (and he did not differentiate between female and male performers). Concerned with the affective qualities of Scottish songs, he sought the best version of a song to collect and revise as needed and obtained his material (song and music texts) from a wide range of sources (oral, manuscript, print) provided by both women and men, independent of claims of authenticity or historicity. Demonstrating a flexible and nuanced approach to national identity, especially in his work with song culture, Burns wrote, collected and contributed songs for the Scottish musical anthologies of James Johnson

(*Scots Musical Museum* [1787–1803]) and George Thomson (*A Select Collection of Original Scotish* [sic] *Airs* [1793–1846])), although these projects involved quite different notions of national culture.[82] As Nigel Leask points out, while 'Both Johnson and Thomson were important pioneers in transforming "popular" into "national" song, […] the latter term has a slightly different inflection in each case. Compared to Johnson's "patriotic inclusivity", Thomson's collection was in its very conception an "act of union" presenting alternative Scottish and English lyrics to each of its elaborately set melodies'.[83] However different, both of these works contain songs found in the *Miscellany*, evidence of the songs' enduring popularity as well as their perceived relevance to later editors of Scottish song collections.[84]

Given the numerous ways in which the *Miscellany* complicated Scottish national identity, the continuing interest in the *Miscellany* after the eighteenth century is striking. References to Ramsay's work in the nineteenth-century periodical press speak to his ongoing influence. His work was sold throughout the British Empire, as witnessed by the numerous advertisements appearing in newspapers and periodicals such as the *Cape Monthly Magazine* (South Africa), *The Friend of India* (India), the *Melbourne Punch* (Australia), and *The Canadian Journal* (Canada). Moreover, his enduring cultural authority is suggested by his inclusion in anthologies such as *Beeton's Great Books of Poetry*, which contained, according to its editor, 'Nearly 2,000 of the Best Pieces in the English Language'.[85] However, with the rise of antiquarianism in the eighteenth century, Scottish song culture experienced a splitting into two streams, one in which songs were historicised and seen as evidence of the past, and another in which they were recognised as popular, contemporary cultural forms. One of the results of this split was the casting of Ramsay and Scottish songs in a nostalgic mode. Rhona Brown has noted the decline in Ramsay's influence beginning in the latter decades of the eighteenth century, with Robert Burns eventually replacing him as the national 'bard'.[86] By the second half of the nineteenth century, the complexity of voices constituting Ramsay's Scotland is reduced to a handful of songs, suggesting a distillation, perhaps a homogenisation, of national identity.[87]

Ramsay's *Miscellany* in its paratextual materials (such as frontispieces, title pages, dedications, prefaces) and collected songs, requires us to query the intersections between song culture, gender and the nation. At the same time, however, collections such as Ramsay's, made up of and animated by voices whose interests are very diverse, also make clear that none of these categories – song culture, gender, nation – is a stable, homogenous form. There is no one Scottish voice which sings for the nation; rather there are many, multi-mediated voices singing many songs of the nation. These voices – female and male – speak diverse languages (Scots language mixed with standard English, and standard English by itself), and represent various landscapes of early eighteenth-century Scotland (rural and urban, local and national, north and south). They sing of sexual inequality and gender inequity, lost dignity, unsparing grief, intense passion, ambition, and joy in lyrics which are sometimes trite, often conventional, and usually engaging. Yet, however diverse, they all speak to (and sing of) the complexity of the Scottish nation as they suggest how that nation is mediated by song.

CHAPTER SIX

Fierce Females and Male Pretenders: Gender, Cultural Memory and Anti-Jacobite Print Culture in the 1745 Rising

Leith Davis and Jasreen Kaur Janjua

Jacobitism – derived from *Jacobus*, Latin for 'James' – was a complex movement in the British Isles that involved issues of religion, culture, dynasty, and nationalism. Its origins go back to the 1688 Revolution, but it played out in a series of armed uprisings in the first half of the eighteenth century.[1] After the death of Charles II in 1685, his Roman Catholic brother, James VII/II proceeded to alarm many of his subjects by introducing a series of pro-Catholic policies. William of Orange's invasion of England in November 1688 was undertaken ostensibly in order to restore the rights and interests of the Protestant religion in Britain.[2] William and his troops marched on London, and in December, James fled to France. After the meeting of the Convention Parliament (22 January–12 February 1689), William and his wife, Mary (James VII/II's Protestant daughter) were declared monarchs of England and Ireland. The Scottish Convention of Estates met in March 1689 to consider whether to offer William and Mary the Scottish crown as well. In April 1689, while James mounted an offensive in Ireland intended to re-assert his kingship, James Graham, Viscount Dundee, rallied a number of clans in the Highlands of Scotland in support of James's cause. Neither campaign was successful, and the conflict in Ireland was particularly bloody.[3] William and Mary were declared joint monarchs of Scotland as well as England and Ireland on 11 May 1689. Upon William's death in 1702, the throne passed to Mary's sister, Anne, who would be the last of the Stuart monarchs.

It was under Anne's rule in 1707 that the Acts of Union joining the kingdoms of Scotland with England and Ireland were passed in the parliaments of Scotland and England. The union added further fuel to the fire for Jacobite adherents. 'After 1707,' F. J. McLynn writes, 'enthusiasm for the House of Stuart [in Scotland] became closely identified with nationalism and a nostalgia for the Scottish past'.[4] Following Anne's death and the accession of the Hanoverian George I in 1714, Jacobites rose in 1715 in a number of different locations within Britain, this time on behalf of James VII/II's son, James. Other conflicts took place in 1708 and 1719.[5] The Jacobites' efforts to overthrow the Hanoverian dynasty ended, however, with the Rising of 1745 led by Charles Edward Stuart (Bonnie Prince Charlie), the grandson of James VII/II. The Jacobites were decimated at the Battle of Culloden on 16 April 1746. After the battle, Charles spent the next five months moving between locations in the Highlands and Islands in an attempt to elude government troops before finally escaping to France in September 1746; he was aided in his flight by loyal Jacobites, including Flora MacDonald (see cover illustration).[6] The battle at Culloden was followed by a concerted effort by the Hanoverian forces to eradicate the clan system and Highland culture.

Although the Jacobites mounted a series of threats to the Hanoverian state from 1689 onwards, including an extensive mobilisation north of the Forth in 1715, it is the final conflict in 1745 that has become the most firmly entrenched in cultural memory. This chapter examines the continuing resonance of 'the 45' in light of its initial mediation, as we consider how the events of the 1745 Rising unfolded during a significant tipping point in the history of media, a shift to an era of 'print saturation'.[7] As Clifford Siskin and William Warner explain, print, although not strictly speaking a 'new medium,' took centre stage in the eighteenth century within an 'already existing media ecology of voice, sound, image, and manuscript writing' in relation to the increasing development of print capitalism.[8] As a result of the increased creation and circulation of printed works during the 1745 Rising, individuals in Britain were able to learn about and see the events of the Rising reflected in printed works in a manner that was far more extensive than during earlier Jacobite conflicts.[9] Newspapers in particular, which had increased exponentially between 1715 and 1745, played an important role in relaying the events of the later Rising,[10] while popular pamphlets such as *A Journal of the Pretender's Expedition to North Britain* (1745) and *Seasonable Considerations on the Present War in Scotland* (1746) purported to give readers accounts of the events in the North almost in real time.[11] In a print marketplace in which post-publication prosecution was a very real threat, however, pro-Hanoverian mediations dominated the presses. Works such as *A Complete and Authentick History of the Rise, Progress and Extinction of the Late Rebellion* (1746) and *The History of the Present Rebellion: Collected from Authentick [Sic] Memoirs, Letters and Intelligences* (1746),[12] for example, drew earlier newspaper accounts into a narrative arc of the Rising favourable for the government, one that consisted of the expansion and 'extinction' of an unnatural rebellion and the justified punishment of the perpetrators.[13] Printed accounts of the trials and execution of the Jacobite prisoners, including three Jacobite lords – Kilmarnock, Cromartie and Balmerino – flooded the marketplace, encouraging the vilification of Jacobite actors.[14] Printed engravings, too, which were becoming cheaper and more easily accessible to more people, injected a visual element into negative public perceptions of the Jacobites.[15] Jacobite cultural memories, because of their treasonous nature, circulated primarily through oral and material culture means or in otherwise coded forms.[16]

Scholars have examined the way in which anti-Jacobite works represented the elimination of Highland culture as necessary for the pathway to modernity in Britain,[17] focusing on the way such works present the Jacobites as 'savage,' 'violent,' and 'backward colonials' in contrast to an 'enlightened' and 'morally superior' British society.[18] This chapter examines two anti-Jacobite works of visual culture and two printed pamphlets that circulated during and in the aftermath of the 1745 Rising: Richard Cooper's satirical engraving of Prince Charles Edward Stuart in 'disguise' (1745) and John Williams's broadside *Prince Charles Edward Stuart Disguised as Betty Burke* (c. 1746); and *A Brief Account of the Life and Family of Miss Jenny Cameron* (1746) and *The Female Rebels: Being some remarkable Incidents of the Lives, Characters, and Families of the titular Duke and Duchess of Perth, the Lord and Lady Ogilvy, and of Miss Florence M'Donald* (1747). We pay particular attention to how gender stereotypes are employed in order to comment on the Rising as well as how the representation of the Rising as 'unnatural' serves to reinforce gender roles.[19]

At the same time, as we demonstrate, gendered images within these four works are also linked to the articulation of counter-memories that in fact call into question the one-sidedness of their anti-Jacobite perspective.[20] Michael Rothberg comments on the existence of competing memories within any mediated cultural memory: 'all places and acts of memory' are 'rhizomatic networks of temporality and cultural reference that exceed attempts at territorialisation [...] and identarian reduction'.[21] Rothberg offers the term *noeuds de mémoire* or 'knots of memory' as a substitute for the concept of *lieux de mémoire* ('sites of memory') popularised by French historian Pierre Nora.[22] The image of memory knots, suggests Rothberg, usefully conveys the possibility of layers and convolutions of competing memories. These knots, Rothberg adds, may 'well have territorializing or identity-forming effects, but those effects will always be contingent and open to re-signification'.[23] The complexity of the 'knots of memory' is evident in the case of works responding to the

1745 Rising in which traces of the more ephemeral or coded Jacobite mediations appear frequently within anti-Jacobite printed texts. Although these mediations confirmed Hanoverian versions of the history of the Rising, they also effected the circulation of pro-Jacobite counter-memories, and they contributed to the complicated discourse on gender circulating in mid-century Britain.

Pro-Hanoverian patriotism is prominent in the satirical image of Charles Edward Stuart produced by Richard Cooper, an Edinburgh engraver (see Figure 1). Created in order to advertise the reward for Charles's capture, this engraving depicts Charles in a tartan coat and breeches with a rumpled plaid wrapped around his lower torso and a dirk and large sword at his side. Pittock notes that in both the 1715 and the 1745 Risings, tartan was 'used to uniform the Jacobite army, irrespective of place of origin'.[24] As Viccy Coltman confirms, tartan served as an 'ideological uniform' for the Jacobites.[25] Eighteenth-century pro-Jacobite portraits of Charles often show him wearing a bonnet with a white cockade – an 'explicit symbol of Jacobite loyalty',[26] but, as Coltman notes, Cooper's engraving was the first known image of Charles in tartan.[27] The representation of Charles as a Highland military leader is called into question in this satirical 'wanted poster,' however, as the engraving presents the Stuart heir as an unnatural combination of masculine and feminine attributes. The bare, muscular calves and the broad shoulders suggest masculine power, but they contrast sharply with the figure's pursed red lips and tiny feet. Moreover, Charles's plaid, which looks more like a skirt than a kilt, is draped in a disorderly fashion, bunched up and ruffled. His bonnet has exuberant pinkish feathers attached to it, playing up the 'foppish' nature of this unflattering image. Instead of placing his hand firmly on his sword, he daintily caresses the pommel with his left hand, while his right hand casually drops a paper inscribed 'Manifesto' just as a woman might let go of a handkerchief. Framed within the borders of the page, Cooper's Charles offers a curtsey to the viewer, suggesting his effeminate, passive nature. At the same time, however, such perceptions are unsettled as Charles is represented as conscious of himself as if on display. He seems to deliberately turn his head to one side to reveal an earring for the viewer as if calculating the effect. His dropping of the paper with his father's 'Manifesto' similarly plays with viewers' expectations. Although the writing on the 'Manifesto' is an illegible scrawl, perhaps reflecting the stereotype of the Jacobites as uncivilised and inscrutable, it also offers a blank slate of possibilities, teasing the viewer to imagine its contents. The inscription accompanying the image further

FIERCE FEMALES AND MALE PRETENDERS 121

Figure 1. Richard Cooper, Prince Charles Edward Stuart, 1720–1788. Eldest son of Prince James Francis Edward Stuart ('Wanted Poster'), 1745
© National Galleries of Scotland.

adds to the dilemma about interpretation, as it notes that the engraving is 'A likeness, notwithstanding the disguise that any person who secures the son of the pretender is entitled to a reward of 30,000 £'. But the words are ambiguous, begging the question of what exactly is the 'disguise' and what the 'likeness'? Is the foppish Charles in disguise as a masculine and martial Highlander or is a masculine, capable Charles in feminine disguise to mask the extent of his power?[28] Cooper's engraving both draws on the discourse of secrecy and disguise associated with the Jacobite cause and amplifies it.

In the aftermath of the defeat at Culloden, the story of Charles's prolonged escape proved a media event in its own right both in newspaper accounts and in popular printed narratives such as *Ascanius, or the Young Adventurer*; *The Wanderer, or Surprizing Escape* and *Young Juba: being the History of the Young Chevalier, from his Birth to his Escape from Scotland at the Battle of Culloden*.[29] Despite their pro-Hanoverian stance of condemning Charles, however, these narrative accounts also manage to celebrate the Stuart leader, representing him as a hero of a grand adventure.[30] A key element in these narratives, one that caught the interest of readers of both ideological persuasions, was the story of how he escaped from Benbecula to Skye by assuming the guise of Flora MacDonald's Irish waiting-maid, Betty Burke. This story became extremely popular, circulating not just in printed narratives, but also in printed engravings.

The broadside *Prince Charles Edward Stuart Disguised as Betty Burke* (see Figure 2), for example, references the cross-dressing episode, depicting Charles as an attractive young woman wearing a frilly gown, a petticoat, a lace-trimmed fichu, and a lace cap. The broadside draws on the anti-Jacobite strategy of feminising Charles while the accompanying six lines of verse in the broadside inform the viewer of his ignominious flight:

> Routed, o'er Hills the young Adventurer flies,
> And in a Cottage sinks to this Disguise.
> Fled his gay Hopes, defeated his fond Scheme,
> His Throne is vanish'd like a golden Dream.
> By manly Thoughts He'd charm His Woes to rest;
> In vain! Culloden still distracts His Breast.[31]

As the text from the broadside indicates, whatever 'golden dream' and 'gay Hopes' Charles had are now 'vanish'd'. His 'manly thoughts' have becoming impotent to 'charm His Woes to rest' while the image of his

Figure 2. *Prince Charles Edward Stuart Disguised as Betty Burke* (c. 1746), © National Library of Scotland License: CC BY 4.0

failure at 'Culloden still distracts His Breast'. The broadside's text complicates the message of impotence, however. Although it emphasises Charles's ignoble flight from both civilisation and masculinity, it also represents that flight in the language of romance, painting an epic picture of a 'young Adventurer' roaming 'o'er Hills' in much the same way that prose works like *Alexis; Or the Young Adventurer* (1746) and *Ascanius* (1746) did.[32] This more positive representation also reflects the perspective of Charles's Jacobite adherents for whom the female outfit could be seen as merely another 'Disguise' that Charles adopted. For Jacobites, the Betty Burke episode was a providential action that enabled Charles to escape through the fingers of his Hanoverian pursuers. The third volume of the ten-volume 'Lyon in Mourning' manuscript, for example, includes scraps of 'a piece of that identical Gown' noted as being that which Charles Stuart wore 'when he was obliged to disguise himself in Female-Dress'.[33] The broadside appears to have been based on the face of Charles in the portrait painted by Allan Ramsay while the Stuart heir was at Holyrood, further emphasising the inscription of a Jacobite counter-memory within this anti-Jacobite mediation.[34]

The images of Charles in Cooper's engraving and the 'Betty Burke' broadside draw attention to the strategy of representing Jacobite men as un-manly in order to minimise the political threat that the Jacobites posed. Female figures, too, were used to promote the Hanoverian political agenda of presenting Jacobitism as an 'unnatural' cause. Carine Martin explores the use of the female figure in anti-Jacobite works of the 1745 Rising, noting that 'women in Hanoverian propaganda often adopt the traits of familiar figures in misogynistic satire such as the virago, the amazon, and the lewd woman'.[35] She suggests that the use of these pre-existing female tropes that were familiar to eighteenth-century readers conveys a perspective on Jacobitism as 'a world turned upside down' in which gender roles were under threat.[36] Hanoverian propaganda, she argues, portrays 'warlike, barbarian' Jacobite females who overstep their domestic boundaries in association with inept, weak men who are confined to the private realm.

The Female Rebels: Being some remarkable Incidents of the Lives, Characters, and Families of the titular Duke and Duchess of Perth, the Lord and Lady Ogilvy, and of Miss Florence M'Donald (1747), for example, works to disparage the Jacobite cause by associating it with the reversal of traditional gender roles. The pamphleteer begins his commentary by critiquing women in general, noting their tendency to excessive behaviour: 'It is remarkable of the fair Sex, that whatever Opinions they embrace, they assert them with greater Constancy and Violence than the generality of Mankind: They seldom observe any Medium in their Passions, or set any reasonable Bounds to those Actions which result from them'.[37] Whenever 'absurd Doctrines' of 'State or Religion' begin to take hold of a populace, 'the Ladies are sure to lead the Van'.[38] The author clearly intends to mock Jacobite women who fail to recognise that the women's realm of activity is separate from that of the political realm and who are still bold enough to express their ideas about politics in public. According to the pamphleteer, Jacobite women, in particular, have allowed their 'weak Heads and warm Hearts'[39] that make them incapable of proper reasoning and more susceptible to emotional outbursts to rule their behaviour. At the same time, this 'unnatural' female behaviour also has implications for male behaviour, as, suggests the author, only weak men allow themselves to subsist under 'Petticoat Patronage'.[40] Although he begins by denigrating women for their support for the Jacobite cause, the author expands his satire to condemn the Jacobite cause in general by suggesting it is a disguise for a more extensive plan by women to overthrow their natural lords. The attempt to re-place a Stuart on the throne, he warns, may be a 'traitorous Conspiracy of our liege Subjects, the Women against their sovereign Lord Man'.[41] The author cautions against the dire consequences of the success of the Jacobite cause for the entire British society, as he indicates that a 'Change of Government might bring along with it more than a simple Change of the legal Constitution'.[42] It might bring along the end of the 'Empire of the Males'.[43]

After discussing the connection between gender and Jacobitism in general, the author shifts perspective to focus on the role of individual 'female rebels' who aided Charles in the '45, Margaret Drummond, Duchess of Perth and Lady Ogilvy, both of whom, it is suggested, are now in danger of making their 'Exit at Tyburn'.[44] The author indicates his design is to shed some 'Light into their Characters' and help the reader understand the 'extraordinary Behaviour' of the two women, whose 'Birth and Education might have induced the Publick to expect a quite different Conduct'.[45] As he indicates, each of the women suffers from fatal gender flaws. The Duchess of Perth, for example, has 'something of Cruelty and Ferocity in her Disposition' which had been evident 'even in her Childhood,' but which has only grown since 'she commenced Warrior' as she has 'not only laid aside the Woman, but even Humanity'.[46] Lady Ogilvy, for her part, having demonstrated extreme cunning in trapping Lord Ogilvy into matrimony, was won over to the cause of Jacobitism through her friendship with the Duchess of Perth, and she encouraged her husband, too, to embrace the 'airy Visions of a Faction'[47] and follow the Stuarts to 'Ruin and Perdition'.[48] According to the author, it is 'no wonder' that Lady Ogilvy lays aside 'all the Softness of her Sex' and chooses rather to 'act the Fury'; she is driven by 'blind Zeal' rather than any rational thought.[49] Both the Duchess and Lady Ogilvy, the author notes, exhibited a far greater desire for 'Revenge, Fire and Sword'[50] than any of the male Jacobite leaders. Not only are they unnatural women; they also give ample evidence of their inhumanity and barbarism as they suggest such schemes as firing prisoners against the walls of the government fortress at Fort William.[51]

Throughout the pamphlet, Jacobite women are presented as warriors who play an active role in the military and political affairs of the state, while Jacobite men are placed in an inferior position to their wives. The Duke of Perth is described as lacking traditional male qualities such as strength, bravery, and confidence. As the author notes, the Duke had 'something of milkiness in his blood, which rendered him unfit for a great command in the field'.[52] When the Duchess of Perth requests that he join forces with Charles, the Duke claims that he is not willing to risk his life and fortune 'only to have the honour of making a sudden Blaze, which the Government would soon extinguish'.[53] While the Duke is hesitant to participate in the Jacobite Rising, the Duchess boldly challenges him: 'if you deserve to be Duke of Perth, exert yourself suitable to your Rank, and shew by your Actions you deserve that title you would assume by daring to fight for it'.[54] The Duke only continues to participate in the Rising because of the pressure exerted by the Duchess. Lord Ogilvy, in contrast, demonstrates 'more Courage and Conduct than could be expected from his Years',[55] but his weakness is evident as he allows himself to be led by his wife.

The ideological perspective of *The Female Rebels* is complicated, however, in the final section which concerns Flora MacDonald. Unlike her unnatural female Jacobite compatriots, Flora is represented as 'more amiable, more feminine, and less shocking to the imagination'.[56] In this account, Flora received an 'early, female Education' and was raised to demonstrate proper feminine qualities such as 'Meekness of Temper, Dignity of Sentiment, and Chastity of Behaviour'.[57] Flora's contribution to the Jacobite cause is made without sacrificing gendered expectations. The author suggests that her crime was being *too* womanly as she demonstrated 'those social and endearing [female] Virtues of Mercy to an unseasonable [sic] Height'.[58] The author does not criticise Flora's actions after the Rising's failure, when she aided Charles in his escape. Instead, he poses a series of rhetorical questions designed to fend off any condemnation of her by suggesting that her actions can be seen as a reflection of her natural qualities as a female and a human being: 'How would she wish to be divested of Humanity? To be deprived of Heaven's darling Attribute Mercy? And to be capable of turning a deaf Ear to the cries of the Distressed?'[59] He responds:

Nothing that's feminine surely would: A surly plodding Statesman, may [...] refuse to be warm'd with the tender Notions of Pity and Compassion to any object, however circumstanced [...] but Woman, while she remains Woman, and possesses the genuine Characteristicks of her Sex, must still be under a Temptation to act as Miss M'Donald has done, or is supposed to have done.[60]

Although *The Female Rebels* condemns Jacobite women such as the Duchess of Perth and Lady Ogilvy who have 'disclaimed all the Softness peculiar to their Sex',[61] it also suggests the intrusion of a counter-memory into the text in the guise of a Jacobite woman who demonstrates traditional gender characteristics. Moreover, in the section on Flora MacDonald, the case of Charles Stuart's distress after Culloden becomes the ultimate test not just for female sensibility but for that of 'Humanity' in general. The author suggests that rather than threatening social bonds, the Jacobite cause, at least now after Culloden, can be used to strengthen them. The section of *The Female Rebels* concerning Flora MacDonald ultimately uses the discourse of gender to elicit sympathy for the Jacobites.

A Brief Account of the Life and Family of Miss Jenny Cameron, the Reputed Mistress of the Pretender's Eldest Son (1746) also represents complex layers involved in the construction of the memory of the '45, although this time the memory concerns only one individual, Jenny Cameron. Cameron first came to the public's attention in the newspaper accounts where she was represented as Charles's lover in order to suggest the Prince's debauched inclinations. The 'Extract of a Letter from a Lady at Preston, to her Friend in Town, dated December 14. Concerning the young pretender and his retinue' which appeared in the 14–17 December 1745 issue of the *London Evening Gazette* and which was widely reprinted in other newspapers, for example, introduces 'anecdotes relating to *Jenny Cameron*'. One of these anecdotes describes Jenny's first appearance before Charles as he was on his way from Lochaber to Perth:

> she jump'd off her horse, and told him with great frankness, that she came like the queen of *Sheba*, to partake of the wisdom of *Solomon*: he answered, And thou shalt, my dear, partake of all that *Solomon* is master of.—He took her in his arms, and retired with her into his tent, and they were some time alone; the rest [...] we are to guess.[62]

References to Cameron, including notices of her capture, appear intermittently in the press in the early months of 1746. *A Brief Account* capitalises upon public interest in the salacious story of Cameron and Charles as the title page refers to her as '*the Reputed Mistress of the Pretender's Eldest Son*'.

The author of *A Brief Account* traces the abnormality of Jenny's gender identity back to her childhood, observing that she displayed early signs of deviating from gendered expectations: her 'natural temper' is characterised as 'hot and violent'[63] and she is brought up with no concerns regarding her appearance: 'there was no Care taken of her Complexion, or her Shape, no Regimen of Diet observed to keep her lean'.[57] Instead, Cameron 'shewed a Disposition more masculine than is really common, even for Boys of her Years'.[64] As a premonition of the rebellious Jacobite female that she will become, Cameron is represented as an uncivilised creature: 'in every Thing Nature [was left] to take its Course, in as wild a Manner as the Animal Creation'; the animalistic side of her is also suggested by the author's remarks that she 'could not be brought to herd with her Sisters'.[65]

In addition to describing Cameron's unusual childhood, *A Brief Account* also relates her sexual promiscuities as a young woman, combining her transgressive sexuality with her transgressive class instincts. After being sent abroad to Edinburgh as punishment for her already rebellious nature, Cameron takes to romping around with her great aunt's maid and footmen, dressing up in 'Men's Apparel' and visiting the 'Bawdy-house'.[66] She subsequently becomes pregnant with the footman's child, and her father, deeply afflicted by this public embarrassment, dies of shock.[67] The author coyly suspends judgment on the question of whether Cameron subsequently suffers a miscarriage 'by Accident, or by some Means used to occasion an Abortion',[68] but the possibility that she caused the loss of her own child adds to her representation as unnatural. Cameron's mother sends her to a nunnery in France to bury the scandal, but to no avail: 'she had experienced so much of the World, and the Conversation of Men, that she could not, with any Patience, think of parting with either.'[69] Cameron's perverse, unnatural impulses are only encouraged within the milieu of the convent as she takes several more lovers, eventually escaping as the mistress of an Irish officer. When she makes the acquaintance of Sir Hugh Cameron of Lochiel who has come to the continent after the 1715 Rising, he arranges to send her back to her brother in Scotland.

Cameron's gendered perversity, consisting of hypermasculinity as well as female promiscuity and unnatural passions, becomes linked with political dissidence as, thirty years later, following an incestuous relationship with her brother, Cameron joins the Jacobite army in 1745, dressing as a 'young gentleman'.[70] The author notes that she

> got together two hundred and fifty Men, and marched at the Head of them to the Pretender's Camp. She was dressed in a sea-green Riding Habit, with a Scarlet Lapel trimmed with Gold; her Hair tied behind in loose Buckles, with a velvet Cape, and scarlet Feather: she rode a bay Gelding, with green Furniture, richly trimmed and fringed with Gold; instead of a Whip, she carried a naked Sword in her Hand; and in this Equipage arrived at the Camp.[71]

Here, Cameron is represented as an active commander gathering together male soldiers and 'march[ing] at [their] head'. Unlike the feminine Charles in Cooper's engraving who timidly fingers the pommel of his sword, Cameron boldly carries 'a naked Sword in her Hand', striking a fearsome pose at the head of an army. As a 'Female Officer'[72] in the Jacobite army, she betrays both her country and her sex.

But, like other anti-Jacobite accounts, *A Brief Account* also inscripts complex memories into its anti-Jacobite invective. Although Cameron is portrayed negatively in terms of her unnatural gendered behaviour and political subversion, the narrator's description of Cameron's spectacular actions during the 1745 Rising also hint at admiration. Indeed, Cameron is given a lengthy stirring speech upon meeting with Charles. Indicating that, while her nephew has been unable to bring the Cameron men to join the Stuart cause, she herself has 'rais'd his Men, and brought them to his H——ss,' she notes that they will 'hazard their Lives in his Cause'.[64] In her speech, Cameron also comments self-consciously on her role as a 'Female Officer' as she asserts that she found that 'so glorious a Cause had raised in her Breast every manly Thought, and quite extinguished the Woman: What Effect then [...] must it have upon those who have no feminine Fears to combat, and are free from the Incumbrance of Female Dress?'[73] In the character's perspective, gender reversal on the part of women in the cause of the Stuarts is not unnatural. It is, rather, a mark of the power of the cause.

Cameron is represented at the end of *A Brief Account* as behaving respectably. Instead of proffering suggestive language, she addresses Charles with 'an Officer-like Salute'.[74] After delivering the men, she leaves his presence; there is no dalliance with Charles in the tent. Although the title page of *A Brief Account* tantalises readers by alluding to the story that Cameron was Charles's mistress, the narrative concludes by going out of its way to contradict the representations of Jenny Cameron that had appeared in the newspaper accounts. Charles had ample political reasons to be grateful to Cameron, notes the author, and she does indeed have a pleasing appearance and a 'singular Humour,' even though she is 'within a Year or two of being fifty'.[75] But the story of her being Charles's lover, notes the author, has 'no other Foundation, than that of a Woman of some Distinction being in the Camp'.[76] As well as contradicting the story of Cameron's sexual connection to Charles, *A Brief Account* also concludes by contradicting the reports of her capture. 'She has been frequently reported to have been taken, but without Foundation'[77] the account notes, concluding with the assertion that: 'where she is now, is as much a Secret, as where the rest of the Rebel Chiefs are'.[78] Cameron, like Charles and other Jacobite leaders, continues to evade government forces. Although *A Brief Account* attempts to vilify Cameron – and, by extension, the Jacobite cause – by associating her with gendered 'unnaturalness' in the earlier part of the text, it ends by representing the continuity of the 'Secret' Jacobite cause despite the government's best efforts to stamp it out.

The subject of Jenny Cameron provided further opportunity for a discussion of gender in another popular narrative that shares textual features with *A Brief Account*: *Memoirs of the Remarkable Life and Surprizing Adventures of Miss Jenny Cameron*. *Memoirs* sets an expanded narrative about Cameron within a paratextual debate on the nature of woman. While the alleged author, Archibald Arbuthnot, 'Minister of *Kiltarlaty*,' begins his prefatory comments with comments such as 'There is scarce one Woman in Ten Thousand but what is a Hypocrite,'[79] his sister, Bel, takes the opportunity of her brother going to smoke with a neighbour to write her own thoughts onto his papers. Refuting her brother's assertions that the inferiority of female powers is proven by the lack of any significant written works by women, Bel asserts that this is just a reflection of the lack of educational opportunities offered to women, adding: 'whenever any of us sets Pen to Paper, we shew as much Brilliancy of Thought, just Reasoning, and sound Judgment as any He of you all.'[80] Bel's perspective on the subject of the narrative remains a mystery, however, as just as she begins her discussion, 'As for *Jenny Cameron*—,' her brother returns and discovers her own transgression. While he suggests that 'the following Memoirs [...] will give incontestable Proofs, that ever Thing which I have affirm'd of her Sex is true; and that whatever my pert Sister has advanc'd in Contradiction thereto, is merely the Fruit of her own Invention,'[81] the incredible story he recounts suggests that he is more guilty of the charge of 'Invention' than his sister. Like *A Brief Account, Memoirs* offers opportunities for readers to come to their own ideological conclusions both about Jacobitism and about gendered expectations.

As we have explored here, the 1745 Rising coincided with a time of media change which scholars refer to as the era of 'print saturation'. This expanded print marketplace favoured the storage and circulation of pro-Hanoverian narratives rather than those promoting Jacobite perspectives, which tended to be non-print or coded.[82] The quashing of the 1745 Rising and the Jacobite cause was accomplished not just through military means, but through an effective media campaign that wrote the disappearance of Jacobitism into the cultural memory of Britain. This media campaign drew substantively on the discourse of gendered norms of behaviour to discredit the Jacobite cause. At the same time, as we have suggested, traces of Jacobite counter-memories continued to circulate even within pro-Hanoverian printed works, indications of the endurance of other forms of mediation and the complexity of 'knots of memory' that exceed attempts to limit their signifying power. The political memory inscribed within these texts was reflected in and in turn reinforced a robust and ongoing debate on gender roles in mid-eighteenth-century Britain.

CHAPTER SEVEN

How to Become an 'Authoress' in Provincial Scotland: Women's Poetry in Manuscript and Print

Juliet Shields

While women have always been under-represented in studies of eighteenth-century Scottish literature, they have tended to be more visible as poets than as novelists, dramatists, or essayists, largely because of the prominent part they played in early modern Scotland's vibrant oral culture. Catherine Kerrigan observes that 'major male collectors of the ballad – Burns, Scott, Hogg, Greig-Duncan – all [...] refer to women as a prime source of their material'.[1] Scotswomen's comparative visibility in preserving and transmitting oral traditions means that scholars have paid more attention to their renditions of popular songs and ballads than to the other modes of poetic creation in which they engaged during the eighteenth century. In this chapter, I begin to redress the imbalance by bringing together manuscript and print collections of poetry by eighteenth-century Scotswomen to examine how they understood authorship. These collections suggest that authorship may have meant something quite different to women situated in provincial Scotland than it did in London, or even Edinburgh. They also demonstrate that authorship had different connotations for elite women, who tended to circulate their poetry in manuscript, and for working-class women, who tended to publish their poetry by subscription. Expanding our own understandings of authorship, then, may reveal that women played a greater part in the literary culture of Enlightenment Scotland than we have hitherto recognised.

In eighteenth-century Scotland, as in much of provincial Britain, authorship was much less closely tied to print publication than it was in London's commercialised literary marketplace, and the relationship between manuscript and print publication seems to have been fluid rather than oppositional. This is particularly true of poetry. In *Women Writers and the Edinburgh Enlightenment*,[2] Pam Perkins discusses late eighteenth- and early nineteenth-century Scotswomen who wrote for a commercial market, albeit in Edinburgh rather than London, and who thus might be considered professional authors. With the exception of Anne MacVicar Grant (1755–1838), Perkins's subjects made their living writing prose, primarily novels. It is significant, then, that Grant initially seems to have regarded the print publication of her poetry as, if not undesirable, certainly unnecessary to her status as an author. When George Thomson (1757–1851), compiler of *A Select Collection of Original Scottish Airs* (1799–1818), expressed interest in Grant's poems, she declared them 'too Slight & too Local for the Publick Eye, being merely a History of the Feelings [and] Domestic Occurrences of a most Obscure individual'.[3] Thomson had learned of Grant's literary talents from her friends, with whom she had shared her poetry in manuscript. While Grant's dismissal of her poems as 'Slight' might seem like a conventional display of feminine modesty, she was evidently happy to circulate her poems within the 'Small circle Whom they were meant to please'.[4] Her objection was to sharing them with an anonymous reading public. Grant turned to print publication only after her husband's death, in the hopes of making some money to support her children.

Many of the verses in Grant's first published work, *Poems on Various Subjects* (1803), are addressed to friends or relations, bearing the marks of their manuscript origins. Grant suggests that she had not intended these 'Memorials dear of loves and friendships past' to be shared with an unknown public when she begs those whose 'modest virtues' she has 'display'd' in print to forgive her: 'for well you know the unstudied lay, / Was only meant to soothe the lonely shade'.[5] Yet, if *Poems on Various Subjects* may have been read by a broader audience than Grant originally had envisioned for her poems, it was hardly a vast and anonymous one, as the book was published by subscription. It is relatively easy to trace the connections from Grant's friends and relations, often named in the poems themselves, to other subscribers on the list. Perkins aptly describes *Poems on Various Subjects* as 'exist[ing] in a hazy state between the private domestic world and the public world of print'.[6] Although Grant went on to publish works in prose – essays, memoirs, and epistles – she did not publish a second poetry collection, instead reverting to her earlier practice of circulating her poetry in manuscript throughout the 1820s and 1830s. Print publication, for Grant, was not necessarily the end goal of writing poetry, nor was it essential to authorship.

Most poetry by eighteenth-century Scotswomen, whether it remains to us in manuscript or in print, existed in the 'hazy state' between private and public described by Perkins; and one of the contentions of this chapter is that, with relatively few exceptions, eighteenth-century Scotswomen seem to have written their poetry for a circumscribed community of readers rather than a broad and anonymous reading public. Regardless of their social status, they appear to have considered poetry not as an elite literary form reserved for those with a classical education, but as an informal genre for entertaining and communicating with friends and relations. However, the medium in which Scotswomen shared their writing was to some extent defined by social class, illustrating Donna Landry's claim that any attempt to recover an eighteenth-century tradition of women's poetry must attend to 'the operations of class difference'.[7] Women whose families belonged to the gentry and aristocracy, such as Elizabeth Rae Keir (1747–1834) and Frances Scott (1750–1817), generally seem to have preferred to share their poetry in manuscript, and their concept of authorship depended upon social circulation rather than print publication. Working-class women including Christian Milne (1773–1816) and Anne Ross (fl. 1798) were more likely to seek print publication by subscription, a method that delimited their readership while conferring a legitimacy on their efforts that their social superiors could afford to eschew.

If, as many historians and literary critics have suggested, one of the hallmarks of the Scottish Enlightenment was its 'quintessentially *social*' orientation, then provincial Scotswomen's poetry was integral to Enlightenment literary culture even if it is largely unread today.[8] Only by examining the authorial practices of these neglected provincial poets can we accurately assess either the extent of women's contributions to the Enlightenment or the achievements of better-known poets such as Grant and Joanna Baillie (1762–1851).

Manuscript Miscellanies

For a long time, scholars assumed that women chose to circulate their works in manuscript out of a respect for the dictates of feminine propriety, which cautioned women against thrusting themselves unnecessarily into the public eye.[9] But in eighteenth-century Scotland, geography and social class perhaps played as significant a part as gender in determining whether a poet chose to circulate her verses in manuscript or in print. Margaret Ezell has pointed out that manuscript circulation might be very much a choice of convenience for those who lived at a distance from London or other major centres of publication: 'manuscript culture permitted and encouraged participation in literary life of groups of people whom print technology effectively isolated and alienated'.[10] While we tend to understand authorship as the individual creation of a printed text, Ezell and Betty Schellenberg have shown that authorship in provincial literary culture depended upon circulation rather than print publication, and that, as a result, textual production was often collaborative.[11]

Two Scotswomen, already mentioned, who circulated their poetry in manuscript form among a readership of friends and family members were Elizabeth Rae Keir and Frances Scott. Although they spent time in London and Edinburgh and mixed with the literary luminaries of their time, Keir's and Scott's poetry is deeply rooted in their experiences living outside of the city among those with more modest literary aspirations. Elizabeth Rae, the daughter of an esteemed dental surgeon, inhabited the outskirts of Edinburgh's intellectual and social elite. She spent most of her youth in Corstorphine, at that time a rural region well outside of Edinburgh, although she made at least one visit to London. In 1779, she married William Keir, a physician at St Thomas' Hospital in London. After her husband's death in June 1783, she returned to Scotland with three children and again took up residence in Corstorphine. Keir was connected by friendship and marriage with the Keiths of Ravelston, through whom she met Alison Cockburn and Walter Scott, among other influential members of Edinburgh society.

Keir published two novels, *Interesting Memoirs* (1785) and *The History of Miss Greville* (1787), but put her name to neither of them. Their publication dates – the first two years after her husband's death – suggest that Keir may have turned to writing in hopes of earning some money to support her children. If so, then she was likely disappointed. While *Interesting Memoirs* was published in London by Strahan and Cadell, and in Edinburgh by Balfour and Creech, the title page of *The History of Miss Greville* explains that the book 'is printed and sold for the author', suggesting that poor sales of her first novel may have required Keir to subsidise the publication of the second. Both novels are sentimental and didactic, filled with long religious and philosophical disquisitions. Despite their solemn tone, their plots are of the Minerva press variety, with abductions, convents, failed family fortunes, unfaithful lovers, and clandestine meetings featuring largely.

By contrast, the two volumes – almost nine hundred manuscript pages – of poems that Keir wrote to her friends, sisters, husband, and children are lively and full of character, revealing a thorough acquaintance with the literature of her time. For instance, writing to her sister in 'Epistle to

Miss Marianne Rae', Keir apostrophises Samuel Johnson, mockingly alluding to his *Journey to the Western Islands of Scotland*:

> Hail Clerk of science! Great Grammerian [*sic*],
> Of Scottish wants, the dread Historian;
> Of erudition so profound,
> His depths no mortal man can sound;
> Yet, soaring above truth and sense,
> Leaves not a tree for our defence.[12]

Keir dismisses as nonsense Johnson's claim that Scotland was notably lacking in trees, and she elsewhere shows her fondness for the poems of Ossian, another of Johnson's bugbears. For instance, 'Epistle to Miss Fraser at Aldoury 3 October 1773' quotes from James Macpherson's (1736–1796) *Fingal: An Ancient Epic Poem* (1763): Keir envisions Miss Fraser as 'Fidelia' wandering through the Highland landscape, 'Where raptured Bards oft to the trembling string / The mournful "tale of other times" would sing'.[13] Keir shows her versatility as a poet in 'On Receiving Burns's Poems from Mrs Cockburn, 1787', one of her rare attempts to write in Scots. Adopting the six-line Standard Habbie favoured by Burns, she recounts:

> When Madam Cockburn, Queen o' hearts!
> Wha willingly her wit imparts,
> (Fu' weel I ken her pawky arts!)
>   Sent me Robert Burns,
> I read, amazed, at sic wild starts,
>   An' beauteous turns.[14]

Despite her admiration for the 'beauteous turns' of Burns's poetry, Keir chides him for his bawdiness, asking him why his verses bring to women's faces:

> blushes that should shame your pen,
> When you sometimes to please the men
> Forget what's decent.[15]

As these examples demonstrate, Keir at her best easily stands comparison with her close contemporaries such as Grant and Baillie. Why, then, didn't she seek to publish her poetry?

Recent research on eighteenth-century manuscript culture indicates that this is perhaps the wrong question to ask. Why would Keir seek to publish her poetry, given that it was written for and read by a circle of friends and family members? The first of Keir's volumes is dedicated to Mrs Maxwell of Carriden, and in her dedicatory letter Keir requests permission 'under the sanction of your name, to introduce [the poems] to that circle of chosen friends for whom alone they are design'd; and to boast that they have obtained the approbation of one, whose candor cannot be bribed, though her judgment may perhaps be biased by partiality'. Declaring her 'dread of censure and aversion [...] to the appellation of learned Lady', Keir asserts her right 'to please myself in retirement with this harmless amusement, and to become Authoress, without danger of becoming ridiculous'. For Keir, becoming an 'Authoress' evidently did not require print publication, but merely the circulation of her manuscript within her 'circle of chosen friends'.[16] Most of the poems in the first volume are addressed to friends, including Jane Kerr, or 'Delia', and Ann and Margaret Keith, although there are also a few addressed to her parents and her sister Marianne. A series of poems at the beginning of the second volume records Delia's unexpected death, and William Keir, Elizabeth's future husband, soon emerges as the primary addressee of her poems. Following William's death in 1783, Keir addressed the majority of her poems to her children, nieces and nephews, and members of the Keith family into which her sister Marianne had married.

Although she may have dreaded 'censure' from unknown readers, Keir seems to have sought out criticism from her chosen circle. 'To Mr. Keir with some verses', written to her future husband, entreats its addressee to read her verses 'as a Critick, not a friend, / Blame where you ought, and where you can, commend'.[17] She urges Keir not to confine his criticisms to poetic style, asking him instead to

> assume the generous, friendly part,
> Trace every winding labyrinth of my heart,
> Bring forth each lurking prejudice to light,
> Disclose each foible that declines the sight,
> Each kind affection cultivate with care,
> And aid the growth of real virtue there.[18]

While happy to reveal her poems and her heart to friends, Keir was averse to broader publicity. In a poem written to her friend Margaret Keith,

Keir humorously imagines local tongues wagging about her predilection for writing poetry:

> 'The silly thing pretends to write!—
> 'Heavens! Could you bear her in your sight?
> 'Nay, not content with prose and letters,
> 'And such like things as please her betters,
> 'I'm told, by those that saw her writing,
> ''Tis poems she is now inditing!'[19]

If it was fear of ridicule or criticism that initially kept Keir from publishing her poetry, her reasons changed as she grew older. 'Ode to the Female Writers of the Present Age', written in the late 1780s, celebrates the 'fair and virtuous throng, / Daughters of science and of song'. In this poem, Keir implies that her husband's early death required her to renounce her 'wish for fame' so that she could devote herself instead to 'a Mother's cares'.[20] Yet Keir remained a prolific poet, and some of her most entertaining verses were written to her children. Moreover, she continued to experiment formally and thematically even though she had no intention of attempting to publish her work. After William's death, the poetry of place emerges as a distinct genre in Keir's manuscript volumes, and geography vies with friendship as an overarching theme. Keir's visits to particular spots in Edinburgh and its environs become a way for her to revisit the past. 'Elegy written in Greyfriar's Church yard', for instance, commemorates Keir's parents, who were buried there. There are no fewer than six poems that allude in their titles to the 'Temple at Ravelstone (*sic*)', a kind of rustic summerhouse on the Keiths' estate where Keir liked to write; and a further handful of poems declare themselves to be written at 'my Rock, Ravelstone (*sic*)'. In contrast to the poems she writes to and for others, these ones tend to be inward-looking. In them, Keir reflects on the differences between her past and present existence and affirms her intention to submit to God's will, even when it seems to bring only suffering. The death of Keir's youngest son David Orme in 1810 seems to have put an end to her interest in writing. Her manuscript volumes contain only three poems following 'Written while watching by the Corpse of my Son David-Orme Keir. Edinburgh 19 May 1810', and these are dated 1812, 1820, and 1825. Quite simply, as she lost her readership, Keir lost the impulse to write.

Lady Frances Scott, later Lady Douglas, also wrote for a select social circle, albeit one that was more elite, and thus less permeable, than Keir's seems to have been. Scott's single manuscript volume is considerably slimmer than Keir's two, and includes poems written between 1774 and 1782, most of which time Scott spent at Dalkeith Palace, home of her elder brother, the Duke of Buccleuch. Prior to this extended sojourn, Scott lived primarily in London, where her intellectual interests had been cultivated almost exclusively by her stepfather Charles Townshend. Whereas Keir's volumes contain clean copies of her poems, bearing few marks of corrections or revisions, Scott's manuscript is decidedly messy, with words, lines, and occasionally entire stanzas crossed out and rewritten. Possibly, these were draft versions of poems to be sent to friends or copied into a shared volume, now lost, known as the Dalkeith Miscellany. Lady Louisa Stuart, one of Scott's closest friends, recalls in in her *Memoire of Frances, Lady Douglas* that at Dalkeith Palace it was for a time 'almost a law that every inmate or visitor should attempt versifying'.[21] Scott's 'To Lady Louisa Stuart with the Dalkeith Miscellany 1777' corroborates Stuart's recollection of the Dalkeith Miscellany as a collaborative effort. Scott invites Stuart,

> Here with indulgent Eye peruse
> The first attempts of many a Muse,
> Nor hope in all our works to find
> Both poetry and sense combined.[22]

As these lines suggest, poetry writing at Dalkeith was a form of entertainment. The contents of Scott's volume reflect this intention: it includes a poem written in the voice of Lord William Gordon's dog, and several that parodically elevate the commonplace into the subject of poetry, such as 'To Lady Pembroke with the Hollow rind of a large Cheese 1778', and 'To Lady Eleonora Home with a Cushion and False Hair, 1777'. Titles such as 'Answer to Lady Louisa Stuart's Vision 1781' and 'Answer to Ld Wm G's invitation—1775' suggest that some of Scott's poems were written as part of an ongoing exchange of verses; and Stuart explains that Scott and Gordon 'were by agreement, the nymph and swain of each other' among the 'band of rhymers at Dalkeith'.[23]

Scott and Stuart affirmed their own friendship through the exchange of verse. Stuart was adamantly opposed to publishing her writing, perhaps, as Jill Rubenstein suggests, because she feared that doing so would lead to the ostracism that her grandmother, Lady Mary Wortley Montagu, had endured.[24] Yet Stuart readily acknowledges in the *Memoire* she wrote for Scott's daughter that 'One of the delights of having a friend was to indulge vanity by showing her my verses'.[25] Scott and Stuart evidently shared an understanding that poetry written for friends should be judged by different standards than that written for an unknown public. Thus, in the poem accompanying the Dalkeith Miscellany, Scott urges Stuart, 'Indulge not the verse by Critic laws / Whose author never sought applause'.[26] That Stuart read Scott's verse with the eyes of a friend rather than a critic is evident in 'To Lady Louisa Stuart—1781', in which Scott demurringly writes:

> Yet, conscious you o'erate [my] lays
> I cannot trust your partial praise,
> But while, half humble, I disclaim
> All title to Poetic Fame
> My Heart exalts—well pleased to find
> Your Friendship can your Judgment blind. [27]

Lady Stuart expresses the same preference for friendly appreciation over critical judgment in her poem, 'To Lady Frances Scott: *Envoi*: of some pieces in verse 1781':

> Go, idle rhymes! To friendship's hand repair
> Safe be your rest and faithful Delia's care;
> [...]
>
> Unawed by sterner glance, contented lie,
> Nor fear contempt from Delia's partial eye.
> For partial will't not be, my Delia, say?—
> —Shall critic censure here have rig'rous sway?
> No—let indifference blemishes deride,
> Thy heart shall now become thy judgement's guide.[28]

For Scott and Stuart, the circulation of their poetry in manuscript offered protection from the judgments of critics who might not respect the concessions that should be made to an author's gender and social class. Scott in particular clearly wanted to write for an audience, and, within a limited circle, to prove her merit. But, more than praise, she seems to have sought the pleasures of intellectual engagement – pleasures that an unknown reading public could not provide.

Publication by Subscription

Scotswomen who belonged to elite social circles may have chosen to restrict their readership by circulating their poetry in manuscript, but they nonetheless regarded themselves as authors. Working-class Scotswomen, like their male counterparts, seem to have been more likely than the elite to regard print publication as an indisputable sign of authorship, without which they might be perceived as lacking legitimacy. However, rather than seeking to disseminate their poetry as widely as possible, they seem to have been contented with publication by subscription, a practice in which legitimate authority was conferred on the poet by the subscribers' interest and confidence in the work, rather than by the fact of print itself. Donna Landry describes 'the publication by subscription of volumes of verse by laboring-class women' as a distinctively eighteenth-century phenomenon,[29] but subscription publication was by no means a practice confined to women. The first edition of Robert Burns's (1759–1796) *Poems, Chiefly in the Scottish Dialect* (1786) was underwritten by 621 subscribers when it was printed by John Wilson in Kilmarnock.[30] The practice of subscription publication in provincial Scotland tended to be determined by geography (distance from centres of commercial publication) and social class at least as much as by gender.

Texts published by subscription existed in an ill-defined state between print and manuscript cultures, between commercial authorship and an older patronage system, and between public and private spheres. This liminality makes them interesting but difficult to study, and our understanding of subscription publication still relies heavily on a bibliographic project run out of the University of Newcastle in the 1970s.[31] Scholarship on the practice of subscription publication has tended to focus largely on London's metropolitan literary marketplace, where subscription publication began as a way to fund expensive printing ventures, large and lavish folios, or works with a small and highly specific audience.[32] Thomas Lockwood explains that in early- to mid-eighteenth-century London subscription publication was sometimes a 'way-station on the road from personal patronage to commercial authorship', but was more often a form of social posturing that could be exploited by writers and subscribers.[33] But in provincial Britain, where commercial publishing was less well developed, subscription publication was perhaps a more innocent practice. The 'relative poverty of the [...] book trade' in the provinces 'made publication by subscription something of an economic necessity'. It spurred the growth of provincial presses, funding 'smaller local publications' including sermons, county histories, or collections of poetry.[34]

In the cases of the working-class poets I examine here, subscription publication was a natural outgrowth of an older system of patronage. Christian Milne and Anne Ross were both household servants, and, like their better-known countrywoman Janet Little (1759–1813), they depended on their employers to function as patrons of sorts.[35] Rather than underwriting the cost of publication themselves, as a patron would, their employers assisted Milne and Ross by procuring subscriptions from among their own acquaintances. The resulting lists of subscribers, however, were naturally much more modest than the subscriptions that a literary luminary such as Hannah More (1745–1833) could obtain for her working-class protégée Ann Yearsley (1753–1806). Yearsley's *Poems on Several Occasions* (1785) boasted over a thousand subscribers including Henry Dundas (1742–1811), Sir Joshua Reynolds (1723–1792), and Horace Walpole (1717–1797); and Yearsley's engagement with this readership, according to Kerri Andrews, was 'heavily mediated' and 'had to be conducted imaginatively through her work'.[36] By contrast, Milne's and Ross's lists sit at about 250 subscribers, and their poems, like Grant's, often refer to particular subscribers or groups of subscribers. Like the elite Scotswomen who circulated their manuscript poetry among friends, then, working-class Scotswomen wrote their works for a circumscribed readership, but one that might include their employers' social circle in addition to their own.

There is no way to know whether Milne and Ross hoped that their volumes would achieve popularity beyond a geographically and socially circumscribed readership, but it was clearly important to them that their poems be in print, rather than circulated in manuscript. The only extant version of Ross's *A Collection of Poems* (1798) claims to be a third edition, 'revised and corrected' and including poems 'never before published'. Could earlier 'editions' have been circulated among Ross's readership in manuscript, allowing her to revise before the poems were printed in final form? Milne's poems are prefaced by a narrative intended to 'indulge the laudable curiosity of the reader, eager, no doubt, to be made acquainted with the history of a female who, without external aid from birth or education' has become a poet. The truth of the narrative and the authenticity of Milne's authorship is certified by local authorities – 'Bishop Skinner of the Scotch Episcopal Church; William Livingston, M.D., Professor of Medicine in Marischal College; Rev. John Thomson, Minister of Footdee; and Messrs. John Ewen and Robert Gibbon, Merchants in Aberdeen' – much as Phillis Wheatley's (c. 1753–1784) authorship of *Poems on Various Subjects, Religious and Moral* (1773) required the authentication of the great men of Boston, including the governor Thomas Hutchinson, and lieutenant-governor Andrew Oliver. Would this certification have been necessary if Milne's collection were intended to be read only by a local community?

Publication by subscription legitimated Milne's and Ross's authorial endeavors, allowing them to see their poetry in print; but it also created dissonance within their work, as some of their poems addressed those of their own social circle while in others they seem to perform for their wealthier subscribers. Reading Milne's and Ross's poetry in conjunction with the subscription lists and other paratextual materials (biographical notices, dedications, etc.) included in their volumes reveals the strategies these women used to address their various audiences and to establish themselves as authors within these local literary cultures.

Christian Milne's *Simple Poems on Simple Subjects* (1805) speaks to a double audience, with poems including 'To the Ship Carpenters of Footdee' and 'Written on my Little Girl's "Introduction to Reading"' written to or about members of her immediate social circle, and others, such as 'To a Gentleman, Desirous of Seeing my Manuscripts' and 'On Seeing the List of Subscribers to this Little Work' addressed to those who helped to see her work into print. Milne slyly plays these audiences against each other, contrasting her social equals' mockery of her poetic aspirations to the encouragement offered by Aberdeen's intellectual elite. Born to a carpenter and a schoolmaster's daughter in 1773, Milne was, in her own words, a 'menial maid' in a succession of houses in Edinburgh and Aberdeen until she married a journeyman ship-builder.[37] In 'Introductory Verses' she recalls the 'Spite' of those who would 'Assert my songs are drawn from printed books', and remembers how 'servitude, with its incessant toil / Harsh damp'd my Muse, when she inclin'd to smile'.[38] Under these conditions, Milne explains in the autobiographical narrative that precedes her poems, 'friendship and patronage, when offered, gave me much more surprize [sic] than the public can feel in perusing the productions of my humble untaught Muse!'[39] Milne was encouraged to publish her poems by 'a gentleman of great professional respectability in Aberdeen', very likely one of the pillars of the community who certified the truth of her autobiography.[40] In addition to the unnamed gentleman, one of Milne's employers, probably Mrs Moir of Aberdeen, seems to have cultivated her poetic talents. 'Introductory Verses' mentions a 'Fair Lady' who:

> [...] deign'd her favours on my verse to pour,
> And told her friends she'd found a Bard obscure.
> They, like herself, to generous acts inclin'd
> Drew forth the offspring of my untaught mind,
> From where they long in embryo had dwelt,
> Such fost'ring hands ne'er hoping to have felt.[41]

Milne likens her patrons to midwives who assisted in the birth of her poems by 'fost'ring' her talents. Without their help, Milne implies, her verses would have remained in embryonic form rather than achieving their full development in print. That print publication was a very meaningful distinction to Milne is evident when she declares,

> Be't known—'mid all who pant for public fame,
> That one more modest ne'er put in a claim
> To be enroll'd an Author, than the mean
> Unletter'd—female bard of Aberdeen![42]

Print publication transforms Milne from a bard, with all the connotations of primitive genius and oral composition the term implies, into an author, however modest.

Whereas Keir and Scott sought to circumscribe the bounds of their readership, Milne and her contemporary Anne Ross sought to expand theirs, relying on their employers to help them obtain enough subscriptions to see their works into print. This system of diffused and commercialised patronage enabled these women to become authors rather than remaining bards. The final poem in *Simple Poems on Simple Subjects*, titled 'On Seeing the List of Subscribers to this Little Work', describes Milne's feelings on reading through her subscription list. She is amazed:

> To see so many names of worth
> Here join'd, to draw their Poet forth
> From her obscure estate![43]

Geographically, the list of subscribers for *Simple Poems on Simple Subjects* is confined primarily to those living in Northeast Scotland, between Dundee and Aberdeen; but as far as the occupations of those listed is concerned, it must be one of the most diverse subscription lists of its time. Several members of the local aristocracy, including the Duchess of Gordon and the Earl of Aberdeen, purchased multiple copies, and the list also includes the Provost of Aberdeen, doctors, clergymen, lawyers, teachers, and university faculty – all of whose names Milne might have considered 'names of worth'. But it is the array of less 'worthy' subscribers that will surprise contemporary readers: a dancing master, a haberdasher, a grocer, a land-surveyor, an organist, a nail manufacturer, a wine merchant, a builder, and several sailors, among others. By purchasing a copy of Milne's book, these subscribers of the middling sort presented themselves as people of literary taste, capable of recognising and nurturing talent. They also declared their upwards mobility, occupying the place of patrons rather than the patronised.

In the notice prefacing her *Collection of Poems*, Anne Ross similarly acknowledges the scope of her subscription list when she thanks 'all those Friends who have not only favoured me with their own names, but been at great pains procuring Subscriptions from others.' Ross's *Collection* is dedicated to 'The Young Ladies who have been so obliging as to interest themselves for me in this publication', and several of the poems are addressed 'To a Young Lady'.[44] Like Milne's book, Ross's *Collection of Poems*, published in Glasgow, lists a geographically circumscribed but socio-economically diverse group of subscribers, including military officers, manufacturers, and merchants. But whereas Milne's book is inscribed to the Duchess of Gordon, whose name appears at the head of the list of subscribers, there is no such grandee heading Ross's list.

It is impossible to tell which of the many young ladies who subscribed might have been Ross's particular patrons, but it seems likely that they did not move in the highest echelons of Scottish society, as the list is devoid of peers, and features only a few members of the gentry. It is, however, smattered with men connected to Glasgow University, whether as students or faculty, and includes Dr Archibald Davidson, Principal of the University. The prevalence of these men among the subscribers suggest that Ross's employers were also affiliated with the university. 'Lines Composed Upon Seeing the Funeral of Professor William Hamilton Pass' reflects Ross's familiarity with university society. She praises Hamilton's 'healing art', and also remarks on the circumstances of his birth – he was 'an only son, an only child [...] giv'n / To aid his parents as the gift of

Heav'n' – details suggesting that she was acquainted with Hamilton's personal history.[45] Like Milne, Ross clearly wrote with a very definite sense of her readership, for a specific, albeit somewhat eclectic audience, rather than for a general public.

Place is as important in defining the readership for Milne's and Ross's poetry collections as for Keir's and Scott's manuscripts. The subscription list for Ross's *Collection of Poems* is dominated by people from Glasgow and Greenock, with a few from Edinburgh and its environs; and the book seems designed to appeal to a local readership, familiar with the geography and society of the western Lowlands. The local appeal of Ross's *Collection* is evident in works such as 'The Banks of Clyde, connected with the Seasons of the Year, and the Different Stages of Life', which she dedicates 'To All Friends on the Banks of the Clyde'. In this poem, Ross observes that, while more learned writers soar on 'Fancy's wing', she:

> humbly […] remain[s] below,
> Near Clutha's flowing tide,
> To celebrate the thing I know,
> And that's the Banks of Clyde.[46]

In referring to the Clyde by its Latin name, Clutha, Ross subtly reveals her own learning and her awareness of the poetic conventions that would transform the simple things she knows into high art even as she affirms her preference for the familiar Clyde.

As these lines demonstrate, Ross's verse tends to be in ballad meter, a verse form suitable to her humble subjects. 'Bread and Cheese. Inscribed to all Friends in the Country' develops the tuneful quality of a ballad as Ross expresses her hopes for her friends' prosperity, symbolised by the homely but nourishing fare of bread and cheese. The poem draws the landed elite into a community with land labourers through this symbol:

> may they ay ha'e butter-milk,
> And routh of bread and cheese,
> And sleeket kye, wi' skins like silk,
> And sheep gaun on the lees.[47]

Like Milne, Ross wrote for two distinct readerships – her own friends and those of her superiors. While the opening stanzas of 'Bread and Cheese' are written in Scots, Ross code-switches throughout the poem so that her diction represents that of the social class she is describing. Thus she uses English when she observes that:

> [...] lairds may claret drink or gin,
> And brandy if they please,
> And bring a roasted turkey in
> Before their bread and cheese.[48]

And she returns to Scots to describe the farm labourer who:

> [...] ca's the pleugh,
> To help him o'er the lees,
> He sings and whistles blythe enough,
> If he have bread and cheese.[49]

Ross's poetry is like the bread and cheese that pleases both gentle and simple, bringing into communion otherwise disparate social strata.

Conclusion

This chapter has focused on the situation of women writing in Scots and English. There are, of course, some useful parallels with the situation of Gaelic women poets, whose emergence into published writing is discussed in detail by Kate L. Mathis in Chapter Eleven. While the women whose poetry I have discussed here may have shared little in common socially, as writers they reveal some marked similarities. All of them wrote for a circumscribed readership, an audience delimited primarily by social ties and secondarily by locale. Whether they published their poetry in print or circulated it in manuscript, their conception of themselves as authors seems to have been grounded in the recognition of the social circles for which they wrote. These similarities throw into relief the anomalousness of Baillie, perhaps the best-known of eighteenth-century Scottish women poets, whose work is often anthologised. Baillie's comparative renown perhaps depends as much on the publication history of her work as on her literary talents. In the context of the women whose writing I have discussed here, Baillie's career is strikingly atypical simply because she lived for most of her adult life in London, the centre of commercial publishing.[50] Like the women I have discussed here, Baillie wrote songs and ballads, but also employed neoclassical forms, and her diction depended upon the tradition in which she worked. But unlike Keir,

Scott, Milne, and Ross, Baillie published her work for an anonymous and disembodied reading public. This simple fact has undoubtedly shaped literary scholars' reception of her poetry and their comparative neglect of Baillie's Scottish contemporaries. While Baillie will always remain an important figure in the history of Scottish women's writing, we can only understand the significance of her work by exploring the practices of other Scottish women poets of her time.

CHAPTER EIGHT

Gaelic Enlightenment to Global Gaelosphere: Gaelic Literature, 1750–1800

Domhnall Uilleam Stiùbhart

This chapter examines Gaelic literature from 1750 to 1800. It traces how, out of the profusion of verbal art circulating in the Gàidhealtachd during the period, a corpus of Scottish Gaelic literature came to be created and written down for a new Scottish Gaelic readership. From the mid-eighteenth century onwards, systematic endeavours to codify and refine a 'pure' written standard of Scottish Gaelic were complemented by initiatives to record and evaluate poetry, songs, and proverbs, some of which were subsequently disseminated in printed anthologies. Thus out of a vast, complex, fluid, processual oral culture, a supposedly representative, hegemonic canon would be fashioned, influenced by a vision of Scottish Gaelic character that reflected contemporary ideologies, value judgements, aesthetic ideals, and moral principles.

Chief among those responsible for the new codified standard of Scottish Gaelic was the poet Alasdair MacDhomhnaill (Alexander MacDonald, c. 1700–c. 1770), known as Alasdair mac Mhaighstir Alasdair. His *Galick and English Vocabulary* (1741), composed for his employers, the SSPCK, is the first dictionary printed in Scottish Gaelic. In the dedication, MacDonald explains that the volume is intended to spread knowledge of English across the region, making its inhabitants 'more useful Members in the Commonwealth', fostering among them Protestantism, loyalty, and industry.[1] For the dictionary to be effective, the Gaelic forms used had to be as accessible as possible. As Ronald Black remarks in an astute article on Scottish Gaelic orthography, Mac Mhaighstir Alasdair's spelling represents a break with the past.[2] Disregarding traditional rules of classical Gaelic, it cleaves closer to spoken vernacular – a pragmatic option in a dictionary intended for schools. It is notable that systematic codification of modern Scottish Gaelic began in a work intended to help spread English among the children of the Gàidhealtachd.

A decade later MacDonald built upon his programme in his *Ais-eiridh na Sean Chánoin Albannaich* (*The Resurrection of the Ancient Scottish Language*, 1751). Given that a principal purpose of the anthology was clearly to rally support in the expectation of a new Jacobite rising, it is perhaps not surprising that, in Mac Mhaighstir Alasdair's words, '[n]o pains have been spared to render the language as plain and intelligible as can be expected.'[3] Ronald Black has drawn attention to the similar, though even more radical, spelling system that was adopted around the same time by the Rev. Alexander MacFarlane or Alasdair MacPhàrlain of Kilninver and Kilmelfort (c. 1715–63) in *Gairm an Dè Mhòir* (1750), his translation of Richard Baxter's popular evangelical tract *Call to the Unconverted*.[4] The Synod of Argyll, encouraged by this volume's success and enthused by MacPhàrlain's subsequent translation of the Paraphrases, which they praised as 'just, exact and beautifull [...] excellently adapted to excite Devotion', sponsored his reworking the Psalms in simplified spelling.[5] These, with the Paraphrases, were printed in Glasgow in 1753. Black designates the two Alasdairs together 'the founding fathers of Gaelic orthography'; contemporary manuscript sources hint at an unlikely collusion between Presbyterian minister and Catholic Jacobite renegade.[6]

These mid-eighteenth-century Scottish Gaelic spelling reforms are not just a matter of orthographical and grammatical arcana. They demonstrate a slow, but profound, reorientation of the language and its speakers' vernacular identity and a cultural integration, best understood within a wider British context. The remodelled written language was closer to spoken norms, easier to read and write, easier to print: the Synod of Argyll was at least partly motivated in promoting orthographical innovations by the many spelling errors increasingly appearing in new editions of older religious texts composed in classically-inflected Gaelic.[7] But the modifications were also more accessible for readers, schoolchildren and congregations alike, ever more fluent in English. The language itself was rebranded within a national Scottish context, as the ancient Scottish tongue. 'Irishisms' in orthography, grammar, or lexis – in other words, the residue of classical Gaelic vocabulary – were increasingly rejected, discarded in favour of a national language that was pure, simple, elegant, and enlightened.[8]

The Gaelic New Testament, Dùghall Bochanan, and Donnchadh Bàn Mac an t-Saoir

The third quarter of the eighteenth century saw the emergence of an increasingly assertive cohort of young Gaelic intellectuals intent on re-creating a specifically Scottish Gaelic language and affirming its fundamental place in Scottish national history. The epics composed by the most prominent of these, James Macpherson (Seumas Bàn MacMhuirich, 1736–96), would leave a decisive mark on Scottish Gaelic literature and influence many other European literatures beside – although he neither wrote in Gaelic, nor claimed to be a creative author. Encouraged by Edinburgh literati, assisted particularly by the author and literary critic Rev. Hugh Blair (1718–1800), at the beginning of the 1760s, Macpherson translated, reworked, and expanded Gaelic Ossianic lays still recited at funeral wakes in his native Badenoch. In *Fingal: An Ancient Epic Poem* (1761) and *Temora: An Ancient Epic Poem* (1763), he rewrote their heroic narratives in English poetic prose, elaborating the profound emotions the characters expressed, arranging them in sublime, sombre settings of immense grandeur calculated to inspire awe and terror in readers. To some extent, Macpherson may have derived this *Gefühlswelt*, this emotional landscape, from the tragic love ballads then fashionable at all levels of society, in Gaelic as well as in English. He may also have been reacting to an increasingly popular sub-genre of English religious devotional poetry whose mixture of the sentimental and the sublime powerfully affected its readers.[9] Ossian helped light the touchpaper of the Romantic movement in literature and the arts whose effects we still experience today: a worldwide audience relished their own 'modern' romantic sensibilities reflected in Macpherson's northern epics supposedly composed one and a half millennia earlier. The Ossian poems also supplied a nascent university-educated Scottish Gaelic intelligentsia with a brand-new origin legend, a counter-narrative vision of a martially glorious, emotionally sophisticated indigenous Highland civilisation located in a prelapsarian past antedating clan animosities and transcending scholarly controversies regarding the origins of the Scottish nation.

The sensational success of Macpherson's Ossianic epics may have expedited the publication of the newly translated New Testament under the SSPCK's auspices in 1767, not least by helping neutralise lingering hostility among society members to sponsoring Gaelic publishing. The work, primarily undertaken by Rev. Seumas Stiùbhart, or James Stuart, of Killin (1701–89) was the first step in a major, generation-long project to supersede with a more accessible, modern vernacular translation the cumbersome classical Gaelic Bible first printed in Roman script in 1690 and accompanied by a lengthy inventory by Rev. Robert Kirk of some 550 words judged unfamiliar to Highland congregations.[10] While the earlier volume was '[a]r na ttabhairt go fírinneach as Greigis go Goidheilg' ('accurately brought over from Greek to [common] Gaelic', Stiùbhart's New Testament was pointedly '[e]idir-theangaicht' o'n Ghreugais chum Gaidhlig Albannaich' ('translated from the Greek to Scottish Gaelic').

Of course, this new translation's preparation was no simple matter. As with Biblical translations elsewhere, the weighty matter of rendering Scriptures in the vernacular entailed agreeing and codifying a new literary standard. The Highland translators built on the earlier language work of Alasdair mac Mhaighstir Alasdair and others, replacing many older norms of classical Gaelic with vocabulary, spelling, and grammar of a new formalised standard: 'Scottish Galic' [sic].[11] But before investigating other, perhaps unexpected consequences of this momentous step, we should consider two major Gaelic poets whose collections were published in Edinburgh at the same time as the New Testament: a benefit on the side, as it were, of the pooling of linguistic expertise then in the Scottish capital.

For nearly a decade, Dùghall Bochanan (Dugald Buchanan, 1716–68), an SSPCK schoolmaster-catechist in Rannoch, had been closely involved with Stiùbhart in the translating and editing processes of the Gaelic New Testament. There are eight pieces in Bochanan's *Laoidhe Spioradail* (*Spiritual Hymns*) of 1767; all but one – a versification of the life and crucifixion of Christ – are devotional or meditative religious poems emphatically directed at the individual reader. They are creations of a highly literate and learned poet. Using forceful, complex imagery, imbued with evangelical sublimity, the hymns confront readers with vertiginous abysses of time and space, unfathomable mysteries concerning the majesty of creation, original sin, mortality, and God's seismic wrath on the Day of Judgement:

> 'N sin fàsaidh rudhadh anns an speur
> Mar fhàir' na maidne 'g èirigh dearg,
> Ag innse gu bheil Ìosa fèin
> A' teachd na dhèidh le latha garbh.
>
> Grad fhosglaidh às a chèil' na neòil,
> Mar dhoras seòmar an Àrd-Rìgh,
> Is foillsichear am Breitheamh mòr
> Le glòir is greadhnachas gun chrìch.
>
> Tha 'm bogha-frois mun cuairt da cheann,
> 'S mar thuil nan gleann tha fuaim a ghuth;

'S mar dhealanach tha sealladh shùl
A' spùtadh às na neulaibh tiugh [...]

Then the sky will begin to glow red / Like the morning horizon, rising scarlet, / Telling that Jesus himself / Is coming afterwards with a day of storms. // Swiftly the clouds will open up from each other, / Like the door of the High King's chamber, / And the great judge will be revealed / With glory and majesty eternal. // The rainbow is about his head, / The sound of his voice like a flood in the glens; / Like lightning the look from his eyes / Pouring from the thick clouds [...][12]

As recently demonstrated by Donald Meek, much of Bochanan's work in fact translates, adapts, reconsiders, and responds to English devotional poetry of his age, particularly, perhaps, the 'publishing phenomenon of massive proportions' that was the devotional poems and hymns of Isaac Watts.[13]

English-language devotional poetry, combining intensely felt, awe-inspiring imagery of the religious sublime with direct, even urgent address to the individual reader, clearly exerted a strong influence upon Gaelic religious verse from the mid-eighteenth century through to the evangelical movement of the century following. Its effects may have been felt beyond religious literature: the genre appears to have exerted a formative influence on the landscape descriptions and sentiment of James Macpherson's Ossian – and through Ossian may have played an intriguing, albeit indirect, role in sparking Highland Romanticism. Dùghall Bochanan had no time for the battlefield heroism of the Ossianic heroes, however. For him:

Cha ghaisg' an nì bhith liodairt dhaoin',
'S cha chliù bhith ann an caonnaig tric;
Chan uaisle inntinn àrdan borb,
'S cha treubhantas bhith garg gun iochd.

Ach 's gaisgeach esan a bheir buaidh
Air eagal beatha, 's uamhann bàis,
'S a chòmhlaicheas le misnich crìdh'
Na h-uile nì ata dha 'n dàn.

It is no heroism to be thrashing people, / No fame to be often in a quarrel; / Savage pride is no nobility of mind, / Nor is bravery brutal and merciless. //

The hero is he who overcomes / Fear of life and terror of death, / Who meets with heartfelt courage / Everything destined for him.[14]

Nevertheless, Dùghall Bochanan and James Macpherson seem to have been influenced by the same English-language tradition of the religious sublime.

The second, very different, Gaelic poetry volume published in Edinburgh while the New Testament was seen through the press was the *Orain Ghaidhealach* (*Highland Songs*) of Donnchadh Bàn Mac an t-Saoir (Duncan Ban Macintyre, 1724–1812).[15] At first sight, Mac an t-Saoir offers a very different poetic persona from Bochanan: a poet of outdoors rather than the study; intensely sociable, not withdrawn; caught up in the present moment, not the prophetic future; a poet of materiality, of the senses, rather than the spirit. After an ignominiously unheroic role as a hapless private in the Argyll government militia in the rout of Falkirk, ruefully recounted in his *Blàr na h-Eaglaise Brice*, he spent the first half of his life employed as stalker and gamekeeper in the elongated sprawl of deer forests stretching from Breadalbane to Glencoe.

His poetry of the hills, above all the great epic in *pìobaireachd* metre 'Moladh Beinn Dóbhrain' ('*Praise of Ben Dorain*'), demonstrates capacious powers of observation and, in Ronald Black's words, 'dazzling fluency' of language and metrics. Far from overawing us with sublime obscurity, Donnchadh Bàn creates his masterwork out of a recursive series of intricate, high-resolution montages, a polyphonic picturesque:

> An t-urram thar gach beinn
>   Aig Beinn Dóbhrain,
> De na chunnaic mi fon ghréin
>   Si bu bhòidhche leam:
> Munadh fada réidh,
> Cuilidh 'm faighte féidh,
> Soilleireachd an t-sléibh
>   Bha mi sònrachadh;
> Doireachan nan geug,
> Coill' anns am bi feur:
> 'S foinneasach an spréidh
>   Bhios a chòmhnaidh ann,
> Greadhainn bu gheal céir,

> Faghaid air an déidh –
> 'S laghach leam an sreud
>   A bha sròineiseach.

The prize above each ben / Is Ben Dorain's, / Of all I've ever seen / To me she was loveliest: / Moorland long and smooth, / Store where deer were found, / The brightness of the slope / Is what I pointed to; / Groves of branching trees, / Woods containing grass: / Well-favoured is the stock / That makes its dwelling there, / A white-buttocked band / With hunt pursuing them – / Lovely to me is the herd / That were snuffle-nosed.[16]

Dissimilar in their nature, their life, their calling, and their art, Bochanan and Mac an t-Saoir nevertheless shared a common burden: both were charged, in different ways, with keeping order at opposite ends of Rannoch Moor, that great simmering cauldron of lawlessness and disaffection in the middle of the southern Gàidhealtachd. One a catechist-schoolmaster, the other a gamekeeper, both employed their poetic gifts to keep the peace. Certainly, a measure of calculated self-deprecation was part of Donnchadh Bàn's appeal – but the bard could also wield caustic satire to devastating effect.[17]

Mac an t-Saoir's allegiance to the established order is incontrovertible: he praises his erstwhile militia comrades for their bravery against the Jacobites at Culloden (and also for their clemency during the subsequent pacification of the western Highlands); he mourns the assassination of Colin Campbell of Glenure in the Appin Murder; a few years later he would eulogise King George and the British Empire.[18] Yet both Bochanan and Mac an t-Saoir came from humble backgrounds. Both appear to share a growing anxiety about the future of the people of the Gàidhealtachd under a new commercial dispensation. In 'An Claigeann' ('*The Skull*'), Bochanan goes well beyond his exemplar, Blair's 'The Grave', in revelling in the apocalyptic reckoning destined to be meted out to vicious landlords:

> No 'n robh thu ro chruaidh
> A' fionnadh do thuath
> 'S a' tanach' an gruaidh le màl;
> Le h-agartas geur
> A' glacadh an sprèidh,
> 'S am bochdainn ag èigheach dàil?

Gun chridh' aig na daoin'
Bh' air lomadh le h-aois,
Le'n claiginnibh maola truagh,
Bhith seasamh ad chòir
Gun bhoineid nan dòrn,
Ged tholladh gaoth reòt' an cluas.

Tha nise do thràill,
Gun urram ad dhàil,
Gun ghearsom, gun mhàl, gun mhòd;
Mòr mholadh don bhàs,
A chasgair thu tràth,
'S nach d' fhuiling do stràic fon fhòid.

Or were you too hard / Flaying your tenantry, / Wearing out their appearance with rent; / With sharp practice / Confiscating their herds, / While their poverty cried out for deferment? // They would not dare, the men / Who were ruined by age, / With their poor, bald skulls, / To stand in your presence / Without their cap in their hand, / Though the frozen wind would pierce their ears. // Now your slave / Has happened upon you, without honour, / Without entry-fee, without rent, without court; / All praise to death / Who slaughtered you early / And didn't suffer your conceit under the turf.[19]

William Gillies proposes that, concealed beneath its ekphrases, Donnchadh Bàn's 'Moladh Beinn Dóbhrain' offers a more subtle critique arising from prospects of dispossession and estrangement. The landscape is depicted holistically, a place where 'flora and fauna, and especially the deer and the men who hunt the deer are all part of a continuum – an ecological system – sustained by and on the mountain.' 'Tha 'n èilid anns an fhrìth / Mar bu chòir dhi bhith': '*The doe is in the deer forest, as she should be*'.[20] It may be that for Donnchadh Bàn, the people too were of, and belonged to, the land.

The New Testament translation project thus enabled the publication of works by two of the major Gaelic poets of the eighteenth century. It also brought into being a network of enthusiastic indigenous intellectuals focused upon their native language and increasingly aware of what was needed to make Scottish Gaelic suitable as a language of education and preaching in the modern era – in other words, as a language of Enlightenment. The printing of the New Testament helped spark and pull together fundamentally important initiatives for the history of language and literature, additional language planning efforts not only to codify Gaelic by standardising its spelling and grammar, but also to collect its vocabulary, proverbs, and poetry, and so create an ideal literary canon illustrative of the supposed essence of Gaelic culture.

Compiling a Dictionary, and Creating a Canon

The Rev. Seumas Stiùbhart and his assistants who supervised the Gaelic translation of the New Testament came mostly from the southern and eastern Gàidhealtachd peripheries.[21] Their native Gaelic dialects thus differed sharply from those of the Hebrides and western Highlands. After the New Testament was printed, the SSPCK requested Dùghall Bochanan to compile an explanatory word-list: readers in the north and west had complained that certain words and expressions in Stiùbhart's translation were either quite alien to them, or used in unfamiliar senses. Bochanan, however, envisaged a considerably much more ambitious undertaking than a mere Biblical concordance. In a letter to the antiquarian Sir John Clerk of Penicuik, one of the commissioners administering the Forfeited Estates, he outlined the case for a comprehensive dictionary drawing upon older printed works in Gaelic, as well as expeditions 'thro the Isles and western Coasts' in order to 'collect the words of the antient & modern Bards, in which alone he could find the Language in its purity'.[22] Bochanan's proposal went far beyond finding exemplars of bardic best practice in order to help codify pronunciation, vocabulary, grammar, dialect, and linguistic register. It broached wider questions regarding how the language – and its speakers – were to be improved, refined, modernised, and made fit for the Era of Enlightenment.

Bochanan's ambitions for a comprehensive dictionary and grammar to complement and enable new theological works in Scottish Gaelic foundered with his untimely death in 1768. But his project was taken up by a patriotic group, mainly composed of enthusiastic young ministers, arising out of a 'Gaulic Society at Edinburgh'.[23] The planned grammar and dictionary of this *gälische Sprachgesellschaft* only survive today in scattered manuscripts, but the project also may have given shape and scholarly direction to their youthful ventures into recording oral song texts.[24] Cèilidhing, visiting, travelling, and corresponding, the clergymen recorded out of the protean mass of songs circulating in Highland oral tradition hundreds of texts. From these was crystallised and refined a Scottish Gaelic poetic canon. In it, pride of place was given to Ossianic lays and the work of 'official' vernacular bards such as Iain Lom MacDhomhnaill (John MacDonald, c. 1624–c. 1710), in tradition King Charles II's Gaelic poet laureate, Màiri nighean Alasdair Ruaidh (Mary MacLeod, c. 1625–c. 1705), and the still living Iain mac Fhearchair (John MacCodrum, c. 1693–1779) in North Uist, poet to Sir Alexander Macdonald of Sleat.[25]

In codifying and legitimising a formal standard of Scottish Gaelic and collecting and constructing a canonical literature as a tangible expression of Gaels' cultural distinctiveness, their claims to early indigenous origins, and thus their distinct role and standing in their nation's history, the activities of the first generation of 'Gaelic activists' are broadly comparable at least in part to similar programmes carried out by intellectual elites of language movements elsewhere in Europe from the mid-eighteenth century onwards.[26] Within the wider British Atlantic world, significant affinities might be traced with the work of indigenous intellectuals and entrepreneurs in, for example, the Creek nation in North America, facing challenges as to how their peoples might 'progress' within existing political constraints and contemporary colonial socio-cultural and economic ideals and prejudices, to find a place, standing, and advantageous circumstances in the new British imperial space being then consolidated and integrated.[27]

The efforts of the Gaelic ministers to codify and refine a standard Scottish Gaelic have, of course, an equivalent much closer to home. The process is, in fact, precisely analogous to the contemporary language shift – among educated Scots throughout the country, Highlanders as well as Lowlanders – from a purportedly 'vulgar' Lowland Scots to a more refined, 'polite', and prestigious standard English. This produced the situation described by the pioneering social historian John Ramsay of Ochtertyre who noted that 'nothing can be more different than the language of Edin[burgh] in 1760 and 1802'.[28] While contemporary literary London proffered a linguistic exemplar for Scottish speakers of English, Scottish Gaels could attend to the legacy of the vernacular bards, the more so given the notional intellectual descent now ascribed to them as heirs of the druids.[29] For the Gaelic literary intelligentsia of the late eighteenth-century, the bard had kept language, culture, and historical memory vigorous at all levels of society in the past. As champions of the vernacular, effectively modern language corpus planners, the educated literati might, perhaps, themselves be heirs to the bards. In particular, of course, they could look to Macpherson's Ossian. Certainly, the poems represented a valedictory elegy to a lost Gaelic civilisation; but they also came freighted with cultural capital, an ancient underpinning for a modern, self-confident linguistic reflorescence. With Ossian, the Scottish Gaelic intelligentsia could assert a native, national Scottish vernacular antiquity which, if not entirely bypassing the classical Gaelic heritage they shared with Ireland, nevertheless played down its historical significance.[30]

Macpherson's claims also generated considerable controversy which may have hastened the printing of the first Gaelic poetry anthology, the *Comh-chruinneachidh Orannaigh Gaidhealach* (1776) or Eigg collection by Raghnall MacDhomhnaill (c. 1730–c. 1810), doubtless using songs collected by his father Alasdair mac Mhaighstir Alasdair. Another outcome of the dispute was the publication in London of a grammatical *Analysis of the Galic Language* (1778) and a two-volume *Galic and English Dictionary* (1780) by the Rev. William Shaw (Uilleam Seathach, 1749–1831) – projects encouraged, enabled, and orchestrated by Shaw's mentor, Samuel Johnson.[31] Having secured financial backing from many wealthy Highland subscribers, Shaw's volumes effectively stymied any chance of the ministers' grammar and dictionary going through the press. Their disappointment triggered legal action in Scotland, as well as a spate of anti-Johnsonian mudslinging in English-language periodicals, for whose editors and readers the Ossianic dispute offered a picturesque, minor-key Scottish iteration of the much more widely debated controversy over Thomas Chatterton's Rowley forgeries.[32]

The ministers may not have been able to publish a Gaelic grammar or dictionary, but their manuscript poetry collections formed the framework for the highly influential *Sean Dain agus Orain Ghaidhealach* (*Old Gaelic Poems and Songs*, 1786), known as the Gillies collection after its ostensible editor and 'project manager', the Perth-based bookseller-publisher and antiquarian John Gillies. The volume certainly drew inspiration from Lowland precedents: the various editions of James Watson's *Choice Collection of Comic and Serious Scots Poems* (1706–11); Allan Ramsay's *Tea-Table Miscellany* (1723); in particular, David Herd's *Ancient and Modern Scottish Songs, Heroic Ballads, &c.* (1769); as well as Gillies' own anthology of popular contemporary songs *The Chearful Companion* (1780). Commercial expectations were doubtless to the fore: the projected rise in Gaelic literacy fostered expectations of a substantial new market for secular books in the language as well as religious material. At the same time, British public and political opinion appeared ever more favourable to Highlanders and Highland culture. Gaels were shedding the lingering taint of Jacobitism as a result of

Highland regimental exploits in the recent worldwide war against France and Spain; Highland Societies – elite-led patriotic cultural and economic political pressure groups – had been established in London (1778) and Edinburgh (1784); and successful lobbying had resulted in the repealing of the anti-tartan Dress Act (1782) and the restoration of the Forfeited Estates (1784).[33] An astute combination of high-status Ossianic ballads, clan panegyric and lament, aristocratic hunting, drinking, and love poetry, satire (including three lampoons aimed at Samuel Johnson), intermixed with popular love song, the Gillies Collection was foundational for the modern Gaelic literary canon.

In Chapter One, I noted the decisive influence exerted by English literature upon Gaelic poets from the late seventeenth century onwards. Even more significant was the colossal effect of contemporary English commercial song, of broadsides, chapbooks, and ballads, on popular Gaelic culture. By the end of the eighteenth century, the Gàidhealtachd was being drawn ever more closely into a multilingual British cultural marketplace in which new songs, music, poems, and stories, fashions in clothes, and emotional styles, were being exchanged, adopted, adapted, and acculturated across linguistic boundaries.[34]

The Late Eighteenth-Century Gàidhealtachd: Tìr nan Òg?

As we might expect, high-status poetry overwhelmingly predominates in the canonical literary collections of Scottish Gaelic at the end of the eighteenth century, collections that were generally dedicated to a wealthy patron and paid for by gentry subscribers. As well as the Eigg (1776) and Gillies (1786) Collections mentioned above, the brothers Alexander and Donald Stewart also collected a two-volume *Cochruinneacha Taoghta de Shaothair nam Bard Gaëlach* (1804), while Patrick Turner created *Comhchruinneacha do dh'Orain Taghta Ghaidhealach* (1813). Popular love songs represent only a relatively small percentage of the contents of these collections, between six and sixteen per cent. But there are also lesser-known commercial Gaelic miscellanies: Donnchadh Lobhdain's (Duncan Lothian's) *Orannaigh Gaedhealach agus Bearla* (1780); Aonghas Caimbeul's *Orain Nuadh Ghaidhleach* (1785); the *Co-chruinneachadh Nuadh do dh'Orannibh Gaidhealach* or Inverness Collection (1806); Griogair MacGriogair's *Eoin Bheag nan Creagaibh Aosda* (1819); and Rev. Duncan MacCallum's *Co-chruinneacha Dhan, Orain* (1821). Composed of varying proportions of traditional and new material, these books were primarily money-making ventures which had to appeal to as many potential purchasers as possible. In this category, popular song constitutes anywhere from a fifth to over a half of all items printed; indeed, a number also print fashionable English hit songs with Gaelic translations. The situation is even more marked in collections of Highland music such as Elizabeth Ross's manuscript 'Original Highland airs collected at Raasay in 1812', Simon Fraser's *Airs and Melodies peculiar to the Highlands of Scotland and the Isles* (1816), and Finlay Dun's *Orain na h-Alban* (1848). It is likely that these compilations can give us a rough idea, free from any literary piety, about what songs contemporary Gaels actually sang and danced to. Airs for popular love songs take up anywhere between a third and a half of their contents. In this respect, we might note the case of the newly founded Highland Society of London (1778). Although its members professed an interest in funding Gaelic scholarship, the best way to earn their goodwill, according to Rev. Donald Mackinnon (Domhnall MacFhionghain) of Claybrooke in a letter he sent in 1779 to the scholar and song collector Rev. Donald MacNicol (Domhnall MacNeacail), was to send them 'the Galic translation of Robin Grey': that is, Lady Anne Lindsay's 'Auld Robin Gray', the hit song of the decade.[35]

Popular love poetry, of course, is emphatically not inevitably of throwaway quality, as demonstrated by the work of Uilleam Ros (William Ross, 1762–90). A schoolteacher in Gairloch, Ross was a highly gifted poet whose originality and versatility remain overshadowed by his searing poems caused by a hapless infatuation with Mòr Ros of Stornoway that, according to tradition, killed him at only twenty-eight years old:

> Tha mise fo mhulad 's an àm,
> Chan òlar leam dràm le sunnd,
> Tha durrag air ghur ann mo chàil
> A dh'fhiosraich do chàch mo rùn;
> Chan fhaic mi 'dol seachad air sràid
> An cailin bu tlàithe sùil;
> 'S e sin a leag m' aigneadh gu làr
> Mar dhuilleach bho bhàrr nan craobh.

I am despondent now, / I cannot drink a dram with pleasure, / A maggot has hatched in my frame / And revealed my secret love to the rest; / I do not see going past on the street / The girl with the gentlest eye; / That is what felled my spirit to the ground / Like foliage from the treetops.[36]

Through close analyses of Ros's work beyond the love poetry, however, William Gillies has laid the foundation for more complex, balanced, and inclusive approaches towards poet and œuvre. It is not only his passionate romanticism that makes Uilleam Ros emblematic of his age; he also exhibits unexpected penchants for salacious burlesque, experimentation with generic boundaries, dialectal caricature, and juxtaposition of high and low linguistic registers.[37] The difficulty of assimilating this candid, sociable, and playful side of Ros to the legend of the lonely, exemplary victim of an all-consuming love passion may have contributed to the poet's uneasy posthumous reputation in oral tradition.

In order better to understand the changes in Gaelic popular literature during the second half of the eighteenth century, we have to consider the material background. Clanship was in terminal decay; gentry and nobility had withdrawn from their tenants and from tenant culture; and the ideal of the aristocratic masculine warrior as protector of his community, and with it the notion of reciprocal obligations assumed by chief and tenantry, were becoming increasingly obsolete tropes. As a result, the older panegyric rhetoric that had shaped so much of vernacular Gaelic oral culture was losing its meaning and raison d'être.[38]

The Gàidhealtachd was rapidly being transformed by the adoption of innovative methods of improved, efficient agriculture; an expanding transport infrastructure; formal, bilingual education; new small-scale manufacturing industries offering waged day-work; more comfortable housing; and fashionable, lighter clothes. The first, water-powered Industrial Revolution, exemplified by the vertical mill-wheel, allowed people – women above all – additional time to work for money, often by spinning flax, instead of spending long hours making bread for the family.[39] The introduction of the potato offered communities instant fast food, bypassing grain preparation altogether.[40] Essentially, there was a new spirit of industriousness afoot: this, and the loss of communal leisure once enjoyed at summer shielings and winter cèilidh houses, meant that fewer people had the time to create, memorise, polish, and perform extensive cultural repertoires as their forebears might have done.

In addition, the striking nationwide decline in infant mortality had cultural as well as demographic consequences. The second half of the eighteenth century saw an extraordinary rise in the number of young people in the Gàidhealtachd.[41] Compared to their parents, this bilingual 'boomer' generation had vastly expanded cultural horizons; many had grown comfortable with the English language, and acculturated to its fashions, pastimes, and attitudes, during work sojourns in the south. Late eighteenth-century Gaelic culture, then, was increasingly a youth culture. For younger, perhaps more individualistic Gaels, communal work songs sung while waulking cloth or turning the quern reeked of bygone poverty and boorish inelegance; clan panegyric evoked only the old-fashioned world of their grandparents. One lasting contribution of this youth culture to literature may have been the development of puirt-à-beul or mouth music: light-hearted, rhythmically complex, rapid-fire verses, designed to be danced to in the absence of a fiddle, late-eighteenth century Gaelic rap composed of ostensibly absurd tongue-twisters frequently, to the knowledgeable ear, drenched in bawdy innuendo:

> 'S ann ort fhéin a tha na casan
>   'S chan e casan Gallda
> Chinn cho gairbhe ris a' chalpa
>   'S ainmeil air an danns' thu. [x2]

> Gogan fhéin an gille gasda
>   Tha e math gu dannsa
> Tha e ruith air feadh nan nighean
>   A' mireag 's a' cainnt riuth'. [x2]

It is you that has the fine legs / And not Lowland legs, / Head as thick as a calf / You're famous at dancing. [x2] // Gogan himself is the lad / He's good at dancing, / He runs among the girls / Flirting and chatting with them. [x2][42]

Rob Donn and Gaelic Satire

In the commercially oriented, often increasingly authoritarian late-eighteenth-century Gàidhealtachd estates, it could be challenging for poets to exercise an independent critical voice. A telling exemplar is the case of Rob Donn MacAoidh (1714–78), a poet of exceptional insight, linguistic vitality, and productivity: well over two hundred songs were recorded from him, a corpus considerably more extensive than that of any of his contemporaries. Rob Donn's character studies and often satirical social commentaries, thoroughly contextualised by

Ian Grimble and recently edited, with accompanying music, by Ellen Beard, offer us unparalleled insights into the communal life of a single district: Dùthaich MhicAoidh, Mackay Country in the far north, already a stronghold of evangelicalism for several generations.[43] Rob Donn's métier was to craft out of daily events instructive, memorable paradigm cases that promoted public ideals of moral integrity and civic virtue; played a civilising role by exposing fallible and foolish behaviour; called out instances of cruelty, greed, hypocrisy, and injustice; and so endeavoured to better society – society as it actually was, rather than an ancestral clannish yesteryear. For its success, Rob Donn's work required a knowledgeable audience conversant with the sophisticated stratagems in his satiric arsenal: imitation, parody, the testing of generic expectations, and multi-faceted irony. For its effectiveness, it also demanded a poet of principle, honest, fearless, and impartial in assigning *deagh chliù* and *droch chliù*, good and bad reputation. The gleeful coda of Rob's satire on Domhnall nan Cluas, 'Donald of the Ears', who had mistakenly accused him of rustling cattle, exults in the power of words set to music, portraying his song's relentless energy and dynamism as it circulates throughout the countryside, eventually engrossing the entire community:

> 'Nuair théid an t-òran cluasach seo
>   A-suas air feadh na tìr,
> Bitheadh e aig na buachaillean,
>   A' cuairteachadh 'n cuid nì;
> Bitheadh e 'm beul nam buanaichean,
>   A' gearradh sios gach raoin;
> Chan eil guth nach bi fuaimneach dha,
>   'S cha chluinn e cluas nach claon.

When this 'eary' song will go / Up throughout the land, / Let the herding lads have it, / Gathering in their cattle; / Let it be in the mouth of the reapers, / Cutting down every field; / No voice that won't be echoing it, / And no ear hearing it but taking heed.[44]

Much research remains to be done, tracing how Rob Donn's ethics and intellectual ideas echo contemporary currents in Rational Christianity and Enlightenment thought, and how they draw upon eighteenth-century sermon cultures and wider modes of satire. A specific concatenation of circumstances catalysed his work's sophistication and won it credit. A framing Presbyterian outlook, combined with apprehension regarding an increasingly commercial society and repressive estate management, added new urgency, piquancy, and moral force to traditional township satire. Rob's occupation as a cattle drover, accompanying herds to crowded Lowland trysts, enabled his songs to circulate among Gaels far beyond Mackay Country. The development of a national public sphere allowed Rob Donn to hear extempore translations from English literature – among them, supposedly, works by Alexander Pope read to him by the local minister Maighstir Murchadh.[45] Finally, we cannot ignore the possible allure for Rob, in composing his songs, of the permanence, higher status, and broader horizons of print, the more so given his increasing insecurity and vulnerability to a hostile estate administration towards the end of his life.

One question, however, might be whether much of Rob Donn's poetry would in fact appeal to literate Gaelic audiences, given that their reading tastes especially were increasingly moulded by the newly developing Age of Sentiment. Even during his lifetime, his best-known work was his handful of love songs.[46] His best work, however, relies on his penchant for dialectic. Idealised panegyric is not this poet's vocation – but idealised panegyric was what appealed to the creators of the canon.

The Age of Clearance

The Age of Sentiment coincided with the commencement of the Age of Clearance on Highland estates. After an initial period of apparently widespread optimism, the absorption and peripheralising of the Scottish Gàidhealtachd within wider British and global economies was accompanied by rising inequalities, socioeconomic dislocation further exacerbated by a series of catastrophic weather events and broken expectations.[47] The clergy's vision of an enlightened Gàidhealtachd, in which ministers acted as instructors and cultural brokers between the authorities and a quiescent tenantry, was in tatters. Many members of the Highland managerial class to which the ministers belonged would cross the Atlantic, joining and often assisting the great waves of Gaelic emigrants seeking their own land, and freedom from landlord oppression. Behind them remained an increasingly proletarianised workforce, particularly in the west, where many island estates were being reorganised into extractive plantation economies based on harvesting kelp.[48]

Writing in 1790 to the clan chief and landlord Francis Humberston MacKenzie concerning the ongoing emigrations from the Isle of Eigg, the agricultural improver George Dempster of Dunnichen remarked:

> The emigration of the whole inhabitants of an island the neglect or oppressions they must feel before forming so violent a resolution the measures they concert for executing their Plan and at last their final Departure—Man woman child & Household Gods—their sucking Infants & aged Parents has something awfull in it and inspires my mind with a kind of sublime & grand Melancholy. It is a species of obscure & aggregate Heroism of the most interesting sort yet it passed under our noses without comment or observation.[49]

Sublime, melancholic, and obscurely heroic though it may have appeared to sympathetic outsiders, the Age of Clearance was a time of growing friction among tenants, as well as between them and the authorities: years of anxiety, growing poverty, and grubby daily compromises. Under such circumstances, a candid, unconstrained voice, speaking out with moral integrity and emotional honesty, offering a clear-eyed critique, could be dangerous for the community as well as troublesome for the landlord. The Clearances were not favourable for major poetry – the more so because, as Rob Donn's case makes clear, Gaelic poets remained dependent on the forbearance of those possessing real power. Lowland shepherds and estate factors – often, it must be said, the main ideologues of Clearance – were condemned, but the landlords enabling them were rarely mentioned. For Somhairle MacGill-Eain, the beginning of 'Òran do na Cìobairibh Gallda' ('Song to the Lowland Shepherds') by Ailean Dall (Allan MacDougall, c. 1750–1828) is 'devastating':

> Thàinig oirnn do dh'Albainn crois,
> Tha daoine bochda nochdte ris,
> Gun bhiadh, gun aodach, gun chluain,
> Tha 'n àird a tuath air a sgrios.
> Chan fhaicear ach caoraich is uain,
> Gaill mun cuairt dhoibh air gach slios;
> Tha gach fearann air dol fàs,
> Na Gàidheil, 's an ceann fo fhliodh.

Misfortune has come upon us in Scotland, / Poor people are naked before it, / Without food, without clothing, without pasture, / The north has been destroyed. / Nothing can be seen but sheep and lambs, / Lowlanders around them on every hillside; / Every piece of land has been emptied, / The Gaels with their heads under chickweed.[50]

Yet, MacGill-Eain continues, there is not (and cannot be) 'a disparaging word of the noble landlords whose pockets were being filled by the high rents paid by the shepherd farmers', including the poet's grotesque patron, himself notorious for clearances, Colonel Alastair Ranaldson Macdonell of Glengarry.[51]

The strongest condemnation of landlords is made in songs by Coinneach MacCoinnich (Kenneth MacKenzie, 1758–c. 1837), a sailor poet from near Inverness whose work may offer us intriguing hints of a Gaelic 'Red Atlantic'. MacCoinnich's *Cumha an Taobh Tuath*, 'The Lament of the North' was composed in the famine year 1783:

> 'S iad nas motha ann an saothair,
>   'S na h-uaislean a' daorach' a' mhàil,
> Dh'fhalbh truas o na daoine,
>   'S tha fuaralachd 'taomadh na h-àit'.
> Cha sheas facal duin' uasail,
>   'S dona 'n teist tha ri luaidh orr' an-dràst',
> 'S ann tha fìrinn is ceartas
>   Na linn seo an itean nan gèadh.

[The tenants] are in worsening travails, / And the nobles increasing the rent, / Pity deserted the people, / With cold indifference surging in in its place. / A nobleman's word is good for nothing, / They have an evil reputation just now, / Truth and justice / At this time are found in the goose quill [pens].[52]

But all the poet can advocate at the end of his song is that his listeners emigrate to the country's erstwhile enemy, 'Aimearaga shuairce', 'kindly America' – kindly not only in an idealised graceful benevolence towards her citizens, but also, perhaps, in the semi-legal sense of showing them favour in an intimately experienced social framework of respect and mutual obligations.[53]

An altogether more threatening, active Highland radicalism does leave its traces in the literature, as a foil for poetry composed by government loyalists. Thus Raibeart Stiùbhart from Highland Perthshire praises the steadfastness of the farmers around Pitlochry: they are gentlemen, 'daoine uaisl'', rather than 'cairde an t-sluaigh', followers of the reformist Friends of the People; Donnchadh Cuiningneach (Duncan Cunningham) from Argyll, meanwhile, relates how he has been scandalised by the words of a disaffected old man in Morvern:

> Ma thig ar cùrsa mun cuairt
> 'S gun tig Bonapart gruamach air ais,
> Gun sgriosar na caoraich bhon t-sliabh,
> Cha mhist leinn na biasdan dhol às [...]
>
> Ma thig am fear seo gun dàil,
> Mar tha pàirt aca 'g ràite gun tig,
> Sgriosar na caoraich gu tràigh,
> 'S bidh gach cìobair air fhàgail air sgeir.

If our time comes around, / And grim Bonaparte comes back, / The sheep will be swept from the hillside, / We won't be the worse of these beasts disappearing [...] // If this man comes without delay, / As some say he will, / The sheep will be swept to the shore, / And every shepherd marooned on a sea-rock.[54]

The promises previously made to Gaels by Jacobite revanchism on the one hand, and by Enlightenment improvement on the other, had not come to pass. In the new nineteenth century, across much of the region, it would be the flourishing evangelical churches that now offered hope. Outstanding verbal art in Gaelic was now more often encountered in prose: the bravura impromptu sermons and prayers of evangelical preachers and elders, offering their listeners epiphanic glimpses of a new metaphysical sublimity.[55] Unlike poets, ministers were able to free themselves from landlord authority, through an institutional alliance with the Lowland urban intelligentsia, under the auspices of the new Free Church of Scotland.

By this time, of course, much of the Gaelic tacksmen class, along with thousands of tenants, had left the Highlands, whether for Lowland towns or further afield. The early-nineteenth-century Gaelic world is increasingly international, a global Gaelosphere drawing upon, and in some ways disquietingly parallel to, the rapidly expanding global Anglosphere.[56] This was a world of increasing power imbalances, commodity exploitation, repression, atrocities, and resistance, with Gaels both perpetrators and victims. It was a world offering new geographical horizons and environments, new beliefs and ideological assumptions, new mentalities, perceptions, and emotional landscapes, new work patterns, fashions, and leisure requirements – and an increasingly hybrid, bilingual culture, ever more mass-literate, though perhaps occasionally less adept when handling oral culture. This is the threshold to modern Gaeldom.

PART 3: POSSIBILITIES OF GENRE

CHAPTER NINE

Scottish Theatre in the Long Eighteenth Century

Ian Brown

Oliver Cromwell's 1650 defeat of General Leslie at the Battle of Dunbar came about, it is commonly said, through the Presbyterian clergy's pre-battle evangelical purging of the best of Leslie's officers. Despite the false Stuart dawn of Charles II's coronation at Scone on New Year's Day 1651 – leading only to further defeat at Worcester that year – for Scotland Dunbar effectively marked the end of the Wars of the Three Kingdoms (1639–1652). Ensuing Cromwellian rule in Scotland deprived the country of its separate political institutions and led, until the 1660 Stuart Restoration, to the imposition of a Puritan regime with little sympathy for Scottish sensitivities. As in England, any dramatic form, let alone playhouse theatre, was banned, something the Scottish Kirk had never achieved post-Reformation, not least in terms of folk drama in the country and seasonal quasi-theatrical celebrations in town. Yet, even under such an attempted Cromwellian blanket ban, exceptions existed. Theatre in various forms, though not primarily playhouse theatre, had deep roots in Scottish culture. English puritanism would not eradicate those. Rather, a reassertion – reacting initially against ten years of Cromwellian rule – of drama's role in Scotland can be seen to have helped theatre develop through the long eighteenth century. This evolution was partly energised by the religio-politico-cultural conflict between what in the eighteenth century became the Moderate and the Popular wings of the Kirk, the former influenced by those seventeenth-century periods when the Kirk was effectively Episcopalian, the latter being more evangelical. Theatre was an important element in the discourses that arose from this conflict, to which Enlightenment thinking in Scotland responded.

First, one must review the theatrical situation at the beginning of the long eighteenth century. Earlier scholars viewed its health pessimistically.

In 1927, for example, Anna Jean Mill's important study of medieval Scottish drama concluded that 'the dramatic history of Scotland in the period following the Reformation is that of the gradual extinction of the once flourishing but now effete medieval drama in its several forms. [...] The drama as a popular institution and a force in the national life was now dead.'[1] Such views prevailed into much of the twentieth century and sometimes can still be heard, even from theatre critics who should know better: Mark Brown, regular *Sunday Herald* reviewer, for example, claimed in 2017 that 'Scotland's Calvinist Reformation brought the curtain down on theatre for centuries'.[2] The evidence is quite to the contrary: above all, Bill Findlay's magisterial 1998 *A History of Scottish Theatre* provides ample evidence of more vibrant theatre cultures than Mill's doom-laden, but influential, conclusion suggests.[3] By 1997, meantime, John McGavin, discussing sixteenth- and seventeenth-century Haddington, could note the early seventeenth-century Presbytery's failure to suppress annual local plays in two nearby villages, Samuelston and Saltoun. What McGavin observes is a shift 'from urban to rural drama [... and] from unthinking pleasures to pleasures pointedly enjoyed in opposition to the kirk. [... The Presbytery's] flurries of activity against rural drama, our only evidence that such drama took place, were all it could manage in the circumstances.'[4] Certainly, the reformed church sought to manage theatrical activity into at least the 1700s: J. McKenzie notes that 'Kirk Sessions and Presbyteries exercised a stricter control, banning Sunday performances, censoring plays, and restricting the choice of subject'.[5] McKenzie here suggests an emphasis on control rather than the pre-Reformation Catholic church's suppression of theatre (one playwright, John Kyllour, was burned at the stake in 1539; another, James Wedderburn, was driven into exile around 1540;[6] and, although the eminent Sir David Lyndsay was untouchable, the script of his *Thrie Estaitis* was burned at the cross in Edinburgh after his death in 1555, the year the Catholic church promoted a parliamentary act banning theatre, which fell by the way post-Reformation). Margo Todd confirms that the Kirk's focus was chiefly on control rather than outright suppression:

> Protestantism may have succeeded in part *because* the sessions enforced their legislation against festivity lightly, flexibly and sporadically. Where a heavy hand might have strengthened the opposition to Reformed doctrine as well as discipline, the elders' sense of the inutility of quashing the useful and harmless allowed for a more gradual but secure cultural reconstruction.[7]

It is also important to remember the place of other dramatic modes. Gaelic-speaking communities had their own theatrical traditions throughout our period, though none of playhouse theatre. Michael Newton has discussed these, although, given the folk nature of the theatre he describes, there is little textual evidence available.[8] Nonetheless, whatever else its social and creative functions, such performances asserted the identity of Gaelic as a language of dramatic discourse, and was a particular contributing element throughout the eighteenth century alongside other prevailing versions of Scottish identities. A further aspect of theatrical performance affirming community identity involved annual ceremonies performed in many towns, often related to marking boundaries. While many of those now most famous are of later invention (or re-invention), many have long ancestry, like that in Linlithgow, still held on the first Tuesday after the second Thursday in June. This actually gave rise to a play, John Finlayson's *The Marches Day*, published in 1771. Urban performativity was further reinforced by the street theatre of chapbook sales throughout the Enlightenment period, a topic discussed by Janet Sorensen with particular reference to the interaction of the performance of chapbook salespeople and their clients, who would themselves perform privately or in social contexts.[9] Meanwhile, Robert Burns's (1759–1796) *The Jolly Beggars* (1785), often described as a cantata, highlights intergeneric crossing of borders between poetry, music, and theatrical performativity, not only in such formal achievements, but in the general context of quasi-dramatic song which existed in both folk and drawing-room forms throughout the century. A further aspect of eighteenth-century dramatic activity, widespread amongst Lowland upper and professional classes, was amateur acting. As Alasdair Cameron has pointed out, this 'ranged from the country-house performances of Charles Frank of Dughtrig [*recte*, Bughtrig] [...] to benefits for deserving causes in the cities, and village entertainments'.[10] Kate Newey observes of such theatre:

> The issue of writing for *private* performance destabilises the dualisms of public/private, work/home, and masculine/feminine. [...] The publication and extensive marketing of scripts challenges claims about the private nature of such work. [...] home performance can blur the neat categorisation of social space into public and private arenas.[11]

Drama in seventeenth- and eighteenth-century Scotland had many strands. In Tracy Davis and Ellen Donkin's words, it was a 'myriad of public and private forms'.[12]

A key driver in Scottish theatrical development by the middle of the seventeenth century and into the next was a form the Kirk not only controlled, but actively encouraged: school and university drama, both in Latin and English. As McKenzie observes, school 'plays were [...] used [...] for imparting religious instruction or for revealing the errors of the Roman Catholic faith'.¹³ Glasgow Grammar School's 1643 education plan, for example, requires that 'when the scholars have committed to memory dialogues, speeches, and particularly comedies, they are to assume the characters of the speakers, rehearsing in an imitative fashion in order to acquire the arts of good pronunciation and acting'.¹⁴ In an age without artificial voice-amplification indoors or out, and given the need to hold the attention of crowds being addressed, the use of theatre in this educational way for those who might hold public positions later was part of the humanist tradition. Plays thus performed were not necessarily in any sense juvenile: those George Buchanan (1506–1582) wrote for his Bordeaux pupils in 1539–43 are possibly the most internationally influential of any Scottish playwright, produced across Europe for most of the next three centuries and underlying the seventeenth-century French neoclassical drama of Pierre Corneille (1606–1684) and Jean Racine (1639–1699). On returning to post-Reformation Scotland Buchanan wrote for court performances. Drama was so embedded in post-Reformation school life that across Scotland pupils performed classical plays or occasional scripts by their masters at least annually for magistrates', ministers' or patrons' visitations or festive occasions. Even under Cromwellian anti-theatrical rule, Aberdeen Town Council actually required in 1659 quarterly visitations where various classical or renaissance pieces were played.

This commitment – not to suppress, but to require – theatre in schools continued well into our period. Meanwhile, in 1711 Aberdeen required a public theatre to 'be erected in some publict place of the toune, as the counsell shall think fit and there some publict action to be acted by the schollars of the said school' and other councils, like Haddington, Lanark, Paisley and Selkirk, also paid for public performances.¹⁵ Across Scotland – from Forres to North Berwick, Montrose to Dumfries, even in the tiny village of Lundie in Angus, where in 1688, the dominie William Bouok was disciplined for the acting of 'a comoedie wherein he mad [sic] a mock of religious duties and ordinances'¹⁶ – theatre in schools was endemic in pupils' education and culture.

Theatrical engagement among the educated young did not cease on leaving school. In 1720, Glasgow university authorities tried to stop students' playing *Tamerlane* [probably Nicholas Rowe's 1701 play], objecting, *inter alia*, to men performing in women's clothes. Supported by some staff, the students resisted. A compromise permitted the play, but not on university premises. The play was presented on 30 December, in – perhaps its inspirational home – the Grammar School.[17] Given this dynamic role in Scottish society, despite any Cromwellian or later evangelical Presbyterian attempts to suppress it, drama retained the potential to be a key locus for religio-politico-cultural debate and discourse throughout the period. When Scotland developed playhouse theatre or Scots wrote for the London stage, the drivers were primarily the professions, including lawyers and ministers, the very people to have seen or participated in school drama. Such people, if they found the experience positive, would have developed skills that could service the country-house theatre to which Cameron refers, and would tend towards supporting playhouse theatre.

While theatrical performance's inclusion in school curricula was aimed at developing rhetorical skills, inclusion, *ipso facto*, implied theatre was a proper locus for politico-cultural debate. Moreover, theatre itself occasioned controversy. As in 1659, when Aberdonian civic authorities opposed central government, theatre was often seen as anti-authority. After all, the conflicts it explored were often those within the very authorities themselves, whether local council or institutional, as in the 1720 case of Glasgow University staff's differing views. It is no surprise, then, that the first playhouse productions in Scotland after the 1660 Restoration were highly political in implication, both in their dramaturgy and given their context.

By 1662, Edinburgh playhouse theatre was established under Scottish noble patronage at the Tennis Court Theatre at Holyrood, which had been run down in the Cromwellian period and now became the performative site of a reassertion of royal authority. There, for example, William Clark's (sometimes spelled Clarke; fl. 1663–1699?) *Marciano, or The Discovery* (1663), implicitly celebrating the Restoration through the defeat of a thinly-disguised Cromwellian character, explored issues of loyalty, betrayal, and the need for established order. Marciano says 'When men begin to quarrel with their Prince, / No wonder if they crush their fellow Subjects',[18] while Clark's preface talks of theatre as 'this innocent and usefull recreation' and of 'hell-hounds, assassinats of our liberties [who] snatch'd the very reins of Government [… and voted] down all Scenick Playes [… to suffer] in the same sentence with Monarchy'.[19] In the same decade, the trend developed of Scottish playwrights seeking London production. There, though theatre was often tightly controlled, court-sponsored drama flourished. Thomas Sydserf or St Serfe (fl. 1667–1689?), the Bishop of Galloway's (later of Orkney) son who fought under Montrose, was early among these with *Tarugo's Wiles* (1667; Edinburgh première, 1668), influenced by the early work of Molière (1622–1673) and Spanish romance. He returned to Edinburgh in 1667 to manage, until 1689, the Tennis Court Theatre. As compared with the variety of other Scotland-wide theatrical manifestations, such productions represented elite practice with elite costs: Sir John Foulis of Ravelston's Account Books between 1669 and 1672 show his family regularly attended theatre in and around Edinburgh, his expenditure suggesting sometimes eye-watering prices.[20]

Such elitism was highlighted during the residence of James, Duke of York and Albany (the future James VII/II) at Holyrood (1679–82). By then, the return of Stuart authority with all that meant – politically, socially, and theologically – had been architecturally asserted by the 1671–78 expansion of the old palace in Sir William Bruce's design, establishing the grand building we now know, set splendidly in the amphitheatre between Arthur's Seat and Calton Hill. So, in the immediate post-Restoration period, Scottish theatre was bound up with the royalist post-Restoration settlement: in the newly expanded building, James encouraged masques and plays, bringing over a company of Irish actors for a time, while in 1681 his daughter Anne, later queen, appeared in Nathaniel Lee's *Mithridates, King of Pontus* (1678) before the Duke and his court.[21] His pro-Catholic milieu's theatrical activity at the beginning of the Killing Time (the period from roughly 1680 to 1688 when Presbyterian Covenanters resisted the Episcopalian direction in which Charles II and his brother-successor James VII/II were leading the Church of Scotland, atrocities being committed by both sides) can only have reinforced any radical Presbyterian's sense that theatre was suspect.

Of course, this was not the only way of experiencing plays. Country-house theatre employed, *inter alia*, 'closet drama' plays, whether published, or circulated in manuscript. Such drama offered another means of cultural discourse. Following William of Orange's arrival and James VII/II's flight in 1688, there was a dearth of Edinburgh playhouse theatre for some decades. Nonetheless, closet drama remained a lively element in politico-religious debate, not least because it allowed uncensored performance, especially after the 1737 Theatre Act's empowerment of the Lord Chamberlain as British-wide theatre censor. Archibald Pitcairne's (1652–1713) *The Assembly* (1692) circulated in manuscript until it was published in 1722. This attacked Presbyterian General Assembly pedantry, ministerial lechery and both Williamite and Jacobite political sectarianism's obscurantism.

Meantime, Scottish playwrights turned again to the London stage. Catherine Trotter's (1679–1749) *Agnes de Castro* (a baroque version of a plot Jo Clifford (1949–) returned to in 1989 under the title *Ines de Castro*, the play being adapted as opera by James MacMillan in 1996) was probably played in 1695, followed by her verse-tragedy *Fatal Friendship* (1698), a comedy, *Love at a Loss* (1700) and two more verse-tragedies, *The Unhappy Penitent* (1701) and *The Revolution in Sweden* (1706), the latter of which asserts the importance of liberty in the face of authoritarian oppression. David Crawford (1665–1726), already a novelist, had *Courtship A-la-mode* (1700) presented at Drury Lane and *Love at First Sight* (1704) at Lincoln's Inn Fields. Newburgh Hamilton (1691–1761) followed with his comedies, *The Petticoat-Plotter* (1712) and *The Doating Lovers* (1715) and his lyrics for Handel's *Samson* (1743). Such playwrights were integrated into post-Restoration London theatrical practice; their example was followed by a later, more clearly post-Union, generation, including James Thomson (1700–48) and David Mallet (Malloch) (c. 1705–65). These offered more politically explicit themes, often linked to Hanoverian court politics, however masked by foreign settings. Terence Tobin notes Thomson's first play *Sophonisba* (1730), dedicated to Queen Caroline, is a contemporary political allegory: the 'heroine's dominant passion is to prevent her native Carthage (Britain) from becoming subservient to tyrannic Rome (France)'.[22] Though its baroque bravura was mocked, Thomson returned with *Agamemnon* (1738), now dedicated to the Princess of Wales; Orestes was read as Frederick, Prince of Wales, Clytemnestra his mother as Queen Caroline, and Aegisthus as Walpole. When *Edward and Leonora* (1739), dedicated to Frederick, began Covent Garden rehearsals, the Lord Chamberlain banned its performance for its implied references to the royal family's civil war, though it was published in print. Mallet had written *Eurydice* (1731), which was accused of being a coded Jacobite play. This accusation possibly arose from the playwright's Perthshire family background of Catholicism and Jacobite sympathy, which his name-change from Malloch to Mallet, besides providing a form easier for Londoners to pronounce, may have sought to mask. His next play *Mustapha* (1739), somehow evading the censor, implicitly attacked Walpole and the Queen's encouragement of George II's hostile post-1737 treatment of Frederick;[23] by mid-century Mallet was seen 'as a writer of the Patriot Opposition',[24] which Samuel Johnson later saw as the 'last refuge of a scoundrel', but which saw Frederick as beau ideal of patriotic 'non-partisan' government. Mallet (dialogue) and Thomson (lyrics) collaborated on *The Masque of Alfred* (1740) whose wise Anglo-Saxon (a key identity in Whig iconography of the time) Patriotic paragon hero emerges from disguise and drives out the Danes. The play concludes with Thomson's 'Rule Britannia' sung in duet by Alfred and his queen Eltruda, advocating a global naval rather than continental military policy. Its political significance is reflected in the fact that its proposed 9 February Drury Lane première was cancelled so that it could be premièred at the Prince of Wales's Cliveden retreat on 1 and 2 August.[25] Thomson achieved European fame with his greatest dramatic success: *Tancred and Sigismunda* (1745), dedicated to Frederick. Set in Sicily, it deals with 'a favourite motif, the conflict of public duty and private feelings'[26] – a recurrent Thomson theme – in a tale of love and betrayal in the, at least nominally, public interest. Thomson's preface to the published text asserts the importance of drama in influencing public and private lives: 'But of all the different Species of Writing, none has such an Effect upon the Lives and Manners of Men, as the Dramatick'.[27]

The plays of Thomson and Mallet can be seen to participate in what I have called 'The (Rule) Britannia Project'.[28] This, whose first major step was, arguably, John Arbuthnot's (1667–1735) personifications, 'John Bull' (England) with his sister 'Peg' (Scotland), is the process by which, after the 1707 ratifications of the 1706 Treaty of Union, a number of Scottish cultural figures developed concepts of 'Britain', preferring the more 'polite' language, English, a process including David Hume's despatching his manuscripts to have 'scotticisms' removed. In the context of this post-Union project, the Scottish religio-politico-cultural conflicts discussed hitherto are complicated by the issue of Scottish identities within the Union. It can be argued that those playwrights who focus on London production, neglecting Scottish politics for court politics, are distanced from national debates within the context of the developing Enlightenment in Scotland. It is hard to disagree, especially given their plays' themes, except, perhaps, to observe that they take as given the acceptance of specifically Scottish identities within an amalgamated British one. In Scotland, however, theatre and related performance artists, from the Aberdonian Jacobite chapbook seller and street-singer Charles Leslie (c. 1677–1782), 'Mussel-mou'd Charlie', to playwrights from Allan Ramsay (1686–1758) on, were involved in the issue of Scottish post-Union identities.

In this politico-cultural debate Ramsay was profoundly engaged, not only as poet and bookseller, but as a leader in Scottish playhouse theatre.

After the Williamite chill (when, following the recognition of William III and Mary II as joint monarchs in 1689, a more severely Calvinist regime was re-established in the Church and civic life in Scotland), professional public theatre returned around 1715 in Edinburgh's Carrubber's Close, but only as a venue for 'musicians, acrobats, clowns and other strolling players', later being associated particularly with the actor-manager, singer, and rope-dancer, Signora Larina Violante.[29] Meantime, in 1715 a visiting English company played Shakespeare's *Macbeth* and a number of Restoration plays at Holyrood and in the old Magazine House nearby in the Canongate, their stay causing some presbytery protest.[30] Nonetheless, however stuttering the development of early eighteenth-century playhouse theatre in Scotland, playhouse development after the first quarter of the century was, despite some few setbacks on the way, continuous, spreading through most of Scotland by the end of the century. Ramsay was key in this progress as playwright, producer, and salesman (he employed such apparently modern practices as two-for-one offers and season ticket reductions). When an English actor, Anthony Aston (d. 1731), initially welcomed by council and social elite, arrived in 1725, Ramsay was his friend. Yet, despite 'blythesome Tony' Aston's observing he had played for the king and his court in London, in 1727 the Kirk's *Admonition and Exhortation* attacked theatre on theological grounds of immorality.[31] In 1728 Ramsay's response, *Some Few Hints, in Defence of Dramatical Entertainments*, appeared, strongly defending 'Dramatick Actions […] which in all Ages and Nations, have always been esteem'd the most noble and improving Diversions'.[32] Aston, meantime, ran into trouble. Donald Campbell suggests he failed to pay dues to the Master of the Revels in Scotland, responsible for licensing plays, companies and playhouses, a post whose independence Scots had fought for,[33] while Adrienne Scullion suggests the culminating issue was nuisance to neighbours of his venue, Skinner's Hall.[34] Whatever the trigger, his company folded in December 1727, and the next April Aston, who had also offered lessons in English pronunciation to the Edinburgh bourgeoisie, no doubt part of the (Rule) Britannia Project, skipped town, leaving many unpaid debts. That October, an Edinburgh Company of Players was established at Taylor's Hall, though that company lasted only about six months.

While much of the material available for performance was in English, Ramsay broke this anglicising model, writing for the stage in Scots. An early version of *The Gentle Shepherd* being published in 1725, he rewrote the play for his friend, the Haddington Grammar School master John Leslie, whose pupils performed the 1729 première of the ballad-opera version we are familiar with in Taylor's Hall. This explores issues of social order, public duty versus personal emotion, and restoration and reconciliation after conflict. Ramsay's Jacobite sympathies underpin its themes, while the use of Scots as dramatic language asserts Scottish identities after and within the Union at the time of the Vernacular Revival (or reinvention) in the early eighteenth century when, perhaps in direct reaction to the Treaty of Union of Scotland and England, some leading writers returned to using Scots language in poetry and drama after a period of anglicisation following the Union of the Crowns in 1603. The play certainly contributed to cultural debates about appropriate social structures and the nature of Scottish civilisation in which later Enlightenment writers would engage. Its production, in Edinburgh's main commercial theatre venue, also marks a clear link between the tradition of school theatre and the development of professional theatre in Scotland. In 1731, Leslie became Dalkeith's schoolmaster and Vanbrugh's *The Provok'd Husband* was performed there, only three years after its Drury Lane première.

In 1730, meantime, a Company of Edinburgh Players was again established, now with a patent, meaning the civic authorities did not challenge them, as they had Aston's company. With Ramsay as producer, it ran until 1736. Then, he obtained the Carrubber's Close theatre as home for his own permanent company, which included some Edinburgh Players,[35] opening in November 1736 as 'The New Theatre' with Ramsay's prologue proclaiming, 'Long has it been the business of the stage / To mend our manners, and reform the age'. The *Kulturkampf* between what was now becoming defined as the Moderate and Popular wings of the Kirk continued,[36] but it was not specifically this that closed Ramsay's company after seven months, though it formed part of the background. The 1737 Licensing Act, which established the censorship role of the Lord Chamberlain – which lasted until 1968 – forbade buildings to present spoken drama without a Royal Patent approved by parliament. Ramsay's theatre had to close and, perhaps because of magistrates' nervousness of public gatherings following the 1736 Porteous Riots, attempts to reopen it in 1738 and 1739 failed, as did Lord Glenorchy's 1739 attempt, opposed by Council, Kirk and University, to introduce a patent theatre Bill in Parliament. Opposition then to theatre in Edinburgh can be seen to arise not only from powerful cliques in the Kirk, but from issues like public order, class bias perhaps related to high costs of theatre-going (which, while lower than Restoration prices, were still at least equivalent to, if not more than, modern West End prices), and, perhaps, cultural and linguistic resistance to anglicisation. While Ramsay's pioneering continued to have impact, not least through *The Gentle Shepherd* – the century's most successful pastoral play in British and North American theatre – at this point Ramsay seems to have resiled from theatre involvement.

A device to evade the patent theatre system's impact was already in place. Music concerts, not covered by the act, were presented, followed by plays performed nominally for nothing. Thus, in 1741 Thomas Este (d. 1745) relaunched theatre performances in Taylor's Hall in the Cowgate. This stratagem proving effective, on 16 November 1747, complementing Taylor's Hall, the Canongate Concert Hall opened (in fact, a theatre, a name it soon assumed). Still advertised as *gratis*,[37] John Home's (1722–1808) *Douglas* opened at the Canongate Theatre on 14 December 1756. Arguably this was, for theatre, the century's crucial breakthrough. Although Home had written a play before, *Agis* (1746/7), David Garrick at London's Drury Lane had rejected it as being 'about an obscure ancient monarch'.[38] In writing *Douglas*, Home, minister of Athelstaneford, consulted progressive Moderate friends. Circulating drafts to literary sympathisers in 1754 for comment, he asked for their 'corrections'. He sought Hugh Blair's (1718–1800) and William Robertson's (1721–1793) views on his 'judgement' and the view of Lord Elibank (1703–1778) and several women friends, including Andrew Fletcher's nieces and great-nieces, on 'taste'; Katherine Glover notes this 'specifically gendered role for the Fletcher women as arbiters of taste'.[39] Home was supported by his relative David Hume (1711–1776), who, with other leading Enlightenment thinkers, engaged in a script-reading at the Edinburgh home of Sarah Ward who would first play Lady Randolph. This process looks remarkably like a modern 'play-development workshop'. Hume played Glenalvon; Robertson, Randolph; Alexander Carlyle (1722–1805), Old Norval; Home, Douglas; Adam Ferguson (1723–1816), Lady Randolph; and Blair, Anna. The only savant of this cast not a minister was David Hume. Also present, no doubt offering views, were law-trained Lords Elibank (1703–78), Kames (1696–1782), Monboddo (1714–1799) and Milton (1692–1766). The play – presented in the year Hume had faced Popular threats of excommunication, seen off by the efforts of the Moderate wing, and ten years after Culloden – explores issues of civil turmoil, hidden identities, and political loyalty and faithlessness. While modern critics might cavil at Hume's view that the play shows 'the true theatric genius of Shakespeare and Otway, refined from the unhappy barbarism of the one and licentiousness of the other',[40] there is no doubt that for many years the play was seen as a work of genius and central cultural importance. It was a hit throughout the rest of the century and well into the nineteenth, being picked up by Garrick in 1757, who now also presented *Agis*.

The development of *Douglas* drew together various strands of eighteenth-century Scottish theatre, including non-professional actors, initially, as in large-house drama, reading of closet drama, and mid-century development of professional playhouse drama. It also marked a triumph of Moderate thinking in the Kirk. While the local presbytery censured ministers, including Carlyle, who attended the play and issued on 5 January 1757 another *Admonition and Exhortation* declaring playhouses immoral, those censured mostly simply apologised, staying in post, and the *Admonition* had little impact.[41] Home himself resigned in June, avoiding any disciplinary action, heading south to make some success in London theatre. Evangelicals were in retreat. Although the playhouse form, as Barbara Bell notes of the Scottish patent houses later in the century, 'had been the province of a small number of socially confident groups, notably the nobility, professions such as the law and above all, the military',[42] theatre in all its forms had played a prominent role in the process of resisting puritanical Evangelicalism.

By the end of the 1750s, playhouse theatre was an established element in Edinburgh's social life, attended not only by the elite, but, when an attractive success came along, by merchants and their wives. The *View of the Edinburgh Theatre during the Summer Season, 1759*, probably written by James Boswell, shows, not nightly productions, but three professional performances a week of two plays, a full-length and a one-act play, programmes changing from night to night, from Wednesday, June 20 until Monday, August 20. The playwright Jean Marishall (fl. 1765–89) in her novel *The History of Miss Clarinda Cathcart, and Miss Fanny Renton* (1765) reinforces the sense that playgoing was now a well-established elite Edinburgh pursuit: her characters, having just reached the city, are reported as being 'at the play'; four pages later they are there again.[43] The plays to be seen included, beside imports from London theatre, new Scottish plays. *Patriotism* (1763) by the advocate John/James(?) Baillie (fl. 1760–70) is a political farce in support of Prime Minister Bute. Andrew Erskine's (1740–1793) *She's Not Him, and He's Not Her* (1764) is a cross-dressing love farce. John Wilson's (1720–1789) *Earl Douglas; or, Generosity Betray'd* (1764) features the 1440 Black Dinner during James II's minority where the sixth Earl of Douglas and his brother, who were under safe-conduct, were assassinated. Wilson was part of a playwriting movement presenting Scottish themes, including history, his play exculpating James as innocent victim, like the Douglases, of scheming politicians, while

Chancellor Crichton and Regent Livingston oppose the nobility which embodies Scotland's liberties.

The 1767 Act authorising the building of Edinburgh's New Town included a clause permitting a patent theatre. When the Canongate Theatre season next opened – as the Theatre Royal, Edinburgh – Boswell's prologue celebrated, linking 'enlighten[ment]' with the Hanoverian settlement:

> This night lov'd GEORGE's free enlighten'd age,
> Bids *Royal Favour* shield the SCOTTISH STAGE;
> His Royal Favour ev'ry bosom cheers;
> The Drama now with dignity appears.[44]

On 9 January 1769, the new Theatre Royal in 'Shakespeare Square' at the north-east end of the new North Bridge opened, facing the site of Register House (built 1774–87) on the edge of the New Town. On 8 March 1773, its first play by a Scot, Henry Mackenzie's (1745–1831) *The Prince of Tunis*, opened. Hugh Blair had responded favourably to a 1771 draft, particularly admiring the third-act line, 'Scaring the dimply cupids from their Seats', and enjoying the 'good poetry' and 'animated and high style'.[45] While Tobin argues that 'the tragedy resembles Shakespearean burlesque',[46] it also played in London. Mackenzie went on to write for both Edinburgh and London stages, including *The Shipwreck* (1784) and *Force of Fashion* (1789), his first comedy. Around him flourished more plays by Scots, some romantic, some classical, some historical, featuring figures like Mary, Queen of Scots and William Wallace, and some, in the new fashion, Ossianic. The existence of a canon of Scottish eighteenth-century drama beyond the century-long hits, *The Gentle Shepherd* and *Douglas*, seems undeniable; the fact also is that this canon has been much neglected, perhaps not least because it was written for a pre-Stanislavskian declamatory acting style now very foreign to modern readers and playgoers. Of the plays of eighteenth-century English-language dramatists really only those of four Irishmen, George Farquhar (1677–1707), Charles Macklin (1690–1797), Oliver Goldsmith (1728–1774) and Richard Sheridan (1751–1816), and scarcely any by Scots, with the exception of Ramsay and Home, or English, with the exception of John Gay (1685–1732), are, for whatever reason, now much remembered. That does not mean they did not exist.

Indeed, the development of Scottish playhouse theatre's status in our period was remarkable. From being banned after 1650, through the Tennis

Court Theatre's establishment after the 1660 Restoration and then the late seventeenth-century religio-cultural conflicts, and despite such temporary setbacks as the burning of the first playhouse in Glasgow in 1762, a presumably evangelical arson attack overcome by the efforts of theatre supporters, by the end of the eighteenth century, there were nine permanent theatres spread throughout Scotland, in Edinburgh (two), Aberdeen, Glasgow, Dundee, Dumfries, Paisley, Ayr, and Greenock. Yet, this underrates the prevalence and impact of playhouse theatre and its touring analogues. For example, after the soldier and aspiring playwright Archibald Maclaren (1755–1826) returned on recruiting duty from service fighting the American Revolution, his first play, *The Conjurer; or, The Scotsman in London* (1781), was printed, presumably having been performed, in Dundee. He established links with George Sutherland, a member of the Edinburgh Theatre Royal company under Henry Ward, which was touring in the Angus area, performing in temporary theatre spaces in towns like Arbroath and Montrose. On demobilisation in 1783, Maclaren appears to have taken roles in the Edinburgh Theatre Royal company from time to time 'where he was allowed some merit in the performance of Scotch, Irish, and French characters; but his own "Highland Drover" was the part in which he was inimitable'.[47] Sutherland, a friend of Robert Burns, was to be a prime mover in the establishment of the Theatre Royal, Dumfries in 1790. Meantime, Maclaren became a prolific playwright, usually of shorter pieces, including two plays, *The Humours of Greenock Fair* (1788) and *The Highland Drover* (1790) which included Gaelic dialogue. In the former, the Gaelic was effectively translated in characters' replies, but in the latter there is substantial untranslated dialogue, evidence that at least in theatres in towns fringing the Gàidhealtachd, like Inverness, Dundee, Perth and Greenock, to which the play was toured, there was a commercially viable audience for drama in that language.[48] Maclaren returned between 1794 and 1798 to army service, while still writing plays, before on his final discharge moving to London and striving, not especially successfully, to make a living writing for London theatres. The action of many of those later plays drew on Scottish historical material or legend.

Maclaren's career shows that too much focus on patent theatres can lead one to miss the complexity of the theatre scene by the end of the century. By then, actors and writers like him might move professionally between patent theatres and companies touring to smaller towns and act as instigators of the development of playhouse theatre in large regional towns. Bell offers, further, an example of how local magnates might arrange for productions in their area: '*The Monthly Mirror* of 1798 reported that the Greenock company of comedians were having a deal of success at Inverary, where the Duke of Argyle had fitted up a theatre for them.'[49] Bell also highlights the geographical extent of quasi-playhouse production available by the end of our period:

> The 1805 advertisement for the Theatre, Banff, (*The Aberdeen Journal*, 4 September 1805) is for a small company "The Cynosure; or, North Scots Company of Comedians, Smith, Bennett & Co." who are pleased to let the populace of Banff know that they have refitted the Trades Hall with new scenery, dresses, etc., and will open shortly for a brief season. The company also present their compliments to previous patrons in Fochabers, Elgin, Forres, Nairn, Dingwall and Tain "with a grateful sense of past favours"; [...] far from offering an alternative to the type of piece seen in the Theatres Royal, they undertake to play "the most fashionable and favourite pieces that have been performed [...] on the London stages".[50]

The wide variety of theatrical forms discussed at the start of this chapter, of course, remained, as did links between closet drama, amateur country-house performance, and professional theatre. These links are strong in the case of Christian Carstairs's (fl. 1763–1786) boundary-transgressing (though relatively short), anti-slavery, class- and gender-challenging *The Hubble-Shue* (1786?). Of this Gioia Angeletti comments:

> the genre obscurity of this apparently ludicrous dramatic experiment [...], owing to its unusual blending of comedic, satirical, and surreal elements, its rambling storyline and inconsequential illogical speeches, looks forward to the theatre of the absurd.[51]

Another woman playwright, Eglantine Wallace (c. 1754–1803), wrote more directly socially critical plays like *Diamond Cut Diamond* (1787), attacking forced marriages, and the anti-aristocratic *The Whim* (1795), both banned from the stage, although *The Ton* (1788), 'attacking aristocratic corruption and arguing for female education and divorce'[52] was received riotously at Covent Garden. Links between closet drama and professional theatre are exemplified most, perhaps, by Joanna Baillie's (1762–1851) experience. Her first volume of plays was published in 1798, including *Count Basil*, exploring the Count's conflict between love and military duty, his loving at the wrong time leading to betrayal of his colleagues and subsequent suicide. Most of Baillie's work emerged in the next century, usually, like *De Montfort* (1800), with its Byronic hero, and *The Family Legend* (1810), which engaged with early-modern Scottish clan rivalry, focused on historical material. Despite her reputation as a closet dramatist whose introductions contain fascinating and important discussions of subjects like emotional expression, the impact of stage lighting, and performance style, many of her plays were professionally performed. A friend and correspondent of Walter Scott, Baillie exchanged ideas on aspects of theatre and theatricality with him. Baillie's and Maclaren's plays, not to mention predecessors like Wilson's, anticipate the development of nineteenth-century Scottish historical drama in the form of the 'National Drama'.

One should always bear in mind, too, how the range of theatrical activity in our period extended beyond what would now be considered dramatic. In a period when equestrianism was central not just to the gentry or military, but to the economy, 'circus' was found in larger towns and cities. This was not a travelling show in the modern sense, but a venue where, while performances on the model developed from 1768 in London's Astley's Amphitheatre were presented at certain times, during the rest of the year people were taught to ride and horses were trained, put at livery, bought and sold. Circus performance in this context was a hybrid of illegitimate theatre with displays of horsemanship. The more 'theatrical' presentations would include all sorts of fantastic feats and amazing spectacles, where novelty ruled and conventions were occasionally stretched to breaking point, in contrast to the more word-based, static pieces seen in playhouse theatre. It was a part of the movement, alongside text-based illegitimate houses and strolling companies, which raised 'national' expectations of the patent houses, and their ability to produce sensational effects. The *Caledonian Mercury* of 1790, for example, has a series of advertisements for a 'Circus' under a Mr Jones which sometimes has a theatrical title and whose repertoire consisted of horsemanship, novelty acts, some burletta, music, singing and pantomimes or spectacles.

Bell draws attention to another example, which makes clear the threat such entertainments might be seen to offer playhouse theatre:

> on 9 February 1800 the *Royal Circus,* whose energetic efforts were causing Stephen Kemble, then manager of the Edinburgh Theatre Royal, so much concern, brought forward 'An Entire New Splendid Scotch Spectacle' of Hallowe'en; or, The Castles of Athlin and Dunbaine (1799).[53]

She summarises the position of Scottish playhouse theatre at the end of the eighteenth century as:

> inherently weak and consequently fragmented, hemmed about with conventions and regulations that made the job of the manager a difficult one. Whilst increasing numbers of towns and cities possessed purpose-built theatres or spaces capable of being 'fitted up' for short-term engagements, nowhere saw theatre all the year round and even in the largest cities, the theatres were open for perhaps three or four nights per week. [...] In smaller towns and villages the travelling companies often followed the agricultural or civic calendars, arriving for the Assizes, Race Weeks or Agricultural Shows at the same time each year.[54]

Nevertheless, Alasdair Cameron could confidently assert that by 1800 'throughout Scotland, the theatre was becoming the most popular form of organised entertainment in the country'.[55] Ticket prices had become more affordable, as theatres had grown in size. Scottish themes and Scots language were welcomed as reinforcing Scottish identities within the Union and its developing imperial projects. Scots actors like Henry Erskine Johnston (1775?–1845), 'The Scottish Roscius', whose gigantic portrait is featured on the main stairs of London's Garrick Club, had established a cross-border reputation, while Charles Mackay (1787–1857) would develop a continuing tradition of Scottish cross-generic acting, playing both seriocomic roles like Bailie Nicol Jarvie and the 'dame' role of Meg Dods in nineteenth-century National Drama. His standing was such that he was branded 'The Real Mackay', a phrase later Americanised to 'The Real McCoy'. By now, even a theatre worker could embody genuine quality and public acclaim. While there were still those who, like Cromwell, condemned theatre, they were a small minority. During the long eighteenth century, attitudes in Scotland to theatre were transformed.

CHAPTER TEN

'Will No One Tell Me What She Sings?': Scots Pastoral Poetry

David Radcliffe

In the eighteenth century, concepts of pastoral were intimately bound up with shifting ideas about progress. So long as grammar school education began with Virgil's eclogues, the idea of a progress from pastoral to georgic to epic was deeply ingrained. But as ideas of literary progress came to be linked to ideas of national prowess, Virgil's preeminence was challenged by vernacular pastoralists: Edmund Spenser, William Shakespeare, and John Milton. Later still, with discussions of literary progress taking a biographical turn, poets abandoned formal imitation for personal styles based on the melancholia of Spenser's Colin Clout, the wit of Shakespeare's Jaques, and the enthusiasm of Milton's Penseroso. Eighteenth-century pastoral modes became so ubiquitous and so mutable as to go largely unnoticed – save perhaps in the north where poets contemplated the progress of Scottish literature in a series of pastorals concerned with tradition, education, political economy, and nationality. It is to this series of writers, extending from Allan Ramsay (1684–1758) to James Hogg (c. 1770–1835), that we might turn for insight into eighteenth-century Scottish pastoral. Or we might begin with William Wordsworth (1770–1850).

'Will no one tell me what she sings?' he asks in 'The Solitary Reaper', a lyric written on a tour in Scotland that engages defining issues for Scottish pastoral, such as language. The reaper might be singing in Scots, but since the *Ossian* controversy was heating up in 1805 as a result of the *Report of the Committee of the Highland Society of Scotland, Appointed to Inquire into the Nature and Authenticity of the Poems of Ossian*, she is more likely singing in Gaelic, the language of the oral ballads from which James Macpherson (1736–1796) crafted his heroic pastorals. If Gaelic, the woman is likely illiterate, in conformity with the pastoral norm of a learned writer speaking through the words of uneducated speakers. The words being unintelligible, however, the poet speculates whether she sings of 'old, unhappy, far-off things' or 'familiar matter of today'. And if unfixed in time, he suggests, so unfixed in place, ballads being ballads, be they Arabian or Hebridean. Locality and nationality were subjects of keen debate not only in the *Ossian* controversy, but in pastoral poetry generally, so much so that the very notion of 'Scottish' pastoral was fraught. 'The Solitary Reaper' engages another point of controversy by making the singer a labourer as opposed to an Arcadian shepherdess. Her relation to nature and to culture is very different than that of the leisured traveller listening to her song.

Wordsworth properly underscores the connection between ballads and pastoral verse, but ballads were never just ballads. Topical pastorals had very obvious connections to place and time as one sees in the tide of verse flowing through eighteenth-century broadsides, pamphlets, and newspaper columns. In 'A Pastoral Poem upon the Union' (1707) Albia rails at the Jacobites: 'Those unclean Birds, that hover in the Air, / All High-Church Cormorants and Burrards (*sic*) are'. In 1801, a century later, James Hogg took aim at the Pitt administration's proposal to tax sheepdogs in 'Dusty, or, Watie an' Geordie's Review of Politics; an Eclogue'. In 1757, 'J. B—e, Kincardineshire' complains of Native American assaults on British settlements in 'A Pastoral': 'exulting o'er our prostrate lands, / Grim with red rage and death, unnumber'd bands.' In 'A Pastoral, suited to the Times' (1776) the prophetic words of a 'weird-wife' direct public anger at a different target: 'Hegh! Dany, man, an' are we a' gaen' aff / To beat the wild Americans to caff?' If the shepherd-gossips concentrate on the political here-and-now, such 'familiar matter of today' is more broadly contextualised by being delivered in an antique literary form.[1]

Only one of the topical pastorals attained general and lasting significance: *The Prophecy of Famine. A Scots Pastoral* (1763), a burlesque of Virgil's 'messianic' eclogue by the English poet Charles Churchill (1732–1764), in which Famine informs a pair of ragged borderers of all the good things awaiting them southwards. The primary target is patronage under the Bute administration which the satirist mocks in a long catalogue of things the English find objectionable about Scots: manners, dress, food, sexuality, music, and religion. The list of particulars covers the very topics identified with the 'spirit of place' in nascent cultural discourse – not that Churchill displays any concern with anthropology as had James Macpherson, his second target, or as would Robert Burns (1759–1796) in 'The Cotter's Saturday Night' (1786), which might be regarded as one of the many responses to Churchill. *The Prophecy* is cleverer in abusing the *Poems of Ossian:* by selecting for imitation the one heroic pastoral in classical literature, Churchill mocks Macpherson's mangling of the Virgilian hierarchy of genres.

Macpherson's conflation of pastoral and heroic modes was indeed unusual; it was much more common to mingle pastoral with georgic, as in James Thomson's (1700–1748) Spenserian burlesque *The Castle of Indolence* (1748) where pastoral Indolence squares off against georgic Industry. In classical literature pastoral and georgic were contrary genres, the one concerned with shepherds, leisure, and simplicity, the other with farmers, labour, and knowledge. But in eighteenth-century pastoral, 'simple' persons from all walks of life appear as speakers: seamen, drivers, chairmen, gamesters, auctioneers, actors, clergymen, prostitutes, and politicians. As these characters suggest, pastoral writers were taking a new interest in money and the division of labour, a turn paralleling the interest georgic poets were taking in such non-agricultural topics as the progress of science and international trade. Under the sway of georgic, landscapes in pastoral might become very particularised, while under the influence of pastoral, landscapes in georgic poetry were sometimes thoroughly idealised. Some were inclined to lump the genres together as 'descriptive verse', but sophisticates knew better: it matters that Wordsworth's Scottish singer is a reaper and not a shepherdess just as it matters that the landscape in which she sings is in no way particularised.

The pastoral juxtaposition of simplicity and sophistication proved particularly attractive to Scottish poets writing about the effects of political economy on persons in humble life – for example, Hogg railing at a London government taxing dogs as though they were a luxury like hair-powder. But it was in urban pastoral that the theme of commerce was usually handled, the best urban pastoralists being two Scots: Andrew Erskine (1740–1793) and Robert Fergusson (1750–1774). The 'Street-Walkers' in Erskine's *Town Eclogues* (London prostitutes from Yorkshire and Kent, respectively) are at once urban sophisticates and country innocents; their sentiments about money and morality distill the essence of commerce into a dialogue equally sad and hilarious. Distillation is the theme of Fergusson's 'A Drink Eclogue', a pastoral singing (or rather flyting) contest pitting the high (Brandy) against the low (Whisky) where the topic of art-versus-nature is deftly introduced when the adjudicating landlady reveals that Brandy is sophisticated in more ways than one. Taking materialism to the limit, Fergusson sings elsewhere of the labours of Edinburgh's paving stones: 'For what use was I made, I wander, / It was na tamely to chap under / The wight of ilka codroch (rustic) chiel, / That does my skin to targits peel.'² For all their specificity of place, time, and language, the themes and modes of these poems are as old as pastoral itself.

Echoes of antiquity are one example of the strong patterning pastoral poets used to render simplicity artful; others include demotic or highly literary diction, shaping dialogue into intrusive stanzas and metrical forms, and copious allusions to poets and poetry. Strong patterning reached its apex in the pastoral ballads popularised by Dublin-born John Cunningham (c. 1729 -1773) in the 1760s and 1770s. This mode, derived from William Shenstone (1714–1763) out of Nicholas Rowe's (1674–1718) original 'Pastoral Ballad', combined a dramatically constricted range of diction, themes, and images with a most insistent anapestic meter, as in Cunningham's elegy for Shenstone (1763):

> No Verdure shall cover the Vale,
> No Bloom on the Blossoms appear,
> The Sweets of the Forest shall fail,
> And Winter encompass the Year;
> No Birds in our Hedges shall sing,
> (Our Hedges so vocal before!)
> Since he that should welcome the Spring,
> Can greet the gay Season no more.³

Neither the poet nor the landscape are at all particularised, yet the trite metaphors (songbirds for poets, winter for death) resonate powerfully through association. Cunningham and his scores of imitators set their little dramas in a timeless, idealised nowhere called 'the plain'. The cosmopolitan Cunningham, a provincial actor who performed in Edinburgh, was in his way as much a Scottish type as Robert Fergusson – whose poetry was never so popular because it was so much more local.

Eighteenth-century readers identified Scottish pastoral with Allan Ramsay whose *Gentle Shepherd* (1725) set in train the series of works which led to the identification of Scotland with pastoral verse. Departing from convention, Ramsay arranged his play as a sequence of eclogues serving for scenes, an artfully rustic form of strong patterning. So too the diction: Scots, at once a classical tongue and a vulgar dialect, was an ideal medium for developing pastoral frisson between art and nature, high and low – a frisson embodied in Ramsay's hero Patie, the 'gentle' shepherd who turns out to be the squire's son and heir. The theme of reclaiming a legacy propelling the story is doubled in Ramsay's programme for renewing the tradition of writing literary poetry in Scots. Patie is not 'simple' in the conventional sense of being naive; his innocence takes the form of a moral purity which in the context of the story renders him genteel, but which in the context of later cultural nationalism would make him a figure for virtue rooted in the manners and beliefs of Scottish peasants.

Ramsay's fiction turns on the seeming paradox that Patie's manners are *not* those of his social peers. For example, 'he delites in Books— He reads, and speaks / With Fowks that ken them, *Latin* Words and *Greeks*'.[4] This is a fine bit of pastoral equivocation since it is apparently Patie's nature, not his nurture, that leads him to read just the authors his father, the exiled cavalier, would have had on his shelf: Shakespeare, Ben Jonson (1572–1637), William Drummond of Hawthornden (1585–1649), and Abraham Cowley (1618–1667) – not exactly a syllabus for Scottish nationalism. But such, with the important addition of the classical Scots poets, were just the writers Ramsay, a man of humble origins, *did* read and from whom he was instructed in the artfully oblique ways of pastoral wit. Ramsay was a self-educated man, as much cosmopolitan as national in his outlook, and in that respect typical of what would develop out of his engagements with tradition. Pastoral may take rural simplicity as its subject but as a literary form it is the very antithesis of innocence.

The *Poems of Ossian* (1760–65) by James Macpherson, another writer of humble origins, 'translate' Gaelic ballads, or memories of ballads, into a brilliantly original form. Macpherson's bardic enterprise should be considered in the light of what his Aberdeen professor Thomas Blackwell (1701–1757) had written about Homer: 'We find that without *Virtue* there can be no *true Poetry:* It depends upon the *Manners* of a Nation, which form their Characters, and animate their Language.'[5] Macpherson projects uniformity of manners, character, and language by means of the strong patterning that typifies pastoral writing. The *Ossian* poems began with the *Fragments* (1760) printed as though they were a collection of pastoral monologues and dialogues. The longer works are, like the *Gentle Shepherd*, concatenations of what are in effect eclogues, though pointedly ignoring distinctions between pastoral, georgic, and epic verse. Since, prior to divisions of labour, manners, character, and language would be uniformly simple, in Ossianic characters, songs, memories, landscapes, visions, supernatural beings, and the very weather are all figuratively interchangeable. The result is strong patterning with a vengeance:, Blackwell's speculations about Homeric times fashioned into what the anthropologist Ruth Benedict would later call 'patterns of culture'.[6]

Repetition is not used, as in georgic poetry, to mark distinctions but to reveal the holism underlying a way of being in the world. But what world? The Ossianic landscape is as idealised as 'the plain' in Cunningham's pastoral ballads, and indeed the rhythms, diction, and imagery of the one are as hypnotically constricted and monotonous as the other.

The contrast between local and idealised pastoral can be seen in a pair of once popular works by poets, like Macpherson, with connections to Marischal College: Alexander Ross (1699–1784) and James Beattie (1735–1803). Ross's *The Fortunate Shepherdess* apparently underwent a long and tortuous gestation before it was published in 1768. It is a 4,000-line pastoral romance written in response to the *Gentle Shepherd*, though the relation between the two works is complicated. Ramsay rejected the form of pastoral romance while adopting its moral conventions; Ross adopts the form while rejecting its idealism. Both are written in Scots, though Ross writes in the dialect of northeast Scotland, particularising his language as well as his landscape. The story derives from Spenserian romance, as the names of the characters indicate. The eponymous shepherdess, Helenore, turns out, like Patie, to be of gentle birth, but unlike Patie's, her behaviour is sometimes less than genteel and indeed she is referred to as 'Nory' throughout. Her lover, Rosalind [sic] is known as Lindy. Ross deliberately violates convention by marrying Lindy to a woman he had betrayed (along with Nory) and Nory to a less-than-disinterested local squire who turns out to be her cousin.

This unexpected outcome leaves readers of Ross in a situation familiar to readers of Hogg: are we dealing with a semi-literate raconteur or a hyper-literate subverter of the conventions of polite literature? The latter may well be the case, since the conclusion of Ross's tale is a doubly clever play on pastoral topics. Helenore and Rosalind (Nory and Lindy, rather) behave in ways less than honourable, but if the poet seems sympathetic to their pragmatic choices, we should not be too quick to take this as endorsement of a plebeian outlook. One cannot but notice that in the unexpected (yet carefully prepared) denouement the more honourable characters come off better than the more slippery ones. Such Spenserian double-crossings imitate, while undermining, Ramsay's pastoral engagements in the *Gentle Shepherd*. Ross's demotic diction is used to better effect than Ramsay's more literate Scots, the forcefulness of his vulgar tongue becoming the chief source of strong patterning in his meandering story. Less obvious are narrative and verbal repetitions that may be either clumsiness or sly evocations of oral balladry. Ross's seeming artlessness may indicate a writer, like Ramsay, well versed in pastoral deviousness.

Or not: it was apparent sincerity, not concealed wit, that kept the *Fortunate Shepherdess* popular for more than a century.

Like Ross's poem, Beattie's *The Minstrel, or, the Progress of Genius* (1771, 1774, begun 1766) bears the marks of a long and complicated gestation; begun as a Spenserian burlesque, it evolved into something more like autobiography. Beattie told the Dowager Lady Forbes that Edwin, the minstrel, is 'a picture of myself as I was in my younger days' and wrote to Elizabeth Montagu of his difficulty in proceeding with the poem due to the 'imperfection of the plan'. Much as Book VI of the *Faerie Queene* ('of Courtesie') stands behind *The Fortunate Shepherdess*, so 'December' in the *Shepheardes Calender* (1579) seems to have inspired *The Minstrel*: 'Whilom in youth, when flowrd my joyfull spring [...]'. Edwin, Beattie's minstrel, owes something to Ramsay's Patie, but more to Spenser's eidolon, particularly the melancholia that marks him as 'no ordinary boy'. Colin Clout, 'Somedele ybent to song', is instructed in 'arte more cunning' by a 'good olde shephearde'; just so, Edwin encounters an old Hermit (apparently another self-portrait) who encourages the youth to pursue a classical education, at which the boy balks. Beattie stalled, leaving unwritten a third canto in which the minstrel 'was to employ himself in rousing his countrymen to arms'.[7]

This suggests that the 'progress of genius' was to have followed the Virgilian model from pastoral to georgic to epic verse. But that design would run contrary to a second in which Edwin's character was to manifest the simplicity of the rural countryside and elder times in which he lived, as in Blackwell's account of Homer. If virtue is to be looked for in 'the lowly vale of shepherd life',[8] the genius of the place would not be improved by giving Edwin a humanist education. If genius refers to a spirit of the age, Edwin's minstrelsy is no more compatible with academic instruction than Homer's. To the extent that Edwin's simplicity implies ignorance, education would be a boon; to the extent that it portrays the holistic unity of his unsullied place and time, its progress could only represent a fall from grace: 'Perish the lore that deadens young desire!'[9] Then too, if Edwin was 'no vulgar boy',[10] it would be problematic to assert that his literary genius accorded with his situation in life.

For writers striving to imagine a harmonious union of topography, manners, religion, poetry, and social order, the notion of kinds and degrees of literacy was problematic – in becoming a *docta poeta* Edwin would cease to be Edwin, or Scottish, or medieval. Neither was the progress of civilisation, which depended upon divisions of labour within a society and exchanges of ideas across societies, consistent with emergent concepts of culture and nationalism. Readers versed in cultural discourses have long felt that Beattie's first canto ought to be more particularised, more Scottish, while the second should substitute for Latin humanism modern aesthetic education – the education of the heart – the better to propagate a common social vision. Beattie was at bottom a cosmopolitan humanist not inclined to regard demotic poetry as literature, though others, from similar moral motives, were taking a keen interest in untutored insight. Poets who wrote in Scots such as Ramsay, Ross, and Fergusson began to be valued less for their wit than their language, and, as if on cue, Robert Burns, deeply read in Beattie as well as the vernacular pastoralists, stepped forward as a real-life, modern Edwin, closing the gap between orality and literacy.

Tellingly, Burns did not, like his mentors, compose pastoral eclogues. He imitated selectively, combining elements of pastoral with other forms, as indeed Ramsay, Ross, and Beattie had previously done. For example, 'The Cotter's Saturday Night', an ode written in a heroic variant of the Spenserian stanza, connects high themes with low persons through dialect verse and particularised description. Where Churchill turned to heroic pastoral to mock Macpherson and Scottish poverty, Burns illustrates how the bardic function survives in bible-reading and hymn-singing, binding demotic Scotland into a powerful unity based on a common literature and historical memory. Like the georgic pastorals, Burns illustrates the connection between political economy and persons in humble life, but with the roles reversed: not only are these simple persons literate, they shape the national character through their manners and beliefs. 'The Cotter's Saturday Night' engages with Scottish pastoral in a variety of ways: from Ramsay, the reclamation of a legacy, with Covenanters substituted for Cavaliers; from Macpherson, the union of place, persons, memory, and song; from Beattie, the identification of moral virtue with rural simplicity. In the patriarchal Cotter, one sees the Virgilian roles assigned to shepherd, farmer, and soldier conflated into a single imposing character.

Burns's memorable self-portrait as a 'rustic bard' in 'The Vision' was inspired, so he told Mrs Dunlop, by Alexander Ross's address to Scota in *The Fortunate Shepherdess* ('Come Scota, thou that anes upon a day / Gar'd Allan Ramsay's hungry heart-strings play').[11] Scota becomes 'Coila', Ayrshire, rendering matters more geographically specific. Burns writes in the Habbie stanza (his favourite mode of strong patterning) as had Beattie in the Scots verses he addressed to Ross ('Thy hamely auld-world muse provokes / Me for a while / To ape our guid plain country folks /

In verse and style').[12] Coila's account of the bard's education echoes *The Minstrel* point for point, though unlike illiterate Edwin young Burns was a reader: 'I oft would gaze, / Fond, on thy little, early ways, / Thy rudely-caroll'd, chiming phrase, / In uncouth rhymes, / Fir'd at the simple, artless lays / Of other times.'[13] Like Beattie imitating Ross imitating Ramsay, Burns underscores his relationship to Scottish pastoral. 'Other times' suggests that he included Macpherson in that tradition, as does the description of Coila's visionary garb which 'seem'd, to my astonish'd view, / A well-known Land.'[14] The distinction between simple speaker and sophisticated poet is articulated in the shift from Scots to English in the second 'duan'; yet, Burns equivocates by using the cultish image of Coila to identify the farmer cultivating his land with the poet cultivating his mind. This is cleverly managed, all the more because the learned poet makes it transparently clear that his woodnotes wild derive from close study of the best literary models. He may not have written eclogues, but Robert Burns was deeply versed in the ways of pastoral poetry, traditional and contemporary.

Still, Burns left the concept of a progress of genius as articulated by Beattie as problematic as ever for, like Edwin, 'he was no vulgar boy'. If poetical genius is the product of a pattern of circumstances woven into the fabric of a particular place and social order, why was Burns such a one-off even among the untutored bards and dialect poets appearing at the end of the eighteenth century? The relation of demotic to literary poetry became more complicated as the proliferation of books gave the labouring classes better access to knowledge and literary poets better knowledge of traditional materials. In 'A Historical Essay on Scotish [*sic*] Song' (1794), Joseph Ritson championed illiteracy: 'The genuine and peculiar natural song of Scotland, is to be sought – not in the works of Hamilton, Thomson, Smollett, or even Ramsay; but – in the productions of obscure or anonymous authors, of shepherds and milk maids, who actually felt the sensations they describe; of those, in short, who were destitute of all the advantages of science and education, and perhaps incapable of committing the pure inspirations of nature to writing: and in this point of view, it is believed, the English have nothing equal in merit, nor in fact any thing of the kind.'[15] This idea that there is something 'peculiar' about the 'natural song of Scotland' is just what Wordsworth denies in 'The Solitary Reaper', but it is affirmed by Hector Macneill in *The Pastoral, or Lyric Muse of Scotland* (1808): 'Not a bank, or stream, or hill, or dale is unnoticed; and, while the general theme is rural occupations peculiar to pastoral life, we are in a manner constrained to believe that the poet describes scenes and circumstances with which he was not only familiarly acquainted, but intimately connected.'[16]

Macneill (1746–1818) was, like Burns, the son of a tenant farmer with much reading but no classical education. His three-canto poem attempts to 'complete' *The Minstrel* by tracing a progress of genius in the untutored poetry of the border poets: 'They sung contentment's rural strains / Around the "Braes o' Yarrow;" / On "Ettrick banks" was heard the reed / That piped to pastoral leisure.'[17] The first canto recapitulates *The Minstrel*, describing how an anonymous shepherd-bard invented Scottish pastoral by imitating the songs of birds and then coming under the tutelage of the Scottish Muse. The second, corresponding to Beattie's unwritten third, describes the poet venturing into 'the banner'd hall / Of plundering chief' to pacify the Borders; at the sound of his lyre, 'the *Minstrel* crew / Blush'd, conscience struck! – in haste withdrew'.[18] The third canto illustrates this proposition in a ballad imitation of Macneill's composition. The spirit of barbarism is laid to rest in lyric stanzas modelled on Dryden's 'Alexander's Feast' (1697) and the primal status of pastoral asserted in stanzas modeled on Collins' 'The Passions. An Ode for Music' (1747). At the centre of the poem, the 'moral Muse' presents to the untutored borderers a visionary progress of poetry in a catalogue of future Scottish poets: Ramsay, Thomson, Home, Beattie, Burns, and Joanna Baillie (1762–1851) (*Plays on the Passions* [1798–1812]). If this were Burns, one might suspect irony in what amounts to an enumeration of the literary origins of Macneill's own origin-fable, but literalism seems intended: 'The Shepherds listening, felt ambition's flame '.[19] This passage concedes what the poem otherwise denies: that untutored bards *do* learn their craft by emulating literary models, as was certainly the case with Macneill himself, whose slippery argument elides border poetry with Scottish poetry and both with doctrines of aesthetic education he regards as universal.

James Hogg's perplexing *Pilgrims of the Sun* (1815) does not attempt to complete *The Minstrel* but to explode it, in part by implicitly asserting the extensive reading of 'untutored' poets like Macneill or himself. It is useful to compare Hogg's programme with that of George Gordon, Lord Byron's (1788–1824) *Childe Harold's Pilgrimage* (1812). In his semi-autobiographical poem Byron (like Ross, Macpherson, and Beattie, the product of an Aberdeen education) embraces the supposed deficiencies of *The Minstrel*: *Childe Harold* was conceived as a fragment; the burlesque Beattie dropped is retained, with Edwin's simplicity refashioned as satirical candour. Beattie's rejection of Scottish nationalism becomes in Byron a worldly cosmopolitanism for which the particularities of Highland and Albanian manners appear as distinctions without a difference. But if Byron challenges nativist assumptions, so too the Enlightenment alternative: *Childe Harold* is a progress poem in which, like *The Minstrel*, progress makes no progress. Such contrariness is just what Hogg hails in his dedication of his *Pilgrims* to Byron: 'Thy soul that dares each bound to overfly, / Ranging through Nature on erratic wing—'.[20] Hogg's poem is a Menippean satire less in the manner of Byron than of Jonathan Swift's (1667–1745) *Gulliver's Travels* (1726), a patchwork of modes and imitations whose design is to defeat attempts to discover design.

Like Macneill, whose third canto is in ballad quatrains, Hogg writes in mixed measures, evoking balladry in the first and fourth parts, imitating John Milton's *Paradise Lost* (1667) in the second, and Alexander Pope's (1688–1744) *Moral Essays* (1731–1735) in the third. The disconcerting shifts in metre and style are very unlike the elisions Macneill uses to conflate locality and universalism, pastoral and epic, and orality and literacy. Here the seams are intended to be seen: Hogg is at once a border poet and a poet crossing borders, daring 'each bound to overfly', but chiefly boundaries dividing nature from the supernatural and orthodoxy from heterodoxy. In recasting his saintly Kilmeny from the *Queen's Wake* as the votaress Mary Lee of Carelha', Hogg gives her an enquiring mind: 'She learned to read, when she was young, / The books of deep divinity'.[21] Weary of this world, 'she pined the next to see', and so encounters a shape-shifting fairy who elsewhere appears as an angel, a minstrel, and a shepherd. The conversations of Mary Lee with her tutor recall the scenes of instruction in *The Minstrel* and *Pastoral or Lyric Muse of Scotland*, but how changed! Taking locality to new heights, the characters visit a wildly various series of worlds where nonetheless manners correspond to passions, and passions to landscape. The universe, it seems, is as various as Scotland – physically, morally, and theologically. The travellers return in the last canto and after an improbable series of events are united in matrimony, make mysterious appearances after death, and then vanish as the chronology approaches modern times.

James Hogg was unique in being both a professional shepherd and professional writer. In *Pilgrims of the Sun*, he stands astride these opposing worlds, refusing to be assimilated into either. Where Ritson associates shepherds and milkmaids with nature, Hogg is more inclined to discover in rural Scotland the untrammelled supernatural. Fairies make appearances in Ross and Beattie, but Hogg makes superstition – simplicity rendered sublime – a central component of his literary programme.

Literary imitation, a hallmark of untutored poetry long after it was deprecated in more polite literature, is also characteristic of Hogg's oeuvre. As Alexander Pope had once recommended, he steals boldly – from Macneill for instance, in making his fairy-tutor Cela the primal shepherd: 'The first who attuned the pastoral reed / On the mountains of Ettrick, and braes of Tweed; / The first who did to the land impart / The shepherd's rich and peaceful art'.[22] If Hogg's strong-patterning-through-imitation is shocking, it is how pastoral had always worked: what Virgil, Spenser, and Milton had done in writing artful poems about simple persons, Hogg does, with a knowing complexity and eye for paradox. His originality lies in using demotic traditions to unsettle the verities of polite ideas about education – soaring, like Byron, on 'erratic wing'.[23]

There is very little in pastoral poetry that can be regarded as essential, certainly not sheep, shepherds, or blushing lovers, save perhaps the reworking of traditions, old or new, demotic or literary. In using pastoral poetry to unsettle conventional ideas about nature and art, Hogg was doing in his novel way what Ramsay, Macpherson, Ross, Beattie, and Burns had all done before, and so underscoring the strong continuity between eighteenth-century Scottish pastoral and emergent debates about culture and civilisation.

CHAPTER ELEVEN

Gaelic Women's Poetry

Kate Louise Mathis

> Don Ollamh Colm Ó Baoill, le meas is miadh.
> *For Professor Colm Ó Baoill, with respect and esteem.*

The eighteenth century is remarkable for the increasing visibility of Scottish Gaelic women poets' work within the manuscript collections that flourished in its latter half,[1] and for 'the arrival of women in Gaelic print',[2] including the earliest single-authored anthology assembled by a female poet in 1785.[3] Items of verse that appear to have been composed much earlier than the time of their preservation – in print or by collection – become visible in consequence, having also, sometimes simultaneously, been 'pressed into service' as *òrain luaidh* and *luinneagan*,[4] work-songs that accompanied daily tasks. Contemporary social historian John Ramsay of Ochtertyre (1736–1814) indicates that these songs were:

> sung by the women, not only at their diversions, but also during almost every kind of work, where more than one person [was] employed, [such] as milking cows and watching the folds, fulling of cloth, grinding of grain with the *quern*, or hand-mill, hay-making, and cutting down corn.[5]

Despite the 'degree of suspicion and mistrust' with which the act of composition was sometimes regarded,[6] women poets, both named and anonymous, exhibit command of a wide range of subjects, styles, and types of verse, many of which – chiefly elegy and eulogy, conventional to the panegyric code[7] – develop earlier poets' style, subject, and purpose. Black and Carruthers' observation that 'what the new century brings to Gaelic verse is above all the deepening and broadening of the pre-existing tradition of highly codified vernacular verse'[8] is applicable to women's poetry and song as much as to their male contemporaries' work. Innovation, however, is also apparent, while larger corpora attributable to named women poets permit fuller appreciation of these women's (non-professional) careers, sometimes as part of local or national networks, as well as the range of material composed. There is greater evidence, too, for women poets' engagement with the century's turbulent politics and its sometimes terrible effect upon their own and their families' lives, while recognition of the social and economic decline of Gàidhealtachd communities, engendered by the post-Culloden breakdown of clan chieftains' traditional roles, heralds nineteenth-century poets' systematic critique of the longer-term impact of landlordism and clearance.[9] In contrast, the minutiae of personal lives emerge – fashions in dress, fondness for snuff or hot chocolate[10] – alongside praise of education,[11] guidance for courtship and appropriate sexual conduct,[12] and detailed contemplation of spiritual belief and changing doctrine. Gaelic women's poems are addressed to husbands or sweethearts; to family; to other women;[13] to figures of contemporary authority; and, although rarely, to themselves, but, as with older examples, 'the public nature of [women's] poems tends to throw the focus outward, onto events and actions, rather than inwards to thoughts [and] feelings', even in the strongest of emotional states.[14]

In common with the 'great majority of post-Classical [post-1600] Gaelic songs', women's poetry was composed 'without recourse to writing' until at least the early 1900s.[15] Moreover, the act of preservation in writing – or, thereafter, in print – tended to exclude the agency of poets themselves; even items of verse attributed to named women remained vulnerable to collectors' or editors' imprecision or lack of contemporary knowledge (and/or to subsequent singers' distance from attributed songs reshaped by years of circulation and performance in the oral tradition).[16] While anonymous items that employ a female voice are more likely to be accepted as women's compositions than hitherto,[17] the propensity for male and female poets to adopt opposite-gendered voices in their work – including those of traditional *personae* such as Oiséan or Deirdre – remains problematic for the definition and criticism of 'women's poetry' in Gaelic.[18] Initially, however, most problematic in this regard is the lack of preserved examples: prior to the eighteenth century, only the Book of the Dean of Lismore (compiled c. 1512×1542) includes contemporary verse attributed to named women authors.[19] Women's compositions are absent from the Fernaig manuscript, compiled c. 1688×1693 by Donnchadh 'nam Pìos' MacRath (Duncan MacCrae of Inverinate),[20] whose wife's and sister-in-law's poems were not included,[21] while neither Rev. Alexander Pope's (c. 1739) nor Jerome Stone's (c. 1755) formative collections of heroic ballads attribute items to female authorship or even recitation.[22]

The later 1700s, therefore, witnessed a significant rise in preservation of named poets' work, and of verses whose titles presume the authenticity of their female voice (e.g. 'Oran le mnaoi d'a leannan', 'A woman's song to her sweetheart') – in other words, the formation of a canon of early modern women's poetry in Gaelic. The process, however, was largely inadvertent, detached from the context in which that work had been composed, and, as noted, largely outwith the control of the women themselves. The Ossianic controversy, which ossified the perception of James Macpherson (Seumas Bàn MacMhuirich, 1736–96) and Gaelic literature for more than a century,[23] galvanised collection and publication of 'genuine' Gaelic verse, but fostered, in consequence, a 'new sense of what Gaelic poetry should be about, in an age when traditional patrons and 'clan' audiences no longer existed'.[24] The most prolific of the century's collectors, Revs. Donald McNicol (Domhnall MacNeacail, 1735–1802), Ewen MacDiarmid (Eoghain MacDiarmaid, d. 1801), and James McLagan (Seumas MacLathagain, 1728–1805),[25] whose interest and activity predated Macpherson's sudden fame, inherited the 'mantle of the traditional Gaelic scholar', the patronised, Classically trained poets and scribes whose influence had declined by 1700.[26] With few exceptions, however, they upheld the culture of clanship and the chieftain's hall:

> their concept of what was important and most worthy of preservation […] valued age and antiquity over recent and contemporary times, heroic and martial over agricultural and peasant society, [and] gentlemanly and aristocratic tastes and pursuits over those of the rest.[27]

While, in general, women's poetry is neither segregated from nor subordinated to men's, and collectors' consistency of method with regard to the recognition of women's work does not appear to have differed,[28] the type of material their collections preserve prioritises, for example, 'encomiastic and rhetorical' verse above òrain luaidh.[29] These same collectors' tastes and their 'partial view' – of men's as well as women's compositions[30] – also formed the basis of the anthologies published by John Gillies (1786), the Stewart brothers (1804), Eoin Young (1806), and Patrick Turner (1813).[31]

Nonetheless, the scale of these collections, especially McLagan's, is unprecedented, and their collectors' 'collaborative scholarship and mutual criticism'[32] preserved, then propelled into print, more than a hundred items that employ a female voice, about a third of whose authors are named. Richard Sharpe observes that McLagan and his colleagues mediated 'between the living literature [in the oral tradition] and the preserved text',[33] but it should not be overlooked that none of the women whose work their collections preserve – at least what is possible to date – were alive at the time. McLagan's text of Margaret Stevenson's tirade against the Dis-Clothing Act of 1746 was copied in 1775, the year of Margaret's death,[34] but those others whose names are attached to their work in his and his colleagues' collections had flourished on average at least half a century before, and typically much longer. The best represented are Màiri nighean Alasdair Ruaidh (Mary MacLeod, c. 1625–c. 1705), panegyrist of the MacLeods of Dunvegan and Berneray, and Sìleas na Ceapaich (Cicely MacDonald, c. 1660–c. 1729), Jacobite satirist, devout Catholic, and social critic.[35] McLagan's collection includes six of Màiri's poems, four of which are attributed, and five or six by Sìleas, two with attribution;[36] his copies were probably acquired from Donald McNicol,[37] and Màiri's work, at odds with McLagan's usual practice, is mostly grouped together.[38] Uniquely for his collection, McLagan includes a tune to which Màiri's praises for MacLeòid of Dunvegan should be sung,[39] and attempts a translation into English of Sìleas's critique of the battle of Sheriffmuir.[40]

Perhaps predictably, foreshadowing McNicol's and McLagan's interest, items of verse by Màiri nighean Alasdair Ruaidh and Sìleas na Ceapaich also enjoy the distinction of being recorded sooner than many contemporaries' work, within about forty years of their respective deaths.[41] In 1776, some of their work enters print, about forty-five years after Sìleas's death and seventy years after Màiri's.[42] In the closing decades of the eighteenth century, the gap between time of composition and time of mediated preservation, latterly in print, decreases, but many poets' work continues to circulate primarily in the oral tradition, which neither collection nor publication supersede. Margaret Stevenson's polemic, for example, may have been preserved in manuscript within thirty years, but it remained unpublished until 1911.[43] Only the work of Sìleas's near-contemporary Mairghread nighean Lachlainn (Margaret Maclean, c. 1660–c. 1751)[44] is recorded any closer to the time of its composition,[45] but publication awaited Turner's anthology more than fifty years later,[46] due perhaps to her poems' exclusive preservation by MacLean sources beforehand, not the collections of McNicol, McLagan, or Ewen MacDiarmid. Not merely sufficient, the oral tradition was fundamental to ensuring preservation of poets' identities, reputations, and at least some of their work, as McNicol himself observed in 1779:

[it] was so closely interwoven with the custom and constitution of the country that it could not be separated from them; and it was handed down from one generation to another, not by Bards and Seannachies only, but by the general voice and consent of a whole nation.[47]

The fact that Turner, as well as the Stewarts and Young, include items preserved initially by McLagan that lack attribution – which Turner, in 1813, supplies – underlines the role that circulation in the oral tradition continued to hold: Turner, for example, associates an elegy for Aonghas Óg MacDonald of Glengarry (d. 1746), preserved anonymously by McLagan, to 'Bean Achadh-uaine'.[48] It is sometimes unclear, however, if attribution were omitted formerly due to lack of knowledge or, in contrast, when a poet's work was too well known to require it; the latter items were typically attributed on reaching print, such as Young's text of Sìleas na Ceapaich's elegy for Alasdair Dubh, 10th MacDonald of Glengarry (d. 1721), which McLagan had not ascribed.[49] Other texts, normally anonymous, but also those with attribution, make their first traceable appearance in print, such as the Stewarts' copies of Sìleas na Ceapaich's 'Cumha Lachlainn Daill' (*Lament for Lachlan Dall*) and 'An aghaidh na h-obar nogha' (*Against the oobie noogie*).[50] Texts preserved in manuscript with neither title nor attribution may also be labelled on their entry into print: Gillies entitles an anonymous complaint of desertion, of which McLagan's collection, his likeliest source, preserves three unlabelled copies, 'Oran a rinn Oigh d'a Leannan' (*A girl's song to her sweetheart*).[51] Perhaps conversely, however, secure attribution in manuscript does not guarantee publication, such as 'Air Alasdair Butter, a chaidh mharbhadh 'n Cùilfhodair' (*Concerning Alasdair Butter, who died at Culloden*), attributed by McLagan to the otherwise unknown Mairea Strong, which remains unpublished (see below).[52]

Consistency of attribution also varied, if collectors – and, subsequently, editors of print anthologies – obtained multiple copies of similar texts or received new information. Normally confined to details other than authorship, such as McLagan's revised annotation to his copy of Aonghas Óg's lament that his death had occurred in Falkirk, not Stirling,[53] particular items' formerly clear presentation as female-voiced or authored could sometimes be affected. McLagan's collection preserves two copies of an elegy labelled, firstly, 'Caoidh oig-mhna ann deis a leannain a mharbhadh le h Athair & le brathairin' (*A young woman's lament for her sweetheart's killing by her father and brothers*), but latterly 'MᶜDhughail Mhic Ruaridh'

('*Son of Dougal, son of Ruairidh*'), prioritising its subject, not its unnamed composer (Gillies's printed version adopts the former).⁵⁴ Similarly, McLagan's original title for his only copy of a seventeenth-century elegy, 'Cumha le mhnaoi do dh' fhear do Chlainn Ghriogair' ('*A wife's lament for a man of Clan Gregor*'), has been scored out and replaced by 'Do Ghilleaspuig McCalum Sealgair sa Bhein mhoir' ('*To Archibald McCalum, hunter in Beinn Mhor*').⁵⁵ The correction revises its subject's identity, but obscures its composer's, whose status as his widow, clear from her text itself and otherwise unchanged, is better attested by the older name. On its publication in 1786, Gillies's combined title 'Oran do Ghilleaspuig Mac Calum sealgair a bha sa Bheinne-mhoir, le Mhnaoi fein' ('*A song to Archibald MacCallum, a hunter in Beinn Mhor, by his own wife*') restores the poet's connection to her subject.⁵⁶

Misattribution, however, could also occur at this stage – entry into print – such as Gillies's adoption of a colophon to one poem as the title of another: McLagan's copy of a lament by Teàrlach Òg MacFhionghuin ('Fear a' Chinn Uachdaraich') was published, in consequence, with incorrect attribution to a female poet, an error repeated by subsequent editors.⁵⁷ Similarly, misunderstanding of Gaelic poets' frequent adoption of opposite-gendered voices, especially for items arranged as dual- or multi-voiced dialogue, could result in the mistaken presumption of female authorship by a subsequent audience, even with precise attribution to the contrary in print. A documented contemporary example is Iain mac Ailein's (c. 1660–1741) dramatised conversation between two women, Mairearad and Marsaili, debating the appeal of a chaste or extravagant life, printed by the Eigg collection in 1776.⁵⁸ Its title in the latter asserts both its (male) authorship and the women's status clearly: 'Oran a roinn Eon M Gilleon do dhios Inghin Dhoniùl mhic Doniùl duibh' ('*A song made by John MacLean for two daughters of Donald son of Mac Dhòmhnaill Dhuibh*').⁵⁹ Anne Grant of Laggan (1755–1838), however, referred to the poem as 'a dialogue, very curious in its kind, between two young maidens, one of whom is determined to dedicate her life to recluse devotion, [while] the other argues in favour of active duties and the pleasures of liberty'. From her own book's date of publication in 1811 Grant's source, identified vaguely as 'one of the collections of old poetry', cannot be other than the Eigg collection itself, yet if she has grasped the essence of the poem's subject she has overlooked its title, its clearly designated male authorship and, therefore, its exemplary ventriloquised style.⁶⁰

Grant's discussion of the poem is, nonetheless, an unusual example of contemporary interest in Gaelic women's poetry for its own sake; she was also familiar with at least some of the work of Sìleas na Ceapaich, whom she described as 'an eminent poetess'.[61] As a fortunate consequence of some collectors' heightened self-interest, post-Ossian, in declaring the authenticity of their sources, visibility of women's roles as tradition bearers also increases: in 1803, for example, McLagan obtained a ballad from Isabel Stewart, 'a middle-aged woman, in Easter Inverack, a widow', who identified another woman, Catherine McArthur of Glenlyon, as her own source.[62] Similarly, the ultimate source for Turner's copies of poems by Sìleas na Ceapaich was the now-lost manuscript compiled by Iain Bàn MacDonald of Inch (c. 1765–c. 1850), who had obtained them from the recitation of Sìleas's former servant, sadly unnamed.[63] Acknowledgement of this kind, however, remains incidental, nor is it stimulated by increasing numbers of female tourists visiting the Gàidhealtachd as the century turns, even those rarities such as Dorothy Wordsworth (1771–1855) who were not inspired chiefly by Macpherson's *Ossian*.[64] Until the publication of John MacKenzie's *Sar Obair nam Bard Gaelach* in 1841, the first collection that included its poets' biographies in English, opportunities for non-Gaels to engage critically with Gaelic poetry were limited to certain anthologies' dedications or prefatory remarks; even *Sar Obair*, moreover, did not provide translations of its texts. The first such preface, which accompanied *Ais-Eiridh na Sean Chánoin Albannaich* (*The Resurrection of the Ancient Scottish Tongue*) by Alasdair mac Mhaighstir Alasdair (Alexander MacDonald, c. 1695–c. 1770) in 1751, expressed the hope that its appearance would awaken public interest in:

> a greater collection of poems of the same sort [...] with a translation into English verse and critical observations on the nature of such writings, to render the work useful to those that do not understand the Gaelic language.[65]

As Ronald Black has observed, the publication in 1776 of *Comhchruinneachidh Orannaigh Gaidhealach* (the 'Eigg collection') by Mac Mhaighstir Alasdair's son Raghnall looks, at least in part, 'like the son's attempt to fulfil the father's ambition'.[66] It also includes the first selection of Gaelic poetry attributed to women: Màiri nighean Alasdair Ruaidh and Sìleas na Ceapaich are both represented, alongside a small number of anonymous female-voiced texts and the first printed examples of female-voiced *òrain luaidh* (inspired perhaps by Mac Mhaighstir Alasdair's determined rejection of 'the demands of the panegyric code' throughout his own career).[67] Nonetheless, what Raghnall does not include – in common with McLagan's and his colleagues' collections – is the work of contemporary women. In certain cases, this is unsurprising: two poets, Anna Chaimbeul, Bean a' Bharra (Anna Campbell of Barr, c. 1715–c. 1785) and Màiri nighean Iain mhic Eoghain (Mary MacDonald, fl. 1740s), were satirised by Mac Mhaighstir Alasdair in his own work, Màiri by a mock-elegy that alleges she engaged in prostitution,[68] Anna by four poems including his masterpiece 'An Airce' ('*The Ark*').[69] Both women are accused of sexual misconduct,[70] but their real offense was that both had authored verses, neither now extant, that 'slandered the Prince, or otherwise mocked the Jacobite cause'.[71] Mac Mhaighstir Alasdair was also acquainted with Margaret Stevenson (née Campbell), collected by McLagan, apparently Anna's mother,[72] whose own polemic was also overlooked for publication. The effect of his contempt on these particular women's subsequent visibility is hard to discern.[73] In 1834, the poet Duncan Kennedy opined that Mac Mhaighstir Alasdair's criticism of Anna Campbell had significant impact, ensuring that, instead of composing further panegyric and becoming the equal of Màiri nighean Alasdair Ruadh or Mairearad nighean Lachlainn, she 'turned her whole thoughts to futurity and sacred subjects' instead.[74]

The decade that followed the Eigg collection and 'the arrival of women in Gaelic print'[75] saw John Gillies's publication of his own anthology in 1786, including seven texts with direct attribution to women (two identified, five anonymous), and eight that are female-voiced; all of the latter and all but one of the former are derived from McLagan.[76] Gillies's volume also includes a copy of an unattributed spiritual text 'M' anam, iomuigh thusa samhach' ('*My soul, go quietly on*'),[77] composed by Mary MacPherson, Mrs Clark (Màiri Nic a' Phearsain, Bean Torra Dhamh, c. 1740–c. 1815), whose source may have been a pamphlet printed in 1785 with the patronage of Mrs Grant of Rothiemurchus.[78] Its lack of attribution by Gillies suggests that the pamphlet was also anonymous, and the extent to which Mary herself was involved in its production is unclear; around 1802, she would attempt to find a publisher for a collection alleged to have numbered some thirty items composed in English as well as Gaelic, but was unsuccessful.[79] Only seven remain extant – all in Gaelic – printed anonymously in the 1830s and with increasing recognition in the later 1800s.[80] Copies of three poems may have been preserved in her own hand, potential contenders for the earliest known autograph copies of verses in Gaelic by a female poet.[81] In addition to its tender, sometimes deeply sensual praise of God,[82] Mary's poetry criticises the 'abuse of power and wealth' by figures of authority neglectful of their social obligations,[83] envisaging a 'reformed society [whose] leaders conduct themselves according to God's law':[84]

> An-sin gach duine chuir san eucoir,
> Buainidh e le deuraibh goirte,
> 'S bidh an duais gu truagh mar thoill iad [...]
> Ach na fireanaich gu aoibhneas,
> Crùn is oighreachd gheibh gach neach dhiubh
> 'S còmhnaidh ait an teach na soillse [...]

Then all those who sowed unjustly, / They will reap with bitter tears, / And their prize will be as sad as they've deserved [...] / But the righteous will go to happiness, / A crown and inheritance all of them will have / And pleasant lodging in the house of brightness.[85]

Also in 1785, the publication of *Orain nuadh Ghaidhealach* (*New Gaelic songs*) saw Marairead Cham'ron (Margaret Cameron, fl. c. 1770–1805) become the first female poet to print her own work in Gaelic with clear attribution.[86] Only five male poets – Mac Mhaighstir Alasdair (1751), Donnchadh Bàn Mac an t-Saoir (Duncan Ban MacIntyre, 1768), Lachlann MacLachlainn (Lachlan MacLachlan, 1770), Donnchadh Lobhdain (Duncan Lothian, 1780), and Peter Stuart (1783) – had preceded her.[87] Two other single-authored collections by male poets were published the same year,[88] in what Ronald Black has described as a mood of optimism among Gaels that followed the repeal of the Dis-Clothing Act in 1782, and the authorised return in 1784 of many estates confiscated after Culloden.[89] In contrast to Mac Mhaighstir Alasdair's *Ais-Eiridh*, however, whose publication reacted to the Rising's defeat and 'coincided with the prohibition of various aspects of Gaelic culture'[90] – which *Ais-Eiridh* celebrates boldly – Marairead's poetry defines the Prince's attempt to regain his throne as imprudent idealism, suggesting that his followers' dispossession and even execution was deserved:

> Chaill an sinnsir sud le 'n gòraich,
> 'S cha chion aithne bh' orr' na folum,
> 'Mhain nach gèille iad le m' Beò-shlaint,
> Ach le Tearlach an aghaidh Dheòrsa.
>
> Chaidh cuid do 'n Fhraing, 's cuid do 'n Òlaind,
> Chaidh cuid san fhairge sìos le doilinn

> Chaidh cuid eile 'reuba beò dhiubh,
> A leth a' Phrionnsa a dh' fhalbh air fògra.

Those ancestors lost with their foolishness, / And they weren't lacking in knowledge or education, / Merely that they wouldn't yield their livelihood, / But stood with Charles against George. // Some went to France and some to Holland / Some went down in the sea with dolor. / Some others were torn asunder, / Because of the Prince who left in exile.[91]

'Moladh do na Fineachaibh Gaidheileach a fhuair an Oighreachdan, ann Bliaghna 1784' ('*A song to the clans who had their lands restored, in the year 1784*'), which opens her collection, sets its tone, positioning Marairead – born a Campbell – in the company of other Gaelic poets who 'learned to love George', although not unconditionally.[92] It suggests, more specifically, that she is willing to support policies and individuals, such as James Graham, later 3rd Duke of Montrose (1755–1836), providing new opportunities for Gaels loyal to the house of Hanover to maintain their traditional culture without further sanction:

> 'S gu ma slàn do Dhiùc Mhontròs,
> A thug an t-ac' a-mach o 'n Bhòrd,
> Do na Gàidheil air am breacain bhòidheach,
> Cead dol do 'n Chlachan leo' Di-Dòmhnaich.

And good health to the Duke of Montrose, / Who took the act out from the Board, / Permission for the Gaels in the beautiful tartan / To go to the church on Sunday.[93]

Heightening the poem's ambivalence towards the Stuarts, the Duke's ancestor James Graham, 1st Marquis of Montrose (1612–50), is praised as 'clach-bhun' a' chaisteil nach gabh a' gluasad' ('*the foundation stone of the castle that won't be moved*'), and extolled as 'an curaidh 's an saighdear gailbheach' ('*the hero and the fierce soldier*') who restored Charles II to his rightful place. Since, despite the defiance of *Ais-Eiridh*, Gillies's anthology and even the Eigg collection 'concentrated on an earlier heroic past' and – like the collectors on whom Gillies depends – avoided material that engaged directly with the Jacobite cause,[94] Marairead's tepid support for Hanover precedes into print a significant number of women's poems that celebrated the Stuarts and advocated for their cause explicitly. Her pragmatism, however, is representative of eulogy addressed to chieftains such as Simon Fraser, 12th of Lovat (1726–1782), whose public display of loyalty to the British Government despite his ninety-year-old father's execution after Culloden resulted in his estates' return – and, thereby, an ease to his tenants' suffering – a decade prior to the Act of Restoration.[95] Moreover, Marairead's expectation of mutual respect between the Gaels and Hanover anticipates nineteenth-century poets' complaints that Highland regiments' faithful service in the British military deserved a better return than their communities' treatment during Clearance.[96]

The ability to control her work, its attribution, and its presentation in print ensures that Marairead Cham'ron's experience is atypical to those whose work was collected, classified, and published without their involvement. The twenty original poems in her collection remain the second-largest single corpus composed by a woman in Gaelic until 1891, and several of its texts, such as 'Moladh do na Fineachaibh [...] am bliadhna 1784', were composed only months in advance of their publication. Some address unusual subjects, such as 'Oran mu clag Challasraid' ('*A song about Callander's bell*'),[97] and 'Fearas-chuideachd mu chaonaig bh' aig Clann Domhnuil' ('*Banter about Clan Donald's skirmish*'), which dramatises a game of shinty between rival teams as a clan conflict on the 'pitch' of battle.[98] Finally, her book's appendix of 'sean orain' ('*old songs*') contains an elegy for Dòmhnall, 11th MacDonald of Clanranald (d. 1618) composed by its subject's wife Mairi nighean Aonghais,[99] inclusion of which renders Marairead the first female poet to select another woman's work for publication. Nonetheless, despite her collection's remarkable context, its general tone is eulogistic,[100] with frequent recourse to the panegyric code, and her emphasis on affairs and individuals of mainly local interest ('the aristocracy and lesser gentry of Lochaber and south Perthshire')[101] is also typical of her mediated contemporaries' style, tone, and subject. Self-publication does not result in radical departure from established norms, to which anticipation of financial return may even have encouraged greater deference; in Marairead's case, this is possible, since her collection was also reprinted in 1805 in hopes of alleviating straightened financial circumstance towards the end of her life.

The reception of *Orain nuadh Ghaidhealach* is largely invisible; in 1915, its first edition is described as 'exceedingly rare' and its second as 'very rare'.[102] It is possible to speculate, however, that its publication raised awareness of Gaelic women's poetry, at least to the extent that printed collections after the 1780s appear to include larger numbers, with editors more diligent in their recognition of female-authored texts. From seven items attributed directly to women in the Eigg collection and seven in Gillies's, the Stewarts' anthology (1804) contains thirteen and Young's (1806) fifteen, while Turner's (1813) includes sixteen, all of whose authors are identified by name. The Stewarts' and Turner's are also the first collections to include overtly Jacobite poetry by Sìleas na Ceapaich, supporting 'King James' in 1715,[103] and an impassioned declaration for his son's campaign attributed by Turner to 'te mhuinntir Lochabar' ('*a woman of Lochaber*'),[104] urging the clans to rally to Charles as the 'star' of their cause's constellation:

> Sgrìos le claidhe' gun dearmad,
> Air gach cealgaire bréige,
> Tha o dhuine gu duine,
> A cuir bun anns an eucoir;
> Nis o 'n thàinig an Rìonnag,
> Teannaibh uile ri chéile,
> 'S leibh clach-mhullach a' chabhsair,
> Anns gach àite ga 'n d' théid sibh.

Let your swords bring unstinting destruction / On every deceitful liar / Who has, from one man to another, / Put his trust in injustice; / Now that the Star has arrived, / Gather together, / The top-most stone of the causeway is with you, / In every place you might go.[105]

In 1810 and 1831, moreover, *Orain nuadh Ghaidhealach* was joined by two other single-authored collections of Gaelic women's compositions. *Laoidhean Spioradail air an cnuasachadh le Mairearad Chaimbeul* (*Reflections on spiritual hymns, by Margaret Campbell*), published in 1810, has been suggested as the work of Marairead Cham'ron herself, i.e. of the same poet as the 1785 collection reverting to her maiden name in later life.[106] While several other Gaelic poets –including Anna Campbell (Bean a' Bharra) in the 1750s – turned from composing secular to religious verse, the dramatic alteration between collections in tone and style as well as content casts doubt on the likelihood of Marairead Cham'ron as the author of both.[107] Donald MacLean alleges, on no clear authority, that 'the authoress [of *Laoidhean Spioradail*] lived at Inverlochy',[108] but if Mairearad Chaimbeul is not the same woman as Mrs Cameron, the detail of her life is otherwise unknown. Her hymnbook's preface, however, which also confirms that she was literate in English – though perhaps not to the extent of translating her own songs – claims a reluctance with regard to publication of these particular texts that may support the adoption of another name when they were printed:

> It was once the intention of the Author of the following Gaelic Compositions to have got several of them translated into English to gratify the wishes of such subscribers to her performance as do not understand the original. That intention however has since been departed from, in consequence of the suggestion of some friends who [...] did not judge it expedient to hazard a literal version of effusions which, at one period, were never intended for publication.[109]

As Anne Macleod Hill observes, 'associating her[self] with the Presbyterian Campbells, rather than the Camerons, who were at heart still Jacobite and Episcopalian', would have been a pragmatic choice for the current poet – were she and Marairead Cham'ron one and the same – appealing once again to the most appropriate audience for her songs. Moreover, the possibility that a significant life event underlay the starkness with which the hymns of *Laoidhean Spioradail* are expressed would place Marairead Cham'ron in the company of Mary MacPherson (Bean Torra Dhamh), alleged to have wasted her youth in selfish pleasure until 'the Lord was obliged to break [her] leg', drawing attention to her 'sinful and lost condition'.[110] Sìleas na Ceapaich's religious poetry was also shaped by 'severe illness and a near-encounter with death',[111] including the remarkable 'Còmhradh ris a' Bhàs' ('*Conversation with Death*'), a dialogue in which Sìleas assumes the voice of Death and debates, with herself, the likelihood that alteration to the behaviour believed to have caused her illness may yet be effected while she lives:

> (Bàs)
> [...] Nì mi do leagail o 'n àrdan;
> Fàgaidh mi do chasan caol is
> Nì na daolagan dìot fàrdach.
>
> (Sìleas)
> Ochòin, ma tha thu dha rìreadh,
> 'S nach faigh mi sìneadh no dàil bhuat,
> Feuch an toir thu orm ìsleadh,
> Gus an dèan mi sìth ri m' Àrd-righ.

> [Death] [...] I shall humble your pride; / I shall leave your legs scrawny and / The worms will make you their home. // [Sìleas] Alas! If you are in earnest / And I am to get no reprieve or respite from you, / Try to make me humble / So that I may make peace with my High King.[112]

The oldest extant copy of 'Còmhradh ris a' Bhàs' was collected 1800×1804 by Rev. Dr Alexander Irvine (1772–1824), from the recitation of John MacDonald of Dalchosnie (d. 1809). The manuscript, though still preserved without her involvement and almost a century after her death, is the largest deliberate gathering of Sìleas's poetry prior to its modern edition by Colm Ó Baoill, entitled 'Òrain Ghaidhleach agus Laoidhean le Silis ni' mhic Raonail' (*'Gaelic songs and hymns by Sileas, daughter of [Mac] Mhic Raghnaill'*).[113]

Laoidhean Spioradail contains thirty-four hymns, the joint-largest female-authored collection in Gaelic until 1891, when Màiri Mhòr nan Òran ('Big Mary of the Songs', c. 1821–1898) published her work.[114] *Co-chruinneach dh' orain thaghte Ghaeleach* (*A Choice Collection of Songs in Gaelic*), published in 1831, also contains thirty-four poems attributed to Mairearad Ghriogarach (Margaret Gow, née MacGregor, c. 1751–?1831). The collection may have been printed posthumously or in the year of Mairearad's death, and was published, perhaps at her behest, by her husband's grandson Donnchadh Gobha, a.k.a., Mac an Tòisich (Duncan Gow, a.k.a., Macintosh, 1804–c. 1846). Alongside Mairearad's, the volume contains poems by her half-brother, her daughter Anna, and several by Donnchadh Gobha; as Michel Byrne has observed, the collection represents a *duanaire* (family compilation), found often in manuscript and brought here into print.[115] Mairearad's grandfather Donald MacGregor was also a poet, some of whose work was preserved by James McLagan, Mairearad's parish minister in Blair Atholl until his death in 1805.[116] Despite their date of publication, most of her poems refer to the closing decades of the eighteenth century and address similar subjects to Marairead Cham'ron's, celebrating those of importance to local clan politics. Her welcome to Colonel Alexander Robertson of Struan (1741–1822) opens the collection; composed in English, it affirms the extent of the education that Mairearad received in her youth, attending a school in Perth referred to by another of her poems. Praise of other women's education occurs in several older eulogies, such as 'Oran Do Bhean Chladh-na-macraidh, Leis An Aigeannach' (*'A song to the mistress of Clenmacrie, by "The Boisterous Lass"'*),[117] but Mairearad may be the first to praise her own:

'S mòr an stàth tha san ionnsach, bheir e tionnsgal don dràic,
'S neach sam bith ga bheil tur cha leig à chuimhne e gu bràth.

Schooling is of great benefit, it gives purpose to the slovenly, / And anybody with good sense will hold on to it for life.[118]

Like Bean Torra Dhamh's work, Mairearad's poems also foreshadow the devastation of Gàidhealtachd communities throughout the nineteenth century, expressing concern at non-traditional management of the Menzies estate in her native Rannoch. A trio of songs addressed to her brothers Iain and Dòmhnall, who had settled in America, also situates her collection in the era of tremendous social change entailed by increasing emigration. Iain's reluctant military service during the Revolutionary Wars (1775–1783) permits Mairearad to condemn the depersonalised nature of modern combat, a rarity in Gaelic verse despite its frequent elegising of the human cost of armed conflict, and atypical even in terms of popular contemporary criticism.[119] 'Òran do Bràithrean bha an Cog' America' ('*A song to her brothers fighting in America*'), for example, denounces war as an evil 'above and beyond individual human beings': accepting that her brothers may deserve to lose their lives for taking part, Mairearad 'does not presume to ask the King of Heaven to spare [them], only that He gives them a moment to repent before they die'.[120] It is hard to recognise the woman whose tender farewell to a child she had fostered occurs in the same book, yet 'Do Leanabh-Altraim a bha aice' ('*To an infant whom she nursed*') delights in the genteel life that awaits the girl on returning home:

> Ma bhios tu làthair ri dol a Phèaslaidh
>   Cha bhi thu dhèidhlàimh 's piuthar d' athar ann,
> Bidh tì 's seàclad 'feithi' ghnàth ort
>   Ga lìon 'n-àird dhut ann a glainneachan;
> 'S tu fuaghal 's a' fàithm ann an uinneag àrd,
>   Sgrìobha is dannsa 's e 's ceàrd is mathas dut,
> Mur paigh thu *bhisat* ann an tìmibh
>   Do *mhissa* prìseil bhios a' tathaich ort.

If you live to go to Paisley, / You will not be neglected since your father's sister is there, / Tea and chocolate will always be waiting for you / And be poured into glasses for you. // As you sew and hem by a high window, / Writing and dance will be excellent occupations for you, / Unless you pay a visit now and again / To a refined young Miss who will socialise with you.[121]

This poem, and others in Mairearad's collection, provides a glimpse of the urbanised environments in which Gaelic women had begun to participate as the century closed,[122] in contrast to the 'hardships and precariousness of farming life'.[123] Addressing her fosterling, Siùsaidh, with genuine fondness, Mairearad also celebrates the income that her nursing has provided during the winter, 'seach bhith gam chramb ri snìomh chalanais' (*'rather than growing stiff from spinning the flax'*).[124] The poems by Anna Ghobha (Ann Gow, 1788–c. 1851), Mairearad's daughter, make similar reference to the typical necessity of balancing seasonal work in the Lowlands with various tasks at home; Anna herself, as her poems attest, was renowned for her skill in weaving tartan, especially for officers' uniforms.[125]

The poems of Mairearad Ghriogarach and her contemporaries, both named and anonymous, demonstrate a significant degree of continuity with their predecessors', while establishing the range of themes – chiefly protest, social critique and social commentary – that will also preoccupy the nineteenth century's poets and gradually dominate their work.[126] Both personal and public, as before, the voices of Gaelic women grow louder in the eighteenth century and their lives as poets, but also as performers, printers, and literate subscribers to others' published work, become more visible and better preserved.[127] Their poems, whether written, printed, self-published, or sung, find new audiences at home in the Gàidhealtachd and, increasingly, abroad. Dispersal of close family members such as Mairearad Ghriogarach's brothers becomes commonplace: initially elective and chiefly to seek employment, often in Highland regiments,[128] emigration is referred to indirectly by the earliest collections, such as an anonymous woman's protest that her sweetheart's decision to sail for Jamaica concealed his desire to end their affair.[129] In contrast, 'Le Oigmhnaoi a chaidh mhealladh' (*'By a young woman who was deceived'*), the only female-voiced text in Gillies's collection that does not derive from McLagan's, complains that its composer's brothers cannot pursue the careless MacLean by whom she has fallen pregnant since, in Jamaica, he is too far away.[130] By 1773, when songs of emigration are observed by Samuel Johnson on his visit to Raasay,[131] women poets themselves have begun to travel and record their experience. McLagan preserves an unnamed woman's vivid description of 'shiubhal thonn àrd borb' (*'sail[ing] high, savage waves*'), and her destination's intemperate climate and its native species, which cannot compare to her home's:

> An àit' nan luibh cùbhraidh b' àbhaist
> Bhith fodham tlàth mun chrodh,
> 'S e gheibh mi droigheann geur is deannt
> 'S an nathair chàm fom chòt.
>
> *Instead of the fragrant, pleasing herbs which used / To be beneath my feet as I attended the cattle, / I now find sharp brambles and nettles / And a coiled snake under my coat.*[132]

Its composer may have been a MacFarlane, resettled in Jamaica on the estate of their chieftain's brother.[133] Another woman, possibly from Skye, addressed her infant daughter in a lullaby that may have been composed in North Carolina; its author fears that contemporary unrest, perhaps the Revolutionary Wars, will mar the child's future life.[134] Its transmission is complex, but suggests circulation primarily in print and latterly in Scotland.[135] In contrast, the work of Anna Gillis (fl. 1780s–c. 1812) was published in Cape Breton in the early 1900s, following its preservation locally by the oral tradition. Anna is credited with a poem made prior to her family's emigration from Morar, perhaps in 1786, and another made several years later that praises the freedom and abundance of their new home.[136]

The changes wrought by emigration to women's lives were profound, and far greater numbers left the Gàidhealtachd than related that experience in verse. More numerous, in fact, are those who complain of others' desertion, even temporarily,[137] while poems composed by those left behind are most likely to lament the deaths of male relatives on military service who have perished abroad, as Duncan Kennedy observed c. 1781 with reference to the terrible impact of the Revolutionary Wars:

> 'S iomadh mac tha gun athair is athair gun mac
> On là thòisich air teugmhail gu reubadh fad as
> Dh' fhàg bràithrean dhe dubhach is peathraichean 'gal
> Is màithraichean brònach a' clò-bhualadh bhas.
>
> *There are many fatherless sons, and many sonless fathers / Since the long-distance war of destruction was begun / It has left brothers upset and sisters crying / And mothers sorrowful, beating their palms.*[138]

Except for the panegyric code, of which it is also part, the imagery of women's lament provides the strongest element of continuity in Gaelic verse. Eighteenth-century elegies for the dead, chiefly casualties of war, may respond to new conflicts and political contexts, but their subjects are mourned on similar terms and in similar ways to older examples.[139] Dòmhnall, son to Maighread Fhriseil, Baintighearna Ghiuthsachain (Mrs Fraser of Culbokie, fl. c. 1740–1790s), served on commission in the Austrian army during the French Revolutionary Wars (1793–1802) and died in battle (1792×1795). His mother's lament begins, conventionally, by describing the moment that she learned of his death – at Christmas – but, as Maciver observes, the distance at which it occurred disrupts the progress of Maighread's grief, preventing her from attending his burial; she is even unaware of his grave's location. The poem concludes with her blessing:

> Ach ma thiodhlaic sibh mo mhac
> 'S gu 'n d' fhalaich sibh le ùir a chorp;
> Leigidh mise mo bheannachd le feachd,
> Air an làimh chur dlighe 'bhàis ort.

But if you buried my son, / And hid his corpse with soil; / I will give my benediction to the regiment [?] / And the hand that placed the rites of death on you.[140]

A widow of Culloden, whose elegy was printed by the Stewarts, was also excluded from tending her subject's grave, but refers to his burial as the most recent cause of the weeping that began – as would Maighread's – with word of his death:

> Bha mi greis ann am barail
> Gum bi mhaireann mo chéile
> 'S gun tigeadh tu dhachaigh
> Le aighear 's le faoilteachd;
> Ach tha 'n t-àm air dol thairis.

I believed for a while / That my husband was living / And that you would come home / With a joke and a greeting; / But the time has gone past.[141]

A number of elements of the panegyric code are employed to praise his bravery, devotion, and appearance in life ('mar ghealbhradain do chosan', '*like bright salmon your legs*'), some of which are shared by the superb list of laudatory kennings in Sìleas na Ceapaich's exemplary lament for Alasdair Dubh, 10th MacDonald of Glengarry (d. 1721). Preserved by MacDiarmid and McLagan, it was printed initially in the Eigg collection in 1776. Concerning Alasdair's unwavering opposition to the Stuarts' detractors, whom he faced at Sheriffmuir in 1715, Sìleas declares:

> Bu tu 'n lasair dhearg 'gan losgadh,
> Bu tu sgoltadh iad gu 'n sàiltibh,
> Bu tu curaidh cur a' chatha,
> Bu tu 'n laoch gun athadh làimhe;
> Bu tu 'm bradan anns an fhìor-uisg
> Fìreun air an eunlaith 's àirde.

> *You were a red torch to burn them, / You would cleave them to the heels, / You were a hero for waging battle, / You were a champion whose arm never flinched. / You were the salmon in fresh water, / The eagle in the highest flock.*[142]

Also conventionally, Sìleas acknowledges the grief of Alasdair's wife, whose condition she compares to hers on hearing word of his death: by coincidence, however, Alasdair's lament was composed on the eve of her own husband's *jahrzeit*. She also refers with empathy to other widows of the battle, including, unusually, those of the opposite side.[143] The latter's suffering is overlooked by Mairghread nighean Lachlainn's complex lament, printed by Turner, for Sir John MacLean of Duart (1670–1716), otherwise a mutual cry of bitter regret from the women of Mull, voiced by Mairghread, for their chieftain's loss and their clan's increasing dispossession.[144] Sir John survived Sheriffmuir but died four months later; his body, like Dòmhnall Friseil's, could not be returned to its ancestors' traditional place of rest:

> Och, is mis' th' air mo sgaradh
> Nach tug iad thu thairis
> Dhol air tìr air an Ealaidh
> Dhol fo dhìon anns a' charraig
> Ann an réilig nam manach
> Mar ri t' athair 's do sheanair
> 'S ioma treunlaoch a bharrachd,
> Far am faodamaid teannadh mu d' chàrnan.

> *Och, I am distraught / That they brought you not over / To the land on the Ealadh / To be sheltered in rock / In the graveyard of the monks [of Iona] / With your father and grandfather / And many other brave heroes / Where we could gather around your cairn.*[145]

Like Sìleas na Ceapaich's lament, Mairghread addresses the grief of Catrìona, ''n deagh bhean mhaiseach sa chì mi' (*'the good lovely wife whom I see here'*), who also mourns Sir John. Perhaps Sir John's wife, Catrìona may also have been someone else's;[146] nonetheless, her description by Mairghread suggests she is grieving profoundly and, perhaps, creating her own lament. The women's collective loss of a chieftain who will not return however much he is sought is enhanced by Mairghread's allusion to Sir John as 'mar Mhaol Ciarain' (*'like Maol Ciarain'*); a poet, whose father sought the cause of his death without reprieve, the scale on which Maol Ciarain was mourned became a standard measurement for others' unmitigated grief.[147] In 1689, an elegy to a victim of Killiecrankie employs the same allusion in its opening lines, which declare:

> Och! a's och! gur mi 'n t-Oisian
> 'S mi mar choslas Maol-chiarain
> Tha mo chridh' air a' dhochnadh
> Mar gun gòirtaicheadh sgian e;
> Air a lìonadh do thùrsadh.

> *Alas, and alas! I am like Oiséan, / And like Maol Ciarain; / My heart is wounded / As if a knife had pierced it, / Overwhelmed by grieving you.*[148]

The poet, another widow and another MacDonald of Keppoch, whose identity is otherwise uncertain,[149] is alleged by McLagan to have lost her father and two of her brothers on the field that day, in addition to her husband:

> Ge b' e chuir orm an umhail
> Mi bhi dubhach mu d' dhéibhinn,
> Cha d' fhios iad mo ghalar,
> 'S cha mho dh' fhairich iad fhéin e;
> Bean gun bhrathair gun athair
> Gun fhear-tighe gun chéile,
> Gun aon solas foi 'n chruinne
> Mur duine bheir déirc dhomh.

Whoever took heed of me, / Distressed on your behalf, / They did not know my malady / And had not felt its grip themselves; / A woman lacking brother, lacking father, / Without either husband or friend, / Without one comfort in all the world, / Save someone should give me alms.[150]

The elegy, apparently the only extant female-voiced response to Killiecrankie, heralded a century of impassioned lament and a century of turbulent politics, whose most significant events were observed, critiqued, rejoiced at, and regretted by many other Gaelic women's words. The canon of their poems that began to form in the eighteenth century was not inclusive and, inevitably, many items have been lost, while others that belong to the 1700s emerge in later centuries instead. While its longer-term sustainability became despaired of, even by those whose pioneering collections it had benefitted most, the oral tradition continued to ensure their performance and survival.[151]

In memoriam Professor Richard Sharpe (1954–2020)

Acknowledgements

I am indebted to Michel Byrne and Ruairidh Maciver for sharing their research on the poetry of Mairearad Ghriogarach and Anna Ghobha, and for providing a selection of in-progress translations. Unattributed translations (and remaining errors) are my own, with many thanks to Kathleen Reddy, Priscilla Scott, Duncan Sneddon, and Aonghas MacCoinnich for assistance; and to Sìm Innes, Geraldine Parsons, Thomas Clancy, Martin MacGregor, Alasdair Whyte, Anne Macleod Hill, Peadar Ó Muircheartaigh, Domhnall Uilleam Stiùbhart, Michael Newton, Jamie Kelly, and Elina Koristashevskaya. The editors' support and patience is acknowledged with gratitude.

CHAPTER TWELVE

Common Sense Philosophy and Sentimental Fiction: Eighteenth-Century Scottish Women Novelists

JoEllen DeLucia

In an era when British women novelists were out-publishing their male contemporaries, Scottish women contributed relatively little to this outpouring of female-authored fiction.[1] This imbalance registers in one of the more risible passages of the eighteenth-century Scottish writer Jean Marishall's (fl. 1765–1788) memoir, *A Series of Letters* (1789):

> My mother, who had a great share of common sense and a good heart, was not much given to reading, nor do I believe at that time had ever heard of a female author in her life. On reading my letter, she burst into tears concluding that I had lost my senses. My father, brother, and sister had the greatest difficulty in the world to compose her; assuring her there was not a single word in the epistle which in the least indicated insanity. A lady coming in was immediately shown the letter; and she corroborated a circumstance which my brother and sister had in vain endeavoured to make my mother believe, viz. that there was nothing more common in England than ladies writing novels.[2]

Scottish women novelists, who like Marishall did write novels in the late eighteenth and early nineteenth centuries, fit awkwardly within British women's literary history. In an era dominated by melancholy sentimental fiction, writers such as Marishall, Elizabeth Hamilton (1756?–1816), and Mary Brunton (1778–1818) were critical of the sentimental tradition, often incorporating humour and satiric elements alongside the melancholy emotions that characterise much fiction from the period. Critics have understood sentimental fiction as primarily a commercial form that through formulaic plots, intertexuality, and pastiche reworked the 'virtue in distress' narrative as a means of satisfying the desires of female consumers and codifying the morality of the emerging bourgeoisie. Many of the best-known Scottish novels adapt the 'virtue in distress' plot made famous by Samuel Richardson and reproduced by countless imitators, but they also ridicule the form. They trade in laughter and derision instead of tears.

The earliest of the Scottish novels surveyed in this essay, Marishall's *The History of Miss Clarinda Cathcart, and Miss Fanny Renton* (1765), exemplifies many of these traits. Although the author claims in her memoir that it was a 'better novel' than the 'nonsense' typically found in circulating libraries,[3] she adopted the formulaic plot of the sentimental fictions that flooded the print market and published with the fashionable London circulating library proprietor John Noble. At the same time, her satiric heroine and direct attacks on sentimental fiction make the novel a parody instead of a sincere engagement with the genre. *Clarinda Cathcart*'s use of ridicule creates a foundation for understanding later novels by Scottish women, such as Mary Brunton's *Self-Control* (1811) and Elizabeth Hamilton's *Memoirs of Female Philosophers* (1800). Like Marishall, Brunton and Hamilton borrow heavily from sentimental fiction but use satire and ridicule to maintain distance from the genre's emotions and formulaic plots.

The critique of tearful affects mounted by these Scottish novelists seems particularly important if we understand the sentimental novel as developing in a fictional register the Scottish Enlightenment's theories of sympathy and sentiment, as historians and literary critics such as G. J. Barker-Benfield and Claudia Johnson have argued.[4] After all, these novelists' connections to the intellectual culture of the Scottish Enlightenment are much more direct than that of their English contemporaries: the subscription list of Jean Marishall's play *Sir Harry Gaylove, or Comedy in Embryo* (1772) includes David Hume (1711–1776), Adam Smith (c. 1723–1790), Adam Ferguson (1723–1816), Thomas Blacklock (1721–1791) (who also wrote the play's prologue), James Beattie (1735–1803), Lord Kames (1696–1782), and Thomas Reid (1710–1796); Mary Brunton's husband was a professor of Oriental Languages at the University of Edinburgh, and they were known to study philosophy and history together, particularly the works of Thomas Reid and William Robertson (1721–1793); and Elizabeth Hamilton's correspondence with the Common Sense philosopher Dugald Stewart (1753–1828) and her study of Lord Kames and Reid has been well-documented by scholars.[5] These novelists' close ties to Scottish intellectual culture make their investment in satirising or reforming the sentimental novel significant for both literary historians and those interested, more generally, in the gender dynamics of the Scottish Enlightenment. They expand our understanding of the emotional register of sentimental culture, drawing attention to ludicrous sentiments, particularly discussions of ridicule and absurdity in the work of Kames, James Beattie, and Thomas Reid. Scottish women writers' turn to ridicule provides a new means of gauging the aesthetic and social value of comic distance and laughter as opposed to the tearful attachments that dominate current understandings of the sentimental novel and Scottish moral philosophy; finally, the comic vantage they provide on the 'virtue in distress' plot also raises questions about women writers' contributions to cultural debates about women's social and legal vulnerability.

Ridicule as a Moral Sentiment

Importantly, Marshall and her successors' reliance on ridicule as a moral corrective shifts attention away from the theories of sentiment and sympathy developed by David Hume and Adam Smith and towards Lord Kames's exploration of ridicule in his rhetorical theory and James Beattie and Thomas Reid's common sense defense of ridicule as both a useful emotion and a tool of moral judgement. As Mark Towsey argues, Thomas Reid's common sense philosophy and its critique of Hume's scepticism made him popular with Scottish male and female readers who were looking to reconcile their faith with contemporary philosophy and natural science. Reid's common sense philosophy may have particularly appealed to women, not only because it was compatible with conventional ideas about religion, but also because it did not require specialised training or knowledge. Reid positioned ridicule as a means of critiquing Hume's scepticism in his *Essays on the Intellectual Powers of Man* (1785),[6] but his ideas about humour's philosophical application circulated in lectures throughout his teaching career, which began in the 1750s, and were popularised in James Beattie's *Essay on Truth* (1771). Beattie's work featured 'scathing[ly] sarcastic' attacks on Hume and was enthusiastically embraced by Scottish readers.[7] In fact, Towsey argues that many Scottish female readers only knew Hume through their reading of Beattie.[8] Notably, Reid also influenced Beattie's defense of humour's social utility in his *An Essay on Laughter and Ludicrous Composition* (1779).

In Reid's *Essays*, he describes the first principles or innate moral ideas that separated his approach from Hume's scepticism as 'purely natural, and therefore common to the learned, and the unlearned; to the trained, and the untrained'.[9] He goes on to describe these first principles as bestowed by the 'author of nature' or 'Supreme Being' and dependent on the 'ripeness of understanding and the freedom from prejudice, but nothing else'.[10] Reid's definition of common sense recalls Marshall's own description of her mother as 'not much given to reading', but having 'a great share of common sense and a good heart'. Reid's direct influence can also be seen in the advice she gives her nephew in her *Series of Letters*. She encourages him to embrace 'common sense' and 'good principles' in order to guard against a 'mind [...] staggered with doubts'.[11] In an explicit attack on Hume, she argues that a man of good and common sense will never 'become a slave to his passions'.[12] In common sense philosophy, as in Marshall's writing, ridicule marks deviations from the first principles as absurd. Reid magnifies ridicule's importance by linking it directly to his first principles and using it to create a moral foundation for his philosophy, circumventing the uncertainties introduced by sceptics such as Hume. According to Reid, the sentiment of ridicule combines both judgement and sensation. His definition cites Anthony Ashley Cooper, Lord Shaftesbury's *Sensus Communis; An Essay on the Freedom of Wit and Humour, in a Letter to a Friend* (1709) and develops Shaftesbury's idea that ridicule can be used to appeal to common sense and counteract what Reid understands as the absurdities that scepticism introduces.[13] He goes on to say that 'opinions which contradict first principles are distinguished from other errors by this; that they are not only false, but absurd: And, to discountenance absurdity, Nature hath given us a particular emotion, to wit, that of ridicule, which seems intended for this very purpose of putting out of countenance what is absurd, either in opinion or practice'.[14] Reid describes ridicule as a 'weapon' that 'when properly applied, cuts with as keen an edge as argument'.[15]

Before the publication of Reid's *Essays*, Beattie and Kames were also exploring ludicrous sentiments and their social function. In his *Essay on Laughter*, Beattie positions laughter as a tool of moral judgement; he begins his essay by separating 'sentimental laughter' from 'animal laughter', writing:

> the one always proceeds from a sentiment or emotion, excited in the mind, in consequence of certain objects or ideas being presented to it, of which emotion we may be conscious even when we suppress laughter;— the other arises, not from any sentiment, or perception of ludicrous ideas, but from some bodily feeling, or sudden impulse, on what is called the animal spirits, proceeding, or seeming to proceed from the operation of causes purely material.[16]

According to Beattie, sentimental as opposed to animal laughter functions to process and identify disorder and resolve, what he calls 'incongruous combination[s]' of objects and ideas.[17] Like Reid, Beattie saw ridicule as a means of registering 'moral disapprobation'.[18] Although he warns against applying humour to serious crimes and vices, he claims that 'Our follies, and vices of less enormity, may [...] be exhibited in very laughable colours; and if we can be prevailed upon to see them in a ridiculous light, that is, both to laugh at and to despise them, our reformation may be presumed to be in some forwardness: and hence the utility of ridicule, as an instrument of moral culture'.[19] Kames, whose extensive correspondence with Reid has been recognised as mutually influencing the development of both writers' ideas, shares Reid and Beattie's sense of laughter as reforming objects, circumstances, or ideas that are 'out of rule' or improper.[20] In his *Elements of Criticism* (1762), he describes ridicule and the laughter it inspires as 'unbending the mind'.[21] A complex sentiment, ridicule is both 'mirthful and contemptible', a feeling in which 'the pleasant emotion of laughter [...] is blended with the painful emotion of contempt; and the mixed emotion is termed the emotion of ridicule. The pain a ridiculous object gives me, is resented and punished by a laugh of derision.'[22] Although there are differences in their approaches, all three philosophers saw ridicule as producing contempt for depraved ideas and immoral behaviours, policing the boundaries of 'moral culture', and discrediting ideas and actions that encourage moral uncertainty.

Putting the fiction of Marshall, Brunton, and Hamilton in dialogue with Scottish Enlightenment accounts of ridicule complicates literary scholars' understanding of the Age of Sentiment. The emotion of ridicule has received little attention because, as Giovanni Grandi argues, Reid and also Kames (and to this I would add Beattie and other members of Reid's Aberdeen circle, including George Campbell [1719–1796] and Alexander Gerard [1728–1795]) were 'unique' amongst their Scottish peers in understanding ridicule and humour, more generally, as philosophically useful.[23] Although the specific ways in which they understood laughter and ridicule were often quite different, they all saw laughter as resolving moral contradictions, helping to maintain social order – guarding against the disorder associated with scepticism. Scottish readers' and writers' turn to ridicule provides an additional vantage on Simon Dickie's recent work, which has invited eighteenth-century scholars to return to comic literature as a way of complicating overly polite depictions of the eighteenth century created in part by scholars' intense focus on the sentimental novel at the expense of other forms.[24] Reid's belief in the moral function of ridicule and Scottish women novelists' application of ludicrous sentiments in their fiction expands the emotional register of the period and our understanding of the sentimental novel, 'unbending', to borrow from Kames, the genre.

Absurdity and the Sentimental Novel

When literary historians do comment on novels by Scottish women, they often note their peculiar relationship to other fiction of the period. Claire Grogan has described Elizabeth Hamilton's work as employing 'familiar genres in unfamiliar ways' and, in a discussion of the 'hybridity' of Brunton's *Self-Control*, Anthony Mandal dubs it a 'brilliant mess, all things and no-thing'.[25] In an essay surveying Brunton, Hamilton, Jane Porter (1776–1850), and Susan Ferrier (1782–1854), Carol Anderson and Aileen M. Riddell describe Scottish women novelists as 'anti-Romantic', reading Ferrier and Brunton's turn to satire as a possible reaction to Scotland's depiction as a 'land of Romance' in much period fiction.[26] However, when read in the context of eighteenth-century Scottish intellectual culture, a context that emphasises fiction's interactions with Scottish theories of sentiment, the generic instability associated with Hamilton's and Brunton's works gestures toward the influence of common sense philosophy on the sentimental tradition. The satiric framework created around these sentimental fictions works to tame the immoral elements of the sentimental plot, which is structured by motifs inherited from an earlier romance tradition. In these Scottish novels, the duelling suitors, abductions, ravishments, and hyper-sensitive heroines the genre inherits from romance become ludicrous and absurd. The satiric approach of these novelists points up the more ridiculous elements of this commercial form; at the same time, humour works to dismiss or relegate to the anachronistic world of romance sentimental fiction's public and well-documented considerations of rape and the very real legal and social vulnerability of women.[27]

Like many other sentimental fictions, Marshall's epistolary *Clarinda Cathcart* borrows the form and the plot of Samuel Richardson's (1689–1761) *Pamela; or, Virtue Rewarded* (1740) and *Clarissa; or, The History of a Young Lady* (1748). Yet, the comic effect she creates through borrowed plot elements and direct references to Richardson creates an awkward distance between her novel and the sentimental tradition. Early on in a letter to her friend, Clarinda embraces the designation 'tragi-comic epistle' for her letter-writing style,[28] adapting an absurd tone and mixing incongruous sentiments, as common sense philosophers suggest, to register her disapproval of the improbable events that structure the sentimental plot in which she eventually finds herself immersed. In addition, she demonstrates contempt for the sentimental novel by mocking her story's commercial potential, the unoriginality of her ideas, and even the woman writer's desire for publicity and fame.[29] In one letter she suggests to a friend that 'some girl, who is wiser than the rest, with a little addition of her own, will dispose of them to a bookseller';[30] she tells another friend that she will 'expect to see it advertised, The History of Miss Clarinda Cathcart, and Miss Fanny Renton' and accuses the same friend jokingly of 'think[ing] her ambitious of such a task'.[31] Clarinda spends the first volume contrasting her more plausible boredom in the country with the ridiculous adventures of other sentimental heroines; however, the second volume's plot begins to mirror that of the novels Clarinda both imitates and mocks. She finds herself improbably caught between two suitors, Fanny's brother, the kind and admirable Sir Harry Renton, and the rakish Lord Darnly. In describing her situation, Clarinda employs the paradox of Buridan's ass, describing herself as an 'ass between two bundles of hay'.[32] Because the novel has already established the superiority of Harry Renton to Lord Darnly, the paradox is falsely applied and might best be understood as mocking sentimental novels that establish a false equivalence between the incongruous figures of the reformed rake and the more virtuous and also likeable suitors encountered by their heroines. This impression is compounded when, finding herself unable to write an appropriate response to either suitor, Clarinda uses sentimental tropes to ridicule her indecision. She writes herself and her suitors into contemporary fiction, playfully imagining Sir Harry taking 'the lover's leap' and Lord Darnly 'drown[ing] himself', leaving her to flee to a 'huge rock at the sea-side', which commands a view of 'the gentlemen's seats for many miles around'.[33] Once on this precipice, she imagines herself as a heroine, using the third-person to describe a 'disconsolate Clarinda', who 'beats her breast' and 'plunges headlong into the sea'.[34] Although none of this happens, right after she formally and without any real qualms accepts Sir Harry's proposal, Lord Darnly, taking a page from sentimental fiction himself, hires someone to stop her carriage and abducts Clarinda and a companion. Disconcertingly, Clarinda takes the same satiric approach to her capture as she did to her courtship. Instead of being overcome by fear or sadness at the damage her abduction might do to her reputation, she uses humour to maintain a distance between herself and her dangerous circumstances, all the while trying to escape and undermine the conventional sentimental plot that now literally imprisons her.

Once her reality and the plot of sentimental fiction converge, she moves from mocking sentimental fiction as incompatible with her lived reality to demonstrating the absurdity of sentimental heroines' responses to their dangerous circumstances. She parodies the heroines' responses as a means of distancing herself from her increasingly perilous narrative. She navigates the 'virtue in distress' plot by using what she has learned reading sentimental fiction to avoid its traps and escape Darnly without damage to her person or reputation, maintaining moral order by transforming the immoral acts she experiences into bad fiction. When Darnly first offers her food, she writes with a wink to popular fiction, 'I was too deep read in novels, Nancy, to venture to take any of his wine'.[35] When he removes her to a remote country seat, she describes 'a middle-aged, ugly looking woman' meeting them at the door, and she imagines her as a Richardsonian 'Miss Jewkes, I suppose' – a characterisation that discredits Darnly's assistant, transforming her into a parody of her fictional counterpart.[36] After days under Darnly's control, she begins to lose faith in her difference from her fictional counterparts and decides to stop resisting and behave in the desperate, unreasonable, and ridiculous ways fiction mandates:

> I began to think, Nancy, I was destined for a heroine, and wanted of all things, to act up to the character. I could think of no scheme of my own invention, likely to relieve us. At last I fixed on one that had succeeded with a sister in romance, I forget whom—I rummaged in my pocket and found a blank cover; so taking out my pencil, I wrote the following words, without telling Betsy what I meant, till it was finished.[37]

Not surprisingly, this secret message fails, reinforcing the futility and ludicrousness of sentimental strategies. Fortunately, soon after, she is rescued by a friend of the Renton family. She goes on to marry Sir Harry without equivocation and bizarrely accepts an apology from Lord Darnly who admits that if she had not been rescued his 'passion would have made [him] force what [he] could not gain by persuasion'.[38] In this final moment, it appears that the comic distance she maintained from her own abduction and near-rape enables her to countenance Lord Darnly's reappearance in her social circle and his apology for the 'trifling misfortune' they shared.[39] Her 'tragic-comic' frame allows him to be a ridiculous sentimental villain instead of a real rapist. Humour functions here to turn the violent acts and ludicrous circumstances that disrupt Clarinda's reality into immoral fictions that can be tolerated because they are absurd and therefore laughable – plots to which only heroines in silly sentimental fictions are vulnerable. Marshall's Scottish successors borrowed from her critique of sentimental fiction and also turned in their different ways to ridicule in order to maintain moral order and transform unpalatable violence, particularly violence against women, into absurd and improbable fictions.

Although not as consistently satirical as Marshall's novel, the title of Mary Brunton's *Self-Control* acts as a tongue-in-cheek rejoinder to the tearful affections of popular fiction. Far from overflowing with emotion, its heroine Laura Montreville forcefully restrains her laughter and her tears, turning instead to self-denial and self-harm, whether it be through repressing her desire for the rakish Colonel Hargrave or denying herself food in London so her sick father can eat. Ridicule in *Self-Control* is displaced onto the third-person narrator, who turns the heroine into an object of ridicule, mocking Laura's earnestness and restraint. Despite Laura's differences from the typically effusive sentimental heroine, her experiences (like Clarinda's before her) are structured by a standard sentimental plot. Laura finds herself caught between two suitors, who like Lord Darnly and Sir Harry seem so dissimilar that Laura's internal conflict becomes laughable: the dangerous and violent Colonel Hargrave and the gentle and honorable Montague De Courcy. Like Clarinda, Laura is also abducted and nearly raped by Hargrave; at the end of the novel, Hargrave kidnaps her and removes her to the wilds of Quebec. Trapped in a remote cabin, Laura only barely escapes his aggressions by stealing away in a canoe and, miraculously, making her way back to Scotland. Despite the similar plots, in stark contrast to Marshall's novel, Hargrave and De Courcy are more avid novel readers than Laura. In fact, Colonel Hargrave's flaws, which include duelling, criminal conversation with his friends' wives, and the repeated seduction and rape of lower-class women, are attributed to his education by fiction. When he was a child, Hargrave's mother discovered that he had a 'turn for reading' and she provided him with an endless supply of novels.[40] As Brunton writes,

> it was very easy to supply the young man with romances, poetry, and plays; and it was pleasing to mistake their intoxicating effect for the bursts of mental vigour. A taste for works of fiction, once firmly established, never after yielded to the attractions of sober truth; and, though his knowledge of history was neither accurate nor extensive, Hargrave could

boast of an intimate acquaintance with all the plays, with almost all the poetry, and as far as it is attainable by human diligence, with all the myriads of romances in his mother tongue.[41]

Although provided with a much sounder education than his rival, De Courcy, at one point, worries that Laura will never be able to overcome her first attachment to Hargrave and learn to love him. In response, his sensible mother quips, 'from what Romance have you learned that sentiment?'.[42] Compared with her suitors, Laura is woefully underread. When a friend asks her to name her favourite character from popular fiction, Laura admits that her 'acquaintance with these accomplished personages is so limited that I can scarcely venture to decide; but, I believe, I prefer the hero of Miss Porter's new publication – Thaddeus of Warsaw'.[43] Choosing a more sober historical fiction – and one by a fellow Scotswoman no less – Laura claims to admire Jane Porter's novel because its hero is 'inflexibly upright'.[44] Whereas fiction leads Hargrave to violate moral and social codes and leads De Courcy to expect Laura to behave unreasonably, the Scottish fiction selected by Laura models maintaining 'uprightness' at all costs.

Laura's own uprightness and restraint function to reform sentimental fiction and her suitors, whose characters have been distorted by their reading. Her inversion of the gendered roles assigned by the sentimental formula, in which typical heroines have an excess of feeling, appear in Colonel Hargrave's repeated description of her as cold and tyrannical. At the same time, her masculine virtues of fortitude and self-command, a stoicism that recalls Porter's Thaddeus, become key to her attractiveness, and this is even reflected in her physiognomy. Struck by the combination of her Roman and masculine facial features, De Courcy works to reconcile her 'maiden loveliness' to her complete lack of 'sensual' characteristics (74).[45] In one of the more comical pieces of dialogue, he comments to his mother 'had Lavater seen her, he could scarcely believe her human'.[46] Even the narrator enjoys poking fun at Laura's failure to conform to the sentimental mode. A talented artist, Laura paints classical figures throughout the novel. When confronted with a need to represent pleasure, she 'could not portray what she would have shrunk from beholding – a female voluptuary […] after all her toil, even the form of Pleasure came sober and matronly from the hand of Laura'.[47] Later in the novel, after De Courcy refuses to invite Hargrave to his home, Laura compliments him, commenting 'it is not for friends of Virtue to remove the ancient Landmarks'.[48] The narrator comments, 'Though this was one of the stalest pieces of morality that ever De Courcy had heard Laura utter, he could scarcely refrain from repaying it by clasping her to his heart'.[49] Laura's stoic morality stands in stark contrast to the tears and frequent fainting fits of her fictional counterparts. The narrator ridicules Laura's behaviour because it is incongruous within the context of sentimental fiction; instead of deviating from the formula by laughing, as her predecessor Clarinda did, in the face of abduction and near-rape, Laura refuses to succumb to emotion and abandon her moral principles, even incredibly (and somewhat ridiculously) managing to make her way back from Quebec to Scotland. Her common sense and self-control, which is often so severe as to be laughable, distances her from sentimental fiction, forcing the reader to question the incompatibility of the novel's heroine with the ridiculous circumstances created by her suitors' imitation of immoral sentimental fictions.

Relying on ridicule as a tool for reform, Elizabeth Hamilton's *Memoirs of Modern Philosophers* aligns direct criticism of sentimental fiction with the common sense critique of sceptical philosophy, making explicit the connections between the two that are largely implied in Brunton and Marshall's novels. Interestingly, Hamilton transforms Reid and Beattie's critique of Humean scepticism into an attack on William Godwin's (1756–1836) atheism and associated vision of political anarchy. She targets Godwin, who in the novel is personified by the philosopher and avowed atheist Mr Myope. The 'virtue in distress' plot, which she borrows from sentimental fiction, structures her attack on Godwin's scepticism and his notorious *An Enquiry Concerning Political Justice* (1793). The two heroines of the novel, Bridgetina Botherim (Hamilton's cruel send-up of Mary Hays) and Julia Delmond, are ruined by a steady diet of sentimental fiction and new philosophy. Bridgetina has read 'every book in the circulating library' and describes herself as never 'tak[ing] the trouble of going through all the dry stuff [...] history and travels, sermons and matters of fact? I have a better taste! You know very well I never read anything but novels and metaphysics'.[50] Influenced by a poorly educated father, Julia's failures are traced to her father's predilection for 'volumes of romances' and the 'works of many free-thinking philosophers'.[51] Their consumption of Godwin's sceptical philosophy and popular sentimental fiction lead both Bridgetina and Julia to renounce filial duty and gratitude. When Julia meets Vallaton, the man who later ruins her, she falls in love with his rigid adherence to the new philosophy and abandons her flawed but loving father. Vallaton, a thief and murderer who has changed identities several times, makes a living writing defences of the new philosophy, which provides him with a series of absurd justifications for his immoral behaviour. Julia's reading of sentimental fiction and romance also leads her to excuse some of his more extraordinary behaviours. She creates a false history for him, one that assigns him an unlikely aristocratic parentage, based on 'her remembrance [of] all the similar events in her most favourite novels; in these instructive books the discovery of the hero's parents had always appeared to her a catastrophe particularly interesting, and the idea that she should now have it in her power, not only to witness, but to be a principal actor in so tender a scene, filled her heart with extacy'.[52] Conversely, when Julia receives a proposal from another and more respectable suitor, she immediately and without any real cause sees him as Richardson's Solmes, leaving her vulnerable to abduction by the corrupt Vallaton.

Sentimental fiction also inspires Bridgetina to concoct a love story for her and the sensible Henry Sydney, who remains decidedly insensible to her charms. After accosting Henry in public with her ungovernable passion, she finds that he has left the room in embarrassment and anger. Bridgetina responds with a series of delusional questions, 'Was his sensibility too great to bear that sad—sad scene of separation? It was not his own feelings but mine, of which he was thus tender. Ah! The delightful excess of morbid sensibility!'[53] Later in the novel she reads to him a prepared speech intended to entice him to abandon social conventions and run away with her to Africa. The novel does not include the speech, but it lists the philosophical concepts she alludes to and these include, 'Moral sensibility, thinking sensibility, importunate sensibility, mental sensation [...] congenial sympathy, congenial sentiment [...] melancholy emotions [and] frenzied emotions'.[54] This time Henry not only fails to 'acknowledge the force of her arguments' but also 'laugh[s] at their absurdity'[55] – a response that would surely have been approved of by Reid and his common sense school. Bridgetina's speech warrants one of the most extensive footnotes in the novel. The note might have listed many of the popular philosophical treatises of the age, works by Hume, Smith, Rousseau, and even Godwin in his later work; however, Hamilton instead associates these concepts with gothic and sentimental fiction:

> for the benefit of Novel-writers.—We here generously present the fair manufacturers in this line with a set of phrases, which if carefully mixed up with a handful of story, a pretty quantity of moonshine, an old house of any kind, so that it be in sufficient decay, and well tenanted with bats

and owls, and two or three ghosts, will make a couple of very neat volumes. Or should the sentimental be preferred to the descriptive, it is only leaving out the ghosts, bats, owls, and moonlight, and the above phrases will season any tender tale to taste.[56]

The novel substitutes Bridgetina's speech with a catalogue of popular philosophical variants of feeling and sentiment and an accompanying footnote on popular fiction, aligning sentimental and gothic plots with the heightened emotional states studied by eighteenth-century moral philosophers. Importantly, the maintenance of Bridgetina's delusions depend upon her inability to laugh at herself or sense others laughing at her, making her immune to the type of reform and shame Reid believed laughter initiated in the wrongdoer. Earlier in the novel, she says to Julia, 'I do not care for wit and humour […] they may serve to amuse the vulgar, but you know they are quite exploded by the new philosophy. […] The energies of philosophical authors are all expanded in gloomy masses of tenebrific shade. The investigators of the *mind* never condescend to make their readers laugh'.[57] Ultimately, not only does Hamilton make Bridgetina ridiculous, but she links her ridiculousness and her own lack of humour to her reading and subsequent misapplication of sentimental fiction and sceptical philosophy to the world.

Despite Hamilton, Brunton, and Marshall's contributions to Scottish Enlightenment culture and sentimental fiction, their turn to satire and ridicule has most often been read, if read at all, in relationship to Jane Austen. These novels clearly recall *Northanger Abbey* (1803/1817), and Austen's known reading of and admiration for Mary Brunton's work is one of the reasons we have modern editions of *Self-Control*.[58] This approach has created a position for these writers within histories of women's writing,[59] but only as a footnote in studies of Austen. It does not aid our understanding of them as active participants in Scottish intellectual culture. In teasing out the conversations between their novels and Scottish common sense philosophy, this essay hopes to open up a new line of inquiry that both acknowledges the impact of common sense philosophy on sentimental fiction and returns humour to its rightful place as an important sentiment in late eighteenth-century women's fiction. Significantly, humour provides a barrier between the novels' heroines and the perils of their sentimental plots. Marshall uses humour to insulate her heroine from her dangerous circumstances, making her appear less vulnerable than she might have otherwise; at the same time, Clarinda's flippant attitude toward her near-assault unsettles our affective expectations. Similarly, humour in Brunton drives a wedge between the stoic heroine and her dangerously passionate and overly sensitive suitors, but the narrator's critical commentary often leaves the reader wondering if they should laugh or cry at Laura's horrible, yet frequently ridiculous, circumstances. In Hamilton's work, humour prevents readers from sympathising with the plights of the main characters and also functions to undermine female philosophers such as Mary Hays and, in passages I have not had space to consider, align her critique of the new philosophy with sickeningly racist depictions of African cultures. By considering these Scottish novelists' defence of ridicule as both aesthetically and philosophically productive, we complicate our understanding of sentimental culture and, at the same time, add uglier and less sympathetic feelings to our histories of eighteenth-century women's writing.

CHAPTER THIRTEEN

Scottish Enlightenment Inquiry in Gaelic Poetry: 'Air Fàsachadh na Gàidhealtachd Albannaich'

Sìm Innes

The extent to which Scotland's eighteenth-century Gaelic poets and intellectuals engaged with Scottish Enlightenment inquiry is an ongoing debate. It has been claimed, rather curiously, that 'Gaelic speakers played almost no part in the Scottish Enlightenment'.[1] On the other hand, Robert Crawford notes that 'Gaelic culture both fed and was fed by the Scottish Enlightenment'.[2] Richard Sher points out that 'the authors of the Scottish Enlightenment came from virtually every part of Scotland, including a surprisingly large number from the Highlands'.[3] Donald Meek has argued that the Gaelic literary activities of men such as Dùghall Bochanan (Dugald Buchanan, 1716–68) should be considered 'in the context of the Scottish Enlightenment'.[4] There has also been some mention of the poet Alasdair mac Mhaighstir Alasdair (Alexander MacDonald, c. 1695–c. 1770) as 'bard of the Gaelic Enlightenment'.[5] The Reverend John Walker (1731–1803) noted that the Highlands were 'best defined by the boundary of the Gaelic language', and at the time the area was 'presumed to be considerably more than one-third, and to constitute perhaps nearer one-half of the whole kingdom'.[6] When combined with parish surveys this means that in the middle of the eighteenth century the Gaelic-speaking Highlands contained somewhere between a fifth and a quarter of the Scottish population.[7] Yet the involvement of the eighteenth-century Gaelic literati in a 'Gaelic Enlightenment' and their engagement with the wider Scottish Enlightenment are both under-researched topics.[8]

In this chapter, an investigation of one anonymous Gaelic poem from the manuscript collection of the Reverend James McLagan (Seumas MacLathagain, 1728–1805) will allow for further insight into Highland literary engagement with Scottish Enlightenment thinking.[9] The McLagan collection is made up of 250 discrete paper manuscripts.[10] McLagan, Gaelic-speaking chaplain to the Black Watch (the 42nd Regiment of Foot) and subsequently minister at Blair Atholl, was educated at the University of St Andrews.[11] A combination of personal fieldwork collection and items received in correspondence from a network of other gentleman scholars has resulted in a collection of around 630 items, mostly Gaelic songs and poetry.[12] McLagan claimed to have been collecting since his pre-1750s school days, and the manuscripts themselves tell us that this was a life-long endeavour, with some items dated to as late as 1803.[13] McLagan's corpus seems to have been a vital source for the Gillies collection of Gaelic poetry, published in Perth in 1786.[14]

The poem to be discussed in the present chapter is given the title 'Air Fàsachadh na Gàidhealtachd Albannaich' ('On the Desolation of the Scottish Highlands') and has 'A Bheinn-neamhais ard nan neul' ('O towering Ben Nevis of the clouds') as its first line.[15] I will refer to it as the 'Ben Nevis poem' henceforth. It is one of only four poems that together constitute manuscript 210 of the McLagan collection. Each of the four poems provides comment on the impact of social, cultural, and economic change on the eighteenth-century Highlands.[16] Our poem takes us on a tour of Highland sites known for martial and poetic history, from a starting point at Ben Nevis. The first point of call is nearby Inverlochy Castle, 'a lùchairt uaigneach Inbhir Lòchaidh, is bristeach sian-bhuailte do bhalla!' ('O solitary courtyard of Inverlochy, your wall is brittle and weather-beaten').[17] The poem is, thus, a lament asking for meditation on the ruins of each site and its associated people. From Inverlochy we stay in Lochaber and take in Keppoch, Glengarry and Loch Arkaig before heading south to Glencoe. From Glencoe we go further south, into Argyll, to visit Dùn Mac Sniachan, Dunstaffnage, Dunollie and Finlaggan. In doing so, we will see that the poem arguably extends the purported positive aspects of pre-commercial society (such as the hunter stage, to be discussed in more detail below) into the eighteenth century. A close reading of the poem demonstrates an intellectual standpoint ready to embrace the positive aspects of representations of the Highlands as a barbarous society. Yet it also rejects the ubiquitous notion that the Highlands were free from the corrosive impact of luxury. The poem appears at once rooted in the real-life experience of improvement and its theoretical underpinning from Scottish Enlightenment writings. Before focusing on the presentation of luxury, an examination of the verse on Dùn Mac Sniachan will allow us to situate the poem within an environment of cutting-edge scholarly endeavour.

The poem's previous editor and translator noted that the verse on Dùn Mac Sniachan had caused some difficulty.[18] It is hoped that the emendations suggested here will bring further clarity. This verse, on Dùn Mac Sniachan, at Benderloch on Ardmucknish Bay, demonstrates the poem's indebtedness to textual sources. By the eighteenth century Dùn Mac Sniachan had come to be identified with the ancient lost Scottish city of Beregonium.[19] Beregonium was described by Hector Boece in his *Scotorum Historiae a Prima Gentis Origine* (Paris, 1527), and in Bellenden's Scots translation of Boece, *Hystory and Croniklis of Scotland* (Edinburgh, 1537), as a crucial royal palace in Scotland's history.[20] In these sixteenth-century histories the exact location of Beregonium was not clearly described. The Boece/Bellenden edition notes of King Fergus:

Castelum condidit Berogomum, ubi ius dici voluit in Louquhabria ad Albionis plagam occidentalem in Hebridum insularum prospectu, ut illuc et insulani et Albiani Scoti facilius ad iurisdictionem iustitiaeque administrationem coirent.

Efter this, he beildit the castel of Berigone in Lochquhaber. This castell standis in the west part of Scotland, fornent the Ilis; quhare he exercit his lawis to that fine, that his pepil micht be drawin their the more esaly, for exercitioun of justice.[21]

However, in Boece and Bellenden the exact location of Beregonium in relation to Inverlochy and Evonium/Dunstaffnage is somewhat unclear since all three are described as being in close proximity.[22] By the eighteenth century the location of Beregonium had settled down and various writers commented on its link to Dùn Mac Sniachan. Thomas Pennant's (1726–1798) *Tour in Scotland, 1772* (1774, 1776) has, 'A mile from Connel, near the shore, is *Dun-mac-Sniochain*, the ancient Beregonium, or *Berogomum*. The foundation of this city, as it is called, is attributed, by *Apocryphal* history, to Fergus II'.[23] In the 1790s the report on the united parishes of Ardchattan and Muckairn by the Reverend Ludovick Grant for Sir John Sinclair of Ulbster's (1754–1836) *Statistical Account of Scotland* stated, 'in this district stood the famous city of Beregonium, it was situated between two hills, one called Dun MacSnichan, "the hill of Snachan's son", and the other, much superior in height, is named Dun bhaile an righ, "the hill of the king's town"'.[24] The relevant verse of the Ben Nevis poem appears in the McLagan manuscript as follows below. It is accompanied by a new suggested translation. The significance of a number of the new translation choices will be discussed in some detail.

Diplomatic edition
Dun-mac-sniachain a bha,
Cala nan long o shean,
Ball-tathaich nan ceannuich an alluid
's an d'fhag foi-theine cús d'fhuil-siachraidh
ball-tathaich nan ceannuich an alluid

New translation
Dùn Mac Sniachan as was,
Harbour of ships of old,
Repair of uncouth merchants
in which sub-[terranean] fire
left an overabundance of pumice.

Intriguingly, Bellenden's translation of Boece may provide some insight into the problematic 'ball-tathaich nan ceannuich an alluid'.[25] In Bellenden we read of Inverlochy as having been the 'repair of uncouth marchandis' and there is a separate discussion of Highlanders and 'marchandis of uncouth realms'.[26] We noted above that Inverlochy, Dunstaffnage and Beregonium are linked in Boece. If we were to emend the line to 'Ball-tathaich nan ceannaichean allaidh', it then looks very much like a translation of 'repair of uncouth marchandis'.[27] Bellenden uses 'uncouth' in its Scots-language sense of 'foreign'.[28] If the emendation of 'alluid' to 'allaidh' is accepted then it might suggest a misunderstanding of 'uncouth' (meaning 'foreign') given that, with allaidh, it has been translated as 'savage/wild'. An alternative way to understand the phrase is to see it as containing one or two unusual archaisms. 'An alluid' might otherwise be understood to represent 'anall-ód/a n-allód' ('in ancient times').[29] This phrase, known from poetry, is found in Alasdair mac Mhaighstir Alasdair's *Leabhar a theagasc Ainminnin / A Galick and English Vocabulary* (1741): 'an allod' ('anciently') and thus our poet would have had access to a Scottish source for this literary archaic phrase.[30] It is also feasible, then, that the line, if emended to 'ball-tathaich nan ceannaich' an allod', should be understood as 'repair of merchants in ancient times'. Eighteenth-century dictionaries also give 'ceannaich' as a noun meaning 'strife, contention'.[31] Therefore, if emended to 'ball-tathaich nan ceannaich' an allod', the phrase could also be understood to mean 'hotbed of contentions in ancient times'. The use of archaic vocabulary could be a stylistic choice here, used to match the description of an ancient site. It seems that no matter which of these proposed emendations and translations is preferred, merchants or contentions, they reveal the poet's knowledge of historical writing, in Scots or Latin, on the site of Beregonium.

The fourth line also appears to give us a glimpse into the poet's reading material since it includes a Gaelic word for pumice stone, 'fuil-sìofraith'.[32] This word for pumice also appears, as *'fuilsíofri'*, in Alasdair mac Mhaighstir Alasdair's *Leabhar a theagasc Ainminnin/A Galick and English Vocabulary* (1741).[33] 'Fuil síofraí' would appear to translate literally as 'fairy blood'.[34] Although, used in our poem and by Mac Mhaighstir Alasdair for pumice, it seems that the term is otherwise, as 'fuil sìochaire', known in Scottish Gaelic either for bloodstone (heliotrope) or red crotal lichen.[35] In *A Tour in Scotland* Pennant noted that at the hill of Dùn Mac Sniachan/Beregonium, 'are dug up great quantities of different sorts of pumices, or scoria, of different kinds [...]. The hill is doubtless the work of a volcano'.[36] Tom Furniss has outlined Pennant's pioneering contri-butions, including his writing on Dùn Mac Sniachan, 'to the gradual realization of the extent to which Scotland's landscape had been formed by volcanic activity in the distant past'.[37] The *Statistical Account* report from the 1790s also notes the accumulation of pumice and the 'volcanic appearance' of Dùn Mac Sniachan.[38] Therefore, our Gaelic poet is clearly cognisant of this information about the pumice at Dùn Mac Sniachan and we could conjecture that their source is Pennant, or indeed that Pennant and the poem share a common source. Although the poem is unattributed there is good reason to believe that McLagan himself may be the poet: McLagan and Pennant shared a link to the family of the Stewarts/Stuarts of Killin and Luss; the McLagan manuscripts also contain an English-language prose account 'Of Berigonium' (*sic*), describing eighteenth-century discoveries at Dùn Mac Sniachan, including the pumice.[39]

The poem's use of 'foi-theine' ('sub-fire') as cause of the pumice at Dùn Mac Sniachan/Beregonium might also signal that the poet was aware of contemporaneous scholarly geological debates in Scotland. James Hutton (1726–97) had lectured at the Royal Society of Edinburgh on his *Theory of the Earth* in 1785; the resulting lectures were published in their *Transactions* in 1788, followed by an extended two-volume version published in 1795. In the first version, from the *Transactions* in 1788, Hutton put forward that, 'A volcano is not made on purpose to frighten superstitious people into fits of piety and devotion, nor to overwhelm devoted cities with destruction; a volcano should be considered as a spiracle to the subterranean furnace, in order to prevent the unnecessary elevation of land, and fatal effects of earthquakes'.[40] Hutton comments on known active volcanoes in high mountain ranges before noting, 'It is not meant to allege that, it is only upon the summit of a continent volcanos should appear. Subterraneous fire has sometimes made its appearance in bursting from the bottom of the sea'.[41] Thus, with mention of a 'foi-theine' at Dùn Mac Sniachan the poet communicates his/her awareness of the burgeoning study of Scotland's geological past and present.

Perhaps notable by its absence in the Dùn Mac Sniachan verse, however, is any mention of Ossianic lore. By at least the early nineteenth century the site of Beregonium/Dùn Mac Sniachan had also come to be associated with Selma, Fingal's stronghold in James Macpherson's (Seumas Bàn MacMhuirich, 1736–1736) Ossianic works.[42] As we shall see below this is not the only instance in the Ben Nevis poem of mention of a geographical location associated with Ossian that avoids any reference to that material. It is clear, however, that the use of Beregonium in the poem, in a way that appears to reflect both older writing on its importance and more recent writings on potential volcanic activity at the site, is evidence of a poem grounded in the contemporary intellectual curiosity of the late eighteenth century.

Barbarous Society and Luxury

In lamenting what has been lost, the poem repeatedly returns to the status of Highlanders as hunters, warriors, and poets. These traits as objects of praise have a long history in Gaelic literature.[43] However, this representation is also deeply rooted in eighteenth-century writings of the Scottish Enlightenment. Keppoch is described in the poem as 'Ceapach nam bàrd 's nam fìor laoch' ('*Keppoch of the poets and great heroes*'). A number of well-known Gaelic poets came from Keppoch, such as Gilleasbuig na Ceapaich (Archibald MacDonald, d. 1682), Iain Lom MacDhomhnaill (John MacDonald, c. 1624–c. 1710) and Sìleas na Ceapaich (Cicely MacDonald, c. 1660–c. 1729).[44] In the poem, Glencoe is referred to as 'Gleann Comhann nam bàrd 's nan sealgair' ('*Glencoe of the poets and hunters*'). We can identify a number of Gaelic poets connected to the MacDonalds of Glencoe (Clann Iain Abraich or the MacIains).[45] Furthermore, Gaelic poets from the area were still active in the eighteenth century. For instance, the Gaelic poetry of Ailean Dall MacDougall (c. 1750–1828), born in Glencoe, was published in 1798.[46] Anne Grant of Laggan (1755–1838), in a letter dated 1773, notes that the MacDonalds of Glencoe 'were all, as the country people say, born poets; and this belief was so well established, that, if a Mac Jan [*sic*] could not rhyme, his legitimacy was called in question: whatever his other merits might be, he was no genuine Mac Jan'.[47]

While the MacDonalds of Glencoe were indeed renowned for poetry, the mention of Glencoe in the Ben Nevis poem may also be an oblique reference to Ossian. In the eighteenth century, Glencoe was identified with Macpherson's 'streams of Cona' ('Glencoe' is an Anglicisation of 'Gleann Comhann' and hence the association Comhann/Cona). It thus came to be accepted as the 'birthplace of Ossian', an association which gained further traction once it had become a part of the travelogue tour of the likes of Pennant and Thomas Garnett (1766–1802).[48] It is intriguing, however, that this poem avoids explicit reference to Ossianic lore, given that Donald Meek has shown that for many Highlanders Macpherson's English-language material became 'an inspirational body of literature with which they were pleased and proud to interact'.[49] Our poet seems to have been wary of such direct interaction, perhaps in light of the burgeoning debate over the origins of Macpherson's publications. Rather, the poem, using the vista from Ben Nevis, begins by pointing to areas of Lochaber renowned for poetry as well as warrior and hunter abilities, avoiding talk of Fionn and his warrior band. The renown of Highland localities for fighting, hunting, and producing poetry fixes the poem within a different, although related, debate.

For many savants of the Scottish Enlightenment, the Gaelic-speaking Highland part of the Scottish population was at once 'object of interest and subject of improvement'.[50] The Highlands were considered to be only at the early barbarous stages of societal progress in popular stadial views of history. Adam Smith (1723–1790) described barbarous societies as consisting 'of hunters, of shepherds, and even of husbandmen in that rude state of husbandry which precedes the improvement of manufactures, and the extension of foreign commerce'.[51] Of course, as has been noted by Thomas Devine, in reality Highlanders undertook all sorts of commercial activity and enterprise in the eighteenth century and 'the familiar image of an archaic pre-Culloden Highlands lacking the capacity to adjust to a changing world requires substantial modification if not complete rejection'.[52] Yet, when the reality of Highland commercial activity was ignored or suppressed, then the Highlands, or the 'Arcadia of Scotland', could provide a window onto the past, allowing a Lowland Scot to observe a 'contemporary ancestor'.[53] In Smith's formulation, the stages of progress were: the Age of Hunters, the Age of Shepherds, the Age of Agriculture and, finally, the Age of Commerce.[54] As noted by Penny Fielding, 'Because these stages were not globally uniform, they could all coexist within the same present, available to the gaze of the enlightened observer, though not necessarily to the pre-commercial societies themselves'.[55]

The inherent dichotomy in this understanding of the Highlands necessitated that both the best and the worst qualities of the past could be seen in the eighteenth-century Gàidhealtachd. The best qualities of barbarous societies, in contemporaneous Scottish writing on societal progression, included martial ability and creativity, due to the absence of increased and repetitive labour. The natural creative talents of the savage included epic poetry,[56] since his environment, free from the stability and corrosive luxury of the 'Age of Commerce', nurtured the 'elemental creativity and instinctive spontaneity of his uncorrupted mind'.[57] We see a number of these themes in David Hume's (1711–1776) (anonymously-published) *A True Account of the Behaviour and Conduct of Archibald Stewart Esq.* (1748) where he contends that:

> When men have fallen into a more civilized Life, and have been allowed to addict themselves entirely to the Cultivation of Arts and Manufactures, the Habit of their Mind, still more than that of their Body, soon renders them entirely unfit for the Use of Arms, and gives a different Direction to their Ambition. Every Man is then desirous to excel his Neighbour in Riches or Address, and laugh at the Imputation of Cowardice or Effeminacy. But the barbarous Highlander, living chiefly by Pasturage, has Leisure to cultivate the Ideas of military Honour; and hearing of nought else but the noble Exploits of his Tribe or Clan, and the renowned Heroes of his Lineage, he soon fancies that he himself is born a Hero as well as a Gentleman.[58]

Nevertheless, despite the positives, the Highlands were simultaneously, as a barbarous society, 'an embarrassing anachronism, and as a retarded primitive society should be regarded by the literati of Scotland's improving Lowlands with as much attention as they would give to the tribal societies of North American Indians'.[59]

This dichotomy was temporally further complicated by the appearance of James Macpherson's Ossianic poems, from 1760 onwards. If accepted as authentic, they could highlight the native genius of Gaelic barbarous society. However, since the epic was framed as belonging to 'ancient' Highland society, it could imply that contemporaneous Highland society had suffered decline or decay. Indeed, Hume reflects the idea of decay in a letter to John Wilkes in 1754, admonishing him for not having visited the Highlands since:

> You woud [sic] there have seen human Nature in the golden Age, or rather, indeed, in the Silver: For the Highlanders have degenerated somewhat from the primitive Simplicity of Mankind. But perhaps you have so corrupted a Taste as to prefer your Iron Age, to be met with in London & the south of England; where Luxury & Vice of every kind so much abound.[60]

Thus, the Highlands, perceived as a pre-commercial society, could provide a window onto both the positive and negative aspects of the past. Yet Ossian provided another window onto the past of that past within the present, and the comparison was unfavourable. According to Henry Home, Lord Kames (1696–1782), 'Compared with their forefathers, the present highlanders make a very inconsiderable figure'.[61]

Therefore, the focus on martial, hunting and poetic ability in the Ben Nevis Gaelic poem chimes with the best aspects of barbarous societies. Through nomination of areas of the Highlands known for Gaelic poets into the eighteenth century, such as Keppoch and Glencoe, the poet extends those positive aspects into the present. The poem also echoes the notion of decay since it situates the beginning of the 'seargadh Garbh-chrìoch' ('withering of the Highlands') during the reign of King Cinaed mac Alpín (810–858) in the ninth century. In this reckoning, the normal advance of societal progress has been allowed to decline, or been inhibited, through the movement of the Gaelic royal court to the Lowlands.

The tour of formerly important Highland sites in the poem culminates with the speaker describing the view from Ben Nevis of a solitary Highland hunter. The poem then moves to discuss the reasons for depopulation, 'Dhìthich beusa Shagson sinn: Lean gach triath a struidheas mòr' ('Saxon customs have destroyed us: every chieftain has pursued his own great opulence'). The poem notes the result of this as: 'Theich an sluagh do Mhòr-Thìr Choluim' ('The population fled to Columbia').[62] Thus, the poem ends by returning us to the recent history of negative luxury adopted by the Highland nobility. The description of luxury as 'beusa Shagson' ('Saxon customs') is likely not post-Union anti-Englishness. Rather it may reflect anxiety over the impact and cost of an education in England pursued by many sons of Highland nobles. For instance, Stana Nenadic has highlighted the struggle concerning the English education, at Eton and Oxford, of the young Sir James MacDonald of Sleat, 8th Baronet (d. 1766). In 1759 those against an English education for the baronet wrote that:

> an education pursued solely in England might give him ideas of expense, which are very improper for his fortune which is but moderate and considerably loaded with debt [...] by such a plan of education he becomes an entire stranger in his younger days to his own country and countrymen.[63]

The pursuit of luxury by the Highland nobility is a unifying theme of the four poems in the individual manuscript of the McLagan collection in which we find the Ben Nevis poem. 'Òran an t-Sealgair' opines that after the '45 the triath ('chief') became overly fond of 'sàimh' ('luxury') and 'faoineas' ('foolishness/ vanity'). The song on Loch Lomond notes, 'Is leasach' neònach air tìr bhith ga fàsach de dhaoin'' ('It's a strange improvement for the land to be cleared of its people') before taking aim at a triath's love for: 'cluiche' (sport), 'earradh' (clothing), 'biadh' (food), 'sult' (excess), 'sògh' (affluence) and 'caitheamh' (spending). The final poem, 'Òran na Banaraich' is the only song of the four not to mention the 'triath' but nonetheless laments the appearance of 'cearrachd agus sàimh' ('gaming and luxury'). The thematic nature of this collection of four poems might suggest a literary coterie composing on particular topics.

The arrival of luxury was seen to be a key marker of the advanced commercial stages of society and the nature and impact of luxury was a crucial Scottish Enlightenment debate.[64] Writings on luxury pivoted on the potential for increased luxury to improve arts, culture, and inquiry, but also to lead to inequality and depopulation in the countryside.[65] Improvement might lead to luxury for the rich but repetitive and increased labour for the poor, resulting in the poor losing both their creativity and their ability to fight. The Highlands, as a barbarous society, were largely presented as lacking luxury. For instance, Henry Home, Lord Kames (1696–1782), notes in *Sketches of the History of Man* (1774):

> Where luxury is unknown, and where people have no wants but what are suggested by uncorrupted nature; men and women live together with great freedom, and with great innocence. [...] Men and women among the Spartans bathed promiscuously, and wrestled together stark naked.

Tacitus reports, that the Germans had not even separate beds, but lay promiscuously upon reeds or heath along the walls of the house. The same custom prevails even at present among the temperate Highlanders of Scotland; and is not quite worn out in New England.[66]

Thus, the Ben Nevis poem, and indeed the other poems in this particular manuscript, shows us that some eighteenth-century Gaelic poets were keenly aware of the debates on luxury and societal progress and co-opted or rejected parts of the rhetoric as it suited their own purposes. This should be unsurprising, given that Adam Ferguson (1723–1816), a key thinker on the impact of improvement, was a Gaelic-speaker. Indeed, it has been argued that Ferguson's own status as a Gaelic-speaking Highlander and his awareness of the economic situation of the Highlands had a major impact on his thinking in *An Essay on the History of Civil Society* (1767), which contains a section on luxury and 'Corruption incident to Polished Nations'.[67] Ferguson writes that '*barbarian*, in use with one arrogant people, and that of *gentil*, with another, only serve to distinguish the stranger, whose language and pedigree differed from theirs'.[68] Thus, David L. Blaney and Naeem Inayatullah note that Ferguson does not 'fully polarize the savage and civilized'.[69]

Of course, Gaelic poets did not need to wait for writing such as Ferguson's or Smith's to warn of the impact of luxury on Highland communities. Ruairidh MacGilleMhoire, known as An Clàrsair Dall (Roderick Morrison, The Blind Poet, c. 1645–c. 1714) mocks the new young chief of the MacLeods for his extravagant spending at the end of the seventeenth century in 'Òran do MhacLeòid Dhùn Bheagain' ('Song to MacLeod of Dunvegan').[70] Traditionally in Gaelic poetry the liberality and generosity of the chieftain's household was praised, including celebration of the consumption of wine.[71] A wider study of how this trope evolved in Gaelic poetry, in light of the emergence of the notion of corrosive luxury, is needed.

Despite the oft-repeated notion that luxury had not reached the Highlands, we do also see some acknowledgement in contemporary English-language sources of the very real 'evolving relationships through five generations with luxury consumption' in Highland families from c. 1680 to 1830.[72] Nenadic points out, for instance, that Johnson and Boswell were 'disappointed to find that southern "politeness" and the metropolitan "world of goods" had greatly eroded what they had come to observe'.[73] The Ben Nevis Gaelic poem, 'Air Fàsachadh na Gàidhealtachd Albannaich', and indeed the other poems that accompany it in the manuscript, also all deal with the impact of luxury, cultivated by the Highland nobility in the eighteenth century. It has been shown here that the poem is rooted in writing about the history, geology, culture and economy of the Highlands. It shows tacit acceptance of the Enlightenment idea that Highland society was only at the initial barbarous stages of societal progress, but explains that this is due to a particular set of historical circumstances. It co-opts the positive aspects of the representation of a part of Scotland, to some, stuck in the past; in order to highlight what has been lost due to luxury. It was noted above that Hume was of the opinion that the eighteenth-century Scottish Gael heard of 'nought else but the noble Exploits of his Tribe or Clan'.[74] This close reading and editorial work on one anonymous Gaelic poem from the eighteenth-century McLagan collection shows this to be erroneous. It shows a Gaelic poet, and presumably audience, deeply engaged with key contemporary Scottish Enlightenment texts and debates.

PART 4: ENVIRONMENTS OF SPACE
AND TIME

CHAPTER FOURTEEN

Eighteenth-Century Scottish Poetry and Ecology

Eric Gidal

It has been over 130 years since Professor John Veitch published his two-volume study *The Feeling for Nature in Scottish Poetry* (1887), which identified the works of Allan Ramsay (1684–1758), James Thomson (1700–1748), James Beattie (1735–1803), Robert Fergusson (1750–1774), and Robert Burns (1759–1796) as marking an eighteenth-century revival of native expression rooted in the landscapes and seascapes of Scotland. By Veitch's account, natural affinities fell into decline during the sixteenth and seventeenth centuries, when 'the language of Scotland had begun to lose its vernacular character' and 'we find a distinct decadence, and even abandonment, of the native language by Scottish writers'.[1] But the feeling for Nature, by which Veitch means 'the outward world of the senses, as this lies before us untouched by the hand of man',[2] would return in the hands of eighteenth-century and romantic-period poets who had the 'courage, in a conventional time both in English and Scottish poetry, to recognise and be true to the manners, the simple everyday life, the rural character, and the scenery of [their] native land'.[3] Veitch's identification of natural feeling with poetries of vernacular expression, rural scenery, and national sentiment now appears less a critical model for ecological reflection and more a symptomatic reaction to an industrialising economy. But Scottish poetry of the eighteenth century continues to offer compelling case studies for ecocriticism, written and published as it was during a period of rapid changes in land use, resource extraction, industrial production, urban growth, and rural depopulation. Furthermore, these poetries grappled with environmental changes in ways that rehearse many of the same questions facing ecological literary studies today.

As Veitch's equation of nature and nation suggests, for Scottish poetry of the modern era, the question of place is often paramount, if always as much a problem as a basis for expression. This is no less true in the eighteenth century, when the 1707 Acts of Union, the Jacobite Risings of 1715 and 1745, and the Highland Clearances, agricultural reforms, and infrastructural expansions that followed in their wake marked the lands and waters of Scotland as highly contested political territories, cultural regions, and economic zones.[4] At the same time, major and minor authors of the Scottish Enlightenment – our retrospective term for the philosophical, economic, literary, and scientific networks that connected Edinburgh, Glasgow, and Aberdeen during this period – grappled with divisions between national pride and cosmopolitan allegiances, romantic nostalgia and social progress, that were persistently mapped onto questions of physical and historical geography.[5] Whether or not it expresses a 'feeling for Nature' in temperament or range, eighteenth-century Scottish poetry inevitably registers changes to the lands, airs, and waters through the no-less contested medium of language, be it English, Scots, or Gaelic, and thus provides a record of human-nature relations across measurable dimensions of time and space. At our own moment in global history when the breakdown of discrete ecosystems seems a *fait accompli*, and when the intersection of world systems and earth systems has reached a moment of transformational crisis, it is a useful exercise to return to this body of work so as to gain some orientation within an unfolding catastrophe.[6]

Eighteenth-century Scottish poets repeatedly constructed the 'natural' in opposition to normative English traditions, spatialising divisions of language and style in terms that often obscured, even as they depended upon, Scotland's increasingly networked economy. Fiona Stafford has observed how poetry of the period frequently grafts ideological tensions between originality and convention onto the equally ideological categories of nature and culture.[7] She suggests Scottish poets from Ramsay to Burns, as much caught up in, as contributing to, the eighteenth-century fascination with the vernacular, the colloquial, and 'original genius', valorised native idioms and forms in dialogue with an English literary tradition they sought to absorb and make their own. These movements, as Janet Sorensen has framed them, 'between familiar and strange, place and class, low and common, "foreign" and national', mediated the category of the 'natural' as both grounded and transitive, and thereby contributed to what Alan Bewell has identified as the globalisation of local natures in the Romantic period through translation, mobility, and exchange.[8] Burns's exclamation in his 'Epistle to J. L[aprai]K, An Old Scotch Bard' to 'Gie me ae spark o' Nature's fire, / That's a' the learning I desire',[9] privileges a rural Scots vernacular over a normative urban English tradition as the proper source of authentic poetry, while the epigraph to his *Poems, Chiefly in the Scottish Dialect* (1786), though written in more conventional diction, presses on this association all the same:

> The Simple Bard, unbroke by rules of Art,
> He pours the wild effusions of the heart:
> And if inspir'd, 'tis Nature's pow'rs inspire;
> Her's all the melting thrill, and her's the kindling fire.[10]

Burns opposes Nature to Art as a source of freedom and passion, uniting the natural with the local and the wild. These manoeuvres speak to political and cultural imperatives of the nation, attempting, as Leith Davis has argued, 'to include geographical peripheries (Scotland) and economic peripheries (the laboring classes) in the cultural realm of the British nation'.[11] At the same time, they also consolidate a romantic model of Nature as a place apart, both superior and anterior to commercial modernity. 'O NATURE!', Burns declaims in his address 'To W. S[impso]n, Ochiltree', 'a' thy shews an' forms / To feeling, pensive hearts hae charms!':[12]

> The warly race may drudge an' drive,
> Hog-shouther, jundie, stretch an' strive,
> Let me fair NATURE'S face descrive,
>   And I, wi' pleasure,
> Shall let the busy, grumbling hive
>   Bum owre their treasure.[13]

Despite such ambitions, Burns's poetry contains few extended descriptions of 'NATURE'S face', though his letters periodically express fashionable enthusiasms for solitary walks, sublime exaltation, and natural piety.[14] Burns's poetic encounters with the natural world are more commonly satirical than descriptive, as in the poems 'To a Mouse, on turning her up in her Nest, with the Plough, November 1785' or 'To a Louse, On Seeing one on a Lady's Bonnet at Church', or else they are bawdy and seductive, as in his 'Song, Composed in August' in which, among 'westlin winds, and slaught'ring guns',[15] he woos his 'charmer' to the fields:

> But PEGGY dear, the ev'ning's clear,
>   Thick flies the skimming Swallow;
> The sky is blue, the fields in view,
>   All fading-green and yellow:
> Come let us stray our gladsome way,
>   And view the charms o' Nature;
> The rustling corn, the fruited thorn,
>   And ilka happy creature.[16]

On the other end of the moral spectrum, Nature can appear as the site of allegory. The mountain daisy Burns tears up with a plough is likened to 'the fate of artless Maid, / Sweet *flow'ret* of the rural shade' ('To a Mountain-Daisy, On turning one down, with the Plough, in April—1786'.) and to 'the fate of simple Bard, / On Life's rough ocean luckless starr'd', and, extending the *memento mori* sentiment to the poem's reader: 'Ev'n thou who mourn'st the *Daisy's* fate, / *That fate is thine* – no distant date'.[17]

But simply to search for Burns's scattered representations of 'NATURE'S face' is to remain confined within the parochial regionalism his verse and its reception has as much complicated as upheld, whereas to place Burns within a truly ecological context requires a broader range of environmental history. The very publication sites of Burns's *Poems* in both the Kilmarnock and the Edinburgh editions register, in Stafford's estimate, 'both his regional origins and his larger importance as the poet of Scotland',[18] and his status as what Penny Fielding terms an 'icon of locality' positioned him both as an 'original genius' and 'poet of nature', terms derived less from ecological encounters than from 'macro-structures' of geographical inscription, environmental determinism, and geospatial linguistics.[19] Nigel Leask has demonstrated extensively how Burns's production of 'naïve pastoral' and the 'Heaven-taught ploughman', engages rather than repudiates the modernising culture of improvement that was transforming every aspect of Scottish life in the eighteenth century. Such transformations included not only agricultural economy, but also, in Leask's words, 'the rise of manufactures, country banking, and the booms and busts of the new credit economy, war, and empire, accompanied by religious and cultural enlightenment', all in an increasingly globalised system that connected Scotland to tobacco, sugar, and cotton production from India to the Caribbean.[20]

Burns's more ecological poems, then, may be those that look beyond the rural experiences of his native Ayrshire towards the bifurcated role of natural systems within a commercially, and ecologically, global terrain, such as his 'On a Scotch Bard Gone to the West Indies', which mourns the departure of a rowdy alter-ego for Jamaica:

> Fareweel, my *rhyme-composing billie*!
> Your native soil was right ill-willie;
> But may ye flourish like a lily,
>   Now bonilie!
> I'll toast you in my hindmost *gillie*,
>   Tho' owre the Sea!²¹

Burns's plans to relocate in Jamaica before the successful reception of his *Poems* has inspired recurrent debate over his attitude towards the pervasive slave trade.²² We need not enter into Burns's political opinions, however, to see that this poem offers a measure of the intersection of Ayrshire economy with that of the Atlantic world, specifically the plantation ecology of the Caribbean. The passage of a Scotch bard from his 'native soil' to '*Jamaica bodies* [...] owre the Sea', moves along routes of slave energy and extractive agriculture that were enriching the tobacco lords of Glasgow and supplying cotton to the mills of Lanarkshire.²³ In this sense, the poem registers numerous aspects of what John R. McNeill has described as 'the ecological Atlantic', in particular the expansion of Scotland's environmental footprint to the 'ghost acreage' of the West Indies, an extraction of energy from American soils and African slaves that allowed Scotland, along with the rest of Atlantic Europe, in McNeill's words, 'to sidestep the constraints of the pre-industrial organic energy regime until the subterranean forest, coal, helped to shatter them'.²⁴ From the perspective of the history of energy, Burns's relation to the transatlantic world may be measured not only along the circulation of ideas and cultural receptions that Sharon Alker, Leith Davis, and Holly Faith Nelson have helped to chart, but also by way of what David McDermott Hughes has characterised as the 'human, somatic fuel' of slavery and the 'institutional and cultural pipeline[s]' that 'disembedded energy from ethics'.²⁵ To map the arc of such a history, Burns's lyrical apostrophe may be placed alongside his fellow Scot James Grainger's (1721–66) earlier West Indies georgic, *The Sugar Cane* (1764) and John McGrath's (1935–2002) later ceilidh-inspired activist theatre, *The Cheviot, The Stag and the Black, Black Oil* (1973), to form a poetic archive of energy transfer in the Atlantic world. To read Burns in this context is to recognise what Leask has identified as a poetics of dispossession in a world of globalised 'improvement' from the position of what the historical ecologist Jason Moore calls the 'world-ecology perspective [...] in which the relations of capital, power, and nature form an evolving, uneven and patterned whole in the modern world'.[26] Such a world-ecology perspective does not so much contest as complement a more bioregional emphasis on a poetics of the local. It reminds us, to quote Tom Lynch, Cheryll Glotfelty, and Karla Armbruster, that 'a localised sense of place is incomplete unless augmented by a sense of how that place is integrated into the wider biosphere and the global network of cultures and economies', even as 'a sense of the global is likewise incomplete without an awareness that the globe is an amalgamation of infinitely complex connections among variously scaled and nested places'.[27] And if Ayrshire offers one such nested locale for geohistorical reflection, another may be found further to the north, across the Highland line.

By some accounts, Scottish environmental poetics begins and ends in the Highlands, that land 'on the other side of sorrow' whose dramatic topography and tragic history have conspired to create either a locale for indigenous expressions of attentive care and impassioned allegiance or an evacuated terrain for the projection of sublime aesthetics and romantic nostalgia.[28] The English poet William Collins' (1721–1759) 'Ode on the Popular Superstitions of the Highlands of Scotland, Considered as the Subject of Poetry' (1749) would seem to embody these tensions, written on the occasion of the playwright John Home's (1722–1808) return from London to the north, where, Collins imagines, 'ev'ry Vale / Shall prompt the Poet, and his Song demand' and where 'Fairy People', 'Airy Minstrels', and 'Runic Bards' provide 'Themes of simple, sure Effect', for 'Scenes like these, which, daring to depart / From sober Truth, are still to Nature true, / And call forth fresh delight to Fancy's view'.[29] Collins's division between 'sober truth' and the fantastic forms of nature is at once spatial and temporal – 'For not Alone they touch the Village Breast, / But fill'd in Elder Time th' Historic page'[30] – an overlay even more pronounced in James Macpherson's (1736–1796) Ossianic poetry of the 1760s, which Hugh Blair (1718–1800) announced as 'genuine remains of ancient Scottish poetry', even as Macpherson insisted it was 'still sung in the north, with a great deal of wild simplicity'.[31] Macpherson promoted Ossianic poetry as both a remnant of an early stage of society, one, in Matthew Gelbart's words, 'closest to nature [and] so, of course [...] most disinterested and noble', yet still present in the 'pure and original' traditions of the Highlands, a bifurcated assessment that informed visions of the lands and waters, as well as of the people, of this northern region throughout the eighteenth century.[32]

T. C. Smout has located the 'roots of green consciousness' in an analogous bifurcation between promotions of the Highlands as a space for physical recreation, spiritual refreshment, and wilderness refuge and the more utilitarian attitudes of crofters, fishermen, landowners, and industrialists.[33] But Meg Bateman, Michael Newton, James Hunter, and John Murray among others have countered these easy dichotomies by celebrating native Gaelic voices of natural communion dating back at least to the eighth century and including the verse of such eighteenth-century poets as Alasdair mac Mhaighstir Alasdair / Alexander MacDonald (c. 1695–c. 1770) and Donnchadh Bàn Mac an t-Saoir / Duncan Bàn MacIntyre (1723?–1812).[34] Hunter, in terms not dissimilar from Veitch's in the nineteenth century, highlights these poets' great love and deep reading of a northern land: their 'ability to merge – indeed identify – with [their] surroundings', and their 'equally striking capacity to evoke these surroundings by means of a wealth of meticulously noted detail'.[35] Hence a work like Mac Mhaighstir Alasdair's 'Oran an t-Samhraidh' ('*Song of Summer*'), composed in the early 1740s, can be read as a lyrical encounter between human consciousness and a vibrant ecosystem:

> An dèis dhomh dùsgadh san mhaidean
> 'S an dealt air a' choill,
> Ann am maidean ro shoilleir,
> Ann a lagan beag doilleir,
> Gun cualas a feadan
> Gu leadarra seinn,
> 'S mac-talla nan creagan
> Da fhreagra bròn-bhinn.
>
> Bidh am beithe deagh-bholtrach,
> Urail, dosrach nan càrn,
> Ri maoth-bhlàs driùchd Cèitein,
> Mar ri caoin-dheàrrsadh grèine,
> Brùchdadh barraich roi gheugaibh
> San mhìos cheutach-sa Mhàigh:
> Am mìos breac-laoghach buailteach,
> Bainneach, buadhach gu dàir.
>
> Bidh gach doire dlùth uaignidh
> 'S trusgan uaine umpa a' fàs;
> Bidh an snodhach a' dìreadh

As gach freumhaich as ìsle
Roi na cuislinnean snìomhain
Gu mìodachadh blàth;
Cuach is smeòrach san fheasgar
Seinn a leadain 'nam bàrr.

On waking this morning, / with the dew on the woods, / on this very bright morning, / in a shady wee hollow / I heard then the chanter / with elegance played, / and the rocks' Echo sounded / their sweet-sad reply. // The fine-scented birch-tree, / new-branched over the cairn, / wet with tender warm May-dew / warm with sun's kindly shining, / exudes foliage from twiglets / in this lovely month, May: / month of dappled calves folded, / month for mating and milk. // Each grove, close and secret, / has its mantle of green, / the wood-sap is rising / from the roots at the bottom, / through arteries twisting / to swell out the growth; / thrush and cuckoo at evening / sing their litany above.[36]

As a sampling of ecopoetics, there is much here to admire. Mac Mhaighstir Alasdair parallels the vitality of a birch tree's budding leaves with the nurturing of a mother cow and the flowing of sap with the song of thrush and cuckoo, all through a poetic voice in affective sympathy with rocks that echo the 'chanter' of seasonal rebirth. The poem offers an expression of cohabitation in both thought and emotion, one we might describe as 'storied matter' that the poet as much records as sings.[37] Yet Derick Thomson observes that its central conceit may be adapted from a song collected in Ramsay's 1724 *Tea-Table Miscellany*:

> As early I walked, on the first of sweet May,
> Beneath a steep mountain,
> Beside a clear fountain,
> I heard a grave lute soft melody play,
> Whilst the echo resounded the dolorous lay.[38]

and its subject matter from James Thomson's *Spring* (1728):

> Moist, bright, and green, the Landskip laughs around.
> Full swell the Woods; their every Musick wakes,
> Mix'd in wild concert with the warbling Brooks
> Increas'd, the distant Bleatings of the Hills,
> The hollow Lows responsive from the Vales,
> Whence blending all the sweeten'd Zephyr springs.[39]

If there is a network of agents at play in Mac Mhaighstir Alasdair's verse, it includes not only the biosphere of the northern Highlands, but a mediasphere of print circulation and Lowland markets, Gaelic poetry and neoclassical verse. These multiple contingencies do not devalue the power or accomplishments of the poetry – Mac Mhaighstir Alasdair is said to have composed these lines on the shore of Loch Sunart, and there is little doubt that he is working as much in Gaelic as in English poetic traditions – but it underscores how such traditions, like the lands they described, were already products of centuries of cross-fertilisation and cannot be delineated by absolute standards of native authenticity and foreign impositions.[40]

Donnchadh Bàn Mac an t-Saoir's 'Moladh Beinn Dóbhrain' ('*Praise of Ben Dorain*') is frequently cited as a masterpiece of eighteenth-century Gaelic poetry, formed on the basis of a pibroch with themes and variations that, as Murray has put it, 'transfers the bardic tradition of praise poetry to the natural world':[41]

>   An t-urram thar gach beinn
>   Aig Beinn Dóbhrain,
>   De na chunnaic mi fon ghréin
>   Si bu bhòidhche leam:
>   Munadh fada réidh,
>   Cuilidh 'm faighte féidh,
>   Soilleireachd an t-sléibh
>   Bha mi sònrachadh;
>   Doireachan nan geug,
>   Coill' anns am bi feur:
>   'S foinneasach an spréidh
>   Bhios a chòmhnaidh ann,
>   Greadhainn bu gheal céir,
>   Faghaid air an déidh –
>   'S laghach leam an sreud
>   A bha sròineiseach.

The prize above each ben / Is Ben Dorain's, / Of all I've ever seen / To me she was loveliest: / Moorland long and smooth, / Store where deer were found, / The brightness of the slope / Is what I pointed to; / Groves of branching trees, / Woods containing grass: / Well-favoured is the stock / That makes its dwelling there, / A white-buttocked band / With hunt pursuing them – / Lovely to me is the herd / That were snuffle-nosed.[42]

Recalling both his own youth as a cattle herder and his community's relation with the land through a fine attention to specific landmarks, toponyms, and features, Donnchadh Bàn recreates the sensuous experience of a deer hunt in language whose very richness crystallises the geographical and cultural distance between his native glen and his position in the City Guard of Edinburgh, where he was posted at the time of this poem's first publication. Bateman has praised Donnchadh Bàn's poetry for persistently refuting any distinction between man and nature: 'where nature thrives, so does man; where crops are planted, so too are songs sung; culture simultaneously implies agrarian and human culture'.[43] Smout likewise argues that 'the Gaelic poets were in every sense poets of the people, and their language is of a direct delight in nature [...] the popularity of Duncan Bàn Macintyre's songs in Perthshire and Argyll paralleled in some ways the appeal of Robert Burns to the tenants and farm servants of Ayrshire: his view of nature and life, like that of Burns, struck a chord among ordinary unlettered people'.[44] And Iain Crichton Smith has celebrated Donnchadh Bàn's poetry for 'the authentic feel of authoritative genius, the detailed obsession, the richly concentrated gaze, the loving scrutiny, undiverted by philosophical analysis, [which] has created a particular world, joyously exhausting area after area'.[45] Without departing from this critical admiration, we can nonetheless attempt to query the aesthetic prioritisations of authenticity, feeling, authority, and genius and the necessity of departing from 'philosophical analysis' to 'create a particular world'. It is, after all, possible to read Donnchadh Bàn's lines as an accomplished invocation of a rural and mountainous existence without ignoring the perilous history of subsistence farming, clan rivalry, and estate and township economics that would have made agrarian existence in his native Glen Orchy unstable at best by mid-century.[46] The 'woodland where grass grows' would have already been depleted during Donnchadh Bàn's lifetime to feed the demands of the nearby Bonawe ironworks, leaving the area particularly susceptible to the economic expansion of large-scale sheep farming in the second half of the century,[47] an economic and ecological transition recorded in his later 'Cead Deireannach nam Beann' (Final Farewell to the Bens) (1802):

> Bha mi 'n dé 'san aonach
>   'S bha smaointean mór air m' aire-sa,
> Nach robh 'n luchd-gaoil a b' àbhaist
>   Bhith siubhal fàsaich mar rium ann;
> 'S a' bheinn as beag a shaoil mi

> Gun dèanadh ise caochladh,
> On tha i nis fo chaoraibh
>   'S ann thug an saoghal car asam.
>
> 'N uair sheall mi air gach taobh dhìom
>   Chan fhaodainn gun bhith smalanach,
> On theirig coil is fraoch ann,
>   'S na daoine bh' ann, cha mhaireann iad;
> Chan 'eil fiadh r' a shealg ann,
> Chan 'eil eun no earb ann,
> Am beagan nach 'eil marbh dhiubh,
>   'S e rinn iad falbh gu baileach as.

> *Yesterday I was on the moor, / and grave reflections haunted me: / that absent were the well-loved friends / who used to roam the waste with me; / since the mountain, which I little thought / would suffer transformation, / has now become a sheep-run, / the world, indeed, has cheated me. // As I gazed on every side of me / I could not but be sorrowful / for wood and heather have run out, / nor live the men who flourished there; / there's not a deer to hunt there, / there's not a bird or roe there, / and the few that have not died out / have departed from it utterly.*[48]

This elegiac vision of a world transformed, though site-specific, is a mode that was increasingly common by the turn of the nineteenth century in Gaelic, Scots, and English, as the pressures of agricultural consolidation and global commerce were altering lands on either side of the Highland Line. Indeed, we may read Donnchadh Bàn's 'Cead Deireannach nam Beann' alongside Burns's 'On a Scotch Bard Gone to the West Indies' as two signatures of an increasingly unified system of global mobility, resource extraction, and ecological degradation. To do so is not to deny the linguistic, cultural, social, and – yes – bioregional distinctions between these poets and their work, but rather to understand each in relation to an economic history of Scottish and global environmental change.

This is the perspective of what Ursula K. Heise has denoted 'eco-cosmopolitanism', an approach that focuses less on *reterritorialisation*, 'a reconnection with the local [and] an attempt to realign culture with place', and more on *deterritorialisation*, which 'foregrounds how cultural practices become detached from place [and] how these practices are now imbricated in [...] larger networks'.[49] Garry MacKenzie has adapted Heise's argument in relation to modern Scottish island poetry and 'debates about whether environmental concerns should best be understood through proximity to place or through embracing global networks of communication and ideas'.[50] As my examples thus far demonstrate, these questions are no less pertinent to the poetry of the eighteenth century. 'The challenge for environmentalist thinking', Heise argues, 'is to shift the core of its cultural imagination from a sense of place to a less territorial and more systemic sense of planet'.[51] And one such sense of planet may be located in the poetry of James Thomson, specifically his georgic masterwork *The Seasons* (1726–1730).

In many critical accounts, Thomson is a decided outlier in the ranks of eighteenth-century Scottish poets, a self-consciously *British* poet whose adaptations of English traditions mark him as 'unnatural', 'inorganic', or 'disconnected' in contrast to the vernacular Scottish and Gaelic works we have been surveying.[52] Yet Burns held no such views, eulogising Thomson as 'sweet Poet of the Year, / [...] While Scotia, with exulting tear, / Proclaims that *Thomson* was her son',[53] and Mary Jane W. Scott has meticulously traced the Scottish influences on Thomson's *Seasons*, from his natural descriptions to his absorption of Scottish religious, philosophical, and political themes and details of his own rural childhood in Roxburghshire.[54] His overt representations of Scotland in 'Autumn', specifically of the northern islands, belie the utility of such issues, however, as they offer a strong example of how a break from what Stafford terms 'local attachments' and Heise, citing Zygmunt Bauman, an 'ethic of proximity' was already providing poets of the eighteenth century the capacity to understand Scotland within the integrative scales of intersecting earth and world systems. Here I follow not only David Fairer's reclamation of georgic as a mixed genre best able to express 'non-hierarchical, practical, functioning system[s]' but also Tobias Menely's reading of georgic as a model 'of the relation of planetary energy input to the generation of social surplus'.[55] Thomson's turn to the outer islands 'where the *Northern* Ocean, in vast Whirls, / Boils [...] and the *Atlantic* surge / Pours in among the stormy *Hebrides*',[56] poses a sequence of questions that positions Scotland at the intersection of migratory as well as oceanic and atmospheric currents:

> Who can recount what Transmigrations there
> Are annual made? What Nations come and go?
> And how the living Clouds on Clouds arise?
> Infinite wings! Till all the Plume-dark Air,
> And rude resounding Shore are one wild Cry.[57]

Thomson never visited the Hebrides, Orkney, or Shetland, making these lines less poetic description than systems analysis. He draws on accounts of stork and geese migration in Richard Bradley's *Philosophical Account of the Works of Nature* (1721) as well as Martin Martin's *Late Voyage to St. Kilda* (1698) and *Description of the Western Islands of Scotland* (1703, 1716), and portrays an archipelago intersected by 'transmigrations' of birds, of fish, of thermal currents, and of hydrological cycles.[58] He pauses to paint a self-consciously pastoral vision of 'the plain harmless Native' on St Kilda, with 'his small Flock, / And Herd diminutive of many Hues', who:

> Tends on the little Island's verdant Swell,
> The Shepherd's sea-girt Reign; or, to the Rocks
> Dire-clinging, gathers his ovarious Food;
> Or sweeps the fishy Shore; or treasures up
> The Plumage, rising full, to form the Bed
> Of Luxury.[59]

But the very terms of this tableau suggest less isolation than interconnection, a 'native existence' sustained by currents and cycles of global circulation. Here Thomson draws directly from Martin's detailed accounts of oceanic tides and migratory patterns that supported the inhabitants of St Kilda as well as their trade in seabird oil and feathers with the mainland. The result is a poetic representation of energy and nutrient cycles sustained by atmospheric currents, migratory routes, and circuits of trade, one we can only assess in retrospect since the island was finally evacuated in 1930.[60]

This poetics of interconnection becomes more extensive as Thomson expands the scale of his reflections by means of the Muse's aerial perspective, who, 'High-hovering o'er the broad cerulean Scene, / Sees CALEDONIA, in romantic View':

> Her airy Mountains, from the waving Main,
> Invested with a keen diffusive Sky,
> Breathing the Soul acute; her Forests huge,
> Incult, robust, and tall, by Nature's Hand
> Planted of old; her azure Lakes between,
> Pour'd out extensive, and of watery Wealth
> Full; winding deep and green her fertile Vales;
> With many a cool translucent brimming Flood

> Wash'd lovely, from the *Tweed* (pure *Parent-Stream*,
> Whose pastoral Banks first heard my *Doric* reed,
> With, silvan *Jed*, thy tributary Brook)
> To where the North-inflated Tempest foams
> O'er *Orca's* or *Betubium's* highest Peak.[61]

This view may be 'romantic', but it is also remarkably effective at portraying Scotland as an integrated ecological system. And as a naturalised political body and expansive commercial empire, for this aerial panorama of mountains, forests, lakes, and vales transitions effortlessly in Thomson's verse to a tribute to the Scots themselves, 'a People, in Misfortune's School / Train'd up to hardy Deeds', 'A manly Race, / Of unsubmitting Spirit, wise and brave', and an aspirational quest for economic improvement:

> OH is there not some Patriot, in whose Power
> That best, that godlike Luxury is plac'd,
> Of blessing Thousands, Thousands yet unborn,
> Thro' late Posterity? some, large of Soul,
> To chear dejected Industry? to give
> A double Harvest to the pining Swain?
> And teach the labouring Hand the Sweets of Toil?
> How, by the finest Art, the native Robe
> To weave; how, white as Hyperborean Snow,
> To form the lucid Lawn; with venturous Oar,
> How to dash wide the Billow; nor look on,
> Shamefully passive, while *Batavian* Fleets
> Defraud us of the glittering finny Swarms,
> That heave our Friths, and croud upon our Shores;
> How all-enlivening Trade to rouse, and wing,
> The prosperous Sail, from every growing Port,
> Uninjur'd, round the sea-incircled Globe;
> And thus, in Soul united as in Name,
> Bid BRITAIN reign the Mistress of the Deep?[62]

By the pastoral standards of romantic ecocriticism, it is difficult to view such lines as expressing an environmental ethics. Thomson's programme of economic improvement, agricultural reform, wool and linen manufacturing, and fisheries development exemplifies what Fredrik Albritton Jonsson has described as a cornucopian rhetoric of civil cameralism, less a promotion of local knowledge and bioregional integrity than an advocacy of national investment and international trade.⁶³ Peter Womack has denigrated Thomson's lines as ideological obfuscation, misrepresenting political and economic interests as natural systems, but Denys Van Renen has recently argued for a reading of *The Seasons* as 'an essential precursor text in an era of unprecedented movements of peoples and goods and the concomitant disruption of ecologies', and of these lines as promoting 'a sensibility attuned to the interconnectedness of trade, ecology, time, and labor'.⁶⁴ As he delineates projects of improvement within a dynamic prospect of mountains and floods, migrations and harvests, Thomson makes explicit the recursive interconnections that bind commerce and ecology in a globalising economy. Framing a pastoral and patriotic portrait of subsistence living in the northern islands within a national program for expansive trade exemplifies the capacity of such georgic verse to construct what the historical ecologist Carole L. Crumley has identified as the 'integrative scale' of landscape ecology, 'enabling the simultaneous study of both the physical environment and human activity'.⁶⁵

From English-language georgic through Gaelic-language song and Scots-language apostrophes, we can view a range of poetic and cultural responses to a globalising economy and the consequent transformations to the airs, waters, and places of the northern archipelago. While a commitment to localised particularities is a feature of much Scottish poetry in the century after union, and understandably so, ecocriticism in the twenty-first century cannot remain so regional in its focus if it is to respond to the challenges of our age. I align these reflections with Timothy Clark's mandate for ecocriticism to move beyond repairing the 'cultural imaginary' of human-nature relations towards a 'reexamination of inherited notions of the human, the cultural and "identity" in the first place'.⁶⁶ This approach to eighteenth-century Scottish poetry is less concerned with questions of complicity or resistance and more with describing the manifold signatures of ecological transformation that are our legacy from that ambitious time.

CHAPTER FIFTEEN

The Poems of Ossian and the Birth of Modern Geology

Dafydd Moore

James Macpherson's (1736–1796) *The Poems of Ossian* was one of the literary sensations of its age. Between 1759 and 1763 Macpherson produced three volumes of prose poetry: *The Fragments of Ancient Poetry Collected in the Highlands of Scotland* (1759); *Fingal* […] *and Other Poems* (1761/62) and *Temora* […] *and Other Poems* (1763). The latter two were explicitly labelled as the poetic remains of a hitherto lost third-century Gaelic epic poet Ossian, edited and translated by Macpherson. *Ossian* was both influential and controversial: while debates about the poem's provenance rumbled on, at least two generations of antiquarians, poets and novelists from across the world were influenced (sometimes in reaction against) the sublime tales of tragic heroism and frustrated desire played out against a louring Highland landscape.

Since the mid-1980s there has been a significant revival of interest in Macpherson's work (including a volume in this series), and his place within the canon of eighteenth-century Scottish literature seems assured.[1] While the question of the poems' authenticity has remained a topic of exclusive interest to some, the majority of scholarship has sought to explore the poems in relation to the intellectual, cultural and political climate of the Scottish Enlightenment and Scottish Gaeldom in the aftermath of the Jacobite risings, and the reception of the poems, both across Britain and Ireland and the rest of the world. This chapter offers a hitherto overlooked example of the ways in which *Ossian* can be considered in relation to its intellectual and cultural milieu, and addresses some of the broader issues such consideration raises.

The question of landscape and geography and its relationship with *Ossian* has been a longstanding one, stretching from (what to our eyes seem slightly naïve or wrong-headed) nineteenth-century attempts to use *Ossian*'s topographical descriptions within the context of the authenticity dispute, to more recent readings of the Ossianic in terms of the broader cultural and identity politics of travelling, tourism and landscape.[2] The focus of this chapter is different: not features of topographical description *per se*, but rather the poems' sense (fleeting though it may be), and perhaps even contribution to, a changing understanding of geology and geological time. In this way it contributes to the wider project of accounting for, and provides another index of, *Ossian*'s paradoxical combination of the familiar and the unfamiliar, the uncanniness to which its enduring fascination is often ascribed.

The sense of being poised between the old and the new, between tradition and innovation, has been a key element of responses to the poems from their first appearance. At the time Charles Churchill (1732–1764) sneered about 'that *old, new, Epic Pastoral*, FINGAL', while a little later Walter Scott noted (perhaps only slightly less facetiously) that 'Fingal has all the strength and bravery of Achilles, with the courtesy, sentiment, and high breeding of Sir Charles Grandison'.[3] Modern critics, less invested in the question of Ossian's provenance, have seen such accommodations as important explanations both for the Scottish Enlightenment project of which the poems were a part and also the imaginative grip the poems exerted over several generations of readers the world over. John Dwyer, in a comment that in effect paraphrases and glosses that of Scott, suggests that the poems' power lies in the way that they provide a 'cultural seam between two ethical domains', while Ken Simpson similarly suggests that Macpherson's achievement consists of his ability 'to graft on to the heroism of the traditional epic the compulsive pathos of the age of sensibility'.[4] For Dwyer and others, this marriage of ancient and modern virtue explains the sponsorship, and some would say co-creation, of *Ossian* by key Scottish Enlightenment literati, figures who in a number of ways were tussling with the meaning and practice of virtue in a commercial state whose political centre had moved south in 1707 and in whom 'zeal for improvement (and [...] theories of progress) coincided with a hearty regret for the independence and simplicity of the past'.[5]

Ian Duncan has revised the terms of this equation without upsetting its fundamental emphasis on *Ossian* as a mediating point by suggesting that the 'affective power of Ossian derived as much from the representation of modernity as a peculiar temporal relation, a kind of negative dialectic between past and present, as from the primitive framing of a modern ideology of conduct'.[6] Robert Crawford sees this in action in the juxtaposition of primitive bardic verse and Enlightenment literary criticism, claiming that 'in its blend of primitivism and sophistication the evolving Ossianic text creates the modern poet'.[7] Eric Gidal is the most recent of a line of critics, then, who have considered *Ossian* as the interface between past and present, pre-modern and modern, in terms of the representation of the bardic voice of a lost civilisation in the form of a printed book by Ossian: the poems are 'a memorial record of a vanishing moment within the landscape of industrial modernity and a product of the urbanised communicative networks facilitating the shaping of that new terrain'.[8]

An *Ossian* that looks both backward and forward and that is both new and strangely familiar, has also emerged from commentary on the style and construction of the poems. For all the apparent innovation in Macpherson's measured prose, it hardly represents the shock of the new: not only are the poems redolent (as Macpherson himself pointed out) of the King James Bible, Shakespeare, Milton, Homer and Virgil, but they fall easily into iambics, as *Ossian*'s many versifiers showed in the thirty years following the poems' publication. The sensibility articulated in those lines can be interpreted in terms both of that of the epic voice of the past and also that of a personal, internalised poetic sensibility that would come to dominate the future. As Potkay puts it, 'does Ossian sense a daemon in the viewless winds, or is he apostrophising his dead father? Are we witnessing a confident animism, or the modern suspicion that our fathers are everywhere?'[9] This chapter explores some of these issues of familiarity and innovation, and perhaps shadows some of the larger questions to do with *Ossian*'s Enlightenment modernity, through a focus on one speech, and a couple of phrases, at the end of one of *Ossian*'s more celebrated poems.

The poem 'Carthon' appeared in the 1761/2 *Fingal* collection. It offers a microcosm of the Ossianic world and contains examples of all that is most significant about Macpherson's style and manner of proceeding. It opens, characteristically, with the aged Ossian:

> A tale of the times of old! the deeds of days of other years!—The murmur of thy streams, O Lora, brings back the memory of the past. The sound of thy woods, Garmallar, is lovely in mine ear. Dost thou not behold, Malvina, a rock with its head of heath? […] The deer of the mountain avoids the place, for he beholds the gray ghost that guards it: for the mighty lie, O Malvina, in the narrow plain of the rock. A tale of the times of old! the deeds of days of other years![10]

Ossian is both inspired by this landscape and re-animates it, unlocking the meaning in its stones and re-peopling it with the events of the past.[11] The story he tells is a tragic *bel inconnu* romance, familiar within Gaelic literature[12] (it is a version of the Gaelic tale upon which W. B. Yeats (1865–1939) based 'Cuchulain's Fight with the Sea', though it is a motif that appears in many folk traditions). In Macpherson's telling, Clessammor, Fingal's maternal uncle, visits and settles at Balclutha, marrying the daughter of the king. He is forced to flee after a quarrel, leaving his wife, who unbeknownst to him is pregnant, behind. She dies in childbirth, and when a short time later Fingal's father storms the city and fires it, the child Carthon survives to vow revenge on the Fingalians. But when as an adult Carthon invades Morven he is killed in combat by Clessammor. That they are father and son is revealed only as Carthon lies mortally wounded:

> His words reached the heart of Clessammor: he fell, in silence, on his son. The host stood darkened around: no voice is on the plains of Lora. Night came, and the moon, from the east, looked on the mournful field: but still they stood, like a silent grove that lifts its head on Gormal, when the loud winds are laid, and dark autumn is on the plain.
>
> Three days they mourned above Carthon; on the fourth his father died. In the narrow plain of the rock they lie; and a dim ghost defends their tomb.[13]

The predominant note of the poem is human *vanitas* and the remorseless effects of time's passage. Early in the poem Clessammor relates the story of his youth and love in Balclutha, a story which prompts one of Fingal's best-known speeches, an echo (as the footnote points out), of the prophecy of the destruction of Babylon as told in Isaiah 13:

> I have seen the walls of Balclutha, but they were desolate. The fire had resounded in the halls: and the voice of the people is heard no more. The stream of Clutha was removed from its place, by the fall of the walls.— The thistle shook, there, its lonely head: the moss whistled to the wind [...] Desolate is the dwelling of Moina, silence is in the house of her fathers.—Raise the song of mourning, O bards, over the land of strangers. They have but fallen before us: for, one day, we must fall.—why dost thou build the hall, son of the winged days? Though lookest from thy towers today; yet a few years, and the blast of the desert comes; it howls in thy empty court and whistles round thy half worn shield.[14]

At the end of this speech Fingal speculates as to whether the 'sun of heaven shalt fail', whether its 'brightness is for a season, like Fingal'. This notion is picked up at the end of the poem in Ossian's 'address to the sun', one of the most famous and frequently cited passages in all of *Ossian*:

> O thou that rollest above, round as the shield of my fathers! Whence are thy beams, O Sun! thy everlasting light? Thou comest forth, in thy awful beauty, and the stars hide themselves in the sky; the moon, cold and pale, sinks in the western wave. But thou thyself movest alone: who can be a companion of thy course? The oaks of the mountain fall: the mountains themselves decay with years; the ocean shrinks and grows again: the moon herself is lost in heaven; but thou art for ever the same; rejoicing in the brightness of thy course […] but thou art perhaps, like me, for a season, and thy years will have an end. Thou shalt sleep in thy clouds, careless of the voice of the morning.—Exalt then O sun, in the strength of thy youth! Age is dark and unlovely; it is like the glimmering light of the moon, when it shines through broken clouds, and the mist is on the hills.[15]

There are multiple echoes and remembrances in the passage, not just of the words Ossian has previously placed in his father's mouth. In a poem about filial relationships – Fingal and Ossian, Clessammor and Carthon – it is not difficult to hear the sun/son pun working in this paragraph. There may be something more broadly messianic at play, reinforced for those readers aware of the metaphorical association of the sun with the 'King across the Water' in Gaelic Jacobite verse, as in this example from Alasdair mac Mhaighstir Alasdair's 'Oran a Rinneadh Sa Bhliadhna 1746':

> Seo a' bhliadhna chòrr
> An tilg a' ghrian le meadh-bhlàths biadhchar
> Gathain chiatach òirnn [16]

This is the wonderful year / When the sun with soft and fertile warmth / His lovely beams shall shed on us.[17]

For those without this frame of reference, Macpherson's footnotes also draw the reader's attention to parallels in book four of *Paradise Lost* at the beginning and to an image drawn from Virgil at the end.

Within all of this, however, I want to focus on one image from the middle of the speech: 'The oaks of the mountain fall: the mountains themselves decay with years; the ocean shrinks and grows again'. The notion that mountains were not permanent was not an entirely unfamiliar one in 1762. The possibility is provided for in Isaiah (though Macpherson does not draw this parallel himself, even though he had already referenced Isaiah 13 earlier in the poem):

> The voice of him that crieth in the wilderness, Prepare ye the way of the Lord, make straight in the desert a highway for our God.
>
> Every valley shall be exalted, and every mountain and hill shall be made low: and the crooked shall be made straight, and the rough places plain.[18]

What is today called geological erosion was a recognised principle in early modern geological accounts of the history of the earth, even if it was forced into the service of an unfamiliarly theological frame of reference. This, famously, is Thomas Burnet (1635–1715) in his *Telluris Theoria Sacra* or *Sacred Theory of the Earth* (1691) invoking the idea of erosion to prove the relative youth of the planet:

> If this present state and form of the earth had been from Eternity, it would have long ere this destroy'd it self, and chang'd it self: the Mountains sinking by degrees into the Vallies, and into the Sea, and the Waters rising above the Earth [...] For whatsoever moulders or is washt away from them, is carried down into the lower grounds, and into the Sea, and nothing is ever brought back again by any circulation.[19]

However, within twenty years of 'Carthon' there would be the beginnings of a geological revolution, emanating from the Edinburgh social and intellectual circle of which Macpherson was, if only temporarily, a part. In March and April of 1785, James Hutton (1726–1797) read papers to the Royal Society of Edinburgh outlining ideas that would appear in their first published form in 1788 in the first volume of the *Transactions of the Royal Society of Edinburgh* before eventually being published in 1795 in the two-volume *Theory of the Earth with Proofs and Illustrations*. Hutton's ideas were distilled and popularised following his death by his friend John Playfair (1748–1819) in his *Illustrations of the Huttonian Theory of the Earth* in 1802.

Hutton is seen, in the English-speaking world at least, as a founder of modern geology and uniformitarianism in particular. Uniformitarianism is the principle that geological phenomena are the result of the same set of physical laws operating across and throughout time. While

Burnet conceived of a process of erosion, he explicitly ruled out any accompanying principle of deposition and uplift believing, as he put it in the above quoted passage, that 'nothing is ever brought back again'. Hutton in contrast theorised both sides of this equation, demonstrating it through the identification of the observable phenomenon of the 'unconformity': a disjunction in the geological record usually caused by a plane of erosion amidst strata of deposition. More importantly, whereas for Burnet, working within a broadly millenarian perspective (though one of his purposes was to give a lie to the notion of imminent apocalypse), the process of erosion implied a timescale sanctioned by biblical understandings of the age of the world (because otherwise the topography 'would have long ere this destroyed itself'), for Hutton the cycle of erosion, deposition, and uplift suggested the complete opposite. In the closing lines of the 1788 text he famously pronounced:

> if the succession of worlds is established in the system of nature, it is in vain to look for anything higher in the origin of the earth. The result, therefore, of our present enquiry is, that we find no vestige of a beginning,—and no prospect of an end.[20]

The sense of geological time implied by Hutton's theory is its most important innovation. He bequeaths the notion of geological or 'deep' time, a perspective of profound importance for modernity as a whole given what it maintains about the appropriate place and timespan of humanity – the Anthropocene – within the age of the planet.[21] Everyone has their favourite analogy for the puny span of humanity's existence on Earth relative to the age of the planet (along the lines of, if the Earth has been around a year, *homo sapiens* turns up just in time to see in the New Year), but it is an awareness that has its roots in Hutton and what Stephen Jay Gould terms the 'cardinal transition' in the history of scientific thought.[22] The most vivid pictorial rendering of Hutton's perspective came in John Clerk of Eldin's (1728–1802) now famous illustration of the Jedburgh unconformity.[23] The top twenty-five per cent of the drawing is of a coach meeting a rider on the modern-day road, while the remaining seventy-five per cent of the picture is taken up with the geological strata, including the plane of unconformity, beneath their feet, a giddying abyss of previous time, to paraphrase Playfair's recollection of the impact of being shown this feature and having it explained to him by Hutton in the field. As Gidal puts it, also quoting Playfair, it is a 'compelling illustration of the "high antiquity and great revolutions of the globe" underlying the quotidian existence of human affairs'.[24] The effect is similar to the sublime impact of considering the depth of a body of water (discussed by Edmund Burke [1729/30–1797] in his 1757 *A Philosophical Enquiry Into the Origins of Our Ideas of the Sublime and Beautiful*). To that extent the closest modern equivalent might be the original poster for (and psychological effect engendered by) the movie *Jaws*: what makes us fear for the swimmer in that poster is only in part and most obviously the (patently exaggerated and oversized) shark heading in her direction, teeth displayed for the benefit of the viewer. It is the sheer depth of water that really forces home her vulnerability and helps to account for the more unsettling sense of dread upon which the film as a whole plays.

Returning to possible parallels between Hutton and *Ossian*, Gould notes that 'the discovery of deep time combined the insights of those we would now call theologians, archaeologists, historians and linguists – as well as geologists', and that Hutton was fortunate to be 'a full time intellectual at a time when Edinburgh was the thinking capital of Europe'.[25] This is suggestive in considering a relationship between Ossianic and Huttonian thought, and indeed Gidal draws a parallel between these 'near contemporary writings' as 'early forays in an experimental strain of Scottish geopoetics' that can be traced into the work of contemporary poets and artists.[26] That said, direct connections are hard to find. While Macpherson and Hutton may have had a number of mutual friends, they had them at rather different times. Macpherson was active in Edinburgh in the early 1760s but had moved to London by the time of the third (if one counts the *Fragments*) Ossian volume *Temora* in 1763 – and the distance was more than merely geographical, given the strains in Macpherson's relationships with some of his erstwhile friends by the middle of the decade. While there is evidence of Hutton's interest in geological matters from the 1750s (and it is almost certain that the ideas he first formalised to the Edinburgh Society in 1785 were familiar to his circle considerably beforehand), he did not move to Edinburgh and play a full role in the city's intellectual scene until 1770.

Specifically, in terms of the passage from 'Carthon' under discussion, the geological metaphors can be traced back both to the Book of Isaiah and Burnet, while Ossian's conviction that 'the ocean shrinks and grows again' may merely be a reference to the rising and falling tides. On the other hand, the stately quality of this description reaches for an idea and scale of rhythm that feels something other and more than the diurnal nature of the tide. A Huttonian frame of reference would interpret this phrase, juxtaposed with the idea of the mountains wasting, as a reference to the cyclical nature of geomorphological processes, the changes in sea level that accompany the cycle of erosion, deposition and uplift. It would be rather silly to claim that Macpherson was in some ways pre-figuring or intuiting Hutton's leap forward in geological understanding. It is possible to see *Ossian* as exemplifying a poetic sensibility that was being formed by – and giving significant voice to – a cultural and intellectual milieu that was also responsible for Hutton's later scientific thinking. *Ossian*, a prolonged and insistent mediation on the passage of time, is part of the cultural sensibility that allows for the imaginative leap in the direction of the idea of 'deep time', the distinctive element of this geomorphological understanding and, according to Gould, a 'turning point in human knowledge'.[27] After all, *Ossian*'s view is essentially the long one. The aged poet looks back to the times of glory through what seems to him an almost unbridgeable gulf and, if he draws one message from it, it is of the passing of all things, the fact that those things which seem so permanent and strong and real are but fleeting moments in the long march of history. This is the overwhelming message of 'Carthon', with its meditations on the vanity of human wishes and the likely permanence or otherwise of what seem to be the ageless features of the natural environment, the mountains, oceans, and even the celestial bodies. Indeed, there is a long and respectable tradition of Macpherson criticism, stretching back to Hugh Blair (1718–1800) and William Hazlitt (1778–1830), which has emphasised what Tom Normand calls 'the wretched bequest of Ossian's dream, a world of unresolved conflict and perpetual despair'.[28]

Yet, however acute this reading is, we also miss something if we do not also catch the note of heroic defiance that comes with Ossian's sense of 'deep time'. Fingal's central speech in 'Carthon' ends, after all, on a note not of despair, but of daring, and a statement of a belief in the things that can escape time's oblivion:

> They have but fallen before us: for, one day, we must fall.—why dost thou build the hall, son of the winged days? Thou lookest from thy towers today; yet a few years, and the blast of the desert comes; it howls in thy empty court and whistles round thy half-worn shield—And let the blast of the desert come! We shall be renowned in our day. The mark of my arm shall be in the battle, and my name in the song of the bards.—Raise the song; send round the shell: and let joy be heard in my hall.—When thou, sun of heaven, shalt fail! If thou shaft fail, thou mighty light! If thy brightness is for a season, like Fingal; our fame shall survive thy beams.[29]

The past is, after all, not entirely dead to us, or totally opaque, even if our view is but fleeting; and the voices of the past are not entirely silenced. And there is a peculiar power to *Ossian* that comes from precisely this tension, for example in 'Cath-Loda':

> Whence is the stream of years? Whither do they roll along? Where have they hid, in mist, their many-coloured sides? I look into the times of old, but they seem dim to Ossian's eyes, like reflected moon-beams, on a distant lake [...] Dweller between the shields; thou that awakest the failing soul, descend from thy wall, harp of Cona, with thy voices three! Come with that which kindles the past: rear the forms of old, on their own dark-brown years![30]

Similarly, Ossian's farewell at the end of 'Berrathon' (the final poem in the *Fingal* volume, then placed last in the two volumes of *Works*), articulates an awareness both of the remorseless passage of time and the ability of song to transcend the passing of all other things:

> Did thy beauty last, O Ryno? Stood the strength of car-borne Oscar? Fingal himself passed away; and the halls of his fathers forgot his steps.— And shalt thou remain, aged bard! when the mighty have failed?—But my fame shall remain, and grow like the oak of Morven; which lifts its broad head to the storm, and rejoices in the course of the wind.[31]

The poems themselves embody this tension: fragments of a lost whole re-assembled and made 'compleat' (in his word) by the editor and translator, Macpherson. They are testaments to the ravages of time and the vicissitudes of fifteen centuries; they represent the yawning chasm of a literary past that offers glimpses of alternative histories, traditions and lost worlds; and they mark the ability for things to endure and reach across that chasm. They are then a literary version of Hutton's geological unconformities, which testify simultaneously both to the almost incomprehensible vastness of earth's history, and yet also to its legibility, and the ability of science to recover an understanding of those lost worlds. Both represent a version of the Enlightenment sublime.

Ultimately, then, it is less Macpherson's sense of a dynamic restless Earth that is suggestive of developments in geology than it is his conception of time and history; the articulation of this conception in the subjectivity of Ossian (whose sense of the vastness of time is then as anachronistically modern as his fine manners); and, crucially, the placing of that sense in the context of landscape, rocks, and ruins. That subjectivity is the result of a wide range of influences and factors, only some of which this chapter has gestured towards: antiquarian speculation, Jacobite iconography and historiography, stoic philosophy, biblical scholarship, and aesthetic theory. The interaction of these elements goes to make up the Ossianic sensibility and create a compelling expression of a wider Scottish Enlightenment perspective that, in turn, provided fertile ground and an enabling sensibility for Hutton's later geological speculations.

CHAPTER SIXTEEN

Crossing Borders: Travel Writing and Eighteenth-Century Scotland

Alex Deans

Sir, I am now just enter'd *Scotland*, and that by the ordinary Way from *Berwick*. We tread upon *Scots* Ground, after about three Miles riding beyond *Berwick*; the little District between, they say, is neither in *England* or *Scotland* [...]

Daniel Defoe, *A Tour thro' the Whole Island of Great Britain*[1]

The entrance into Scotland has a very unpromising look; for it wanted, for some miles, the cultivation of the parts more distant from England: but the borders were necessarily neglected: for, till the accession of James VI. and even long after, the national enmity was kept up, and the borderers of both countries discouraged from improvements by the barbarous inroads of each nation [...]

Thomas Pennant, *A Tour in Scotland, 1769*[2]

Conflict lay close to the surface for many travellers to Scotland in the eighteenth century. In his perennial *A Tour thro' the Whole Island of Great Britain* (1724–27), Daniel Defoe (c. 1660–1731) inserts the transitional space of a 'debateable land' north of the Tweed, that elides a potentially hostile interface between England and Scotland.[3] Descriptions of border regions invite attention to both the continuities and disparities between neighbours, appearing as ready-made sites of national comparison which express separation as readily as union. In addition to the complexity of Great Britain as a political entity in this period, such moments shed light on travel writing's reflexive unfolding of place and history within a narrative of spatial progress.[4] In his *Tour of Scotland, 1769* (1771), the Welsh traveller Thomas Pennant (1726–1798) follows a gentlemanly imperative of impartiality in his scrupulously even ascription of Anglo-Scottish hostility when describing the border landscape passed over by Defoe as neither Scottish nor English. The passage suggests the sense in which much eighteenth-century travel writing reflected the period's obsession with land itself, as productive property that carried the moral and economic obligation of improvement, even as it increasingly competed with colonial sources of wealth as an object of national interest. The impoverishing legacy of past conflict is illustrated for Pennant by the more developed state of agriculture further north of Berwick and away from the border. Having described a germinal scene of rural modernisation, Pennant writes: 'I speak in the present tense; for there is still a mixture of the old negligence left amidst the recent improvements, which look like the works of a new colony in a wretched impoverished country'.[5] Pennant's language hints at something more complex and fraught beneath the apparently straightforward linking of Scotland's material progress with the relatively recent security of Hanoverian Great Britain. Further along the road, Pennant writes that 'the country relapses', as if the forward movement of the traveller warrants an analogous form of progress in the condition of the landscape.[6] Despite his very different perspective, Pennant echoes the ineluctably spatial figuration of national development in Defoe's introduction to the Scottish section of his *Tour*: 'they are where we were, I mean as to the Improvement of their Country and Commerce; and they may be where we are'.[7]

A complex relationship between the forms and meanings of progress (historical and spatial) suffuses eighteenth-century travel writing about Scotland. On one level, many eighteenth-century travel writers viewed their own efforts in observing and recording what Defoe called 'the present State of Things' – often alongside their own suggestions for ameliorative schemes – as important contributions to a shared project of national improvement. The broad premise of the travel text as a narrative description of a journey, in contrast to the parallel genre of the topographical survey, lends an experiential structure to the miscellany of subjects in which travellers were interested; it also amplifies the disruptive potential of encounter, and with it the radical diversity of place. If the border between England and Scotland was one site where travel revealed disjuncture, profounder still were the internal disparities encountered by travellers who crossed from Scotland's Lowlands into the Gaelic-speaking Highlands. Indeed, the story of the Scottish tour in the eighteenth century is partly one of the rise of the Highland tour as a fashionable practice of British domestic travel, rivalling excursions to less remote locations (from a metropolitan perspective) such as Wales and the Lake District.[8]

Ina Ferris has described travel writing at the end of the eighteenth century as 'less a genre than a generic possibility: a loose discursive field, diverse and disordered'.[9] In this sense too, eighteenth-century travel writing about Scotland tended to range across borders, incorporating the fields of antiquarianism, natural history, and political economy as well as elements of literary culture into its expansive purview. This chapter considers travel writing about Scotland primarily by British writers, though there is much to be said about voyages and travels abroad by Scottish writers such as James Bruce's *Travels to Discover the Source of the Nile (1790)*, and such material is often closely related to that discussed here in terms of form, content and theme.[10] Similarly, while this chapter focuses on non-fictional narratives arising from journeys undertaken within Scotland during the period, such works clearly share some affinity with topographical or place writing about Scotland more generally, from ballads, poems and novels with a loco-descriptive or travel element, such as Tobias Smollett's *The Expedition of Humphry Clinker* (1769), to works of survey or description like John Sinclair's *Statistical Account of Scotland* (1791–99). Though beyond the scope of this chapter, such works can and have been productively studied alongside travel texts *per se* under the wider banner of the spatial humanities.[11] Published accounts by women tourists in this period are few and far between in comparison to those by men, though as Betty Hagglund has shown, numbers begin to rise when manuscript sources are taken into account.[12] For this reason, and because of the often complex relationship between printed and unpublished travels in general, manuscript represents an important area of research for those interested in the eighteenth-century Scottish tour, though for purposes of space and accessibility, this chapter focuses on published texts.

Dividing Lines

Betty A. Schellenberg notes that the way in which Daniel Defoe's *Tour Thro' the Whole Island of Great Britain*, by 'plac[ing] Scotland and England in a progressive historical sequence', has the effect of painting the Union itself as a work in progress, and that this incompleteness is reflected by the peripheral status of the Scottish material in the text itself, separated from the main body with a discrete introduction.[13] If the central conceit of Defoe's *Tour* is one of circulation, in which the movement and perspective of the traveller and the flow of trade described work to centralise London as a starting point and destination, Scotland and particularly its Highlands, do not seem to conform to this image of national space as a circuit of commerce and consumption. While Defoe's *Tour* does contain an account of the Highlands, it simultaneously reflects his lack of direct experience of the region and its irrelevance to the national image which Defoe is constructing around the primacy of business and trade. Describing a crossing over the River Ness, Defoe writes:

> When you are over this Bridge you enter that which we truly call the North of *Scotland*, and others the North *Highlands*; in which are several distinct Shires, but cannot call for a distinct *Description*, because it is all one undistinguish'd Range of Mountains and Woods, overspread with vast, and almost uninhabited Rocks and Steeps fill'd with Deer innumerable, and of a great many Kinds.[14]

In part, Defoe's lack of original information on the Highlands reflected the obstacles presented to tourists by the region's lack of infrastructure. But it may also suggest a discursive limit as much as a lack of information, in the sense that the polite mode of Defoe's tour (underlined by its epistolary conceit and London addressee), everywhere seeking comparisons with metropolitan business and manners, is not equipped to deal with the radically different cultural and economic scene presented by the Highlands.

Defoe's Lowland Scottish contemporary, the traveller John Macky (d. 1726), provides an equally distanced account of the Highlands in his 1723 *A Journey through Scotland,* skirting the eastern fringes of the region on his own narrative and slipping into topographical generalities when describing the western interior. In both accounts, the Highlands exist as a wilderness to be skimmed rather than investigated, implying not only that the writer's knowledge of the Highlands is murky and indistinct, but that these are the native qualities of the region itself. In Defoe's evocation of an 'undistinguished' and 'uninhabited' landscape, we can perhaps already see the 'aesthetics of negation' which Peter Womack attributes to later Romantic writing on the Highlands, that would see the region refracted through the lenses of the Burkean sublime and James Macpherson's (1736–1796) *Poems of Ossian* (1760–63), as well as the economic imperatives already registering here.[15] However it may be too simplistic to see tourists and travel writing as merely complicit in the production of a Romantic Highlands that displaced the authentic culture and traditions of the Gaels, and thus as the ideological concomitants of economic practices that would empty the landscape through clearance and emigration.

For all that Defoe chastises the 'Northern Vanity' that confines tours by Scottish authors like Macky to 'describing the Seats of the Nobility and Gentry' to avoid the nation's shortcomings, national differences seem hardly to register when both writers cross the Highland line.[16] The negational character of much Highland description is captured by the traveller Martin Martin (d. 1718) in his *Description of the Western Isles of Scotland* (1703) when he writes that

> Foreigners, sailing thro the Western Isles, have been tempted, from the Sight of so many Wild Hills, that seem to be covered all over with Heath, and fac'd with High Rocks, to imagin [*sic*] the Inhabitants, as well as the Places of their residence, are barbarous [...] The like is supposed by many that live in the South of *Scotland*, who know no more of the Western Isles than the Natives of *Italy*.[17]

A native of Skye and Gaelic-speaker, Martin made a number of journeys in the Hebrides around the turn of the eighteenth century, under the encouragement of the Scottish Geographer Royal Robert Sibbald (1641–1722) and Hans Sloane (1616–1743) of the Royal Society in London. The resulting *Voyage to St. Kilda* (1698) and *Description of the Western Isles* (1703) depicted a society and culture that were endangered, even prior to the shocks of Culloden and the rise of commercial landlordism. Martin's credulity towards the phenomenon of second sight and Hebridean superstition in general may have undermined his authority as an observer.[18] However, Martin was explicit in his aim to approach the Hebrides as a source as well as object of knowledge, writing that 'The Inhabitants of these Islands do for the most part labour under the want of knowledge of Letters, and other useful Arts and Sciences; notwithstanding which defect, they seem to be better vers'd in the Book of Nature, than many that have greater opportunities of improvement'.[19] Accordingly, Martin recounts numerous botanical remedies and uses of plant and animal resources such as seal flesh and skin, gathered from locals during his travels in the Hebrides. A fieldworker rather than a literary observer like Defoe, Martin addressed developing cosmopolitan knowledge networks in which there was an increasing synergy between the study of the natural world and that of human society and history through empirical observation. In doing so, he asserted the dualistic potential of local knowledge to reveal information about the wider world through the character of a particular place and its people. In this sense, Martin anticipates the paradoxical way in which Thomas Pennant, in Penny Fielding's words, 'privileges the local as a source of authentic knowledge communicated by individual subjects and subsumes it into a larger structure'.[20] Though not always written as travel texts, Martin's works were a vital touchstone for later travellers to the Hebrides including Pennant and Samuel Johnson (1709–1784), and a necessary corrective to Defoe's dismissive view of the Highlands as characterless wilderness, and early-eighteenth Scottish place-writing as parochial in scope and audience. If Martin's lament that his own work lacks 'a politer turn of phrase' is partly a rhetorical turn designed to stress the unvarnished and, thus, authentically empirical nature of his descriptions, it nonetheless reflects a point of stylistic difference with other writers.[21] While Defoe's *Tours* presented national information as a strand of polite literature suitable for the leisured reader, Martin's reflected a burgeoning interest in a localising type of natural enquiry; two traditions that would be increasing integrated by travellers later in the eighteenth century.

Local Knowledge

In summer 1772, the botanist and future head of the Royal Society Joseph Banks (1743–1820) visited the small island of Staffa on the return leg of a voyage to Iceland with the naturalist Daniel Solander (1733–1782). Banks had risen to celebrity for his role on the *Endeavour* voyage to the South Pacific under James Cook a few years earlier, and an emphasis on discovery and encounter reminiscent of colonial travels further afield animates his account of the island, culminating in a revelatory moment in one of its basaltic sea caves:

> We asked the name of it. Said our guide, the cave of *Fhinn*; What is *Fhinn*? said we. *Fhinn Mac Coul*, whom the translator of *Ossian*'s works has called *Fingal*. How fortunate that in this cave we should meet with the remembrance of that chief, whose existence, as well as that of the whole *Epic* poem is almost doubted in *England*.[22]

Banks's account of Staffa, published as part of Thomas Pennant's *Voyage to the Hebrides 1772* (more on which below), touches on several of the powerful new currents animating an expansion in Scottish and particularly Highland travels in the decades after Culloden. Banks's interest in Staffa reflected a broader application of cosmopolitan natural history networks to overlooked domestic resources in a manner that echoed the example of naturalist Carl Linnaeus in Sweden. In a discussion of the dynamic between travels and authorship, Bill Bell and Charles Withers reference the status of 'the book as an object of, and means to, communicative action in science, literature and exploration'.[23] Here they echo James Secord's conception, in turn adapted from Jürgen Habermas, of 'knowledge-making itself as a form of communicative action,' in which 'Questions of trust, testimony and communitarian objectivity are simultaneously questions of how knowledge travels, to whom it is available, and how agreement is achieved'.[24] Secord's model helps to underline the role of the first-person travel narrative as a method of simultaneously transmitting and legitimating new knowledge. Banks's account of Staffa records an act of discovery through an encounter with a local source as much as it does the site of Fingal's Cave and its etymon.

Like many of his contemporaries, Banks found the ethnographic attraction of Britain's ancient literature hard to resist. The *Poems of Ossian* by James Macpherson (1736–1796), intellectually underwritten by the Scottish literati and Enlightenment conjectural history, painted the post-conflict Highlands in a new light as the classical ground of Gaelic epic tradition, whose authenticity seemed ripe for confirmation or refutation by travellers in search of sources. As Fiona Stafford notes, in the early 1760s Macpherson himself, with the encouragement of the Scottish literati, had toured the Hebrides in search of poetic fragments and traditions preserved in oral culture and manuscript.[25] The reformulation of the Gaelic language and its speakers as the vessel of an ancient tradition in a region of ecological interest created the conditions for major departures from the work of earlier tourists, Martin Martin excepted, who had tended to view both as an obstacle to the work of rendering the nation in smooth gradations of deviance from a normative metropolitan centre. Frederick Albritton Jonsson has described the Highland tour of this period as a 'time machine for the adherents of stadial history', while the Gael was seen, in Charles Withers' words, as a 'contemporary ancestor'.[26] In the era of Carl Linnaeus (1707–1778) and *Ossian*, the formulation of Highland primitivity as a political and symbolic threat to the integrity of the Union was inverted and recast as living evidence of Britain's noble 'cultural origins'.[27] All of this took place in the context of unparalleled state intervention into the Highlands. In addition to the military road network and chain of forts constructed in response to Risings of 1715 and 1745, a large number of forfeited Jacobite estates fell under state ownership and administration.[28] As Jonsson argues, these Annexed Estates constituted an ecological 'laboratory for the Enlightenment', where new forms of agricultural practice and social organisation were attempted.[29]

If the collapse of such schemes was later a factor in justifying the mass clearance of Highlanders, the 1760s were characterised by optimistic projections and searches for natural wealth. Scottish naturalists such as John Walker and James Robertson produced tours and reports of their attempts to discover mineral and plant resources in the Highlands, blazing a trail for the leisured elite and middle-class tourism of the following decades.[30]

Improving Visions: Pennant and Johnson

The achievement of Thomas Pennant was in mobilising the knowledge networks and civic spiritedness associated with Enlightenment projection to produce commercially successful travel volumes. As Jonsson writes: 'Pennant's best-selling tours of Scotland repackaged the business of strategic surveying into a form of polite entertainment.'[31] The success of Pennant's *A Tour in Scotland 1769* (first published in 1771) encouraged a second visit in 1772, to take in the Hebrides and parts of the west Highlands and east coast omitted from his earlier travels, resulting in the two-part *Tour in Scotland and Voyage to the Hebrides, 1772* (first published 1774–1776). As suggested by the incorporation of his friend Joseph Banks's account of Staffa, Pennant's 1772 tour of Scotland was not simply a single author's account of his travels, but the result of a temporally and spatially expansive process which reveals the necessarily social and material nature of knowledge production and print. Pennant travelled with the clergymen-botanists John Lightfoot (1735–1788) and John Stuart (1743–1821) – the latter a Gaelic-speaker – in addition to the artist Moses Griffith (1747–1819). As well as reflecting the role of visual representation in the work of natural history and antiquarianism, Pennant's employment of Griffith (a servant whom he had trained to be his personal draughtsman) suggests the growing appetite for pictures of Scottish scenes and views among those who could afford to purchase Pennant's extensively illustrated volumes.

In advance of his 1772 expedition, Pennant circulated printed queries soliciting information on natural history and antiquities from local sources, and afterwards corresponded extensively with figures such as Reverend Donald MacQueen of Skye (1712–1785) and the aforementioned John Stuart, who provided detailed information on the economy, natural history and culture of the Highlands and Hebrides. Pennant's interest in locale was matched by a strong vein of social critique running through his 1772 *Tour*. While descriptions of the interiors of 'Highland huts' were a recurring trope of the genre, Pennant's account of a cottage on Islay and its inhabitants is particularly unsparing. There he finds 'A set of people worn down with poverty: their habitations scenes of misery, made of loose stones; without chimnies, without doors, excepting the faggot opposed to the wind at one or other of the appertures, permitting the smoke to escape through the other, in order to prevent the pains of suffocation'.[32] This is less an aestheticisation of the Highlander as a noble savage unchanged since antiquity, and more an indictment of the grinding poverty Pennant observed throughout the Hebrides, which he attributed both to the region's lack of improvement and the greed of clan chiefs turned commercial landlords. Yet, in keeping with the spirit of projection, Pennant is broadly optimistic about the economic future of the Highlands within the Union. Having observed 'a fleet of at least hundred boats' fishing for herring in the '*Alpine* wildness and magnificence' of Loch Hourn, Pennant reflects warmly that 'there is no part of our dominions so remote, so inhospitable, and so unprofitable, as to deny employ and livelihood to thousands'.[33] Here the 'wild and romantic' scenery of the Highlands seems to ennoble as much as inhibit the vision of productive human activity, a vision which would be further pursued in tours by Scottish improvers such as James Anderson and John Knox.[34]

Hot on the heels of Pennant's *Voyage to the Hebrides 1772*, the more widely known and celebrated tour of Samuel Johnson and James Boswell in 1773 was notoriously sceptical towards the Ossianic craze that had so captured the imagination of Joseph Banks and others. According to Boswell, their journey was inspired by Martin Martin's *Description*, which 'impressed us with a notion that we might contemplate a system of life almost totally different from what we had been accustomed to see'.[35] Boswell seems to allude here to one of the most famous passages in Johnson's earlier account of their tour, in which he writes, 'We came thither too late see what we expected, a people of peculiar appearance, and a system of antiquated life'.[36] In part, Johnson's lament serves as an implicit rebuke to the stadialist 'time travellers' discussed by Jonsson and Withers, as well as to the broader tenor of Scottish Enlightenment social theory and its underwriting of Macpherson's *Ossian*. For Johnson, it was contradictory to see Gaelic culture as both authentically ancient and extant: a double-edged perspective that allowed him to remark incisively on the decline of Gaelic culture, but which also drew justified accusations of anglophone chauvinism from Gaels such as the Reverend Donald McNicol.[37] Johnson was critical of Lowland Scottish attempts to impose improvement on the Highlands, further dismantling the traditional clan structure of the region's society in the process. Echoing Martin Martin, Johnson writes, 'To the southern inhabitants of Scotland, the state of the mountains and the islands is equally unknown with that of *Borneo* or *Sumatra* [...] They are strangers to the language and the manners, to the advantages and wants of the people whose life they would model, and whose evils they would remedy'.[38] In part, Johnson's criticisms represented an English Tory resistance to the improving spirit of the eighteenth-century Scottish elite, but they also prophesied the more brutal phase of Highland improvement represented by the clearances of the later-eighteenth and nineteenth centuries and lodged a claim for the legitimacy of Highland social and cultural difference within the Union, in opposition to the attempted remaking of the region in a Lowland image of commercial society.[39]

Before concluding this section however, it is worth noting the way in which anxieties regarding the effects of modernisation were latent in the Scottish tour as a genre. Returning to his first tour of 1769, Pennant uses a moment of geographical transition as he crosses the divide between Highlands and Lowlands, to implicitly reflect on the historical transition which the former region was undergoing:

> The country from *Luss* to the Southern extremity of the lake continually improves; the mountains sink gradually into small hills; the land is highly cultivated, well planted, and well inhabited. I was struck with rapture at a sight so long new to me: it would have been without alloy, had it not been dashed with the uncertainty whether the mountain virtue, hospitality, would flourish with equal vigor in the softer scenes I was on the point of entering on; for in the *Highlands* every house gave welcome to the traveller.[40]

The passage recalls the inherent metaphor of spatiotemporal movement as historical progress which we saw in Pennant's earlier account of the Anglo-Scottish border. If the traveller's forward progress is aligned with improvement, it is equated here with the loss of what is left behind, in time as well as space, and qualified by uncertainty about the destination. If this speaks in part to Enlightenment thinking about the spatialised nature of historical development, it is also a function of the travel narrative as a genre that lends itself to reflection, comparison and contemplation in a way that the rival forms of the survey or chorographic synthesis do not.

Leisure

If Johnson's scepticism towards *Ossian* and criticism of Lowland Scotland made his legacy a difficult torch to bear, Pennant's *Tours* had a direct sequel in the works of the clergyman Charles Cordiner (c. 1746–1794), whose *Antiquities and Scenery of the North of Scotland, in a Series of Letters to Thomas Pennant* and *Remarkable Ruins and Romantic Prospects of North Britain*, followed Pennant and Griffith's example in their illustration of tourist sites. In the 1780s, the improving and 'naturalist-antiquary' concerns of Pennant and other virtuosi were easily parlayed into the stuff of leisured tourism, as both a literary and travel practice.[41] Of central importance here were William Gilpin's *Observations, Relative Chiefly to Picturesque Beauty*, which arguably consecrated the aesthetic appeal of the Highland landscape, by no means secure in the accounts of earlier travellers who equated the appeal of terrain with its level of cultivation. However, the picturesque was complex both in the protocols by which it conformed and often distorted physical scenery in verbal and visual representation, and in its particular modulation of the tourist-as-subject, which tended to emphasise the integrity of sensory experience over the class-based authority of the gentleman virtuoso.

This logic applied both to scenery *per se* and to scenes in the narrative sense of composed episodes of experience. Thus in *Letters on a Tour through Various Parts of Scotland* (1794), the traveller John Lettice (1737–1832), having memorably described Buachaille Etive Mòr at the entrance to Glencoe as 'the carcase of a mountain pealed, sore and hideously disgustful', retires to the inn at King's House, where he imagines travellers reciting Ossianic verse, inspired by Macpherson's connection of its characters to the locale.[42] Continuing the thematic alignment of mountains and ancient poetry, Lettice elsewhere describes an encounter with 'a young female Highlander' near the base of Cruachan. Inserting a translation of the Gaelic legend of the mountain's inhabitant, 'Bera the aged', Lettice notes that the woman is 'not unprovided with Gaelic songs', and asks himself, 'who knows, but I may have been listening to a descendant of one of the old bards? long may have been the line of her fathers, and old Ossian, himself, her great progenitor!'[43] The ethnographic trope of Gael as 'contemporary ancestor' manifests here as a device of literary personification rather than philosophical analogy, while Lettice (as below) breaks into Ossianic syntax. Before Lettice is able to quiz his interlocutor on the authenticity of *Ossian* however, the road splits, and 'The songstress bidding us adieu, took that, which branched off to the left; and, soon disappearing, in the hazy dusk of the evening, she descended into the vale of her kindred, to sing of the loves of the chiefs; the glory days of old'.[44] The passage basks in the mixture of moral sincerity and self-irony characteristic of sentimental literature, but it also harks forwards to William Wordsworth's poem, 'The Solitary Reaper' (the product of another Highland tour), in its use of a female figure to symbolise the alien sublimity of Gaelic culture to the anglophone traveller.[45]

Lettice's touristic sensibility reflected the increasing accessibility and popularity of the Scottish tour as a leisure pursuit concerned with aesthetic enjoyment, in contrast to the improvement and knowledge-focused travels of Pennant and others. Sarah Murray's (1744–1811) *Companion and Useful Guide to the Beauties of Scotland* (1799) helped to formalise this shift by explicitly advising the reader on how to conduct their own tour: 'informing them of those objects which are worthy of notice, and at the same time acquainting them where, and by what means they can get at them in the safest and most comfortable manner'.[46] That this statement of purpose forms part of an opening apologia requesting clemency from reviewers, reflects the particularly male-dominated nature of the eighteenth-century Scottish tour as a genre, and a sense that in order to avoid censure Murray must strictly limit her claims as an author, particularly in comparison to the virtuosic sweep of earlier gentleman travellers. One apparent product of this concern is the structure of the volume, which separates the 'Guide' from the 'Description', distinguishing its advertised knowledge content on the logistics of travel from the more experiential narrative that follows. But this restraint of authority also has the effect of concentrating description on the physical exertions and risks encountered by Murray in her own person. There are numerous passages like the following, in which Murray describes her efforts to gain a view of the Bracklinn Falls near Callander:

> I crept through the wood and broken rock, until I got upon a huge projecting tower, in front of the chasm, where the pent up water rushes through the narrowest passage. In getting, however, to that point, I was obliged to step over several rents in the rocks, of at least a foot wide, the depth of them not to be seen; but the grand beauties of the cascade, and the deep glen below, seen from that station, made me full amends for my temerity in getting to it.[47]

If, in the case of the travel text as a form of 'communicative action', a first-person voice performed the function of testimony in relation to new natural or antiquarian knowledge, then here the object of testimony is the emotion and sense of aesthetic appreciation that the experience of travel provides.[48] Hagglund describes Murray as 'writing both within and in opposition to the prevailing travel writing conventions of the late eighteenth century'.[49] In part, Murray's text signals the autonomy of the Scottish tour as a leisure practice not necessarily linked to the Enlightenment concerns of knowledge production and improvement. Her scramble above the Bracklinn Falls also suggests the sense in which this model of tourism brought with it a different form of spatial affect from that found in earlier travels, one that was anchored in the sensibility of the individual tourist rather than locale itself. Murray's sublimation of the touristic tropes of discovery and encounter, following Gilpin and others, into a series of *Beauties* ripe for recreation by the readers of her *Guide* seems a suitable place to end this necessarily selective account of the transformations of the Scottish tour in the long eighteenth century.

CHAPTER SEVENTEEN

Scots and the Language of the Sea in Tobias Smollett's *Roderick Random* and William Falconer's *The Shipwreck*

Janet Sorensen

In Tobias Smollett's *The Adventures of Roderick Random*, both Roderick and his father share what the preface refers to as 'the disposition of Scots, addicted to travel'.[1] This Scots proclivity for travel, the preface explains, is why the 'chief personage' of the work was a North-Briton. Despite this facetious claim, neither character is especially given to wanderlust, but rather both find themselves, as was the case for many Scots of the eighteenth century, driven to travel, including, most predominantly, sea travel, because of the exigencies of their circumstances. While a romance device of defiant and doomed love sets Roderick's father on his seaborne ventures, more prosaic and material conditions send Roderick to sea. Like many Scots of the time, he is forced to head to London and hopes of better economic opportunities and finds the navy the most promising among them after a series of disappointments.[2] And, like many Scots, the press gang captures him before he can secure a suitable appointment, forcing him into terms of maritime labour not of Roderick's choosing.

Britain was a seafaring nation in the eighteenth century, and the ships of its global maritime expansion were heavily populated with Scots. Some of them were writers. This chapter examines writings of two of the most popular of those mariner Scots writers in the eighteenth century, Tobias Smollett's (1721–1771) novel *The Adventures of Roderick Random* (1748) and William Falconer's (1732–1769) poem *The Shipwreck* (1762). It asks how maritime experience shaped this Scots imaginative writing, not only in its representations of life at sea, but also in its use of those representations, particularly at the level of language, to make a place for Scots within the British national imaginary. For both of these Scottish writers, imaginative representations of mariners and their language often negotiated the pressing questions of distance and proximity posed by increasingly mobile Scots to their status as Britons. Scots' mobility was one point of attack in the often Scotophobic culture of eighteenth-century south

Britain, with disparaging images of Scots on the move, descending locust-like on London. Examining Smollett's and Falconer's works reveals how they repurposed representations of distance and mobility in sailors and sea language to cultivate sympathetic relations with itinerant Scots characters.

Although *Roderick Random* depicts life on board a naval vessel interestingly and in great detail, the narrator initially figures life at sea as a dropping out of sight. Pregnant with Roderick, whose forced itinerancy will eventually take him away to sea, his mother has a premonitional dream that, 'she was delivered of a tennis-ball, which the devil struck so forcibly [...] that it disappeared'.[3] Deeply melancholic after his father's murderous neglect of his wife, and then sailing off, we later learn, to the West Indies, Roderick's own father, the narrator explains, 'disappeared'. Tom Bowling, Roderick's kind uncle, a ship's lieutenant, disappears from Roderick's life – and the narrative action – to return to his ship after a brief, consolatory visit with Roderick, and then disappears from the radar altogether, as it were, when he must go on the run after a violent encounter with his captain. His fellow sailor tells Roderick 'we could never after get sight of him'.[4]

Smollett sets these disappearing acts, however, within the emerging form of the novel, a genre in which, as Ian Watt observes, the writer's 'aim is *to bring his object home* to us in all its concrete particulars'.[5] In a new age of mobility, bringing the object home presented a particular challenge. Smollett's seafaring Scots might figure the outer edges of that mobility, inhabiting, at points, a remote and, to most, invisible distant space. Yet Smollett deploys emerging novelistic techniques to bring them home to readers. One, perhaps counterintuitive, technique of 'bringing his object home' is Smollett's representation of technical maritime argot. In what Margaret Cohen has called a 'maritime picaresque', Roderick is the travelling picaro, yet Roderick's father and uncle are also sea travellers.[6] And they know and, in his uncle's case, speak almost exclusively that maritime argot.

Crucially, Smollett, the first Scot to represent a seafaring Scots protagonist in prose fiction, chooses to represent his mobile Scottish characters Roderick and Tom Bowling speaking nautical language, but not Scots language. In representations of his Scottish characters' speech and Roderick's thoughts, Smollett uses Standard English. When Tom and Roderick speak a non-standard language, it is maritime language, a specialised, often quite technical, language. It is not, then, in their Scots language that Smollett marks their remoteness and movement, but in technical nautical language. In the developing context of a standard English print world, an English based on the practices of England's home counties, both Scots and maritime languages could signify an outsiders itinerant's language – a language that marks their distance from 'home'. Yet Smollett completely switches out his Scots characters' non-standard Scots language for non-standard technical nautical language. And as their specialised nautical language – and not their Scots language – is made central to depicting and indeed differentiating these remote Scottish others of British society, it also becomes the way in which these Scots can be brought home to British readers.

Smollett, of course, was not the first to depict technical sea language in print. He draws from a variety of sources, from journalism to song and drama, all of which depicted mariners' language as a source of entertaining outsiderness. Smollett adopts these representations of sea language and the outsiderness attributed to their speakers – and not representations of their Scots language – in part to position his Scots-speakers as those earlier works did, as curious outsiders, novel figures whose oddness and cultural distance are on display in their outlandish language. Early in the eighteenth century popular journalistic works such as Ned Ward's (1667–1731) *A Trip to Jamaica* (1698) and *The Wooden World Dissected* (1706), for instance, had offered images of sailors humorously alien in their language.[7] *The Wooden World Dissected* describes the language of the master of a man-of-war as 'fuller of crabb'd terms than a Moorfield's conjurer', and offers some examples of those 'crabb'd terms' with 'equinoctial, edyptick, azimaths'.[8] Ward represents sailors' language as distinguishing them from the narrator and from readers, situating its speakers, even when on shore, as inhabitants of a foreign wooden world with its own incomprehensible technical jargon.

In Ward's texts, nautical jargon repeatedly baffles landlubbers in ways not unlike Smollett's own representations of Scots speaking to English listeners. When Strap, Roderick's pal and loyal servant, addresses a London carman, Roderick describes how Strap 'was answered by a stare accompanied with the word, "Anan!" Upon which I came up in order to explain the question, but had the misfortune to be unintelligible likewise, the carman damning us for a lousy Scotch guard'.[9] Like Scots in London, even when nearby and visible, sailors remain remote and strange with their odd jargon.

Anticipating novelistic techniques of displaying the strangeness of different pockets of British society while bringing them home to readers, Ward's texts brandish sailors' technical argot as a strange curiosity that is nonetheless part of – usually unseen – British life.[10] His journalistic work introduces the strange but also makes it familiar. Such techniques of linguistic representation – depicting the strange language of compatriots, emphasising their strangeness through that unusual language, while also incorporating them into a diverse Britain – make their way into Smollett's prose fiction. It is significant, however, that in *Roderick Random*, as I have noted, it is not representations of Scots, but of sea language that function in this way. Neither Strap's nor Roderick's nor Tom Bowling's Scots is represented on the page. What is represented, instead, is their sea language. And crucially, the book's protagonist encounters the technical sea jargon that is represented on the page as a foreign language that he, like the reader, must learn and assimilate. Roderick, who becomes familiar enough with the language to use it, initially shares the readers' alienated response to this unusual jargon, which Roderick refers to as 'the confused noise of the ship's crew'.[11] When he first encounters this maritime world and its language, Roderick emphasises the division he experiences between a new nautical life and his own status as a landlubber:

> I was [...] carried on board a pressing tender [...] thrust down into the hold, among a parcel of miserable wretches [...] I desired one of my fellow-captives [...] to take a handkerchief out of my pocket and tie it round my [bleeding] head. He [...] went to the grating of the hatchway, and with astonishing composure sold it to a bum-boat woman.* [12]

Smollett's footnote in the original texts reads: '*a bum-boat woman is one who sells bread, cheese, greens, liquor, and fresh provision to the sailors, in a small boat that lies along-side of the ship'.[13] Roderick's – and readers' – distance from the naval world into which he is pressed is marked both through a paratextual note and through spatial imagery that emphasises Roderick's initial separation from this world, as he finds himself confined below deck and separated by 'gratings'. Here is an initial partition between remote, moving sea world and home, marked in image and language. While English readers might perceive Roderick's Scottishness and Scots language as inherent markers of difference and distance, they share Roderick's encounter with the new and strange nautical language.

Throughout his sea journey Roderick emphasises the distinct status of that technical sea language. When he describes how 'my uncle ordered the studding-sails to be hoisted, and the ship to be cleared for engaging', he makes a point to note that this is the language of a separate group: 'but finding that (to use the seamen's phase) we were very much wronged by the ship which had us in chace [sic] [...] he commanded the studding-sails to be taken'.[14] Yet he also comes to master this language enough to translate it, explaining at one point that 'the cock-pit [...] is the place allotted for the habitation of the surgeon's mates'.[15] Like Scots, maritime language would be a strange language for many British readers, yet *Roderick Random* depicts maritime language as an initially strange, but also assimilable, language, as modelled through its Scots protagonist's relation to it.

This technical maritime language functions on a variety of levels in fiction of the period and in Smollett's text. Technical sea language not only established and negotiated itinerant outsiders, but could also signal the credibility of print representations of what was for readers an otherwise remote, out-of-sight existence. Defoe's use of technical maritime language in *Robinson Crusoe*, *Colonel Jack*, and *Captain Singleton*, for instance, is central to his realism; his technical terms are among the 'vivid details' by which readers attach his characters 'much more completely to their environments'.[16] They are part of the relentlessly referential language that underwrites a sense of transparent representation of the real in emerging realist fiction. In this calling up of a real world, technical sea language encourages readers to imagine and to credit the remote oceanic experience.

It is critical, for instance, that Roderick uses technical naval language – 'the admiral discovered four ships to leeward, and made signal for our ship and four more to chase' – moments before describing how he was 'well-nigh blinded with brains' in the ensuing battle.[17] The spatially and experientially remote experience of violent sea battle is brought home to readers in part by calling up that world through nautical, referential language. Smollett's novelistic representation of technical sea language, then, does more than differentiate sailors from readers, if only to bring them together through explanation and assimilation. It also allows readers to imagine and credit the existence of those remote figures, a means of making the distant present. Remote sailors are made real through representations of their specialised and often technical language, even as that language is also a reminder of their distance from the land-bound.

While Scots language too might add to the authenticity or reality effects emerging in prose fiction at this time, culturally it did not possess the same authority as technical and scientific jargon. With the Royal Society, since the seventeenth century, issuing directions for the recording of technical information on sea voyages, nautical jargon had a cultural imprimatur that Scots did not. And while both Scots and mariners' jargon could signal comic meaning, mariners' jargon did not suffer the institutionalised delegitimisation that Scots did, with books and lectures aimed at eliminating it from 'proper' language. Nautical jargon, alternatively, had another, authorised existence in the scientific discourse of the day.

At times, fiction might even 'humanise' that sanctioned, scientific technical sea language as Margaret Cohen argues. She notes how passages of technical sea language also function as what Philippe Hamon has called 'narration-description' – dissolving fiction's traditional distinctions between plot and description by narrating specialised objects in action. This narration-description, Cohen observes, has the effect of 'naturaliz[ing] technological language, both humanizing and dramatizing it'.[18] The humanisation of technical sea language allows it, by the time of Smollett's *Roderick Random*, to create affective connections between readers and mariners. These qualities are part of what makes the strangeness of technical sea language – as opposed to the strangeness of Scots – a language through which to facilitate affective relations between readers and Smollett's Scots characters.

We see this humanising of the technical when Roderick integrates nautical language into the high emotion of a deadly storm at sea, describing how

> Some clung to the yards, endeavouring to unbend the sails that were split into a thousand pieces flapping in the wind; others tried to furl those which were yet whole, while the masts, at every pitch, bent and quivered like twigs, as if they would have shivered into innumerable splinters!— While I considered this scene with equal terror and astonishment, one of the main-braces broke, by the shock whereof two sailors were flung from the yard's arm into the sea.[19]

As we will see too in Falconer's *The Shipwreck*, the alien, dry quality of technical language works in a complex way in such passages, as the scene and action invest that language with feeling, even sublimity, and with sympathy for powerless sailors. Similarly, when Roderick recounts a fierce battle in Carthagena, he begins with technical sea language,

'Our ship [...] immediately weighed, and in less than half an hour came to an anchor before the castle of Bocca Chica, with a spring upon our cable. The cannonading (which indeed was terrible!) began. The surgeon, after having crossed himself, fell flat on the deck.'[20] The following battle sees many casualties, including Roderick's friend's loss of his hand, 'shattered to pieces with grape shot'.[21] Not only elevated by associations with the prestige of technical language, nautical language is here sutured to adventure and to the emotions – and suffering – of warfare.

Alternatively, it is worth noting that while *Roderick Random* does not include representations of Scots language, it does include depictions of Welsh dialect, associated not with the charged heights of naval battle, but with the petty domestic aspects of shipboard life. Roderick's Welsh shipmate, Mr Morgan, shows inordinate concern with his rations, exclaiming, 'Cot is my life! All the pork is gone', soon after Roderick begins to observe him, and later offering the wisdom that 'Prandy was the best menstruum for onion and sheese' and praising Glamorgan's 'produce of goats and putter [butter]'.[22] While the text adapts the placeless language of technical ship terms to high emotions wrought by battles and storms, it attaches local language, such as Morgan's Welsh pronunciation, to a domestic, sentimental sphere. Long after being separated from Morgan, without hope of seeing him again, it is by the smell of Morgan's humble concoction of onions and 'putter' that Roderick recognises and is reunited with his old Welsh shipmate and friend.

Scots language, associated in early eighteenth-century songs and literature with pastoral idylls and local colour, could easily have served in this domestically sentimental way in Smollett's text, but, of course, by not appearing on the page it never does. *Roderick Random*, however, manages to summon such local, domestic feelings for a Scot too, but without the comic triviality attached to Morgan and his foodstuffs. The text does so by displacing Scots language for mariners' lingo to call up more noble sentimental feelings for a Scottish character. To trace the sentimental connections this language makes possible, we must start where Smollett's novel starts in its representations of nautical language, with Roderick's kind-hearted Uncle Tom Bowling. There are times when Bowling's maritime language is explicitly sentimental. This loyal tar, who is the only familial connection to offer unstinting support to Roderick, deploys maritime language repeatedly as a language of feeling, as when he consoles Roderick, upon finding his grandfather has bequeathed to him nothing of his vast estate – 'Come along, Rory, I perceive how the land lies, [...] let's tack about'.[23]

Although a Scot, Bowling speaks with no hint of Scots, but rather is restricted to sea language to describe any and all experiences: either when responding to Roderick's disappointment or when Roderick's sneering cousin's dogs attack him, and Bowling indignantly observes in nautical language that the dogs attempted to 'board me without provocation' and threatens to 'rub [the cousin] down with an oaken towel'.[24] Ward's *Wooden World* had highlighted sailors' confined use of language to such 'crabbed terms' – their perspective, as reflected in their language, so limited as to translate all experiences into their own highly particular experience and peculiar idiom. Underscoring their limited sense of the world and of their obliviousness to any wider sense of things, despite their world travels, Ward compares sailors in their ship to worms living cosily in a nut.[25]

Such depictions of sailors and their language as comically limited have parallels in representations of Scots and their language in this period. John Wilkes would parody the language of Scots speakers, for instance, making his characterisations of their language and worldview as parochial the butt of jokes for political purposes, and such representations were widespread in the period.[26] But several elements distinguish representations of the limited view of maritime jargon from that attributed to Scots, making that nautical jargon a possible means of attachment to eighteenth-century characters, including Scottish characters. First, while the sailor's language functions on one level as a barrier between the sailor and the 'all wondering' operator or reader, it also functions as a sign of a kind of linguistic camaraderie in the face of global movement. Elizabeth DeLoughrey has argued that 'the perpetual circulation of the ocean dissolved local phenomenology', but Smollett's sailors' technical maritime language, and especially their use of that language figuratively, in a colloquial and idiomatic sense, strangely recuperates a local phenomenology.[27] Representations of their language conjure a community produced out of movement, and out of the specialised experience and technical expertise needed to facilitate that movement. Second, as representations of maritime language, such as those of Bowling's speech, often depict the language as figurative, its technical terms operate not only as we have seen as technical referential names. The language becomes a riddle of sorts, which might be puzzled out by English readers. Unlike an unknown Scots term such as 'thrang' or 'fient', figurative allusions in technical sea language such as 'board' need only be transposed into the land-situation use for English readers to be in on the joke. When Bowling complains that Roderick's cousin's dogs tried to 'board' him, he refers to the unlawful trespassing and attack of an enemy on a ship. Learning the meaning of the word 'board' in its sea context allows the reader to see the humour when it is transplanted to land. What initially positions the language as outside English also makes it the instrument of creating insiders. Smollett's use of technical maritime language in his novel works on several levels. It shifts between reality-effect-producing opacity and riddle-solving clarity, suggesting that mariners have their own distinctive community, somewhere out there, beyond the horizon, which might at times be brought home to readers. Smollett uses the 'confined' characterisation of technical sea language to create insiders through the logic of riddle solving, and also to solicit sentimental relations to a kind of – surprisingly – local language that is unconnected to any place but a ship.

It is not Roderick, but Bowling, who became the sentimental icon in the afterlives of Smollett's text, and significantly, while Roderick is marked as a Scot by his long red hair (also embedded in his name, Roderick suggesting the Scottish Gaelic word for red), Bowling is always first and foremost a sailor, immediately recognisable as such when first introduced in the text with his 'soldier's coat altered for him by the ship's taylor [sic], a striped flannel jacket, a pair of red breeches japanned with pitch'.[28] It is, then, not the Scot, but the sailor, who also happens to be a Scot, who was to become the remote and mobile figure who could also be a figure of attachment for Britons. Bowling, whose own name is a technical sea term of movement, sings of going through the world.[29] And yet this nautical-jargon-speaking character on the move proved a highly moving subject – he was such a powerfully sentimental figure that his character migrated to the stage, to print engravings, and even to a well-known song by Charles Dibdin.

While mapping maritime jargon onto the sentimental figure of Bowling is one means of bringing home the remote Scot on the move, more crucial might be the way in which maritime language marked sailors as not of this world – disinterested, unpropertied – making them ideal sentimental subjects in a different sense. If both Scots and sailors were suspiciously on the move, sailors, unlike the Scots, were depicted as divested of local attachments and material interests in their movement. Roderick aims to succeed in the world, to find a place for himself, even if he is long disappointed in those aims. In contrast, Bowling has no such aspirations. He is instead a lateral mover over the world's oceans, happily placeless and propertyless. When, by the novel's end, Roderick comes into the fortune that his father has made in his ocean-borne movement to the West Indies, Bowling determines 'to go to sea again', bestowing whatever fortunes he might make upon Roderick.[30] This propertylessness is significant for, as Catherine Gallagher has noted, under David Hume's influential model of sympathy, 'property is an important break on the dynamic of sympathy'.[31] In the sea-jargon-speaking Bowling we find a figure for the sailors' distanced, unencumbered language, with its linguistically marked removal from life on land. This language, then, also has the effect of making them disinterested figures, potentially ideal for sentimental attachment. Further, Scottish moral philosophy, with its increasing emphasis on tamping down emotion to elicit sentimental exchange, might suggest that, far from working against sentimental exchange, the distance, and the distancing effect of the mariner's technical language, are essential to effective sympathetic exchange. The very remoteness of sailors, emphasised in the stubborn, distancing technicality of their language, might make them especially available for sympathy.

Smollett's technical maritime language, and its positioning of sailors as separate and distant, might be exactly what was needed to bring those Scots travellers home to readers. Its use in this way was powerful enough, I would argue, to influence another popular Scots writer who was also a mariner, the poet William Falconer. Falconer's 1762 verse account of a British commercial wreck in Greek waters, *The Shipwreck*, was a wildly popular poem with classical influences, a significant achievement for its poor, young Scots author who began life at sea as a teenager.[32] Unlike Smollett, Falconer was a lifelong seaman without the benefits of education Smollett enjoyed. Yet he too managed to solicit sympathy for a man not unlike himself – distant, peripatetic – through his depiction of, not Scots, but mariners. This Edinburgh native reproduces no Scots language on the page but includes an abundance of the technical language of the ship.

Republished repeatedly throughout the eighteenth and early nineteenth centuries, the poem recounts a doomed merchant ship departing from Crete for Britain. Filled with classical allusions and generically indebted to both georgic and epic predecessors, Falconer's poem steers well clear of any comic associations with maritime language. Instead, the tone is at all points serious, beginning with solemn descriptions of Greek waters and coasts, tying its time-spanning genre to a space-traversing voyage. It gestures toward the perspective-expanding mode of world travel with an initial fold-out plate of a map of Greek waters – and the ship's course through them – and with opening passages describing the landscape of Crete. That expansiveness is met by, or perhaps produces dialectically, an emphasis on the highly particularised world of technical sea language.

The other fold-out plate is a diagram of a ship, labeling in great detail all of its technical parts. The focus on the technical aspect of sailors' language counteracts any cosmopolitanism or classical learnedness in these sailors, re-situating these world travellers as an arcane group limited by language, much as the ship diagram suggests limitations in space. Nonetheless, although Falconer claims to have intended the poem for 'gentlemen of the sea', it was a best-selling poem amongst those unacquainted with the sea. I want to suggest that in the wake of Smollett's Bowling, the poem's popularity might have derived in part from its connection of technical sea language and sentiment.

Sometimes described as a georgic poem, *The Shipwreck* offers that genre's representations of real maritime labour, and these generic characteristics contribute to the realistic sense of the poem. Georgic, with its stagings and usually failed negotiations of immediacy and distance, made it an especially apt genre for the representation of maritime workers. Georgic poetry could also make use of technical language in its efforts to bring home the experiential to readers. Although written in verse, this text's diction, specifically its technical writing, bolsters, as it had in Smollett's novel, the sense of the real. Lord Byron would celebrate the use of technical language as making possible the 'strength and reality of the poem'.[33]

As in *Roderick Random*, the technical sea language functions on multiple levels to bring its remote wanderers home to readers. Part of the surprising appeal of this poem, and its heavy use of technical jargon, might also have been the poem's work at educating the uninitiated into this particular language. In 1769 Falconer's *Universal Dictionary of the Marine* also became a best-selling work, going through multiple editions and similarly introducing non-specialists to this terminology. One of *The Shipwreck*'s most distinctive traits is its copious footnoting to explain technical terms – these sometimes take up much of the page. The popularity of this poem, with its extensive footnotes, as well as of Falconer's *Universal Dictionary of the Marine*, suggests a wide interest in the highly particular language of those at sea, and not simply as an impenetrable argot, but as a peculiar language that at once modelled a highly particular, distinct community and was at the same time available for readerly consumption and perhaps even imitation and imagined participation.

Oddly, Falconer also manages to make these technical terms a central part of a sentimental poem. Falconer states as his aim for the poem 'to wake to sympathy the feeling heart' despite – or maybe in part because – he loads it with technical maritime terms like 'bowsprits' and 'for-cat-harpings' and challenging footnotes.[34] Falconer's poem's sentimentalism – the poem includes a melancholic back story of one sailor's thwarted love and finally depicts the dramatic death at sea of most of the crew – emerges in its fullest when the technical language begins to appear alongside the description of the deadly storm's emergence. It is only after the onset of the storm that passage after passage describing the impact of that massive storm on a floundering ship, the master's commands, and the sailors' actions feature an abundance of those highly specialised terms. In some of its first technical language, for instance, the poem describes the sailors' actions at the beginning of the storm, 'Impell'd by mighty pressure, down she lies; / 'Brail up the mizzen quick!' the Master cried: / 'Man the clue-garnetts, let the main-sheet fly!' / In thousand shiv'reng shreds it rends on high!'.[35] As in Smollett's entwinement of heroic exploits with technical words and the specialised parts of the ship they name, Falconer repeatedly imbues the technical maritime language with doughty action, the arcane and thingish with movement and emotion.

Absent in the initial canto describing Crete and sea marvels, such as dolphins, the technical language appears at the moment of heightened emotional feeling – the onset and duration of what proves to be a deadly storm. It is the impassioned medium of exchange of a small community in deep danger, a language revalued by its association with sentiments of terror and grief. In this context, this otherwise dry language offers, I would argue, something akin to what we might think of as a model of affective national language. Sea language becomes a distinct language connected to and connecting a group under attack, a group undeniably embodied in its feelings and expressions both of wide-eyed fear and human interdependence. The sea language in Falconer's poem and dictionary, then, works toward establishing a model of a highly restricted affective community which outsiders, in familiarising themselves with the language, might briefly glimpse and tentatively join through textual consumption.

Falconer's technical language, however, works in a different sentimental register as well. While Smollett provides occasional maritime language to mark his characters as outsiders (for whom sentiment, nonetheless, is cultivated), Falconer inundates his reader with technical terms. Extensive footnotes explain some of the terms, and there is the diagram for consultation, but reading the poem itself would prove fairly rough going for the non-specialist attempting to imagine exactly what action is taking place. It poses a stubborn, distancing particularity at the moments of highest feeling – the crashing destruction of the ship, the loss of lives. We might say this language in the mouths of sailors at their moments of highest suffering modulates and 'brings down' the emotion in the way that Adam Smith, in his *Theory of Moral Sentiments* (1759), had argued needed to happen in order to elicit sympathy. Counter-intuitively, technological language in these moments comes to work with and not against the sentimental relation of sailor and reader.

Literary reviews of the period emphasised both the poem's appeal to pathos and its use of technical sea terms. The *Critical Review* praised its 'great number of pathetic touches, which will not fail to interest the reader of sentiment' and the *Monthly Review* admiringly asked, 'who, except a poetical sailor [...] educated by Neptune, would ever have thought of versifying his own sea language? What other poet would ever have dreamt of reef-tackles, halyards, clue-garnets, buntlines, lashings, lanyards, and fifty other terms equally obnoxious to the soft sing-song of modern poetasters?'[36] In this poem, whose coded 'obnoxious' language works against what is described as an increasingly feminised language of poetry, a masculine technical language describes scenes of sentiment while it tempers the danger of feminisation, always an undercurrent of sentiment.

Although the sailors that people Falconer's nautical poem are not Scots, the poem takes on the question of Scottishness and its relation to Britain. The ship's name is the Britannia, and the poem features long passages elaborating the grand paintings of personified England and Scotland on the ship's two sides, including characterisations of the two respective kingdoms. Yet Scots language is entirely missing from this Scottish-authored poem. What appears instead is the technical sea language of those mariners on the move and the particular language aimed to facilitate that movement – and mariners' survival in the face of deadly force.

Although he is far less known today, Falconer's poem, through to the middle of the nineteenth century, was every bit as canonical as Smollett's work, reproduced alongside Milton and Pope in collections of great British authors.[37] Like Smollett, Falconer takes up the disappearing quality of itinerant others. Yet Falconer turns their disappearance not into an occasion to be recuperated in later domestic sentiment, but into a final act eliciting elevated and profound sentiments. As one might expect in a poem entitled *The Shipwreck*, many of the sailors and most of the technical world they inhabit ultimately disappear into a battering, black sea. The dead – figure of the ultimate propertylessness – are also the figure for the deepest kind of sympathy in Falconer's poem. The itinerant Scot, switched out for the globe-travelling sailor, not least through the language associated with him, elicits the most powerful sympathy in his disappearance.

CHAPTER EIGHTEEN

Ottobah Cugoano and Scotland's Minority Imperialist Culture

Michael Morris

> The poor negroes in the West-Indies, have suffered enough by such religion as the philosophers of the North produce; Protestants, as they are called, are the most barbarous slave-holders, and there are none can equal the Scotch floggers and negroe-drivers […]
> —Quobna Ottobah Cugoano (1787)[1]

In 1787, an unusual publication appeared in London: *Thoughts and Sentiments on the Evil and Wicked Traffic of the Slavery and Commerce of the Human Species, Humbly Submitted to the Inhabitants of Great Britain, by Ottobah Cugoano, a Native of Africa*. This publication is now recognised as 'the first piece of black writing published in Britain which can be considered as both unequivocally political and unequivocally abolitionist'.[2] 'Part autobiography, part political treatise, and part Christian exegesis', it is remarkable for its detailed refutation of pro-slavery arguments, and for its move from 'abolitionist' calls to end the slave-trade, to 'emancipationist' demands to end colonial slavery.[3] Therefore, Cugoano's striking accusation that eighteenth-century Scotland produces the most vicious philosophers and overseers deserves attention, linking as it does the apparently distant worlds of Enlightenment and Plantation. Part of the explanation for this charge would be that the slaver who brought Cugoano to Britain was a Highlander, Alexander Campbell Esq. Vincent Carretta observes that this was 'probably' Alexander Campbell of Grenada (1739–1795), originally from the isle of Islay in Argyll.[4] On the one hand, scholars of slavery tend to mention Campbell in passing; on the other, he has become a figure of interest for historians who have begun to investigate the 'intrinsic links' between the eighteenth-century Highlands and the Caribbean, though the connection with Cugoano has been missed.[5] This chapter will fill in the details of the contextual reasons that suggest Alexander Campbell was the owner, it will demonstrate the structural significance of Scots in Cugoano's life, and it will examine the ways that Scotland and the Highlands are registered in the text at three key stages. Furthermore, taking the Cugoano–Campbell relationship as a starting point, I would like to begin to develop the suggestion that eighteenth-century Scotland can be thought of as the inauguration of Scotland's 'Minority Imperialist Culture'.

Given the sustained critical attention to Scotland and empire over the past couple of decades it is unsurprising that a number of terms which look to capture the nature of that relationship have been proposed.[6] The main issue boils down to the nature of the power and role of England within the United Kingdom in comparison to the power and role of the British empire; to what extent does anglocentrism overlap with colonialism? In *Gaelic Scotland and the Colonial Imagination* (2016), Silke Stroh skilfully notes 'the sense of internal hierarchy which was built into pan-British national identity constructs from the beginning, and which contemporary "postcolonial" Scottish literature and criticism writes against'. But, 'Postcolonial approaches pertain not only to Scottish-English relations, but also to ethno-cultural divisions within Scotland, especially those between the Anglophone Lowlands and the traditionally Gaelic-speaking Highlands'.[7] Following Stroh, the term I would like to propose, 'Minority Imperialist Culture', is intended to capture three main aspects. Firstly, it recognises the 'minor' position of Scotland within the United Kingdom, and the Highlands within Scotland, in terms of population, wealth and often, though not always, prestige. Throughout the seventeenth century an expansionistic Scotland jostled for position amongst the colonising nations in the New World though its capabilities did not match its ambitions. Since Darien (1695–1700), there has been no independent Scottish parliament which directed a specifically 'Scottish Empire'. Yet since the Union of Parliaments in 1707, Scots have been influential architects of the UK state and its *British* empire. 'Minority' does not mean that Scotland played a 'minor' role in state and empire building, and in no way excuses or minimises Scotland's profound investment in imperial violence. Rather, 'Minority' emphasises the participation in and attachment to these processes, with the understanding that Britain's internal hierarchies have always been a matter of contestation and negotiation. 'Minority' then is related to 'four-nations history' and the concept of the 'Atlantic archipelago' in which the internal histories of the four nations ought to be read 'independently if interconnectedly'.[8] The eighteenth century saw the interdependent development of mergers and hierarchies around the archipelago 'from the Channel Islands to the Shetlands, from the Wash to Galway Bay, with ties to North America and down to the Caribbean'.[9] The term 'Minority' registers the pressures of anglocentrism at the same time as recognising the often profound investments in nation, state and empire building. Of course, Gaelic-speaking Highlanders had an extra layer to negotiate in terms of 'Mìorun mòr nan Gall' – 'The great ill-will of the Lowlander'[10] – as they jostled for position in the burgeoning British state, its dominions and plantations. Britain has rarely achieved an entirely stable platform of common belonging; lines of inclusion and exclusion have constantly been drawn and re-drawn.

Secondly, I say 'imperial' rather than 'colonial' to emphasise that it is Scotland's engagement in what Immanuel Wallerstein calls a 'world-system' of global capitalism that brings into sharper focus the combination of depredations overseas and inequalities at home which discussions of postcolonialism and Scotland have been keen to recognise. In 2003, Liam Connell recommended this distinction between a Marxist understanding of 'imperialism' and a looser use of 'colonialism'.[11] More recently a re-energised Marxist intervention in the field of world literature has critiqued the 'civilisational' mode of postcolonialism for neglecting that the motor of modern world empire has been global capitalism.[12] This invites a world-systems perspective on the contests over the creation of the British state post-1707 and the Jacobite attempts for the throne; improvement and enclosure; the agricultural revolution; and the spectrum of labour conditions on which that world-system relied: from chattel enslavement through indentured, bonded, apprentice, convict and waged labour. Eighteenth-century Scotland is marked by its position in the world-system as a minority state in an expanding empire in which the Caribbean slave economy plays a fundamental role.

Thirdly, Scotland's cultural sphere mediates these 'combined and uneven' conditions which foster economic inequality and social hierarchies. It is important to stress that the practices and ideologies of empire have always been contested in Scotland, as they are in every imperial culture. We might therefore read the flourishings of Enlightenment and Romanticism (recently backdated to earlier in the eighteenth century) as alternating cultural responses to this unruly world-system.[13] Scotland's autonomous civil society and its institutions, such as schools, universities, and churches, are in part funded by imperial wealth and largely dominated by endorsements of empire, at the same time as they can register anxieties, doubts and critiques of that same empire.[14] Literature, as ever, is shaped by its socio-economic conditions, but not determined by it. Scotland's 'Minority Imperialist Culture' constantly negotiates anglocentrism and is dominated by Scoto-British endorsement of empire and the disavowal of imperial violence, at the same time as it stages certain moments of protest.

Brycchan Carey, Markman Ellis, and Sara Salih observe that 'The "long eighteenth century" might also be called the age of slavery, abolition, and emancipation, bracketed as it is by the foundation of the Royal Adventurers into Africa in 1660, the Abolition of the Slave Trade Act in 1807, and the emancipation of slaves in British colonies in 1838'.[15] As part of the current moves to measure the role of Scotland in the 'Age of Slavery', recent research has emphasised the significance of Caribbean slavery to the Highland economy. Prior to the Union of 1707, David Worthington notes a seventeenth-century network of Highland sugar merchants dealing through the Dutch empire.[16] Iain MacKinnon and Andrew Mackillop demonstrate how 'slavery derived wealth', including the compensation payments paid to slavers in the 1830s, was used to purchase Highland estates including some which were subsequently cleared.[17] Highland networks expanded across the Atlantic, but Karly Kehoe notes that it was the acquisition of the Ceded Islands from France (Grenada, the Grenadines, Dominica, Saint Vincent and Tobago) following the Seven Years War (1763) which 'gave Highlanders the opportunity to really establish a footing in the Caribbean'.[18] In the context of 'Improvement' and the fallout from Culloden, Kehoe argues:

> Far from being passive bystanders or mere victims during a period of acute socio-economic upheaval at home, many Highlanders demonstrated significant agency by their willingness to engage in a deeply exploitative, slave-based economy that would lead to an expanded culture of enterprise and prosperity in the Highlands.[19]

Grenada was the most important of these islands. and its French colonists were soon outnumbered by British, particularly Scottish and Highland arrivals. The Scots, along with governor Robert Melville, born in Monimail in Fife, were notorious for their 'profoundly anti-Catholic bias'.[20] As part of the Argyll Campbell slaving interest in the Caribbean, Alexander Campbell became one of the wealthiest and most prominent figures in the Ceded Islands. In 1790 he was called, along with fellow Scot James

Baillie of Dochfour (1737–1793), to testify before a Select Committee gathering evidence against the Abolition of the Slave Trade. Campbell reports that he first went to the Caribbean in 1754 spending time in Barbados, Saint Kitts, Dutch Saint Eustatia, Antigua and French Martinique, as well as Virginia and South Carolina. In 1763, Campbell 'purchased two sugar estates [on Grenada], with upwards of 300 slaves, which cost me upwards of £40,000 sterling'. Since then, he purchased 'fourteen different properties in Grenada, the Grenadines, Saint Vincent, and Tobago', growing 'sugar, coffee, cocoa, and cotton'. He reports that he has purchased 'upwards of 1,200 new Negroes'; each year he has owned between 500 to 1,000 enslaved people; he states 'I am currently in possession of upwards of 900 slaves'.[21] In contrast to Cugoano's picture of barbarous 'Scotch floggers', Campbell asserts that in the Caribbean enslaved Africans work less than labourers in Europe, punishments are lenient, and overseers are respectable:

> It is only men of some education and ability that are fit for such employments, and they are very often the sons of gentlemen from this country, Scotland, and Ireland, who go out from this country as overseers [...] and if their conduct is humane and proper, they are generally as much respected as the proprietor of the estate.[22]

Despite the serene picture Campbell paints, five years later he would be murdered alongside his friend the Berwickshire-born governor of Grenada Ninian Home, in Fedon's Rebellion in which enslaved people joined forces with disaffected French colonists in open revolt.

In a biographical note, Cugoano explains that he was high-born amongst the 'chief men in the kingdom of Agimaque and Assinee' in modern-day Ghana around 1757, but was kidnapped at thirteen years of age by African slavers and sold to Europeans in 1770 and, after, 'being about nine or ten months in the slave gang at Grenada, and about one year at different places in the West Indies, with Alexander Campbell Esq; who brought me to England in the end of the year 1772'.[23] The movement around several islands corresponds to Campbell's statement to the Select Committee that he 'visited the other islands once a year' and Mark Quintanilla notes he was resident in London from 1773 to 1778. There, he won a court case securing tax relief for West India planters and petitioned parliament for harsher policies against the Caribs of St Vincent.[24] Carretta notes the significance of Cugoano arriving in late 1772, given the Steuart v Somerset case had concluded that June.[25] Lord Mansfield, born in Perthshire, ruled in favour of the enslaved James Somerset against slave owner Charles Steuart. Steuart was born in Orkney, became a prominent customs official in Boston, and brought Somerset from Massachusetts to England in 1769.[26] The (perhaps deliberate) ambiguity of Mansfield's verdict resulted in broad and narrow interpretations – it was popularly believed to have ended slavery, though others, including John Millar, noted it focussed only on outlawing unwilling re-transportation out of England.[27] In 1773, Joseph Knight would start the long legal process which eventually went further to outlaw slavery under Scots law (1778). The Mansfield verdict which Cugoano hails as a 'noble decision'[28] meant that Campbell could not remove him from the country against his wishes. It was common practice to give the enslaved aggrandised names and Campbell gave him a Scottish name, 'I was called Steuart by my master',[29] the name of the deposed royal house of Scotland. He was advised to get baptised in the (mistaken) belief that 'I might not be carried away and sold again'.[30] His baptism record at St James' church shows 'John Stuart – a Black Aged 16',[31] a name he continued to use throughout his life in Britain with a variety of spellings. Thus, the structure of Cugoano's life – his enslavement, freedom and Christian identity – is entangled in Scotland's Minority Imperialist Culture and his 1787 anti-slavery text registers Scotland and the Highlands at a number of key points.

The immediate intervention that Cugoano's *Thoughts and Sentiments* makes is in the dispute provoked by James Ramsay's *Essay on the Treatment and Conversion of African Slaves in the British Sugar Colonies* (1784). Ramsay (1733–1789) was born in Fraserburgh to an Episcopalian family and attended the University of Aberdeen where the anti-slavery intellectual James Beattie (1735–1803) became a life-long friend. The Scottish Enlightenment thinkers, such as Beattie, emerged from and reacted to Scotland's Minority Imperialist Culture and, as such, slavery was a central concern through David Hume (1711–1776), James Steuart (1713–1780), James Millar (1762–1827), and Adam Smith (bap. 1723–1790). Michael Guenther sums up the consensus: 'Set against the backdrop of Europe's transition from feudalism, [Adam] Smith presented the abolition of slavery and serfdom as a necessary condition for the advent of a commercial economy'.[32] This is what James Oakes names 'the bourgeois critique of slavery'.[33] For fifteen years, between 1762 and 1777, Ramsay was vicar and surgeon on the sugar island of St Kitts. On return he became

Anglican vicar at Teston in Kent, and forefather of British abolitionism; it is said he inspired Clarkson, Wilberforce and Pitt towards anti-slavery.[34] As a surgeon, Ramsay was concerned with medical treatment; as a vicar, he was concerned with the conversion of enslaved Africans to Christianity. This 'would be the most probable means of making slaves diligent and faithful; for it would awaken conscience within them, to be a strict overseer, and a severe monitor, whom they could not evade'.[35] Ramsay criticises the polygenist ideas found in Kames and Robertson to maintain an orthodox Christian monogenesis that encourages humane treatment of all 'God's children'.[36] Indeed, he rebukes David Hume for his notorious footnote on the 'natural inferiority of negroes'.[37]

Given the Enlightenment consensus against slavery, pro-slavery apologists such as Edward Long found Hume's anti-black racism particularly congenial and his footnote was quoted widely. Ramsay rebukes 'the Caledonian' Hume for his 'Northern pride' saying that had he been born amongst the Romans he would have been satisfied even to be considered 'on a footing of equality with the sable Africans'.[38] Ramsay's phrase 'northern pride' may be playing to his audience now that he is installed as Anglican Vicar of Teston. Alternatively, there may be a sly joke here as the Highlander Ramsay is more 'northern' than the Edinburgher Hume. The West India lobby had long been able to dismiss condemnations of slavery as the mistaken impressions of metropolitan theorists therefore Ramsay's *Essay* provoked a fierce response as it presented an eyewitness account from a respectable source, portraying relentless labour combined with routine punishments from a cruel planter class.[39] The most significant of these were James Tobin, a planter on Nevis, and Gordon Turnbull, a Scottish planter on Cugoano's Grenada, who published *An Apology for Negro Slavery: Or, The West-India Planters Vindicated from the Charge of Inhumanity* in 1786. Turnbull demonstrates his own Enlightened education in his refutation of Ramsay's depiction. He quotes Montesquieu (1689–1755), Alexander Pope (1688–1744) and Tobias Smollett (1721–1771), and concurs with Hume's footnote, as he argues that planters are not 'tyrants', but are 'remarkable for their urbanity of manners, liberality of sentiment, and generosity of disposition'.[40] Their slaves are grateful to be removed from the savagery of Africa to the pastoral scene of the West Indies. Although 'the negroes are much happier [in the West Indies] than the peasantry in most parts of the globe', he makes his own recommendations for improvements and regulations without the unnecessary step of abolition:[41] 'Negro slavery is', after all, 'part of the great chain of being'.[42]

Tobin and Turnbull provoked responses from Britain's two leading black intellectual abolitionists: Ottobah Cugoano and Olaudah Equiano.

Cugoano's *Thoughts and Sentiments* is not a straightforward text and is best understood in relation to Julia Kristeva's description of intertextuality: '[A]ny text is constructed of a mosaic of quotations; any text is the absorption and transformation of another.'[43] These quotations are not always acknowledged and unaltered. This mosaic includes sections from Methodist John Wesley's *Thoughts on Slavery* (1774), Thomas Clarkson's abolitionist *Essay on the Slavery and Commerce of the Human Species, Particularly the African* (1786), and a lengthy section on the Spanish conquistadors is drawn unacknowledged from William Robertson's *History of America* (1777). The text counters point-by-point religious, racial, and economic justifications for slavery and damaging misconceptions of life in West Africa and the Caribbean. For example, David Hume in 'Of National Characters' (1748) had written that:

> You may obtain anything of the *Negroes* by offering them strong Liquors; and may easily prevail with them to sell, not only their Parents, but their Wives and Mistresses, for a Cask of Brandy.[44]

Cugoano provides a detailed description of being captured by African 'kidnappers and slave-procurers' whom he condemns as 'African villains', but mobilises a discourse of sensibility to counter the attitudes of the likes of Hume: 'What man of feeling can help lamenting the loss of parents, friends, liberty. [...] Those people brought away annually from Guinea, are born as free, and are brought up with as great a predilection for their own country, as the sons and daughters of fair Britain.'[45] He provides a nuanced picture of West Africa portraying the wider social system in comparison to Highland clanship:

> Their different chieftains, which bear a reliance on the great chief, or king, exercise a kind of government something like that feudal institution which prevailed some time in Scotland. In this respect, though the common people are free, they often suffer by the villainy of their different chieftains, and by the wars and feuds which happen among them.[46]

This comparison between West African and Scottish Highland clanship became a popular trope with Cugoano's comrade Olaudah Equiano describing dress in Ibo-land as 'a long piece of calico, or muslin, wrapped loosely round the body, somewhat in the form of a Highland plaid'.[47] To counter the distortions of the likes of Hume, at this point Cugoano draws a line of inclusion between the Scottish Highlands and West Africa, playing on the Minority position of the Highlands to explain the political tensions which produce prisoners–of-war and enslaved people as a result of a recognisable and proximate social system for his British audience.

Although earlier readings of Cugoano focussed on black identity narrative or use of sentiment, more recent scholarship has struggled to pin down the politics of the intervention. The text registers the role of slavery in a world-system, serviced by African sellers, which also creates poverty and misery for poor whites in Britain – though their position is not worse than enslaved people as Turnbull argued. The 'emancipationist' demands certainly push the text towards the 'radical' end of the political spectrum, though comments on British society remain fairly conventional. Jonathon Holt positions the text more securely in the context of 'liberal' politics of the 1780s, noting its demands that the British empire turn its military power towards making anti-slave trade interventions, and spreading Christianity across Africa.[48] Indeed, in a discussion of criminal laws of civilisation, Cugoano makes an observation on rebellion breaking forth of the 'pretenders' against the 'Sovereign':

> Even in a late rebellion there were many suffered in Britain, which, if they had been preserved to this mild reign, they would have been as good neighbours, and as faithful subjects as any other.[49]

This coded reference to the Jacobite rebellion of 1745 maintains a Hanoverian perspective which is perfectly compatible with the majority of his London readership, and perhaps his Campbell former master.

To return, then, to the striking statement that Scots make the most barbarous slave-holders with which we started. It is certainly possible to take this at face-value as an honest assessment of what Cugoano saw in the Caribbean islands where Scots formed a significant proportion of the white population. At the same time, it is a statement which rewards some unpacking in relation to Minority Imperialism. If the regal loyalty of the text is Hanoverian, its religious loyalty is Anglican and the statement appears in Cugoano's closing section which urges the religious conversion of Africans. This ought to be performed by the best of Anglican missionaries. At this point, Cugoano turns to address Gordon Turnbull – that 'erroneous philosopher' – and quotes his opinions on the conversion of enslaved Africans:

> But if the slave is only to be made acquainted with the form, without the substance; if he is only to be decked out with the external trappings of religion; if he is only to be taught the uncheering principles of gloomy superstition; or, if he is only to be inspired with the intemperate frenzy of enthusiastic fanaticism, it were better that he remained in that dark state, where he could not see good from ill.[50]

Cugoano turns Turnbull's words back upon himself:

> These words intemperate, frenzy, enthusiastic and fanaticism[... better fit] this author's brutish philosophy; and he may subscribe to it, and the meaning of these words, with as much affinity to himself, as he bears a relation to a *Hume* or to his friend *Tobin*. The poor negroes in the West Indies have suffered enough by such religion as the philosophers of the North produce; Protestants, as they are called, are the most barbarous slave-holders, and there are none can equal the Scotch floggers and negroe-drivers, and the barbarous Dutch cruelties. Perhaps as the Church of Rome begins to sink in its power [...] its followers [...] may blush and abhor the very mention of the cruelty that their ancestors have committed; and we find slavery itself more tolerable among them, than it is in the Protestant countries.[51]

The quotation in its context, if no less disturbing, gives a sense of its purpose. At this point, Cugoano draws a line of exclusion between the 'pious and wise' Anglican Church, and the rival Protestant churches in Scotland and the Netherlands, as well as the Catholic Church. Their errors in religious approach are evidenced by their role in slave societies.

Cugoano responds to Scotland's minority imperialism by rolling Turnbull and Hume (and Tobin) together as 'brutish philosophers'. This shifts the role of 'brute' from enslaved African to Scottish planters and philosophers. This is compatible with a Wilkesite discourse of Scotch tyranny against English liberty, familiar from the 1760s. Cugoano is able to counter Turnbull by associating his pro-slavery Scottishness with an extreme Presbyterian 'frenzy', recalling memories of Covenanters, which his Anglican fellows found 'intemperate'. This reading of Cugoano's life and text reveals Scotland's eighteenth-century Minority Imperialist Culture and its penetrating influence in the Atlantic slave economy, and the way that enslaved people responded to it. Figures such as Cugoano must be at the centre of efforts to recover the memory of that past and their discursive strategies deserve close attention revealing as they do the shifting lines of inclusion and exclusion of the archipelago in an Atlantic context.

Endnotes

Introduction

1 John Robertson, *A Union for Empire: Political Thought and the British Union of 1707* (Cambridge: Cambridge University Press, 1995); Colin Kidd, *Union and Unionisms: Political Thought in Scotland, 1500–2000* (Cambridge: Cambridge University Press, 2008).
2 The signing of the Solemn League and Covenant in 1643 in Edinburgh provided an initial challenge to monarchical power, but Edinburgh also became a key Royalist stronghold as the first place in Britain to declare Charles II monarch after his father Charles I's execution in 1649. See I. J. Gentles, *The English Revolution and the Wars in the Three Kingdoms, 1638–1652* (Abingdon: Routledge, 2014); A. Woolrych, *Britain in Revolution: 1625–1660* (Oxford: Oxford University Press, 2002).
3 Keith Brown, *Kingdom or Province?: Scotland and the Regal Union 1603–1715* (New York: Macmillan, 1992), p. 137. The official Treaty of Union, however, was not passed until 1657.
4 Clare Jackson, *Restoration Scotland, 1660–1690: Royalist Politics, Religion and Ideas* (Rochester, NY: Boydell, 2003).
5 Alasdair Raffe, *Scotland in Revolution, 1685–1690* (Edinburgh: Edinburgh University Press, 2018). We use the term '1688 Revolution' in this volume, although there is considerable debate about the nature of that event, as Kevin Sharpe suggests: 'Perhaps no historiographical interpretation of a period or reign had such a near monopoly for centuries afterwards as the so-called Whig interpretation of 1688 and the reign of William III' (*Rebranding Rule: The Restoration and Revolution Monarchy, 1660–1714* (New Haven: Yale University Press, 2013), p. 343). See, for example, Tim Harris and Stephen Taylor, *The Final Crisis of the Stuart Monarchy: The Revolutions of 1688–91 in their British, Atlantic and European Contexts* (Woodbridge: Boydell Press, 2013); Tim Harris, *Revolution: The Great Crisis of the British Monarchy,*

1685–1720 (London: Penguin, 2006); Jonathan Israel, *The Anglo-Dutch Moment: Essays on the Glorious Revolution and Its World Impact* (New York: Cambridge University Press, 1991); Steve Pincus, *1688: The First Modern Revolution* (New Haven; London: Yale University Press, 2009); Leith Davis, *Mediating Cultural Memory in Britain and Ireland: From the 1688 Revolution to the 1745 Jacobite Rising* (Cambridge: Cambridge University Press, forthcoming); and the essays in *Restoration: Studies in English Literary Culture, 1660–1700* 39, nos. 1–2 (2015).

6   David Armitage, 'The Scottish Vision of Empire: The Intellectual Origins of the Darien Venture', in *A Union for Empire: Political Thought and the British Union of 1707*, ed. John Robert (Cambridge: Cambridge University Press, 1995), pp. 97–118; Douglas Watt, *The Price of Scotland: Darien, Union and the Wealth of Nations* (Edinburgh: Luath Press, 2007).

7   Karin Bowie, *Scottish Public Opinion and the Anglo-Scottish Union, 1699–1707* (Woodbridge: Boydell Press, 2007); Christopher Whatley, *Scots and the Union: Then and Now* (Edinburgh: Edinburgh University Press, 2014); Alvin Jackson, *The Two Unions: Ireland, Scotland, and the Survival of the United Kingdom, 1707–2007* (Oxford and New York: Oxford University Press, 2012).

8   Alexander Murdoch, *Making the Union Work: Scotland, 1651–1763* (London and New York: Routledge, 2020); Allan I. Macinnes, Kieran German, and Lesley Graham, *Living with Jacobitism, 1690–1788: The Three Kingdoms and Beyond* (London: Pickering & Chatto, 2014).

9   Daniel Szechi, *Britain's Lost Revolution?: Jacobite Scotland and French Grand Strategy 1701–1708* (Manchester: Manchester University Press, 2015); Daniel Szechi, *1715: The Great Jacobite Rebellion* (New Haven: Yale University Press, 2006); Murray Pittock, *The Myth of the Jacobite Clans: The Jacobite Army in 1745* (Edinburgh: Edinburgh University Press, 2009).

10 Murray Pittock, *Poetry and Jacobite Politics in Eighteenth-Century Britain and Ireland* (Cambridge: Cambridge University Press, 1994).

11 Murray Pittock, *Culloden (Cùil Lodair)* (Oxford: Oxford University Press, 2016).

12 Alasdair Raffe, *The Culture of Controversy: Religious Arguments in Scotland, 1660–1714* (Woodbridge: Boydell Press, 2012), p. 3.

13 See Jackson, *Restoration Scotland*. Raffe, in *The Culture of Controversy*, indicates that the rift between Episcopalians and Presbyterians developed during the Restoration as the two religions differed on two 'particularly important principles' (p. 34). First, Presbyterians believed that Christ, not the monarch, was the head of the church. Second,

Presbyterians asserted a 'hierarchy of committees, in which ministers of equal authority were assisted by lay elders' (pp. 35–36). Raffe suggests that the 'small numbers of Roman Catholics and Quakers' in Scotland at this time 'played only minor roles in religious controversy, except in a few localities, and as figures of fear and hatred for presbyterians and episcopalians alike' (p. 3).

14 Kelsey Jackson Williams, *The First Scottish Enlightenment: Rebels, Priests, and History* (Oxford: Oxford University Press, 2020), p. 17.

15 Valerie Wallace, *Scottish Presbyterianism and Settler Colonial Politics: Empire of Dissent* (Cham, Switzerland: Springer International Publishing, 2018), pp. 3–4. Richard B. Sher, *Church and University in the Scottish Enlightenment: The Moderate Literati of Edinburgh* (Edinburgh: Edinburgh University Press, 1985).

16 Roger Emerson and Mark Spencer, 'Several Contexts of the Scottish Enlightenment', in *The Cambridge Companion to the Scottish Enlightenment*, ed. Alexander Broadie and Craig Smith (Cambridge: Cambridge University Press, 2019), pp. 9–32 (p. 10).

17 Innes, p. 234.

18 For discussion of these practices in a literary context, see Alex Benchimol and Gerard Lee McKeever, *Cultures of Improvement in Scottish Romanticism, 1707–1840* (Abingdon, Oxon: Routledge, 2018). Eric Gidal, *Ossianic Unconformities: Bardic Poetry in the Industrial Age* (Charlottesville: University of Virginia Press, 2015); Nigel Leask, *Robert Burns and Pastoral: Poetry and Improvement in Late Eighteenth-Century Scotland* (Oxford: Oxford University Press, 2010).

19 Nicholas Phillipson, 'Forward', in *Cultures of Improvement in Scottish Romanticism, 1707–1840*, ed. Benchimol and McKeever, pp. 16–17 (p. 16).

20 Deans, p. 278.

21 T. M. Devine, *The Scottish Clearances: A History of the Dispossessed, 1600–1900* (Harmondsworth: Penguin, 2018).

22 See Murray Pittock, *Enlightenment in a Smart City: Edinburgh's Civic Development, 1660–1750* (Edinburgh: Edinburgh University Press, 2019).

23 Craig Lamont, *The Cultural Memory of Georgian Glasgow* (Edinburgh: Edinburgh University Press, 2021).

24 Corey Andrews, *Literary Nationalism in Eighteenth-Century Scottish Club Poetry* (Lewiston, NY: Edwin Mellen, 2004). See also: James Gerard Livesey, *Civil Society and Empire: Ireland and Scotland in the Eighteenth Century Atlantic World* (New Haven: Yale University Press,

2009); Christopher J. Berry, *The Idea of Commercial Society in the Scottish Enlightenment* (Edinburgh: Edinburgh University Press, 2013).

25   Just to point to a few examples: Francis Hutcheson was professor of moral philosophy at the University of Glasgow (1694–1746); Thomas Reid (1710–1796) was natural and moral philosopher at King's and Marischal Colleges in Aberdeen; David Hume (1711–1776) was a philosopher and historian who eventually became keeper of the Advocates' Library; William Robertson (1721–1793) was a historian and Church of Scotland minister; Adam Smith (bap. 1723–1790) held the chair in moral philosophy at the University of Edinburgh; philosopher and historian Adam Ferguson (1723–1816) became chair of natural philosophy at the University of Edinburgh; James Hutton (1726–1797) was a geologist; James Beattie (1735–1803) was professor of moral philosophy and logic at Marischal College; and Dugald Stewart (1753–1828) held the chair in mathematics at the University of Edinburgh, then replaced Adam Ferguson as chair of moral philosophy.

26   Alexander Broadie and Craig Smith, *The Cambridge Companion to the Scottish Enlightenment*, 2nd edn (Cambridge: Cambridge University Press, 2019), p. 1.

27   Adam Smith, 'The Four Stages of Society', in *The Scottish Enlightenment: An Anthology*, ed. Alexander Broadie, (Edinburgh: Canongate Press, 1997), pp. 475–87 (p. 479).

28   Robert Crawford, *The Scottish Invention of English Literature* (Cambridge: Cambridge University Press, 1998).

29   Kenneth McNeil, *Scottish Romanticism and Collective Memory in the British Atlantic* (Edinburgh: Edinburgh University Press, 2020), p. 7.

30   Richard B. Sher, *The Enlightenment and the Book: Scottish Authors and Their Publishers in Eighteenth-Century Britain, Ireland, and America* (Chicago: University of Chicago Press, 2007).

31   Stephen W. Brown and Warren McDougall (eds), *The Edinburgh History of the Book in Scotland. Volume II, Enlightenment and Expansion, 1707–1800* (Edinburgh: Edinburgh University Press, 2012).

32   Rhona Brown, *Robert Fergusson and the Scottish Periodical Press* (Farnham: Ashgate, 2012). Alex Benchimol, Rhona Brown, and David Shuttleton, *Before Blackwood's: Scottish Journalism in the Age of Enlightenment* (London: Pickering and Chatto, 2015). See also: Mark Towsey, *Reading the Scottish Enlightenment: Books and Their Readers in Provincial Scotland, 1750–1820* (Leiden: Brill, 2010) and *Reading History in Britain and America, c. 1750–c. 1840* (Cambridge: Cambridge University Press, 2019).

33 See also Derick Thomson, *An Introduction to Gaelic Poetry* (Edinburgh: Edinburgh University Press, 1989).
34 William Warner, *Protocols of Liberty: Communication Innovation and the American Revolution* (Chicago: University of Chicago Press, 2013), p. 26.
35 Paula McDowell, *The Invention of the Oral: Print Commerce and Fugitive Voices in Eighteenth-Century Britain* (Chicago: University of Chicago Press, 2018).
36 Eve Tavor Bannet, *Empire of Letters: Letter Manuals and Transatlantic Correspondence* (Cambridge; New York: Cambridge University Press, 2005), p. xvii.
37 Julie Orr, *Scotland, Darien and the Atlantic World, 1698-1700* (Edinburgh: Edinburgh University Press, 2018).
38 Douglas Mack, *Scottish Fiction and the British Empire* (Edinburgh: Edinburgh University Press, 2006), p. 6. See also: Angela McCarthy and John Mackenzie, *Global Migrations: The Scottish Diaspora since 1600* (Edinburgh: Edinburgh University Press, 2016); T. M. Devine, *To the Ends of the Earth: Scotland's Global Diaspora, 1750-2010* (Washington: Smithsonian, 2011).
39 See, for example, Michael Morris, *Scotland and the Caribbean, c. 1740-1833: Atlantic Archipelagos* (London: Routledge, 2015); Douglas Hamilton, *Scotland, the Caribbean and the Atlantic World, 1750-1820* (Manchester: Manchester University Press, 2005); T. M. Devine, *Recovering Scotland's Slavery Past: The Caribbean Connection* (Edinburgh: Edinburgh University Press, 2015); Colin Calloway, *White People, Indians, and Highlanders: Tribal Peoples and Colonial Encounters in Scotland and America* (Oxford: Oxford University Press, 2008); Nikki Hessell, *Romantic Literature and the Colonised World: Lessons from Indigenous Translations* (Cham, Switzerland: Springer International Publishing, 2018). The 2nd World Congress of Scottish Literatures in Vancouver, Canada, focused on the theme of 'Dialogues and Diasporas', included the creation of a research cohort on 'Indigenous/Scottish Connections'.
40 T. M. Devine, *Clanship to Crofters' War: The Social Transformation of the Scottish Highlands* (Manchester: Manchester University Press, 1994); Stana Nenadic, *Lairds and Luxury: The Highland Gentry in Eighteenth-Century Scotland* (East Linton: John Donald, 2007).
41 Thomas Clancy, 'Scottish Literature Before Scottish Literature', in *The Cambridge Companion to Scottish Literature*, ed. Gerard Carruthers and Liam McIlvanney (Cambridge: Cambridge University Press, 2012), pp. 13-26 (p. 13).

42　Jamie Kelly, 'Revisiting the Language Issue: The Society in Scotland for Propagating Christian Knowledge (SSPCK) and Highland Education, c. 1660–1754', *Journal of the Northern Renaissance*, 12 (2021) www.northernrenaissance.org/revisiting-the-language-issue-the-society-in-scotland-for-propagating-christian-knowledge-sspck-and-highland-education-c-1660-1754 [accessed 18 February 2021]. As Kelly points out, the first printed works in Gaelic were ecclesiastical, as the Synod of Argyll approved a translation of the first fifty of the psalms into Gaelic in 1659.

43　Gerard Carruthers, *Scottish Literature* (Edinburgh: Edinburgh University Press, 2009), p. 50. See also the University of Glasgow, 'Bridging the Continental Divide: Neo-Latin and Its Cultural Role in Jacobean Scotland, As Seen in the *Delitiae Poetarum Scotorum* (1637)' www.dps.gla.ac.uk [accessed 1 July 2021].

44　See Steven J. Reid and David McOmish, *Neo-Latin Literature and Literary Culture in Early Modern Scotland* (Leiden; Boston: Brill, 2016); Jack MacQueen, 'From Rome to Ruddiman: The Scoto-Latin Tradition', in *The Edinburgh History of Scottish Literature I: From Columba to the Union (until 1707)*, ed. Thomas Owen Clancy and Murray Pittock (Edinburgh: Edinburgh University Press, 2006), pp. 184–208; F. W. Freeman, *Robert Fergusson and the Scots Humanist Compromise* (Edinburgh: Edinburgh University Press, 1984).

45　Robert McColl Millar, *A Sociolinguistic History of Scotland* (Edinburgh: Edinburgh University Press, 2020), p. 100.

46　*The Cambridge Companion to Scottish Literature*, ed. Gerard Carruthers and Liam McIlvanney (Cambridge: Cambridge University Press, 2012), p. 4. As Nelson and Alker point out in their chapter in this volume, this *Cambridge Companion* leaps from a chapter on Renaissance Scottish literature up to the 1650s to a chapter on 'The Aftermath of Union'.

47　David Daiches, *The Paradox of Scottish Culture: The Eighteenth-Century Experience* (London: Oxford University Press, 1964). For examples of works that commence with 1707, see Marshall Walker, *Scottish Literature since 1707* (London and New York: Longman, 1996); Leith Davis, *Acts of Union: Scotland and the Literary Negotiation of the British Nation, 1707–1832* (Stanford: Stanford University Press, 1998); Evan Gottlieb, *Feeling British: Sympathy and National Identity in Scottish and English Writing, 1707–1832* (Lewisburg: Bucknell University Press, 2007); Benchimol and McKeever, *Cultures of Improvement, 1707–1840*. Although the four-volume *History of Scottish*

Literature produced by the University of Aberdeen devotes its second volume, edited by Andrew Hook, to literature between 1660 and 1800 (Aberdeen: University of Aberdeen Press, 1987), the more recent three-volume *Edinburgh History of Scottish Literature* uses 1707 as a dividing year between Volume I (*From Columba to the Union*) and Volume II (*Enlightenment, Britain and Europe*), although the editors recognise 'that any system of literary periodisation in a complex, multi-cultural society like Scotland through the ages will inevitably have an element of arbitrariness' (p. 9).

48 Leith Davis, Ian Duncan, and Janet Sorensen, *Scotland and the Borders of Romanticism* (Cambridge: Cambridge University Press, 2004), p. 3.

49 See also Murray Pittock, *Scottish and Irish Romanticism* (Oxford: Oxford University Press, 2008), which begins with a consideration of Allan Ramsay.

50 Tobias Smollett, *The Expedition of Humphrey Clinker* (London: Johnston, 1771), Vol. 3, p. 5. The term 'Scottish Enlightenment' was first used in W. R. Scott, *Francis Hutcheson: His Life, Teaching and Position in the History of Philosophy* (Cambridge: Cambridge University Press, 1900); see Broadie and Smith, p. 3.

51 Dan Edelstein, *The Enlightenment: A Genealogy* (Chicago: University of Chicago Press, 2010), p. 3.

52 *The Scottish Enlightenment and Literary Culture*, ed. Ronnie Young, Ralph McLean, and Kenneth Simpson (Lanham MD: Bucknell University Press, 2016), p. 1.

53 Silvia Sebastiani, *The Scottish Enlightenment: Race, Gender, and the Limits of Progress* (Basingstoke: Palgrave Macmillan, 2013).

54 Silke Stroh, *Gaelic Scotland in the Colonial Imagination: Anglophone Writing from 1600 to 1900* (Evanston, IL: Northwestern, 2017).

55 Alexander Broadie (ed.), *The Cambridge Companion to the Scottish Enlightenment* (Cambridge: Cambridge University Press, 2003), p. 3.

56 Pamela Perkins, *Women Writers and the Edinburgh Enlightenment* (Amersterdam: Rodopi, 2010); JoEllen DeLucia, *A Feminine Enlightenment: British Women Writers and the Philosophy of Progress, 1759–1820* (Edinburgh: Edinburgh University Press, 2015). See also: Katie Barclay and Deborah Simonton, *Women in Eighteenth-Century Scotland: Intimate, Intellectual and Public Lives* (Burlington, VT: Ashgate, 2013).

57 David Allan, '"Winged Horses, Fiery Dragons and Monstrous Giants": Historiography and Imaginative Writing in the Scottish Enlightenment', in *The Scottish Enlightenment and Literary Culture*, pp. 19–36; Pamela Perkins, 'Regulating Reality by Imagination: Fact,

Fiction and Travel in the Scottish Enlightenment', in *The Scottish Enlightenment and Literary Culture*, pp. 37–52; Ralph McLean, 'Hugh Blair and the Influence of Rhetoric and Belles-Lettres on Imaginative Literature', in *The Scottish Enlightenment and Literary Culture*, pp. 137–52.
58 Clifford Siskin and William Warner, *This Is Enlightenment* (Chicago and London: University of Chicago Press, 2010), p. 10.
59 Sebastiani, *Scottish Enlightenment*, pp. 6, 15. As an antidote to perpetuating the parameters of Enlightenment, Sebastiani suggests that 'by contextualizing the relationship between texts, it is possible to dig beneath what may appear to be stable surfaces of meaning. Every text, when set within a larger field of discourse (geographic and of gender), is destabilized in its interaction with others' (p. 6).
60 Stiùbhart, p. 25.
61 Andrews, p. 41.
62 Ibid., p. 55.
63 Davis, p. 56.
64 Nelson and Alker, p. 76.
65 Ibid., p. 74.
66 Ibid., p. 76.
67 Pink, p. 96.
68 Ibid.
69 Ibid., p. 97
70 Michael Rothberg, 'Introduction: Between Memory and Memory: From Lieux de Mémoire to Noeuds de Mémoire', *Yale French Studies*, 2010, 3–12.
71 Shields, p. 134.
72 Ibid., p. 132.
73 Stiùbhart, p. 157.
74 Ibid., p. 169.
75 Brown, p. 183.
76 Ibid., p. 170
77 Radcliffe, p. 189.
78 Ibid., p. 198.
79 Mathis, p. 199
80 Ibid., p. 202.
81 Ibid.
82 Ibid.
83 DeLucia, p. 220.
84 Ibid., p. 221.

85 Innes, p. 235.
86 Gidal, p. 247.
87 Moore, p. 262.
88 Ibid., p. 266.
89 Ibid., p. 269.
90 Deans, p. 273.
91 Ibid.
92 Ibid., p. 284.
93 Sorensen, pp. 285–86.
94 Morris, p. 300.
95 Ibid., p. 308.
96 Ibid., p. 309.
97 See the 'Editing Burns for the 21st Century' and 'The Collected Works of Allan Ramsay' projects at the Centre for Robert Burns Studies, University of Glasgow.
98 See, for just several examples, Gerard Lee McKeever, '*Regional Romanticism: Dumfriesshire and Galloway, 1770-1830*' regionalromanticism.glasgow.ac.uk; Murray Pittock and Craig Lamont, 'Edinburgh's Enlightenment, 1680–1750' www.gla.ac.uk/schools/critical/research/researchcentresandnetworks/robertburnsstudies/edinburghenlightenment/themap/#d.en.412385; and Juliet Shields, 'Scottish Women Writers on the Web' www.scottishwomenwritersontheweb.net [accessed 1 July 2021].

1. Adaptation, Integration, and Renewal: Scottish Gaelic Literature, 1650–1750

1 For previous assessments of early modern Scottish Gaelic literature, see John MacInnes, 'Gaelic poetry' (unpublished PhD thesis, University of Edinburgh, 1975); Domhnall Uilleam Stiùbhart, 'An Gàidheal, a' Ghàidhlig, agus a' Ghàidhealtachd anns an t-seachdamh linn deug' (unpublished PhD thesis, University of Edinburgh, 1997); Derick Thomson, *An Introduction to Gaelic Poetry* 2nd edition (Edinburgh: Edinburgh University Press 1989), pp. 19–217 and 'Gaelic poetry in the eighteenth century: The breaking of the mould', in Andrew Hook (ed.), *A History of Scottish Literature vol. 2 1660-1800* (Aberdeen: Aberdeen University Press, 1987), pp. 175–90; Ronald Black, 'Alasdair mac Mhaighstir Alasdair and the new Gaelic poetry', in Susan Manning (ed.), *The Edinburgh History of Scottish Literature Volume Two: Enlightenment, Britain and Empire (1707-1918)* (Edinburgh: Edinburgh University Press, 2007), pp. 110–124; Thomas Clancy, 'Gaelic Literature

and Scottish Romanticism', in Murray Pittock (ed.), *The Edinburgh Companion to Scottish Romanticism* (Edinburgh: Edinburgh University Press, 2011), pp. 49–60; William Gillies, 'Some Eighteenth-century Developments in Scottish Gaelic poetry', in Anders Ahlqvist and Pamela O'Neill (eds), *Language and Power in the Celtic World* (Sydney, NSW, 2011), pp. 61–96; Carla Sassi (ed.), *The International Companion to Scottish Poetry* (Glasgow: ASLS, 2016), passim.

2 Robert Dodgshon, *From Chiefs to Landlords: Social and Economic Change in the Western Highlands and Islands c. 1493–1820* (Edinburgh: Edinburgh University Press, 1998) and *'No Stone Unturned': A History of Farming, Landscape and Environment in the Scottish Highlands and Islands* (Edinburgh: Edinburgh University Press, 2015); Allan I. Macinnes, *Clanship, Commerce and the House of Stewart, 1603–1788* (East Linton: Tuckwell Press, 1996); Andrew MacKillop, *More Fruitful than the Soil: Army, Empire and the Scottish Highlands, 1715–1815* (East Linton: Tuckwell Press, 2001).

3 John Gregorson Campbell, *The Gaelic Otherworld: John Gregorson Campbell's Superstitions of the Highlands and Islands of Scotland and Witchcraft and Second Sight in the Highlands and Islands*, ed. Ronald Black (Edinburgh: Birlinn, 2005), pp. 530–53, 575–78; Michael Hunter (ed.), *The Occult Laboratory: Magic, Science and Second Sight in Late 17th-Century Scotland* (Woodbridge: Boydell Press, 2001), pp. 64, 125–26.

4 John Shaw, 'Scottish Gaelic Traditions of the *Cliar Sheanchain*', in Cyril J. Byrne, Margaret Harry, and Pádraig Ó Siadhail (eds), *Celtic Languages and Celtic Peoples: Proceedings of the Second North American Congress of Celtic Studies* (Halifax, NS, D'Arcy McGee Chair of Irish Studies, Saint Mary's University, 1992), pp. 141–58 and idem, 'What Alexander Carmichael Did Not Print: The *Cliar Sheanchain*, 'Clanranald's Fool' and Related Traditions', *Béaloideas*, 70 (2002), pp. 99–126.

5 John MacInnes, *Dùthchas nan Gàidheal: Collected Essays of John MacInnes*, ed. Michael Newton (Edinburgh: Birlinn, 2010), pp. 265–319; also Ronald Black (ed.), *An Lasair: Anthology of 18th Century Scottish Gaelic Verse* (Edinburgh: Birlinn, 2001), pp. xix–xxvii, 525–27; and M. Pía Coira, *By Poetic Authority: The Rhetoric of Panegyric in Gaelic Poetry of Scotland to c. 1700* (Edinburgh: Dunedin Academic Press, 2012).

6 Cristian Bratu, 'Mirrors for Princes (Western)', in Albrecht Classen (ed.), *Handbook of Medieval Studies: Terms – Methods – Trends* (2 vols, Göttingen: De Gruyter, 2010), pp. 1921–49.

7   See Jacqueline Rose, 'The Problem of Counsel in Medieval and Early Modern England and Scotland', in Jacqueline Rose (ed.), *The Politics of Counsel in England and Scotland, 1286–1707* (Oxford: Oxford University Press, 2016), pp. 1–44.
8   For background, see Macinnes, *Clanship*, pp. 88–121 and *The British Confederate: Archibald Campbell, Marquess of Argyll, c. 1607–1661* (Edinburgh: John Donald, 2011), pp. 10–15, 28–30, 198–224.
9   *Òrain Iain Luim: Songs of John MacDonald, Bard of Keppoch*, Annie M. MacKenzie (ed.), (Edinburgh: Scottish Gaelic Texts Society, 1964), p. 22; Andrew Pettegree, *The Invention of News: How the World Came to Know about Itself* (New Haven: Yale, 2014), pp. 67–84, 121–34, 139–58, 194–200, 208–29.
10 Angus Matheson, 'Traditions of Alasdair mac Colla', *Transactions of the Gaelic Society of Glasgow*, 5 (1958), pp. 9–93.
11 Colm Ó Baoill (ed.), *Màiri nighean Alasdair Ruaidh: Song-maker of Skye and Berneray* (Edinburgh: Scottish Gaelic Texts Society, 2014), p. 162.
12 See Marc Caball and Kaarina Hollo, 'The Literature of Later Medieval Ireland, 1200–1600: From the Normans to the Tudors', in Margaret Kelleher and Philip O'Leary (eds), *The Cambridge History of Irish Literature, Volume 1: to 1890* (Cambridge: Cambridge University Press, 2006), pp. 74–139; MacInnes, 'Gaelic Poetry', pp. 305–22; Martin MacGregor, 'Creation and Compilation: The *Book of the Dean of Lismore* and Literary Culture in Late Medieval Gaelic Scotland' and William Gillies, 'Gaelic Literature in the Later Middle Ages: The *Book of the Dean* and Beyond', in Thomas Owen Clancy and Murray Pittock (eds), *The Edinburgh History of Scottish Literature Volume 1: From Columba to the Union* (Edinburgh: Edinburgh University Press, 2007), pp. 209–18, 219–25; Virginia Blankenhorn, *Tradition, Transmission, Transformation: Essays on Scottish Gaelic Poetry and Song* (Oxford: Peter Lang, 2019), pp. 159–89.
13 William J. Watson (ed.), *Bàrdachd Ghàidhlig* (Inverness: Northern Counties Printing and Publishing Company, 1918), pp. xlv–liv; MacInnes, 'Gaelic Poetry', pp. 214–70 and 'Bàird is Bleidirean', in MacInnes, *Dùthchas nan Gàidheal*, pp. 341–56; Blankenhorn, *Tradition, Transmission, Transformation*, pp. 22–31, 38–40, 191–230.
14 Thomson, *Introduction to Gaelic Poetry*, pp. 106–7; MacInnes, 'Gaelic Poetry', pp. 25–27, 72–75, 134–35, 305–22.
15 Donald E. Meek, 'The Gaelic Ballads of Medieval Scotland', *Transactions of the Gaelic Society of Inverness*, lv (1986–88), pp. 47–72 and 'Development and Degeneration in Gaelic Ballad Texts', in Bo

Almqvist, Séamas Ó Catháin, and Pádraig Ó Héalaí (eds), *The Heroic Process: Form, Function and Fantasy in Folk Epic* (Dún Laoghaire: Glendale Press, 1987), pp. 131–60; Anja Gunderloch, 'The Heroic Ballads of Gaelic Scotland' in Sarah Dunnigan and Suzanne Gilbert (eds), *The Edinburgh Companion to Scottish Traditional Literatures* (Edinburgh: Edinburgh University Press, 2013), pp. 74–85.

16 See Pádraig Ó Macháin, 'Scribal Practice and Textual Survival: The Example of Uilliam Mac Mhurchaidh', *Scottish Gaelic Studies*, XXII (2006) pp. 95–122; Maolcholaim Scott, 'Politics and Poetry in Mid-Eighteenth Century Argyll: *Tuirseach andiugh críocha Gaoidhiol*', in Colm Ó Baoill and Nancy R. McGuire (eds), *Rannsachadh na Gàidhlig 2000* (Aberdeen: An Clò Gàidhealach, 2002), pp. 149–62.

17 William Matheson (ed.), *The Blind Harper: The Songs of Roderick Morison and his Music* (Edinburgh: Scottish Gaelic Texts Society, 1970), pp. 151–62.

18 Daniel E. O'Sullivan, 'Contrafacture', in Classen (ed.), *Handbook of Medieval Studies*, 1478–81; Friedrich Gennrich, *Die Kontrafaktur im Liedschaffen des Mittelalters* (Langen bei Frankfurt: Summa musicæ medii ævi, 1965), pp. v, 4–11.

19 Although the author herself discounts the influence of English, see Allison Ann Whyte, 'Scottish Gaelic Folksong 1500–1800' (unpublished BLitt dissertation, University of Glasgow, 1971), pp. 36–37, 41, 74, 136; Stiùbhart, 'An Gàidheal', pp. 213–16.

20 *An Ceud Chaogad do Shalmaibh Dhaibhidh, Ar a dtarring as an Eabhra, A Meadar dhana Gaodhilg* (Glasgow, 1659), p. [4].

21 Domhnall Uilleam Stiùbhart, 'Highland Rogues and the Roots of Highland Romanticism', in Christopher MacLachlan (ed.), *Crossing the Highland Line: Cross-currents in Eighteenth-Century Scottish Writing* (Glasgow: ASLS, 2009), pp. 171–73.

22 Ibid., pp. 173–74.

23 Blankenhorn, *Tradition, Transmission, Transformation*, pp. 231–76; Martin MacGregor, '"Surely one of the Greatest Poems Ever Made in Britain": The Lament for Griogair Ruadh MacGregor of Glenstrae and Its Historical Background', in Edward J. Cowan and Douglas Gifford (eds), *The Polar Twins* (Edinburgh: John Donald, 1999), pp. 114–53 and '"Tha mulad air m' inntinn": A Third Song by Marion Campbell of Glen Lyon?', *Aiste*, 5 (2019), pp. 1–49; MacInnes, 'Gaelic Poetry', 219–26; Kate L. Mathis, 'An Ulster Tale in Breadalbane? Personæ and Literary Allusion in the Poetry of Mòr Chaimbeul', *Aiste*, 2 (2008), pp. 43–69; Stiùbhart, 'Highland Rogues', pp. 163–70.

24 Matheson (ed.), *Blind Harper*, pp. lxxiii–lxxvi.
25 Ibid., pp. 58, 131–36.
26 Macinnes, *Clanship, Commerce and the House of Stuart*, pp. 122–58; Stiùbhart, 'An Gàidheal', pp. 250–310.
27 See especially Angela Bourke, '"A bhean úd thall!"': Macallaí Idirghaelacha i bhFilíocht Bhéil na mBan', *Scottish Studies*, 37 (2014), pp. 37–47; Máire Ní Annracháin, 'Metaphor and Metonymy in the Poetry of Màiri nighean Alasdair Ruaidh', in Sharon Arbuthnot and Kaarina Hollo (eds), *Fil Súil nGlais: A Grey Eye Looks Back* (Brig o Turk: Ceann Drochaid, 2007), pp. 163–74; also Alan Bruford, 'Workers, Weepers and Witches: The Status of the Female Singer in Gaelic Society', *Scottish Gaelic Studies*, XVII (1996), pp. 61–70; Anne Frater, 'The Gaelic tradition up to 1750', in Douglas Gifford and Dorothy McMillan (eds), *A History of Scottish Women's Writing* (Edinburgh: Edinburgh University Press, 1997), pp. 1–14; Anne Frater and Michel Byrne, 'Gaelic Poetry and Song', in Glenda Norquay (ed.), *The Edinburgh Companion to Scottish Women's Writing* (Edinburgh: Edinburgh University Press, 2012), pp. 22–34; Colm Ó Baoill, '"Neither out nor in": Scottish Gaelic Women Poets, 1650–1750', in Sarah M. Dunnigan, C. Marie Harker, and Evelyn S. Newlyn (eds), *Women and the Feminine in Medieval and Early Modern Scottish Writing* (Basingstoke: Palgrave Macmillan, 2004), pp. 136–52.
28 Ó Baoill (ed.), *Màiri nighean Alasdair Ruaidh*, pp. 1–16, 86–107, 124–46, 239–43.
29 Macinnes, *Clanship, Commerce and the House of Stuart*, pp. 135–37; see MacInnes, 'Gaelic Poetry', pp. 81–89.
30 Colm Ó Baoill (ed.), *Mairghread nighean Lachlainn: Song-maker of Mull* (Llandysul: Scottish Gaelic Texts Society, 2009), pp. 72–73, 158–60; Black (ed.), *An Lasair*, pp. 388–93.
31 Ó Baoill (ed.), *Màiri nighean Alasdair Ruaidh*, pp. 3–5, 15–16, 21; idem. (ed.), *Mairghread nighean Lachlainn*, pp. 14, 20–1, 32–33.
32 Colm Ó Baoill (ed.), *Bàrdachd Shìlis na Ceapaich* (Edinburgh: Scottish Gaelic Texts Society, 1972), pp. lxiii–lxiv, 12–15, 126–27, 226.
33 Ibid., p. 72; Black (ed.), *An Lasair*, pp. 405–07; Macinnes, 'Gaelic Poetry', pp. 321–22.
34 Ó Baoill (ed.), *Bàrdachd Shìlis na Ceapaich*, pp. lxiv–lxv, 44–49, 58–63, 84–107, 116–21, 154–55, 165–75, 181–82, 234–36, 244–50.
35 Macinnes, *Clanship*, pp. 159–209; Daniel Szechi, *The Jacobites: Britain and Europe, 1688–1788* (Manchester: Manchester University Press, 2019 [1994]).

36 Eric R. Cregeen, 'The Tacksmen and Their Successors: A Study of Tenurial Reorganisation in Mull, Morvern and Tiree in the early eighteenth century', *Scottish Studies*, 13 (1969), pp. 93–144; Ronald Black, *The Campbells of the Ark*, 2 vols (Edinburgh: Birlinn, 2017), I, pp. 246–47, 478–79.

37 Domhnall Uilleam Stiùbhart, 'The Genesis and Operation of the Royal Bounty Scheme 1725–30', *Records of the Scottish Church History Society*, 33 (2003), pp. 140–41.

38 Campbell, John Lorne (ed.), *Highland Songs of the Forty-Five* (Edinburgh: Scottish Gaelic Texts Society, 1984), p. 14.

39 Ibid.; see also *An Lasair*, pp. 36–77, 164–201, 377–94, 440–67; William Gillies, 'Gaelic songs of the "Forty-Five"', *Scottish Studies*, 30 (1991), pp. 19–58.

40 Campbell (ed.), *Highland Songs of the Forty-Five*, pp. 106–115; Angus MacLeod (ed.), *The Songs of Duncan Ban Macintyre* (Edinburgh: Scottish Gaelic Texts Society, 1952), pp. 2–7, 421–22; Black (ed.), *An Lasair*, pp. 174–79.

41 Ronald Black, *Mac Mhaighstir Alasdair: The Ardnamurchan Years* (Coll: Society of West Highland & Island Historical Research, 1986), 'Mac Mhaighstir Alastair in Rannoch: A Reconstruction', *Transactions of the Gaelic Society of Inverness*, lix (1994–96), pp. 341–419, 'Sharing the Honour: Mac Mhaighstir Alastair and the Lowlands', in *Crossing the Highland Line*, pp. 45–56; and *Campbells of the Ark*, I, pp. 41–78; II, pp. 141–46, 176–78, 182–84; Camille Dressler and Domhnall Uilleam Stiùbhart (eds), *Alexander MacDonald: Bard of the Gaelic Enlightenment* (Kershader: Islands Book Trust, 2012); Revs. Angus Macdonald and Archibald Macdonald (eds), *The Poems of Alexander MacDonald* (Inverness: Northern Counties Newspaper and Publishing Co., 1924); Derick S. Thomson (ed.), *Alasdair mac Mhaighstir Alasdair: His Political Poetry* (Inverness: Bookmag, 1989) and 'Mac Mhaighstir Alasdair's Nature Poetry and Its Sources', in *Gaelic and Scots in Harmony* (Glasgow: University of Glasgow Celtic Department, 1990), pp. 95–115; *Alasdair Mac Mhaighstir Alasdair: Selected Poems,* Derick S. Thomson (ed.) (Edinburgh: Scottish Gaelic Texts Society, 1996).

42 See Natasha Sumner, 'James Thomson's *The Seasons*, Gone Gaelic: The Emergence of a Poetic Trend', in *Proceedings of the Harvard Celtic Colloquium* 30 (2010), 236–258.

43 Angus MacLeod (ed.), *Sàr Òrain: Three Gaelic Poems* (Glasgow: An Comunn Gàidhealach, 1933), pp. 54, 102–04; Black (ed.), *An Lasair*,

pp. 469–73; Peadar Ó Muircheartaigh, 'Birlinn Chlann Raghnaill: Long a Fuair Foscadh in Éirinn', *Comhar Taighde*, 6 (2020) [online]; Thomson (ed.), *Alasdair mac Mhaighstir Alasdair: Selected Poems*, pp. 150, 163; EUL Mackinnon (1924), Box 9, fo.714.

44 Alastair Mac-Dhonuill, *Ais-eiridh na Sean Chánoin Albannaich* (Edinburgh, 1751), pp. vii–viii.

45 See Nathan Grey, '"A Publicke Benefite to the Nation": The Charitable and Religious Origins of the SSPCK, 1690–1715' (unpublished PhD thesis, University of Glasgow, 2011); Jamie J. Kelly, 'The Society in Scotland for Propagating Christian Knowledge, 1709–1745' (unpublished PhD thesis, University of Glasgow, 2020) and 'Revisiting the Language Issue: The Society in Scotland for Propagating Christian Knowledge (SSPCK) and Highland Education, c. 1660–1754', *Journal of the Northern Renaissance*, 21 (2021); Domhnall Uilleam Stiùbhart, 'The Genesis and Operation of the Royal Bounty Scheme 1725–30', *Records of the Scottish Church History Society*, 33 (2003), pp. 63–141.

2. Poems in the Scots Register, 1650–1800

1 See 'Register', defined as 'term used in stylistics to refer to a variety of language used in specified kinds of social situations' in *Oxford Dictionary of Literary Terms*, ed. Chris Baldick, 4th edn (Oxford: Oxford University Press, 2008).

2 Ibid. Baldick notes that tone is 'a very vague critical term usually designating the mood or atmosphere of a work'.

3 *Scottish Literature in English and Scots*, ed. Douglas Gifford, Sarah Dunnigan, and Alan MacGillivray (Edinburgh: Edinburgh University Press, 2002), p. 64.

4 Ibid., p. 67.

5 Ibid., p. 69.

6 Ibid., pp. 77–79.

7 Ibid. For more on Scottish ballads, see Roderick Watson, *The Literature of Scotland: The Middle Ages to the Nineteenth Century*, 2nd edn (New York: Palgrave Macmillan, 2007), pp. 135–147.

8 'The Gaberlunzie Man', in *Scottish Literature: An Anthology*, ed. David McCordick, 3 vols (New York: Peter Lang, 1996–2001), I, 783–84 (p. 783), l. 24.

9 Ibid., p. 784, l. 70.

10 Ibid., l. 72.

11 'The Jolly Beggar', in Ibid., I, 786–87 (p. 787), ll. 23–24.
12 Ibid., l. 30.
13 For more on this tradition, see Linda Hutjens, 'The Disguised King in Early English Ballads', in *Literature and Culture in Early Modern England*, ed. Matthew Dimmock and Andrew Hadfield (London: Routledge, 2009), pp. 74–90.
14 *Scottish Poetry of the Seventeenth Century*, ed. George Eyre-Todd, Abbotsford Series of Scottish Poets, 7 vols (London/Bristol: Routledge/Thoemmes Press, 1997), V (1895), 251.
15 Ibid.
16 Robert Sempill, 'Habbie Simson', in *Scottish Literature*, ed. McCordick I, 780–82 (pp. 780, 781), ll. 25, 39–40.
17 Francis Sempill, 'Maggie Lauder', in Ibid., I, 813–14 (p. 813), ll. 2, 10.
18 Ibid., ll. 7, 8, 19, 28.
19 Ibid., ll. 31–32.
20 Ibid., ll. 35–36.
21 Francis Sempill, 'Hallow Fair', 815–17 (p. 815), l. 1.
22 For discussion of this poem and its sources, see Corey E. Andrews, 'Footnoted Folklore: Robert Burns's "Halloween"', in *Robert Burns and Friends*, ed. Patrick Scott and Kenneth Simpson (Columbia: University of South Carolina Libraries, 2012), pp. 24–37.
23 *Scottish Poetry*, ed. Eyre-Todd, V, 260. For more on the Sempills of Beltrees, see Watson, pp. 147–49.
24 Christopher Harvie, *Scotland: A Short History* (Oxford: Oxford University Press, 2002), p. 121.
25 *A Choice Collection of Comic and Serious Scots Poems, Both Ancient and Modern*, ed. James Watson (Edinburgh, 1706), p. i.
26 Ibid.
27 T. F. Henderson, *Scottish Vernacular Literature: A Succinct History*, 3rd edn, (Detroit: Gale, 1969), (1910), pp. 398, 399. See also Watson, *Literature of Scotland*, p. 172.
28 Allan Ramsay, 'Lucky Spence's Last Advice', in *Before Burns: Eighteenth-Century Scottish Poetry*, ed. Christopher MacLachlan (Edinburgh: Canongate, 2002), pp. 25–29 (p. 25 fn).
29 Ibid., l. 7
30 Ibid., l. 24.
31 Allan Ramsay, 'Elegy on Lucky Wood in the Canongate, May 1717', in ibid., 30–33 (p. 30), ll. 13–18.
32 Ibid., pp. 33, l. 78.

33 Allan Ramsay, 'Elegy on John Cowper Kirk-Treasurer's Man', in ibid., pp. 45–48 (p. 45 fn. 1).
34 William Hamilton of Gilbertfield, 'The Last Dying Words of Bonnie Heck, a Famous Greyhound in the Shire of Fife', in *Scottish Literature*, ed. McCordick I, 852–54 (p. 852), ll. 11, 13, 15.
35 Ibid., p. 854, ll. 80, 81, 83–84.
36 Ibid., l. 81.
37 Ibid., ll. 83–84.
38 *The Letters of Robert Burns*, ed. J. DeLancey Ferguson and G. Ross Roy, 2nd edn, 2 vols (Oxford: Clarendon, 1985), I, 136. This is Burns's famed autobiographical letter to Dr John Moore dated 2 August 1787.
39 Henderson, p. 398.
40 Lady Grizzel Bailie, 'There Ance Was a May', in *Scottish Literature*, ed. McCordick I, 840–41, (p. 840), ll. 1, 5.
41 Ibid., p. 841, ll. 37–40.
42 Elizabeth Wardlaw, 'Hardyknute', in *Scottish Literature*, ed. McCordick I, 859–866.
43 Ibid., p. 866, ll. 333–34.
44 For more on this aspect of Wardlaw's poem, see Justin Sider, '"Modern Antiques", Ballad Imitation, and the Aesthetics of Anachronism', *Victorian Poetry* 54 (2016), 455–75.
45 Wardlaw, 'Hardyknute', p. 866, ll. 309–10.
46 Alan I. Macinnes, *A History of Scotland* (London: Macmillan, 2019), pp. 115–16. Macinnes describes the reprisals of the British government as 'a final solution to the Jacobite problem […] by active terrorism' (p. 115).
47 Tobias Smollett, 'The Tears of Scotland', in *Scottish Literature*, ed. McCordick I, 1026–27 (p. 1026), ll. 1, 24.
48 This was a popular subject, for another version of the song was written in English by Alison Rutherford Cockburn (1712–1794).
49 John Skinner, 'Tullochgorum' in *Scottish Literature*, ed. McCordick I, 1020–23 (p. 1020, l. 12) See also Robert Fergusson, 'Elegy on the Death of Scots Music' in *Scottish Literature*, ed. McCordick II, 29–30 and Robert Burns, 'Epistle to John Lapraik, an Old Scotch Bard' in *Scottish Literature*, ed. McCordick II, 82–84.
50 William Julius Mickle, 'The Sailor's Wife', in *Scottish Literature*, ed. McCordick I, 1125–27 (p. 1126), ll. 9–12.
51 Alexander Ross, *Helenore; or The Fortunate Shepherdess, a Pastoral Tale*, ed. Alexander Thomson (Dundee: Alexander Thomson, 1812), pp. xxxvii–xxxix.

52 Ibid., p. viii.
53 Peter Zenzinger, 'Cultural Paradoxes in Alexander Ross's Fortunate Shepherdess', *Studies in Scottish Literature*, 35 (2007), pp. 271–94 (pp. 271, 273).
54 Ibid., p. 274.
55 *Letters of Robert Burns*, ed. J. DeLancey Ferguson and G. Ross Roy, I, 170. The quotation is from Burns's letter to James Hoy, 6 November 1787.
56 MacLachlan, p. 330. For more on Fergusson, see *'Heaven-taught Fergusson': Robert Burns's Favourite Scottish Poet*, ed. Robert Crawford (East Linton: Tuckwell, 2003).
57 For discussion and analysis of Fergusson's poems for the Cape Club, see Corey Andrews, *Literary Nationalism in Eighteenth-Century Scottish Club Poetry* (Lewiston: Edwin Mellen, 2004), pp. 115–215.
58 Robert Fergusson, 'The Daft-Days', in *Before Burns*, ed. MacLachlan, pp. 222–24 (p. 224), ll. 1–2.
59 Ibid., ll. 6–7.
60 Ibid., ll. 19–21.
61 Ibid., p. 223, ll. 34, 43, 50, 48.
62 Ibid., ll. 44.
63 Ibid., ll. 55–56.
64 Ibid., pp. 223–24, ll. 60–61.
65 Ibid., p. 224, ll. 64–65.
66 Ibid., p. 322.
67 Examples of his English verse include the satires 'To Samuel Johnson: Food for a New Edition of his Dictionary', in *Before Burns*, ed. MacLachlan, pp. 268–69 and 'The Sow of Feeling', in *Before Burns*, ed. MacLachlan, pp. 277–79.
68 Robert Fergusson, 'Auld Reikie', in *Before Burns*, ed. MacLachlan, pp. 211–221 (p. 211), ll. 25–26.
69 Ibid., p. 212, ll. 33.
70 Ibid., ll. 34.
71 Ibid., p. 213, ll. 67–68.
72 Ibid., ll. 77.
73 Ibid., ll. 85.
74 Ibid., ll. 95–8.
75 Ibid., ll. 101.
76 Ibid., p. 214, ll. 119–20.
77 Ibid., p. 215, l. 148.
78 Ibid., ll. 157.
79 Ibid., p. 216, ll. 182–84.

80 Ibid., ll. 187–90.
81 Ibid., p. 219, ll. 279–85.
82 Ibid., p. 330.
83 For discussion of this aspect of Burns's influence, see Corey E. Andrews, *The Genius of Scotland: The Cultural Production of Robert Burns, 1785–1835* (Leiden: Brill Rodopi, 2015), pp. 191–236.
84 Robert Burns, 'Holy Willie's Prayer', in *The Poems and Songs of Robert Burns*, ed. James Kinsley, 3 vols (Oxford: Clarendon, 1968), I, 74–78 (p. 75), l. 25.
85 Burns, 'The Death and Dying Words of Poor Mailie, the Author's Only Pet Yowe', in *Poems and Songs*, ed. Kinsley, I, 32–34 (p. 32), ll. 17–20.
86 Burns, 'Epistle to John Lapraik, an Old Scotch Bard', in *Poems and Songs*, ed. Kinsley, I, 85–89 (p. 86), ll. 49–51.
87 Ibid., p. 87, ll. 73–74.
88 Burns, 'To a Mouse', in *Poems and Songs*, ed. Kinsley, pp. 127–128 (p. 127), ll. 7–12.
89 Ibid., l. 15.
90 Ibid., l. 19
91 Ibid., l. 23.
92 Ibid., p. 128, l. 37–40.
93 Ibid., l. 43–44.
94 An excellent biographical study of Burns's motivations in writing Scottish songs can be found in J. DeLancey Ferguson, *Pride and Passion: Robert Burns, 1759–1796* (New York: Oxford University Press, 1939), pp. 234–77.
95 Janet Little, *The Poetical Works of Janet Little, the Scottish Milkmaid* (Air: Printed by John Wilson, 1792); John Mayne, *The Siller Gun* (London: Thomas Cadell, 1836); John Lapraik; *Poems on Several Occasions* (Kilmarnock: Printed by John Wilson, 1788); David Sillar, *Poems* (Kilmarnock: Printed by John Wilson, 1789); Ebenezer Picken, *Poems and Epistles, Mostly in Scottish Dialect* (Paisley: Printed by John Neilson, 1788).
96 For analysis of this process, see Andrews, *The Genius of Scotland*, pp. 145–90.

3. Presenting the National Past: The Uses of History in Scottish Literature, 1650–1707

1 For a fuller consideration of this topic, see Leith Davis, 'The Aftermath of Union', in *The Cambridge Companion to Scottish Literature*, ed.

Gerard Carruthers and Liam McIlvanney (Cambridge: Cambridge University Press, 2012), pp. 56–70.

2   Louisa Schein, 'Importing Miao Brethren to Hmong America: A Not-So-Stateless Transnationalism', in *Cosmopolitics: Thinking and Feeling Beyond the Nation*, ed. Pheng Cheah and Bruce Robbins (Minneapolis: University of Minnesota Press, 1998), pp. 163–91 (p. 164).

3   Suvir Kaul, *Eighteenth-Century British Literature and Postcolonial Studies* (Edinburgh: Edinburgh University Press, 2009), p. 17. See also: Leith Davis, 'Transnational Articulations in James Macpherson's Poems of Ossian and The History and Management of the East-India Company', *The Eighteenth Century*, 60 (2019), 441–60.

4   See Keith Brown, *Kingdom or Province?: Scotland and the Regal Union 1603–1715* (New York: Macmillan, 1992), p. 137. The official Treaty of Union, however, was not passed until 1657.

5   Alvin Jackson, *The Two Unions: Ireland, Scotland, and the Survival of the United Kingdom, 1707–2007* (Oxford and New York: Oxford University Press, 2012), p. 46.

6   See Nicola Royan and Dauvit Broun, 'Versions of Scottish Nationhood, c. 850–1707', in *The Edinburgh History of Scottish Literature I: From Columba to the Union (until 1707)*, ed. Thomas Clancy and Murray Pittock (Edinburgh: Edinburgh University Press, 2007), pp. 168–83 (pp. 172–73). Royan and Broun examine the complicated textual history of Fordun's text, including its integration into Walter Bower's *Scotichronicon*, and discuss the different ideological interpretations of Boece by the Catholic John Leslie in *De Origine, Moribus, Ac Rebus Gestis Scotiae Libri Decem* (1578) and the Gaelic-speaking Calvinist George Buchanan in *Rerum Scoticarum Historiae* (1582). Where Leslie emphasised the power of the monarch, Buchanan focused on the implicit argument that the king's power derives from the people.

7   Royan and Broun point out that 'Barbour's presentation of Robert Bruce as hero and as king came to dominate accounts of the king and his journey to the throne', while *The Wallace* borrows episodes from *The Bruce*, but was also aimed toward a less elite audience (pp. 175–76).

8   See David Allan, 'Prudence and Patronage: The Politics of Culture in Seventeenth-Century Scotland', *History of European Ideas*, 18 (1994), 467–80; Alvin Jackson, *The Two Unions*; Colin Kidd, *Union and Unionism: Political Thought in Scotland, 1500–2000* (Cambridge:

Cambridge University Press, 2008); and *Scots and Britons: Scottish Political Thought and the Union of 1603*, ed. Roger Mason (Cambridge: Cambridge University Press, 1994).

9   Thomas Urquhart, *Ekskybalauron: Or, The Discovery of a Most Exquisite Jewel* (London: Printed by J. Cottrel, 1652), n.p.

10 See Jeremy J. Smith, 'The Inventions of Sir Thomas Urquhart', in *The Impact of Latin Culture on Medieval and Early Scottish Writing*, ed. Alessandra Petrina and Ian Johnson (Kalamazoo: Medieval Institute Publications, 2018), pp. 223–48.

11 Thomas Urquhart, *Logopandecteision, or, An Introduction to the Universal Language* (London: 1653), p. 10.

12 Thomas Urquhart, *Pantochronochanon: Or, A Peculiar Promptuary of Time* (London: Printed for Richard Baddele, 1652), pp. 13–14.

13 Urquhart, *Ekskybalauron*, n.p.

14 Ibid.

15 Ibid., p. 214.

16 Ibid., pp. 252–53.

17 Urquhart, *Logopandecteision*, p. 10.

18 Ibid.

19 Ibid., p. 22.

20 Thomas Urquhart, *The First Book of the Works of Mr. Francis Rabelais* (London: Printed [by Thomas Ratcliffe and Edward Mottershead] for Richard Baddeley, 1653).

21 Alexander Ross, *Som Animadversions and Observations Upon Sr Walter Raleigh's Historie of the World* (London: Printed by William Du-Gard for Richard Royston, 1648), p. 2.

22 Alexander Ross, *The History of the World: The Second Part* (London: Printed for John Saywell, 1652), n.p.

23 Ibid., Preface, n.p.

24 Ibid.

25 Ibid.

26 David Allan, '"An Ancient Sage Philosopher": Alexander Ross and the Defence of Philosophy', *The Seventeenth Century*, 16 (2001), 68–94 (p. 68).

27 Robert Crawford, *Scotland's Books: The Penguin History of Scottish Literature* (London: Penguin, 2007), p. 209.

28 Crawford, p. 211.

29 *New Penguin Book of Scottish Verse*, ed. Robert Crawford and Mick Imlah (Harmondsworth: Penguin, 2001), p. 215.

30 Ibid., p. 215.
31 Ibid.
32 Ibid., p. 217.
33 George Mackenzie, *Aretina, or The Serious Romance* (Edinburgh: Printed for Robert Broun, 1660), p. 13.
34 Ibid., pp. 7–8.
35 See Irene Basey Beesemyer, 'Sir George Mackenzie's Aretina of 1660: A Scot's Assault on Restoration Politics', *Scottish Studies Review*, 4 (2003), 41–68.
36 Mackenzie, p. 128.
37 Ibid., p. 130. See M. R. G. Spiller, 'The First Scots Novel: Sir George Mackenzie's Aretina (1660)', *Scottish Literary Journal*, 11 (1979), 1–20 and Clare Jackson, 'The Paradoxical Virtue of the Historical Romance: Sir George Mackenzie's *Aretina* (1660) and the Civil Wars', in *The Celtic Dimensions of the British Civil Wars*, ed. John R. Young (Edinburgh: John Donald, 1997), pp. 205–25.
38 Mackenzie, p. 271.
39 Ibid., p. 338.
40 Ibid., p. 340.
41 See Kelsey Jackson Williams, *The First Scottish Enlightenment: Rebels, Priests, and History* (Oxford: Oxford University Press, 2020), pp. 24–32, for Mackenzie's contributions to Scottish legal and literary culture; he was, for example, responsible for the founding of the Advocates' Library in 1682. In addition, as Colin Kidd points out, Mackenzie's 'interpretation of Scottish history' in his *A Defence of the Antiquity of the Royal line of Scotland* (1685) published upon James VII/II's accession to the throne would form 'the core of Scottish Jacobite ideology' following the 1688 Revolution. Colin Kidd, *Subverting Scotland's Past: Scottish Whig Historians and the Creation of an Anglo-British Identity 1689–1830* (Cambridge: Cambridge University Press, 1993), p. 27.
42 See the chapters by Ian Brown and by Sharon Alker and Holly Faith Nelson in this volume *passim*.
43 As Jeffrey Stephen points out, the Presbyterians themselves were split in response to the Revolution Settlement. The Cameronians, for example, rejected the Revolution Settlement because of its 'failure to renew the covenants' and because they saw it as an Erastian settlement (*Scottish Presbyterians and the Act of Union 1707* (Edinburgh: Edinburgh University Press, 2007), p. 5). See also Clare Jackson, *Restoration Scotland, 1660–1690: Royalist Politics, Religion and Ideas* (Rochester, NY: Boydell, 2003), p. 49.

44 See Kidd, *Subverting Scotland's Past*, p. 28. Notably, an English translation of Buchanan's *Rerum Scoticarum Historiae* was published in 1690. See George Buchanan, *The History of Scotland. Written in Latin by George Buchanan*, trans. F. Fraser (London: Printed by E. Jones, for A. Churchil, 1690).

45 See John Coffey, 'The Problem of "Scottish Puritanism," 1590–1638', in *Enforcing Reformation in Ireland and Scotland, 1550–1700*, ed. Elizabethanne Boran and Crawford Gribben, St Andrews Studies in Reformation History (Aldershot, England and Burlington, VT: Ashgate, 2006), pp. 66–90 (p. 88).

46 Jack MacQueen, 'From Rome to Ruddiman: The Scoto-Latin Tradition', in *The Edinburgh History of Scottish Literature I*, ed. Clancy and Pittock, pp. 184–208 (p. 203). See also Steven J. Reid and David McOmish, *Neo-Latin Literature and Literary Culture in Early Modern Scotland* (Leiden and Boston: Brill, 2017).

47 F. W. Freeman, *Robert Fergusson and the Scots Humanist Compromise* (Edinburgh: Edinburgh University Press, 1984), pp. 14–15.

48 MacQueen, p. 203. See also Freeman.

49 John MacQueen and Winifred MacQueen, *Archibald Pitcairne: The Latin Poems* (Royal Van Gorcum: Arizona Center for Medieval and Renaissance Studies, 2009), p. 1.

50 Archibald Pitcairn, *The Assembly: A Comedy, by a Scots Gentleman* (London: 1722).

51 Five copies survive, one in Philp's handwriting. See L. B. T. Houghton, 'Lucan in the Highlands: James Philp's *Grameid* and the Traditions of Ancient Epic', in *Neo-Latin Poetry in the British Isles*, ed. L. B. T. Houghton and Gesine Manuwald (London: Bloomsbury Academic, 2012), pp. 190–207 (p. 190).

52 James Philip, *The Grameid: An Heroic Poem Descriptive of the Campaign of Viscount Dundee in 1689 and Other Pieces*, ed. Alexander Murdoch (Edinburgh: Printed at the University Press by T. and A. Constable for the Scottish History Society, 1888), p. 1.

53 Ibid., p. 23.

54 Murray Pittock, *Poetry and Jacobite Politics in Eighteenth-Century Britain and Ireland* (Cambridge: Cambridge University Press, 1994), p. 40.

55 Murray G. H. Pittock, 'Philp [Philip], James, of Almerieclose (1654/5–1732), Jacobite Poet', *Oxford Dictionary of National Biography* (Oxford University Press, 2004) doi.org/10.1093/ref:odnb/68270 [accessed 1 May 2020].

56 Ibid., p. 2.
57 Colm Ó Baoill, 'Sìleas na Ceapaich', in *The Edinburgh History of Scottish Literature I*, pp. 305–14 (p. 305), and Colm Ó Baoill, 'A History of Gaelic to 1800', in *Edinburgh Companion to the Gaelic Language*, ed. Moray Watson and Michelle McLeod (Edinburgh: Edinburgh University Press, 2010), pp. 1–21 (p. 15).
58 See John Brewer, *The Sinews of Power: War, Money and the English State, 1688–1783* (London: Unwin Hyman, 1989).
59 *Scotland's Right to Caledonia (Formerly called DARIEN and the Legality of its Settlement, asserted in Three several Memorials presented to His Majesty in May 1699 by the Lord President of the Session and Lord Advocate, on behalf of the Company of Scotland, Trading to Africa and the Indies* (Edinburgh: 1700), p. 12.
60 *An Ode Made on the Welcome News of the Safe Arrival and Kind Reception of the Scottish Colony at Darien in America* (Edinburgh: Printed by James Watson, 1699).
61 Alexander Pennecuik, *Caledonia Triumphans: A Panegyrick to the King* (Edinburgh: Printed by the Heirs and Successors of Andrew Anderson, 1699).
62 Ibid.
63 Walter Herries, 'Epistle Dedicatory', in *A Defence of the Scots Abdicating Darien Including An Answer To the Defence of the Scots Settlement There* (Edinburgh: 1700), n.p.
64 George Ridpath, *An Enquiry into the Causes of the Miscarriage of the Scots Colony at Darien or an Answer to a Libel Entituled A Defence of the Scots Abdicating Darien. Submitted to the Confideration of the Good People of England* (Glasgow: 1700), pp. 34–35. See also Andrew Fletcher, *A Short and Impartial View of the Manner and Occasion of the Scots Colony's Coming Away from Darien in a Letter to a Person of Quality* (Edinburgh: 1699).
65 See Karen Cullen, *Famine in Scotland: The 'Ill Years' of the 1690s* (Edinburgh: Edinburgh University Press, 2010).
66 See Karin Bowie, *Scottish Public Opinion and the Anglo-Scottish Union, 1699–1707* (Woodbridge: Boydell Press, 2007) and Christopher Whatley, *Scots and the Union: Then and Now* (Edinburgh: Edinburgh University Press, 2014).
67 See Chapter One of Leith Davis, *Acts of Union: Scotland and the Literary Negotiation of the British Nation, 1707–1832* (Stanford: Stanford University Press, 1998).

68 Andrew Fletcher, *Speeches by a Member of the Parliament, Which Began at Edinburgh the 6th. of May 1703* (Edinburgh: 1703), pp. 6–7.
69 James Hodges, *The Rights and Interests of the Two British Monarchies* (London: 1703), p. 7.
70 Christopher Whatley, *The Scots and the Union: Then and Now* (Edinburgh: Edinburgh University Press, 2014), p. 13.
71 *James Watson's Choice Collection of Comic and Serious Scots Poems*, ed. Harriet Harvey Wood, 2 vols (Aberdeen: Scottish Text Society, 1977 and 1991), II, xix.
72 James Watson, 'The Publisher to the Reader', in *A Choice Collection of Comic and Serious Scots Poems* (Edinburgh: 1706), 4.
73 See Leith Davis, 'Imagining the Miscellaneous Nation: James Watson's Choice Collection of Comic and Serious Scots Poems', *Eighteenth-Century Life*, 35.3 (2011), 60–80.
74 James Watson, *A Choice Collection of Comic and Serious Scots Poems*, Part 2 (Edinburgh: 1709), 4.
75 George Mackenzie, *Lives and Characters of the Most Eminent Writers of the Scots Nation*, 3 vols. (Edinburgh: Printed for J. Watson, 1708–22), I, p. 18.
76 Ibid., 1:1.
77 Allan Ramsay, 'Christis Kirk on the Green' (Edinburgh: 1718).
78 Allan Ramsay, *The Ever Green, Being a Collection of Scots Poems, Wrote by the Ingenious Before 1600* (Edinburgh: printed by Mr Thomas Ruddiman for the publisher, 1724), p. iv.
79 Ibid., p. vii.
80 Allan Ramsay, *Scots Songs* (Edinburgh: Printed for the Author, 1718); Allan Ramsay, *Tea-Table Miscellany* (Edinburgh: Thomas Ruddiman, 1724).
81 Allan Ramsay, *Edinburgh's Address to the Country* (Edinburgh: 1718), p. 5.
82 Ibid., p. 8.
83 Ibid., p. 7.

4. Literary Print Culture in Restoration Scotland, 1660–1688

1 Many studies of Scottish literature over the past few decades foreground the navigation of Anglo-Scottish relations in literature and therefore focus on cultural production after the Union; such works include Leith Davis's *Acts of Union: Scotland and the Literary Negotiation of the British Nation, 1707–1830* (Stanford: Stanford University

Press, 1998) and Juliet Shields's *Sentimental Literature and Anglo-Scottish Identity, 1745–1820* (Cambridge: Cambridge University Press, 2010). Rivka Swenson's *Essential Scots and the Idea of Unionism in Anglo-Scottish Literature, 1603–1850* (Lewisburg, PA: Bucknell University Press, 2016) does begin with the reign of James VI/I, but her insightful study of pre-Union writing foregrounds the works of Francis Bacon rather than those of Scottish writers. In defence of *The Cambridge Companion to Scottish Literature*, ed. Gerard Carruthers and Liam McIlvanney (Cambridge: Cambridge University Press, 2012), its editors acknowledge in their introduction that '[t]raditionally, Scotland's seventeenth century has been viewed as a cultural wasteland' and attempt to address this issue with the chapter on Renaissance Scottish literature, which covers Scottish literature up to the 1650s (p. 4).

2 For the purpose of this short study, we work with a narrow definition of published literature: poetry, plays, and the rather nebulous category of prose fiction. This means that findings will be biased toward literature written in support of the Stuarts since works more critical of the Stuarts, especially in the 1660s and 1670s, were more likely to circulate in manuscript or to appear in non-literary or partially literary prose genres. The study also does not address the importation to and circulation in Scotland of books issued by publishers from England or the Continent.

3 See Joad Raymond, *Pamphlets and Pamphleteering in Early Modern Britain* (Cambridge: Cambridge University Press, 2003) and Nigel Smith, *Literature and Revolution in England, 1640–1660* (New Haven: Yale University Press, 1997).

4 John Morrill, 'The Causes and Course of the British Civil Wars', in *The Cambridge Companion to Writing of the English Revolution*, ed. N. H. Keeble (Cambridge: Cambridge University Press, 2001), pp. 13–31 (p. 23); Charles Carlton, 'Civilians', in *The Civil Wars: A Military History of England, Scotland, and Ireland 1638–1660*, ed. John Kenyon and Jane Ohlmeyer (Oxford: Oxford University Press, 1998), pp. 272–305 (p. 277). For a detailed account of the wars in Scotland, see Edward Furgol, 'The Civil Wars in Scotland', in *The Civil Wars*, ed. Kenyon and Ohlmeyer's, pp. 41–67. See also, John R. Young, ed., *Celtic Dimensions of the British Civil Wars* (Edinburgh: John Donald, 1997); John L. Roberts, *Clan, King and Covenant: History of the Highland Clans from the Civil War to the Glencoe Massacre* (Edinburgh: Edinburgh University Press, 2000); David Scott, *Politics and War in*

the Three Stuart Kingdoms, 1637–49 (New York: Palgrave Macmillan, 2004); Ian Gentles, *The English Revolution and the Wars in the Three Kingdoms 1638–1652* (Harlow: Pearson Longman, 2007); R. Scott Spurlock, *Cromwell and Scotland: Conquest and Religion 1650–1660* (Edinburgh: John Donald, 2007); and Stuart Reid, *Crown Covenant and Cromwell: The Civil Wars in Scotland 1639–1651* (Barnsley: Frontline Books, 2012).

5   Spurlock, pp. 104, 47, 50, 72.
6   Ibid., p. 72.
7   David L. Smith, 'Parliaments and Constitutions', in *The Oxford Handbook of the English Revolution*, ed. Michael J. Braddick (Oxford: Oxford University Press, 2015), pp. 243–59 (p. 252).
8   Alastair J. Mann, *The Scottish Book Trade, 1500–1720: Print Commerce and Print Control in Early Modern Scotland* (East Linton: Tuckwell, 2000), p. 14.
9   Ibid., p. 31.
10 Ibid., pp. 127–28.
11 Ibid., pp. 134, 201.
12 Two representative religious works published in the year of the Restoration which are inflected by the political are *A Testimony to the Truth of Jesus Christ, or To the Doctrine, Worship, Discipline, and Government of the Kirk of Scotland, and To the Nationall Covenant of Scotland, and To the Solemn League and Covenant of the Three Nations, England, Scotland, and Ireland* (Edinburgh: Printed by a Society of Stationers, 1660); and James Ramsey's *Moses Returned from Midian; or, Gods Kindnesse to a Banished King; His Office, and His Subjects Duty. As it was Delivered in a Sermon, Preached at Linlithgow, on the Day of Thanksgiving for His Majestie our Soveraigns Happy Restauration* (Edinburgh: Printed by Gedeon Lithgow, 1660).
13 Steven N. Zwicker, 'Is There Such a Thing as Restoration Literature', *Huntington Library Quarterly*, 69 (2006), 425–50 (pp. 432–33).
14 Alastair J. Mann, 'The Anatomy of the Printed Book in Early Modern Scotland', *The Scottish Historical Review*, 80 (2001), 181–200 (p. 194).
15 Robert Crawford, *Scotland's Books: A History of Scottish Literature* (Oxford: Oxford University Press, 2009), p. 12.
16 Ibid., p. 11.
17 Jonquil Bevan, 'Scotland', in *The Cambridge History of the Book in Britain*, 7 vols (Cambridge: Cambridge University Press, 2002), IV: 1557–1695, ed. John Barnard and D. F. McKenzie, pp. 687–700 (p. 692).

18 Steven J. Reid, 'A Latin Renaissance in Reformation Scotland? Print Trends in Scottish Latin Literature, c. 1480–1700', *The Scottish Historical Review*, 95 (2016), 1–29 (p. 20); see also *Neo-Latin Literature and Literary Culture in Early Modern England*, ed. Steven J. Reid and David McOmish (Leiden: Brill, 2016).
19 Mann, *The Scottish Book Trade*, p. 116.
20 Ibid., p. 102.
21 Crawford, p. 11.
22 Cited from the title page of Richard Bernard, *The Isle of Man: or, The Legal Proceeding in Man-shire against Sin* (Glasgow: Robert Sanders, 1674); see also nos. 24 and 25 of the first part of 'The Contents [...]', n. pag.
23 Richard L. Greaves, 'Bernard, Richard (*bap.* 1568, *d.* 1642)', in *Oxford Dictionary of National Biography* (Oxford: Oxford University Press, 2009). doi.org/10.1093/ref:odnb/2249 [accessed 23 June 2018].
24 This work was published anonymously. Anthony à Wood, *Athenæ Oxonienses*, new edn., vol. 4 (London: Lackington, Hughes, Harding, Mavor, and Jones et al., 1820), pp. 232–33, n3.
25 'Introduction' to *Adam Bell, Clim of the Clough, William of Cloudesley*, in *Robin Hood and Other Outlaw Tales*, ed. Stephen Knight and Thomas H. Ohlgren (Kalamazoo: Medieval Institute Publications, 1997) d.lib.rochester.edu/teams/text/adam-bell-clim-of-the-clough-william-of-cloudesley-introduction [accessed 27 February 2019].
26 There were also a few anonymous English broadsides of a more comic nature republished in Scotland, including the anti-feminist piece *Fore-warn'd, Fore-arm'd: or, A Caveat to Batchelors, in the Character of a Bad Woman* (Edinburgh: Printed by J. van Solingen and J. Colmar, 1685).
27 Andrew Cambers, *Godly Reading: Print, Manuscript and Puritanism in England, 1580–1720* (Cambridge: Cambridge University Press, 2011), p. 182; Richard L. Greaves, 'Wild, Robert (1615/16–1679)', in *Oxford Dictionary of National Biography* (Oxford: Oxford University Press, 2008). doi.org/10.1093/ref:odnb/29395 [accessed 23 June 2018]; Charles Clay Doyle, 'Birkenhead, Sir John (1617–1679)', in *Oxford Dictionary of National Biography* (Oxford: Oxford University Press, 2004). doi.org/10.1093/ref:odnb/2455 [accessed 23 June 2018].
28 Greaves, 'Wild, Robert'; Tony Claydon, *Europe and the Making of England, 1660–1760* (Cambridge: Cambridge University Press, 2007), p. 139.

29 Elkanah Settle, *An Heroick Poem on the Coronation of the High and Mighty Monarch, James II. King of England, &c* (Edinburgh: Re-Printed by the Heir of Andrew Anderson, 1685), pp. 3, 8. Settle was not always a conservative or Tory, as Abigail Williams explains in 'Settle, Elkanah (1648–1724)', in *Oxford Dictionary of National Biography* doi.org/10.1093/ref:odnb/25128 [accessed 23 June 2018]. His allegiance varied with the political winds.
30 John Dryden, *Britannia Rediviva: A Poem on the Birth of the Prince* (Holyrood House: P. B. Enginier, 1688), p. 7.
31 Ibid., p. 4.
32 Aphra Behn, *A Congratulatory Poem to Her Most Sacred Majesty* (Edinburgh: Re-Printed by the Heir of Andrew Anderson, 1688), pp. 2, 7. According to Emma Major, this royalist interpretation reads the Stuart infant's birth as a sign of the hope for 'a united Britain': '"That glory may dwell in our land": The Bible, Britannia, and the Glorious Revolution', *The Oxford Handbook of the Bible in Early Modern England, c. 1530–1700,* ed. Kevin Killeen, Helen Smith, and Rachel Judith Willie (Oxford: Oxford University Press, 2015), pp. 427–48 (p. 444).
33 The early English tales republished do raise the issue of challenging unjust authority, but in a relatively benign and carnivalesque manner.
34 As Roderick Watson remarks, 'the Scotsman's many descriptions of split brains and arms hewn away recreate the details of combat as if from a foot-soldier's point of view', a narrative that would surely resonate with Scottish men and women who had endured a lengthy internecine war: *The Literature of Scotland: The Middle Ages to the Nineteenth Century*, 2nd edn (Houndmills: Palgrave Macmillan, 2007), p. 47.
35 Sally Mapstone, review of *James Watson's Choice Collection of Comic and Serious Scots Poems,* ed. Harriet Harvey Wood, *The Review of English Studies*, 45 (1994), 604–05 (p. 605).
36 In 'Animal Rights, Legal Agency, and Cultural Difference in *The Testament of the Buck*', *Theorizing Legal Personhood in Late Medieval England,* ed. Andreea D. Boboc (Leiden: Brill, 2015), pp. 270–90, Jamie Taylor explains that the 'literary testament' poem was 'popular in England and Scotland between the fourteenth and sixteenth centuries'. In *The Testament of the Buck*, as with *The Meir of Collingtoun*, the wounded animal 'produces a legal testament to bequeath parts of his own body to various recipients' (p. 270).
37 *The Chearfull Acclamation of the City of Edinburgh* (Edinburgh, c. 1660).

38 As Charles Carlton records, after the Scottish army abandoned Charles I to his fate with the English 'in return for payments of debts worth £400,000', 'Newcastle's fishwives screamed "Judas! Judas!" taunting the Scots for agreeing to leave Charles behind': *Charles I: The Personal Monarch*, 2nd edn (London: Routledge, 1995), p. 309.
39 Gillian H. MacIntosh, *The Scottish Parliament under Charles II, 1660–1685* (Edinburgh: Edinburgh University Press, 2007), p. 7.
40 Variants of Clark's name include Clarke, Clerke, and Clerk.
41 Irene Basey Beesemyer, 'Sir George Mackenzie's *Aretina* of 1660: A Scot's Assault on Restoration Politics', *Scottish Studies Review*, 4 (2003), 41–68 (pp. 41–42).
42 William Clark, title page of *Marciano; or, The Discovery of a Tragi-Comedy* (Edinburgh: n. pub., 1663). John Leslie 'also chaired the Scottish Privy Council, presided over the Treasury and was General of the Scots military': Clare Jackson, *Restoration Scotland, 1660–1690: Royalist Politics, Religion and Ideas* (Woodbridge: Boydell Press, 2003), p. 78. In her earlier chapter 'Restoration to Revolution, 1660–1690', in *The New British History: Founding a Modern State, 1603–1715*, ed. Glenn Burgess (London: I. B. Taurus; New York: St. Martin's, 1999), pp. 92–114, Jackson notes that at this time '[i]n Scotland, effective political power was increasingly vested in the office of parliamentary High Commissioner' (p. 98).
43 Clark, pp. 3–7 (p. 4).
44 George Mackenzie, 'An Apologie for Romances', *Aretina; or, The Serious Romance* (Edinburgh: Robert Broun, 1660), pp. 5–11 (p. 7).
45 Clark, pp. 3–4.
46 Ibid., pp. 65–66.
47 Mackenzie, pp. 333–34.
48 As Beesemyer contends, 'While praising the individual Stuart monarchs with predictable royalist rhetoric, *Aretina* grapples with problems of kingship, indicating that Mackenzie had reservations, not about the overall monarchical schema he so ultimately champions, but its implementation' (p. 45).
49 The second Earl of Southesk 'first […] took part with the Covenanters, but subsequently […] became a Royalist', spending some time waiting on the future Charles II in exile in 1650. He did serve for a time as 'one of the Commissioners for negotiating a Treaty of Union with England' when he returned from the Continent in 1652: 'Appendix to Seventh Report', *Seventh Report of the Royal Commission on Historical Manuscripts: Part I, Report and Appendix* (London: George Edward

Eyre and William Spottiswoode, 1879), p. 717; see also *Burke's Genealogical and Heraldic History of Peerage and Baronetage of the British Empire,* 21st edn (London: Harrison, 1859), p. 932a.

50 Peter C. Herman, *Destabilizing Milton: 'Paradise Lost' and the Poetics of Incertitude* (New York: Palgrave Macmillan, 2005), pp. 113, 112.

51 Parliamentarians also routinely turned to the Jobean narrative to make sense of their pre- and post-Restoration sufferings, as Maurice J. O'Sullivan details in *The Books of Job* (Newcastle: Cambridge Scholars Publishing, 2007).

52 Arthur Nasmyth, 'The Epistle Dedicatory', *Divine Poems, in Three Parts* (Edinburgh: Printed for James Miller, 1665), n. pag.

53 Variants of Sydserf's name include Sydeserf, Sydserff, and St. Serfe.

54 Sydserf routinely makes his political affiliations and sympathies known. For example, in *Variety of News for all Pallats, as Certainties, Probabilities, &c.* (Edinburgh: n. pub., 1661), he writes, 'There is nothing of greater truth then the blessings that accompanies His *Majesties* happy Government'; Charles II has 'already made His Subjects in *Great Britain,* forget their by-past miseries' (p. 1).

55 Markman Ellis writes that Charles II 'suppressed' Sydserf's royalist newspaper 'in the interests of toleration'; see his introduction to *Tarugo's Wiles,* in *Eighteenth-Century Coffee House Culture,* ed. Markman Ellis, 4 vols (New York: Routledge, 2016), III, 43–44 (p. 44). This conclusion is based on *The Letters and Journals of Robert Baillie, A.M.,* ed. D. Laing, 3 vols (Edinburgh: Bannatyne Club, 1841–42), III (1842), p. 468, via Terence Tobin's article 'Thomas St Serfe [Sydserf] 1624–69', *Theatre Notebook,* 27 (1973), 74–77.

56 We are, for the first time, attributing the anonymous *The New Claret-Club* (n.p.: n. pub., 1669) to Thomas Sydserf. Its internal substance and style make a very strong case for this attribution.

57 The first quotation is from Sydserf; he describes the setting after the 'Dramatis Personæ' (*Tarugo's Wiles: or, The Coffee-House* [London: Printed for Henry Herringman, 1668], n. pag.); Ellis, introduction to *Tarugo's Wiles,* in *Eighteenth Century Coffee House Culture,* III, p. 43.

58 At the end of *The New Claret-Club,* the following advertisement appears: 'Tarugo's Wiles, *or the* Coffe[e]-house. *A Comedy acted at his Royal Highness Theatre in* London*, newly re-printed with additions; to be sold by the Book-sellers in* Edinburgh' (p. 8).

59 Thomas Sydserf, "To the Right Honourable, and most Noble Lord, George Marquesse of *Huntley,* Earl of *Eigney,* and Lord *Strathbogy,*" in *Tarugo's Wiles* (n. pag.). As an apparent afterthought, Sydserf

writes in the same dedicatory epistle that though he 'dedicate[s]' the play to the Marquess's 'recreation', it has 'like most other Playes [...] its useful moralities', though nowhere are these 'moralities' enumerated.

60 It is also very possible that the work may not have been published by a Scottish publisher because the London publisher, Henry Herringman, 'England's foremost publisher of belles lettres from 1661 to 1699', would not allow it to be published in Scotland to maximise his profits: Don-John Dugas, *Marketing the Bard: Shakespeare in Performance and Print, 1660–1740* (Columbia: University of Missouri Press, 2006), p. 110. He may have held the copyright to *Tarugo's Wiles*.

61 [Sydserf], *The New Claret-Club*, p. 4. The character Peter Prudence, however, offers some hope that comedy might appeal to the Scots, suggesting that if puppet shows, 'dumb trifles', can entertain them, why not comedy? (p. 4).

62 Andrew R. Walking, *Masque and Opera in England, 1656–1688* (Aldershot: Ashgate, 2016), p. 126.

63 Alasdair Raffe, *The Culture of Controversy: Religious Arguments in Scotland, 1660–1714* (Woodbridge: Boydell Press, 2012), p. 124.

64 *Historical Notices of Scotish Affairs, Selected from the Manuscripts of Sir John Lauder of Fountainhall*, Volume First. 1661–1683 (Edinburgh: T. Constable, 1848), p. 361; George Good, *Liberton in Ancient and Modern Times* (Edinburgh: Andrew Elliot, 1893), p. 18. Good writes that Paterson 'petitioned the Presbytery of Dalkeith, 10th October 1683, to have the sentence relaxed. Compliance was delayed, however, "until it shall be made more apparent that he is reformed in his life and conversation"'.

65 Ninian Paterson, *The Fanatick Indulgence Granted, ANNO 1679* (Edinburgh: Printed by David Linsday, and his Partners, 1683), p. 2. For a helpful overview of the use and evolution of the term 'fanatics' in a Restoration Scottish context (1660s-1680s), see Raffe, pp. 122–27.

66 Ibid., pp. 2, 3, 7.

67 Ninian Paterson, 'A Welcome to His Royal Highness JAMES Duke of *Albanie*, to the Kingdom of *Scotland*', in *The Fanatick Indulgence*, 12–14 (p. 12).

68 Ibid., p. 13.

69 Ninian Paterson, *A Poem on the Test* (Edinburgh: n. pub., 1683), pp. 3–4.

70 Ibid., pp. 9, 5.

71　Ninian Paterson, *To the Memorie of the much Honoured, And much Lamented Thomas Robertson Bailie and Builder of Edinburgh; Who Departed this Life, September 22. 1686. A Funeral Elegie* (Edinburgh: Printed by J. Reid, [1686]).

72　Ninian Paterson, *On that Devout, and Industrious Gentelman [sic], George Monteith, Merchant in Edinburgh* (Edinburgh: n. pub., 1685), n. pag.

73　M. L., *Albion's Elegie* (Edinburgh: Printed by the Heir of Andrew Anderson, 1680), pp. 4 and 7.

74　See, for example, the following stanza in *Albion's Farewel*, "Then Farewell MONARCH *of one Heart, / Whereof all* SCOTLAND *claims a part, / except some clownish Boo'rs*" (p. 13).

75　M. L., 'To His Royal Highness', *Albion's Congratulatory* (Edinburgh: Printed by the Heir of Andrew Anderson, 1680), n. pag.

76　It is possible he is the Edinburgh actor who was convicted for attacking Thomas Sydserf in 1669, but there is no evidence to prove or disprove this claim.

77　M.M., *On the Death and Horrid Murther of the Most Reverend Father, in God, James Archbishop of Saint-Andrews, Lord Primate of Scotland* (Edinburgh, 1679).

78　Thomas N. Corns, *A History of Seventeenth-Century English Literature* (Malden, MA: Wiley Blackwell, 2014), p. 325.

5. Gender and National Identity in Allan Ramsay's *The Tea-Table Miscellany* and Eighteenth-Century Scottish Song Culture

1　An edition of *The Collected Works of Allan Ramsay* is currently under way at the Centre for Robert Burns Studies at the University of Glasgow which will pave the way for important new critical assessments of the poet, collector and cultural figure. www.gla.ac.uk/schools/critical/research/researchcentresandnetworks/robertburnsstudies/edinburghenlightenment [accessed 10 February 2021].

2　Murray Pittock, *Scottish and Irish Romanticism* (Oxford: Oxford University Press, 2008); Steve Newman, *Ballad Collection, Lyric, and the Canon: The Call of the Popular from the Restoration to the New Criticism* (Pittsburgh: University of Pennsylvania Press, 2007); Leith Davis, 'Imagining the Miscellaneous Nation: James Watson's Choice Collection of Comic and Serious Scots Poems', *Eighteenth-Century Life*, 35.3 (2011), 60–80 (p. 76). See also Leith Davis, 'At "Sang About": Scottish Song and the Challenge to British Culture', in *Scotland and the Borders of Romanticism*, ed. by Leith Davis, Ian Duncan and Janet Sorensen (Cambridge: Cambridge University Press, 2004), pp. 188–203.

3   I draw in particular on the work of Michèle Cohen who examines 'why tongues (languages) and the tongue (of the speaking subject) came to be critical sites for the representation, articulation and production of national and gender identities'. Cohen is specifically interested in 'how the play of tongues – English, French and Latin – was implicated in the shaping of the English gentleman'. See *Fashioning Masculinity: National Identity and Language in the Eighteenth Century* (London; New York: Routledge, 1996), p. 1.

4   *An Excellent New Song, Intituled, Valiant Jockie His Ladies Resolution. To be Sung to its Own Proper Tune* [Edinburgh, s.n, 1700], (ll. 1–2). *Early English Books Online* www.proquest.com/eebo [accessed 1 June 2020].

5   Ibid., ll. 7, 28.

6   *The Sorrowful Maiden for the Want of Tocher-good. To an Excellent Old tune.* [Edinburgh, s.n. 1700], (ll. 33–34). *Early English Books Online* www.proquest.com/eebo [accessed 1 June 2020].

7   *A Dialogue Between Ald* [sic] *John M'clatchy, and Young Willie Ha, about the Marriage of his Daughter Maggy M'clatchy* [Edinburgh, s.n., 1700?]. *Early English Books Online* www.proquest.com/eebo [accessed 1 June 2020].

8   Joseph Ritson, 'A Historical Essay on Scotish [sic] Song', in *Scotish* [sic] *Song: In Two Volumes*, 2 vols, ed. by Joseph Ritson (London: Printed for J. Johnson, in St. Pauls Church-Yard; and J. Egerton, Whitehall, 1794), I, pp. xii–cxix (p. lx). *Eighteenth Century Collections Online* link.gale.com/apps/doc/CW0106653651/ECCO?u=sfu_z39&sid=ECCO&xid=cc5f7939&pg=1 [accessed 15 May 2020].

9   Ibid., p. lx.

10 Thomas D'Urfey, 'Song', in *Wit and Mirth: Or, Pills to Purge Melancholy*, ed. by Thomas D'Urfey, with an Introd. by Cyrus L. Day, 'This edition is a facsimile reproduction of the 1876 reprint of the original edition of 1719–1720', 6 vols (New York: Folklore Publishers, 1959), I, pp. 324–25. Allan Ramsay, 'Song: She raise and loot me in', in *The Tea-Table Miscellany: or, a Collection of Choice Songs, Scots and English*, ed. by Allan Ramsay, 10th edn, 4 vols (London: Printed for A. Millar; and sold by him, and by J. Hodges, 1740), II, pp. 123–24, ll. 8, 25, 32, 40. *Eighteenth Century Collections Online* link.gale.com/apps/doc/

CW0112760608/ECCO?u=sfu_z39&sid=ECCO&xid=62932b55&pg=1 [accessed 15 April 2012].

11 Pittock notes Ramsay's mixing of old and new materials, suggesting that in doing so, Ramsay was "a song-collector of a type familiar in the Romantic period, one who edited and rewrote material alike" (*Scottish and Irish,* p. 33). The change of content is also reflected in the change of title; originally titled *The Tea-Table Miscellany*, by 1726 its title was *The Tea-Table Miscellany, or a Collection of Scots Sangs.* By 1737 the work became *The Tea-Table Miscellany: Or, A Collection of Choice Songs, Scots and English*, a title it would retain throughout the eighteenth and nineteenth centuries.

12 In 1725, Ramsay opened the first circulating library in Britain, leading some of his contemporaries to accuse him of channelling the culture of the British metropole into the Scottish capital. See K. A. Manley, *Books, borrowers, and shareholders: Scottish circulating and subscription libraries before 1825: a survey and listing* (Edinburgh: Edinburgh Bibliographical Society; in association with the National Library of Scotland, 2012), pp. 185–87.

13 According to Burns Martin, Vol. II was brought out in 1726, Vol. III in 1727, and Vol. IV in 1737, *Bibliography of Allan Ramsay* (Glasgow: Jackson, Wylie and Co., 1931), pp. 11–13.

14 Ibid., pp. 114, 14. These statistics are based on Martin's *Bibliography of Allan Ramsay*. While I have used the word 'edition' here to describe the numerous printings of *The Tea-Table Miscellany*, Martin notes that the word 'edition' was used in the eighteenth-century to signify what we would now refer to as an 'impression'. Thus, while the imprints of the 'editions' published during the eighteenth century numbered no higher than nineteen, Martin lists twenty-seven 'editions' published between 1723 and 1799.

15 Thomas Crawford, *Society and the Lyric: A Study of the Song Culture of Eighteenth-century Scotland* (Edinburgh: Scottish Academic Press, 1979), p. 7.

16 Ramsay, *The Tea-Table Miscellany*, 10th edn, I, imprint, ll. 1–6.

17 Newman, p. 58.

18 Ramsay, *The Tea-Table Miscellany*, 10th edn, I, frontispiece and imprint.

19 Ramsay, Dedication, in *The Tea-Table Miscellany*, 10th edn, I, pp. v–vi (p. v).

20 Ibid., p. v, ll. 1, 4.

21 Ibid., p. v, ll. 6, 7–8.
22 Ibid., p. v, ll. 9, 15–16.
23 Ramsay, 'Song', in *The Tea-Table Miscellany*, 10th edn, I, p. 35, ll. 1, 5–8.
24 Ibid., p. 35, ll. 9–12, 1, 14, 13.
25 Ibid., p. 35, ll. 15–16.
26 *Oxford English Dictionary*, 'die'.
27 Ramsay, Preface, in *The Tea-Table Miscellany*, 10th edn, I, pp. vii–x (pp. viii–ix).
28 Ibid., p. ix.
29 Jeff Strabone, *Poetry and British Nationalisms in the Bardic Eighteenth Century: Imagined Antiquities* (Springer International Publishing: Imprint: Palgrave Macmillan, 2018), p. 77. Springer Literature, Cultural and Media Studies eBooks 2018 English/International link.springer.com/book/10.1007/978-3-319-95255-0 [accessed 12 February 2020].
30 Ramsay, Preface, in *The Tea-Table Miscellany*, 10th edn, I, p. ix.
31 Kathleen Wilson, *The Island Race: Englishness, Empire and Gender in the Eighteenth Century* (London: New York: Routledge, 2003), pp. 40–41.
32 William Thomson, *Orpheus Caledonius: Or, A Collection of Scots Songs*, ed. by William Thomson, 2 vols (London: Printed for the Author, at his House in Leicester-Fields, 1733), I, The Subscribers Names, pages unnumbered.
33 Ramsay, Preface, *The Tea-Table Miscellany*, 10th edn, I, p. x.
34 Ramsay, 'Dumbarton's *Drums*', in *The Tea-Table Miscellany*, 10th edn, I, p. 49, ll. 5–6, 7, 8–10.
35 Ibid., ll. 11–15.
36 Ibid., ll. 17, 19–20.
37 Ibid., ll. 21–25.
38 See '*O'er the Moor to* Maggy' for further evidence of a consenting, flexible masculinity. The male speaker will become what his beloved desires, as long as she loves him: 'My bonny *Maggy*'s love can turn / Me to what shape she pleases, / If in her breast that flame shall burn, / Which in my bosom blazes' (Ramsay, *Tea-Table Miscellany*, 10th edn, I, pp. 64–65 [p. 65], ll. 21–24).
39 Ramsay, 'Magie's Tocher', in *The Tea-Table Miscellany*, 10th edn, I, pp. 26–28.
40 Ramsay, 'Lass with a Lump of Land', in *The Tea-Table Miscellany*, 10th edn, II, p. 114, ll. 7, 23–24.

41 Ramsay, 'This is no mine ain House', in *The Tea-Table Miscellany*, 10th edn, I, pp. 90–91 (p. 91), ll. 13–16.
42 Ibid., ll. 17–20.
43 Ibid., p. 90, l. 6.
44 Allan Ramsay, '*Norland* Jocky *and Southland* Jenny', in *The Tea-Table Miscellany*, 10th edn, II, pp. 182–183 (p. 182), ll. 1–2.
45 Ibid., p. 183, ll. 5–6, 11–12.
46 Ibid, ll. 13–14.
47 Ibid., ll. 17–20, 21–24.
48 While both 'Dumbarton's *Drums*' and '*Norland* Jocky *and Southland* Jenny' feature women who have economic capital (or access to economic capital), there are songs in which women without capital still have a strong sense of personal worth and agency. For an example, see 'Song', in which the female speaker declares, 'ALTHO' I be but a country lass, / Yet a lofty mind I bear—O, / And think my sell as good as those / That rich apparel wear—O' (Ramsay, *Tea-Table Miscellany*, 10th edn, II, pp. 169–70 [p. 169], ll. 1–4).
49 Ramsay, '*The Highland Laddie*', in *The Tea-Table Miscellany*, 10th edn, I, pp. 85–86 (p. 85), ll. 1–4.
50 The *OED* defines the adjectival form of 'manly' as 'having those qualities or characteristics traditionally associated with men as distinguished from women or children; courageous, strong, independent in spirit, frank, upright, etc.'. The *OED* cites Ramsay's *Christ's-kirk on the Green* (1718): 'The manly Miller haff and haff, Came out to shaw good Will' (II.17).
51 Ramsay, '*The Highland Laddie*', in *The Tea-Table Miscellany*, 10th edn, I, pp. 85–86 (p. 85), ll. 10, 11–12, 13–14, 15, 16.
52 Ibid., ll. 17–20.
53 Ibid., ll. 21–24.
54 Ramsay, '*Sandy and* Betty', in *The Tea-Table Miscellany*, 10th edn, II, p. 145, l. 2.
55 Ibid., ll. 3–4.
56 Ibid., ll. 5–6.
57 Ibid., ll. 9–12.
58 Ibid., ll. 13–16.
59 Ibid., ll. 17–24.
60 In 'Spoken to Mrs. N.', the opening piece of Ramsay's 1721 volume of *Scots Songs* (published two years before his *Miscellany*), the speaker declares that even the most banal lyrics when combined with music

and the female voice transform in performance. Allan Ramsay, 'Spoken to Mrs. N.', in *Scots Songs* (Edinburgh: Printed for the Author, [1721]), pp. 245-260 (p. 245). *Eighteenth Century Collections Online* link.gale.com/apps/doc/CW0112760608/ECCO?u=sfu_z39&sid=ECCO&xid=62932b55&pg=1 [accessed 1 April 2019].

61 David McGuinness and Aaron McGregor, 'Ramsay's Musical Sources: Reconstructing a Poet's Musical Memory', *Scottish Literary Review*, 10 no. 1 (Spring/Summer 2018), 49–71 (p. 50). muse.jhu.edu/article/696243 [accessed 1 April, 2019].

62 Ibid., p. 50.

63 Ibid., pp. 51, 54. The song texts of Ramsay's *The Gentle Shepherd* are, by 1733, included in the *Miscellany*.

64 For example, Ramsay is cited as the author of the song texts ('The Words by Allan Ramsey' [sic]) on the imprint of Robert Bremner, *Thirty Scots Songs Adapted for a Voice & Harpsichord*, ed. by Robert Bremner, 2 vols (London: Printed and sold by R. Bremner, [1770?]).

65 Anon. Preface, in *The Merry companion: or, Universal songster: Consisting of a new collection of above 500 celebrated songs, with their tunes prefix'd to each song.* […] 2nd edn (London: Printed for Ward and Chandler, 1742), Preface pages unnumbered. *Eighteenth Century Collections Online* link.gale.com/apps/doc/CW0116703748/ECCO?u=sfu_z39&sid=ECCO&xid=8180e3d0&pg=1 [accessed 20 October 2009]

66 Paula McDowell, 'Media and Mediation in the Eighteenth Century', in *Oxford Handbooks Online* www.oxfordhandbooks.com [accessed 1 June 2018].

67 David Herd, *Ancient and Modern Scottish Songs, Heroic Ballads, etc.*, ed. by David Herd, 2nd edn, 2 vols (Edinburgh: Printed by John Wotherspoon, for James Dickson and Charles Elliot, 1776). *Eighteenth Century Collections Online* link.gale.com/apps/doc/CW0111765520/ECCO?u=sfu_z39&sid=ECCO&xid=4341870a&pg=1 [accessed 1 October 2009]. John Pinkerton, *Scottish Tragic Ballads*, ed. by John Pinkerton (London: Printed by and for J. Nichols, 1781). *Eighteenth Century Collections Online* link.gale.com/apps/doc/CW0111174561/ECCO?u=sfu_z39&sid=ECCO&xid=53b3fe83&pg=1 [accessed 1 October 2009].

68 Pinkerton, 'On the Oral Tradition of Poetry', in *Scottish Tragic Ballads*, pp. ix-xxvii; Pinkerton, 'On the Tragic Ballad', in *Scottish Tragic Ballads*, pp. xxviii-xxxvii (p. xxxvii).

69 Pinkerton, Notes, in *Scottish Tragic Ballads*, pp. 87-124, (p. 97, 'Hardyknute: Part I', V., l. 188).

70 Ibid., p. 99, 'Hardyknute: Part I', V., l. 305.
71 Ibid., pp. 99–100, 'Hardyknute: Part I', V., l. 305.
72 Ibid., p. 100.
73 Ritson, Preface, in *Scotish* [sic] *Song*, I, p. i–x; Ritson, 'A Historical Essay on Scotish[sic] Song', I, pp. xi–cxix.
74 Janet Sorensen, 'Alternative Antiquarianisms of Scotland the North', *Modern Language Quarterly*, 70 no. 4 (December 2009), 415–41. In her discussion of eighteenth-century song collectors and publishers, Sorensen describes Ritson as '[a]n antiquarian dedicated to the most rigorous standards of authentication' (p. 417).
75 Ritson, Preface, in *Scotish* [sic] *Song*, I, p. i.
76 Ramsay, Preface, in *The Tea-Table Miscellany: Or, a Complete Collection of Scots Sangs*, ed. by Allan Ramsay, 3 vols (Dublin: Printed by E. Smith, and sold by the Booksellers of *Great-Britain* and *Ireland*, 1729), I, pp. v–viii (p. v).
77 Sorensen, p. 416.
78 Ibid., p. 425.
79 Preface, in *Ancient and Modern Scottish Songs, Heroic Ballads, etc.*, ed. by David Herd, 2nd edn, 2 vols (Edinburgh: Printed by John Wotherspoon, for James Dickson and Charles Elliot, 1776), I, pp. v–ix (p. v). *Eighteenth Century Collections Online* link.gale.com/apps/doc/CW0111765520/ECCO?u=sfu_z39&sid=ECCO&xid=4341870a&pg=1 [accessed 1 October 2009].
80 Ibid., p. ix.
81 *Robert Burns's Commonplace Book, 1783–1785*, ed. by David Daiches (Oxford: Clarendon, 1985) pp. 37–38.
82 James Johnson, *The Scots Musical Museum: Consisting of Upwards of Six Hundred Songs, with Proper Basses for the Pianoforte*, ed. by James Johnson, 6 vols (Edinburgh: Printed by James Johnson & Co., 1787–1803). George Thomson, *A Select Collection of Original Scotish* [sic] *Airs*, ed. by George Thomson, 6 vols (London: Preston, 1793–1846).
83 Nigel Leask, *Robert Burns and Pastoral: Poetry and Improvement in Late Eighteenth-Century Scotland* (Oxford; New York: Oxford University Press, 2010), p. 254.
84 James Johnson's *The Scots Musical Museum*, for example, contains 625 songs, 112 of which appear in Ramsay's *The Tea-Table Miscellany* 10th edn (1740). Of the 112 songs, Johnson attributes 46 to Ramsay.
85 *Beeton's Boy's Own Magazine*, 1 November 1868.
86 Rhona Brown, 'The Afterlives of Allan Ramsay in the British Periodical Press, 1720–1879', *Scottish Literary Review* 10 no. 1 (Spring/

Summer 2018), 95–115 (p. 104). muse.jhu.edu/article/696245 [accessed 5 May, 2019].

87 In 1864, William Black, in his review of Ramsay's work and influence, lists four songs as 'the most widely-known': '"Lochaber no More", "Bessy Bell and Mary Gray", "The Lass of Patie's Mill", and "The Flower of Yarrow"' (*Once a Week*, 19 November 1864, p. 614).

6. Fierce Females and Male Pretenders: Gender, Cultural Memory and Anti-Jacobite Print Culture in the 1745 Rising

1 Paul Monod suggests that Jacobitism was not just a political movement; it was part of the 'cultural totality' of seventeenth- and eighteenth-century British society ('Jacobite Rhetoric', in *Jacobitism and the English People* (Cambridge: Cambridge University Press, 1989), pp. 1–70).

2 See *The Prince Of Orange His Declaration Shewing the Reasons Why He Invades England: With a Short Preface, and Some Modest Remarks On It* (London: Published by Randal Taylor, 1688).

3 See Steven Pincus, *1688: The First Modern Revolution* (New Haven: Yale University Press, 2009); Tim Harris, *Revolution: The Great Crisis of the British Monarchy, 1685–1720* (London: Penguin, 2007).

4 F. J. McLynn, 'Issues and Motives in the Jacobite Rising of 1745', *The Eighteenth Century*, 23, (1982), pp. 97–133 (p. 117).

5 See Daniel Szechi, *1715: The Great Jacobite Rebellion* (New Haven: Yale University Press, 2006) and *Loyalty and Identity: Jacobites at Home and Abroad*, ed. Paul Monod, Murray Pittock, and Daniel Szechi (New York: Palgrave Macmillan, 2010).

6 A copy of the transcription of Flora MacDonald's declaration of how she helped Charles escape is available at *National Archives* www.nationalarchives.gov.uk/education/resources/ [accessed 30 January 2021].

7 See, for example, Paula McDowell, *The Invention of the Oral: Print Commerce and Fugitive Voices in Eighteenth-Century Britain* (Chicago: The University of Chicago Press, 2017); The Multigraph Collective, *Interacting with Print: Elements of Reading in the Era of Print Saturation* (Chicago: University of Chicago Press, 2017).

8 Clifford Siskin and William Warner, 'This Is Enlightenment: An Invitation in the Form of an Argument', in *This Is Enlightenment*, ed. Clifford Siskin and William Warner (Chicago: University of Chicago Press, 2010), pp. 1–36 (p. 10).

9   For the theoretical parameters argument, see Leith Davis, *Mediating Cultural Memory in Britain and Ireland: From the 1688 Revolution to the 1745 Jacobite Rising* (Cambridge: Cambridge University Press, forthcoming).
10 According to Bob Harris, there were now eighteen papers produced within the nation's capital, including 'eight weeklies, four thrice-weekly evening papers, and six dailies,' and 'nearly forty' papers in the English provincial towns as well as four Scottish papers ('"A Great Palladium of Our Liberties": The British Press and the 'Forty-Five', *Historical Research*, 68.165 [1995], 67–87).
11 *Seasonable Considerations on the Present War in Scotland* (London: Printed for M. Cooper, 1746) and *A Journal of the Pretender's Expedition to North Britain* (London: Printed for J. Collyer, 1745).
12 *A Complete and Authentick History of the Rise, Progress and Extinction of the Late Rebellion and of the Proceedings Against the Principal Persons Concerned Therein* (London: Printed for M. Cooper, 1746) and John Marchant, *The History of the Present Rebellion: Collected from Authentick [Sic] Memoirs, Letters and Intelligences* (London: Printed for R. Walker, 1746).
13 See Geoffrey Plank, *Rebellion and Savagery: The Jacobite Rising of 1745 and the British Empire* (Philadelphia: University of Pennsylvania Press, 2006).
13 See Plank.
14 See, for example, *An Authentick Narrative of the Whole Proceedings of Court at St. Margaret's Hill, Southwark, in the Months of June, July and August, 1746* (London, 1746) and *The Tryals of William, Earl of Kilmarnock, George, Earl of Cromertie [sic], and Arthur Lord Balmerino, for High Treason* (London, 1746).
15 See Stana Nenadic, 'Print Collecting and Popular Culture in Eighteenth-Century Scotland', *History*, 82, (1997), 203–22 and Diana Donald, *The Age of Caricature: Satirical Prints in the Reign of George III* (New Haven: Yale University Press, 1996). Eirwen Nicholson points out that prints could be viewed for free in public spaces such as print-shop windows, taverns, and town squares so people did not have to purchase them to gain access to prints ('Consumers and Spectators: The Public of the Political Print in Eighteenth-Century England', *History*, 81, (2019), pp. 5–21).
16 See Murray Pittock, *Material Culture and Sedition, 1688–1760: Treacherous Objects, Secret Places* (Houndmills: Palgrave Macmillan, 2013);

Neil Guthrie, *The Material Culture of the Jacobites* (Cambridge: Cambridge University Press, 2013); and Davis, *Mediating Cultural Memory*.

17 Murray Pittock, *The Myth of the Jacobite Clans: The Jacobite Army in 1745* (Edinburgh: Edinburgh University Press, 2009).

18 Murray Pittock, 'Culloden in British Memory: Objects, Artefacts, and Representations of the Conflict', in *Culloden: Great Battles* (Oxford: Oxford University Press, 2016), pp. 137–58; Monod, *Jacobitism and the English People*.

19 With the important exceptions such as Carine Martin and Rosalind Carr, the issue of gender in anti-Jacobite propaganda has not been addressed. Carine Martin, '"Female Rebels": The Female Figure in Anti-Jacobite Propaganda', in *Living with Jacobitism, 1690–1788: The Three Kingdoms and Beyond*, ed. Allan I. Macinnes, Kieran German, and Lesley Graham (London: Pickering & Chatto, 2014), pp. 85–98; Rosalind Carr, 'Women, Land and Power: A Case for Continuity', in *Women in Eighteenth-Century Scotland: Intimate, Intellectual and Public Lives*, ed. Katie Barclay and Deborah Simonton (Farnham: Ashgate, 2013), pp. 193–210. See also Maggie Craig, *Damn' Rebel Bitches: The Women of the '45* (London and Edinburgh: Mainstream, 1995).

20 Foucault describes a counter-memory as a memory that 'opposes history given as continuity or representative of a tradition' ('Nietzsche, Genealogy, History', in *Language, Counter-Memory, Practice: Selected Essays and Interviews*, ed. Donald F. Bouchard, trans. Donald F. Bouchard and Sherry Simon (Ithaca: Cornell University Press, 1977), pp. 139–64, (p. 160)). In terms of the Jacobite-Hanoverian conflict, individuals or groups can create counter-memories that oppose the Hanoverian 'tradition' and the histories that take this tradition to be official.

21 Michael Rothberg, 'Introduction: Between Memory and Memory From Lieux de mémoire to Noeuds de mémoire', in *Yale French Studies*, 118/119 (2010), 3–10 (p. 7).

22 See Pierre Nora and Lawrence D. Kritzman, *Realms of Memory: Rethinking the French Past* (New York: Columbia University Press, 1996) for the concept of *lieux de mémoire*.

23 Rothberg, 'Between Memory and Memory', p. 7.

24 Pittock, *Material Culture and Sedition, 1688–1760*, p. 83.

25 Viccy Coltman, *Art and Identity in Scotland: A Cultural History from the Jacobite Rising of 1745 to Walter Scott* (Cambridge: Cambridge University Press, 2019), p. 143.

26 Pittock, *Material Culture and Sedition*, p. 169.
27 Coltman, p. 161.
28 See Murray Pittock, 'Marginal Societies in Britain', in *Inventing and Resisting Britain: Cultural Identities in Britain and Ireland, 1685–1789*, ed. Jeremy Black (London: Macmillan Press, 1997), p. 55.
29 See *Ascanius, or the Young Adventurer* (London: printed for G. Smith, near Temple Bar, 1746) for the 63-page verion; a longer version was 'Printed for T. Johnson, in Salisbury Court' in the same year; *The Wanderer, or Surprizing Escape* (London: Printed for J. Robinson, 1747); *Young Juba: Being the History of the Young Chevalier, from his Birth to his Escape from Scotland at the Battle of Culloden* (London, 1748).
30 In part this is because they model themselves on the popular Jacobite narrative, *Alexis; or, The Young Adventurer. A Novel* (London: Printed for T. Cooper, 1746).
31 John Williams, 'Prince Charles Edward Stewart, 1720–1788. Eldest son of Prince James Francis Edward Stewart, 1746', in *National Galleries Scotland* www.nationalgalleries.org/art-and-artists/37273/prince-charles-edward-stewart-1720-1788-eldest-son-prince-james-francis-edward-stewart [accessed 5 May 2020]
32 *Alexis; or, The Young Adventurer. A Novel* (London: Printed for T. Cooper, 1746) and *Ascanius* (1746).
33 NLS Adv.MS.32.6.18.
34 See Coltman, p. 151.
35 Martin, '"Female Rebels"', p. 86.
36 Ibid., p. 89.
37 *The Female Rebels* (Edinburgh and London, 1747), p. 5.
38 Ibid., p. 5.
39 Ibid.
40 Ibid., p. 6.
41 Ibid., p. 7.
42 Ibid.
43 Ibid., p. 8.
44 Ibid., p. 11.
45 Ibid.
46 Ibid., p. 29.
47 Ibid., p. 47.
48 Ibid.
49 Ibid., p. 48.
50 Ibid.

51 Ibid., p. 51.
52 Ibid., p. 21.
53 Ibid., pp. 59–60.
54 Ibid., p. 54
55 Ibid., p. 48.
56 Ibid., p. 53.
57 Ibid., pp. 59–60.
58 Ibid., p. 54.
59 Ibid.
60 Ibid., pp. 55–56.
61 Ibid., p. 53.
62 *London Evening Gazette*, 14–17 December 1745.
63 *A Brief Account of the Life and Family of Miss Jenny Cameron, the Reputed Mistress of the Pretender's Eldest Son* (London: T. Gardner, 1746), p. 17. A second edition was published by Gardner later in the same year. The 1 August 1746 issue of the *Gentleman's Magazine* included a notice about this publication under 'Poetry and Entertainment'. It was published using the pseudonym of Archibald Arbuthnot. Another version was published by Robert Goadby of Yeovil.
64 Ibid.
65 Ibid.
66 Ibid., p. 24.
67 Ibid., p. 27.
68 Ibid., p. 27.
69 Ibid.
70 Ibid., p. 52.
71 Ibid., pp. 60–61.
72 Ibid., p. 62.
73 Ibid., p. 63.
74 Ibid., p. 61.
75 Ibid., p. 62.
76 Ibid.
77 Ibid., p. 63.
78 Ibid. In the reprinted version of *A Brief Account* included in *The Trials of Simon Fraser*, the author wishes for mercy for her in the end.
79 Archibald Arbuthnot [pseud.], *Memoirs of the Remarkable Life and Surprizing Adventures of Miss Jenny Cameron* (London: printed and sold by R. Walker, 1746), p. iv. Gale Primary Sources www.gale.com/intl/primary-sources [accessed 2 Feb 2020].
80 Ibid., p. xi.

81 Ibid., p. xii.
82 On 'stored' memories, see Aleida Assmann, *Cultural Memory and Western Civilization: Functions, Media, Archives* (Cambridge: Cambridge University Press, 2011).

7. How to Become an 'Authoress' in Provincial Scotland: Women's Poetry in Manuscript and Print

1 Catherine Kerrigan, 'Introduction', *An Anthology of Scottish Women Poets* (Edinburgh: Edinburgh University Press, 1991), pp. 1–11 (p. 2). The fact that only two of the poets I discuss in this essay – Grant and Baillie – are included in Kerrigan's anthology suggests just how much remains to be explored in this field. On women's place in Scotland's culture of song, see also Mary Ellen Brown, 'Old Singing Women and the Canons of Scottish Balladry and Song', in *A History of Scottish Women's Writing*, ed. Douglas Gifford and Dorothy McMillan (Edinburgh: Edinburgh University Press, 1997), pp. 44–57.
2 Pam Perkins, *Women Writers and the Edinburgh Enlightenment* (Amsterdam: Rodopi, 2010).
3 Edinburgh University Library (UL), Laing Collection, La.II.357, 43^v, 29 August 1801.
4 Edinburgh UL, Laing Collection, La.II.357, 42^r, 20 June 1801.
5 Anne MacVicar Grant, *Poems on Various Subjects, by Mrs Grant, Laggan* (Edinburgh: printed for the author, 1803), pp. 17–18.
6 Perkins, p. 161.
7 Donna Landry, *The Muses of Resistance: Laboring-Class Women's Poetry in Britain, 1739–1796* (Cambridge: Cambridge University Press, 1990), p. 2.
8 Ruth Perry, 'Balladry and the Scottish Enlightenment', in *The Scottish Enlightenment and Literary Culture*, ed. Ralph McLean, Ronnie Young, and Kenneth Simpson (London: Rowman and Littlefield, 2016), pp. 77–94 (p. 85), italics in original.
9 See for example Mary Ellen Lamb, *Gender and Authorship in the Sidney Circle* (Madison: University of Wisconsin Press, 1990).
10 Margaret J. M. Ezell, *Social Authorship and the Advent of Print* (Baltimore: Johns Hopkins University Press, 1999), p. 12.
11 Betty Schellenberg's study of literary coteries in Northern England bears out Ezell's claim that the decision to circulate works in manuscript was often a matter of convenience. See *Literary Coteries and the Making of Modern Print Culture* (Cambridge: Cambridge University Press, 2016), pp. 205–36.

12 National Library of Scotland (NLS), Acc. 8363, vol. I, p. 52.
13 NLS, Acc. 8363, vol. I, p. 259.
14 Ibid., vol. II, p. 237.
15 Ibid., p. 239.
16 Ibid., vol I, n.p.
17 Ibid., p. 42.
18 Ibid., p. 43.
19 Ibid., p. 112.
20 Ibid., vol. II, p. 273.
21 Lady Louisa Stuart, *Memoire of Frances, Lady Douglas*, ed. Jill Rubenstein (Edinburgh: Scottish Academic Press, 1985), p. 79.
22 NLS MS 3814, p. 20.
23 Stuart, *Memoire of Frances, Lady Douglas*, ed. Rubenstein, p. 79.
24 Jill Rubenstein, 'Introduction', in Stuart, *Memoire of Frances, Lady Douglas*, ed. Rubenstein, pp. 1–23 (p. 4).
25 Stuart, *Memoire of Frances, Lady Douglas*, ed. Rubenstein, p. 71.
26 NLS, MS 3814, p. 20.
27 Ibid., p. 63.
28 Bodleian MS. Eng. Poet. D.202, fol.7.
29 Landry, p. 11.
30 On the publication history of *Poems Chiefly in the Scottish Dialect*, see Gerard Carruthers, 'Burns and Publishing', in *The Edinburgh Companion to Robert Burns*, ed. Gerard Carruthers (Edinburgh: Edinburgh University Press, 2009), pp. 10–11.
31 The parameters of the Book Subscription List Project, an early example of computational analysis in literary studies, are described in P. J. Wallis, 'Book Subscription Lists', *The Library*, XXIX (1974), 256–86 (pp. 273–75).
32 F. J. G. Robinson and P. J. Wallis, *Book Subscription Lists: A Revised Guide* (Newcastle upon Tyne: H. Hill, 1975), p. ii.
33 Thomas Lockwood, 'Subscription Hunters and their Prey', *Studies in the Literary Imagination*, 34 (2001), 122–35 (p. 132).
34 Robinson and Wallis, p. ii.
35 On Little's relationship to her employer's family at Loudon Castle, see Leith Davis, 'Gender and the Nation in the Work of Robert Burns and Janet Little', *Studies in English Literature, 1500–1900*, 38 (1998), 621–45 (pp. 629–32).
36 Kerri Andrews, *Ann Yearsley and Hannah More, Patronage and Poetry: The Story of a Literary Relationship* (London: Pickering and Chatto, 2013), p. 7. On the subscription list for Yearsley's *Poems*, see also Mary

Waldron, *Lactilla, Milkwoman of Clifton: The Life and Writings of Ann Yearsley, 1753–1806* (Athens: University of Georgia Press, 1996), p. 62.
37 Christian Milne, *Simple Poems on Simple Subjects* (Aberdeen: printed for the author, by J. Chalmers & co., 1805), p. 34.
38 Milne, p. 34.
39 Ibid., p. 19.
40 Ibid., pp. 18–19.
41 Ibid., pp. 34–35.
42 Ibid., p. 7.
43 Ibid., p. 155.
44 Anne Ross, *A Collection of Poems*, 3rd ed. (Glasgow: R. Chapman, 1798), n.p.
45 Ibid., p. 88.
46 Ibid., p. 7.
47 Ibid., p. 59.
48 Ibid., p. 59.
49 Ibid., p. 60.
50 On the importance of London to Baillie's development as a poet, see Judith Bailey Slagle, *Joanna Baillie: A Literary Life* (Madison, NJ: Fairleigh Dickinson University Press, 2002), pp. 60–64.

8. Gaelic Enlightenment to Global Gaelosphere: Gaelic Literature, 1750–1800

1 Alexander McDonald, *A Galick and English Vocabulary* (Edinburgh, 1741), p. v.
2 Ronald Black, 'Gaelic Orthography: The Drunk Man's Broad Road', in Moray Watson and Michelle Macleod (eds), *The Edinburgh Companion to the Gaelic Language* (Edinburgh: Edinburgh University Press, 2010), pp. 234–35; see Glasgow University Library, MS Gen 9; Edinburgh University Library, Mackinnon (1924), Box 9, fos. 258–84.
3 Alastair Mac-Dhonuill, *Ais-eiridh na Sean Chánoin Albannaich* (Edinburgh, 1751), p. x.
4 Black, 'Gaelic Orthography', pp. 235–36.
5 NRS CH2/557/6 p. 315.
6 Black, 'Gaelic Orthography', pp. 236–37; see NRS GD95/2/7 p. 258.
7 NRS CH2/557/6, pp. 321, 332.
8 Ibid., pp. 229–33, 238–40, 241, 243, 248; John MacInnes, 'Gaelic Poetry' (unpublished PhD thesis, University of Edinburgh, 1975), p. 123; Susan Ross, 'The Standardization of Scottish Gaelic orthography 1750–2007' (unpublished PhD thesis, University of Glasgow, 2016), pp. 67–69;

see also Donald E. Meek, 'Religion, Riot and Romance: Scottish Gaelic Perceptions of Ireland in the 19th Century', in Cathal Ó Háinle and Donald E. Meek (eds), *Unity in Diversity: Studies in Irish and Scottish Gaelic Language, Literature and History* (Dublin: School of Irish, Trinity College, 2004), pp. 173–93.

9 David B. Morris, *The Religious Sublime: Christian Poetry and Critical Tradition in 18th-Century England* (Lexington: University of Kentucky Press, 1972), pp. 155–70.

10 Richard Sharpe and Mícheal Hoyne, *Clóliosta: Printing in the Irish Language, 1571–1871: An Attempt at Narrative Bibliography* (Dublin: Dublin Institute for Advanced Studies, 2021), pp. 162–70, 174–77; Dòmhnall Eachann Meek (ed.), *Laoidhean Spioradail Dhùghaill Bhochanain* (Glasgow: Scottish Gaelic Texts Society, 2015), pp. 28–36, 83–85; NRS RH 15/105/1.

11 Black, 'Gaelic Orthography', pp. 134–45; also Donald E. Meek, 'The Pulpit and the Pen: Clergy, Orality and Print in the Scottish Gaelic World', in Adam Fox and Daniel Woolf (eds), *The Spoken Word: Oral Culture in Britain, 1500–1800* (Manchester: Manchester University Press, 2003), pp. 94–96.

12 Meek (ed.), *Laoidhean Spioradail Dhùghaill Bhochanain*, pp. 144–45, 185–6; Ronald Black (ed.), *An Lasair: Anthology of 18th Century Scottish Gaelic Verse* (Edinburgh: Birlinn, 2001), pp. 481–85.

13 Meek (ed.), *Laoidhean Spioradail Dhùghaill Bhochanain*, pp. 43–44, 47, 50–53, 85–92.

14 Ibid., pp. 208–09.

15 Angus Macleod (ed.), *The Songs of Duncan Ban Macintyre* (Edinburgh: Scottish Gaelic Texts Society, 1952), pp. xv, xxvii, 455–56.

16 Black (ed.), *An Lasair*, pp. 266–67, 490–93.

17 See Macleod (ed.), *Songs of Duncan Ban Macintyre*, pp. 86–101, 316–25, 396–405.

18 Ibid., pp. 20–33, 58–63, 68–77.

19 Meek (ed.), *Laoidhean Spioradail Dhùghaill Bhochanain*, pp. 234–35.

20 William Gillies, 'The Poem in Praise of Ben Dobhrain', *Lines Review*, 61 (December 1977), pp. 42–48. See also Meg Bateman, 'The Environmentalism of Donnchadh Bàn: Pragmatic or Mythic?', in Christopher MacLachlan (ed.), *Crossing the Highland Line: Crosscurrents in Eighteenth-Century Scottish Writing* (Glasgow: Association of Scottish Literary Studies, 2009), pp. 126–36; Anja Gunderloch, 'Donnchadh Bàn's *Òran do Bhlàr na h-Eaglaise Brice*: Literary Allusion and Political Comment', *Scottish Gaelic Studies*, xx (2000), pp. 97–116.

21 Dugald Buchanan: Strathyre, Perthshire; Rev. James Fraser: Pitcalzean, Nigg, Ross-shire; Rev. Archibald MacArthur: Glenlyon, Perthshire; Rev. Alexander MacFarlane: Pollochro, Stirlingshire; Rev. John MacPherson: Strath, Isle of Skye; Rev. James Stuart: Glenfinglas, Perthshire.
22 GD95/2/8 pp. 305, 338–41, 346; Meek (ed.), *Laoidhean Spioradail Dhùghaill Bhochanain*, p. 292.
23 GUL MS Gen 1042/64 fo.1^v.
24 GUL MS Gen 1042/122 fos.1^{r-v}; NLS Adv. MSS 73.3.5, 7–12, 22–3; EUL Mackinnon (1924), Box 9 fos. 410–596; Ronald Black, 'The Gaelic Academy: The Ingliston Papers', *Scottish Gaelic Studies*, xv (1988), pp. 111–12; MacInnes, 'Gaelic Poetry', pp. 27–35, 49–56, 71–116; Celestine Savonius-Wroth, 'Bardic Ministers: Scotland's Gaelic-speaking Clergy in the Ossian Controversy', *Eighteenth-Century Studies*, 52 (2019), pp. 225–43; Victoria Henshaw, 'James Macpherson and his Contemporaries: The Methods and Networks of Collectors of Gaelic poetry in Late Eighteenth-century Scotland', *Journal for Eighteenth-Century Studies*, 39 (2016), pp. 197–209; also Bernhard Maier, '"This Unique and Valuable Volume": Donald Macintosh's *Gaelic Proverbs*, 1785–2010', *Scottish Gaelic Studies*, xxvii (2010), pp. 31–43.
25 See William Gillies, '"The Mavis of Clanranald": Engaging with John MacCodrum', in Anders Alqvist and Pamela O'Neill (eds), *Germano-Celtica: A Festschrift for Brian Taylor* (Sydney: Sydney Series in Celtic Studies, 2017), pp. 123–51.
26 See Miroslav Hroch *European Nations: Explaining their Formation*, trans. Karolina Graham (London: Verso, 2015), pp. 195–228; also Tomasz Kamusella, *Creating Languages in Central Europe during the last Millennium* (Basingstoke: Palgrave Macmillan, 2015); Viktorija Šeina, 'Nation-building canons: Historical and Methodological Considerations', in Aistė Kučinskienė, Viktorija Šeina, and Brigita Speičytė (eds.), *Literary Canon Formation as Nation-Building in Central Europe and the Baltics: 19th to early 20th Century* (Leiden: Brill, 2021), pp. 1–24.
27 Claudio Saunt, *A New Order of Things: Property, Power, and the Transformation of the Creek Indians, 1733–1816* (Cambridge: Cambridge University Press, 1999), pp. 1–63; also Christopher Bayly, *The Birth of the Modern World 1780–1914: Global Connections and Comparisons* (Oxford: Blackwell, 2004), pp. 1–119; James Sidbury and Jorge Cañizares-Esguerra (eds), 'Forum: Ethnogenesis', *William and Mary Quarterly*, 68 (2011), pp. 181–246.

28 NLS MS 1637 fo.150; see James G. Basker, 'Scotticisms and the Problem of Cultural Identity in Eighteenth-century Britain', in John Dwyer and Richard B. Sher (eds), *Sociability and Society in Eighteenth-Century Scotland* (Edinburgh: Mercat Press, 1993), pp. 81–95; Charles Jones, 'Nationality and Standardization in Eighteenth-century Scotland', in Raymond Hickey (ed.), *Eighteenth-Century English: Ideology and Change* (Cambridge: Cambridge University Press, 2010), pp. 221–34.

29 James Macpherson, *An Introduction to the History of Great Britain and Ireland* (London, 1772), pp. 195–96, 199–203 and 'A Dissertation Concerning the Æra of Ossian', in *The Poems of Ossian* (2 vols, London, 1773), pp. 225–31; Rev. Donald MacNicol, *Remarks on Dr. Samuel Johnson's Journey to the Hebrides* (London, 1779), pp. 105–06, 236–57, 263–70, 283–90, 323–26.

30 Lesa Ní Mhunghaile, 'Ossian and the Gaelic world', in Dafydd Moore (ed.), *The International Companion to James Macpherson and the Poems of Ossian* (Glasgow: Scottish Literature International, 2017), pp. 26–38; Clare O'Halloran, *Golden Ages and Barbarous Nations: Antiquarianism and Cultural Politics in Eighteenth-Century Ireland, c. 1750–1800* (Cork: Cork University Press, 2004).

31 Kenneth D. MacDonald, 'The Rev. William Shaw: Pioneer Gaelic Lexicographer', *Transactions of the Gaelic Society of Inverness*, l (1976–8), pp. 1–19; Sharpe and Hoyne, *Clóliosta*, pp. 305–07.

32 Daniel Cook, *Thomas Chatterton and Neglected Genius, 1760–1830* (Basingstoke: Palgrave Macmillan, 2013), pp. 93–128; see also NRS CS238/S/10/38.

33 Ronald Black, 'The Gaelic Academy: The Cultural Commitment of the Highland Society of Scotland", *Scottish Gaelic Studies*, xiv(2) (1986), pp. 1–38.

34 Thomas Crawford, *Society and the Lyric: A Study of the Song Culture of Eighteenth-Century Scotland* (Edinburgh: Scottish Academic Press, 1979); William Donaldson, *The Jacobite Song: Political Myth and National Identity* (Edinburgh: Mercat Press, 1988); and 'Poems on the streets', in Jack Lynch (ed.), *The Oxford Handbook of British Poetry, 1660–1800* (Oxford: Oxford University Press, 2016), pp. 3–22; Matthew Gelbart, *The Invention of 'Folk Music' and 'Art Music': Emerging Categories from Ossian to Wagner* (Cambridge: Cambridge University Press, 2007); Karen McAulay, *Our Ancient National Airs: Scottish Song Collecting from the Enlightenment to the Romantic Era* (Farnham: Ashgate, 2013); Domhnall Uilleam Stiùbhart, 'Highland Rogues and the Roots of Highland Romanticism', in Christopher MacLachlan

(ed.), *Crossing the Highland Line* (Glasgow: ASLS, 2009), pp. 161–93; also Alan Bruford, 'The Sea-divided Gael: Some Relationships between Scottish Gaelic, Irish and English Traditional Songs', *Irish Folk-Music Studies*, 1 (1972–3), pp. 4–27; Sorcha Nic Lochlainn, 'Making the Foreign Familiar: The Gaelicisation of the Classical Ballad', *Aiste*, 4 (2014), pp. 58–95.

35 NLS MS 14853 fo.4^v.

36 George Calder (ed.), *Gaelic Songs by William Ross* (Edinburgh: Oliver & Boyd, 1937), p. 172.

37 William Gillies, 'Merely a Bard? William Ross and Gaelic poetry', *Aiste*, 1 (2007), pp. 123–69; idem, '"No bonnier life than the sailor's": A Gaelic Poet Comments on the Fishing Industry in Wester Ross', *Studies in Scottish Literature*, 35–36 (2008), pp. 62–75 and 'The Poetry of William Ross', in MacLachlan (ed.), *Crossing the Highland Line*, pp. 195–215.

38 Allan I. Macinnes, *Clanship, Commerce and the House of Stuart, 1603–1788* (East Linton: Tuckwell, 1996), pp. 210–11, 221–34.

39 Alastair J. Durie, *The Scottish Linen Industry in the Eighteenth Century* (Edinburgh: John Donald, 1979), pp. 88–91, 124–40; John Shaw, *Water Power in Scotland, 1550–1870* (Edinburgh: John Donald, 1984), pp. 1–53, 93–130, 171–220, 267–316, 538–44.

40 Tom Devine, *The Great Highland Famine: Hunger, Emigration and the Scottish Highlands in the Nineteenth Century* (Edinburgh: John Donald, 1988), pp. 12–18.

41 Eric Richards, *The Highland Clearances: People, Landlords and Rural Turmoil* (Edinburgh: Birlinn, 2000), pp. 45–49.

42 Canna House Collections CW0106A.461 (John MacInnes, Iain Pheadair 'ic Sheumais, Baghasdail a Deas, Uibhist a Deas (1903–57)): track 26 of William Lamb (ed.), *Dhannsadh gun Dannsadh: Dance-Songs of the Scottish Gaels* (Cockenzie: Greentrax Recordings, 2019). See William Lamb (ed.), *Keith Norman MacDonald's Puirt-à-Beul: The Vocal Dance Music of the Scottish Gaels* (Isle of Skye: Taigh na Teud, 2012), pp. 21–29, 152–3, 162, 166; also Heather Sparling, *Reeling Roosters and Dancing Ducks: Celtic Mouth Music* (Sydney, NS: Cape Breton University Press, 2014). 'Gogan' is of course a phallic sobriquet.

43 Ian Grimble, *The World of Rob Donn* (Edinburgh: Saltire Society, 1999 [1979]); Ellen L. Beard, 'Rob Donn Mackay: Finding the Music in the Songs' (unpublished PhD thesis, University of Edinburgh, 2016); eadem (ed.), *100 Òran le Rob Donn MacAoidh/100 Songs of Rob Donn Mackay* (Isle of Skye: Taigh na Teud, 2018); Black (ed.), *An Lasair*, pp. 429–32, 478–79, 494.

44 Hew Morrison (ed.), *Songs and Poems in the Gaelic Language by Rob Donn* (Edinburgh: John Grant, 1899), p. 140.

45 See Natasha Sumner, 'How Popean was Rob Donn? A Study in Intertextuality', *Aiste*, 4 (2014), pp. 96–113; Donald John MacLeod, 'The poetry of Rob Donn Mackay', *Scottish Gaelic Studies*, xii (1971), pp. 3–21.

46 See Beard, 'Rob Donn Mackay', pp. 38–39, 162–66, 170–76.

47 Macinnes, *Clanship*, pp. 231–33; Richards, *Highland Clearances*, pp. 32–85.

48 See Kevin Grant, '*Òran an Fheamnaidh* – Song of the Seaweed Gatherer: An Archaeology of Early 19th-century Kelping', *Scottish Archaeological Journal*, 41 (2019), pp. 63–85; also Frank Uekötter, 'Rise, Fall, and Permanence: Issues in the Environmental History of the Global Plantation', in Frank Uekötter (ed.), *Comparing Apples, Oranges, and Cotton: Environmental Perspectives on the Global Plantation*, (Frankfurt: Campus, 2014), pp. 7–25.

49 NRS GD46/17/4 fos.308–9; my thanks to Helen Smailes for this reference.

50 Hugh Cheape, 'A Song on the Lowland Shepherds: Popular Reaction to the Highland Clearances', *Scottish Economic and Social History*, 15 (1995), pp. 85–100; Donald Meek (ed.), *Tuath is Tighearna/Tenants and Landlords: An Anthology of Gaelic Poetry of Social and Political Protest from the Clearances to the Land Agitation (1800–1890)* (Edinburgh: Scottish Gaelic Texts Society, 1995), pp. 47–53, 186–89; Somhairle MacGill-Eain (ed. William Gillies), *Ris a' Bhruthaich: Criticism and Prose Writings of Sorley Maclean* (Stornoway: Acair, 1985), p. 53.

51 Lucille H. Campey, *The Scottish Pioneers of Upper Canada, 1784–1855: Glengarry and Beyond* (Toronto: Natural Heritage Books, 2005), pp. 1–34, 69–75; Marianne McLean, *The People of Glengarry: Highlanders in Transition, 1745–1820* (Montreal and Kingston: McGill-Queen's University Press, 1991); Brian D. Osborne, *The Last of the Chiefs: Alasdair Ranaldson Macdonell of Glengarry, 1773–1828* (Glendaruel: Argyll Publishing, 2001), pp. 159–90.

52 Coinneach Mac'Coinnich, *Orain Ghaidhealach agus Bearla air an Eadar-theangacha* (Edinburgh, 1792), p. 104; see Black (ed.), *An Lasair*, pp. 499–500, 508–12.

53 See Peadar Mac Cuillin, 'Gnéithe de na Focail *suairc* agus *suairceas* sa 18ú hAois', in Aidan Doyle and Siobhán Ní Laoire (eds), *Aistí ar an Nua-Ghaeilge in ómós do Bhreandán Ó Buachalla* (Dublin: Cois

Life, 2006), pp. 193–215; Charles Withers, '"Give Us Land and Plenty of It": The Ideological Basis to Land and Landscape in the Scottish Highlands', *Landscape History*, 12 (1990), pp. 45–54.
54 Donacha Cinicnach, *Orainn Ghaelich* (Glasgow, 1805), p. 42.
55 Meek, 'The Pulpit and the Pen', pp. 96–109.
56 Domhnall Uilleam Stiùbhart, 'A Global Gàidhealtachd? Historical Gaelic Ethnoscapes', in Michel Byrne and Sheila M. Kidd (eds), *Lìontan Lìonmhor: Local, National and Global Gaelic Networks from the 18th to the 20th Century* (Glasgow: Roinn na Ceiltis & na Gàidhlig, Oilthigh Ghlaschu, 2019), pp. 1–19.

9. Scottish Theatre in the Long Eighteenth Century

1 Anna Jean Mill, *Mediaeval Plays in Scotland* (Edinburgh: Blackwood, 1927), p. 112.
2 Mark Brown, 'Not so "In-yer-face": Nielson and the Renaissance in Scottish Theatre', in *The Theatre of Anthony Neilson,* ed. Trish Reid (London: Bloomsbury, 2017), p. 191.
3 Bill Findlay, ed., *A History of Scottish Theatre* (Edinburgh: Polygon, 1998).
4 John McGavin, 'Drama in Sixteenth-Century Haddington', *European Medieval Drama*, 1 (1997), 147–59 (pp. 156–57).
5 J. McKenzie, 'School and University Drama in Scotland, 1650–1760', *Scottish Historical Review*, 34 (1955), 103–21 (p. 103).
6 Findlay, 'Beginnings to 1700', in *Scottish Theatre,* ed. Findlay, pp. 18–19.
7 Margo Todd, *The Culture of Protestantism in Early Modern Scotland* (New Haven: Yale University Press, 2002), pp. 221–22.
8 Michael Newton, 'Folk Drama in Gaelic Scotland', in *The Edinburgh Companion to Scottish Drama*, ed. Ian Brown (Edinburgh: Edinburgh University Press, 2011), pp. 41–46.
9 Janet Sorensen, 'Varieties of Public Performance: Folk Songs, Ballads, Popular Drama and Sermons', in *The Edinburgh History of Scottish Literature*, 3 vols (Edinburgh: Edinburgh University Press, 2007), II: *Enlightenment, Britain and Empire (1707–1918)*, ed. Susan Manning, pp. 133–42.
10 Alasdair Cameron, 'Theatre in Scotland 1660–1800', in *The History of Scottish Literature*, ed. Andrew Hook, 4 vols (Aberdeen: Aberdeen University Press, 1987), II: *1660–1880*, 191–208 (p. 203).
11 Katherine Newey, 'Home Plays for Ladies: Women's Work in Home Theatricals', *Nineteenth Century Theatre*, 26 (Winter 1998), 93–111 (pp. 93–94).

12 Tracy D. Davis and Ellen Donkin, 'Introduction', in *Women and Playwriting in Nineteenth-Century Britain*, ed. Tracy D. Davis and Ellen Donkin (Cambridge: Cambridge University Press, 1999), 1–12 (p. 6).
13 McKenzie, p. 103.
14 Ibid., p. 104.
15 Ibid., pp. 104, 119.
16 Ibid., p. 106.
17 Ibid., pp. 106–07.
18 William Clark, *Marciano; or, The Discovery*, ed. W. H. Logan (Edinburgh: privately published, 1871 [1663]), p. 41.
19 Clark, 'Preface', pp. 5–6.
20 See Findlay, *Scottish Theatre*, pp. 71–72. The figures quoted there, allowing for inflation, by any measure amount to modern expenditure of many hundreds of pounds for some theatre expeditions.
21 Ibid., p. 72–74.
22 Terence Tobin, *Plays by Scots 1660–1800* (Iowa City: University of Iowa Press, 1974), p. 134.
23 Sandro Jung, *David Mallet, Anglo-Scot: Poetry, Patronage and Politics in the Age of Union* (Newark: Delaware University Press, 2008), pp. 17–23, 72–74.
24 Ibid. p. 15.
25 Thomas Arne, *Alfred*, ed. Alexander Scott (London: Stainer and Bell, 1981), p. 175.
26 Tobin, p. 140.
27 James Thomson, *Tancred and Sigismunda* (London: A. Millar, 1745), p. iv.
28 See, for example, Ian Brown, *Scottish Theatre: Diversity, Language, Continuity* (Amsterdam: Rodopi, 2013), pp. 81–82, and also Brown, *Performing Scottishness: Enactment and National Identity* (London: Palgrave Macmillan, 2019), *passim*.
29 Adrienne Scullion, 'The Eighteenth Century', in *A History of Scottish Theatre*, ed. Findlay, pp. 80–136 (p. 93).
30 Ibid. p. 87.
31 See ibid., pp. 89–90.
32 Allan Ramsay, *Some Few Hints* [...] (Edinburgh: [n. pub.], 1728), p. 2.
33 Donald Campbell, *Playing for Scotland: A History of the Scottish Stage 1715–1965* (Edinburgh: Mercat Press, 1996), p. 4.
34 Scullion, 'Eighteenth Century', in *A History of Scottish Theatre*, ed. Findlay, pp. 90, 93.

35 Ibid., p. 93. Scullion cites the Prologue as it originally appears in the *Caledonian Mercury*, 15 November 1736.
36 Murray Pittock has provided a lively account of this in relation to Ramsay's theatre's opening and closing. See *Enlightenment in a Smart City: Edinburgh's Civic Development, 1660–1750* (Edinburgh: Edinburgh University Press, 2019), pp. 180–82.
37 See Findlay (ed.), p. 102.
38 Tobin, p. 163.
39 Katherine Glover, 'The Female Mind: Scottish Enlightenment Femininity and the World of Letters. A Case Study of the Women of the Fletcher of Saltoun Family in the Mid-Eighteenth Century', *Journal of Scottish Historical Studies*, 25 (2005), 1–20 (p. 17).
40 David Hume, *The Philosophical Works of David Hume*, ed. Thomas Grose and Thomas Green, 4 vols (London: Longmans, 1874–75), III, 66.
41 See Scullion, pp. 103–04.
42 Barbara Bell, 'The Scottish Theatrical Landscape Leading into the Emergence of the National Drama', *International Journal of Scottish Theatre and Screen*, 8 (2015), 27–53 (p. 33) ijosts.ubiquitypress.com/articles/abstract/197/ [accessed 12 January 2018].
43 Jean Marishall, *The History of Miss Clarinda Cathcart and Miss Fanny Renton,* 2 vols (London, 1766), II, 162, 166.
44 John Jackson, *The History of the Scottish Stage* (Edinburgh: Peter Hill, 1793), p. 77.
45 Quoted in Tobin p. 50.
46 Ibid., p. 51.
47 Anon., *Memoir of Archibald Maclaren, Dramatist: with a List of his Works* (Edinburgh, 1835), p. 2.
48 For further detailed discussion of Maclaren's work see Ian Brown and Gioia Angeletti, 'Cultural Crossings and Dilemmas in Archibald Maclaren's Playwriting', in *Gael and Lowlander in Scottish Literature: Cross-Currents in Scottish Writing in the Nineteenth Century*, ed. Christopher MacLachlan and Ronald W. Renton (Glasgow: Scottish Literature International, 2015), pp. 41–55, and Ian Brown, 'Theatricality, Bilingualism and Metatheatricality in Archibald Maclaren's The Highland Drover', *International Journal of Scottish Theatre and Screen* 9 (2016), pp. 13–23.
49 Bell, p. 31.
50 Ibid., p. 36.
51 Gioia Angeletti, '"Closeted" Discourses in Private Theatricals: The Mystification of Genre and Audience in Christian Carstairs' *The*

Hubble-Shue', in *Closet Drama: History, Theory, Form*, ed. Catherine Burroughs (New York and London: Routledge, forthcoming).
52 Jane Rendall, 'Wallace, Eglinton', in *The Biographical Dictionary of Scottish Women*, ed. Elizabeth Ewan, Sue Innes, Siân Reynolds, and Rose Pipes (Edinburgh: Edinburgh University Press, 2006), p. 365.
53 Bell, p. 5. I am particularly grateful to Dr Bell for her indispensable help in drafting this paragraph.
54 Ibid., p. 27.
55 Cameron, 'Theatre in Scotland', in *History of Scottish Literature*, ed. Hook, II, 191.

10. 'Will No One Tell Me What She Sings?': Scots Pastoral Poetry

1 'A Pastoral Poem on the Union', *The Observer*, 12 March 1707, n.p.; James Hogg, 'Dusty, or, Watie an' Geordie's Review of Politics; an Eclogue', in *Scottish Pastorals, Poems, Songs, &c.* [...] (Edinburgh: John Taylor, 1801), pp. 9–24; J. B - e, 'A Pastoral. Damon and Thyrsis', *Universal Magazine*, February 1758, pp. 94–96; 'A Pastoral, suited to the Times. In the Caledonian Dialect', *Weekly Magazine or Edinburgh Amusement*, 25 January 1776, pp. 145–46.
2 Andrew Erskine, *Town-Eclogues* (London: T. Cadell, (1773)); Robert Fergusson, 'A Drink Eclogue', *Weekly Magazine or Edinburgh Amusement*, 11 November 1773, pp. 209–10; 'Mutual Complaint of Plainstanes and Causey, in their Mother-tongue', *Weekly Magazine or Edinburgh Amusement* , 4 March 1773, pp. 306–07.
3 John Cunningham, 'Corydon: A Pastoral. To the Memory of William Shenstone, Esq.', *St. James's Chronicle; or The British Evening-Post*, 12 March 1763, n.p.
4 Allan Ramsay, *The Works of Allan Ramsay*, 6 vols (Edinburgh: Scottish Text Society, 1945–74), II: *Poems: 1728* (1953), ed. by Burns Martin and John Oliver, p. 250.
5 Thomas Blackwell, *An Enquiry into the Life and Writings of Homer* (London: n. pub., 1735), p. 57.
6 Ruth Benedict, *Patterns of Culture* (Boston, New York: Houghton Mifflin, 1934).
7 William Forbes, *An Account of the Life and Writings of James Beattie* [...] (Edinburgh: A. Constable, 1806), pp. 207, 352, 203.
8 James Beattie, *The Minstrel, in Two Books: With Some Other Poems*, 8th edn (London: Charles Dilly; Edinburgh: W. Creech, 1784), p. 8.
9 Ibid., p. 35.
10 Ibid., p. 9.

11 Alexander Ross, *Helenore; or, The Fortunate Shepherdess: A Poem in the Broad Scotch Dialect*, ed. John Longmuir (Glasgow: Hugh Hopkins, 1868), p. 135.
12 Ibid., p. 131.
13 Robert Burns, 'The Vision', in *Poems, Chiefly in the Scottish Dialect* (Kilmarnock: John Wilson, 1786), p. 95.
14 Ibid., p. 91.
15 Joseph Ritson, *Scotish [sic] Songs: In Two Volumes* (London: J. Johnson, 1794): I, lxxix–lxxx.
16 Hector Macneill, *The Pastoral, or Lyric Muse of Scotland; in Three Cantos* (Edinburgh: Archibald Constable, 1808), p. 61.
17 Ibid., p. 10.
18 Ibid., pp. 22, 34.
19 Ibid., p. 28.
20 James Hogg, *Midsummer Night Dreams and Related Poems*, ed. J. H. Rubenstein, Gillian Hughes, and Meiko O'Halloran (Edinburgh: Edinburgh University Press, 2008), p. 1. I obviously do not concur with the editors' conclusion that the poem preaches a 'peculiar form of gradualist perfectibility' (p. lviii).
21 Ibid., p. 4.
22 Ibid., p. 48.
23 Ibid., p. 16.

11. Gaelic Women's Poetry

1 Michel Byrne, 'A Window on the Late Eighteenth-century Scottish Highlands', *Proceedings of the Harvard Celtic Colloquium*, 30 (2010), pp. 39–60 (p. 39).
2 Ronald Black, 'Gaelic Secular Publishing', in *The Edinburgh History of the Book in Scotland vol. II: Enlightenment and Expansion, 1707–1800*, ed. Stephen W. Brown and Warren McDougall (Edinburgh: Edinburgh University Press, 2012), pp. 595–612 (p. 602).
3 Marairead Cham'ron, *Orain nuadh Ghaidhealach* (Edinburgh: D. Mac-Phatraic, 1785), reprinted Inverness, 1805 by Eoin Young.
4 William Gillies, 'Traditional Gaelic Women's Songs', in *Alba Literaria: a history of Scottish literature*, ed. Marco Fazzini (Venezia Mestre: Amos Edizioni, 2005), pp. 165–79 (p. 169).
5 'Of the Influence of Poetry and Music Upon the Highlander', in *A Collection of Highland Vocal Airs*, ed. Patrick MacDonald (Edinburgh: for the publisher, 1784), p. 10; cf. NLS MS 1644, Ramsay's manuscript on 'Highlanders and the Highlands', printed in *Scotland and Scotsmen*

in the Eighteenth Century, ed. Alexander Allardyce (Edinburgh: William Blackwood & Sons, 1888), pp. 410–11. The singing of work-songs was also observed by Samuel Johnson in Raasay; *A Journey to the Western Isles of Scotland*, ed. J. D. Fleeman (Oxford: Oxford University Press, 1985), p. 50.

6   Colm Ó Baoill, '"Neither Out nor In": Scottish Gaelic Women Poets 1650–1750', in *Woman and the Feminine in Medieval and Early Modern Scottish Writing*, ed. Sarah M. Dunnigan, C. Marie Harker, and Evelyn S. Newlyn (Houndmills: Palgrave Macmillan, 2004), pp. 136–53 (p. 136).

7   John MacInnes, 'The Panegyric Code in Gaelic poetry and its Historical background', *Transactions of the Gaelic Society of Inverness*, 50 (1976–78), pp. 435–98; *An Lasair: Anthology of 18th Century Scottish Gaelic Verse*, ed. Ronald Black (Edinburgh: Birlinn, 2001), pp. xix–xxvii; M. Pía Coira, *By Poetic Authority: The Rhetoric of Panegyric in Gaelic Poetry of Scotland to c. 1700* (Edinburgh: Dunedic Academic Press, 2012).

8   Ronald Black and Gerard Carruthers, 'The Eighteenth Century', in *The International Companion to Scottish Poetry*, ed. Carla Sassi (Glasgow: Scottish Literature International, 2015), pp. 54–63 (p. 55).

9   Black, *An Lasair*, pp. xxxii–xxxv; *Tuath is Tighearna: Tenants and Landlords*, ed. Donald Meek (Edinburgh: Scottish Gaelic Texts Society, 1995); Sheila M. Kidd, 'Social Control and Social Criticism: The Nineteenth-century Còmhradh', *Scottish Gaelic Studies*, 20 (2000), pp. 67–87; Priscilla Scott, '"Bean-Chomuinn nam Bàrd": Exploring Common Ground in the Lives and Perspectives of the Gaelic Poets, Mary MacPherson and Mary MacKellar', in *Canan & Cultar / Language & Culture: Rannsachadh na Gàidhlig 8*, ed. Wilson McLeod, Anja Gunderloch, and Rob Dunbar (Edinburgh: Dunedin Academic Press, 2016), pp. 71–84.

10 Anne Frater and Michel Byrne, 'Gaelic poetry and song', in *The Edinburgh Companion to Scottish Women's Writing*, ed. Glenda Norquay (Edinburgh: Edinburgh University Press, 2012), pp. 22–35 (p. 24); Byrne, 'A Window', p. 53.

11 Discussed by Black, 'Gaelic Secular Publishing', p. 604; cf. Meg Bateman, 'Women's Writing in Scottish Gaelic since 1750', in *A History of Scottish Women's Writing*, ed. Douglas Gifford and Dorothy McMillan (Edinburgh: Edinburgh University Press, 1997), pp. 659–76 (p. 661).

12 Natasha Sumner, 'Women's Conduct and the Poetry of Sìleas na Ceapaich', *Proceedings of the Harvard Celtic Colloquium*, 32 (2012), pp. 304–24.

13 Anne C. Frater, 'Women of the Gàidhealtachd and their Songs to 1750', in *Women in Scotland, c. 1100–c. 1750*, ed. Elizabeth Ewan and Maureen M. Meikle (East Linton: Tuckwell Press, 1999), pp. 67–83 (pp. 75–78).
14 Frater and Byrne, 'Gaelic poetry', p. 30.
15 *Màiri nighean Alasdair Ruaidh: Song-maker of Skye and Berneray*, ed. Colm Ó Baoill (Glasgow: Scottish Gaelic Texts Society, 2014), p. 17.
16 Discussed by Virginia Blankenhorn, '"Griogal Cridhe": Aspects of Transmission in the Lament for Griogair Ruadh Mac Griogair of Glen Strae', *Scottish Studies*, 37 (2014), pp. 6–37; cf. the 'danger of distortion' observed by Derick Thomson, 'Scottish Gaelic Traditional Songs from the 16th to the 18th Century', *Proceedings of the British Academy*, 105 (2000), pp. 93–114 (p. 113). In rarer cases, secure attribution of presumed authorship may be restored, e.g. Martin MacGregor, '"Surely one of the greatest poems ever made in Britain": The Lament for Griogair Ruadh MacGregor of Glen Strae and its Historical Background', in *The Polar Twins*, ed. Edward J. Cowan and Douglas Gifford (Edinburgh: John Donald, 1999), pp. 114–53.
17 Thomas Owen Clancy, 'Women poets in Early Medieval Ireland: Stating the Case', in *The Fragility of Her Sex?: Medieval Irishwomen in Their European Context*, ed. Christine Meek and Katharine Simms (Dublin: Four Courts Press, 1996), pp. 43–73 (p. 58).
18 Discussion of 'female-voiced' verse may be most precise; see Kate L. Mathis, 'An Ulster Tale in Breadalbane? Personæ and Literary Allusion in the Poetry of Mòr Chaimbeul', *Aiste*, 2 (2008), pp. 43–69, and '"Tha Mulad Air M'Inntinn" and Early Modern Gaelic Dialogue Verse', *Aiste*, 5 (2019), pp. 50–139.
19 NLS Adv. MS 72.1.37; see Martin MacGregor, 'The View from Fortingall: The Worlds of the Book of the Dean of Lismore', *Scottish Gaelic Studies*, 22 (2006), pp. 35–86, and Mícheál B. Ó Mainnín and Nicola Royan, 'Lyric', in *The International Companion to Scottish Literature 1400–1650*, ed. Nicola Royan (Glasgow: Scottish Literature International, 2018), pp. 124–57 (pp. 130–33), contra William Gillies, 'The Book of the Dean of Lismore: The Literary Perspective', in *Fresche Fontanis: Proceedings of the 2008 Medieval and Renaissance Scottish Languages and Literatures Conference*, ed. Janet Hadley Williams and J. Derrick McClure (Newcastle: Cambridge Scholars Publishing, 2013), pp. 179–216 (p. 206); cf. Thomas Clancy, 'A Fond Farewell to Last Night's Literary Criticism: Reading Niall Mór MacMhuirich', in

Cànan & Cultar / Language & Culture: Rannsachadh na Gàidhlig 4, ed. Gillian Munro and Richard V. A. Cox (Edinburgh: Dunedin Academic Press, 2010), pp. 109–27 (p. 114).

20 GUL, MS Gen 85/1/34; *Làmh-Sgrìobhainn Mhic Rath: Dòrlach Laoidhean do Sgrìobhadh le Donnchadh MacRath, 1688*, ed. Calum MacPhàrlain (Dun Dè: Calum S. MacLeoid, 1923).

21 His wife was Seònaid, daughter of Alasdair mac Alasdair 'ic 'Ille-Chaluim, 6th of Ràarsaidh (d. 1648), one of the sisters of Iain Garbh, 7th of Ràarsaidh who drowned in 1671. Elegies for his death are attributed to Seònaid and her sister Sìleas, e.g. in McLagan's collection (GUL 1042, 137, 13a–b; 120, 14b–15b); see Ó Baoill, *Màiri nighean Alasdair Ruaidh*, pp. 269–79; Sorley Maclean, 'Obscure and Anonymous Gaelic Poetry', in *The Seventeenth Century in the Highlands*, ed. Loraine Maclean (Inverness: Inverness Field Club, 1986), pp. 89–105 (pp. 98–99); J. Carmichael Watson, *Gaelic Songs of Mary Macleod* (Edinburgh: Blackie & Son Ltd., 1934), pp. 26–31, 100–01; and Anne Lorne Gillies, *Songs of Gaelic Scotland* (Edinburgh: Birlinn, 2005), p. 153.

22 *Leabhar na Féinne: Heroic Gaelic ballads*, ed. John Francis Campbell (London: Spottiswoode & Co., 1872), sections C, E. Unacknowledged female informants are likely, and women performers' repertoires were later acknowledged, if still the minority; Victoria Henshaw, 'James Macpherson and his Contemporaries: The Methods and Networks of Collectors of Gaelic poetry in Late Eighteenth-Century Scotland', *Journal for Eighteenth-Century Studies*, 39 (2016), pp. 197–209 (p. 199); Anja Gunderloch, 'The Heroic Ballads of Gaelic Scotland', in *The Edinburgh Companion to Scottish Traditional Literatures*, ed. Sarah Dunnigan and Suzanne Gilbert (Edinburgh: Edinburgh University Press, 2013), pp. 74–85 (p. 77–78).

23 Fiona Stafford, 'Romantic Macpherson', in *The Edinburgh Companion to Scottish Romanticism*, ed. Murray Pittock (Edinburgh: Edinburgh University Press, 2011), pp. 27–39 (pp. 28–29); Gunderloch, 'Heroic Ballads', pp. 77–79.

24 William Gillies, 'Some Eighteenth-century developments in Scottish Gaelic poetry', in *Language and power in the Celtic world*, ed. Anders Ahlqvist and Pamela O'Neill (Sydney: Celtic Studies Foundation, University of Sydney, 2011), pp. 61–97 (p. 75).

25 Robert Dunbar, 'Vernacular Gaelic Tradition', in *Edinburgh Companion to Scottish Traditional Literatures*, ed. Dunnigan and Gilbert, pp. 51–63

(pp. 53–54). For MacDiarmid's career, see *The MacDiarmid MS Anthology*, ed. Derick Thomson (Edinburgh: Scottish Gaelic Texts Society, 1992), pp. 2–3.

26 Michael Newton, *We're Indians Sure Enough: The Legacy of the Scottish Highlanders in the United States* (Auburn: Saorsa Media, 2001), p. 26; Sìm Innes and Alessandra Petrina, 'The Sixteenth and Seventeenth Centuries', in *The International Companion to Scottish Poetry*, ed. Carla Sassi, pp. 44–53 (pp. 52–53).

27 William Gillies, 'Clan Donald bards and scholars', in *Cànan & Cultar/ Language & Culture: Rannsachadh na Gàidhlig 4*, ed. Gillian Munro and Richard V. A. Cox, pp. 91–108 (p. 93). Some exceptions are discussed by Thomas Owen Clancy, 'Gaelic Literature and Scottish Romanticism', in *The Edinburgh Companion to Scottish Romanticism*, ed. Murray Pittock, pp. 47–60.

28 Kate L. Mathis, 'Women's poetry in McLagan's collection', in *Seumas MacLathagain agus a Làmh-Sgrìobhainnean/James McLagan and his Manuscripts*, ed. Sìm Innes and Geraldine Parsons (Glasgow: Scottish Gaelic Texts Society, forthcoming).

29 Hugh Cheape, 'The Gaelic Book—The Printed Book in Scottish Gaelic', *International League of Antiquarian Booksellers* ilab.org/articles/gaelic-book-printed-book-scottish-gaelic [accessed December 10, 2020].

30 Ibid.; cf. William Gillies, 'On the Study of Gaelic Literature', in *Litreachas agus Eachraidh/Literature and History: Papers from the Second Conference of Scottish Gaelic Studies, Glasgow 2002*, ed. Michel Byrne, Thomas Owen Clancy, and Sheila Kidd (Glaschu: Roinn na Ceiltis Oilthigh Ghlaschu, 2006), pp. 1–33 (pp. 3–11).

31 *Sean Dain, agus Orain Ghaidhealach/A Collection of Ancient and Modern Gaelic Poems and Songs, Transmitted from Gentlemen in the Highlands of Scotland*, ed. John Gillies (Perth: for the author, 1786); *Cochruinneacha Taoghta de Shaothair nam Bard Gaëlach: A Choice Collection of the Works of the Highland Bards*, ed. Alexander and Donald Stewart, 2 vols (Duneidin: Clodh-bhuailt le T. Stiuart, 1804); *Co-chruinneachadh Nuadh do dh'Orannibh Gaidhealach*, ed. Eoin Young (Inverness: for the author, 1806); *Comhchruinneacha do dh' orain taghta Ghaidhealach*, ed. Patrick Turner (Duneidionn: Clo-bhuailte airson an ughdair le T. Stiubhard, 1813). For context see Black, 'Gaelic Secular Publishing'.

32 Gillies, 'Eighteenth-century Developments', p. 75.

33 Richard Sharpe, 'Manuscript and Print in Gaelic Scotland and Ireland, 1689–1832', *Canan agus Cultur/Language and Culture: Rannsachadh na Gàidhlig 8*, (ed. McLeod *et al.*), pp. 31–55 (p. 40).

34 GUL 1042, 165B, 1a–b, labelled 'No. 2, Le Mrs Sevenson [sic]'; edited and discussed by Black, *An Lasair*, pp. 186–91, 458.

35 Ó Baoill, '"Neither Out nor In"', pp. 138–41, 141–47; Ó Baoill, *Màiri nighean Alasdair Ruaidh*; *Bàrdachd Shìlis na Ceapaich: Poems and Songs by Sìleas MacDonald, c. 1660–c. 1729*, ed. Colm Ó Baoill (Edinburgh: Scottish Gaelic Texts Society, 1972).

36 Ibid., pp. 144, 149, and Colm Ó Baoill, 'Sìleas na Ceapaich', in *The Edinburgh History of Scottish Literature I: From Columba to the Union (until 1707)*, ed. Thomas Owen Clancy and Murray Pittock (Edinburgh: Edinburgh University Press, 2007), pp. 305–14 (p. 308).

37 Ó Baoill, *Bàrdachd Shìlis na Ceapaich*, p. xxviii, and Ó Baoill, *Màiri nighean Alasdair Ruaidh*, p. 134; cf. GUL 1042, 211, 1a, a copy of one of Màiri's songs in the hand of McNicol's brother Archibald.

38 GUL 1042, 120, 3a–8a, which also contains McLagan's only extant copy of Sìleas's lament for Alasdair Dubh, 10th MacDonald of Glengarry (d. 1721).

39 GUL 1042, 122, 4b–5a (copied in 1775), discussed in *Gàir nan Clàrsach / The Harps' Cry: An Anthology of 17th Century Gaelic Poetry*, ed. Colm Ó Baoill and Meg Bateman (Edinburgh: Birlinn, 1994), p. 227; Ó Baoill, *Màiri nighean Alasdair Ruaidh*, pp. 40–60.

40 GUL 1042, 249, a–b (English); cf. 124, 1a–b (Gaelic).

41 Ó Baoill, '"Neither Out nor In"', p. 138; cf. Ó Baoill, *Màiri nighean Alasdair Ruaidh*, e.g. pp. 134, 222, and *Bàrdachd Shìlis na Ceapaich*, pp. xxix–xxx.

42 Raonuill MacDòmhnuill, *Comh-chruinneachidh Orannaigh Gaidhealach, le Raonuill MacDòmhnuill, ann 'n Eilean Eigg* (Duneidiunn: Clo-bhuailt ann le Walter Ruddiman, 1776), pp. 31–33, 37–42, 235–39, 307–10 (Màiri), and pp. 286–88 (Sìleas).

43 *The MacDonald Collection of Gaelic poetry*, ed. Alexander and Angus MacDonald (Inverness: The Northern Counties Newspaper and Printing and Publishing Company, 1911), pp. 348–49.

44 Ó Baoill, '"Neither Out nor In"', pp. 147–49.

45 Around 1768, by Hector MacLean of Grulin's manuscript; see *Mairghread nighean Lachlainn: Songmaker of Mull*, ed. Colm Ó Baoill (Glasgow: Scottish Gaelic Texts Society, 2009), p. 187, and Colm Ó Baoill, *Maclean Manuscripts in Nova Scotia* (Aberdeen: Aberdeen University Department of Celtic, 2001), pp. 36, 47, 49. Mairghread's

work and several other women's is also copied by Hector's kinsman John, Bàrd Thighearna Chola, c. 1815, and published in the latter's anthology in 1818; see Donald E. Meek and Robert Dunbar, 'John MacLean, the Gaelic bard', in *The Edinburgh History of the Book in Scotland Volume 3 Ambition and Industry, 1800-80*, ed. Bill Bell (Edinburgh: Edinburgh University Press, 2007), pp. 232-40.

46 *Comhchruinneacha do dh' orain taghta Ghaidhealach*, pp. 1-22; Turner prints four of Mairghread's poems, grouped together and opening his collection.

47 Donald McNicol, *Remarks on Dr Samuel Johnson's journey to the Hebrides* (London: T. Cadell, 1779), p. 223, refuting at length Johnson's claim that the Gaels were an 'illiterate and ignorant people', unable to analyse their past.

48 *Comhchruinneacha do dh' orain taghta Ghaidhealach*, p. 171; cf. GUL 1042, 137, 14a-15b.

49 *Co-chruinneachadh Nuadh do dh'Orannibh Gaidhealach*, p. 50; cf. GUL 1042, 120, 12a-b, ed. Ó Baoill, *Bàrdachd Shìlis na Ceapaich*, pp. 70-75. Independently of McLagan, the lament was also attributed to Sìleas in the Eigg collection in 1776; *Comh-chruinneachidh Orannaigh Gaidhealach*, p. 286.

50 *Cochruinneacha Taoghta de Shaothair nam Bard Gaëlach*, pp. 357, 366. For discussion, see Ó Baoill, *Bàrdachd Shìlis na Ceapaich*, pp. 165-66, 175-77, and Black, *An Lasair*, p. 374, who emends 'obair nodha' ('new work'), the older interpretation of Sìleas's title, to 'oba nodha' (anglicised as 'oobie-noogie').

51 *Sean Dain*, p. 61, harmonising McLagan's slightly different versions (GUL 1042, 13, 3a-4a; 20, 16b-17b; 99, 3a-4a); Gillies's treatment of multiple-sourced texts is explored by Charles Coventry, 'A Reconsideration of the Gillies Collection of Gaelic Poetry', *Studies in Scottish Literature*, 26.1 (1991), pp. 199-206 (p. 201). The poem is edited by Anja Gunderloch, ''S tric Mo Shùil air an Linne', in *Bile ós Chrannaibh: A Festschrift for William Gillies*, ed. Wilson McLeod et al. (Tigh a' Mhaide: Clann Tuirc, 2010), pp. 167-89. It had also been printed in appendix to Gillies's *History of the Feuds and Conflicts Among the Clans* in 1780, pp. 130-32 (see note 76, below).

52 GUL 1042, 125, 6a-b; it is possible that its title inspired reluctance, despite the fact that the poem, a lively eulogy, makes no further reference to the battle or the Jacobite cause.

53 In GUL 1042, 137, 14a-15b, 'ann Striliadh' is replaced by 'ann Eaglais Bhric'.

54 *Sean Dain*, p. 298; GUL 1042, 69, 7a–8a, and 138a–b.
55 GUL 1042, 97; McLagan's copy is similar to Rev. Ewen MacDiarmid's, copied prior to 1770 (GUL GB 247 MS Gen 583, p. 174), which is untitled; see Thomson, *MacDiarmid MS Anthology*, p. 276. The alteration may have been prompted by publication of a tune, 'Oran do Ghilleaspuic, Mac Calum Sealgair' ('*A song to Archibald, Mac Calum the hunter*'), in the MacDonald brothers' *Collection of Highland Vocal Airs* in 1784 (no. 102).
56 *Sean Dain*, p. 53. The elegy's context is discussed by Joanna Martin and Kate L. Mathis, 'Elegy and Commemorative Writing', in *The International Companion to Scottish Literature, 1400–1650*, ed. Nicola Royan, pp. 173–99 (pp. 196–97).
57 GUL 1042, 76, 2b–3a; printed in Gillies, *Sean Dain*, pp. 128–32; cf. Young, *Co-Chruinneachadh nuadh do dh'Orannibh Gaidhealach*, p. 171, and *The Gaelic Bards from 1715 to 1765*, ed. Alexander Maclean Sinclair (Charlottetown: Haszard & Moore, 1892), p. 78. For discussion of the error – and the poet's actual career – see Colm Ó Baoill, 'Some notes on "An Aigeannach"', *Scottish Gaelic Studies*, 13.1 (1978), pp. 103–11.
58 Its source was Hector MacLean of Grulin's unattributed copy (MG15G/2/2, Public Archives, Halifax, Nova Scotia, pp. 8–9). For the manuscript, see Michael Linkletter, 'The Gaelic collection of the Public Archives of Nova Scotia', in Byrne *et al.*, *Litreachas & Eachdraidh: Rannsachadh na Gàidhlig 2*, pp. 148–60 (p. 79); cf. Colm Ó Baoill, 'Raghnall Dubh and Hector Maclean', *Scottish Gaelic Studies*, 12.2 (1976), pp. 209–20. The attribution to Iain mac Ailein is retained by *Sar Obair nam Bard Gaelach: The Beauties of Gaelic Poetry and Lives of the Highland bards*, ed. John Mackenzie, 4th edn (Edinburgh: Maclachlan & Stewart, 1877), pp. 393–94, but not by Maclean Sinclair's influential collection of MacLean poets; *Na Baird Leathanach: The Maclean bards, Vol. 1: The Old Maclean Bards* (Charlottetown: Haszard and Moore, 1898), p. 85.
59 MacDòmhnuill, *Comh-chruinneachidh Orannaigh Gaidhealach*, pp. 175–78. 'Mac Dhòmhnaill Dhuibh' refers to Cameron of Lochiel; see discussion of the dialogue by Black, *An Lasair*, pp. 402–03, and Mathis, '"Tha Mulad Air M'Inntinn"', pp. 67–68, note 35.
60 *Essays on the Superstitions of the Highlanders of Scotland, vol. 1* (London: Longman *et al.*, 1811), pp. 145–46. Also erroneously, Grant describes the women as friends, not sisters (p. 148). After its inclusion in the Eigg collection, the poem's next publication did not occur until 1841.

61 Anne MacVicar Grant, *Letters Concerning Highland Affairs in the 18th century by Mrs Grant of Laggan*, in *Wariston's Diary and other papers*, ed. J. R. N. MacPhail (Edinburgh: T. & A. Constable for the Scottish History Society, 1896), pp. 251–330 (p. 316). Her discussion centres on Sìleas's elegy for Alasdair Dubh, also printed with attribution by MacDòmhnuill in the Eigg collection (*Comh-chruinneachidh Orannaigh Gaidhealach*, p. 286); see Ó Baoill, *Bàrdachd Shìlis na Ceapaich*, p. 164.
62 McLagan's wife and daughter are also invoked as witnesses to Isabel's performance; GUL 1042, 84, 1a–4a. I am grateful to Sìm Innes for this reference; cf. Derick Thomson, 'Indexes of the Ossianic ballads in the McLagan MSS', *Scottish Gaelic Studies*, 8 (1958), pp. 177–224 (p. 204).
63 Ó Baoill, *Bàrdachd Shìlis na Ceapaich*, p. xxxi; cf. Donald C. Macpherson, 'Moire Mhaighdean', *The Highlander*, July 25 1879, p. 6 (cited by Ó Baoill, *Bàrdachd Shìlis na Ceapaich*, p. 209). Another informant of Iain Bàn's was Iain Lom MacDonald's granddaughter, also printed by Turner.
64 Nigel Leask, *Stepping Westward: Writing the Highland Tour c. 1720–1830* (Oxford: Oxford University Press, 2020), esp. p. 203. Wordsworth's *Recollections of a tour made in Scotland* (1803) does refer briefly to an old woman who 'sang doleful Erse songs' to a crying child; Leask, p. 214.
65 Alastair Mac-Dhonuill, *Ais-Eiridh na Sean Chánoin Albannaich; no, An Nuadh Oranaiche Gaidhealach* (Duneidiunn: for the author, 1751), pp. v-vi. For the preface, see Peter Mackay, 'Negotiations of Barbarity, Authenticity and Purity in Eighteenth and Nineteenth Century Gaelic Literature', in *Within and Without Empire: Scotland Across the (Post) Colonial Borderline*, ed. Carla Sassi and Theo van Heijnsbergen (Newcastle: Cambridge Scholars Publishing, 2013), pp. 30–45 (pp. 36–37); for the collection, see Ronald Black, 'Alexander MacDonald's *Ais-Eiridh*, 1751', *Journal of the Edinburgh Bibliographical Society*, 5 (2010), pp. 45–64.
66 'Gaelic secular publishing', pp. 602–03.
67 Black and Carruthers, 'The eighteenth century', p. 59. He had included in *Ais-Eiridh* (pp. 98–103) 'Oran-luaigh no fúcaidh, a rinn duin'-uasal d' a leannan, air dhi dol thar fairrge' ('*A waulking or fulling song that a gentleman made to his sweetheart after she had gone over the sea*').
68 *Ais-Eiridh*, pp. 153–58 ('Marbhrainn Máiri nian Ean Mhic-Eun, do 'n gairte an Aigionnach').

69 *Ais-Eiridh*, pp. 170–85; Ronald Black, *The Campbells of the Ark, Men of Argyll in 1745: Volume 1, The Inner Circle* (Edinburgh: John Donald, 2017), pp. 325–41.

70 Ronald Black, *Mac Mhaighstir Alasdair: The Ardnamurchan Years* (Inverness: The Society of West Highland and Island Historical Research, 1986), p. 22.

71 Black, *Campbells of the Ark*, pp. 329–30.

72 Black, *Campbells of the Ark*, pp. 327–28. Before Anna's condemnation, Mac Mhaighstir Alasdair suspected her mother of composing the offending song (id., pp. 334–35).

73 He is responsible, if indirectly, for the confusion surrounding several women poets labelled 'An Aigeannach' ('self-willed, boisterous female'), the epithet applied initially to Màiri nighean Iain mhic Eoghain by his mock elegy (as note 68). See discussion by Black, *Campbells of the Ark*, p. 330, and Ó Baoill, 'Some Notes on "An Aigeannach"', and 'Òran do Bhean Chladh na Macraidh', *Scottish Gaelic Studies*, 21 (2003), pp. 59–79.

74 In 1786, Kennedy printed seven of Anna's spiritual songs in *Co'chruinneachadh Laoidhe agus Chantaicibh Spioradail* (Glas-gho: D. MacCnuidhein) pp. 78–84, 95–106, the first Gaelic hymnary; his remarks on her career and the texts' attribution awaited its second edition, *An Laoidheadair Gaelic na Orain spioradail* (Glasgow, n.pub.), in the 1830s (pp. 64–84); see Black, *Campbells of the Ark*, pp. 335–38. His observation follows Rev. Duncan MacCallum's similar complaint in 1821, though it is clear that MacCallum's remark, unlike Kennedy's, was directed at Màiri nighean Iain mhic Eoghain—a MacDonald—not Anna, and that Kennedy had also been misled by Mac Mhaighstir Alasdair's initial use of 'An Aigeannach' (as note 73). See *Co-Chruinneacha Dhan, Òrain, &c. &c.: A Collection of original poems, songs, &c. taken from oral recitation in various parts of the Highlands and Islands of Scotland, during the last twenty years*, ed. MacCallum (Inverness: Dealbh-bhuailt le Seumais Friseal, 1821), p. 27.

75 Black, 'Gaelic secular publishing', p. 602.

76 'Do Mhinistair Cill-an-Inair' (*Sean Dain*, p. 205), also from McLagan's collection via Donald McNicol (GUL 1042, 58, 1b–2a; EUL MS 3096.1.2, pp. 61–63), had been printed in appendix to Gillies's *History of the feuds and conflicts among the clans* (Glasgow: J. & J. Robertson, 1780), pp. 137–38. Addressed to Rev. Alexander Macfarlane, it is unascribed in 1786 but attributed to 'Nighin Chaptain Blann' in 1780 (following McNicol's copy, not McLagan's).

77 *Sean Dain*, pp. 279–81.
78 Black, *An Lasair*, p. 503. The pamphlet is no longer extant, and is not referred to by Donald Maclean, *Typographia Scoto-gadelica; or, Books Printed in the Gaelic of Scotland from the Year 1567 to the year 1914* (Edinburgh: John Grant, 1915), p. 95.
79 Rev. John Kennedy, *Three Gaelic poems by Mrs Clark* (Edinburgh: Maclachlan & Stewart, 1878), p. 8; Rev. Alexander MacCrae, *Mary MacPherson (Mrs Clark), Bean Torra Dhamh: The Religious Poems of Badenoch* (Arbroath: Herald Press, 1935), p. 26.
80 Duncan Lothian, *Deasbaireachd eadar am Papa agus an t-Athleasacha, le Donnacha Loudinn* (Edinburgh: Menzies, 1834), pp. 30–32; Maclean, *Typographia Scoto-gadelica*, p. 95; Rev. John Rose, *Baird na Gàidhealtachd mu thuath: Laoidhean agus dana spioradail* (Inverness: Mackintosh & Co, 1851), pp. 103–08; Rev. Thomas Sinton, 'Gaelic Poetry from the Cluny Charter Chest', *Transactions of the Gaelic Society of Inverness*, 23 (1898–99), pp. 247–81 (pp. 251–61).
81 Rev. Thomas Sinton, *The Poetry of Badenoch* (Inverness: The Northern Counties Publishing Company, 1906), p. 330, describing NLS Acc. 11044 (items from the Cluny charter chest). They may also be part of the otherwise lost manuscript of Mary's poems to which John Rose refers, written by Rev. Mr Stalker; *Baird na Gàidhealtachd mu thuath*, p. 102.
82 Black, *An Lasair*, p. 504.
83 Bateman, 'Women's Writing', pp. 665–66; John MacInnes, 'Gaelic Poetry in the Nineteenth Century', in *Dùthchas nan Gaidheal: Collected essays of Dr John MacInnes*, ed. Michael Newton (Edinburgh: Birlinn, 2006), pp 357–79 (p. 366).
84 Anne Macleod Hill, 'Reformed theology in Gaelic women's poetry and song', in *The History of Scottish Theology II: From the Early Enlightenment to the Late Victorian Era*, ed. David Fergusson and M. W. Elliot (Oxford: Oxford University Press, 2019), pp. 99–111 (pp. 103–05).
85 'Beachd gràis air an t-saoghal' ('The vantage point of grace'), ed. and trans. by Ronald Black, *An Lasair*, pp. 308–17 (ll. 97–99, 105–07).
86 *Orain Nuadh Ghaidhealach, Le Marairead Cham'ron. Ris am bheil coimh-cheangailte, co-chruinneacha do shean oranaibh eile* (Clodh-bhuailt' ann Dun-Eidin le D. MacPhatraic, airson an ughdair, 1785).
87 Discussed by Black, 'Gaelic Secular Publishing', pp. 599–605; see also Black, 'The Gaelic Book', in *Edinburgh History of the Book in Scotland vol. II*, ed. Brown and McDougall, pp. 177–87.

88 MacLean, *Typographia Scoto-gadelica*, pp. 49–50; Aonghas Campbell, *Orain nuadh Ghaidhleach le Aonghas Caimbeul* (Dun-Eidin: R. Fleming air-son a'n ughdair, 1785).
89 'Gaelic secular publishing', p. 605.
90 Mackay, 'Negotiations of Barbarity', p. 31.
91 'Moladh do na Fineachaibh Gaidheileach a fhuair an Oighreachdan, ann Bliaghna 1784', ll. 5–12; trans. Ruairidh Maciver; see discussion in Ruairidh Maciver, 'Concentric Loyalties: Responses to the Military in Gaelic Women's Poetry', *Proceedings of the Harvard Celtic Colloquium*, 36 (2016), pp. 105–25 (p. 112).
92 Michael Newton, 'Jacobite Past, Loyalist Present', *e-keltoi: Journal of Interdisciplinary Celtic Studies*, 5 (2003), pp. 31–62 (p. 42).
93 'Moladh do na Fineachaibh Gàidhealach', ll. 17–20, trans. Ruairidh Maciver. For the Dis-Clothing Act's repeal, see Matthew Dziennik, 'Whig Tartan: Material Culture and its Use in the Scottish Highlands, 1746–1815', *Past and Present,* 217 (2012), pp. 117–47.
94 Coventry, 'Reconsideration', p. 203.
95 'Oran do Mhac Shimidh, air dha Sealbh fhaotuin ann an Oighreachd a shinnsreadh, le Lachlan Mac Shuine', in Young, *Co-chruinneachadh Nuadh do dh'Orannibh Gaidhealach*, pp. 195–96, discussed by Newton, *We're Indians Sure Enough*, p. 84.
96 Wilson McLeod, 'Gaelic Poetry and the British Military Enterprise, 1756–1945', in *Within and Without Empire*, ed. Carla Sassi and Theo Van Heijnsbergen, pp. 61–76 (pp. 64–66).
97 Discussed by Ronald Black, 'Some Notes from my Glasgow Scrapbook, 1500–1800', in *Glasgow: Baile Mòr nan Gàidheal, City of the Gaels*, ed. Sheila M. Kidd (Glasgow: University of Glasgow Press, 2007), pp. 20–54 (pp. 47–48).
98 *Bho Chluaidh Gu Calasraid—From the Clyde to Callander: Gaelic Songs, Poetry, Tales and Traditions of the Lennox and Menteith in Gaelic with English translations*, ed. and trans. Michael Newton (Glasgow: The Grimsay Press, 2010), pp. 230–33.
99 Coincidentally, it was also collected by McLagan (GUL 1042, 70, 1a–4b); the lament is discussed by Martin and Mathis, 'Elegy and Commemorative Writing', pp. 194–95.
100 Maciver, 'Concentric Loyalties', pp. 109–11.
101 Black, 'Gaelic Secular Publishing', p. 605.
102 MacLean, *Typographia Scoto-gadelica*, p. 54.
103 Ó Baoill, '"Neither Out nor In"', pp. 141–42; Kate L. Mathis, 'Presence, Absence, and Audience: The Elegies of Sìleas na Ceapaich "At Home"

and "Abroad"', in *Gender and Mobility in Scotland and Abroad*, ed. Sierra Dye *et al.* (Guelph: University of Guelph Centre for Scottish Studies, 2018), pp. 183–200.
104 Probably a great-granddaughter of Aonghas, 10th MacDonald of Keppoch; see *Highland Songs of the Forty-Five*, ed. John Lorne Campbell (Edinburgh: Scottish Gaelic Texts Society, 1933), p. 21.
105 'Oran air teachd Phrionnsa Thearlaich, Le te mhuinntir Lochabar'; *Comhchruinneacha do dh' orain taghta Ghaidhealach*, pp. 182–86 (ll. 81–88).
106 Nigel MacNeill, *The Literature of the Highlanders* (Inverness: J. Noble, 1892), p. 316. Marairead Cham'ron was born in Glen Orchy, a daughter of Peter Campbell, tacksman of Clashgour. She married Angus MacIntyre of Lochaber in 1771, then a Mr Cameron of Fort William; John Reid, *Bibliotheca Scoto-Celtica, or, An Account of all the Books Which Have Been Printed in the Gaelic Language* (Glasgow, John Reid & Co., 1832), p. 69.
107 Macleod Hill, 'Reformed theology', pp. 201–02.
108 *Typographia Scoto-gadelica*, p. 62.
109 *Laoidhean Spioradail air an cnuasachadh le Mairearad Chaimbeul* (Edinburgh: Mundell, Doig & Stevenson, 1810), p. iii.
110 Rose, *Baird na Gàidhealtachd mu thuath*, pp. 101–02.
111 Ó Baoill, '"Neither Out nor In"', p. 146. See, for example, McLagan's observation beside his copy of 'Laoidh na Maidne' that it was composed 'an deis a bhi tri bliadhna gun bhiagh, gun deoch, gun chaint' ('*after she was three years without food, drink, or speech*'); GUL 1042, 165B, 6a–b.
112 Ed. and trans. Ó Baoill, *Bàrdachd Shìlis na Ceapaich*, pp. 12–15 (ll. 149–55); discussed by Mathis, '"Tha Mulad Air M'Inntinn"', p. 93 (and *passim*).
113 Ó Baoill, *Bàrdachd Shìlis na Ceapaich*, p. xxvi; Kenneth MacDonald, 'Unpublished Verse by Sìlis Ni Mhic Raghnaill na Ceapaich', in *Celtic Studies: Essays in memory of Angus Matheson*, ed. James Carney and David Greene (London: Routledge, 1968), pp. 76–87 (pp. 84–86). For the collector, see Ulrike Hogg, 'The Life and Papers of the Rev. Dr Alexander Irvine', *Scottish Gaelic Studies*, 28 (2011), pp. 97–175.
114 Màiri Nic a' Phearsain, *Dàin agus Òrain Ghàidhlig* (Inbhirnis: A. & U. Mac-Coinnich, 1891), including ninety items of verse. If Marairead Cham'ron and Mairearad Chaimbeul are the same person, the contents of her combined collections number fifty-four texts, with Mairearad Ghriogarach's corpus in second place.

115 Byrne, 'A Window', p. 48.
116 Ibid., p. 53, note 55. Mairearad's own poetry does not appear to be represented in McLagan's collections.
117 Possibly the work of Anna Campbell (Bean a' Bharra) or her sister Barbara; see Black, *Campbells of the Ark*, pp. 329–31, and Ó Baoill, 'Oran do Bhean Chladh na Macraidh'.
118 'Oran le mairiread Ghrigarach is i san sgoil am peart', in *Co-chruinneach dh' orain thaghte Ghaeleach* (Edinburgh: John Elder, 1831), pp. 30–31, ed. and trans. by Michel Byrne, 'A window', p. 54. See also Domhnall Uilleam Stiùbhart, 'Women and Gender in the Early Modern Western Gàidhealtachd', in Ewan and Meikle, *Women in Scotland*, pp. 233–51 (pp. 241–42).
119 See McLeod, 'Gaelic Poetry and the British Military Enterprise', and Matthew Dziennik and Michael Newton, 'Egypt, Empire, and the Gaelic Literary Imagination', *International Review of Scottish Studies*, 43 (2018), pp. 1–40.
120 Macleod Hill, 'Reformed Theology', p. 105; see also Maciver, 'Concentric Loyalties', p. 120.
121 *Co-chruinneach dh' orain thaghte Ghaeleach*, pp. 38–40 (ll. 49–56), ed. and trans. Michel Byrne.
122 Mairearad's reference to tea dates the poem to the turn of the eighteenth century, prior to which it had been almost unknown; see Rev. Robert MacDonald, 'Parish of Fortingal [1838]', *The New Statistical Account of Scotland*, vol. 10 (1845), pp. 527–58 (p. 558). I am grateful to Michel Byrne for this reference.
123 Byrne, 'A Window', pp. 53–54.
124 'Do Leanabh-Altraim a bha aice', ll. 11–12. For other poems addressed to fosterlings, see Anne C. Frater, 'Clann and Clan: Children of the Gaelic Nobility, c. 1500–c. 1800', in *Children and Youth in Premodern Scotland*, ed. Janay Nugent and Elizabeth Ewan (Woodbridge: Boydell Press, 2015), pp. 89–103 (pp. 89–96).
125 E.g. 'Luinneag an Fhoghairidh, le Anna Ghobh, air dhi dol thun an fhogharaidh Ghalld anns a' bhliadhna 1827', pp. 104–05; Paul Cameron, 'Perthshire Gaelic songs and their composers', *Transactions of the Gaelic Society of Inverness*, 17 (1890–91), pp. 126–70 (p. 164). See also Maciver, 'Concentric loyalties', pp. 109–10.
126 Ian Duncan and Sheila Kidd, 'The Nineteenth Century', in *International Companion to Scottish Poetry*, ed. Carla Sassi, pp. 63–74.
127 Black, 'The Gaelic Book', esp. pp. 181–82; Anja Gunderloch, 'Wives and Mothers, Sisters and Daughters: Donnchadh Bàn Macintyre's

Women Subscribers', in *Rannsachadh na Gàidhlig 6: Papers read at Rannsachadh na Gàidhlig 6, held at the University of Aberdeen 23–26 August 2010*, ed. Nancy R. McGuire and Colm Ó Baoill (Obar Dheathainn: An Clò Gàidhealach, 2013), pp. 161–77.
128 Stana Nenadic, 'The Impact of the Military Profession on Highland Gentry Families, c. 1730–1830', *Scottish Historical Review*, 85.1 (2006), pp. 75–99. For the broadest context of Gaels and the British military, see Matthew Dziennik, *The Fatal Land: War, Empire, and the Highland Soldier in British America* (New Haven-London: Yale University Press, 2015).
129 Untitled, beginning ''S gur e mo rùn an t-àrmann'; GUL GB 247 MS Gen 583, pp. 117–18; *MacDiarmid MS Anthology*, ed. Thomson, pp. 213–15.
130 *Sean Dain*, p. 45; discussed by Coventry, 'Reconsideration', p. 119.
131 Margaret MacDonell, *The Emigrant Experience: Songs of Highland Emigrants in North America* (Toronto: University of Toronto Press, 1982), p. 10.
132 'Oran na Banaraich', GUL 1042, 210, 4a–b; ed. and trans. Newton, *Bho Chluaidh Gu Calasraid*, pp. 256-59.
133 Ibid., p. 254.
134 Newton, *We're Indians Sure Enough*, pp. 176–78, 239.
135 Michael Newton, 'Unsettling Iain mac Mhurchaidh's Slumber: The Carolina Lullaby, Authorship, and the Influence of Print Media on Gaelic Oral Tradition', *Aiste*, 4 (2014), pp. 131–55.
136 *The Emigrant Experience*, ed. and trans. MacDonell, pp. 131–37.
137 Maciver, 'Concentric Loyalties', pp. 121–24.
138 'Nuadh Oran, air a Leantuinn', ed. and trans. Newton, *Were Indians Sure Enough*, p. 161, from *An Gaidheal*, 1 (1872), pp. 268–70, 322–24.
139 Martin and Mathis, 'Elegy and Commemorative Writing'.
140 Translated by Ruairidh Maciver, 'Concentric Loyalties', pp. 115–16; cf. Colin Chisholm, 'Unpublished Old Gaelic songs', *Transactions of the Gaelic Society of Inverness*, XII (1886), pp. 118–67 (pp. 135–36).
141 *Cochruinneacha taoghta de shaothair nam Bard Gaëlach*, pp. 440–42, trans. Ronald Black, *An Lasair*, pp. 174–79 (ll. 55–59). Its subject and composer are unclear, despite a range of titles in the Stewarts', Young's, and subsequent collections; id., pp. 444–46.
142 *Bàrdachd Shìlis na Ceapaich*, ed. and trans. Colm Ó Baoill, pp. 70–75 (ll. 831–35).
143 Mathis, 'Presence, Absence, and Audience', p. 199.
144 Ó Baoill, *Mairghread nighean Lachlainn*, p. 168.

145 'Gaoir nam ban Muileach, le Maiririad Ni Lachuinn', originally in Turner, *Comhchruinneacha do dh' orain taghta Ghaidhealach*, pp. 1–8; ed. and trans. Black, *An Lasair*, pp. 60–73 (ll. 201–08).
146 Ibid., p. 393; Ó Baoill, '"Neither Out nor In"', p. 147.
147 Thomas Owen Clancy, 'Mourning Fearchar Ó Maoilchiaráin: Texts, Transmission and Transformation', in *Cànan agus Cultar: Rannsachadh na Gàidhlig 3*, ed. Wilson McLeod et al. (Edinburgh: Dunedin Academic Press, 2006), pp. 57–71.
148 GUL 1042, 152, 1a–2b (cf. 137, 11a–12b), ll. 9–10.
149 Gillies, 'Clan Donald Bards', p. 108. The elegy's subject is a MacDonald of Glengarry, probably a brother of Alasdair Dubh.
150 GUL 1042, 152, 1a–2b, ll. 89–96.
151 [Rev. James McLagan] 'Number XLI: Parishes of Blair Atholl and Strowan', in *Statistical Account of Scotland*, ed. John Sinclair, 21 vols (Edinburgh: William Creech, 1791–99), vol. II, pp. 461–82 (p. 462).

12. Common Sense Philosophy and Sentimental Fiction: Eighteenth-Century Scottish Women Novelists

1 Michelle Levy, 'Women and Print Culture, 1750–1830', in *The History of British Women's Writing*, ed. Jacqueline Labbe, 10 vols (New York: Palgrave Macmillan, 2013), v, 32.
2 Jean Marishall, *A Series of Letters*, 2 vols (Edinburgh: C. Elliot 1789), II, 172–73.
3 Ibid., p. 149.
4 See G. J. Barker-Benfield, *The Culture of Sensibility: Sex and Society in Eighteenth-Century Britain* (Chicago: University of Chicago Press, 1992), and Claudia Johnson, *Equivocal Beings: Politics, Gender, and Sentimentality in the 1790s* (Chicago: University of Chicago Press, 1995).
5 For additional information on Scottish women writers' connections to the Scottish Enlightenment, see Rosalind Carr, *Gender and Enlightenment Culture in Eighteenth-Century Scotland* (Edinburgh: Edinburgh University Press, 2014); Claire Grogan, *Politics and Genre in the Works of Elizabeth Hamilton* (New York: Routledge, 2012); and Pam Perkins, *Women Writers in the Edinburgh Enlightenment* (Amsterdam: Rodopi, 2010).
6 Reid's most sustained defence of ridicule and its philosophical utility was published in his 1785 *Essays on the Intellectual Powers of Man*, very late in his career; however, these essays were based on lectures he had given throughout his career first as a professor

in Aberdeen and then in Glasgow. Most scholars see his later work as developing his influential *An Inquiry into the Human Mind and the Principles of Common Sense*, which was first published in 1764.

7   Mark Towsey, *Reading the Scottish Enlightenment: Books and their Provincial Readers in Provincial Scotland, 1750–1820* (Boston: Brill, 2010), pp. 282–87.
8   Ibid., p. 284.
9   Thomas Reid, *Essays on the Intellectual Powers of Man*, ed. Derek Brookes and Knud Haakonssen (Edinburgh: Edinburgh University Press, 2002), p. 453.
10 Reid, pp. 412, 443, 453.
11 Marshall, *Series of Letters*, II, pp. 135–36.
12 Ibid., p. 136.
13 Reid, p. 428.
14 Ibid., p. 462.
15 Ibid.
16 James Beattie, *Essays: On Poetry and Music, as They Affect the Mind; On Laughter and Ludicrous Composition; On the Utility of Classical Learning* (Edinburgh: William Creech, 1770), p. 329.
17 Beattie, p. 351.
18 Beattie, p. 416.
19 Beattie, p. 425.
20 Henry Home [Lord Kames], *Elements of Criticism*, ed. Peter Jones, 2 vols (Indianapolis: Liberty Fund, 2005), I, 194.
21 Home [Kames], p. 193.
22 Home [Kames], pp. 194–95.
23 Giovanni Grandi, 'Reid on Ridicule and Common Sense', *Journal of Scottish Philosophy*, 6 (2008), 72.
24 See Simon Dickie, *Cruelty and Laughter: Forgotten Comic Literature and the Unsentimental Eighteenth Century* (Chicago: University of Chicago Press, 2011).
25 Claire Grogan, *Politics and Genre in the Works of Elizabeth Hamilton* (New York: Routledge, 2012), p. 25; Anthony Mandal, 'Introduction,' in Mary Brunton, *Self-Control*, ed. Anthony Mandal (New York: Routledge, 2014), pp. xxxiv and xxxv.
26 Carol Anderson and Aileen M. Riddell, 'The Other Great Unknowns: Women Fiction Writers of the Early Nineteenth Century', in *A History of Scottish Women's Writing*, ed. Douglas Gifford and Dorothy McMillan (Edinburgh: Edinburgh University Press, 1997), p. 191.

27 Sentimental fiction's engagement with the psychological consequences of sexual assault has been a major element of scholarship on the genre since Frances Ferguson's 'Rape and the Rise of the Novel', *Representations*, 20 (1987), 88–112.
28 Jean Marishall, *The History of Miss Clarinda Cathcart, and Miss Fanny Renton*, 2 vols. (London: Francis Noble and John Noble, 1765), I, 17.
29 Ibid.
30 Ibid., p. 50.
31 Ibid., pp. 146, 205.
32 Marishall, *Clarinda*, II, 55.
33 Ibid., p. 57.
34 Ibid.
35 Ibid., p. 93.
36 Ibid.
37 Ibid., p. 102.
38 Ibid., p. 137.
39 Ibid., p. 139.
40 Mary Brunton, *Self-Control* (London: Pandora, 1986), p. 41.
41 Ibid., p. 42.
42 Ibid., p. 234.
43 Ibid., p. 66.
44 Ibid.
45 Ibid., p. 74.
46 Ibid. Johann Caspar Lavater's *Essays on Physiognomy* was first translated into English in 1789. Lavater argued that the physical aspects of appearance were indicators of character traits and could be read as a gauge of a person's moral disposition. For more on Lavater's study of physiognomy and character in eighteenth-century fiction more generally, see Deidre Lynch, *The Economy of Character: Novels, Market Culture, and the Business of Inner Meaning* (Chicago: University of Chicago Press, 1998).
47 Brunton, p. 128.
48 Ibid., p. 279.
49 Ibid.
50 Elizabeth Hamilton, *Memoirs of Modern Philosophers*, ed. Claire Grogan (Peterborough, Ontario: Broadview Press, 2000), p. 38.
51 Ibid., p. 78.
52 Ibid., p. 75.
53 Ibid., p. 216.
54 Ibid., p. 308.

55 Ibid.
56 Ibid.
57 Ibid., p. 172.
58 Mandal, 'Introduction,' p. xiii.
59 Although critics such as Pam Perkins have devoted whole studies to the work of Scottish women novelists and they figure prominently in studies of Scottish literature such as Juliet Shields, *Sentimental Literature and Anglo-Scottish Identity, 1745–1820* (New York: Cambridge University Press, 2010) and Rivka Swenson, *Essential Scots and the Idea of Unionism in Anglo-Scottish Literature, 1603–1832* (Lewisburg, PA: Bucknell University Press, 2015), the companions and handbooks that are meant to facilitate our knowledge of British women writers tend to exclude or marginalise even the best known Scottish women novelists.

13. Scottish Enlightenment Inquiry in Gaelic Poetry: 'Air Fàsachadh na Gàidhealtachd Albannaich'

1 Roger L. Emerson, *Essays on David Hume, Medical Men and the Scottish Enlightenment: 'Industry, Knowledge and Humanity'* (Farnham: Ashgate, 2009), p. 40.
2 Robert Crawford, *Scotland's Books: A History of Scottish Literature* (Oxford: Oxford University Press, 2009), p. 306.
3 Richard B. Sher, *The Enlightenment and the Book: Scottish Authors and Their Publishers in Eighteenth-Century Britain, Ireland, and America* (Chicago: University of Chicago Press, 2006), pp. 193–94.
4 Donald E. Meek, 'Evangelicalism, Ossianism and the Enlightenment: The Many Masks of Dugald Buchanan', in *Crossing the Highland Line: Cross-Currents in Eighteenth-Century Scottish Writing*, ed. Christopher MacLachlan (Glasgow: ASLS, 2009), pp. 97–112 (p. 106).
5 *Alexander MacDonald: Bard of the Gaelic Enlightenment / Alasdair mac Mhaighstir Alasdair: Bàrd an t-Soillearachaidh Ghàidhealaich*, ed. Camille Dressler and Domhnall Uilleam Stiùbhart (Kershader, Isle of Lewis: Islands Book Trust, 2012).
6 John Walker, *An Economical History of the Hebrides and Highlands of Scotland*, 2 vols (Edinburgh: Edinburgh University Press, 1808), I, pp. 19–20.
7 Charles Withers, *Gaelic in Scotland 1698–1981: The Geographical History of a Language* (Edinburgh: John Donald, 1984), p. 71.
8 For recent comment see the text of Donald Meek's 2018 O' Donnell Lecture: 'The Gaelic Literary Enlightenment: The Making of the

Scottish Gaelic New Testament and Associated Books, 1750–1820', meekwrite.blogspot.com/2018/06/the-gaelic-literary-enlightenment.html [accessed 2 February 2020].

9   For an overview of the collection see Derick S. Thomson, 'The McLagan MSS in Glasgow University Library: A Survey', *Transactions of the Gaelic Society of Inverness*, 58 (1995), 406–24.

10 Glasgow, University of Glasgow Library Special Collections, MS Gen 1042.

11 Thomson, 'The McLagan MSS', p. 407.

12 For some comment on his methods see Victoria Henshaw, 'James Macpherson and His Contemporaries: The Methods and Networks of Collectors of Gaelic Poetry in Late Eighteenth-Century Scotland', *Journal for Eighteenth-Century Studies*, 39 (2016), 197–209. Henshaw's mention of McLagan's reticence about his own Gaelic, at p. 203, should be treated with caution and not understood to mean that he was not a fluent speaker. On McLagan's collecting in Ireland and the Isle of Man, see Sìm Innes, 'Fionn and Ailbhe's Riddles between Ireland and Scotland', in *Ollam: Studies in Gaelic and Related Traditions in Honor of Tomás Ó Cathasaigh*, ed. Matthieu Boyd (Madison, NJ: Fairleigh Dickinson University Press, 2016), pp. 271–85; Peadar Ó Muircheartaigh, '*Fin as Ossian* revisited: A Manx Ballad in Belanagare and Its Significance', *Zeitschrift für celtische Philologie*, 63 (2016), 95–127.

13 Thomson, 'The McLagan MSS', p. 407; Derick S. Thomson, 'Indexes of the Ossianic Ballads in the McLagan MSS', *Scottish Gaelic Studies*, 8 (1958), 177–224 (p. 204).

14 Charles Coventry, 'A Reconsideration of the Gillies Collection of Gaelic Poetry', *Studies in Scottish Literature*, 26 (1991), 199–206.

15 For an edition and translation of the poem see Michael Newton, *We're Indians Sure Enough: The Legacy of the Scottish Highlanders in the United States* ([n.p.]: Saorsa Media, 2001), pp. 43–47. This chapter makes use of that edition and translation, but notes where I have diverged significantly as a result of preferable alternative readings. For use of this poem for terminology to name the Highlands, see Wilson McLeod, 'Galldachd, Gàidhealtachd, Garbhchrìochan', *Scottish Gaelic Studies*, 19 (1999), 1–20.

16 The other three poems in MS 210 are: 'Òran an t-Sealgair' ('The Hunter's Song') which has 'Chaidh Ghàidhealtachd na fàsaich' ('The Highlands have become a desert') as a first line; 'A Loch Laomainn nan Lùb le Turasaiche' ('O Loch Lomond of the many bends by [a] Traveler'); Òran na Banaraich ('The Milkmaid's Song') which has

'O mo thìr a dh'àraich mi gu mìn' ('O my land, which reared me so gently') as the first line of the chorus. For editions and translations of all three see *Bho Chluaidh gu Calasraid / From the Clyde to Callander: Gaelic Songs, Poetry, Tales and Traditions*, ed. Michael Newton (Glasgow: Grimsay Press, 2010 repr. ; Stornoway: Acair, 1999), pp. 246–59. See also 'A Lennox Song', *The Highland Monthly*, 1 (1890), 342–44 (for the Loch Lomond song). Newton's edition of the final song has 'Oran na Bantraich' ('The Widow's Song'), but this should be emended to 'Oran na Banaraich' ('The Dairymaid's song'). All four poems are only known from the McLagan manuscripts.

17 Newton, *We're Indians*, p. 44.
18 Newton, *We're Indians*, p. 277 (footnote 31).
19 *Collins Encyclopaedia of Scotland*, ed. John Keay and Julia Keay (London: HarperCollins, 2000), p. 77. For a longer overview see *James Hogg: Queen Hynde*, ed. Suzanne Gilbert and Douglas S. Mack (Edinburgh: Edinburgh University Press, 1998), pp. 238–44; for chronology see Denis Rixson, *The Hebridean Traveller* (Edinburgh: Birlinn, 2004), pp. 262–66.
20 For Boece I have used the online hypertext critical edition of the 1575 version: Hector Boethius [Boece], *Scotorum Historia*, ed. Dana F. Sutton (2010), in *The Philological Museum* www.philological.bham. ac.uk/boece/contents.html [accessed 3 February 2020]. For Bellenden I have used *The History and Chronicles of Scotland Written in Latin by Hector Boece*, trans. by John Bellenden, 2 vols (Edinburgh: W. and C. Tait, 1821).
21 Boece, 'Liber I', para. 36; Bellenden, 'The First Buke', Chapter 12, vol. 1.
22 Boece, 'Praeliminaria', para. 15–16; Bellenden, 'The Cosmographe and Discription of Albion', Chapter 7. See also Boece, 'Liber II', para. 39; Bellenden, 'The Secund Buke', Chapter 15.
23 Thomas Pennant, *A Tour in Scotland and Voyage to the Hebrides, 1772*, ed. Andrew Simmons (Edinburgh: Birlinn, 1998), p. 356.
24 *The Statistical Account of Scotland. Drawn up from the Communications of the Ministers of the Different Parishes*, ed. John Sinclair, 21 vols (Edinburgh: William Creech, 1791–99), VI (1793), p. 180.
25 'Ball-tathaich nan ceannuich an allaid' was emended by Newton to 'Balla-tathaich nan ceannsaich an allaidh' to give 'the familiar walls of those who tamed the savages', *We're Indians*, p. 44.
26 Bellenden, 'The Cosmographe and Discription of Albion', Chapter 7 and Chapter 5.

27 I have been unable to find another example of 'ball-tathaich'. Robert Armstrong, in *Gaelic Dictionary* (London: J. Duncan, 1825), p. 902, gives 'àite tathaich' ('place of resort'). *Ball* is usually 'object of/instrument of' and 'tathaich' visitation. It is possible that 'ball-tathaich' is used here as a synonym for 'àite-tathaich' given the appearance of 'a place: locus' as a subsidiary meaning of 'ball' in the 1828 Highland Society of Scotland's *Dictionarium Scoto-Celticum: A Dictionary of the Gaelic Language* […], 2 vols (Edinburgh: W. Blackwood, 1828), I, 90 (from an Ossianic translation context). The spacing of 'ceannaich an alluid' for 'ceannaichean allaidh' is somewhat odd and requires us to accept a genitive plural 'nan ceannaichean' rather than 'nan ceannaiche' which would arguably be more usual in the eighteenth century (for evidence of this see *Corpas na Gàidhlig* dasg.ac.uk/corpus/ [accessed 3 February 2020]).

28 'Uncouth, Unco', *Dictionary of the Scots Language / Dictionar o the Scots Leid* www.dsl.ac.uk/entry/dost/uncouth [accessed 3 February 2020].

29 'Anall', *The Electronic Dictionary of the Irish Language* www.dil.ie/3340 [accessed 3 February 2020].

30 Alistair MacDomhnuill, *Leabhar a Theagasc Ainminnin* […] (Edinburgh: Raibeard Fleming, 1741), p. 184.

31 William Shaw, *A Galic and English Dictionary* (London: [n. pub], 1780), n.p. Shaw's dictionary gives 'ceannaich' as a word for 'strife'; it also appears in Armstrong, p. 106, as 'strife; contention for supremacy or superiority'.

32 Newton gives 'fuil-siachraidh' ('pithless blood'), presumably using the Gaelic word 'siachaireach' ('pithless'). *We're Indians*, p. 44.

33 MacDomhnuill, p. 56.

34 It seems that by the modern period the distinction between Old Irish 'síabair' ('phantom') and 'sídaige/síthaige' ('fairy') had broken down somewhat. Later spellings and variants include: 'síofra', 'siafra', 'siabhra', 'siabhrach' 'sìochaire', 'sìbhreach', 'sìthiche', and so on. 'Fuil síofraí', as we see it in Mac Mhaighstir Alasdair's 1741 vocabulary seems more like Irish than Scottish Gaelic. 'Fuilsiofri' for 'pumice' does appear in Edward O' Reilly, *Sanas Gaoidhilge-Sagsbhearla, An Irish-English Dictionary* […] (Dublin: J. Barlow, 1817), n.p. It also appears in Shaw, n.p. However, I am unaware of other Irish examples. In the Ben Nevis poem, as it appears in the manuscript, the form used is 'fuil-siachraidh', and is therefore closer to Scottish Gaelic usage.

35 For 'fuil sìochaire' meaning 'blood stone', see *The Gaelic Otherworld: John Gregorson Campbell's Superstitions of the Highlands and Islands of Scotland and Witchcraft and Second Sight in the Highlands and Islands*, ed. Ronald Black (Edinburgh: Birlinn, 2005), p. 108. For 'fuil sìochaire' and 'fuil nan sluagh' meaning 'red crotal lichen', see Alexander Carmichael, *Carmina Gadelica* […], 2nd edn, 6 vols (Edinburgh: Oliver and Boyd, 1928–54; Edinburgh: Scottish Academic Press, 1971), II (1928), ed. Ella Carmichael Watson, p. 357; Carmichael, *Carmina Gadelica* […], VI: *Indexes* (1971), ed. Angus Matheson, pp. 54, 75.
36 Pennant, p. 358.
37 Tom Furniss, '"As if created by fusion of matter after some intense heat": Pioneering Geological Observations in Thomas Pennant's Tours in Scotland', in *Enlightenment Travel and British Identities: Thomas Pennant's Tours in Scotland and Wales*, ed. Mary-Ann Constantine and Nigel Leask (London: Anthem Press, 2017), pp. 163–81 (p. 170).
38 *The Statistical Account*, VI, 180.
39 I hope to expand on McLagan's possible authorship and the relationship between the Gaelic poem and the prose account in English elsewhere. 'Of Berigonium' is part of Glasgow, University of Glasgow Library Special Collections, MS Gen 1042/14.
40 James Hutton, 'Theory of the Earth', *Transactions of the Royal Society of Edinburgh*, 1 (1788), 209–304 (p. 275).
41 Hutton, p. 275.
42 John Sinclair *et al.*, *The Poems of Ossian in the Original Gaelic* […], 3 vols (London: G. and W. Nicol, 1807), III, 498. For more on this see Nigel Leask, 'Fingalian Topographies: Ossian and the Highland Tour, 1760–1805', *Journal for Eighteenth-Century Studies*, 39 (2016), 183–96 (p. 191).
43 John MacInnes, 'The Panegyric Code in Gaelic Poetry and its Historical Background', *Transactions of the Gaelic Society of Inverness*, 50 (1978), 435–98.
44 Keith Norman MacDonald, *MacDonald Bards from Mediaeval Times* (Edinburgh: Norman Macleod, 1900), pp. 8–13, 15–19.
45 Tradition links the sixteenth-century poet Dòmhnall mac Fhionnlaigh nan Dàn to Glencoe: Robert A. Rankin, 'Oran na Comhachaig: Text and Tradition', *Transactions of the Gaelic Society of Glasgow*, 5 (1958), 122–171 (pp. 127–28), and *Òran na Comhachaig le Dòmhnall mac Fhionnlaigh nan Dàn*, ed. Pat Menzies (Glasgow: SGTS, 2012). For seventeenth-century Gaelic poets connected to the MacDonalds of Glencoe see MacDonald, pp. 20–22.

46 Ronald Black, 'The Poetry of Ailean Dall', in *Gael and Lowlander in Scottish Literature: Cross-Currents in Scottish Writing in the Nineteenth Century*, ed. Christopher MacLachlan and Ronald W. Renton (Glasgow: ASLS, 2015), pp. 22–40.
47 [Anne MacVicar Grant], *Letters from the Mountains; Being the Real Correspondence of a Lady between the Years 1773 and 1807*, 4th edn, 3 vols (London: Longman, Hurst, Rees, and Orme, 1809), I, 79–80.
48 Leask, p. 187.
49 Donald Meek, 'The Sublime Gael: The Impact of Macpherson's Ossian on Literary Creativity and Cultural Perception in Gaelic Scotland', in *The Reception of Ossian in Europe*, ed. Howard Gaskill (London: Thoemmes, 2004), pp. 40–66 (p. 65).
50 Charles Withers, 'The Historical Creation of the Scottish Highlands', in *The Manufacture of Scottish History*, ed. Ian Donnachie and Christopher Whatley (Edinburgh: Polygon, 1992), pp. 143–56 (p. 148).
51 Adam Smith, *The Glasgow Edition of the Works and Correspondence of Adam Smith*, 8 vols (Oxford: Clarendon Press, 1975–2001), II: *An Inquiry into the Nature and Causes of the Wealth of Nations* (vol. 2, 1976), ed. William B. Todd, pp. 782–83.
52 Thomas M. Devine, 'A Conservative People? Scottish Gaeldom in the Age of Improvement', in *Eighteenth Century Scotland: New Perspectives*, ed. T. M. Devine and J. R. Young (East Linton: Tuckwell Press, 1999), pp. 225–36 (p. 229).
53 'Scotch Arcadia' dates to 1771, from Tobias Smollett, *The Expedition of Humphry Clinker*, ed. Evan Gottlieb, 2nd edn (New York: Norton, 2015), p. 263; 'contemporary ancestor' is from Withers, 'Creation of the Scottish Highlands', in *Manufacture of Scottish History*, ed. Donnachie and Whatley, p. 147.
54 Smith, *Works and Correspondence of Adam Smith*, V: *Lectures on Jurisprudence* (1978), ed. R. L. Meek, D. D. Raphael, and Peter Stein, p. 14. This dates to 1762.
55 Penny Fielding, *Scotland and the Fictions of Geography: North Britain 1760–1830* (Cambridge: Cambridge University Press, 2008), p. 72.
56 On epic and the Scottish Enlightenment see Colin Kidd, 'The Scottish Enlightenment and the Matter of Troy', *Journal of the British Academy*, 6 (2018), 97–130 (p. 109).
57 David Allan, '"Winged Horses, Fiery Dragons, and Monstrous Giants": Historiography and Imaginative Literature in the Scottish Enlightenment', in *The Scottish Enlightenment and Literary Culture*, ed. Ralph

McLean, Ronnie Young and Kenneth Simpson (Lewisburg, PA: Bucknell University Press, 2016), pp. 19–36 (p. 31).

58 [David Hume], *A True Account of the Behaviour and Conduct of Archibald Stewart Esq.* (London: M. Cooper, 1748), pp. 6–7.

59 Colin Kidd, 'Gaelic Antiquity and National Identity in Enlightenment Ireland and Scotland', *English Historical Review*, 109 (November 1994), 1197–1214 (p. 1206).

60 *The Letters of David Hume*, ed. J. Y. T. Greig, 2 vols (Oxford: Oxford University Press, 1932), I: *1727–65*, p. 195.

61 [Henry Home, Lord Kames], *Sketches of the History of Man. In Two Volumes*, 2 vols (Edinburgh: W. Creech, 1774), I, p. 308. This is discussed by Fredrik Albritton Jonsson, *Enlightenment's Frontier: The Scottish Highlands and the Origins of Environmentalism* (New Haven: Yale University Press, 2013), p. 30.

62 Newton emends this to give 'Theich an sluagh de Mhòr-Thìr Choluim' ('The population has fled from King Malcom's mainland'): *We're Indians*, p. 46. However, this should be understood as a Gaelic rendering of Columbia, commonly used as a name for North America in the eighteenth century.

63 Stana Nenadic, *Lairds and Luxury: The Highland Gentry in Eighteenth-Century Scotland* (Edinburgh: John Donald, 2007), p. 53.

64 Christopher J. Berry, *The Idea of Luxury: A Conceptual and Historical Investigation* (Cambridge: Cambridge University Press, 1994); Berry, *The Idea of Commercial Society in the Scottish Enlightenment* (Edinburgh: Edinburgh University Press, 2013).

65 Berry, *The Idea of Commercial Society*, p. 160.

66 [Kames], p. 207.

67 Adam Ferguson, *An Essay on the History of Civil Society*, ed. Fania Oz-Salzberger (Cambridge: Cambridge University Press, 1995), pp. 231–47. For the debate on the impact of his own Highland identity on his thinking, see Duncan Forbes, 'Adam Ferguson and the Idea of Community', in Douglas Young, *Edinburgh in the Age of Reason: A Commemoration* (Edinburgh: Edinburgh University Press, 1967), pp. 40–47; Jack A. Hill, *Adam Ferguson and Ethical Integrity: The Man and His Prescriptions for the Moral Life* (Lanham, MD: Lexington Books, 2017), p. 9.

68 Ferguson, p. 195.

69 David L. Blaney and Naeem Inayatullah, *Savage Economics: Wealth, Poverty, and the Temporal Walls of Capitalism* (Abingdon, Oxon: Routledge, 2010), pp. 91–92.

70 For an edition and translation see Ruaidhri Mac Mhuirich, *The Blind Harper (An Clàrsair Dall): The Songs of Roderick Morison and his Music*, ed. William Matheson (Edinburgh: SGTS, 1970), pp. 58–73. We might note that the 'Augustan elements' of this song are pointed out by Ronald Black and Gerard Carruthers, 'The Eighteenth Century', in *The International Companion to Scottish Poetry*, ed. Carla Sassi (Glasgow: Scottish Literature International, 2015), pp. 54–63 (p. 55).
71 MacInnes, p. 456.
72 Nenadic, p. 1
73 Nenadic, p. 2.
74 [Hume], pp. 6–7.

14. Eighteenth-Century Scottish Poetry and Ecology

1 John Veitch, *The Feeling for Nature in Scottish Poetry*, 2 vols (Edinburgh: Blackwood, 1887), II, 2.
2 Ibid., I, 7
3 Ibid., II, 24–25.
4 On Scottish poetry and the question of national space, see Christopher Whyte, *Modern Scottish Poetry* (Edinburgh: Edinburgh University Press, 2004), pp. 5–17; on the question of place in earlier Scottish literature, see Penny Fielding, *Scotland and the Fictions of Geography: North Britain 1760–1830* (Cambridge: Cambridge University Press, 2008); on the basic contours of eighteenth-century Scottish economic history, see T. M. Devine, C. H. Lee, and G. C. Preden, *The Transformation of Scotland: The Economy Since 1700* (Edinburgh: Edinburgh University Press, 2005).
5 Here again see Fielding, in particular pp. 13–39, but also Charles W. J. Withers, *Geography, Science and National Identity: Scotland since 1520* (Cambridge: Cambridge University Press, 2001), and Roger Emerson, who singles out Scottish geography, 'which made Scots poor but which also endowed them with the means of improvement and posed questions which the enlightened studied and sought to answer', as pre-eminent among the contexts for the Scottish Enlightenment in 'The Contexts of the Scottish Enlightenment', in *The Cambridge Companion to the Scottish Enlightenment*, ed. Alexander Broadie (Cambridge: Cambridge University Press, 2003), pp. 9–30, (p. 9). On the role of Scottish writers in imagining their nation from the eighteenth century to the present day, see Cairns Craig, *Intending Scotland: Explorations in Scottish Culture since the Enlightenment* (Edinburgh: Edinburgh University Press, 2009).

6 On environmental history in the context of world systems and earth systems analysis, see *The World System and the Earth System: Global Socioenvironmental Change and Sustainability since the Neolithic*, ed. Alf Hornborg and Carole Crumley (Walnut Creek, CA: Left Coast Press, 2007); for the comparable long-view history of Scotland, see Robert J. Price, *Scotland's Environment during the last 30,000 Years* (Edinburgh: Scottish Academic Press, 1983).

7 Fiona Stafford, 'Scottish Poetry and Regional Literary Expression', in *The Cambridge History of English Literature, 1660–1780*, ed. John Richetti (Cambridge: Cambridge University Press, 2005), pp. 340–62.

8 Janet Sorensen, *Strange Vernaculars: How Eighteenth-Century Slang, Cant, Provincial Languages, and Nautical Jargon Became English* (Princeton: Princeton University Press, 2017), p. 142; Alan Bewell, *Natures in Translation: Romanticism and Colonial Natural History* (Baltimore: Johns Hopkins University Press, 2016).

9 Robert Burns, 'Epistle to J. L[aprai]k, An Old Scotch Bard', in *The Poems and Songs of Robert Burns*, ed. James Kinsley, 3 vols (Oxford: Clarendon, 1968), I: pp. 85–89 (p. 87), ll. 73–74.

10 Burns, in *Poems and Songs*, III: p. 970.

11 Leith Davis, *Acts of Union: Scotland and the Literary Negotiation of the British Nation, 1707–1830* (Stanford: Stanford University Press, 1998), p. 108.

12 Burns, 'To W. S[impso]n, Ochiltree', in *Poems and Songs*, I: pp. 93–98 (p. 95), l. 79–80.

13 *Ibid.*, p. 96, ll. 91–96.

14 See, for example, Burns's letters to Miss Alexander, 18 November 1786; to Mrs Dunlop, 1 January 1789; to Capt. Grose, June 1790, and to Mrs Dunlop, 15 December 1793, in which he praises Cowper as the poet of 'God and Nature'. *The Letters of Robert Burns*, ed. J. de Lancey Ferguson, 2 vols (Oxford: Clarendon Press, 1931), I, 50–51, 282–84; II, 22–24, 223–25.

15 Burns, 'Song, composed in August', in *Poems and Songs*, I: pp. 4–6 (p. 4), l. 1.

16 Ibid., p. 5, l. 25–32.

17 Burns, 'To a Mountain-Daisy, On turning one down, with the Plough, in April – 1786', in *Poems and Songs*, I: pp. 228–29 (p. 229), ll. 31–32, 37–38, 49–50.

18 Fiona Stafford, *Local Attachments: The Province of Poetry* (Oxford: Oxford University Press, 2010), pp. 179–80.

19 Fielding, pp. 40–70.

20 Nigel Leask, *Robert Burns and Pastoral* (Oxford: Oxford University Press, 2010), pp. 10–11. On the culture of improvement see more recently the collection of essays in *Cultures of Improvement in Scottish Romanticism, 1707–1840*, ed. Alex Benchimol and Gerard Lee McKeever, (London: Routledge, 2018).
21 Burns, 'On a Scotch Bard Gone to the West Indies', in *Poems and Songs*, I: 238–39 (p. 239), ll. 55–60.
22 See, for example, Alex Benchimol, 'Let Scotland Flourish by the Printing of the Word: Commerce, Civic Enlightenment and National Improvement in the Glasgow Advertiser, 1783–1800', in *Cultures of Improvement*, ed. Benchimol and McKeever, pp. 67–69; Gerard Carruthers, 'Robert Burns and Slavery', *The Drouth*, 26 (2008), 21–26; Leith Davis, 'Burns and Transnational Culture', in *The Edinburgh Companion to Robert Burns*, ed. Gerard Carruthers (Edinburgh: Edinburgh University Press), pp. 150–63; Nigel Leask, 'Scotland's Literature of Empire and Emigration', in *The Edinburgh History of Scottish Literature*, 3 vols, II: *Enlightenment, Britain and Empire (1707–1918)*, ed. Susan Manning (Edinburgh: Edinburgh University Press, 2007), pp. 153–62.
23 Burns, 'On a Scotch Bard Gone to the West Indies', p. 239, ll. 49, 54
24 J. R. McNeill, 'The Ecological Atlantic', in *The Oxford Handbook of the Atlantic World: 1450–1850*, ed. Nicholas Canny and Philip Morgan (Oxford: Oxford University Press, 2011), pp. 289–304 (p. 303).
25 David McDermott Hughes, 'Plantation Slaves, the First Fuel', in *Energy Without Conscience: Oil, Climate Change, and Complicity* (Durham, NC: Duke University Press, 2017), pp. 29–40, (pp. 36, 40). On Burns and the transatlantic world, see *Robert Burns and Transatlantic Culture*, ed. Sharon Alker, Leith Davis, and Holly Faith Nelson (Farnham: Ashgate, 2012), in particular, Murray Pittock's 'Slavery as a Political Metaphor in Scotland and Ireland in the Age of Burns', pp. 19–30.
26 *Anthropocene or Capitalocene?: Nature, History, and the Crisis of Capitalism*, ed. Jason W. Moore (San Francisco: PM Press, 2016), p. xii.
27 *The Bioregional Imagination: Literature, Ecology, and Place*, ed. Tom Lynch, Cheryll Glotfelty, and Karla Armbruster (Athens: University of Georgia Press, 2012), p. 9.
28 The phrase 'on the other side of sorrow' is taken from Sorley Maclean's 1939 poem 'The Cuillin' and provides the title for James Hunter's defense of Gaelic environmental traditions, *On the Other Side of Sorrow: Nature and People in the Scottish Highlands* (Edinburgh: Mainstream, 1995).

29 William Collins, 'An Ode on the Popular Superstitions of the Highlands of Scotland, Considered as the Subject of Poetry', in Thomas Gray and William Collins, *Poetical Works*, ed. Roger Lonsdale (Oxford: Oxford University Press, 1977), pp. 168–73 (pp. 168, 169, 172), ll. 13–14, 20, 25, 41, 33, 188–90.
30 Ibid., p. 172., ll. 174–75.
31 James Macpherson, *The Poems of Ossian and Related Works*, ed. Howard Gaskill (Edinburgh: Edinburgh University Press, 1996), pp. 5, 474.
32 Matthew Gelbart, *The Invention of 'Folk Music' and 'Art Music': Emerging Categories from Ossian to Wagner* (Cambridge: Cambridge University Press, 2007), pp. 60–66.
33 T. C. Smout, 'The Highlands and Roots of Green Consciousness' in *Exploring Environmental History: Selected Essays* (Edinburgh: Edinburgh University Press, 2011), pp. 21–51.
34 Meg Bateman, 'The Environmentalism of Donnchadh Bàn: Pragmatic or Mythic?', in *Crossing the Highland Line: Cross-Currents in Eighteenth-Century Scottish Writing*, ed. Christopher MacLachlan (Glasgow: ASLS, 2009), pp. 123–36; Michael Newton, *Warriors of the Word: The World of the Scottish Highlanders* (Edinburgh: Birlinn, 2009); Hunter, *Other Side of Sorrow*; John Murray, *Literature of the Gaelic Landscape: Song Poem and Tale* (Caithness: Whittles, 2017).
35 Hunter, p. 73.
36 Reprinted from *Gaelic Poetry in the Eighteenth Century*, ed. and trans. Derick S. Thomson (Aberdeen: ASLS, 1993), pp. 22–23.
37 Serenella Iovino and Serpil Oppermann, drawing upon Karen Barad, Jane Bennet, and David Abram, among others, define 'storied matter' in their introduction ('Stories Come to Matter') to *Material Ecocriticism* (Bloomington, IN: Indiana University Press, 2014), as 'a material "mesh" of meanings, properties, and processes, in which human and nonhuman players are interlocked in networks that produce undeniable signifying forces' (pp. 1–2).
38 *Gaelic Poetry*, ed. and trans. Thomson, p. 20.
39 James Thomson, *The Seasons*, ed. James Sambrook (Oxford: Clarendon Press, 1981), p. 12, ll. 197–202.
40 Wilson McLeod, *Divided Gaels: Gaelic Cultural Identities in Scotland and Ireland c. 1200–c. 1650* (Oxford: Oxford University Press, 2004). For a fuller treatment of Thomson's influence on Gaelic poetry of the seasons and the question of adaptation, see Natasha Sumner, 'James Thomson's "The Seasons", Gone Gaelic. The Emergence of a Poetic

Trend', *Proceedings of the Harvard Celtic Colloquium* 30 (2010), pp. 236–258. See also, Thomas Owen Clancy, 'Early Gaelic Nature Poetry Revisited', in Georgia Henley and Paul Russell (eds.), *Rhetoric and Reality in Medieval Celtic Literature: Studies in Honor of Daniel F. Melia* (Hamilton, NY: Colgate University Press, 2014), pp. 8–19.
41 Murray, p. 116.
42 Ronald Black (ed.), *An Lasair: Anthology of 18th Century Scottish Gaelic Verse* (Edinburgh: Birlinn, 2001), pp. 226–67.
43 Bateman, 'Environmentalism of Donnchadh Bàn', in *Crossing the Highland Line*, ed. MacLachlan, pp. 124, 128.
44 T. C. Smout, *Nature Contested: Environmental History in Scotland and Northern England Since 1600* (Edinburgh: Edinburgh University Press, 2000), p. 18.
45 Quoted in Hunter, pp. 84–85.
46 Robert A. Dodgshon, *From Chiefs to Landlords: Social and Economic Change in the Western Highlands and Islands, c. 1493–1820* (Edinburgh: Edinburgh University Press, 1998). A more idealised portrait of life in Glen Orchy during MacIntyre's lifetime is offered by Angus MacLeod in his introduction to *The Songs of Duncan Ban Macintyre*, (Edinburgh: Scottish Gaelic Texts, 1952) pp. xvii–xliv.
47 Mairi Stewart, 'Using the Woods, 1600–1850 (2) Managing for Profit', in *People and Woods in Scotland: A History,* ed. T. C. Smout (Edinburgh: Edinburgh University Press, 2003), pp. 105–27.
48 Macleod (ed.), *Songs of Duncan Ban MacIntyre*, pp. 390–91.
49 Ursula K. Heise, *Sense of Place and Sense of Planet: The Environmental Imagination of the Global* (Oxford: Oxford University Press, 2008), pp. 53, 55.
50 Garry MacKenzie, 'Utopias, Miniature Worlds and Global Networks in Modern Scottish Island Poetry', *Green Letters: Studies in Ecocriticism*, 17 (2013), 200–10, (p. 202).
51 Heise, p. 56.
52 Rhona Brown and Gerard Carruthers, 'Commemorating James Thomson, *The Seasons* in Scotland, and Scots Poetry', *Studies in the Literary Imagination*, 46 (2013), 71–89, (p. 71). See also Gerard Carruthers, '"Poured out extensive, and of watery wealth': Scotland in Thomson's *The Seasons*', in *Crossing the Highland Line*, ed. MacLachlan, pp. 21–30.
53 Burns, 'Address, To the Shade of Thomson, on crowning his Bust, at Ednam, Roxburgh-shire, with Bays' in *Poems and Songs* II: pp. 577–578 (p. 578) ll. 17, 19–20.

54 Mary Jane W. Scott, *James Thomson, Anglo-Scot* (Athens: University of Georgia Press, 1988).
55 David Fairer, '"Where Fuming Trees Refresh the Thirsty Air": The World of Eco-Georgic', *Studies in Eighteenth-Century Culture*, 40 (2011), 201–18 (p. 205); Tobias Menely, 'Late Holocene Poetics: Genre and Geohistory in *Beachy Head*', *European Romantic Review*, 28 (2017), 307–14 (p. 308).
56 Thomson, p. 178, ll. 862–65.
57 Ibid., ll. 866–70.
58 Alan Dugald McKillop, *The Background of Thomson's* Seasons (Minneapolis: University of Minnesota Press, 1942), pp. 131–36.
59 Thomson, pp. 178–179, ll. 871–78.
60 Andrew Fleming, *St Kilda and the Wider World: Tales of an Iconic Island* (Oxford: Windgather Press, 2005).
61 Thomson, pp. 179–180, ll. 879–93.
62 Thomson, p. 190, ll. 910–28.
63 Fredrik Albritton Jonsson, *Enlightenment's Frontier: The Scottish Highlands and the Origins of Environmentalism* (New Haven: Yale University Press, 2013), pp. 121–46.
64 Peter Womack, *Improvement and Romance: Constructing the Myth of the Highlands* (Houndmills: Macmillan, 1989), pp. 68–70; Denys Van Renen, '"Sick Nature Blasting": The Ecological Limits of British Imperialism in Thomson's *The Seasons*', *Journal of Scottish Historical Studies*, 38 (2018), 121–42, (pp. 123, 140).
65 Carole L. Crumley, 'Historical Ecology: Integrated Thinking at Multiple Temporal and Spatial Scales', in *World System and the Earth System*, ed. Hornborg and Crumley, p. 17. On recursive interconnection as a model of ecological critique, see Alf Hornborg's introduction to that collection of essays, 'Introduction: Conceptualizing Socioecological Systems', pp. 1–12.
66 Timothy Clark, *Ecocriticism on the Edge: The Anthropocene as a Threshold Concept* (London: Bloomsbury, 2015), p. 20.

15. The Poems of Ossian and the Birth of Modern Geology

1   *The International Companion to James Macpherson and the Poems of Ossian*, ed. Dafydd Moore (Glasgow: ASLS, 2017). For a *very* selective start to what is now a considerable body of work (and with an emphasis upon essay collections as a way to cover the ground), see: Fiona Stafford, *The Sublime Savage: James Macpherson and the Poems of Ossian* (Edinburgh: Edinburgh University Press, 1987); *Ossian*

Revisited, ed. Howard Gaskill (Edinburgh: Edinburgh University Press, 1991); *From Gaelic to Romantic: Ossianic Translations*, ed. Fiona Stafford and Howard Gaskill (Amsterdam: Rodopi, 1998); *Ossian and Ossianism*, ed. Dafydd Moore, 4 vols (London: Routledge, 2004); *The Reception of Ossian in Europe*, ed. Howard Gaskill (London: Continuum, 2004); Dafydd Moore, 'James Macpherson', *Oxford Online Bibliography of British and Irish Literature* (2012) 10.1093/OBO/9780199846719-006 [accessed 15 February 2021]; 'Forum on *Ossian in the Twenty-First Century*' ed. Sebastian Mitchell, *Journal of Eighteenth-Century Studies*, 39 (2016), pp. 157–250.

2   For examples of the former, see Archibald Geikie on the Ossianic landscape in his *Landscape in History and Other Essays* (New York: Macmillan, 1905) pp. 113–119, and, most notoriously, Peter Hately Waddell, *Ossian and the Clyde: Fingal in Ireland, Oscar in Iceland, or Ossian Historical and Authentic* (Glasgow: James MacLehose, 1875). For more recent commentary see Sebastian Mitchell, 'Landscape and the Sense of Place in *The Poems of Ossian*', in *The International Companion to James Macpherson and the Poems of Ossian*, ed. Dafydd Moore, pp. 65–75; Nigel Leask, 'Fingalian Topographies: Ossian and the Highland Tour, 1764–1810', *Journal for Eighteenth-Century Studies*, 39 (2016), 183–96; Paul Baines, 'Ossianic Geographies: Fingalian Figures on the Scottish Tour, 1760–1830', *Scotlands*, 4 (1997), 44–61; as well as Gidal cited below.

3   Charles Churchill, 'The Prophecy of Famine: A Scots Pastoral', in *Poems by C. Churchill in 2 Volumes*, 3rd edition (London, 1766), vol. 1, pp. 95–124 (p. 103); Walter Scott, 'Report of the Committee of the Highland Society of Scotland, &c.', *The Edinburgh Review*, July 1805, pp. 429–62 (p. 446).

4   John Dwyer, 'The Melancholy Savage: Text and Context in *The Poems of Ossian*', in *Ossian Revisited*, ed. Gaskill, pp. 164–206 (p. 169); Ken Simpson, *The Protean Scot: The Crisis of Identity in Eighteenth-Century Scottish Literature* (Aberdeen: Aberdeen University Press, 1988), p. 55.

5   Adam Potkay, *The Fate of Eloquence in the Age of Hume* (Ithaca: Cornell University Press, 1994), p. 9.

6   Ian Duncan, 'The Pathos of Abstraction: Adam Smith, Ossian, and Samuel Johnson', in *Scotland and the Borders of Romanticism*, ed. Leith Davis, Ian Duncan, and Janet Sorensen, (Cambridge: Cambridge University Press, 2004), pp. 38–56 (pp. 46–47).

7   Robert Crawford, *The Modern Poet: Poetry, Academia, and Knowledge since the 1750s* (Oxford: Oxford University Press, 2001), p. 44.

8   Eric Gidal, *Ossianic Unconformities: Bardic Poetry in the Industrial Age* (Charlottesville, VA: University of Virginia Press, 2015), p. 14. See also James Mulholland, *Sounding Imperial: Poetic Voice and the Politics of Empire 1730–1820* (Baltimore: Johns Hopkins University Press, 2013).
9   Potkay, pp. 213–14.
10 James Macpherson, *Fingal: An Ancient Epic Poem in Six Books, Together with Several Other Poems, Composed by Ossian the Son of Fingal. Translated from the Galic Language by James Macpherson* (London: Becket and De Hondt, 1761/2), p. 127.
11 For this point see, for example, Katie Trumpener, *Bardic Nationalism: The Romantic Novel and the British Empire* (Princeton: Princeton University Press, 1997), pp. 70–71.
12 There were several late medieval and early modern versions, including in verse, some of which are found in Scotland, e.g., in the Book of the Dean of Lismore: see, for instance, Neil Ross, *Heroic Poetry from the Book of the Dean of Lismore* (Edinburgh: Scottish Gaelic Texts Society, 1939), pp. 168–75.
13 Macpherson, *Fingal* p. 140.
14 Ibid., p. 132.
15 Ibid., pp. 141–42.
16 Derick S. Thomson (ed.), *Alasdair Mac Mhaighstir Alasdair: Selected Poems* (Edinburgh: Scottish Gaelic Texts Society, 1996), p. 125
17 'Song Composed in the Year 1746', *Highland Songs of the Forty-Five*, ed. and trans. John Lorne Campbell (Edinburgh: John Grant, 1933), pp. 95–106 (p. 96).
18 Isaiah, 40.3–4 (KJV).
19 Thomas Burnet, *The Theory of the Earth: Containing an Account of the Original of the Earth, and of All the General Changes Which It Hath Already Undergone, or Is to Undergo till the Consummation of All Things*, 3rd edn (London: Walter Kettilby, 1697), Book 1, p. 25.
20 James Hutton, 'Theory of the Earth', *Transactions of the Royal Society of Edinburgh*, 1 (1788), 209–304 (p. 304).
21 Of increasing importance perhaps given current interest in the idea of the Anthropocene – a new geological age recognising humanity's geological impact on the environment.
22 Stephen Jay Gould, *Time's Arrow and Time's Cycle: Myth and Metaphor in the Discovery of Geological Time* (London: Penguin, 1987, repr. 1991), p. 3.
23 Gould reproduces the image (*Time's Arrow*, pp. 60–61) and, amongst other venues, it adorns the handsome dust jacket of Gidal's *Ossianic Unconformities* and can be readily studied via the internet.

24 Gidal, p. 5.
25 Gould, pp. 4, 64. For this first point see Paolo Rossi, *The Dark Abyss of Time: The History of the Earth and the History of Nations from Hooke to Vico*, trans. Lydia G. Cochrane (Chicago: University of Chicago Press, 1984).
26 Gidal, p. 15.
27 Gould, p. 61.
28 Tom Normand, 'Calum Colvin's Ossian / Oisein Chaluim Cholvin', in Calum Colvin, *Ossian: Fragments of Ancient Poetry / Bloighean de Sheann Bhàrdachd Oisein* (Edinburgh: National Galleries of Scotland, 2002), pp. 11–64 (p. 36).
29 *Fingal*, p. 132.
30 James Macpherson, *Temora, An Ancient Epic Poem in Eight Books: Together with several other Poems, composed by Ossian, the Son of Fingal. Translated from the Galic Language by James Macpherson* (London: T. Becket and P. A. de Hondt, 1763), p. 203 (misnumbered '103' in original).
31 *Fingal*, p. 270.

16. Crossing Borders: Travel Writing and Eighteenth-Century Scotland

1 Daniel Defoe, *A Tour Thro' the Whole Island of Great Britain Divided into Circuits or Journeys*, 4 vols (London: 1724–1727), IV, p. 5.
2 Thomas Pennant, *A Tour in Scotland, 1769* (Chester: 1771), p. 40.
3 On the historical and conceptual significance of this phrase see Claire Lamont and Michael Rossington's 'Introduction' in *Romanticism's Debatable Lands* (Basingstoke: Palgrave Macmillan, 2007), pp. 1–9.
4 On the relationship between literature and the politics of Britishness in this period see for example: Katie Trumpener, *Bardic Nationalism: the Romantic Novel and the British Empire* (Princeton: Princeton University Press, 1997); Leith Davis, *Acts of Union: Scotland and the Literary Negotiation of the British Nation, 1707–1832* (Stanford: Stanford University Press, 1998); Janet Sorensen, *The Grammar of Empire in Eighteenth-Century British Writing* (Cambridge: Cambridge University Press, 2000); Ian Duncan, Davis and Sorensen, 'Introduction' in *Scotland and the Borders of Romanticism*, ed. Leith Davis, Ian Duncan, and Janet Sorensen (Cambridge: Cambridge University Press, 2004), 1–19; Ian Duncan, *Scott's Shadow: The Novel in Romantic Edinburgh* (Princeton: Princeton University Press, 2007); Murray Pittock, *Scottish and Irish Romanticism* (Oxford: Oxford University Press, 2008); Penny

Fielding, *Scotland and the Fictions of Geography: North Britain, 1760–1830* (Cambridge: Cambridge University Press, 2008); Juliet Shields, *Sentimental Literature and Anglo-Scottish Identity, 1745–1820* (Cambridge: Cambridge University Press, 2010).
5   Pennant, pp. 40–41.
6   Ibid.
7   Defoe, IV, p. 3.
8   On domestic travel in this period see for example Zoe Kinsley, *Women Writing the Home Tour, 1682–1812* (Aldershot: Ashgate, 2008) and *Travel Writing and Tourism in Britain and Ireland*, ed. Benjamin Colbert (Basingstoke: Palgrave Macmillan, 2012). Studies of travel writing about Scotland and the Highlands specifically include: John Glendening, *The High Road: Romantic Tourism, Scotland, and Literature, 1720–1820* (Houndmills: Macmillan, 1997); Tom Furniss, *Discovering the Footsteps of Time: Geological Travel Writing about Scotland, 1700–1820* (Edinburgh: Edinburgh University Press, 2018); Nigel Leask, *Stepping Westward: Writing the Highland Tour c. 1720–1830* (Oxford: Oxford University Press, 2020), and Martin Rackwitz, *Travels to Terra Incognita: The Scottish Highlands and Hebrides in Early Modern Travellers' Accounts c. 1600 to 1800* (Münster: Waxmann, 2007).
9   Ina Ferris, 'Mobile Words: Romantic Travel Writing and Print Anxiety', *Modern Language Quarterly*, 60 (1999), 451–68 (p. 452).
10 See Nigel Leask, *Curiosity and the Aesthetics of Travel Writing: 'From an Antique Land', 1770–1840* (Oxford: Oxford University Press, 2002).
11 See, for example, Eric Gidal, *Ossianic Unconformities: Bardic Poetry in the Industrial Age* (Charlottesville: University of Virginia Press, 2002). In a different vein, see Martha Adams Bohrer, 'Tales of Locale: *The Natural History of Selborne* and *Castle Rackrent*', *Modern Philology*, 100 (2003), 393–416.
12 Betty Hagglund, *Tourists and Travellers: Women's Non-fictional Writing about Scotland, 1770–1830* (Bristol: Channel View Publications, 2010), pp. 18–19.
13 Betty A. Schellenberg, 'Imagining the Nation in Defoe's *Tour Thro' the Whole Island of Great Britain*', *English Literary History*, 62 (1995), 295–311 (p. 306).
14 Defoe, IV, p. 197.
15 Peter Womack, *Improvement and Romance: Constructing the Myth of the Highlands* (Houndmills: Macmillan, 1988), pp. 80–81.
16 Defoe, IV, p. 2.

17 Martin Martin, *A Description of the Western Isles of Scotland* (London: 1703), p. 345.
18 On Martin's significance see Charles W. J. Withers, *Geography, Science and National Identity: Scotland since 1520* (Cambridge: Cambridge University Press, 2001), pp. 87–96.
19 Martin, pp. iv-v.
20 Fielding, p. 9.
21 Martin Martin, *Voyage to St. Kilda* (Glasgow, 1818 edition), IV, cited in Withers, p. 90.
22 Thomas Pennant, *A Tour in Scotland and Voyage to the Hebrides 1772* (Chester: 1774), p. 302.
23 Charles W. J. Withers and Bill Bell, *Travels into Print: Exploration, Writing and Publishing with John Murray, 1773–1859* (Chicago: Chicago University Press, 2015), p. 3.
24 James A. Secord, 'Knowledge in Transit', *Isis*, 95 (2004), pp. 654–72 (p. 661).
25 See Fiona Stafford, *The Sublime Savage* (Edinburgh: Edinburgh University Press, 1988), pp. 113–32.
26 Frederick Albritton Jonsson, *Enlightenment's Frontier: The Scottish Highlands and the Origins of Environmentalism* (New Haven; London: Yale University Press, 2013), p. 50; Charles W. J. Withers, 'Contested Visions: Nature, Culture and the Morality of Landscape in the Scottish Highlands', in *Nature and Identity in Cross-Cultural Perspective*, ed. A. Buttimer and L. Wallin (Dordrecht; Boston; London: Kluwer Academic Publishers, 1999), pp. 271–86 (p. 275).
27 John Bonehill, 'New scenes drawn by the pencil of Truth': Joseph Banks's northern voyage', *Journal of Historical Geography*, 43 (2014), 9–27 (p. 10).
28 See Jo Guldi, *Roads to Power: Britain Invents the Infrastructure State* (Cambridge, MA: Harvard University Press, 2012), and Annette M. Smith, *Jacobite Estates of the Forty-Five* (Edinburgh: John Donald, 1982).
29 Jonsson, p. 2
30 See John Walker, *The Rev. Dr. John Walker's Report on the Hebrides of 1764 and 1771*, ed. Margaret M. Mckay (Edinburgh: Donald, 1980) and D. M. Henderson and J. H. Dickson, *A Naturalist in the Highlands: James Robertson, His Life and Travels in Scotland, 1767–1771* (Edinburgh: Scottish Academic Press, 1994).
31 Jonsson, p. 50.
32 Pennant, *A Tour in Scotland and Voyage to the Hebrides*, pp. 261–62.
33 Ibid., pp. 396–98.

34 See James Anderson, *An Account of the Present State of the Hebrides and Western Coasts of Scotland* (Edinburgh, 1785) and John Knox, *A Tour Through the Highlands of Scotland, and the Hebride Isles, in 1786* (London: 1787).
35 *To the Hebrides: Samuel Johnson's Journey to the Western Islands of Scotland and James Boswell's Journal of a Tour to the Hebrides*, ed. Ronald Black (Edinburgh: Birlinn, 2007), p. 17.
36 Ibid., p. 124.
37 See Donald McNicol, *Remarks on Dr Johnson's Journey to the Hebrides* (London, 1779).
38 Black, p. 186.
39 On the history of the Highland Clearances see James Hunter, *The Making of the Crofting Community* (Edinburgh: John Donald, 1976), and Eric Richards, *The Highland Clearances: People, Landlords, and Rural Turmoil* (Edinburgh: Birlinn, 2005).
40 Pennant, *A Tour in Scotland, 1769*, pp. 196–97.
41 On the 'naturalist-antiquary' model, see Maria Toscano, 'The figure of the naturalist-antiquary in the Kingdom of Naples', *Journal of the History of Collections*, 19 (2007), 225–37.
42 John Lettice, *Letters on a Tour through Various Parts of Scotland* (London: 1794), pp. 298–303.
43 Ibid., pp. 257–258.
44 Ibid., p. 259.
45 See Davis, pp. 132–33.
46 Sarah Murray, *A Companion and Useful Guide to the Beauties of Scotland* (London: 1799), p. vii.
47 Ibid., pp. 156–57.
48 For an alternative view on the concept of testimony in relation to the Highlands in this period see Matthew Wickman, *The Ruins of Experience: Scotland's 'Romantick' Highlands and the Birth of the Modern Witness* (Philadelphia: University of Pennsylvania Press, 2007).
49 Hagglund, p. 60.

17. Scots and the Language of the Sea in Tobias Smollett's *Roderick Random* and William Falconer's *The Shipwreck*

1 Tobias Smollett, Preface, *The Adventures of Roderick Random*, ed. Paul Gabriel Boucé (Oxford: Oxford Worlds Classics, 1981), p. xxxv.
2 The union between Scotland and England brought an increase in maritime trade in Scotland and this trade, along with the

expan-sion of the Royal Navy in the eighteenth century, demanded more sailors from Scotland. For a detailed history of the numbers and experiences of Scots sailors see Gordon Jackson, 'Scottish Sailors', in *Those Emblems of Hell: European Sailors and the Maritime Labour Market, 1570–1870*, ed. Paul Van Royen (Oxford: Oxford University Press, 2017).

3 Smollett, *Roderick Random*, p. 1.
4 Smollett, *Roderick Random*, p. 141.
5 Ian Watt, *The Rise of the Novel* (Berkeley: University of California Press, 1957), p. 29 (italics mine).
6 Margaret Cohen, *The Novel and the Sea* (Princeton: Princeton University Press, 2011), p. 8.
7 Ned Ward, *A Trip to Jamaica* (London, 1698) and *The Wooden World Dissected* (London, 1706).
8 Ward, *The Wooden World Dissected*, pp. 48 and 49, respectively.
9 Smollett, *Roderick Random*, p. 62.
10 For a discussion of these novelistic techniques see my *Strange Vernaculars: How Eighteenth-Century Slang, Cant, Provincial Languages, and Nautical Jargon Became English* (Princeton: Princeton University Press, 2017).
11 Smollett, *Roderick Random*, p. 162.
12 Ibid., p. 139.
13 Ibid., p. 139.
14 Ibid., p. 407.
15 Ibid., p. 143.
16 Watt describes the ability of details to call up environments in *The Rise of the Novel*, p. 26.
17 Smollett, *Roderick Random*, pp. 166, 167, respectively.
18 Cohen, *The Novel and the Sea*, p. 75.
19 Smollett, *Roderick Random*, p. 163.
20 Ibid., p. 181.
21 Ibid., p. 181.
22 Ibid., pp. 146, 147, 151, respectively.
23 Ibid., p. 11. Boucé notes that 'Bowling' 'may refer either to a ship 'bowling along', or to a rope used to keep the sail taut and steady'. 'Notes' to Tobias Smollett, *Roderick Random*, p. 438.
24 Ibid., p. 11.
25 Ward, *The Wooden World Dissected*, p. 5.
26 The first issue of Wilkes' periodical publication *The North Briton*, for instance, announced, 'I will endeavor to write *plain English*, and to

avoid the numerous *Scotticisms* the BRITON abounds with' (Smollett was editor of *The Briton*) *The North Briton*, No. 1 June 5, 1762.
27 Elizabeth DeLoughrey *Routes and Roots: Navigating Caribbean and Pacific Island Literature* (Honolulu: University of Hawai'i Press, 2007), p. 55.
28 Smollett, *Roderick Random*, p, 8.
29 In the text, Bowling sings the opening lines of Pepusche's 'The Sailor's Ballad', which includes the line 'A light heart and a thin pair of breeches / Goes through the world brave boys'. See 'Notes' in *Roderick Random,* ed. Boucé, p. 438.
30 Smollett, *Roderick Random*, p. 432.
31 Catherine Gallagher, *Nobody's Story* (Berkeley: California University Press, 1994), p. 168.
32 For extensive background information on Falconer see *A Critical Edition of the Poetical Works of William Falconer*, ed. William R. Jones (Lewiston: Edwin Mellen, 2003).
33 Cited in *A Critical Edition of the Poetical Works of William Falconer*, ed. William R. Jones, p. 31.
34 *A Critical Edition of the Poetical Works of William Falconer*, ed. Jones. This edition includes the first three editions of *The Shipwreck*. The passage cited is from the 1769 edition, p. 279.
35 Falconer, *The Shipwreck* (London, 1762), p. 176.
36 *Critical Review* 13 (1762), p. 440 and *Monthly Review* 27 (1762): p. 198, respectively.
37 See for instance, *Roach's Beauties of the Poets of Great Britain* (5 vols), (London, 1793) or, later, and across the Atlantic, *British Poets in Chronological Order from Falconer to Sir Walter Scott* (Philadelphia, 1848).

18. Ottobah Cugoano and Scotland's Minority Imperialist Culture

1 Quobna Ottobah Cugoano, *Thoughts and Sentiments on the Evil and Wicked Traffic of the Slavery and Commerce of the Human Species, Humbly Submitted to the Inhabitants of Great Britain, by Ottobah Cugoano, a Native of Africa* [London: n. pub., 1787], ed. Vincent Carretta (London: Penguin, 1999) p. 109.
2 Ryan Hanley, *Beyond Slavery and Abolition: Black British Writing, c. 1770–1830* (Cambridge: Cambridge University Press, 2019), p. 171.
3 Brycchan Carey, 'Quobna Ottobah Cugoano: A Former Slave Speaks Out', *Brycchan Carey, Author and Academic* brycchancarey.com/cugoano/index.htm [accessed 25 June 2019].

4   Vincent Carretta, 'Introduction', in Quobna Ottobah Cugoano, *Thoughts and Sentiments on the Evil of Slavery* [1791], ed. Vincent Carretta (New York: Penguin Classics, 1999), ix–xxviii (p. x).
5   Douglas Hamilton, *Scotland, the Caribbean and the Atlantic World 1750–1820* (Manchester: Manchester University Press, 2005), p. 68. David Alston '"Very rapid and splendid fortunes"? Highland Scots in Berbice (Guyana) in the Early Nineteenth Century', *Transactions of the Gaelic Society of Inverness*, 63 (2006), pp. 208–36.
6   Katie Trumpener broadly follows the sociologist Michael Hechter (*Internal Colonialism: The Celtic Fringe and British National Development, 1536–1966* (Berkeley: University of California Press, 1977)) in conceiving of Scotland as an 'internal colony', a victim of English imperialism as a precursor to later global depredations (*Bardic Nationalism: The Romantic Novel and the British Empire* (Princeton: Princeton University Press, 1997)). Murray Pittock gives a 'liberal empire' line to argue that the position of Scotland (and Ireland) in relation to Britain means they engage 'fratriotically' i.e. sympathetically and fraternally with the nations they colonise (*Scottish and Irish Romanticism* (Oxford: Oxford University Press, 2008)). The introduction to *Scottish Literature and Postcolonial Literature* opts for a vision of 'dual relationship of congruence and conflict' between the two categories (*Scottish Literature and Postcolonial Literature: Comparative Texts and Political Perspectives*, ed. Michael Gardiner, Graeme MacDonald, and Niall O'Gallagher (Edinburgh: Edinburgh University Press, 2011), p. 3). For Carla Sassi and Theo van Heijnsbergen, Scotland's subjugated position in the United Kingdom combined with its subjugating role in the Empire requires a dualistic formulation, Scotland is both 'within and without empire' (*Within and Without Empire: Scotland Across the Postcolonial Borderline* (Newcastle: Cambridge Scholars Publishing, 2013)).
7   Silke Stroh, *Gaelic Scotland in the Colonial Imagination: Anglophone Writing from 1600 to 1900* (Illinois: Northwestern University Press, 2016), p. 5.
8   John Pocock, 'British History: A Plea for a New Subject', *Journal of Modern History*, 47, (1975), 601–21 (p. 609).
9   John Kerrigan, *Archipelagic English: Literature, History, and Politics 1603–1707* (Oxford: Oxford University Press, 2008), p. vii.
10 Dauvit Broun and Martin MacGregor, *Mìorun Mòr nan Gall, 'The great ill-will of the Lowlander'?: Lowland perceptions of the Highlands, Medieval and Modern* (Glasgow: University of Glasgow Centre for

Scottish and Celtic Studies, 2009). See also Sheila Kidd, on Gaelic connections with the West Indies, 'Turtaran is faclairean: Ceanglaichean eadar Gàidheil na h-Alba agus Gàidheil nan Innseachan an Iar', *Aiste*, 3 (2010), 19–48 at clog.glasgow.ac.uk/ojs/index.php/aiste/article/view/24 (accessed 11 May 2021) and, on Gaels in the East Indies, '"Fo ghrèin loisgich nan Innsean": na h-Innseachan an Ear tro shùilean Gàidhealach', *Transactions of the Gaelic Society of Inverness*, LXVI (2014), 141–73, at eprints.gla.ac.uk/104219/ (accessed 11 May 2021).
11 Liam Connell, 'Modes of Marginality: Scottish Literature and the Uses of Postcolonial Theory', *Comparative Studies of South Asia, Africa and the Middle East*, 23 (2003), 41–53.
12 Warwick Research Collective, *Combined and Uneven Development: Towards a New Theory of World-Literature* (Liverpool: Liverpool University Press, 2015).
13 See, for example, Silvia Sebastiani, *The Scottish Enlightenment: Race, Gender and the Limits of Progress*, trans. Jeremy Carden (New York: Palgrave MacMillan, 2012).
14 In September 2018, The University of Glasgow published a report by Simon Newman and Stephen Mullen into the slave money which came into the university: 'Slavery, Abolition and the University of Glasgow: Report and Recommendations of the University of Glasgow History of Slavery Steering Committee', *University of Glasgow*, www.gla.ac.uk/media/Media_607547_smxx.pdf [accessed 25 June 2019]. In April 2019, Dollar Academy in Clackmannanshire began to investigate its slavery links in consultation with Graham Campbell, Geoff Palmer and Lisa Williams. 'History', *Dollar Academy* www.dollaracademy.org.uk/about/history [accessed 25 June 2019].
15 *Discourses of Slavery and Abolition Britain and its Colonies, 1760–1838*, ed. Brycchan Carey, Markman Ellis, and Sara Salih (Houndmills: Palgrave Macmillan, 2004), p. 1.
16 David Worthington, 'Sugar, Slave-Owning, Suriname and the Dutch Imperial Entanglement of the Scottish Highlands before 1707', *Dutch Crossing: Journal of Low Country Studies*, 44 (2020), 3–20.
17 Iain MacKinnon and Andrew MacKillop, 'Plantation slavery and landownership in the west Highlands and Islands: legacies and lessons', Land and the Common Good Discussion Paper Series (November 2020) www.communitylandscotland.org.uk/wp-content/uploads/2020/11/ANNEX-report-data-references.pdf [accessed 22 February 2021]. Alexander Campbell's native Islay forms a case study given Daniel Campbell's purchase of the island in 1726 (p. 10).

18 Karly Kehoe, 'From the Caribbean to the Scottish Highlands: Charitable Enterprise in the Age of Improvement, c. 1750 to c. 1820', *Rural History*, 27 (2016), 37–59 (p. 38).
19 Ibid., p. 39.
20 Hamilton, p. 156.
21 Evidence of Alexander Campbell Esq. *Minutes Of The Evidence Taken Before A Committee of the House of Commons, Being A Select Committee, Appointed on the 29th Day of January 1790, For the Purpose of taking the Examination of such Witnesses as shall be produced on the Part of the several Petitioners who have petitioned the House of Commons against the Abolition of the Slave Trade* ([n.p.]: [n. pub.], 1790), p. 135.
22 Ibid., p. 147
23 Cugoano, *Thoughts and Sentiments on the Evil and Wicked Traffic of the Slavery and Commerce of the Human Species* [1787]. The biographical note appears on a separate advertisement and is included in most modern versions: see, for example, the edition edited by Vincent Carretta (London: Penguin, 1999), p. 4.
24 See *Campbell v Hall*, ruled by Judge Mansfield. Mark Quintanilla, 'The World of Alexander Campbell: An Eighteenth-Century Grenadian Planter', *Albion*, 35 (2003), 229–56 (p. 241).
25 Carretta, p. xi.
26 Mansfield was born William Murray to Scottish nobility in 1705 in Scone Palace, Perthshire, his parents were staunch Jacobites. Orcadian Steuart purchased Somerset in 1749.
27 Historians have disputed the case since. See Ruth Paley, 'After Somerset: Mansfield, Slavery and the Law in England, 1772–1830', in *Law, Crime and English Society 1660–1830*, ed. Norma Landau (Cambridge: Cambridge University Press, 2002), pp. 165–84. See also John W. Cairns, 'John Millar and Slavery', in *MacCormick's Scotland*, ed. Neil Walker (Edinburgh: Edinburgh University Press, 2012), pp. 73–106.
28 Cugoano, *Thoughts and Sentiments on the Evil of Slavery; or, the Nature of Servitude as Admitted by the Law of God* [1791], ed. Vincent Carretta (London: Penguin, 1999), p. 116.
29 Cugoano, *Thoughts and Sentiments on the Evil and Wicked Traffic of the Slavery and Commerce of the Human Species* [1787], ed. Vincent Carretta (London: Penguin, 1999), p. 7.
30 Ibid.
31 Ibid., p. 152, n. 5.

32 Michael Guenther, 'A Peculiar Silence: The Scottish Enlightenment, Political Economy, and the Debates Over Early American Slavery', *Atlantic Studies*, 8 (2011), 447–83 (p. 458).
33 James Oakes, 'The Peculiar Fate of the Bourgeois Critique of Slavery', in *Slavery and the American South*, ed. Winthrop D. Jordan (Jackson: University Press of Mississippi, 2003), pp. 29–53.
34 Folarin Olawale Shyllon, *James Ramsay: The Unknown Abolitionist* (Edinburgh: Canongate, 1977). J. Watt, 'Ramsay, James (1733–1789)', *Oxford Dictionary of National Biography*, doi-org.proxy.lib.sfu.ca/10.1093/ref:odnb/23086 [accessed 10 February 2021].
35 James Ramsay, *Essay on the Treatment and Conversion of African Slaves in the British Sugar Colonies* (London: J. Phillips, 1789), p. xi.
36 See Henry Homes, [Lord Kames], *Sketches of the History of Man*, 2 vols (Edinburgh: W. Creech, 1774 (also London: T. Cadell and Dublin: James Williams) and William Robertson, *History of America* (London: W. Strahan, 1777) (also Edinburgh: J. Balfour and Dublin: Price, Whitestone, W. Watson, R. Cross *et al.*). For a discussion of the implications of the monogenesis and polygenesis debate, see Colin Kidd, *The Forging of Races: Race and Scripture in the Protestant Atlantic World, 1600–2000* (Cambridge: Cambridge University Press, 2006).
37 Hume's footnote in his essay 'Of National Characters' cuts across the thrust of the argument he is making for cultural relativity. Although the 1748 version did not contain the footnote, in 1753 he inserted 'I am apt to suspect the negroes and in general all the other species of men (for there are four or five different kinds) to be naturally inferior to the whites. There never was a civiliz'd nation of any other complexion than white, nor even any individual eminent either in action or speculation'. In the 1777 version he altered the footnote to remove the overtones of polygenesis, but maintained the original meaning. *Essays and Treatises on Several Subjects*, 2nd edn, 4 vols (London: A. Millar; Edinburgh: A. Kincaid and A. Donaldson, 1753), I, p. 291; *Essays and Treatises on Several Subjects*, 2 vols (London: T. Cadell; Edinburgh: A. Donaldson and W. Creech, 1777), I, p. 550
38 Ramsay, p. 199.
39 These include attacks in parliament from, for example, Crisp Molyneux. See also James Tobin's *Cursory Remarks upon the Reverend Mr. Ramsay's Essay on Treatment and Conversion of African Slaves in the Sugar Colonies* (London: G. and T. Wilkie, 1785). Ramsay countered such attacks in *Reply to Personal Invectives and Objections Contained in Two Answers, Published by Certain Anonymous Persons, to an Essay*

on the Treatment and Conversion of African Slaves, in the British Colonies (London: James Phillips, 1785).
40 Gordon Turnbull, *An Apology for Negro Slavery: Or, The West-India Planters Vindicated from the Charge of Inhumanity* (London: Stuart & Stevenson, 1786), p. 58.
41 Ibid., p. 29.
42 Ibid., p. 32.
43 Julia Kristeva, 'Word, Dialogue and Novel', in *The Kristeva Reader*, ed. Toril Moil (New York: Columbia University Press, 1986), pp. 34–62.
44 David Hume, 'Of National Characters', in *Three Essays, Moral and Political* (London: A. Millar; Edinburgh: A. Kincaid, 1748), pp. 1–28 (p. 26).
45 Cugoano [1787], p. 27.
46 Ibid., p. 28.
47 Olaudah Equiano, *The Interesting Narrative and Other Writings*, ed. Vincent Carretta (London: Penguin Classics, 2003), p8. One of Equiano's owners was also a Mr Campbell in Virginia. There is an unresolved debate over whether Equiano was born in Ibo-land as he claims and, therefore, his description is drawn from memory; or born in South Carolina, as his naval records state, which would make his description constructed via the accounts of others. See Vincent Carretta, 'Response to Paul Lovejoy's "Autobiography and Memory: Gustavus Vassa, alias Olaudah Equiano, the African"', *Slavery & Abolition*, 28 (2007), 115–19. For the comparison of Highland and African clanship, see the section on 'The African/Scottish Other' in John Corbett, 'The Missionary's Positions: David Livingstone as a British Scot in Africa', *Scotlands*, 5.1 (1998), 79–92 (pp. 83–85).
48 Jeffrey Hole, 'From Sentiment to Security: Cugoano, Liberal Principles, and the Bonds of Empire', *Criticism*, 59 (2017), 175–99.
49 Cugoano [1787], p. 55.
50 Turnbull, quoted in Ibid., p. 109.
51 Ibid., p. 109.

Further Reading

Alker, Sharon, Leith Davis and Holly Faith Nelson (eds), *Robert Burns and Transatlantic Culture* (London: Routledge, 2017)

Alston, David, *Slaves and Highlanders: Hearing Silenced Histories of the Caribbean* (Edinburgh: Edinburgh University Press, forthcoming)

Andrews, Corey E., *The Genius of Scotland: The Cultural Production of Robert Burns, 1785–1834* (Leiden: Brill Rodopi, 2015)

Bannet, Eve Tavor, and Susan Manning (eds), *Transatlantic Literary Studies, 1660–1830* (Cambridge: Cambridge University Press, 2014)

Benchimol, Alex, Rhona Brown, and David Shuttleton (eds), *Before 'Blackwood's': Scottish Journalism in the Age of Enlightenment*, The Enlightenment World, 29 (London: Pickering and Chatto, 2015)

Black, Ronald, 'Alasdair mac Mhaighstir Alasdair and the New Gaelic Poetry', in Susan Manning (ed.), *The Edinburgh History of Scottish Literature*, II: *Enlightenment, Britain and Empire (1707–1918)*, (Edinburgh: Edinburgh University Press, 2007), 110–24

Black, Ronald, 'The Gaelic Book' and 'Gaelic Secular publishing', in Stephen W. Brown and Warren McDougall (eds), *The Edinburgh History of the Book in Scotland,* II: *Enlightenment and Expansion, 1707–1800* (Edinburgh: Edinburgh University Press, 2012), 177–87, 595–612

Black, Ronald (ed.), *To the Hebrides: Samuel Johnson's Journey to the Western Islands of Scotland and James Boswell's Journal of a Tour to the Hebrides* (Edinburgh: Birlinn, 2007)

Black, Ronald and Gerard Carruthers, 'The Eighteenth Century', in Carla Sassi (ed.), *The International Companion to Scottish Poetry* (Glasgow: Scottish Literature International, 2015), pp. 54–63

Blaszak, Marek, 'The Evolution of Sailor Hero in the Eighteenth-Century British Novel: A Study of Defoe and Smollett' in Malgorzata Martynuska and Elzbieta Rokosz-Piejko (eds), *Revolution, Evolution and Endurance in Anglophone Literature and Culture* (Frankfurt am Main: Peter Lang Publishers, 2017)

Broadhead, Alex, *The Language of Robert Burns: Style, Ideology, and Identity* (Lewisburg, PA: Bucknell University Press, 2014)

Broun, Dauvit, and Martin MacGregor, *Mìorun Mòr nan Gall, 'The great ill-will of the Lowlander'?: Lowland Perceptions of the Highlands, Medieval and Modern* (Glasgow: University of Glasgow Centre for Scottish and Celtic Studies, 2009)

Brown, Ian, and Gerard Carruthers (eds), *Performing Robert Burns: Enactments and Representations of the 'National Bard'* (Edinburgh: Edinburgh University Press, 2021)

Brown, Rhona, *Robert Fergusson and the Scottish Periodical Press* (Farnham, Surrey, England: Ashgate, 2012)

Carruthers, Gerard, *The Edinburgh Companion to Robert Burns* (Edinburgh: Edinburgh University Press, 2009)

Carruthers, Gerard, *Robert Burns* (Tavistock, Devon, England: Northcote House, 2005)

Christian, George S., *Beside the Bard: Scottish Lowland Poetry in the Age of Burns* (Lewisburg, PA: Bucknell University Press, 2020)

Christian, George S., 'Gendering the Scottish Nation: Rereading the Songs of Lady Nairne', *European Romantic Review*, 29 (2018), 681–709

Cohen, Margaret, *The Novel and the Sea* (Princeton: Princeton University Press, 2012)

Coyer, Megan J., and David E. Shuttleton (eds), *Scottish Medicine and Literary Culture, 1726–1832* (Amsterdam: Rodopi, 2014)

Crawford, Robert, *Devolving English Literature*, 2nd edn (Oxford: Clarendon Press, 2001)

Crawford, Robert, *Scotland's Books: A History of Scottish Literature* (Oxford: Oxford University Press, 2009)

Davis, Leith, *Acts of Union: Scotland and the Literary Negotiation of the British Nation, 1707–1830* (Stanford: Stanford University Press, 1998).

Davis, Leith, *Mediating Cultural Memory in Britain and Ireland: From the 1688 Revolution to the 1745 Jacobite Rising* (Cambridge: Cambridge University Press, forthcoming).

Davis, Leith, Ian Duncan, and Janet Sorensen, *Scotland and the Borders of Romanticism* (Cambridge: Cambridge University Press, 2004).

DeLucia, JoEllen, *A Feminine Enlightenment: British Women Writers and the Philosophy of Progress* (Edinburgh: Edinburgh University Press, 2015)

Devine, T. M., *Scotland's Empire: The Origins of Global Diaspora* (London: Penguin, 2004)

Devine, T. M., *The Great Highland Famine: Hunger, Emigration, and the Scottish Highlands in the Nineteenth Century* (Edinburgh: John Donald, 1988)

Devine, T. M., *The Scottish Clearances: A History of the Dispossessed, 1600–1900* (London: Allen Lane, 2018)

Devine, T. M., C. H. Lee and G. C. Peden, *The Transformation of Scotland: The Economy Since 1700* (Edinburgh: Edinburgh University Press, 2005)

Fielding, Penny, *Scotland and the Fictions of Geography: North Britain 1760–1830* (Cambridge: Cambridge University Press, 2008)

Fox, Adam, 'Approaches to Ephemera: Scottish Broadsides, 1679–1746', in Kevin D. Murphy and Sally O'Driscoll (eds), *Studies in Ephemera: Text and Image in Eighteenth-Century Print* (Lewisburg, PA: Bucknell University Press; Lanham, MD: Rowman and Littlefield Publishers, 2013), pp. 117–141

Fox, Adam, 'Jockey and Jenny: English Broadside Ballads and the Invention of Scottishness', *Huntington Library Quarterly: Studies in English and American History and Literature*, 79 (2016), 201–20

Frater, Anne, and Michel Byrne, 'Gaelic Poetry and Song', in Glenda Norquay (ed.), *The Edinburgh Companion to Scottish Women's Writing* (Edinburgh: Edinburgh University Press, 2012), pp. 22–35

Furniss, Tom, *Discovering the Footsteps of Time: Geological Writing about Scotland, 1700–1820* (Edinburgh: Edinburgh University Press, 2019)

Gaskill, Howard (ed.), *Ossian Revisited* (Edinburgh: Edinburgh University Press, 1991)

Gidal, Eric, *Ossianic Unconformities: Bardic Poetry in the Industrial Age* (Charlottesville: University of Virginia Press, 2015)

Gillies, William, 'Some Eighteenth-Century Developments in Scottish Gaelic Poetry', in Anders Ahlqvist and Pamela O'Neill (eds), *Language and Power in the Celtic World: Papers from the Seventh Australian Conference of Celtic Studies* (Sydney: Celtic Studies Foundation, University of Sydney, 2011), pp. 61–97

Gillies, William, 'Traditional Gaelic Women's Song', in Marco Fazzini (ed.), *Alba Literaria: A History of Scottish Literature* (Venezia Mestre: Amos, 2005), pp. 165–79

Hagglund, Betty, *Tourists and Travellers: Women's Non-Fictional Writing about Scotland, 1770–1830* (Bristol; Buffalo; Toronto: Channel View Publications, 2010)

Hewitson, Jim, *The Scots at Sea: Celebrating Scotland's Maritime History* (Edinburgh: Saint Andrew Press, 2004)

Jackson, Clare, *Restoration Scotland, 1660–1690: Royalist Politics, Religion and Ideas* (Woodbridge: Boydell Press, 2003)

Jones, William (ed.), *A Critical Edition of the Poetical Works of William Falconer* (Lewiston, NY: Edwin Mellen, 2003)

Jonsson, Frederik Albritton, *Enlightenment's Frontier: The Scottish Highlands and the Origins of Environmentalism* (New Haven; London: Yale University Press, 2013)

Kerrigan, John, *Archipelagic English: Literature, History, and Politics 1603–1707* (Oxford: Oxford University Press, 2008)

Kidd, Colin, *Subverting Scotland's Past: Scottish Whig Historians and the Creation of Anglo-British Identity 1689–c.1830* (Cambridge: Cambridge University Press, 1993)

Kidd, Colin, *The Forging of Races: Race and Scripture in the Protestant Atlantic World, 1600–2000* (Cambridge: Cambridge University Press, 2006)

Lamont, Craig, *The Cultural Memory of Georgian Glasgow* (Edinburgh: Edinburgh University Press, 2021).

Leask, Nigel, *Robert Burns and Pastoral: Poetry and Improvement in Late Eighteenth-Century Scotland* (Oxford: Oxford University Press, 2010)

Leask, Nigel, *Stepping Westward: Writing the Highland Tour c. 1720–1830* (Oxford: Oxford University Press, 2020)

McAulay, Karen, *Our Ancient National Airs: Scottish Song Collecting from the Enlightenment to the Romantic Era* (Farnham, Surrey, England: Ashgate, 2013)

McAuley, Louis Kirk, *Print Technology in Scotland and America 1740–1800* (Lewisburg, PA: Bucknell University Press, 2013)

McLean, Ralph, Ronnie Young, and Kenneth Simpson (eds), *The Scottish Enlightenment and Literary Culture* (Lewisburg, PA: Bucknell University Press; Lanham, MD: Rowman and Littlefield, 2016)

McCue, Kirsteen, '"An Individual Flowering on a Common Stem": Melody, Performance, and National Song', in Philip Connell and Nigel Leask (eds), *Romanticism and Popular Culture in Britain and Ireland*, (Cambridge: Cambridge University Press, 2009), pp. 88–106

McCue, Kirsteen, 'Lowland Song Culture in the Eighteenth Century', in Sarah Dunnigan and Suzanne Gilbert (eds), *The Edinburgh Companion to Scottish Traditional Literatures* (Edinburgh: Edinburgh University Press, 2013), pp. 94–104

McCue, Kirsteen, 'The Culture of Song', in David Duff (ed.), *The Oxford Handbook of British Romanticism* (Oxford: Oxford University Press, 2018), pp. 643–59

McGuirk, Carol, *Reading Robert Burns: Texts, Contexts, Transformations* (London: Routledge, 2014)

McIlvanney, Liam, *Burns the Radical: Poetry and Politics in Late Eighteenth-Century Scotland* (East Linton: Tuckwell, 2002)

McLane, Maureen N., *Balladeering, Minstrelsy, and the Making of British Romantic Poetry* (Cambridge: Cambridge University Press, 2011)

McNeil, Kenneth, *Scotland, Britain, Empire: Writing the Highlands, 1760–1860* (Columbus: Ohio State Press, 2007).

Mann, Alastair J., 'The Anatomy of the Printed Book in Early Modern Scotland', *The Scottish Historical Review*, 80 (2001), 181–200

Mann, Alastair J., *The Scottish Book Trade, 1500–1720: Print Commerce and Print Control in Early Modern Scotland* (East Linton: Tuckwell, 2000)

Manning, Susan, *Fragments of Union: Making Connections in Scottish and American Writing* (New York: Palgrave, 2001)

Meek, Donald E., 'The Pulpit and the Pen: Clergy, Orality, and Print in the Scottish Gaelic World', in Adam Fox and Daniel Woolf (eds), *The Spoken Word: Oral Culture in Britain, 1500–1850* (Manchester: Manchester University Press, 2002), pp. 84–119

Menely, Tobias, and Jesse Oak Taylor (eds), *Anthropocene Reading: Literary History in Geologic Times* (University Park: Penn State University Press, 2017)

Mitchell, Sebastian (ed.), *Ossian in the Twenty-first Century* (= *Journal for Eighteenth-Century Studies*, 39 (2016)), pp. 157–311

Moore, Dafydd (ed.), *Ossian and Ossianism*, 4 vols (London: Routledge, 2004)

Moore, Dafydd (ed.), *The International Companion to James Macpherson and Ossian* (Glasgow: Scottish Literature International, 2017)

Moore, Jason W., *Capitalism in the Web of Life: Ecology and the Accumulation of Capital* (New York: Verso, 2015)

Newman, Steve, *Ballad Collection, Lyric, and the Canon: The Call of the Popular from the Restoration to the New Criticism* (Philadelphia: University of Pennsylvania Press, 2007)

Ó Baoill, Colm, '"Neither Out nor In": Scottish Gaelic Women Poets 1650–1750', in Sarah M. Dunnigan, C. Marie Harker, and Evelyn S. Newlyn (eds), *Woman and the Feminine in Medieval and Early Modern Scottish Writing* (Houndmills: Palgrave Macmillan, 2004), pp. 136–53

Orr, Julie, *Scotland, Darien and the Atlantic World, 1698–1700* (Edinburgh: Edinburgh University Press, 2018)

Pittock, Murray (ed.), *Allan Ramsay Special Number* (= *Scottish Literary Review*, 10 (2018)), 1–168

Roy, G. Ross, *Selected Essays on Robert Burns*, ed. by Patrick Scott, Elizabeth Sudduth, and Jo DuRant (Columbia: University of South Carolina Libraries, 2018)

Sandrock, Kirsten, *Scottish Colonial Literature: Writing the Atlantic, 1603–1707* (Edinburgh: Edinburgh University Press, 2021)

Sergeant, David, and Fiona Stafford (eds), *Burns and Other Poets* (Edinburgh: Edinburgh University Press, 2012)

Sher, Richard B., *The Enlightenment and the Book: Scottish Authors and Their Publishers in Eighteenth-Century Britain, Ireland, and America* (Chicago: University of Chicago Press, 2006)

Shields, Juliet, *Nation and Migration: The Making of British Atlantic Literature, 1765–1835* (Oxford: Oxford University Press, 2016)

Shields, Juliet, *Sentimental Literature and Anglo-Scottish Identity, 1745–1820* (Cambridge: Cambridge University Press, 2010)

Simpson, Kenneth, *The Protean Scot: The Crisis of Identity in Eighteenth Century Scottish Literature* (Aberdeen: Aberdeen University Press, 1988)

Smout, T. C., *Nature Contested: Environmental History in Scotland and Northern England since 1600* (Edinburgh: Edinburgh University Press, 2000)

Sorensen, Janet, *Strange Vernaculars: How Eighteenth-Century Slang, Cant, Provincial Languages, and Nautical Jargon Became English* (Princeton: Princeton University Press, 2017)

Stafford, Fiona, *The Sublime Savage: James Macpherson and the Poems of Ossian* (Edinburgh: Edinburgh University Press, 1988)

Stafford, Fiona, and Howard Gaskill (eds), *From Gaelic to Romantic: Ossianic Translations* (Amsterdam: Rodopi, 1998)

Stuart, Laura A. M. and Janay Nugent, *Union and Revolution: Scotland and Beyond, 1625–1745* (Edinburgh: Edinburgh University Press)

Thomson, Derick, *An Introduction to Gaelic Poetry* (Edinburgh: Edinburgh University Press, 1989)

Thomson, Derick, 'The McLagan MSS in Glasgow University Library: A Survey', *Transactions of the Gaelic Society of Inverness*, 58 (1993–1994), 406–24

Watson, Roderick, *The Literature of Scotland: The Middle Ages to the Nineteenth Century*, 2nd edn (Houndmills: Palgrave Macmillan, 2007), pp. 114–60

Notes on Contributors

Sharon Alker is Mary A. Denny Professor of English and General Studies and Chair of Humanities and Fine Arts at Whitman College. She has published on a range of British literature and is currently co-editing John Galt's *Sir Andrew Wylie* and James Hogg's *Uncollected Works*. She recently published *Besieged: Early Modern British Siege Literature, 1642–1722* (2021), co-written with Holly Faith Nelson.

Corey E. Andrews is Professor of English at Youngstown State University. He has published two books on eighteenth-century Scottish poetry, especially the life and works of Robert Burns; his criticism has also focused on Scottish abolitionist verse and labouring-class poetry. His current research examines the influence of poetic tributes, celebrations, and biographies upon Robert Burns's legacy in nineteenth-century Britain.

Ian Brown is Honorary Senior Research Fellow in Scottish Literature at the University of Glasgow and Professor Emeritus in Drama at Kingston University, London. Widely published on aspects of theatre, literature and cultural policy, he has edited a wide range of volumes. A playwright and poet, his most recent monograph is *Performing Scottishness: Enactment and National Identities* (2020).

Leith Davis is a Professor in the English Department and Director of the Centre for Scottish Studies at Simon Fraser University, Canada. She has published widely on Scottish and Irish literature of the long eighteenth-century. Her most recent book, *Mediating Cultural Memory in Britain and Ireland: From the 1688 Revolution to the 1745 Jacobite Rising*, is forthcoming with Cambridge University Press.

Alex Deans is a Postdoctoral Research Fellow in English Studies at the University of Stirling. He has published articles and book chapters on ecology and landscape in long-eighteenth-century travel writing about Scotland, Romantic-period political economy, and labouring-class reading and authorship.

JoEllen DeLucia is Professor of English at Central Michigan University and the author of *A Feminine Enlightenment: British Women Writers and the Philosophy of Progress, 1759–1820* (2015). She has also published on eighteenth-century travel writing, print culture, gothic fiction, and moral philosophy.

Eric Gidal is Professor of English at the University of Iowa and Editor of *Philological Quarterly*. His recent scholarship includes *Ossianic Unconformities: Bardic Poetry in the Industrial Age* (2015), articles on Scottish and French romanticism, and co-authored studies of Scottish literary and environmental history that apply methods of computational linguistics and geographical information science.

Sìm Innes is Lecturer in Celtic and Gaelic at the University of Glasgow. He works on Scottish Gaelic literature and folklore, from medieval to modern, and has a particular interest in the transmission, borrowing and translation of culture and ideas. In recent years he has worked on the eighteenth-century Gaelic manuscripts collected by the Rev. James McLagan, of the Black Watch and Blair Atholl, now held by Archives and Special Collections, University of Glasgow Library.

Jasreen Kaur Janjua graduated from Simon Fraser University with her MA in English Literature, focusing on eighteenth-century British and Scottish literature and history. She was the 2017–18 recipient of the David and Mary Macaree Graduate Fellowship in Scottish Studies and is currently completing the Professional Development Program in Education at SFU.

Kate Louise Mathis received her doctorate from the University of Edinburgh in 2011 and has taught in the Celtic departments of Aberdeen, Edinburgh, and Glasgow. She has published widely on Gaelic women's poetry and elegy, and the reception of medieval Gaelic Ulster Cycle characters in Scotland. She was previously Scottish Gaelic research assistant for the Leverhulme-funded project 'Women's Poetry in Ireland, Scotland, and Wales, 1400–1800'.

Dafydd Moore is currently Professor of Eighteenth-Century Literature at the University of Plymouth in the UK. He has published widely on James Macpherson and the Poems of Ossian, most notably *Enlightenment and Romance in the Poems of Ossian* (2003); *Ossian and Ossianism* (four volumes, 2004) and *The International Companion to James Macpherson and the Poems of Ossian* (2017).

Michael Morris is Senior Lecturer in the School of Humanities at the University of Dundee. His research and publications are on Scotland's relationship with slavery and the black Atlantic, including *Scotland and the Caribbean, c. 1740–1833: Atlantic Archipelagos* (Routledge, 2015).

Holly Faith Nelson is Professor and Chair of the Department of English and Creative Writing at Trinity Western University in Langley, BC, Canada. She has published widely on the literature of the seventeenth and long eighteenth centuries, with a specialty in Scottish literature. Her latest book, coauthored with Sharon Alker, is *Besieged: Early Modern British Siege Literature, 1642–1722* (2021).

Emma Pink received her PhD from Simon Fraser University in 2016. She is interested in the intersections of gender, national identity, and material culture in Scottish, Irish, and English eighteenth- and nineteenth-century songs. Her current project examines illustrated editions of Thomas Moore's *Irish Melodies*.

David Hill Radcliffe is a literary historian, coder, and digital humanist at Virginia Tech; he has written on Spenser, eighteenth-century poetry, and the romantics, and has complied the databases *Spenser and the Tradition: English Poetry 1679–1830* and *Lord Byron and his Times*. He is currently at work on a database called *Social Networks in Georgian Britain* which tracks relationships among 35,000 persons living during the long eighteenth century.

Juliet Shields is Professor of English at the University of Washington, where she teaches classes on eighteenth- and nineteenth-century British literature. Her research interests include, gender, print culture, migration, and race in the British Atlantic world, and her most recent book is *Scottish Women's Writing in the Long Nineteenth Century: The Romance of Everyday Life* (2021).

Janet Sorensen teaches at the University of California, Berkeley and has published research on eighteenth-century Scots language and literature. Her most recent book is *Strange Vernaculars: How Slang, Cant, Provincial Languages and Nautical Jargon Became English* (2017).

Index

1688 Revolution, 3, 64–65

Aberdeen
    intellectual culture, 143, 145, 196, 224, 247
    Restoration publishers, 78
    school drama, 173
Abolition of the Slave Trade Act, 302
abolitionists, 306
advice to princes/kings, 91–92
Aesop, 79
agricultural improvement. *see* improvement
Alasdair Dubh, 10th MacDonald of Glengarry, 217
Aldis, H. G., *List of Books*, 76, 77
Alexis; Or the Young Adventurer, 124
amateur acting, 172, 184
amhran metre, 30, 32, 33
Anderson, Andrew, 78
Anderson, James, 280
Anderson, Patrick, *Copie of a Barons Court*, 83–84
Andrews, Kerri, 142
Angeletti, Gioia, 184
Anglicanism, 307–08
anglicisation, 177, 179
anglocentrism, 300, 301, 302
Anne, Queen, 68, 117, 175
Annexed Estates, 278
anonymous publications, 203
anthologies, 48
Arbuthnot, John, 177
Armstrong, Dr John, 48
Ascanius, 124
Aston, Anthony, 178
Austen, Jane, *Northanger Abbey*, 232

Bacon, Francis, *The Wisdom of the Ancients*, 79
Bailie, Lady Grizzel, 'There Ance Was a May', 47
Baillie, Joanna, 147–48
    Count Basil, 184–85
    De Montfort, 185
    The Family Legend, 185
Baillie, John/James, *Patriotism*, 181
Baillie of Dochfour, James, 302–03
baird, 29
Balfour and Creech, 135
ballads
    discourse of sacred mystery, 85
    Jacobite themes, 49

ballads (*cont.*)
    Lowland street, 31
    and pastoral verse, 188
    Pinkerton on, 112–13
    political, 78
    Scots register, 42–43
    women poets, 47–48
Banks, Joseph, account of Staffa, 277, 278, 279
Barbour, John, *The Bruce*, 58, 83
Bateman, Meg, 252, 255
Battell of Bodwell-bridge, or The Kings Cavileers Triumph, 78
Baxter, Richard, 150
Beard, Ellen, 164
Beattie, James, 48, 49, 221, 304
    Essay on Laughter, 223–24
    Essay on Truth, 222
    The Minstrel, or, the Progress of Genius, 193–94, 196
    rejection of Scottish nationalism, 196
Beeton's Great Books of Poetry, 115
Behn, Alphra, *Congratulatory Poem to Her Most Sacred Majesty*, 81
Bell, Barbara, 181, 183–84, 185–86
Bell, Bill, 278
Bellenden, John, Scots translation of Boece, 236, 237
Ben Nevis poem, 235–45
Beregonium (ancient city), 236–39
Bernard, Richard (Rector of Balcomb), *The Isle of Man*, 79
'Betty Burke' broadside, 122
Bevan, Jonquil, 77
Bible, New Testament
    classic Gaelic, 151–52
    Gaelic translation, 152, 156–57
Birkenhead, Sir John, *New Ballad of a Famous German Prince and a Renowned English Duke*, 80–81
Black, Ronald, 38, 149, 150, 199, 205
Blacklock, Thomas, 221
Blair, Hugh, 180, 182, 251
Blair, Robert, 48
Blind Harper. *see* MacGilleMhoire, Ruairidh (An Clàrsair Dall)
Blind Harry, *Wallace*, 53, 58, 82–83
Bochanan, Dùghall, 157, 234
    'An Claigeann' ('*The Skull*'), 155–56
    Spiritual Hymns (*Laoidhe Spioradail*), 152–54
Boece, Hector, *Scotorum Historia*, 57–58, 236
The Bonny Highland Laddie, 31
Book of Isaiah, 268
Book of the Dean of Lismore, 200
border poets, 196, 197
border regions, travel writings on, 273
Boswell, James, 181, 182, 244
Bouok, William, 173
Bowling, Tom (fictional character), 293
Bradley, Richard, *Philosophical Account of the Works of Nature*, 258
Bremner, Robert
    The Songs in the Gentle Shepherd, 111
    Thirty Scots Songs for a Voice & Harpsichord, 110
Brief Account of the Life and Family of Miss Jenny Cameron (pamphlet), 127–30

British empire, Scots and, 301–02
broadsides
　political, 78, 80, 122–23
　songs published as, 97–98
Brown, Mark (theatre critic), 171
Brown, Rhona, 115
Bruce, James, *Travels to Discover the Source of the Nile*, 274
Brunton, Mary
　Self-Control, 225, 228–30, 232, 233
　ties to Scottish intellectual culture, 221
Buchanan, George, 69
　Georgii Buchanani Scoti, Poetarum, 83
　school drama, 173
Bunyan, John
　The Holy War, 79
　Pilgrim's Progress, 79, 80
Burke, Edmund, 112, 268
Burnet, Thomas, *Sacred Theory of the Earth*, 266, 267
Burns, Robert, 44, 247
　'Address to the Unco Guid', 53
　'Ae Fond Kiss', 54
　'Auld Lang Syne', 54
　'The Cotter's Saturday Night', 188
　'The Cotter's Saturday Night,', 194
　'Death and Dr. Hornbook', 53
　'Death and Dying Words of Poor Mailie, the Author's Only Pet Yowe', 53–54
　English, poems in, 53
　'Epistle to John Lapraik, an Old Scotch Bard', 53–54
　on Fergusson, 52
　on Hamilton's work, 47
　'The Holy Fair', 53
　'Holy Willie's Prayer', 53
　and improvement, 249
　The Jolly Beggars, 172
　Keir on, 136
　'To a Mouse', 54, 248
　Poems, Chiefly in the Scottish Dialect, 53, 141, 248
　　publication sites, 249
　poetic register, 42
　'A Red, Red Rose', 54
　on Ross's songs, 50
　'On a Scotch Bard Gone to the West Indies,', 250, 256
　Scots verse and song, 52–53
　Scottish songs, work with, 114–15
　and Sempill, 44
　'Song, Composed in August', 248–49
　'Tam o' Shanter', 54
　on Thomson, 257
　'The Vision', 194–95
Byron, George Gordon, 295
　Childe Harold's Pilgrimage, 196–97

Caledonian Mercury, 185
Calvinism, 84, 178
Cambridge Companion to Scottish Literature, 73
Cameron, Alasdair, 172, 186
Cameron, Jenny, 127–30
Cameron, Margaret, *Orain nuadh Ghaidhealach* (*New Gaelic songs*), 207–10
Camerons, 211
Campbell, Agnes, 78
Campbell, Alexander (Highland slaver), 299 300, 302–03

Campbell, Donald, 178
Campbell, Margaret, 210–11
Campbell of Barr, Anna, 206, 210
canonical Gaelic literature, 158, 160
Caribbean slavery. *see* slavery, slaves
Carlton, Charles, 75
Carretta, Vincent, 303–04
Carruthers, Gerard, 7, 199
Carstairs, Christian, *The Hubble-Shue*, 184
'Carthon' (poem), *Fingal* collection, 263–65, 268–70
caterans, 31–32
Catholicism, pre-Reformation, 171
cattle raiders, 31
censorship, 175, 176
Cham'ron, Marairead. *see* Cameron, Margaret
chapbook sales, 172
Charles Edward Stuart, Prince, 38, 118
    Betty Burke episode, 122–24
    and Jenny Cameron, 129–30
    Cooper's engraving, 120–22
Charles I, 58
Charles II, 58, 62, 85, 170
Chearfull Acclamation of the City of Edinburgh (1660), 78, 85
chivalric codes, 113
Church of Scotland. *see* Presbyterianism
Churchill, Charles
    on *Ossian*, 262
    The Prophecy of Famine, 188–89
circus, 185
Clan Donald, 27

Clan Gregor, 32
clans, clanship
    classic Gaelic poets and, 201
    demise of clanship system, 25, 199
    and the panegyric code, 26, 162
Clark, Timothy, 260
Clark, William
    The Grand Tryal, or, Poetical Exercitations upon the Book of Job, 88
    Marciano, 86–87, 174
Clarkson, Thomas, *Essay on the Slavery and Commerce of the Human Species*, 306
classical Gaelic, schools of, 28–29
Clearances, Highland, 165–69, 213, 279, 281
Clerk of Eldin, John, 267
Cliar Sheanchain (poet-band), 26
closet drama, 175, 184–85
Cockburn, Alison, 135
Cohen, Margaret, 286, 290
Collins, William, 251
colonialism, 300
    see also slavery, slaves
Coltman, Viccy, 120
commerce, 189, 240, 241
common sense philosophy, 222–23, 225, 230, 232
Commonwealth, 57, 75, 85–86
communal leisure, loss of, 162
Company of Edinburgh Players, 179
Company of Scotland Trading to Africa and the Indies, 66, 67
contrafacture, 30
Cooper, Richard, engraving of Charles Edward Stuart, 119, 120–22

Cordiner, Charles
  Antiquities and Scenery of the North of Scotland, 282
  Remarkable Ruins and Romantic Prospects of North Britain, 282
Corneille, Pierre, 173
Counter-Reformation, 27
country-house theatre, 175, 184
Covenanters, 77, 90, 308
Craig, James, 4
Crawford, David, 176
Crawford, Robert, 77
  on *Ossian*, 262
  Scotland's Books: A History of Scottish Literature, 73
Crichton Smith, Iain, 255
Critical Review, 297
Cromwell, Oliver, 57, 170
  see also Commonwealth
Cugoano, Ottobah
  biographical note, 303–04
  and Campbell, 300
  Thoughts and Sentiments, 299, 306–09
Cuiningneach, Donnchadh (Duncan Cunningham), 168
Culloden, Battle of, 2, 38–39, 118, 122, 216
cultural nationalism, 68–69
Cunningham, John, 190

Daiches, David, *The Paradox of Scottish Literature*, 8
Dalkeith Palace, 139
Darien colony, 66–68, 300
Davidson, Dr Archibald, 145
Davis, Leith, 96, 248
Defoe, Daniel
  maritime language, use of, 289
  Tour thro' the Whole Island of Great Britain, 272, 273, 274–75, 277
demotic poetry, 195, 198
Dempster of Dunnichen, George, 166
devotional poetry, English language, 153
dialectic, Donn and, 165
Dickson, David, *True Christian Love*, 84
Dis-Clothing Act, repeal of, 207
dispossession, poetics of, 250–51
Domhnall Donn, 31
Donnchadh MacRath (Duncan MacRae) of Inverinate, *Lamh-sgriobhainn Fhearnaig*, 66
Drummond of Hawthornden, William, 42
  A Pleasant History of Roswall and Lillian, 84
  Polemo-Middinia Inter Vitarvam et Nebernam, 84
Dryden, John, 80
  Britannia Rediviva, 81
  Hind and the Panther, 81
  Medall. A Satyre Against Sedition, 81
duanaire (family compilation), 212
'DUMBARTON'S *Drums*', 103–05
Dumfries, Theatre Royal, 183
Dun, Finlay, 161
Dùn Mac Sniachan, verse, 235–36
  and Beregonium, 236–39
Dunbar, Battle of, 170
Dunbar, William, 42
Duncan, Ian, 262
Dundas, Henry, 142

Dundee, John Graham of
    Claverhouse, Viscount, 64
D'Urfey, Thomas
    'Scotch songs', 97–98
    *Wit and Mirth; Or, Pills to
        Purge Melancholy*, 97
Dùthaich MhicAoidh, Mackay
    Country, 164
Dwyer, John, 262

Early English Books Online
    (EEBO), 76, 77
eclogues, 52
ecocriticism, 260
economy, Highland, slavery and,
    302
ecopoetics, 252–53
Edinburgh
    'Auld Reikie', 51–52
    Canongate Theatre, 180
    Carrubber's Close theatre, 178,
        179
    Company of Players, 178, 179
    '*Edina*', 85
    English company play
        Macbeth, 178
    improvement, 4
    literary society, 135
    Macpherson, and Hutton in,
        268
    New Town, 4, 182
    playhouse theatre, 181
    post-Union, Ramsay's poem,
        71–72
    Restoration publishers, 78
    Skinner's Hall, 178
    Taylor's Hall, 178, 179, 180
    Tennis Court Theatre,
        Holyrood, 174, 175, 178
    Theatre Royal, and Company,
        182, 183
    Tolbooth (prison), 69
education, 79, 212–13, 243
Eigg collection, 159, 204, 205–06,
    217
    female-authored texts, 210,
        217
elegy, 32, 44, 52, 138, 190
    Gaelic women poets, 34–35,
        203–04, 209, 216–19
    mock-elegy, 46, 47, 53
Elibank, Lord, 180
Elliott, Jean, 'The Flowers of the
    Forest', 49
emigration, 166, 213, 214–15
'encomiastic and rhetorical' verse,
    201
English language
    anonymous publications, 78
    poems in, 48–49, 51, 53
    see also anglicisation
English literature, 5
Enlightenment, 4, 164, 180,
    280–81
    sense and cognition, 114
    and slavery, 299, 304–05
    see also Scottish
        Enlightenment
environmental poetics, 251
epics, 151, 154, 241, 261, 278
Episcopal Church, 94
Equiano, Olaudah, 306–07
erosion, geological, 266
Erskine, Andrew
    *She's Not Him, and He's Not
        Her*, 181
    Town Eclogues, 189
Erskine Johnston, Henry, 186

Este, Thomas, 180
eulogy, 32, 33
    to education, 212–13
    Gaelic women poets, 208–09
    and the panegyric code, 26, 209
evangelicalism, 164, 168, 181
Excellent New Song, Intituled, Valiant Jockie: His Ladies Resolution, 97
Exclusion Crisis (1679–1681), 91
Eyre-Todd, George, 43, 44
Ezell, Margaret, 134–35

Falconer, William
    The Shipwreck, 285, 294–98
    Universal Dictionary of the Marine, 295
Fedon's Rebellion, 303
The Female Rebels (pamphlet), 124–27
Ferguson, Adam
    Essay on the History of Civil Society, 244
    and Marshall, 221
Ferguson, David, *Nine Hundred and Fourty Scottish Proverbs*, 79
Fergusson, Robert, 5, 44
    'Auld Reikie', 51–52
    'The Daft-Days', 50–51, 54
    'A Drink Eclogue', 189
    elegies and mock-elegies, 52
    and national music, 49
    Scots poems on social occasions, 52
Fernaig manuscript, 200
Ferrier, Susan, 225
Ferris, Ina, 274

Fielding, Penny, 241, 249
filidhean, 26, 29
Findlay, Bill, *History of Scottish Theatre*, 171
Finlayson, John, *The Marches Day*, 172
Fletcher, Andrew, 68, 180
folk tales, in English
    Frier and the Boy, 80
    History of Adam Bell, Clim of the Clough, and William of Cloudesley, 80
    Tom Thumb, 80
folk theatre, 172
footnotes, 295, 296–97
Fordun, John, *Chronica Gentis Scotorum*, 57
Forfeited Estates (1784), 49, 160
Foulis of Ravelston, Sir John, 175
Fraser, Simon, 161, 209
Free Church of Scotland, 168
French Revolutionary Wars, 213, 215–16
Furniss, Tom, 238

'The Gaberlunzie Man', 43
Gaelic
    classical, 28–29
    language of dramatic discourse, 172
    see also Scottish Gaelic
Gaelic epic tradition. *see* epics
Gaelic women poets, 199–219
Garrick, David, 180, 181
Gay, John, *Trivia, or the Art of Walking the Streets of London*, 51
gender in Ramsay's *Miscellany*, 100–10

geological ('deep') time, 267, 269
geological erosion, 266
geology, modern, 266, 270
George I, 35, 117
George II, 176
georgic poets/poetry, 189, 260, 295
Gidal, Eric, 262–63, 267–68
Gillies, John. *see* Gillies Collection
Gillies, William, 156, 162
Gillies Collection, 159, 160, 201, 206
    Chearful Companion, 159
    female-authored texts, 210
    'A girl's song to her sweetheart', 203
    McLagan's corpus as source, 235
    'A song to Archibald MacCallum', 204
Gillis, Anna, 215
Glasgow
    improvement, 4
    intellectual culture, 145, 247
    playhouse theatre, 183
    Restoration publishers, 78, 79
    school/university drama, 173–74
Glencoe, 239, 240
global capitalism, 301
Glover, Katherine, 180
Godwin, William, 230
Goodman, John, *Winter-Evening Conference Between Neighbours*, 79–80
Gould, Stephen Jay, 267, 268
Gow, Ann, 214
Gow, Margaret. *see* Ghriogarach, Mairearad

Grainger, James, *The Sugar Cane*, 250
Grant, Anne MacVicar, *Poems on Various Subjects*, 133
Grant, Ludovick, *Statistical Account* report, 236
Grant of Laggan, Anne, 204–05, 239–40
Greaves, Richard L., 80
Griffith, Moses, 279
Grimble, Ian, 164
Ghriogarach, Mairearad (Margaret Gow, née MacGregor)
    'Do Leanabh-Altraim a bha aice' ('To an infant whom she nursed'), 213–14
    eulogies to women's education, 212–13
    'Òran do Bràithrean bha an Cog' America' ('A song to her brothers fighting in America'), 213
Grogan, Claire, 225

Habbie stanza, 43–44, 53, 194–95
Hagglund, Betty, 274, 284
Hamilton, Elizabeth, 225
    Memoirs of Modern Philosophers, 230–32, 233
    ties to Scottish intellectual culture, 221
Hamilton, Newburgh
    The Doating Lovers, 176
    The Petticoat-Plotter, 176
Hamilton of Gilbertfield, William
    'The Last Dying Words of Bonnie Heck', 47
    Wallace, 47
Hamon, Philippe, 290

Hanoverian dynasty, 118, 208
Hays, Mary, 233
Hebrides, travel writing, 276–77
Heise, Ursula K., 256–57
Henderson, T. F., 45, 47
Henryson, Robert, 42
　The Testament of Cresseid, 83
Herd, David, *Ancient and Modern Scottish Songs*, 111, 114
Herries, Walter, *Defence of the Scots Abdicating Darien*, 67
Highland culture
　British public opinion and, 159
　elimination of, 119
　and Union/Britain, 278
　see also Scottish Enlightenment
'The Highland Laddie', 107–09
Highland Societies, 160, 161
Highland tour, rise of, 273, 282–84
Highlands
　Annexed Estates, 278
　demographics, 3, 234
　Minority position of, 307
　Romantic writing on, 275
　see also Clearances, Highland; economy, Highland
historicisation, 111
Hogg, James
　'Dusty, or, Watie an' Geordie's Review of Politics; an Eclogue', 188
　Pilgrims of the Sun, 196, 197–98
　Private Memoirs and Confessions of a Justified Sinner, 53
　use of Scots register, 55
Hogmanay Rhyme, 26

Home, Henry. *see* Kames, Lord
Home, John
　Agis, 180, 181
　Douglas, 180–81
horsemanship, 185
humanism, 173, 194
Hume, David, 177, 180, 221, 245
　critique of, 222–23, 230
　letter to Wilkes, on decay, 242
　'Of National Characters', 306
　Ramsay on, 305
　on sympathy and sentiment, 222, 294
　True Account of the Behaviour and Conduct of Archibald Stewart Esq., 241
Hunter, James, 252
Hutton, James
　in Edinburgh, 268
　and Ossianic thought, 268–69, 270
　Theory of the Earth and *Transactions*, 238–39, 266, 267

Iain Dubh, 66
Iain Lom. *see* MacDhomhnaill, Iain Lom
Iain mac Ailein, 204
Iain mac Fhearchair (John MacCodrum), 158
iambic love songs, 30–31
iambics, 263
illiteracy, Ritson on, 195
imperialism, 67
improvement, 3–4, 244, 249
　agriculture, 162, 166, 273
　'Ben Nevis poem' and, 235
　economic, Thomson on, 259–60

improvement (*cont.*)
   and Highland engagement in slavery, 302
   manufacturing, 162
   transport, 162
   travel writers on, 279–81
   and the world-ecology perspective, 250–51
   see also Scottish Enlightenment
Industrial Revolution, 4, 162
infant mortality, decline in, 162
Innes, Sìm, 3
intertextuality, 306
Ireland, 117
Irish (language), 24

Jacobites, Jacobitism, 35, 65, 117–19, 176
   1715 Rising, 48
   1745 Rising, 2, 39, 48, 118, 278
   anti-Jacobite works, 119, 120–24
   as ballad theme, 49
   and Gaelic women poets, 206, 210
   poetry, 35–39
   tartan and, 120
   see also Culloden, Battle of
James, Duke of York and Albany, 91, 92, 175
   see also James VII/II
James Francis Stuart (*later* the Old Pretender), 81
James VII/II, 64, 74, 117
   and patronage, 76
   poetry, persona of, 44
Jaws (movie), 268
Johnson, James, Scottish musical anthology, 114–15
Johnson, Samuel, 136, 159, 176, 214, 244, 280–81
'The Jolly Beggar', 43
Jonson, Ben, 42
Jonsson, Frederick Albritton, 278

Kames, Lord, 221, 222, 242
   Elements of Criticism, 224
   Sketches of the History of Man, 243–44
Kaul, Suvir, 57, 59
Kehoe, Karly, 302
Keir, David-Orme, 138
Keir, Elizabeth Rae, 134, 135–38
   'Elegy written in Greyfriar's Church yard', 138
   'Epistle to Miss Fraser at Aldoury 3 October 1773', 136
   'Epistle to Miss Marianne Rae', 135–36
   History of Miss Greville, 135
   Interesting Memoirs, 135
   'Ode to the Female Writers of the Present Age', 138
   'On Receiving Burns's Poems from Mrs Cockburn', 136
Keir, William, 137
Keith, Margaret, 137
Kennedy, Duncan, 206, 215
Keppoch, poets from, 239
Kerr, Jane ('Delia'), 137
Kirk (church), 170, 171
   Admonition and Exhortation, 178, 181
   Moderate thinking in, 181
   opposition to theatre, 179
Kirk, Robert, *Psalma Dhaibhidh an Meadrachd*, 77
knowledge-making, 278

INDEX 431

Knox, John, 280
Kristeva, Julia, 306

lament, women's, 215–16, 217
    see also elegy
landlords, 167, 199, 280
Landry, Donna, 141
Lapraik, John, 55
'The Lass of Peatie's Mill', 70
'*Lass with a Lump of Land*', 105
'The Last Time I Came O'er the Moor', 70
Latin, 65, 77
Latin literature, 79, 91
Latitia Caledonica, or, Scotlands Raptures, upon the Thrise Happy Return of her Sacred Soveraign Charles the Second, 78
Leask, Nigel, 115, 249, 250–51
Lee, Nathaniel, *Mithridates, King of Pontus*, 175
Leslie, Charles, 177
Leslie, John, 178–79
Lettice, John, *Letters on a Tour*, 282–83
Licensing Act, 1737, 179
Lightfoot, John, 279
Linnaeus, Carl, 277
literacy, Gaelic, 159
literary imitation, 198
literary progress, ideas of, 187
Little, Janet, 55, 69, 142
Livingston, Michael, 91
    Albion's Congratulatory, 93
    Albion's Elegie and *Albion's Farewel*, 93
    Augustis, ac Praepotentibus Heroibus, 93
    panegyrical verse, 93

local knowledge, travel writing, 276–77, 277–79
locality, 197
Lockwood, Thomas, 141
London, subscription publication, 141
London Evening Gazette, 127
Long, Edward, 305
Lord Chamberlain, censorship role, 179
Lowland Scots, 158, 300
lullaby, 33
luxury
    debates on, 243–44
    Highland nobles' pursuit of, 242–43
Lyndsay, Sir David
    History of the Noble and Valiant Squyer Meldrum, 83
    Thrie Estaitis, 171
    Works, 83

Mac an t-Saoir, Donnchadh Bàn, 154–56
    'Cead Deireannach nam Beann' ('Final Farewell to the Bens'), 255–56
    'Moladh Beinn Dóbhrain' ('Praise of Ben Dorain'), 154–55, 156, 254–55
    Orain Ghaidhealach (*Highland Songs*), 154
mac Colla, Alasdair, 28
Mac Mhaighstir Alasdair, Alasdair, 37–39, 234
    Ais-eiridh na Sean Chánoin Albannaich (*The Resurrection of the Ancient Scottish Language*), preface, 39, 150, 205, 207

Mac Mhaighstir Alasdair,
    Alasdair (*cont.*)
    'An Airce' ('*The Ark*'), 206
    Birlinn Chlann Raghnaill ('Clan
        Ranald's Galley'), 38–39
    *Galick and English
        Vocabulary*, 149, 237–38
    'Oran a Rinneadh Sa
        Bhliadhna 1746', 265
    Oran an t-Samhraidh and
        Oran a' Gheamhraidh,
        songs, 38
    '*Song of Summer*', 252–54
Mac Mhaighstir Alasdair,
    Raghnall, Eigg collection,
    205–06
MacAoidh, Rob Donn. *see* Rob
    Donn
MacCodrum, John. *see* Iain mac
    Fhearchair
MacCoinnich, Coinneach,
    Cumha an Taobh Tuath, 'The
    Lament of the North', 167
MacDhomhnaill, Iain Lom (John
    MacDonald), 158, 239
    'Oran Cumhaidh air Cor na
        Rìoghachd', 61–62
    songs, 27
MacDhomhnaill, Raghnall, 159
MacDiarmid, Ewen, collector,
    201, 217
MacDonald, Alexander. *see* Mac
    Mhaighstir Alasdair, Alasdair
MacDonald, Archibald, 239
MacDonald, Flora, 118, 126–27
MacDonald, Iain Bàn, of Inch, 205
MacDonald, Mary, 206
MacDonald of Keppoch, Cicely.
    see Sìleas na Ceapaich
MacDonalds of Glencoe, 239–40

Macdonell of Glengarry, Alastair
    Ranaldson, 167
MacDougall, Ailean Dall, 239
    'Òran do na Cìobairibh
        Gallda', 166–67
MacGill-Eain, Somhairle, 166–67
MacGilleMhoire, Ruairidh (An
    Clàrsair Dall), 32, 244
MacGregor, Donald, 212
MacInnes, John, 26
MacIntyre, Duncan Ban. *see* Mac
    an t-Saoir, Donnchadh Bàn
Mackay, Charles, 186
MacKenzie, Garry, 256–57
Mackenzie, George, *Lives and
    Characters of the Most
    Eminent 70 Writers of the
    Scots Nation*, 69–70
Mackenzie, Henry
    Force of Fashion, 182
    The Prince of Tunis, 182
    The Shipwreck, 182
MacKenzie, John, *Sar Obair nam
    Bard Gaelach*, 205
Mackenzie of Rosehaugh, George
    Aretina, 63–64, 86, 87, 88
    'A Poem [...] upon his Majesties
        [*sic*] Happy Return', 62–63
Mackinnon, Rev. Donald, 161
Macky, John, *Journey through
    Scotland*, 275
Maclaren, Archibald
    *The Conjurer; or, The
        Scotsman in London*, 183
    The Highland Drover, 183
    Humours of Greenock Fair, 183
MacLean, Donald, 210
Maclean, Margaret, 202
    lament to a chieftain, 33–34,
        217–18

Macleod, Màiri nighean Alasdair Ruaidh (Mary MacLeod), 28, 158, 202
   An Cronan (*The Croon*), 33
   Fuaim an Taibh (*The Sound of the Ocean*), 33
MacLeod Hill, Anne, 211
MacLeods of Dunvegan, 33, 202, 244
Macneill, Hector, *The Pastoral, or Lyric Muse of Scotland*, 195–96
MacNicol, Rev. Donald, 161
MacPhàrlain, Alasdair, *Gairm an De Mhoir*, 150
Macpherson, James (Seumas Bàn MacMhuirich), 187
   Fingal: An Ancient Epic Poem, 136, 151, 270
   'Berrathon', 270
   'Carthon', 263–65, 268–70
   Fragments, 261
   Poems of Ossian, 158–59, 188–89, 191–92, 239, 240, 241, 251, 261–65, 268–71, 275, 278
   Temora, 151, 268
MacPherson, Mary, 206–07
   '*My soul, go quietly on*', 206
MacQueen, Jack, 65
MacQueen of Skye, Donald, 279
'MAGIE'S Tocher', 105
Mairearad nighean Lachlainn (Margaret Maclean). *see* Maclean, Margaret
Màiri Mhòr nan Òran ('Big Mary of the Songs'), 212
Mallet, David, 48
   Eurydice, 176
   The Masque of Alfred, 177
   Mustapha, 176

Mann, Alastair J., 75–76, 77
   on print culture, 78
Mansfield, Lord, and the Steuart v. Somerset case, 304
manuscript, 65–66, 77
manuscript culture
   attribution in, 203
   duanaire (family compilation), 212
   and women writers, 133, 134–41, 203, 274
Marishall, Jean
   History of Miss Clarinda Cathcart, and Miss Fanny Renton, 181, 221, 225–28, 232–33
   memoir, 220
   Series of Letters, 223
   Sir Harry Gaylove, 221
maritime language, 286–97
Martin, Carine, 124
Martin, Martin
   Description of the Western Islands of Scotland, 258, 276
   Late Voyage to St. Kilda, 258, 276
masques, 175
Master of the Revels in Scotland, 178
Matheson, William, 30, 32
Mayne, John, 44, 55
McDowell, Paula, 111
McGavin, John, 171
McGrath, John, *The Cheviot, The Stag and the Black, Black Oil*, 250
McKenzie, J., 171, 173
McLagan, James, collector, 201, 202–03, 205, 212, 234–35
   'To Archibald McCalum, hunter in Beinn Mhor', 203–04

McLagan, James, collector (*cont.*)
    'Of Berigonium', 238
    'On the Desolation of the Scottish Highlands', 234–35. *see also* Ben Nevis poem
    '*A young woman's lament*' or ('*Son of Dougal, son of Ruairidh*'), 203–04
McLynn, F. J., 117
McNeil, Kenneth, 5
McNeill, John R., 250
McNicol, Donald, collector, 201, 202
    on the oral tradition, 202–03
McNicol, Rev. Donald, 280
Meek, Donald, 234, 240
The Meire of Collingtoun, 83
Melville, Elizabeth Colville, Lady, *Ane Godlie Dream*, 83
Melville, Robert, 302
The Merry Companion: or, Universal Songster, 111
Mickle, William Julius
    The Lusiad, translation, 49
    'The Sailor's Wife', 49
Middle Scots, 69
Mill, Anna Jean, 171
Millar, James, 304
Milne, Christian, 134
    'Introductory Verses', 143, 144
    Poems on Various Subjects, 143
    'On Seeing the List of Subscribers to this Little Work', 144
    Simple Poems on Simple Subjects, 143, 144–45
    subscription publication, 142, 145
Milton, John, 187

mock-elegy, 53, 206
Montgomerie, Alexander, 69
    The Cherrie and the Slae, 83
Montrose, James Graham, third Marquess of, 62, 94, 208
'moral culture', and ridicule, 224–25, 228
More, Hannah, 142
Moreto, Agustín, 90
Morrill, John, 74–75
mourning, cultural work of, 86, 88
mouth music (puirt-à-beul), 163
Murray, Mungo, 91
    On the Death and Horrid Murther, 94
    elegies, 93–94
Murray, Sarah, *Companion and Useful Guide to the Beauties of Scotland*, 283–84
music concerts, 180

Nairne, Carolina Oliphant, Lady, 55
Nasmyth, Arthur, *Divine Poems*, 88–89
'National Drama', 185
national identity, 45, 57
nationhood, and gender, 109–10, 111
natural history/naturalists, 279
    networks, 277–78
    visual representation, role of, 279
Nenadic, Stana, 242–43, 244
Newey, Kate, 172
Newman, Steve, *Ballad Collection, Lyric, and the Canon*, 99
newspapers
    anti-Jacobite narratives, 127

on Charles Edward Stuart's
 escape, 122
 first Scottish, 89
 Ramsay's work, references to,
 115
'*Norland* JOCKY *and Southland*
 JENNY', 106–07
Normand, Tom, 269
novel
 as new genre, 286
 women novelists, 135, 222–33

Ogilvy, Lady, 125–26, 127
orain luaidh, female-voiced, 205
orality, 169
 Gaelic women poets, 200,
  202–03
 in the Gàidhealtachd, 25–26
 and Jacobite cultural
  memories, 119
 and literacy, 197
 oral ballads, 187–88
 ritual lament, 34
 Scottish Gaelic, 66
 Scotswomen and, 132
 and song culture, 99
 travel writers' search for
  traditions, 278
'Òran Mòr MhicLeòid' ('The
 Great Song of MacLeod'), 32
Ossian, 151, 158–59, 240
 controversy, 187, 188, 201
 see also Macpherson, James
  (Seumas Bàn MacMhuirich)
Ovid, 79

pamphlets. *see* print culture
panegyric code, 26, 32, 216–17
panegyrical verse, 78, 93
 see also eulogy

pan-Gaelic identity, 28
pastoral ballads, 190
pastoral drama, 49
pastoral poetry, 187–91
 and ballads, 188
 and the border poets, 196–97
 and Burns, 194–95
 and georgic poetry, 189
 and nature/art, 198
 Ross and Beattie, 192–94
patent theatre system, 179–80,
 183, 185
Paterson, Ninian
 elegies, 92–93
 Epigrammatum Libri Octo, 91
 Fanatick Indulgence Granted,
  Anno 1679, 91, 92
 Latin poetry, 91
 Poem on the Test, 91, 92
patronage, 89, 93, 188
Pennant, Thomas
 social critique of Highland
  poverty, 279–80
 Tour in Scotland, 236, 238,
  240, 272–73, 281
 Voyage to the Hebrides 1772,
  277, 279–80
Pennecuik, Alexander, *Caledonia*
 triumphans, 67
performance, and song culture,
 110, 113, 114
periodicals, Ramsay's work,
 references to, 115
periodicals, Scottish, 5
Perkins, Pam, 132–33
Perth, Margaret of Drummond,
 Duchess of, 125–26, 127
Philip (Philp) of Almerieclose,
 James, *The Grameid*, 65–66
Picken, Ebenezer, 55

Pinkerton, John
    on 'Hardyknute', 112
    introductory essays, 112–13
    Scottish Tragic Ballads, 111
Pitcairne, Archibald, 65
    The Assembly: A Comedy by a Scots Gentleman, 65, 175–76
Pittock, Murray, 120
planters, 305–06
Playfair, John, *Illustrations of the Huttonian Theory of the Earth*, 266
playhouse theatre, 174
    development of, 182–84, 186
    established in Edinburgh's social life, 181
    and 'national' expectations, 185
playwrights, Scottish, and London productions, 174–75, 176–77
Poemata Selecta, 65
political and religious works, Restoration, 76–77
Popish Plot (1678–1681), 91
postcolonialism, 300, 301
Potkay, Adam, 263
poverty, 280
Presbyterianism, 68, 175, 211, 308
    official religion of Scotland, 3
    Psalms, 40
    Revolution and, 64–65
Prince Charles Edward Stuart Disguised as Betty Burke (broadside), 122–24
print culture, 5, 73–95, 165
    on Charles Stuart's escape, 122
    Gaelic women poets, 203
    on Jacobite risings, 118–19
progress, 5, 187
Protestantism, 84, 171, 308
proto-romantic love song, 30
provincial literary culture, women poets in, 132, 135
Psalms, Gaelic translations, 30–31, 40, 150
psalter, 77
puritanism, 170, 181

Q-Celtic, 24
Quakerism, 77
Quarles, Francis, *Enchiridion*, 79
Quintanilla, Mark, 303
Qur'an, English translation of, 61

Racine, Jean, 173
Rae, Elizabeth. *see* Keir, Elizabeth Rae
Ramsay, Allan, the Elder, 44, 45, 247
    'Christis Kirk on the Green', 70
    'Content', 46
    'Edinburgh Address to the Country', 71–72
    'Elegy on Lucky Wood in the Canongate, May 1717', 46
    The Evergreen, 46, 70
    The Gentle Shepherd, 46, 49, 178–79, 180, 190
    Jacobite sympathies, 179
    'Lucky Spence's Last Advice', 46
    mock-elegies, 46
    'The Morning Interview', 46
    Musick for Allan Ramsay's Collection of Scots Songs, 110
    in Scottish playhouse theatre, 178

The Tea-Table Miscellany, 46, 70, 98–111, 115–16, 253
   paratextual materials, 114, 115
'Wealth, or the Woody', 46
Ramsay, Allan, the Younger, 46
Ramsay, James
  Essay on the Treatment and Conversion of African Slaves, 304, 305
  forefather of British abolitionism, 305
Ramsay, John, of Ochtertyre, 158, 199
Rann Challuinn, 26
Raymond, Joad, 74
realist fiction, 289
Reformation, 27
register, 41–42
Reid, Steven, 77
Reid, Thomas, 221
  Essay on Laughter and Ludicrous Composition, 222–23
  on ridicule, moral function of, 224–25
Restoration, 62, 85
Restoration Scotland
  English works, republished, 79–82
  Medieval and Renaissance Scottish works, republished, 82–84
  Scottish works, published, 84–94
revolutions
  American, and French, 2
  see also 1688 Revolution
Reynolds, Sir Joshua, 142
rhetorical skills, 174
Richardson, Samuel, 221
  Pamela and *Clarissa*, 225

ridicule, women novelists' use of, 222–33
Ridpath, George, 67
Ritson, Joseph, 97–98
  Scotish [sic] Song, 111, 113, 195
ritual lament, 33–34
Rob Donn, Gaelic satire, 163–65
Robertson, Thomas, 92–93
Robertson, William, 180
  History of America, 306
romance genre, 86
Romantic movement, 54, 151, 248
romanticism, 162
Ros, Uilleam, love poetry, 161–62
Ross, Alexander
  The Fortunate Shepherdess, 192–93
  Helenore, 49–50
  History of the World, 60
  Qur'an, translation of, 61
  Scots register, 49
  Scots songs, 50
  Som Animadversions and Observations Upon Sr Walter Raleigh's Historie of the World, 60
Ross, Anne, 134
  'The Banks of Clyde', 146
  'Bread and Cheese. Inscribed to all Friends in the Country', 146–47
  Collection of Poems, 142, 145–46
  subscription publication, 142, 145–46
Ross, Elizabeth, 161
Ross, William *see* Ros, Uilleam
Rothberg, Michael, 119–20
Rothes, John Leslie, seventh Earl of, 86, 87, 94

Royal Adventurers into Africa, 302
royal patronage, and Scottish book trade, 75–76
Royal Society of Edinburgh, 239, 266
rural drama, 171

'SANDY *and* BETTY', 109–10
satire, 53, 84, 89–90, 163–65
  see also ridicule, women novelists' use of
scepticism, 223, 230
Schein, Louisa, 56–57
Schellenberg, Betty A., 135, 274
school drama, 173
Scots register, 41–42, 45, 49
  and maritime language, 287, 292
  poetry, 18th cent., 55
  Ramsay's work, 179, 190–91
  Ross's work, 49–50
  vernacular, 65
Scott, Frances, 134, 135
Scott, Lady Frances (*later* Lady Douglas), 139–41
  Dalkeith Miscellany, 139, 140
  'To Lady Louisa Stuart', 140
Scott, Mary Jane W., 257
Scott, Walter, 135, 185, 262
Scottish Enlightenment, 9, 114, 247
  debates on luxury, 243–44
  Gaelic culture and, 234
  on Highland society, 240–41
  and *Ossian*, 262
  on ridicule, 224
  and slavery, 304–05
  and sociability, 4
  social theory, 280
  sympathy and sentiment, 221

Scottish Gaelic, 24
  Bible translation, 151–52
  grammar and dictionary project, 157–58, 159
  Jacobite oral culture, 66
  literary canon, 160
  religious works, 77
  spelling reforms, 149–50
  vernacular prose/poetry, 39
Scottish identities, within the Union, 177
'Scottish' pastoral, notion of, 188
Scullion, Adrienne, 178
Sean Dain agus Orain Ghaidhealach (*Old Gaelic Poems and Songs*, 1786), 159
Secord, James, 278
semi-classical poetry, 29
Sempill, Francis
  'The Banishment of Poverty', 44
  'Fy, Let Us A' to the Bridal', 44
  'Maggie Lauder' and 'Hallow Fair', 44
Sempill, Robert, 'Habbie Simson', 43–44, 46
Sempill, Sir James, *A Pick-tooth for the Pope*, 83
Sempills of Beltrees, 43–45
sentimental novels/tradition, 283
  and women novelists' critique of, 221–33
sermon cultures, 164, 168
Settle, Elkanah, 80
  Heroick Poem on the Coronation of the High and Mighty Monarch, James II, 81
Seven Years War, 302

Shaftesbury, Lord, *Sensus Communis*, 223
Shakespeare, William, 187
Sharp, James, Archbishop of St Andrews, 94
Shaw, Rev. William, 159
Shenstone, William, 51
Sìleas na Ceapaich, 66, 202, 205
   'Còmhradh ris a' Bhàs' ('*Conversation with Death*'), 211–12
   'Cumha Lachlainn Daill' ('*Lament for Lachlan Dall*'), 203
   elegy for Alasdair Dubh, 34–35, 203, 217
   Jacobite poetry, 210
Sillar, David, 55
Sinclair of Ulbster, John, *Statistical Account of Scotland*, 236, 274
'Sir Patrick Spens', 48
Skinner, John, 'Tullochgorum', 49, 50
Skirving, Adam, 'Johnnie Cope', 49
Skye, 122
slavery, slaves, 250, 301–02
   Cugoano–Campbell relationship, 302–04
   emancipation of, British colonies, 302
   Enlightenment consensus against, 305
   and the Mansfield verdict, 304
Smith, Adam, 221, 222, 304
   Lectures on Jurisprudence, 4
   on the stages of progress, 240–41
   The Theory of Moral Sentiments, 297
Smith, David L., 75
Smith, Nigel, 74
Smollett, Tobias
   Adventures of Roderick Random, 285–94
   The Expedition of Humphry Clinker, 274
   'The Tears of Scotland', 49
Smout, T. C., 252, 255
sociability, urban hubs, 4
social class
   women poets and, 134
   working-class poets, 141–47
Solander, Daniel, 277
Somerset, James, 304
songs
   The Bonny Highland Laddie, 31
   broadsides, 97–98
   collections in Scots, 46
   English popular songs, 161
   Gaelic popular love songs, 30
   'Òran Mòr MhicLeòid' ('The Great Song of MacLeod'), 32
   performance, 110, 113, 114
   popular folk songs, 70
   popular Gaelic love songs, 160–61
   Ramsay's *Miscellany*, 98–111
   Ross's, in Scots, 50
   'Rule, Britannia!' 48
   see also ballads; emigration
Sorensen, Janet, 114, 247
The Sorrowful Maiden for the Want of Tocher-good, 97
South Sea Company, 70
Spenser, Edmund, 48, 187, 192
   Shepheardes Calender, 193
Spenserian romance, 192
spiritual/moral literature, 79–80

Spurlock, R. Scott, 75
Stafford, Fiona, 247, 249, 257, 278
Steuart, Charles, 304
Stevenson (née Campbell), Margaret, 202, 206
Stewart, Alexander and Donald, collectors, 201, 203
    Cochruinneacha Taoghta de Shaothair nam Bard Gaëlach, 160
    female-authored texts, 210, 216
    Jacobite poetry, 210
Stewart, Isabel, 205
Stiùbhart, Raibeart, 167–68
Stiùbhart, Rev. Seumas (James Stuart), New Testament Gaelic translation, 151–52, 157
Strabone, Jeff, 102
Strahan and Cadell, 135
Stroh, Silke, *Gaelic Scotland and the Colonial Imagination*, 300
Strong, Mairea, 203
Stuart, Alexander, *Musick for Allan Ramsay's Collection of Scots Songs*, 110
Stuart, House of, 40
    see also Jacobites, Jacobitism
Stuart, John, 279
Stuart, Lady Louisa, 139–40
    'To Lady Frances Scott', 140
    Memoire, 140
subscription publication, 134, 141–47
superstition, 197
Sutherland, George, 183
Swift, Jonathan, 53
    Gulliver's Travels, 197
Sydserf, Thomas
    Bourlasque News from the Antipodes, 89
    Mercurius Caledonius, 89
    New Claret-Club, 89
    Prince of Tartaria his Voyage to Cowper in Fife, 89
    Remarkable Prophesies in Order to the Present Times, 89
    The Scout of Cockeny, 89
    Selenarchia, 89
    Tarugo's Wiles, 90, 175
    The Work Goes Bonnely On, 89

tacksmen, Gaelic, 168
tartan, 49, 120, 160
technical sea language. see maritime language
testimony, 283–84
'The (Rule) Britannia Project', 177
theatre, ban on, 170
Theatre Act, 1737, 175
'This is no mine ain House', 105–06
Thomson, Alexander, 50
Thomson, George, Scottish musical anthology, 115
Thomson, James
    Agamemnon, 176
    The Castle of Indolence, 48, 189
    Edward and Leonora, 176
    The Masque of Alfred, 177
    'Rule, Britannia!' 48, 177
    The Seasons, 48, 257–60
    Sophonisba, 176
    Spring, 253
    Tancred and Sigismunda, 177
Thomson, William, *Orpheus Caledonius: Or, A Collection of Scots Songs*, 103, 110, 111
time. see geological ('deep') time
Tobin, James, 305, 306

Tobin, Terence, 176, 182
Todd, Margo, 171
topical pastorals, 188–89
tourism, and writings, 272–84
transnationalism, 57, 60, 102
transportation and communications, 4
travel writing, British writers, 274–81
travelling companies, 185–86
Treaty of Union, 70, 177
Trotter, Catherine
   Agnes de Castro/Ines de Castro, 176
   Fatal Friendship, 176
   Love at a Loss, 176
   Revolution in Sweden, 176
   Unhappy Penitent, 176
Turnbull, Gordon, *An apology for Negro slavery*, 305–06
Turner, Patrick, collector, 201, 203
   Comhchruinneacha do dh'Orain Taghta Ghaidhealach, 160
   female-authored texts, 210
   Jacobite poetry, 210
Tyler, Evan, 78

uniformitarianism, 266
Union, Acts of (1707), 68, 70–72, 102, 109, 117
Union of Crowns (1603), 1, 42, 58, 68
United Kingdom, Scotland's role within, 300
universities, Scottish, 4–5
university drama, 173–74
urban pastoralists, 189
urban performativity, 172
Urquhart, Thomas
   Ekskybalauron, 58–59
   Logopandecteision, 59–60
   Pantochronochanon, 58
   translation of Rabelais, 60

Veitch, John, *The Feeling for Nature in Scottish Poetry*, 246–47
vernacular Gaelic poetry, 27–30
vernacular pastoralists, 187
vernacular register, 7
Vernacular Revival, 179
verse broadsides. *see* broadsides
Virgil, 187
'virtue in distress' plot, 220–21, 227, 230
visual representation, and natural history, 279
volcanoes, 238–39

Walker, Rev. John, 234
Wallace (1722). *see under* Hamilton of Gilbertfield
Wallace, Eglantine
   Diamond Cut Diamond, 184
   The Ton, 184
   The Whim, 184
Waller, Edmund, 99, 111
Wallerstein, Immanuel, 301
Walpole, Horace, 142
Ward, Ned
   A Trip to Jamaica, 287
   The Wooden World Dissected, 287, 292
Ward, Sarah, 180
Wardlaw, Lady Elizabeth, 'Hardyknute', 47–48
Wars of the Three Kingdoms (1639–1652), 57, 74–75
   in *Aretina*, 63
   and vernacular styles, 27–30

Watson, James
    Choice Collection of Comic and Serious Scots Poems, 45, 69, 97
    'Christ's Kirk on the Green', 69
    'The Life and Death of the Piper of Kilbarchan', 69
    'Ode', 66–67
    People of Scotland's Groans and Lamentable Complaints, 69
    printer, 69–70
    '*ROBERT* the III. King of Scotland', 69
Watson, Roderick, *Literature of Scotland*, 73
Watt, Ian, 286
Watts, Isaac, 153
waulking songs, women's, 33
Wemyss, David Wemyss, second Earl of, 94
Wesley, John, *Thoughts on Slavery*, 306
West Africa, social system, and Highland clanship, 306–07
Whatley, Christopher, 68
Wheatley, Phillis, *Poems on Various Subjects, Religious and Moral*, 143
Whigs, 64–65
Wild, Robert, *Gratulatory Verse upon our Late Glorious Victory over the Dutch*, 80
Wilkes, John, 292
William and Mary, accession of, 64–65, 117
    see also William III

William III, 66
Williams, John (pamphleteer), 119
Wilson, Alexander, 55
Wilson, John, *Earl Douglas*, 181–82
Wilson, Kathleen, 103
Withers, Charles, 278
Womack, Peter, 275
women
    commercial and critical influence of, 102–03
    female tropes, anti-Jacobite works, 124–27
    and the Industrial Revolution, 162
    legal and social vulnerability of, 225
    poets, 132–48
    and ritual lament, 34
    and sociability, 4
    tourism, writing, 274
women novelists, and critique of sentimental fiction, 222–33
Worcester, Battle of (1651), 58
Wordsworth, Dorothy, 205
Wordsworth, William, 'The Solitary Reaper', 187–88, 189, 195, 283
working-class poets, 141–47

Yearsley, Ann, *Poems on Several Occasions*, 142
Young, Eoin, collector, 201, 203, 210
youth culture, Gaelic, 162–63

Zenzinger, Peter, 50
Zwicker, Steven N., 76–77

www.ingramcontent.com/pod-product-compliance
Lightning Source LLC
Chambersburg PA
CBHW051826230426
43671CB00008B/851